The Responsibility to Prot

This book presents the views of various international law and human rights experts on the contested meaning, scope of application, value and viability of R2P; the principle of the Responsibility to Protect. R2P refers to the notion that the international community has a legal responsibility to protect civilians against the potential or ongoing occurrence of the mass atrocity crimes of genocide, large scale war crimes, ethnic cleansing and crimes against humanity. R2P allows for intervention where the individual State is unable or unwilling to so protect its people or is in fact a perpetrator. The book addresses also the controversial issue of whether intervention by States implementing R2P with or without the endorsement of the United Nations Security Council constitutes a State act of aggression or instead is legally justified and not an infringement on the offending State's sovereign jurisdiction. The adverse impact on global peace and security of the failure to protect civilians from mass atrocity crimes has put in stark relief the need to address anew the principle of 'responsibility to protect' and the feasibility and wisdom of its application and this book is a significant contribution to that effort.

This book was originally published as a special issue of *The International Journal of Human Rights*.

Sonja Grover is Professor in the Lakehead University Faculty of Education and its affiliated Northern Ontario School of Medicine, Canada, and an Associate Editor of *The International Journal of Human Rights*. She has published extensively in the area of international law and human rights law with 10 books and 67 peer-reviewed journal articles in this field, as well as two book chapters, two guest edited special issues of *The International Journal of Human Rights* and numerous conference presentations. She has a special interest in children's fundamental human rights under international law.

The Responsibility to Protect

Perspectives on the concept's meaning, proper application and value

Edited by
Sonja Grover

LONDON AND NEW YORK

First published 2017
by Routledge

2 Park Square, Milton Park, Abingdon, Oxfordshire OX14 4RN
711 Third Avenue, New York, NY 10017

Routledge is an imprint of the Taylor & Francis Group, an informa business

First issued in paperback 2018

British Library Cataloguing in Publication Data
A catalogue record for this book is available from the British Library

ISBN: 978-1-138-69006-6 (hbk)
ISBN: 978-0-367-02639-4 (pbk)

Typeset in Times New Roman
by RefineCatch Limited, Bungay, Suffolk

Publisher's Note
The publisher accepts responsibility for any inconsistencies that may have
arisen during the conversion of this book from journal articles to book chapters,
namely the possible inclusion of journal terminology.

Disclaimer
Every effort has been made to contact copyright holders for their permission to
reprint material in this book. The publishers would be grateful to hear from any
copyright holder who is not here acknowledged and will undertake to rectify
any errors or omissions in future editions of this book.

Contents

CONTENTS

Citation Information

The chapters in this book were originally published in *The International Journal of Human Rights*, volume 19, issue 8 (December 2015). When citing this material, please use the original page numbering for each article, as follows:

Chapter 1
Introduction
Sonja Grover
The International Journal of Human Rights, volume 19, issue 8 (December 2015), pp. 999–1001

Chapter 2
Enforcing the responsibility to protect through solidarity measures
Jessica Almqvist
The International Journal of Human Rights, volume 19, issue 8 (December 2015), pp. 1002–1016

Chapter 3
A critical reflection on the conceptual and practical limitations of the responsibility to protect
Joseph Besigye Bazirake and Paul Bukuluki
The International Journal of Human Rights, volume 19, issue 8 (December 2015), pp. 1017–1028

Chapter 4
Redefining the responsibility to protect concept as a response to international crimes
Auriane Botte
The International Journal of Human Rights, volume 19, issue 8 (December 2015), pp. 1029–1043

Chapter 5
R2P, Global Governance, and the Syrian refugee crisis
Alise Coen
The International Journal of Human Rights, volume 19, issue 8 (December 2015), pp. 1044–1058

For any permission-related enquiries please visit:
http://www.tandfonline.com/page/help/permissions

Notes on Contributors

Jessica Almqvist is a Senior Researcher and Lecturer in Public International Law and International Relations, Faculty of Law, Autonomous University of Madrid, Spain. She earned her PhD in Law from the European University Institute in 2002. She is author of the book *Human Rights, Culture and the Rule of Law* (Hart, 2005); and co-editor of *The Role of Courts in Transitional Justice: Voices from Latin America and Spain* (Routledge, 2011). She has also published various book chapters and articles, most recently, 'A Human Rights Appraisal of the Limits to Judicial Independence for International Criminal Justice', in *Leiden Journal of International Law* (2015).

Joseph Besigye Bazirake is a doctoral student at the Institute for Reconciliation and Social Justice, University of the Free State, South Africa. He holds a bachelor's degree in Political Science (International Relations) and a master's degree in Peace and Conflict Studies, both from Makerere University in Uganda. His current research undertakings revolve around social cohesion theories of change in post-apartheid South Africa.

Auriane Botte is a PhD candidate in International Law at the University of Nottingham, UK. She graduated with a degree in Law from the University of Toulouse, France, before continuing her studies in the UK with a master's degree in Conflict Studies at the University of Wolverhampton, UK. She also completed a LL.M (with distinction) in International Criminal Justice and Armed Conflicts at the University of Nottingham. Auriane's research thesis is focused on issues related to ending impunity for core international crimes and looking at a greater integration between International Criminal Justice and the R2P concept. Auriane's research interests broadly cover the fields of International Criminal Justice, International Security Law, United Nations Law and State responsibility.

Paul Bukuluki is an Associate Professor at Makerere University, School of Social Sciences, Uganda. He is also a Guest Professor at the MA Peace Studies Program, University of Innsbruck, Austria. He is a cultural anthropologist with particular interest in peace, recovery and development. He has a master's degree in Peace and Conflict Transformation (University of Innsbruck, Austria) and a PhD in Social and Cultural Anthropology (University of Vienna, Austria). He is specialized in peace and conflict studies, gender, sexual- and gender-based violence research, policy and programming, particularly in conflict and post conflict settings.

Alise Coen received her PhD in Political Science and International Relations from the University of Delaware, USA. She earned her BA in International Relations from the Maxwell School of Citizenship and Public Affairs at Syracuse University, USA. She is currently Assistant Professor of Political Science at the University of Wisconsin-

Sheboygan. Her research focuses on global governance, human rights, religion and politics, and US foreign policy towards the Middle East.

Oscar Gakuo Mwangi is Associate Professor of Political Science at the Department of Political and Administrative Studies, National University of Lesotho, Lesotho. His research interests are in comparative politics, especially in the areas of democratisation and governance, conflict and security, and environmental politics in eastern and southern Africa. His teaching areas are in the fields of comparative politics, international relations and political economy.

David William Gethings is a PhD student in International Conflict Management at Kennesaw State University in Georgia, USA. He received both an MA in Comparative Politics and a Graduate Certificate in Peacebuilding and Human Rights from American University in Washington, DC, USA. His research focuses primarily on political philosophy and human rights and the individual, with a specialization on the Responsibility to Protect. His areas of interest also include political legitimacy, global ethics, the social market economy and the impacts of the digital age.

Sassan Gholiagha is a Researcher at the Chair of Political Science, especially Global Governance in the Department of Social Science, Faculty of Economics and Social Sciences, University of Hamburg, Germany. He works on IR Theory, constructivism, norms research, R2P, the ICC and the use of drones.

Pinar Gözen Ercan is an Assistant Professor and faculty member at the Department of International Relations, Hacettepe University, Ankara, Turkey. Her research engages with responsibility to protect, humanitarian intervention, human rights, international law of the sea and international criminal justice. She is the author of *Debating the Future of 'Responsibility to Protect': The Evolution of a Moral Norm* (forthcoming in 2016) as well as articles and book chapters on the responsibility to protect.

Sonja Grover is Professor in the Lakehead University Faculty of Education and its affiliated Northern Ontario School of Medicine, Canada, and an Associate Editor of *The International Journal of Human Rights*. She has published extensively in the area of international law and human rights law with 10 books and 67 peer-reviewed journal articles in this field, as well as two book chapters, two guest edited special issues of *The International Journal of Human Rights* and numerous conference presentations. She has a special interest in children's fundamental human rights under international law.

Aidan Hehir is a Reader in International Relations at the University of Westminster, UK. He gained his PhD in 2005 and has previously worked at the University of Limerick, Ireland and the University of Sheffield, UK. His research interests include the responsibility to protect, humanitarian intervention and the laws governing the use of force. He is co-convenor of the BISA Working Group on the Responsibility to Protect and is currently working on an ESRC-funded three-year project on 'The Responsibility to Protect and Liberal Norms'. He has published widely, including *Humanitarian Intervention: An Introduction 2nd Edition* (2013) and *International Law, Security and Ethics* (Routledge, 2010 and 2014, co-editor).

Annie Herro is a Lecturer at the Centre for Peace and Conflict Studies, University of Sydney, Australia. She has been researching, teaching and writing about issues relating to peacekeeping and R2P for about seven years. Her work has featured in numerous publications including *Global Change, Peace and Security* and *African Security Review*.

Her first book is entitled *UN Emergency Peace Service and the Responsibility to Protect* (Routledge, 2015).

Lindsey N. Kingston is an Assistant Professor of International Human Rights at Webster University in Saint Louis, USA. She directs the university's Institute for Human Rights and Humanitarian Studies, which includes its undergraduate programme in Human Rights. A topical expert on the issue of statelessness, much of Kingston's work investigates the connections between legal status and the protection of basic human rights. She has conducted fieldwork in locations such as Rwanda, the Canadian Arctic, Eastern Europe and Brazil. She is an editor of *Human Rights Review* and holds a PhD from Syracuse University's Maxwell School of Citizenship and Public Affairs, USA.

Konstantin Kleine is a PhD student at the Graduate Institute of International and Development Studies in Geneva, Switzerland. He has recently graduated from the LL.M programme at the same institute. His research interests include human protection, legal theory and failing states.

Gabriele Lombardo is a PhD student in international order and human rights at the Department of Political Science, University of Rome 'Sapienza', Italy.

Marco Longobardo is a PhD candidate, curriculum of International Law and EU Law, School of Law, University of Rome 'Sapienza', Italy. He is also a teaching assistant at the School of Law of the University of Messina, Italy. From January to June 2015 he was Visiting PhD Fellow at Middlesex University of London, UK.

Conall Mallory is a Lecturer in Law at Northumbria University, UK. He teaches International Law and the Law of the European Union. His recent doctoral dissertation concerned the impact of litigation arising from the Iraq War (2003) on the extra-territorial application of the European Convention on Human Rights. Prior to commencing his PhD he undertook an LL.M in Human Rights Law at Queen's University Belfast, Northern Ireland. He has also interned at Amnesty International.

Hovhannes Nikoghosyan has a PhD in Political Science and is Adjunct Lecturer at the American University of Armenia. Dr Nikoghosyan specializes in human rights and international security, having a keen interest and research experience in human rights and armed conflicts, the United Nations, state sovereignty and intervention, just war theory, international criminal responsibility for *erga omnes* crimes, as well as Responsibility to Protect. He publishes on conflicts and human rights, and is a co-author of the 'Global Problems for Global Governance' report, published by the Valdai Discussion Club in September 2014.

Maggie Powers is a project coordinator at the Columbia University Global Policy Initiative, USA. She focuses on issues of migration, mobility and mass atrocities prevention and serves as the lead coordinator for the initiative's joint project on international migration with the Office of the UN Special Representative of the Secretary-General for International Migration and Development. She is a graduate of Columbia University, USA, with a Master of Arts in Human Rights Studies where she specialized in the normative evolution of the responsibility to protect. She holds a Bachelor of Arts in International Relations and Political Science from Loyola University Chicago, USA.

Heidarali Teimouri is an International Law PhD candidate, School of Law, University of Leeds, UK. His thesis subject is: Responsibility to Protect and International Intervention in Libya in 2011.

Serena Timmoneri is a PhD candidate at the Faculty of Political Sciences, University of Catania, Italy, researching on Responsibility to Protect. She graduated in Political Sciences at the University of Messina in 2009. She also holds a master's degree in Global Politics and Euro-Mediterranean Relations from the University of Catania in 2012 with a thesis on the UN Resolution 'Combating Defamation of Religions'.

Stuart Wallace is a Post-Doctoral Research Fellow at the University of Nottingham, UK. He recently graduated from the University of Nottingham with a PhD in Law. His doctoral dissertation was on the application of the European Convention on Human Rights to Military Operations. He has firsthand experience of working at both the European Court of Human Rights and the International Criminal Court and has taught European Convention on Human Rights Law and European Union Law at the University of Nottingham for a number of years. He also serves as Book Review Editor for the *Human Rights Law Review*.

Introduction

Sonja Grover

Faculty of Education, Lakehead University, Thunder Bay, Ontario. Canada

This special issue of the *International Journal of Human Rights* titled 'R2P: Perspectives on the Concept's Meaning, Proper Application and Value' includes articles that present a wide range of views on various controversial aspects relating to the contested notion of the responsibility to protect (R2P) and its implementation. These aspects include, for instance, the use of force or threat of force by the international community under the R2P rationale, with or without UN Security Council authorisation and/or United Nations General Assembly endorsement, in response to mass atrocity where a state is unable and/or unwilling to address mass atrocity crimes within its own territory or under its territorial jurisdiction. Further, the scope of R2P is considered in various articles in terms of, for instance, its application during peacetime to address mass atrocity crimes; viability when implemented in a failed state; relevance to inter-state conflicts and not just intra-state conflict, potential for application to man-made or natural environmental disasters where the state is unable or unwilling to address the consequent human suffering, arguably committing crimes against humanity in the process, and R2P's application to the global refugee crisis, much of it involving persons fleeing mass atrocity situations. The role of the International Criminal Court (ICC) in reinforcing and clarifying R2P is considered as is the potential utility of a United Nations Emergency Peace Service regarding the prevention R2P obligation of the international community. Also included are articles presenting empirical studies on the emergence of R2P as a contested norm and its varied interpretations in United Nations Security Council (UNSC) and United Nations Human Rights Council discussions. In addition, the often insubstantial legal basis for much of the rhetoric and semantics of R2P is addressed as is the viability of the R2P principle in an age where cosmopolitan civic engagement is more feasible than ever before. More specifically:

Jessica Almqvist examines in an international law context the actual and potential use by states and regional organisations of various coercive measures in implementing R2P where the UNSC has failed to act to prevent or end particular mass atrocities.

Joseph Besigye Bazirake and Paul Bukuluki discuss the roots and evolution of the contested R2P notion, offer an assessment of the viability of R2P and consider particular issues regarding R2P's application in the African context.

Auriane Botte examines the implications of framing R2P as a response to grave, legally defined international crimes *per se* rather than as a response to large-scale threats to life and to international peace and security not characterised in legal terms but rather in political and moral terms open to dispute.

Alise Coen considers R2P in the broader context of various collective efforts to address transnational problems with a particular emphasis on R2P as a framework in addressing the current global refugee crisis created by mass atrocity crimes.

David William Gethings explores perspectives on R2P and democracy in the context of the digital age that fosters 'cosmopolitan civic engagement' – the latter being participation that acknowledges and is directed to meeting citizen responsibilities that extend beyond national borders.

Sassan Gholiagha analyses R2P discourse in the UNSC discussions on Libya and Syria between 2011 and early 2015 as a pathway to understanding the inconsistent application of R2P and the potential for a more robust application of R2P in future.

Pinar Gözen Ercan considers the applicability of R2P to the Gaza situation, various characterisations of the legal status of Gaza and the broader question of whether R2P applies also to inter-state and not just intra-state conflict.

Sonja Grover discusses the semantics of R2P and, with reference to treaty interpretation and R2P-relevant documents' textual analysis, advances the proposition that even when not authorised by the UNSC, the use of force to prevent or end R2P international crimes where all other options have failed does *not* constitute the state act of aggression.

Aidan Hehir examines the international community's response to the situation in Bahrain as a vehicle to explore the contemporary efficacy of R2P and, in the process, challenge the notion that R2P has become a 'lens' through which intra-state humanitarian crises are viewed.

Annie Herro considers the potential utility of a standing UN force or service (United Nations Emergency Peace Service) authorised either by the UNSC or the United Nations General Assembly for short-term deployment directed to R2P's implementation in the prevention of mass atrocity.

Lindsey Kingston considers R2P's scope of application and examines its potential to address institutionalised violence using the plight of the Rohingya in Burma, referred to by the United Nations as 'the world's most persecuted minority', as a case example.

Konstantin Kleine examines the history and scope of the R2P notion and considers the viability of rationales for its application to both man-made and natural environmental disasters.

Gabriele Lombardo considers the malleability of R2P in its current interpretation and application using the Syrian and Libyan situations as case studies.

Marco Longobardo considers various International Court of Justice decisions and the viability of R2P in the context of *erga omnes* and *erga omnes partes* considerations and obligations.

Connall Mallory and Stuart Wallace examine, in the context of European Court of Human Rights jurisprudence, counter-arguments to states' human rights liability concerns allegedly acting as a deterrent to their involvement in United Nations-sponsored R2P coalitions that involve the use of military force.

Oscar Mwangi examines, using Somalia as a case study, the challenges of effective beneficent R2P implementation in the circumstances associated with a collapsed state.

Hovhannes Nikoghosyan considers the international law basis for reaching consensus on whether and when Pillar Three R2P mechanisms should be and can be legitimately implemented in particular state situations as well as the role of the ICC in supporting the international community meeting its Pillar Three R2P obligations.

Maggie Powers provides an empirical study examining UNSC and United Nations Human Rights Council documents referencing R2P and tracks R2P rhetoric and acceptance of the R2P principle as a norm, also post the Libyan intervention.

Heidarali Teimouri uses interactional law theory to consider the inconsistent application of R2P in respect of various mass atrocity situations and suggests that there is at present no shared understanding among states of R2P and its implications.

Serena Timmoneri examines R2P's applicability to peacetime atrocities using North Korea as a case study.

Whether one considers R2P novel in all or only certain respects or but the re-packaging of well-established legal precepts ('old wine in a new bottle' as Stephen Marks and Nicholas Cooper suggest; the old wine being 'just war' and/or 'humanitarian intervention'), it appears that as long as hope lives for an end to human suffering, or at least a humane response to it, so will R2P as a notion. It remains to be seen, however, whether future experience with application of the R2P principle will serve to sustain the hope for sovereignty as responsibility most often realised and for a consistent effective international response to impending or actual mass atrocities wherever and whenever the international community is the only avenue remaining to potentially remedy the situation.

Enforcing the responsibility to protect through solidarity measures[†]

Jessica Almqvist

International Relations, Faculty of Law, Autonomous University of Madrid, Madrid, Spain

Responsibility to Protect (R2P) provides a moral basis for collective action through the UN Security Council in reaction to mass atrocity situations. However, this avenue is not always available. The question then arises whether other actors can and should assume responsibility in such circumstances and, if so, which kinds of measures they may pursue. The present article examines this question with a specific interest in the international reactions to the Syrian crisis since 2011. The analysis proceeds on the assumption that the growing usage of solidarity measures outside the UN framework is a sign of the relative success of R2P in terms of gaining ground among international policy-makers. However, according to the article, if solidarity measures as a way of enforcing R2P are to achieve widespread legitimacy, consideration must be paid to the legal concerns generated by this development. In particular, regard must be had to the compatibility of the measures pursued, including asset freeze, arms embargoes and the arming of rebel forces with the law in force.

1. Introduction

Responsibility to Protect (R2P) provides a moral basis for collective action through the UN Security Council in reaction to ongoing mass atrocity situations. However, this avenue is not always available.[1] The question then arises whether other actors can and should assume responsibility in such circumstances and, if so, which kinds of measures they may pursue. The issue ushers to the forefront in the context of the Syrian crisis since 2011. As the international reactions to this crisis reveal, states and regional organizations do not view the manifest failure of the Security Council to provide a timely and decisive response as impeding them from acting on their own in an effort to end continued atrocities. Rather, what is observed is a growing usage of so-called solidarity measures.

The present study will take stock of this development and assess its legal implications. The analysis proceeds on the assumption that the growing usage of measures outside the

---

[†]Previous versions of this article have been presented in the ISA Human Rights Conference in Istanbul (14-16 June 2014) and in a Lunch Seminar organized by the *Centre Charles de Visscher pour le droit international et europeén*, Catholic University of Louvain (21 October 2014). The author thanks the participants in these events, especially Pierre d'Argent and Melissa Labonte, for helpful comments. The remaining errors are the responsibility of the author.

UN framework is a sign of the relative success of R2P in terms of gaining ground among international policy-makers. However, if solidarity measures as a way of enforcing R2P are to achieve widespread legitimacy, consideration must be paid to the legal concerns generated by this development. Regard must be had to the compatibility of the measures pursued, above all, asset freezing and arms embargoes, but also the arming of rebel forces with the law in force.

2. Collective action through the UN Security Council

The main objective of R2P is to protect civilian populations from atrocity crimes. In this light, its advocates forcefully reject the idea of international passivity as a legitimate stance when faced with ongoing atrocities. However, whereas the core of R2P has remained constant since the time of its original formulation in 2001, its purported scope related to the concrete forms of international engagement have evolved and been revised. In its seminal report on R2P, the Canadian International Commission on Intervention and State Sovereignty famously contemplated the promotion of coercive engagement, also unilateral action, if and when necessary.[2] The Commission opined that 'if the Security Council expressly rejects a proposal for intervention where humanitarian or human rights issues are significantly at stake, or the Council fails to deal with such a proposal within a reasonable time, it is difficult to argue that alternative means of discharging the R2P can be entirely discounted'.[3] Furthermore, if this organ 'fails to discharge its responsibility in conscience-shocking situations crying out for action, then it is unrealistic to expect that concerned states will rule out other means and forms of action to meet the gravity and urgency of these situations'.[4]

This radical claim was thereafter tempered in the process of transforming the concept into a set of concrete proposals that could muster a general support from UN members. Achieving that objective required the reaffirmation of the compatibility between R2P and international law, including the UN Charter. Recognizing the R2P populations from genocide, war crimes, ethnic cleansing, and crimes against humanity, the World Summit held in 2005 proclaimed that the UN is prepared to 'take collective action, through the Security Council, in accordance with the Charter, including Chapter VII … should peaceful means be inadequate and national authorities manifestly fail to protect their populations'. Specifically, the Summit delegates insisted that any military action must be consistent with the prohibition on the use of force (article 2.4), with the understanding that the right to self-defence is the only exception to that prohibition (article 51), and the requirement that the Security Council must authorize all other uses of force (article 42). At the same time, the Summit participants agreed on the need to expand the notion of international security threat (article 39) to cover massive human rights violations in internal conflicts.[5]

This UN agreement endorsed abandoning what in 2001 had been one of the leading ideas: the necessity of unilateral measures, including the use of force, when the Council is unable to act, in favour of a next to exclusive focus on collective action within the UN framework. The fact that the Bush administration had appealed to the concept in 2003 in an effort to convince other Security Council members about the need to intervene in Iraq had become a warning, according to some, of how easily the new concept could become a cloak for armed interventions in general. The duty to respect international law was reinforced.

Since the 2005 World Summit, the UN has attempted to overcome the problem of ambiguity, which was highlighted following the UN consensus in 2005.[6] The concept is now understood as resting on three pillars, i.e. prevention, reconstruction and reaction.[7]

The Secretary-General has reaffirmed that armed force is not ruled out, but that any use of such force, including the deployment of UN-sanctioned multinational forces for establishing security zones, the imposition of no-fly zones, and the establishment of a military presence on land and at sea protection or deterrence purposes are measures to be determined by the Security Council.[8] One example is Council resolution 1973 (2011), which authorized UN members 'to take all necessary measures' in Libya for the purpose of protecting civilians and civilian populated areas under threat of attack.[9] Moreover, though collective action remains central in the implementation process, the responsibility to provide a timely and decisive response in a rapidly unfolding emergency situation is not limited to the Security Council. Not only the UN but also regional, sub-regional, and national decision-makers must focus on saving lives through timely and decisive action.[10]

The effort to translate the somewhat lofty moral ideals associated with R2P into concrete measures has provoked disagreement. In the General Assembly interactive informal dialogue conducted in 2012, delegations stressed the risk of abuse of the use of force, even if authorized by the Council. As India pointed out, NATO's broader objective to induce regime change in Libya had generated considerable unease among UN members.[11] The UK, on the other hand, insisted that the NATO-led intervention in Libya was 'legally and morally right'.[12] Russia pointed to the prevalence of differing opinions, arguing that 'the question remains open of whether the proposed strategy for applying R2P actually enjoys widespread recognition among states'.[13] Several states reaffirmed the importance of the Brazilian claim that the Council must guarantee that its decisions, including the authorization of force, is implemented in a responsible way.[14] Others highlighted the significance of *soft* or non-coercive forms of engagement, such as negotiation, mediation, and good offices, given a growing hesitation towards, even resistance against, armed force, following the Libyan experience.[15] Discussed more positively was the role of regional and sub-regional arrangements as well the significance of the International Criminal Court and economic sanctions.[16]

3. The challenge of the UN Security Council paralysis

The Security Council has responded quite enthusiastically to the new expectations derived from R2P and appealed to the concept in several resolutions. It did so for the first time in January 2006 when reacting to the developments in the Democratic Republic of Congo and Burundi and then again in April the same year when condemning the targeting of civilians in armed conflicts.[17] Shortly thereafter it appealed to R2P when authorizing the deployment of peacekeeping forces in Darfur.[18] The majority of subsequent R2P resolutions concern Libya, although the concept has also been cited in resolutions related to Mali, Yemen, Central African Republic, and South Sudan.[19] In 2014 it adopted at least seven R2P resolutions, recently when denouncing the terrorist acts perpetrated by the Islamic State in Iraq and the Levant.[20]

Nonetheless, a problem resurfaces when morally flavoured arguments promoting Security Council action fail to convince a sufficient number of its members (nine out of 15) or when the permanent members decide to use their veto power (article 27 UN Charter). Some objections to Council-governed responses raise matters of principle, such as those based on convictions, even if on the wane, that respect for state sovereignty is a moral or legal absolute. Others may stem from difficulties of obtaining evidence concerning the gravity of a given situation. A somewhat different problem, which is also related to evidentiary difficulties, is uncertainty about who is mainly responsible for the abuses against civilians – the government or opposition forces and/or other non-actors, such as terrorist groups.

There is a third possibility insofar as the character of the disagreements in the Council are concerned. The most protracted ones are due to the prevalence of strategic interests among permanent members to shield targeted states from becoming the object of military and other coercive measures. Evidently, the strategic interests are unrelated to, or in direct tension with, moral considerations, such as is the case with, for example, an interest in maintaining a friendship with political leaders of governments attacking their own populations. Even if not challenging R2P on moral grounds, these objections to Council action are especially difficult to overcome in practice. Indeed, the P-5 can block any decision, also those incompatible with their strategic interests. In this light, R2P has a moralizing function in Council debates preceding decisions but only up to a certain point: when confronted with competing strategic interests its precepts may have little, if any, impact at all.

When an argumentative strategy based on R2P fails to produce an authorization it might be difficult for those whose moral conscience is great (or said to be so) to accept paralysis. Instead, those who are committed to R2P and posses military power may decide to act on their own, including resorting to the use of force, even if this alternative was expressly discarded in the 2005 consensus. To illustrate, at the beginning of September 2013, a unilateral military intervention into Syria seemed imminent. The absence of a Council authorization was seen as a stumbling block but not impossible to circumvent in practice; a more troubling fact was the widespread popular opposition in the US and the EU. Even so, the US began to build a case in favour of military action and found an important ally in the French government. In the end, the fact that the Syrian government had used chemical weapons together with the work of Russian diplomacy led to the passing of resolution 1288 (2013).[21] In it, the Security Council upholds the 'sovereignty, independence and territorial integrity of the Syrian Arab Republic', and calls for diplomatic peace negotiations and the elimination of the chemical weapons stockpiles held by the Syrian regime.[22] Acting on the basis of Chapter VII and threatening Syria with coercive measures in case of non-compliance, resolution 1288 can hardly be said to represent a 'timely and decisive response' to ongoing atrocities.[23]

Security Council paralysis can be described as a situation in which an established decision procedure fails to produce what in the view of states committed to R2P is an acceptable outcome. Since non-authorization of forcible measures prevents these states from performing what in some cases may be a moral duty, it might be incorrect to understand unilateral and regional coercive forms of engagement in defiance of Council approval as simple law-breaking. To be sure, R2P reflects some of the central ideas behind the moral concept known as the natural duty of mutual aid.[24] It postulates that everyone has a duty to help another when that person is in need or jeopardy. What is special about natural duties is that they have 'no necessary connection with institutions or social practices'. This means, firstly, that the duties are applicable regardless of whether we have made a promise to come to another's aid and, secondly, that the duties hold between persons irrespective of being fellow citizens or foreigners.[25] From this standpoint, there may be legitimate reasons for taking forcible action even if the Council is blocked and in spite of such action in the view of some states amounting to noncompliance with international law.

Those who made it impossible to pass a Council resolution authorizing the use of force have, according to some states, the law 'on their side', even in mass atrocity situations. On the other hand, those who act on duties might find their obligations to respect international law as less important compared with the moral and political consequences of accepting a policy involving not seeking to rescue people who are under attack by their own government and/or other armed actors. Against this background, it is understandable that the argument that all states must respect international law because 'it is the law' strikes as an unsatisfactory response. However, other non-legal considerations for inaction must be considered. One is found in moral discussions on the limits to natural duties.[26] Their application is restricted to situations in which help can be offered without excessive risks or losses.[27] A negative decision could thus legitimately be based on a consideration of the excessive risks of the loss of lives and be reflective of what in truth is a moral and political dilemma. This difficulty is partly acknowledged in a UN report published in 2012. In it, Ban Ki-moon notes that the International Commission of Inquiry on Libya found that NATO had 'conducted a highly precise campaign with a demonstrable determination to avoid civilian casualties' in Libya.[28] Nevertheless, 'notwithstanding these efforts, civilian lives were lost during the air campaign'.[29]

4. Enforcing R2P through solidarity measures

Given the possibility of Security Council paralysis, the question arises whether other actors have responsibilities to enforce R2P in ongoing situations and, if so, by which means?

So-called targeted or smart sanctions, which serve to restrict the availability of resources for persons and entities responsible for ongoing atrocities, are gaining in popularity among states and regional organizations.[30] Such sanctions, including the 'restrictions on arms, police equipment, mercenaries, finances, and travel, are often seen as attractive alternatives to more forceful measures'.[31] These measures are the preferred response by the Security Council to new threats to international security.[32] The approach of the Al Qaida Sanctions Committee, established in 1999, has been followed by several others with a mandate to target people and entities involved in atrocities in internal conflicts, among them, Sudan, Democratic Republic of Congo, Côte d'Ivoire, Libya, Central African Republic and Yemen. The restrictive measures include asset freeze and arms embargoes as well as travel bans.[33]

These measures are also significant outside the UN framework. Both regional organizations and states have resorted to them in reaction to the Syrian crisis. To illustrate, the US[34] and Turkey[35] have imposed sanctions against this country, including nationals (persons and entities), to curb ongoing atrocities. In May 2011, the EU adopted sanctions 'against Syria and against persons responsible for the violent repression against the civilian population in Syria'.[36] Specifically, it imposed travel bans and asset freezes on 13 people. When al-Assad did not accept the EU call for peaceful negotiations, it added 10 people to the list, including the President himself and his family.[37] A few months later, more individuals and entities were listed.[38] As of 6 March 2015, the list includes 218 individuals and 69 entities, including the Syrian Central Bank.[39] In addition to maintaining the travel bans and asset freeze, the EU bans the import of crude oil,[40] and has suspended new investments of the European Investment Bank,[41] as well as gold and minted coin imports. Likewise, it has imposed a ban on luxury goods and on technology, which could be used for internal repression. Early on in the rapidly unfolding emergency situation, the Arab League also imposed asset freeze and travel bans for Syrian officials and VIPs preventing them from travelling to Arab states. It has also adopted arms embargo, banned flights by Arab airlines to Syria, and suspended all dealings with Syrian Central bank and the state-owned Commercial Bank of Syria.[42]

Arms embargo is a type of sanction that can serve to coerce both states and non-state actors to change their behaviour by restricting the resources needed to inflict violence on civilian populations.[43] Throughout the cold war, the UN imposed mandatory embargoes in reaction to different international security threats. Nowadays arms embargoes may be levied independently by regional organizations and states. The UN Secretary General urges third states to deny the means to commit atrocity crimes through cooperation aimed at stemming the flow of arms and light weapons.[44] However, regional and national embargoes may be incomplete. During 2012, the EU, the Arab League, Turkey, and the US maintained arms embargoes in Syria. Meanwhile, Russia and Iran continued to supply weapons to the al-Assad government.[45] In 2013 the situation changed, as the Arab League decided to allow its members to arm the moderate opposition (Syrian Free Army).[46] Also France and the UK wanted to meet the requests from the opposition for military aid in the face of the successive victories of the Syrian government. Their change of stance led to a partial lifting of the EU arms embargo.[47] As of 31 May 2013 until 1 June 2016, the arms embargo is restricted to arms, materials and equipment that might be used for internal repression,[48] and manifests a clearer support to the rebel forces.[49] States that provide weapons to the opposition include Turkey and the US. The provision of weapons was stressed as a problem in the UN dialogue on R2P conducted in 2012. According to the South African delegation, the arming of rebels in Syria is a disturbing trend and a 'complicated response by the international community to the responsibility to protect'.[50]

International involvement in the Syrian crisis intensified during the fall of 2014 as a result of the initiation of airstrikes against the terrorist organization ISIL and other extremist groups associated with Al Qaeda in Iraq and Syria.[51] Also the Arab League vowed to take all necessary measures against the organization and to cooperate.[52] On 23 September, a US-led coalition of states (Bahrain, Jordan, Qatar, Saudi Arabia, and the United Arab Emirate) began airstrikes in Syria. On 26 September, the UK House of Commons voted overwhelmingly in favour of airstrikes in Iraq with the possibility of extending their military engagement to Syria. So far, some Western allies (Australia, and the UK) are not participating in the airstrikes in Syria.[53] However, Canada and Turkey have joined the coalition. In his State of the Union address on 20 January 2015, US President Barack Obama urged Congress to authorize the use of force against ISIL, in part because of the lack of an explicit legal authorization of airstrikes in Syria, in part to establish a political consensus on the scope of the US mission. Additionally, the US has sent troops to train Syrian rebel forces. Turkey, Qatar and Saudi Arabia host this training that commenced during spring 2015.[54]

As of now, the airstrikes in Syria continue amid the reiteration of concerns about their effectiveness. Commentators warn that in practice the ISIL and the Free Syrian Army are nearly indistinguishable from each other.[55] Others stress that the US policy strategy of conducting airstrikes is 'emboldening Damascus and undermining the very rebels it is ostensibly designed to support'.[56] Instead of being weakened, ISIS might instead be gaining strength.[57] According to UN Special Envoy for Syria Staffan de Mistura: 'There is a feeling that no one can win this war. ... The only ones who are losing this war totally at the moment are the Syrian people'.[58]

5. Legal implications of decentralized enforcement

From a legal perspective, the growing importance of regional organizations and states, including the nature and number of the measures is a positive and problematic development. On the one hand, it strengthens the claim about the existence of a legal duty of solidarity. The same development also contributes to the consolidation of post-cold war law on sanctions. At the same time, considering that some of the measures have generated concerns about their lawfulness, the decentralization of R2P actions might end up constituting a challenge to international law and thus as undermining the UN agreement reached in 2005.

5.1 *Strengthening the law on solidarity measures*

A legal inquiry into the role of third actors in relation to atrocities in foreign states generates differing positions. While some jurists view the legal order as a 'self-help' system inclined to promote a general stance of passivity, others insist on the existence of a legal duty of solidarity that requires third states to engage.[59] Consistent with the latter position is the rule pronounced in the ILC draft Articles on State Responsibility of 2001 according to which all states are obliged not to recognize or to assist in grave breaches of peremptory norms, if continuing, and must cooperate in bringing them to an end.[60] In a similar vein, the International Court of Justice (ICJ) has affirmed that in situations of grave violations of human rights and humanitarian law, not only the responsible state, but also third states and international organizations 'are under an obligation not to recognize the illegal situation … not to render aid or assistance in maintaining that situation and to cooperate with a view to putting an end to the alleged violations and to ensuring that reparation will be made therefore'.[61]

Insofar as R2P and the subsequent UN dialogue foster international engagement, including a role for these actors, recent developments add moral weight to solidarity-based interpretations that affirm the existence of positive duties of third actors.[62] Furthermore, the specific meanings of these duties, especially the duty of cooperation, remain somewhat unsettled.[63] In general, it is unclear what counts as 'lawful means' of reacting to ongoing atrocities.[64] Against this background, the international responses to the Syrian crisis can be seen as contributing to a more solid legal understanding of 'cooperation' and 'lawful means'.

5.2 *Consolidating the post-cold war law on sanctions*

The UN Charter contemplates sanctions as coercive measures that may be adopted by the Security Council in reaction to international security threats (article 41). Can sanctions be adopted by states and regional organizations? Whether such measures are 'enforcement actions' according to article 53 and, therefore require Security Council approval prior to their adoption by regional organizations became an issue in 1960. The Organization of American States-imposed sanctions on the Dominican Republic that year led the Security Council to pass a resolution authorizing them.[65] Following the end of the cold war, the regional and unilateral imposition of sanctions has become more frequent. To illustrate, on 27 July 1990, the US imposed sanctions on Iraq.[66] Following the Iraqi invasion into Kuwait on 2 August, the Security Council passed resolution 661 of 6 August 1990, demanding the general imposition of sanctions.[67] On 8 October 1991, the OAS imposed a trade embargo against Haiti and a freeze of government bank accounts. On 16 June 1993, the Security Council passed resolution 841 that imposed oil and arms embargoes, as well as a freeze on the assets of the Haitian regime. In July 1991, the EU (at the time, EC) imposed an arms embargo on the former Socialist Federal Republic of Yugoslavia (Bosnia and Herzegovina). The Security Council followed suit when passing resolution 713, which imposes a general arms embargo.[68] Thereafter, it adopted resolution 757 (1992), which imposes broad trade, finance and political sanctions against Serbia and Montenegro.

Since the end of the cold war, economic sanctions may no longer be seen as 'enforcement actions',[69] and as falling into the same legal category as armed force.[70] Economic sanctions regimes are increasingly established even though there is no prospect of these measures being authorized by the Security Council. Gaining legitimacy instead is the interpretation that non-military measures, which in any case would be permitted under general international law, do not require UN authorization. According to the *Institut de Droit International*, the weight of opinion upholds the right of third states to adopt counter-measures in response to violations of *erga omnes* obligations with a *jus cogens* character. As it proclaims, 'states, acting individually or collectively, are entitled to take diplomatic, economic and other measures' towards any other State which has violated such obligations 'provided such measures are permitted under international law and do not involve the use of armed force in violation of the Charter'.[71]

Nevertheless, the absence of Security Council authorization makes these measures eligible to relabeling in the legal context. These are in essence countermeasures.[72] Unlike UN authorized sanctions which are lawful per se, such measures are inherently unlawful and only justifiable in view of the alleged initial failing to which they are a response. Their eventual legality depends on whether the conditions imposed on the taking of such measures are met in each case. Articles 49 and 50 ILC draft Articles (2001) establish that their lawfulness depends on the specific purpose pursued, which must be to induce compliance, temporal limits, their effectiveness, and respect for the prohibition against the use of force, fundamental human rights obligations, obligations of a humanitarian character prohibiting reprisals as well as other obligations under peremptory norms. Additionally, the measures must be 'commensurate with the injury suffered, taking into account the gravity of the internationally wrongful acts and the rights in question' (article 51). These demanding requirements can be difficult to meet in each case and may give rise to disagreements about the legality of these measures.

Even so, sanctions are attractive since they are politically cheap for those adopting them. They are also convenient for regional organizations, such as the EU, whose international reputation is negatively affected by its relatively weak competences to take external action. Nevertheless, concerns are raised about their conformity with human rights obligations. Considering that targeted sanctions are implemented against individuals without any prior notification, affect their property rights and are typically adopted on grounds not knowable to the affected individuals, the European Court of Justice (ECJ) has annulled several EU decisions regarding asset freeze.[73] So far, some 30 individuals and entities have lodged applications before the ECJ against the EU-imposed restrictive measures in Syria. While some have been dismissed or removed from the docket, others have led to judgments. So far, the General Court has annulled EU Council listing decisions in three cases.[74] The court's view is that the listing decisions are manifestly unfounded due the Council's refusal to provide information about the factual grounds motivating their decisions.[75]

The sanctions regimes create additional dilemmas. One hurdle is timing since it may take several months before sanctions have any effect. Another problem, at least with respect to sectorial sanctions, is the potential collateral damage to the economies of neighbouring countries and trading partners.[76] A third difficulty relates to the ineffectiveness of sanctions in relation to actors who are determined to commit atrocity crimes. However, so far, none of these concerns have led to a reconsideration of the utility of sanctions.

5.3   *The turn to arms as a challenge to international law*

From a legal standpoint, the provision of weapons to rebel or opposition forces is understood as contrary to the principle of non-intervention, at least as defined during the decolonization process. In 1970, the General Assembly condemned intervention as constituting a threat against the personality of the state and its political, economic and cultural elements. Specifically, 'no State has the right to intervene, directly or indirectly, for any reason whatever in the internal or external affairs of any other state', which means that 'no State shall organize, assist, foment, finance, incite or tolerate subversive, terrorist or armed terrorist activities directed towards the violent overthrow of another State, or interfere in civil strife in another State'.[77] In the *Nicaragua* case,[78] the ICJ affirmed that the 'element of coercion, which defines, and indeed forms the very essence of, prohibited intervention, is particularly obvious in the case of an intervention which uses force, either in the direct form of military action, or in the indirect form of support for subversive or terrorist armed activities within another State ... [79] In a more recent case before the ICJ, *Democratic Republic of Congo v. Uganda*, the question resurfaced. The court reaffirmed that international law (continues to) prohibit a State from intervening, directly or indirectly, with or without armed force, in support of the internal opposition in another state.[80]

In the *Nicaragua* case, the court considered whether there might be any *exception* to the established prohibition, i.e. a 'practice illustrative of belief in a kind of general right for States to intervene, directly or indirectly', depending on an understanding that the cause, i.e. political and moral values behind such intervention appears particularly worthy.[81] While the court did not find in this case that the US had sought to justify its intervention as based on an exception,[82] it seemed to leave the door open for the possibility that the interpretation of the customary law principle of non-intervention may evolve and no longer be absolute. Whether the protection of civilian populations against atrocity crimes may constitute such an exception is still too soon to tell. Speaking against this possibility is the fact that, according to a recent survey, at least 22 states (e.g. Saudi Arabia, Syria, the Benelux countries, the Nordic countries, and Spain) have adopted a strong policy against any transfer of weapons or ammunition to Syria.[83] Neither has there been any serious attempt by states committed to arm rebels to justify their policies with reference to R2P goals.

As for the airstrikes against ISIS the first thing to note is that it is uncertain whether the adoption of these measures in the Syrian crisis is at all motivated by a commitment to R2P. Indeed, the states composing the US-led coalition understand the airstrikes in Syria as an exercise of the right to collective self-defence. The trouble is that whereas Iraq has clearly given its consent, the position of Syria is ambiguous.[84] In a Security Council meeting on the situation in Iraq held in September 2014, the representative of the Syrian government reaffirmed that 'any international counter-terrorism effort must be based on full respect for the Charter and the provisions and principles of international law, in particular those upholding the sovereignty of States. Accordingly, there is a need to coordinate upstream with the Syrian Government in the framework of any credible efforts to combat terrorism'.[85] In the same meeting, Russia warned that 'the publicly expressed intentions to strike ISIL's position on Syrian territory without the cooperation of the Government in Damascus are extremely disturbing', amounting to a gross violation of the fundamental norms of international law'.[86] The critical question turns on whether the airstrikes in Syria constitute a lawful exercise of self-defence of Iraq. In relation to this point, legal experts hold that the airstrikes in Syria may still be legal if interpreted as an effort to counter imminent trans-border attacks on Iraq.[87]

In a resolution passed in August 2014, the Security Council affirms that the Islamic State of Iraq and the Levant as well as Al Nusrash Front pose a serious threat to civilian populations in both Syria and Iraq and in this sense acknowledges the existence of a R2P.[88] More specifically, it highlights the devastating humanitarian impact of their presence on the civilian populations, and condemns 'in the strongest terms the terrorist acts of ISIL and its violent extremist ideology, and its continued, gross, systematic and widespread abuses of human rights and violations of international humanitarian law'.[89] With this aim in mind, it calls on 'all States to take all measures as may be necessary and appropriate and in accordance with their obligations under international law to counter incitement of terrorist acts motivated by extremism and intolerance perpetrated by individuals or entities associated with ISIL, ANF and Al-Qaida ... '.[90] However, the resolution is not explicit with respect to the possibility of using armed force. Following the adoption of resolution 1270, Russia affirmed that though it had been adopted under Chapter VII of the UN Charter, 'it cannot be seen as an approval of the use of military action'.[91] No other Council member made statements related to this matter. Insofar as the concrete measures mandated by the resolution were discussed, the focus was on targeted sanctions and the inclusion of six new names on the listing of the Al Qaeda Sanctions Committee.

The airstrikes against ISIS demonstrate the complexity of enforcing R2P goals in relation to a single armed group in a situation involving mass atrocities that are perpetrated by more than one of the parties to conflict, not least the government. What is especially problematic about the military actions in Syria is that they end up favouring President al-Assad. On 8 October 2014, the Syrian government was reported as returning 'with new intensity to its longstanding and systematic attacks on rebellious towns and neighbourhoods'.[92] After four years of conflict, which has killed more than 191,000 people, including well over 10,000 children, the international community remains passive in the face of the continued atrocities perpetrated by the Syrian government. In 2014, the Security Council condemned all parties to the conflict, also stressing the role of Syrian authorities, in the denial of humanitarian access to civilian populations in the country.[93] However, so far, none of these decisions have been accompanied with further initiatives to use armed force in order to compel compliance with their terms and conditions.

6. Conclusion

As has been argued in this article, a manifest failure of the Security Council to provide a timely and decisive response to continuing atrocities does not impede states and regional organizations from acting on their own in an effort to bring them to an end. The responses to the Syrian crisis indicate that a commitment to R2P is interpreted as generating rights and duties to adopt solidarity measures. However, as has also been suggested, international law continues to impose limits to expressions of solidarity with the victims of atrocity crimes and measures geared towards protecting them. By now, the unilateral and regional imposition of sanctions, including arms embargoes, is widely accepted. Also asset freeze is becoming ever more popular in spite of its tension with respect for human rights. By contrast, the provision of arms to rebel forces and the conduct of airstrikes against terrorist organizations (if at all an R2P measure), have provoked negative reactions and disagreements. The main concern is the inconsistency of the provision of arms to rebels and the conduct of airstrikes without consent of affected states with established prohibitions against the use of force and intervention in international law.

That being said, it might be too soon to tell what will be the actual impact of the nature of the responses to the Syrian crisis on R2P and the UN agreement on the need to enforce R2P while keeping with the current law. The power of the R2P rhetoric together with the gravity of the Syrian crisis could ultimately lead to the stretching of legal boundaries of what counts as lawful means in reaction to ongoing atrocities. Possibly, the unilateral or regional usage of the full range of forcible measures in reaction to continuing atrocities may eventually become 'rooted in and partially justified by contemporary trends of the international community'.[94]

Notes

1. See Gareth Evans, 'The French Veto Restraint Proposal: Making it Work', presented at the international colloquium on 'Regulating the use of the veto at the UN Security Council in cases of mass atrocities', organized by the Paris School of International Affairs of SciencesPo and the Ministry of Foreign Affairs of France, 21 January 2015, available at: http://www.globalr2p. org/media/files/vetorestraintparis21jan25i15rev.pdf.
2. *The Responsibility to Protect. Report by the International Commission on Intervention and State Sovereignty* (December 2001).
3. Ibid. para. 6.28.
4. Ibid. para. 6.39.
5. *2005 World Summit Outcome*, A/RES/60/1, 16 September 2005, para. 139. Also see *A More Secure World: Our Shared Responsibility. Report of the Secretary-General's High-Level Panel on Threats, Challenges and Change*, A/59/565, 2 December 2004; and *In Larger Freedom: Towards Development, Security and Human Rights for All. Report of the Secretary-General*, A/59/2005, 21 March 2005, para. 78.
6. Jose E. Alvarez, 'The Schizophrenias of R2P', in *Human Rights, Intervention, and the Use of Force*, eds. Philip Alston and Euan MacDonald (Oxford: Oxford University Press, 2008), 275–284.
7. *Implementing the Responsibility to Protect. Report of the Secretary General*, A/63/677, 12 January 2009.
8. *Responsibility to Protect: Timely and Decisive Response. Report of the Secretary General*, A/66/874-S/2012/578, 25 Jul 2012, para. 32.
9. Ibid.
10. *Implementing the Responsibility to Protect. Report of the Secretary General*, *supra* note 6, para. 50.
11. Statement by India. UN General Assembly Informal Interactive Dialogue on the Responsibility to Protect, September 2012 (hereafter UNGAIID 2012). All statements in this dialogue and cited in this article are available at: http://www.globalr2p.org/resources/278.
12. Statement by the UK. UNGAIID 2012.
13. Statements by the Russian Federation and China, UNGAIID 2012.
14. *Responsibility While Protecting. Elements for the Development and Promotion of a Concept*, A/66/551–S/2011/701, 11 November 2011.
15. See e.g. Statements by The Netherlands and Chile, UNGAIID 2012.
16. Statement by the EU, UNGAIID 2012.
17. UNSC res 1653 /2006 of 27 January 2006. A complete list of resolutions is available at: http://www.globalr2p.org/resources/335.
18. UNSC res 1706 (2006) of 31 August 2006.
19. UNSC res 2139 (2014) of 22 February 2014.
20. Other UN organs appealing to R2P include the General Assembly and the Human Rights Council. See UNGA res 63/308 of 14 September 2009, and HRC res S-19/1 of 4 July 2012. *The Deteriorating Situation in the Syrian Arab Republic, and the Recent Killings in El-houlen.*

21. UNSC res 2118 of 27 September 2013.
22. The OPCW-UN Joint Mission was established to oversee the elimination of the chemical weapons programme of Syria in October 2013 in accordance with UNSC res 2118 (2013), S/213/591 (7 October 2013) and S/213/603, 11 October 2013.
23. The operation was completed on 30 September 2014. See OPCW press release, 1 October 2014.
24. John Rawls, *A Theory of Justice* (Cambridge, MA: Harvard University Press, 2nd ed., 1999), 98–99. Also see Louise Arbour, 'The Responsibility to Protect as a Duty of Care in International Law and Practice', *Review of International Studies* 34, no. 03 (2008): 445–458. For a critique, see e.g. Philip Cunliffe, 'Dangerous Duties: Power, Paternalism, and the "Responsibility to Protect"', *Review of International Studies* 36 Supplement S1 (2010): 79–96.
25. John Rawls, *supra* note 23.
26. See ICISS report (2001), *supra* note 1, which refers to these mentioned limits as "precautionary principles (4.16 ff). Also see High-Level Panel report (2004), *supra* note 4 at 67, and the Secretary-General report (2005), *supra* 4 at 33.
27. John Rawls, *supra* note 43.
28. UN R2P report (2012), *supra* note7, making a reference to the Report of the International Commission of Inquiry on Libya, A/HRC/19/68, 8 March 2012.
29. UN R2P Report (2012), *supra* note 7, para. 55. Also see *Report Unacknowledged Deaths: Civilian Casualties in NATO's Air Campaign in Libya*. Human Rights Watch, 14 May 2012.
30. Margret P. Doxey, *International Sanctions in Contemporary Perspective*, 2nd ed. (New York: St. Martin's, 1996), attesting to the fact that the imposition of sanctions as a substitute to military force has a long history. Also see Michael Reisman, 'Sanctions and International Law', *Intercultural Human Rights Law Review*, 4 (2009): 9–20.
31. *The Role of Regional and Sub-regional Arrangements in Implementing the Responsibility to Protect. Report of the Secretary-General*, A/65/877–S/2011/393, 27 June 2011, para. 36. Also see UN R2P Report (2012), *supra* note 7, para. 31.
32. David Cortright and George Lopez, *The Sanctions Decade: Assessing UN Strategies in the 1990s* (Boulder, CO and London: Lynne Rienner Publishers, 2000).
33. UNSC res 2127 of 5 December 2013 (Central African Republic); and UNSC res 2140 of 26 February 2014 (Yemen).
34. See e.g. Human Rights First, *Syria Sanctions Fact Sheet. Existing Sanctions and Future Steps the Administration Should Take* (June 2012).
35. Turkey imposes economic sanctions on Syria, *BBC News*, 30 November 2011.
36. Council Decision 2011/273/CFSP of 9 May 2011 concerning restrictive measures against Syria and Council Regulation No. 442/2011.
37. Council Implementing Decision 2011/302/CFSP of 23 May 2011 implementing Decision 2011/273/CFSP concerning restrictive measures against Syria.
38. Council Decision 2011/522/CFSP of 2 September 2011 amending Decision 2011/273/CFSP concerning restrictive measures against Syria.
39. Council Implementing Decision (CFSP) 2015/383 of 6 March 2015 implementing Decision 2013/255/CFSP concerning restrictive measures against Syria.
40. Council Decision 2011/782/CFSP of 1 December 2011 concerning restrictive measures against Syria and repealing Decision 2011/273/CFSP.
41. Council Decision 2011/735/CFSP of 14 November 2011 amending Decision 2011/273/CFSP concerning restrictive measures against Syria, para. 4.
42. Decisions of the Arab League adopted on 27 November and 3 December 2011 are available in Arabic at: http://www.sipri.org/databases/embargoes/eu_arms_embargoes/syria_LAS/league-of-arab-states-embargo-on-syria-.
43. For this definition of 'arms embargo', see SIPRI database on arms embargoes, available at: http://www.sipri.org/databases/embargoes.
44. *Fulfilling our collective responsibility: international assistance and the responsibility to protect. Report of the Secretary-General*, A/68/947-S/2014/449, 11 July 2014.
45. Pieter D. Wezeman, 'Arms Transfers to Syria', *SIPRI Yearbook 2013: Armaments, Disarmament and International Security* (Oxford: Oxford University Press, 2013), 269–273.
46. 'Arab League allows members to arm rebels and offers seat to opposition', *Albawaba News* (7 March 2013).

47. Council Decision 2011/273/CFSP of 9 May 2011 concerning restrictive measures against Syria, arts. 1 and 2. Also see Council Decision 2011/782/CFSP of 1 December 2011 concerning restrictive measures against Syria and repealing Decision 2011/273/CFSP.

48. Council Decision 2013/255/CFSP of 31 May 2013 concerning restrictive measures against Syria, para. 1.1. See annex for list of items. Council Decision 2015/837/CFSP of 28 May 2015 amending Decision 2013/255/CFSP extends the application of restrictive measures until 1 June 2015. Further exemptions to the sanctions regime include Council Decision 2013/760/CFSP of 13 December 2013 amending Decision 2013/255/CFSP concerning restrictive measures against Syria, para. 2.

49. OXFAM, 'A Fairer Deal for Syrians'. 190 *Oxfam Briefing Paper*, 9 September 2014: 14. So far, France is the only EU member actually transferring weapons. The UK has supplied non-lethal equipment, assistance and training to the Syrian opposition.

50. Statement delivered by the Permanent Mission of South Africa to the UN, UNGAAID, September 2012.

51. On 4 July 2014, the US bombed an ISIS military base in Syria in an attempt to rescue hostages, including those who were later murdered.

52. 'Arab Meet Vows All-out Efforts to Crush IS Terror', *Arab news* (8 September 2014).

53. Canada, France, UK, Australia, Germany, and The Netherlands have not participated directly in the airstrikes in Syria. See A Fantz, 'Who's Doing What in the Coalition Battle Against ISIS?', *CCN News*, 7 October 2014. See also US Department of Defense, 'Coalition Airstrikes Against ISIL in Syria, Iraq Continue', News Release (3 September 2015), available: http://www.defense.gov/News-Article-View/Article/616186/coalition-airstrikes-continue-against-isil-in-syria-iraq.

54. Pentagon to deploy 400 troops to train Syrian rebels, *Reuters*, 16 January 2015.

55. Syrian Observatory for Human Rights, 'President Obama Urges Congress to Pass a Joint Resolution Authorizing the Use of Force Against ISIL' (22 January 2015).

56. Noah Bonsey, 'What Obama Does Not Understand About Syria', *Foreign Policy* (26 November 2014).

57. Peter Goodman and Erin Banco, 'ISIS Gaining Strength, Warns Iraqi VP Ayad Allaqi', *International Business Times* (22 January 2015).

58. This statement was made in a press briefing in Geneva. See 'In focus: Syria', *UN News Centre* (15 January 2015).

59. Alan Nissel, 'The ILC Articles on State Responsibility: Between Self-help and Solidarity', 38 *NYU Journal of International Law & Politics* (2005–2006): 355; and Bruno Simma, 'From Bilateralism to Community Interest in International Law', in: *Recueil des Cours (Collected Courses of the Hague Academy of International Law)* 1994, no. 6: 217–387.

60. Draft Articles on the Responsibility of States for Internationally Wrongful Acts, UNGA res 56/83 of 12 December 2001, and corrected by document A/56/49(Vol. I)/Corr.4. According to article 40, a breach is serious or grave if it involves a gross or systematic failure of the responsible State to fulfil an obligation arising from a peremptory norm of general international law.

61. *Legal Consequences of the Construction of a Wall in the Occupied Palestinian Territory, Advisory Opinion*, I.C.J. Reports 2004, p. 136, para. 146.

62. For the relevance of R2P in legal analysis, see Carsten Stahn and Catherine Harwood, 'Why Reports about the "Death of R2P" May be Premature: Links between the Responsibility to Protect and Human Rights Fact-finding', *ESIL Reflections* 3, no. 5 (2014); and Anne Orford, 'Rethinking the Significance of the Responsibility to Protect Concept', *ASIL Proceedings 2012*: 27–31.

63. Nina H.B. Jorgensen, 'The Obligation of Cooperation', in *The Law of International Responsibility*, eds. James Crawford, Alain Pellet, and Simon Olleson (Oxford: Oxford University Press, 2010), 695–701.

64. Martti Koskenniemi, 'Solidarity Measures: State Responsibility as a New International Order?' *British Yearbook of International Law* 71 (2001): 337–335, reflecting on article 41.1 ILC draft Articles of 2001, according to which 'States shall cooperate to bring to an end through lawful means any serious breach within the meaning of article 40'.

65. UNSC res 156 of 9 September 1960. Also see Michael Akehurst, 'Enforcement Actions by Regional Agencies, with Special Reference to the Organization of American States', *British Yearbook of International Law* 42 (1967): 174–227.

66. *Congressional Research Service* [CSR], 22 January 1991, 14.

67. Mary Ellen O'Connell, *The Power & Purpose of International Law. Insights from the Theory & Practice of Enforcement* (New York: Oxford University Press, 2011), 243–248.

68. UNSC res 713 of 25 September 1991, para. 6.

69. Peter Malanczuk, 'Countermeasures and Self-Defense as Circumstances Precluding Wrongfulness in the International Law Commission's Draft Articles on State Responsibility', in *United Nations Codification of State Responsibility*, eds. Marina Spinedi and Bruno Simma (New York, Oceana Publications, 1987): 197–286; Ademola Abass, *Regional Organisations and the Development of Collective Security: Beyond Chapter VIII of the UN Charter* (Oxford: Hart Publishing, 2004), 46–52.

70. Mary Ellen O'Connell, *The Power & Purpose of International Law. Insights from the Theory & Practice of Enforcement*, *supra* note 66: 276.

71. International Law Institute, 'Protection of Human Rights and the Principle of Non-intervention in Internal Affairs of States', *Institut de Droit International Annuaire* 63 (1989): 38. Also see Jochen A. Frowein, 'Reactions by Not Directly Affected States to Breaches of Public International Law', *Recueil des Cours* 248 (1994): 388–389.

72. Linos Alexandre Sicilianos, 'Countermeasures in Response to Grave Violations of Obligations Owed to the International Community', in *The Law of International Responsibility*, *supra* note 62: 1141; Pierre-Emmanuel Dupont, 'Countermeasures and Collective Security: The Case of the EU Sanctions against Iran', *Journal of Conflict & Security Law* 14, no. 3 (2012): 301–336; Dennis Alland, 'Countermeasures of General Interest', *European Journal of International Law* 12, no. 5 (2012): 1221–1239.

73. Case C–402/05 P and C–415/05, *P. Kadi and Al Barakaat International Foundation v. Council and Commission* [2008] ECR I–6351; and Case T-85/09 *Kadi v Commission* [2010] ECR II-5177. Also see Joined Cases C-584/10 P, C-593/10 P and C-595/10 P, *Commission and others v. Kadi*, judgment of the Court of Justice, 18 July 2013, paras. 99–100.

74. Joined Cases T-329/12 and T-74/13, *Mazaan Al-Tabbaa v. Council* [2014], judgment of the General Court, 9 July 2014; Case T-572/11, *Samir Hassan v. Council* [2014], judgment of the General Court, 16 July 2014; and Case T-293/12, *Syria International Islamic Bank v. Council*, judgment of the General Court, 11 July 2014.

75. Case T-572/11, *Samir Hassan v. Council* [2014], judgment of the General Court of Justice, 16 July 2014, paras. 86-95; and Joined Cases T-329/12 and T-74/13, *Mazaan Al-Tabbaa v. Council* [2014], judgment of the General Court, 9 July 2014. Also note *Syria International Islamic Bank v. Council*, judgment of the General Court of 11 July 2014, paras. 45–66.

76. UN R2p Report (2011), *supra* note 30, para. 36.

77. *UN Declaration on Principles of International Law concerning Friendly Relations and Co-operation among States in accordance with the Charter of the United Nations*, A/RES/25/2625, 24 October 1970, and *UN Declaration on the Inadmissibility of Intervention in the Domestic Affairs of States and the Protection of Their Independence and Sovereignty*, A/20/2131 (1965), 21 December 1965.

78. *Corfu Channel (Albania v. United Kingdom)*. Merits, Judgment of 9 April 1949, ICJ Reports 1949, p. 4; *Military and Paramilitary Activities in and against Nicaragua (Nicaragua v. United States of America)*. Merits, Judgment. I.C.J. Reports 1986, p. 14; and *Armed Activities on the Territory of the Congo (DRC v. Uganda)*. Merits, Judgment. I.C.J. Reports (2005).

79. *Military and Paramilitary Activities in and against Nicaragua (Nicaragua v. United States of America)*. Merits, Judgment. I.C.J. Reports 1986, p. 14, para. 206.

80. *Democratic Republic of Congo vs. Uganda* (2005), *supra* note 77, para. 164.

81. *Nicaragua vs. United States of America*, *supra* note 78, para. 206.

82. Ibid. para 208.

83. OXFAM, 'A Fairer Deal for Syrians', *supra* note 48.

84. Letter dated 20 September from the Permanent Representative of Iraq to the United Nations addressed to the President of the Security Council, S/2014/691, 22 September 2014. See also Identical letters dated 25 November 2014 from the Permanent Representative of the United Kingdom of Great Britain and Northern Ireland to the United Nations addressed to the Secretary-General and the President of the Security Council, S/2014/851, 26 November 2014.

85. UNSC meeting, S/PV.7271, 16 September 2014: 43.

86. Ibid. p. 19.

87. See e.g. Jennifer Tahran, 'Pesky Questions for International Law: What's the basis for airstrikes in Syria?', *Opinio Juris*, 23 September 2014. Also see Louise Arimatsu and Michael Schmitt, 'The Legal Basis for the War Against ISIS Remains ontentious', *The Guardian*, 6 October 2014.

88. UNSC res 2170 (2014) of 15 August 2014. Also see UNSC res 2178 (2014) of 24 September 2014 (singling out the challenge posed by foreign terrorist fighters).

89. Ibid, para. 1.

90. Ibid, para. 6.

91. UNSC meeting, S/PV.7242, 15 August 2014: 3.

92. A. Barnard and E. Schmitt, 'U.S. Focus on ISIS Frees Syria to Battle Rebels', *New York Times*, 8 October 2014, available online: http://www.nytimes.com/2014/10/09/world/middleeast/us-focus-on-isis-frees-syria-to-battle-rebels.html?_r=0.

93. UNSC res 2139 of 22 February 2014, UNSC res 2165 of 14 July 2004, and UNSC 2191 of 17 December 2004.

94. Antonio Cassese, '*Ex iniuria ius oritur*: Are We Moving Towards International Legitimation of Forcible Humanitarian Countermeasures in the World Community?', *European Journal of International Law* 10, no 1 (1999): 23–30.

A critical reflection on the conceptual and practical limitations of the responsibility to protect

Joseph Besigye Bazirake[a] and Paul Bukuluki[b]

[a]Institute for Reconciliation and Social Justice, University of the Free State, South Africa; [b]Makerere University, School of Social Sciences, Uganda

The Responsibility to Protect (R2P) is without a doubt an iconic representation of the international system's effort to reinterpret the traditional understanding of state sovereignty within a growing trend towards human rights considerations. This article presents the scepticism surrounding the R2P's journey within a conservative and state-centric status quo of international relations, framed on a basic set of 1648 Westphalia treaty ideals. The article analyses the limitations in the conceptualization and actual practice of the R2P, with an incisive examination of its tendency towards becoming the norm. An African introspection based on the application of the R2P also offers an insightful critique of the principle in the changing global order.

Introduction

The twentieth century will be remembered for its ravaging global connectedness, characterized by two world wars, a cold war and unprecedented colonial and post-colonial violence. This period also experienced an increase in caution around inter-state relationships, with a balance of power mechanism regulated within the framework of the United Nations (UN) since 1945. According to the Charter of the United Nations, international law is maintained by the principles of sovereign equality and independence of all states, non-interference in the domestic jurisdictions of states, the prohibition of the use of force by one state (or states) against another, and the universal respect for, and observance of human rights and fundamental freedoms for all.[1] Through the creation of the UN, international relations were concretized within the Westphalia model, in which the right of sovereigns to govern their peoples was expected to be free of outside interference, whether any such external claim to interfere would be based on political, legal or religious principles.[2]

However, human tragedies, such as the genocides in Cambodia, Rwanda, Srebrenica and the Holocaust, exposed a fundamental flaw in the Westphalia model; questioning whether individual states could guarantee their perpetual ability and willingness to protect the human rights of their own citizens. The emergent arguments to rethink the Westphalia sovereign state model[3] are largely a consequence of the changing global dynamics, in which the power structures have been numerically and economically altered, especially by the new post-colonial entrants since the 1960s. These states, particularly in Africa, have also exhibited unprecedented intra-state forms of violence, which would perhaps provide justification for the impetus to revise the hitherto realist framing of the international system.

At the same time, the practice in international relations is only proving to provide a more tilted power imbalance that puts the less developed states at the receiving end of various interventionist models. The trend from humanitarian intervention that permits a waiver on the use of force by states, along with its contested procedural and legal ramifications[4] towards the more recent R2P, presents a similar argument; that any form of state interference within the current international system's status quo would undoubtedly be crammed with the suspicion that they were favouring the interests of the more economically advanced states and their citizens.

Sovereignty and the responsibility to protect

The limitations brought forth by the traditional sovereign status of the nation state, vis-à-vis the consideration of the state as the unrivaled haven for the protection of its citizenry, has birthed debates for alternative ways of dealing with intra-state human tragedies. This is particularly because the Westphalia model of statehood arguably offers an equivocal veil for the potential infliction of mass violence on civilian populations. In this regard, the traditional concepts of sovereignty and non-intervention as embedded in Articles 2.4[5] and 2.7[6] of the UN charter have been occasionally contradicted by state practice. A case in point was the adoption of resolution 688 (1991) by the United Nations Security Council (UNSC) to protect Kurdish populations within the Iraqi territory, which stood out as an unprecedented practice for an externally instituted civilian protection initiative within a state's sovereign boundaries. The UNSC was further stretched out of its traditional stance by the internal tragedies of Somalia and Yugoslavia,[7] which led to a landmark interpretational expansion of Article 39 of the UN charter.[8] This article was operationally expanded to cover the protection of civilians from large scale intra-state violence rather than the implied exclusive domain of interstate aggressions.

It is noteworthy that the premise of the R2P was a derivative of the idea of 'Sovereignty as responsibility' which was advanced by Francis Deng, the special representative of the UN Secretary General for internally displaced persons.[9] Whereas Deng argued that it was the responsibility of host governments to protect their citizens, he also maintained that vulnerable populations were best protected by effective and legitimate states. In this landmark reinterpretation, state sovereignty, by implication, was endorsed as a responsibility held by sovereign states towards their citizenry, rather than a privilege to deter foreign interference per se.

Accordingly, Mamdani[10] notes that with the end of the cold war, a new international order that holds state sovereignty accountable to human rights standards was adopted. In this regard, the state upholds the right of collective self-determination as the key political right of citizens. Mamdani further argues that whereas the Westphalia framing of sovereignty remains the most pronounced approach in the international system, citizenship and sovereignty are not meant to be opposites, but associates. This argument offers insights into the trade-offs that need to be made in order for citizenship rights to prevail within the reinterpretation of sovereignty as advocated by the R2P.

The R2P amidst threats to international peace and security

It is noteworthy that the contradictions around state sovereignty informed the basis on which the United Nations Secretary General (UNSG), Kofi Annan, called for the need to resolve the tensions between sovereignty and fundamental human rights at the 1999 General Assembly. This task was picked up by the International Commission on Intervention and State Sovereignty (ICISS), culminating in a report on the Responsibility to Protect (R2P), whose primary concern was to revisit the understanding of humanitarian intervention in the wake of the Kosovo crisis.[11] The Kosovo crisis had prompted unauthorized NATO interference to stop ethnic cleansing and was labelled legitimate but illegal.[12] This contradiction however, is still reflective of the incongruity between sovereignty and the R2P that the international system has to grapple with, amidst the changing threats to peace.

In this respect, the UNSG also commissioned a group of eminent persons to assess the most urgent global security threats and issue recommendations on how best to mitigate them in preparation for the 60th session of the General Assembly. The resulting report made recommendations on how the world must meet its security challenges, collectively and comprehensively, including the need to embrace and implement the R2P.[13] The report recorded six threats to international peace and security: (1) Economic and social threats, including poverty, infectious disease and environmental degradation; (2) inter-state conflict; (3) internal conflict, including civil war, genocide and other large-scale atrocities; (4) nuclear, radiological, chemical and biological weapons; (5) terrorism; and (6) transnational organized crime. The panel noted that collective security institutions had proved particularly poor at meeting the challenge posed by large-scale, gross human rights abuses and genocide. This was attributed to two challenges: (1) the normative challenge where the concept of state and international responsibility for civilian protection from the effects of war and human rights abuses had not yet overcome the tension between the competing claims of sovereign inviolability and the right to intervene; and (2) the operational challenge that lay in how to stop a government from killing its own civilians, which was recognized as an undertaking that would require considerable military deployment capacity.[14]

The subsequent tenets of the R2P were constructed by ICISS, and later adopted as the UN outcome document in 2005, with a three-tier hierarchy that prescribed a human protection criterion in cases of mass violence. At its foremost level, the R2P stipulates that the state bears the primary responsibility to protect its populations from genocide, war crimes, ethnic cleansing and crimes against humanity. This responsibility entails the prevention of such crimes and violations, including their incitement. At the second level, the document recommends that the international community has a responsibility to assist and encourage the state in fulfilling its primary protection obligations and also stipulates the international community's exercise of R2P by taking up appropriate diplomatic, humanitarian and other peaceful means to help protect populations from these crimes. This responsibility is taken on to a third tier, with the recommendation that the international community must also be prepared to take collective action in a timely and decisive manner and in accordance with the UN Charter, on a case-by-case basis and in cooperation with relevant regional organizations. The third tier ought to be activated in case a state fails to protect its populations or if it is, in fact, the perpetrator of such crimes and may entail coercive measures; including the collective use of force through the UN Security Council.[15]

The absence of a majority of the 2004 UNSG report's outline of threats to international peace and security within the final framework of R2P as endorsed in the 2005 summit document offers a striking contradiction. In the final summit document, R2P is limited to invocation to cases of genocide, war crimes, ethnic cleansing and crimes against humanity. The fact that some threats are not conceivable within the R2P mandate undermines its functional scope in response to the emergent threats to peace and security. Threats such as poverty, infectious disease and environmental degradation, nuclear, radiological, chemical and biological weapons, terrorism and transnational organized crime do not have audience within the R2P's framing and yet these are increasingly standing out as the current era's unrivaled threats to humanity. A counter argument is expressed in the 2009 UNSG report, implying that any attempts to extend R2P to cover other calamities, such as HIV/AIDS, climate change or in response to natural disasters, would undermine the 2005 consensus and stretch the concept beyond recognition or operational utility.[16]

It can however be argued to the contrary, considering that the omitted threats could actually provide a more viable entry point for the prevention of mass atrocities, and would present more meaningful grounds for cooperative actions between the host states and those that would be willing to pursue an externally instituted R2P. Ki-moon's[17] report provides further ambiguity by stating that R2P does not alter, but reinforces, the legal obligations of member states to refrain from the use of force except in conformity with the UN Charter. Such ambiguities can only emphasize the scepticism surrounding R2P's relevance in a conservative international system that operates at the whim of the more powerful states. Such misgivings are well explained by Chesterman's[18] argument that the form in which R2P was endorsed by the world summit essentially provided that the UNSC could authorize, on a case-by-case basis, the same things that it had already been authorizing for more than a decade.

The endorsement of the R2P by world leaders at the 2005 World Summit and its reaffirmation by Security Council resolution 1674 (2006) has not gone far enough in the attempt to concretize the R2P principle and as an emergent norm that can redress the contradiction between the cardinal principles of sovereignty and human rights in the international system. This uncertainty was also the highlight of the 2005 summit in which the R2P was only approved after a 'rancorous and inconclusive' debate about its scope and the question as to whom such a responsibility [to protect] would fall.[19] This can only mean that there is a lot of unfinished business with regard to R2P as an emergent norm, whose primary challenge is rooted in the long standing tradition of state sovereignty as the pivotal structural paradigm of international law.[20]

To further highlight these reservations, Bellamy[21] remarks that there is something inherently militaristic about R2P that diverts attention away from non-military solutions. At the same time, there is a discomforting correlation between the language of R2P and the tag of belligerent human aggressors, against whom protection ought to be sought. In this regard, arguments are increasingly arising to allege that R2P has a tight link to liberal interventionists, who have sought the acceptance of military intervention through a more acceptable language of human rights and morality.[22] Similarly, Mamdani[23] in his reaction to the framing of the R2P also notes that the language of humanitarian action has cut its ties with the language of citizen's rights, resulting in the relegation of the rights of the citizen to the right of the human, which essentially pertains to survival and the need for protection. In this case, Mamdani ironically remarks that the new R2P language refers to its subjects not as bearers of rights – and thus active agents in their own emancipation – but as passive beneficiaries of an external R2P. By this understanding, he seeks to defy the patronizing language of the R2P principle that makes the beneficiaries of such a humanitarian order akin to recipients of charity. He argues that the hype around the R2P principle tends to promote dependence and a system of trusteeship in the international system and he insists that the R2P has always been the sovereign's obligation and it cannot be clothed as a newly introduced principle, but rather one whose terms have been radically altered. This suspicion may be further understood within the *realpolitik* interpretation of the R2P, whose moral and ethical premise is undermined by the prevailing power dynamics in the international system.

Hindrances to the emergence of the R2P Norm

A key challenge of the R2P lies in what Prantl and Nakano[24] identify within the notion of *Normatisation continuum*. By this notion, it is conceded that the three aspects of obligation, precision and delegation, which are prerequisites for the acceptance of norms in the international system, are noticeably absent in the R2P framing. The aspect of obligation for instance, which denotes an ideal-type situation where all actors are legally bound by a set of rules, is limited by the lack of mandate to hold other states accountable to the protection of civilians within the R2P frame. This is because the R2P does not entail any legally binding provisions for the purpose of the compulsion to act, and therefore falls short of the criteria that defines obligation.

Precision on the other hand, which connotes the existence of an unambiguous code of conduct that guides and restrains activities, still lies with pronounced uncertainty under the R2P principle. Whereas a distinction is made between the R2P as an enclave of the host state in the first instance, and the international community only as a second resort, the precision in determining this shift from the host state to the international community is not clearly defined. Notably, paragraph 139 of the outcome document pronounces its stance on collective action to be taken:

> … should peaceful means be inadequate and national authorities *manifestly fail* to protect their populations from genocide, war crimes, ethnic cleansing and crimes against humanity. (emphasis added)

Nonetheless, the consideration of when and how national authorities 'manifestly fail' is ambiguous and may delay or hasten action using R2P, owing to auxiliary considerations that may have little to do with the prevailing circumstances in the host state. It is also important to note that precision was sidelined when the Precautionary principles[25] as suggested in the original ICISS report were omitted from the final 2005 world summit outcome document, making it more difficult to have a precise point of invocation for the R2P. The 2001 ICISS report and the 2004 UNSG report had made specific recommendations to be adopted for states in the use of force criteria for cases of genocide, war crimes and crimes against humanity. The two reports recommended the five criteria drawn from the just war tradition,[26] when considering forceful intervention for the prevention or halting of mass atrocity crimes. These considerations include: the just cause threshold; right intention; last resort; proportional means; and reasonable prospects of success. Such integral considerations in the use of force by states were evidently skipped in the world summit outcome document, and this leaves a lot of room for misuse of R2P owing to the apparent precision gap.

In terms of delegation, Prantl and Nakano[27] further indicate the need for third parties to receive authorization to implement, interpret and apply the rules. In this case, the R2P does not explain how to overcome the stalemate that would arise when major powers in the Security Council have no interest in solving a given crisis.[28] Delegation can therefore prove to be a slow and inconsistent venture; and may turn out to be ineffective owing to the economic and military limitations of some countries, particularly those in Africa, to take on such a mandate at the regional level. This continues to be a problem in the application of the R2P as a principle (and a potentially upcoming norm) in international relations.

To add another twist to the status of the R2P, the 5th committee budgetary meeting in 2007 declined funding for the proposed new special adviser on the R2P and his office. This served as an early blow and negative precedent, impacting the credibility of the R2P principle within the consortium of states. Member state representatives argued that the R2P had actually never been agreed to 'as a norm' during the World Summit to further draw commitment away from the R2P principles. It was noted that the commitment in the world summit document had been limited to the support of the special adviser of the Secretary General on the prevention of genocide as highlighted in Article 140 of the outcome document.[29] Conglomerating the R2P within the provisions of the Genocide Convention was an apparent concession to the reluctance in considering it as an emergent norm in the international relations framework.

The legal status of the R2P was also highlighted among the concerns of civil society organizations in 2008, regarding the non legally-binding status of the UN world summit outcome document. Considering that the endorsement of the R2P by the 2005 world summit document is not recognized as a 'declaration' undermines R2P's foundational stature as a legal instrument.[30] Therefore, the extent to which the 2009 consensus resolution on the implementation of the R2P offers the principle a new legal foundation is yet to be convincingly demonstrated in international relations.

It is undeniable that the circumstances that necessitate civilian protection are still primarily driven by the instigation of the human hand and involve mass atrocities. Despite the 2005 summit outcome's call for an expansion of the UN early warning and assessment of possible genocide, war crimes, crimes against humanity and ethnic cleansing, there is still a challenge in actualizing these measures. The Secretary General noted the efforts of the UN system to address gaps in the early warning mechanism in the 2010 report,[31] although he pointed out the challenges in this regard as: (1) Insufficient sharing of information and analysis among the various offices that collect such information as the Office of the United Nations High Commissioner for Human Rights (OHCHR) and the Office of the United Nations High Commissioner for Refugees (UNHCR), the Department of Peace Keeping Operations and the United Nations Children's Fund (UNICEF); (2) the fact that with the exception of the early warning mechanism to prevent genocide, all other existing mechanisms for the gathering and analysis of early warning information do not view it with the lens of the R2P; and (3) the lack of assessment tools and capacity to ensure both efficiency and system-wide coherence in policy making and development of an early and flexible response tailored to the evolving needs of each situation.

In spite of the tremendous steps undertaken by the UN and regional bodies to develop a more robust early warning mechanism, the R2P still treads along a path that may be more responsive to overt manifestations of atrocities than an approach that can deal with their root causes. This is owing to the challenges in the information and technical gaps as well as the imprecision within the R2P frame of analysis. It is argued in this paper that there is a necessity to be able to acknowledge and seek to address the structural and root causes of conflicts in order to lessen significantly the occurrence of mass atrocities themselves. The justification provided in the 2009 UNSG report that aimed at preventing duplication of what would have already been covered under the conflict prevention framework of the UN can only be taken with some qualms, as conflict prevention mechanisms can coexist without necessarily creating destructive ambiguities, and in so doing, could create a grander platform to mitigate large scale violence. In fact, re-emphasizing the conflict prevention framework within R2P can only increase the chances for a more comprehensive and collective conflict prevention mechanism to minimize the possibilities of mass atrocities. Besides, none of the aspects that make up R2P's framework are novel in themselves, and only echo different aspects of importance in the desire to protect civilians.

As testimony to such ambiguities, the challenges of misinterpretation of the R2P still loom. A case in point involves a situation in which R2P's provisions were conspicuously invoked by the Russian foreign minister in regard to the protection of Russian citizens in

Georgia.[32] This application of R2P went against the tenets of the international system, where the use of force is specifically as a collective response through the UN rather than an individual state's response to situations beyond its own borders. This example also offers a stark example in which the big powers' ability to re-interpret mundane principles in their favour might continue to undermine the validity of the R2P principle.

At the same time, Massingham[33] reiterates that the inclination towards 'responsibility' in R2P eliminates the question of political will, even when he posits the principle as innovative and a progressive development of the law if understood in the sense of a positive duty. The practical challenge for the R2P however still lies in the absence of compulsion for any political will to accept such a duty. The international community therefore runs the risk of seeing more dreaded situations like that of Kosovo, where, according to some, quick reaction could be the result of inherent interests rather than primarily a genuine expression of the R2P, or situations akin to the international reaction to the Rwandan genocide, where states dragged their feet in the absence of their own interests to intervene. In addition, the R2P could be used as an excuse for a state or coalition of states to react based on their inherent grievances (or common interest) under the R2P cover. In the view of some commentators, Libya provides an example of this situation where the invocation of the R2P quickly became a scheme for the overthrow of the Gaddafi regime. The interests of major powers in such cases cannot be overlooked, as this excerpt from president Obama's speech may indicate:

> America cannot use our military wherever repression occurs. And given the costs and risks of intervention, we must always measure our interests against the need for action. But that cannot be an argument for never acting on behalf of what's right ... [34]

The lack of political will was also identified by a roundtable of participants as the biggest challenge in ensuring the protection of civilians from mass atrocities.[35] While states embraced the R2P in 2005, this commitment did not translate into tangible action or readiness at the national and regional levels. This situation, coupled with the perceptible Security Council members' selectivity in the threat to use their veto power in crises involving mass atrocities presents an additional dilemma to the application of the R2P. In spite of the persistent calls for the Council's permanent members to refrain from using their veto power when considering cases of genocide, war crimes and crimes against humanity and ethnic cleansing, the extent to which such a call will be heeded to remains to be seen.

These trends are not surprising as the political will to conduct the R2P would involve risking personnel whose primary mandate would have been to serve and defend their own states and vital interests, ahead of the protection of human rights of people in other countries.[36] The calculation for political will becomes more problematic, owing to what according to some analyses, is the unjustified risk involved for personnel exercising the R2P outside their own boundaries. Other considerations that might come into play involving the erroneous application of the R2P such as the desire to 'punish' aggressors and the desire to 'show off' military supremacy in order to dissuade potential aggressors may all erode the moral intentions inherent in the protective purpose of R2P.

An African introspection of R2P

Colonial history left the African continent susceptible to suspicion of any form of external interference. In recent times, such uncertainties have been heightened by the numerous initiatives to combat terrorism on the continent, particularly after the terror attacks against the US in 2001. African governments have also proved to be prone to the economic influence of external actors; often manifested in the exploitation of the continent's resources and flanked by external support for proxy resource-based wars. It is therefore important to underscore the unique position of the African continent in terms of the social-economic conditions that make it more disposed to becoming the playing field for such precepts as the R2P.

In the first instance, it is notable that African leaders were the pioneering collective that espoused the need for state intervention in respect of grave circumstances. This was ratified in Article 4(h) of the African Union's Constitutive Act[37] five years prior to the 2005 summit that documented the R2P. Nonetheless, Africa as a continent has been host to a number of catastrophic events that would warrant the invocation of R2P but have been met with various contestations, which in most cases have watered down the potential application of the principle. Situations like those that have prevailed in Somalia and the Democratic Republic of Congo have in the past been demarcated as candidates for R2P,[38] but with inadequate responses from the international community and limited effort from within Africa itself.

Perhaps the crisis in the Darfur region of Sudan represented the earliest visible test for the R2P principle. Whereas there had been numerous efforts already underway to tackle the Darfur violence before the 2005 adoption of the summit document, it is significant to note that the international responses were marred by the Sudanese Government's rejection of the intervention by foreign forces. De Waal[39] attributes R2P's failure in the Darfur situation to the inadequate conceptualization and the inflated expectation that physical protection by international troops was possible within the limits of the military strength, coupled with confused advocacy around the issue. Besides that, R2P as a principle could not be used to prevail over the Sudanese government's insistence on its primary responsibility their citizens; even in the face of ambiguities surrounding how effectively such protection was being rendered.

Notably, responses in Sudan were kick-started with UN resolutions passed from 2004, expressing the willingness to authorize a peace operation to oversee the comprehensive peace agreement in Southern Sudan (resolution 1547), and the threat of sanctions on Sudan over the situation in Darfur (resolution 1556). At this point, an argument had been advanced by Philippine's representatives that Sudan had failed in its duty to protect its citizens and that international action was warranted. Representatives from China, Pakistan, and Sudan all rejected any suggestions of intervention, while Brazil and Russia exhibited reluctance to even contemplate the question.[40] This posed one of the earliest demonstrations of the veto challenge that would loom over the application of R2P, within a Security Council that according to Thakur[41] faces a quadruple legitimacy deficit of performance, representation, procedure and accountability.

By October 2004 an initial African Union mission (AMIS) had deployed up to 2200 personnel and was later reinforced by a stronger joint AU-UN force in Darfur (UNAMID) of 15,444 personnel by 2008. The conflict continued to escalate, partly due to the handicap posed by the Sudanese government's non-consent of the operations of these forces. This was also a grim reminder that the norms of non-intervention and sovereignty still resonated more strongly than the emerging R2P principle. Therefore, whereas the R2P language had helped to mobilize international attention on the conflict in Darfur, it failed to activate united or even sufficient political will for states to agree on an explicit and convincing response in line with the R2P framework for action.[42]

The Libyan case also provides an additional example of the inconsistencies in the application of R2P. In the first instance, the early warnings that showed a threat of commission of mass atrocities was conceived with a response within the R2P framing that would have been only warranted if actual mass atrocities had already been underway in Libya. Nonetheless, Evans[43] has described the Libyan R2P case as a classic example that followed the right procedural endorsements; first with resolution 1970 and later, resolution 1973. The prime challenge with the Libyan case was that resolution 1973 that called for 'all necessary measures' to protect civilians, was arguably interpreted by the NATO forces to also involve regime change in the country. Whereas this may have been anticipated to bring about quicker results for civilian protection, it was, from the perspective of many commentators on R2P, undoubtedly working outside the ethos of R2P and was therefore to cause further misgivings about the inconsistent nature in which different mandates could be conscripted in the course of the implementation of the R2P. Mamdani[44] identifies this kind of scenario as being part of a new humanitarian order restrictively applied to the 'rogue and failed' states and as part of an international order that neither acknowledges citizenship rights nor citizens as agents in their own emancipation.

The situation in Kenya that arose after the contested presidential elections of 2007, on the other hand, has been lauded by some commentators as the best R2P example in which preventive diplomacy was effectively implemented. In the aftermath of wide spread ethnically driven post-election violent eruptions in Kenya however, a counter paradigm in the application of the R2P could be denoted; one in which the powerful states are not always meddling in the affairs of the weaker states with disastrous outcomes. The uniqueness of the Kenyan case was that local efforts were also sustained all through till the 2013 elections.[45] However the R2P application in Kenya has also been categorized as *ex post facto*,[46] owing to the fact that the R2P terminology was only conveniently employed following Koffi Annan's already ongoing diplomatic efforts at the time. In this regard, Kuperman[47] has argued that Kenya's relative success in handling the violent aftermath of the 2008 elections can hardly be attributed to a new R2P norm of preventive diplomacy, given that neither the norm nor the preventive diplomacy applied in this case, were novel. This analysis therefore offers an interesting understanding around the limitations that surround the endeavours to spread the R2P framework within international relations as a novel principle. It also highlights the inherent dilemma of the continual approach in international relations that barely pays attention to the contemporary nature of threats to humanity around the world; threats that operate more within the state, rather than as a result of conflict between states.

Conclusion

This article indicates that the R2P and the debates that it generates bring forth an opportunity for the international system to reinvent its priorities in the context of a more globalized world and the changing scope of atrocities against humanity. Whereas the global connectedness highlights the desperate need to revise the long standing nation state protective monopoly over its citizenry, it also presents a case for the utter necessity of considering the changing threats to humanity, whose primary source is no longer located in direct combat between belligerent states.

Contemporary threats are not only increasingly within state boundaries, but also include overwhelming cross-border aspects that result from climate change and a multiplicity of other natural occurrences. As such, the threats to peace have metamorphosed greatly within the last century, characterized by unprecedented numbers of civilian casualties. With such unconventional and yet potent threats to human existence as venereal diseases, poverty coupled with extraordinarily lethal military innovations, the R2P is still far from endorsing the recognition of individuals as full global citizens, whose protection ought not to be compromised.

Even so, the R2P offers the groundwork for challenging and revising the more systematic barriers in the international system towards nurturing the protection of civilians. Aspects that still reflect conservativeness, inherent in the UN and its Security Council ought to be revised to allow for the recognition of the intrinsic need to preserve human life, notwithstanding the power struggles among states. For as long as the status quo in the international system remains largely tagged to the world war reparations of the last century and the ideals of the 1648 Westphalia negotiations, little can be achieved in the face of the twenty-first century realities. In this case, even such initiatives of global life-serving interest as the R2P will be thinned down to fit within the lens of *realpolitk* considerations, at the peril of preventable losses of innocent lives around the world.

Notes

1. R. Amer, 'Non-use of Force, Non-interference and Security: The Case of Pacific Asia', in *The Security-Development Nexus: Peace, Conflict and Development*, ed. R. Amer et al. (London: Anthem Press, 2012), 89–100; B. Simma, ed. *The Charter of the United Nations: A Commentary*, Vol. 2 (Oxford: Oxford University Press, 2002).
2. S. Beaulac, 'The Westphalian Model in Defining International Law: Challenging the Myth.' *Australian Journal of Legal History* 8, no. 2 (2004): 181–214.
3. B. Buzan and R. Little. 'Beyond Westphalia? Capitalism after the "Fall".' *Review of International Studies* 25, no. 5 (1999): 89–104; S.D. Krasner, 'Rethinking the Sovereign State Model.' *Review of International Studies* 27, no. 5 (2001): 17–42.
4. L. Henkin, L. 'Kosovo and the Law of "Humanitarian Intervention".' *The American Journal of International Law* 93, no. 4 (1999): 824–828. doi:10.2307/2555346; T.M. Ocran, 'The Doctrine of Humanitarian Intervention in Light of Robust Peacekeeping.' *Boston College International and Comparative Law Review* 25, no. 1 (2002): 1–9.
5. Article 2.4 of the UN Charter states: All Members shall refrain in their international relations from the threat or use of force against the territorial integrity or political independence of any state, or in any other manner inconsistent with the Purposes of the United Nations.
6. Article 2.7 of the UN Charter states: Nothing contained in the present Charter shall authorize the United Nations to intervene in matters which are essentially within the domestic jurisdiction of any state or shall require the Members to submit such matters to settlement under the present

Charter; but this principle shall not prejudice the application of enforcement measures under Chapter VII.

7. V.P. Nanda, T.F.J. Muther and A.E. Eckert, 'Tragedies in Somalia, Yugoslavia, Haiti, Rwanda and Liberia – Revisiting the Validity of Humanitarian Intervention under International Law – Part II.' *Denver Journal of International Law and Policy* 26, no. 5 (1997): 827–869.

8. Article 39 of the UN Charter states: The Security Council shall determine the existence of any threat to the peace, breach of the peace, or act of aggression and shall make recommendations, or decide what measures shall be taken in accordance with Articles 41 and 42, to maintain or restore international peace and security.

9. A.J. Bellamy, "The Responsibility to Protect and the Problem of Military Intervention." *International Affairs* 84, no. 4 (2008): 615–639.

10. M. Mamdani, *Saviours and survivors: Darfur, Politics and the War on Terror* (New York: Pantheon Books, 2009).

11. ICISS, *The Responsibility to Protect: Report of the International Commission on Intervention and State Sovereignty* (International Development Research Centre, 2001).

12. E. Massingham, 'Military Intervention for Humanitarian Purposes: Does the Responsibility to Protect Doctrine Advance the Legality of the Use of Force for Humanitarian Ends?' *International Review of the Red Cross* 91, no. 876 (2009): 803–831.

13. UNSG Report, 'High-level Panel on Threats, & Change Report.' *A More Secure World* (2004).

14. UNSG Report, 'High-level Panel on Threats, & Change Report.' *A More Secure World* (2004).

15. A.L. Bannon, 'Responsibility to Protect: The U.N. World Summit and the Question of Unilateralism.' *Yale Law Journal* 115, no. 5 (2006): 1157–1165; A.J. Bellamy, 'Whither the Responsibility to Protect? Humanitarian Intervention and the 2005 World Summit.' *Ethics & International Affairs* 20, no. 2 (2006): 143–169, doi:10.1111/j.1747-7093.2006.00012.x; UNGA, 60/1 (24 October 2005),'World Summit Outcome,' UN Doc A/Res/60/1 (2005).

16. B. Ki-moon, 'Implementing the Responsibility to Protect: Report of the Secretary-General.' *UN Document A/63/677,* January 12 (2009): 22.

17. B. Ki-moon, 'Implementing the Responsibility to Protect: Report of the Secretary-General.' *UN Document A/63/677,* January 12 (2009): 22.

18. S. Chesterman, '"Leading from Behind": The Responsibility to Protect, the Obama Doctrine, and Humanitarian Intervention After Libya.' *Ethics & International Affairs* 25, no. 3 (2011): 279–285.

19. M. Kahler, 'Legitimacy, Humanitarian Intervention, and International Institutions.' *Politics, Philosophy & Economics* 10, no. 1 (2011): 20–45.

20. A. Cassese, 'The Fundamental Principles Governing International Relations.' Chap. 5 in *International Law* (New York: Oxford University Press, 2001), 86–116.

21. A.J. Bellamy, 'The Responsibility to Protect and the Problem of Military Intervention.' *International Affairs* 84, no. 4 (2008): 615–639.

22. L. Pingeot and W. Obenland, 'In Whose Name?: A Critical View on the Responsibility to Protect.' *Global Policy Forum Europe* (2014).

23. M. Mamdani, 'Libya: Politics of Humanitarian Intervention.' *Al Jazeera* (2011).

24. J. Prantl and R. Nakano, 'Global Norm Diffusion in East Asia. How China and Japan Implement the Responsibility to Protect.' *International Relations* 25, no. 2 (2011): 204–223.

25. Report of the International commission on Intervention of state sovereignty (December 2001).

26. A. Moseley, 'Just War Theory.' *The Encyclopedia of Peace Psychology.* Available at: http://onlinelibrary.wiley.com/doi/10.1002/9780470672532.wbepp144/full 2003; M. Walzer, *Just and Unjust Wars: A Moral Argument With Historical Illustrations* (New York: Basic Books, 2006).

27. J. Prantl and R. Nakano, 'Global Norm Diffusion in East Asia. How China and Japan Implement the Responsibility to Protect.' *International Relations* 25, no. 2 (2011): 204–223.

28. L. Pingeot and W. Obenland, 'In Whose Name?: A Critical View on the Responsibility to Protect.' *Global Policy Forum Europe* (2014).

29. J. Ranney, 'Responsibility to Protect: Engaging Civil Society.' *The Federalist Debate* no. 2 (2007): 13. http://www.ciise-iciss.gc.ca/report-en.asp (accessed 15 June 2015).

30. J. Ranney, 'Responsibility to Protect: Engaging Civil Society.' *The Federalist Debate* no. 2 (2007): 13. http://www.ciise-iciss.gc.ca/report-en.asp (accessed 15 June 2015).

31. Report of the secretary general on early warning, assessment and the responsibility to protect.

32. M. Payandeh, 'With Great Power Comes Great Responsiblity – The Concept of the Responsibility to Protect Within the Process of International Lawmaking.' *Yale Journal of International Law*, 35, no. 2 (2010): 469–516.

33. E. Massingham, 'Military Intervention for Humanitarian Purposes: Does the Responsibility to Protect Doctrine Advance the Legality of the Use of Force for Humanitarian Ends? *International Review of the Red Cross* 91, no. 876 (2009): 803–831.

34. Barack Obama, "Remarks by the President in Address to the Nation on Libya" (National Defense University, Washington, D.C., March www.whitehouse.gov/the-press-office/remarks-president-address-nation-libya).

35. J. Ranney, 'Responsibility to Protect: Engaging Civil Society.' *The Federalist Debate* no. 2 (2007): 13. http://www.ciise-iciss.gc.ca/report-en.asp (accessed 15 June 2015).

36. N. Dobos, 'Is UN Security Council Authorisation for Armed Humanitarian Intervention Morally Necessary?' *Philosophia* 38 no. 3 (2010): 499–515.

37. In Article 4 of the African Union's charter, African leaders pronounced themselves on the right "of the Union to intervene in a Member State pursuant to a decision of the Assembly in respect of grave circumstances, namely war crimes, genocide and crimes against humanity."

38. G. Evans, 'Interview: The RtoP Balance Sheet after Libya.' Thomas G. Weiss, Ramesh Thakur, Mary Ellen O'Connell, Aidan Hehir, Alex J. Bellamy, David Chandler, Rodger Shanahan, Rachel Gerber, Abiodun Williams and Gareth Evans, *The Responsibility to Protect: Challenges & Opportunities In Light of the Libyan Intervention*, 40 (2011).

39. A. De Waal, 'Darfur and the Failure of the Responsibility to Protect.' *International Affairs* 83, no. 6 (2007): 1039–1054, doi:10.1111/j.1468-2346.2007.00672.x.

40. A.J. Bellamy, 'Responsibility to Protect or Trojan Horse? The Crisis in Darfur and Humanitarian Intervention After Iraq.' *Ethics & International Affairs* 19, no. 2 (2005): 31–54.

41. R. Thakur, 'Outlook: Intervention, Sovereignty and the Responsibility to Protect: Experiences from ICISS.' *Security Dialogue* 33, no. 3 (2002): 323–340.

42. C.G. Badescu and L. Bergholm, 'The Responsibility to Protect and the Conflict in Darfur: The Big Let-down.' *Security Dialogue* 40, no. 3 (2009): 287–309.

43. G. Evans, 'Interview: The RtoP Balance Sheet after Libya.' Thomas G. Weiss, Ramesh Thakur, Mary Ellen O'Connell, Aidan Hehir, Alex J. Bellamy, David Chandler, Rodger Shanahan, Rachel Gerber, Abiodun Williams and Gareth Evans, *The Responsibility to Protect: Challenges & Opportunities In Light of the Libyan Intervention*, 40 (2011).

44. M. Mamdani, 'Libya: Politics of Humanitarian Intervention.' *Al Jazeera* (2011).

45. A.B. Halakhe, '"R2P in Practice": Ethnic Violence, Elections and Atrocity Prevention in Kenya.' *Global Center for the Responsibility to Protect: Occasional Paper Series No*, 4. Available at: https://www.globalr2p.org/media/files/kenya_occasionalpaper_web.pdf (2013) (accessed 15 June 2015).

46. C.G. Badescu and T.G. Weiss, 'Misrepresenting R2P and Advancing Norms: An Alternative Spiral?' *International Studies Perspectives* 11, no. 4 (2010): 354–374. doi:10.1111/j.1528-3585.2010.00412.x.

47. A.J. Kuperman, 'R2P: Catchy Name for a Fading Norm.' *Ethnopolitics* 10, no. 1 (2011): 125–128. doi:10.1080/17449057.2011.552355.

Redefining the responsibility to protect concept as a response to international crimes

Auriane Botte

School of Law, University of Nottingham, University Park, Nottingham, UK

This article assesses whether shifting the focus of responsibility to protect (R2P) as a response to crimes as such would potentially result in a greater support to implement the concept by the Security Council. Ten years ago, the international community endorsed the R2P concept as a response to genocide, war crimes, ethnic cleansing and crimes against humanity. However, the inaction of the Security Council in the situation in Syria sadly illustrates the current lack of consensus among the permanent Member States on the implementation of R2P. This article suggests redefining R2P as a response to core international crimes building upon their unifying effect.

Introduction

In a recent statement issued in April 2015 on the situation in Yarmouk, Syria, the Special Advisers on the Prevention of Genocide and on the Responsibility to Protect (R2P) recalled that 'The Security Council bears particular responsibility to end the bloodshed and to ensure the protection of civilians. Member States must overcome their differences and seek new ways to protect civilians in Syria.'[1] This call for action follows four years of a deplorable lack of consensus among the Security Council to take coercive measures to put an end to the conflict, despite the increasing number of civilian casualties. The Security Council's members have succeeded in reaching a consensus only with regard to the prohibition on the use of chemical weapons and to allow humanitarian access.[2] Russia and China refrained from using their veto on humanitarian access because they considered that the resolution did not pose any threat of a regime change in Syria and from using it on the use chemical weapons because of the strong prohibition attached to it.[3] The fact that the Security Council was only able to reach a consensus on these two issues for these particular reasons raises the question whether one could find a middle ground in shifting the debate from political issues, intrinsically linked with the fear of regime change, to legal issues, covering the commission of international crimes and accountability. This would mean shifting R2P from a political approach to a legal approach.

The R2P was first conceptualized in 2001 in the report of the International Commission on Intervention and State Sovereignty precisely to provide a framework to tackle 'conscience shocking' situations and protect populations from humanitarian catastrophes.[4] R2P was subsequently developed through several reports, including the reports of the High-level Panel on Threats, Challenges and Change, UN Secretary General's reports, the UN General Assembly's informal interactive dialogues and the UN Security Council's practice.

One of the major weaknesses undermining the R2P concept is the lack of consistency in its implementation by the Security Council due to the absence of consensus among the five permanent members. This lack of consistency is caused by diverging opinions on how and in which situations R2P should be implemented, putting Western powers, the UK, France and the US in opposition to the emerging powers, Russia and China. This divide explains why the international community has been unable so far to take any decisive action to address the situation in Syria, despite its commitment to never let a 'new Rwanda' happen again.[5]

It is important to note that 'implementing R2P' is not limited to having resort to military intervention but also encompasses a broad range of measures, including coercive measures under Chapter VII of the UN Charter designed to stop and sanction the commission of mass atrocities.[6] These coercive measures may include, inter alia, economic, political or diplomatic sanctions or a referral to the International Criminal Court (ICC). The veto power is more likely to be used against the adoption of a resolution by the Security Council providing for coercive measures. Consequently, the main question that this article aims to address is: how to facilitate a consensus among the Security Council five permanent members to implement R2P and respond to the commission of mass atrocities?

The new approach to R2P suggested in this article may potentially increase the chances of reaching a consensus among the five permanent members of the Security Council. The article is based on the assumption that the meaning of genocide, war crimes, ethnic cleansing and crimes against humanity, as currently understood, in practice, under the R2P concept, seems to be mainly referring to mass atrocities as 'threats to human life'[7] or threats to international peace and security, not as international crimes in a legal sense. This article argues that redefining R2P as a response to genocide, war crimes, ethnic cleansing and crimes against humanity as international crimes may allow taking advantage of the universal consensus among all States to condemn these specific crimes. This may also have the effect of placing R2P in a legal framework in addition to the moral or political framework in which it currently operates.

Starting from this hypothesis, the first part of the article will identify the signs of the existence of a universal consensus on condemning genocide, ethnic cleansing, crimes against humanity and war crimes in various documents expressing the views of all the States composing the international community. It will then demonstrate that R2P could be currently seen as focusing more on mass atrocities as threats to human life or international peace and security rather than international crimes as such. The second part of the article will examine the different causes behind the lack of consensus at the Security Council on implementing R2P coercive measures. It will focus more specifically on the situation in Syria and the various arguments put forward by Russia and China to justify their use of the veto power. The potential benefits of focusing on mass atrocities as international crimes, in a legal sense, will then be briefly explored, in light of the concerns expressed by Russia and China.

The responsibility to protect and core international crimes

The signs of a universal consensus on genocide, ethnic cleansing, war crimes and crimes against humanity

Genocide, war crimes, ethnic cleansing and crimes against humanity are often referred to as core international crimes because there is a widespread consensus among all States on the fact that these particular crimes are the most serious international crimes.[8] It is widely assumed that the commission of these crimes can never be justified and must give rise to consequences.[9] Examining in more depth the reasons why these specific international crimes should be distinguished from other international crimes or domestic crimes and can draw such widespread condemnation would fall outside the scope of this article. Suffice is to say that core international crimes are associated with the prohibition of acts that are condemned in all societies, in all religions because of the serious threat they pose to the society. Almost all States have introduced the prohibition of these core international crimes into their domestic legislation or, at least, the major underlying acts falling under the scope of core international crimes.[10] For the purpose of the argument, this article will only focus on the evidence demonstrating the existence of this universal consensus on the prohibition of these specific crimes.

Expressions of this universal consensus on condemning the most serious violations of human rights can first be found in the *travaux préparatoires* of the UN Draft Code of Crimes Against the Peace and Security of Mankind that was drafted over the twentieth century by the International Law Commission. In his reports, the Special Rapporteur Doudou Thiam pointed out that genocide, crimes against humanity and war crimes were the only international crimes that would allow reaching a broad consensus because they endanger the 'fundamental interests of Humanity'[11] and they go against the basic 'principles of civilization'.[12] The same conclusion could be drawn from the analysis of the negotiations that took place in 1998 at the Rome Conference to draft the Statute of the ICC to select the few crimes that would fall under the jurisdiction of the ICC.[13] A few years later, the Constitutive Act of the African Union in 2000 explicitly identified war crimes, genocide and crimes against humanity as particularly grave circumstances that would justify an intervention from the African Union.[14] The decision to limit the scope of R2P to genocide, war crimes, ethnic cleansing and war crimes in the World Summit Outcome Document of 2005 also points towards the existence of this universal consensus on condemning these crimes specifically.[15]

Nevertheless, the existence of a universal consensus on the prohibition of core international crimes should be understood as being nuanced. Indeed, the widespread consensus on the prohibition of these crimes may only exist with regard to the 'generic'[16] crimes, that is to say, with regard to the core values defended through the prohibition. In other words, all States agree on prohibiting 'genocide', 'war crimes', 'ethnic cleansing' and 'crimes against humanity' in principle, because of the shocking nature of the crimes. Confronted with a situation involving the widespread commission of atrocities against civilians, all States will be ready to express their indignation at these acts as illustrated by the various statements of States' representatives at the UN meetings, regardless of their own behaviour.[17] Moreover, the States are more likely to deny their involvement in the commission of genocide or crimes against humanity rather than acknowledging their participation in the crimes and defending themselves by arguing that it was justified.[18] However, disagreements emerge when deciding which specific or underlying acts should fall under the scope of the 'generic' crimes, such as rape, imposing measures intended to prevent births within the group, deportation or forcible transfer of population, etc. Disagreements also arise when qualifying the acts committed on the ground as core international crimes.[19] This is due to the fact that the definitions of the specific acts falling under the scope of core international crimes may vary from one State to the other, resulting in different qualification of the same acts by different States.

The above mentioned issues can be illustrated by the situation in Syria and the crimes committed against civilians. The widespread violations of human rights against the population in Syria have been condemned by nearly all the States on several occasions.[20] A resolution issued by the UN General Assembly in August 2012 explicitly condemned the commission of crimes against humanity and stressed that the perpetrators should face accountability.[21] This resolution was voted by 133 States while 12 States voted against, and 31 abstained.[22] The 12 States which voted against were Belarus, Bolivia, China, Cuba, Democratic People's Republic of Korea, Iran, Myanmar, Nicaragua, Russian Federation, Syria, Venezuela and Zimbabwe.[23] The 12 votes against this resolution could be interpreted as expressing a protest against Western powers and the risk of military intervention in Syria rather than contesting the commission of acts amounting to crimes against humanity in Syria.[24] Likewise, despite using their veto to stop the Security Council's resolutions providing for more coercive measures against Syria, Russia and China have also expressed their concerns about the suffering of civilians.[25] One could argue that this may only be a façade and that it does not prove a genuine condemnation of the acts. Nevertheless, Russia and China have also reaffirmed that the most serious international crimes must be condemned and must give rise to accountability outside the specific situation of Syria.[26] The Russian Federation furthermore stressed the necessity to support the values common to all religions.[27] This would tend to show that, at least in principle, ostensibly both Russia and China would agree with the other States on the fact that mass atrocities should never be overlooked. However, the difficulty to reach a consensus on the situation in Syria among the Security Council Member States emphasizes the obstacles that arise with regard to choosing the appropriate approach to adopt to respond to these core international crimes.

R2P 'designed to respond to threats to human life'[28]

As mentioned earlier, the endorsement of the R2P concept by the international community in the World Summit Outcome Document of 2005 relies heavily on the universal consensus on condemning genocide, war crimes, ethnic cleansing and crimes against humanity.[29] The only reason why the R2P concept was broadly accepted is because it was specifically limited to these four international crimes. The scope of R2P as it was first conceptualized in the International Commission on Intervention and State Sovereignty's report in 2001 extended beyond international crimes to large-scale loss of lives caused by natural disasters.[30] However, the High-level Panel on Threats, Challenges and Change in 2004 restricted the scope of R2P to international crimes, namely genocide, other large-scale killing, ethnic cleansing or serious violations of international humanitarian law in its report entitled 'A more secure world: our shared responsibility'.[31] As recalled earlier, the Constitutive Act of the African Union, which provides for a similar concept as the R2P, also limits the scope of Article 4(h) to war crimes, genocide and crimes against humanity.[32] A safe approach was, therefore, adopted by limiting the scope of R2P to mass atrocities that are widely prohibited, excluding more controversial crimes such as the crime of aggression, which was also not included, in 2005, under the ICC's jurisdiction for the same reason.[33] It is important to note that the mass atrocities listed in paragraph 138 and 139 of the World Summit Outcome Document 2005 are meant to refer to the definitions included in the Rome Statute created in 1998.[34] This reference to the Rome Statute is interesting because it means that the clear definitions stated in Articles 6 to 8 of the Rome Statute, completed by the Elements of Crimes, can provide guidance to qualify a series of acts on the ground as core international crimes.[35]

This limitation of the scope of R2P to genocide, war crimes, ethnic cleansing and crimes against humanity has been often criticized as a restriction of the concept and its potential impact.[36] Many scholars have argued that R2P as it was laid out in the World Summit Outcome Document of 2005 was a watered down version of the concept in order to meet the requirements of all the States and obtain a consensus.[37] In this sense, the limitation of R2P to these specific types of mass atrocities is a setback in the development of the concept. In addition to this, criticisms have also been raised about the fact that limiting R2P to the four most serious types of mass atrocities created an artificial threshold.[38] Indeed, this means that the State or the international community have the responsibility to protect the populations only in situations reaching a particular gravity. It could be interpreted as if a similar form of responsibility would not arise for violations of human rights of lesser extent or in other situations that do not reach the threshold of the mass atrocities listed under R2P but in which the population equally suffers and should be protected by the State or the international community.[39] These arguments are valid, to some extent, because limiting the scope of R2P for diplomatic reasons in order to reach a consensus may not suit the greater ideological purposes of R2P to protect the victims from large scale loss of life. However, it should not be forgotten that any definition of a scope inevitably implies creating a threshold. Even if the scope of R2P was extended as it was initially conceptualized, other case scenarios threatening populations would be excluded. Extending further the scope of R2P would result in stretching the concept to breaking point as it would then apply to too many different types of situations risking a dilution of the responsibility of the State and the international community.[40] On the contrary, the limitation of R2P to four international crimes benefiting from a strong universal consensus on their condemnation may be seen as a potential asset for R2P. Regrettably, the development of the concept of R2P through the UN Secretary General's reports, UN General Assembly informal dialogues and the practice of the Security Council appear to have insufficiently tapped into this great potential to strengthen the concept. This may be explained by the pivotal role in implementing R2P allocated in 2005[41] to the Security Council whose mandate is primarily focused on international peace and security, not international justice.[42]

Moreover, one could argue that the R2P concept is mostly designed to prevent the commission of mass atrocities before the populations are endangered.[43] Indeed, the development of the conceptualization of R2P after 2005 has been mainly focused on the preventive aspects of R2P and the necessity to identify the early warnings preceding the commission of mass atrocities.[44] This could be seen as another sign showing that R2P is, above all, a concept developed to remove threats to international peace and security. This is consistent with the spirit of the concept which places the primary responsibility on the State to protect its own population and on the international community to assist the State, in the second place. It promotes capacity building efforts to strengthen the State's ability to tackle situations before they evolve into the commission of mass atrocities. Nonetheless, the increasing number of mass atrocities perpetrated in the world tends to show that focusing only on the preventive aspect of R2P is not sufficient. Not all occurrences of mass atrocities may be prevented on time and an appropriate response may need to be implemented under the Responsibility to React and the Responsibility to Rebuild.[45] In spite of this reality, the Responsibility to Rebuild part of the R2P concept remains underdeveloped.[46]

In addition to the preventive aspect of R2P, the concept is also mainly targeted at protecting the victims more than ensuring accountability of the perpetrators or the responsibility of the State involved in the crimes.[47] The practice has demonstrated that, once the immediate threat to the victims is under control and international peace and security is restored, little attention is given to restoring long-term stability in the country. This can be illustrated by the implementation of R2P in Libya which severely lacked follow-up planned in advance and guiding the approach taken for the intervention. This may appear to be one of the major shortcomings of the conceptualization of R2P which does not encompass, or only to a limited extent, the notion of accountability and International Criminal Justice. When the notion of International Criminal Justice or the ICC is referred to under R2P, it is only seen as a 'tool in the toolbox'.[48] In other words, it is only an option that must be taken into account but it is far from being one of the primary objectives of R2P. The absence of the notion of accountability in R2P is surprising considering that the scope of R2P is genocide, war crimes, ethnic cleansing and crimes against humanity which should be considered as international crimes giving rise to responsibility, not only international threats to peace and security. Moreover, addressing the issues of accountability may also have an influence on preventing future commissions of mass crimes with the potential deterrent effect,[49] although the deterrent effect of International Criminal Justice is controversial.[50] All of the above questions support the assumption that R2P has not been developed, so far, as a response to international crimes as crimes, in a legal sense, but as a response to mass atrocities as threats to peace and security or 'threats to human life'.[51] This explains why the idea of redefining R2P as a response to core international crimes as such should be explored further to be able to rely on the universal consensus on criminalizing core international crimes in order to facilitate a consensus at the Security Council.

Assessing the effect of redefining R2P as a response to core international crimes

Geopolitical interests as R2P's Achilles heel

Following the previous part confirming the primary assumption that R2P is more focused on threats to international peace and security, this next part moves on to test the hypothesis of redefining R2P as a response to core international crimes. The main issue that prevents consistency in the implementation of R2P is the use of the veto power by one or more of the five permanent Security Council's Member States stopping any resolutions going in this direction. Out of the five permanent members of the Security Council having a veto power, only France and the UK are ICC States Parties and strongly support the R2P concept.[52] It can be assumed that neither France nor the UK would use their veto against a resolution deciding measures to stop the commission of mass crimes and ensure accountability for these crimes. The question is, therefore, what would be the best approach to adopt in order to get support from the three remaining permanent members, namely the US, the Russian Federation and China, to a Security Council resolution implementing R2P coercive measures.

When looking at the pattern of the use of veto by the permanent Member States in the last two decades, it appears that the US has consistently used its veto in situations related to the Middle East and the Palestine question.[53] This must be distinguished from the use of the veto power by the Russian Federation and China which was mostly triggered in the various situations where the Security Council was about to intervene in the internal affairs of a State.[54] This can be observed in the situations in the Republic of Bosnia and Herzegovina, Myanmar, Zimbabwe and Syria.[55] The Russian Federation and China also used their veto powers in situations directly involving their national interests and other specific issues, such as in the situations involving Guatemala and Georgia. In defence of the Chinese and Russian positions, it has been argued that the US had actually used its veto power more often than the two emerging powers.[56] However, the analysis of the pattern of the use of the veto clearly demonstrates that the frequency of the use of veto is not relevant. The US may have used its veto more often but it was always on the specific question of the situation in the Middle East and the Palestine.[57] In contrast, Russia and China have used their veto power to defend their vision of the principle of non-interference in any situations in which the issue was raised. Although it should not be assumed that the use of the veto power by the US is more legitimate, Russia and China have impeded the international community from stepping in several situations posing serious threats to civilians. This does not mean that the situation in the Middle East does not pose a threat to civilians but a possible obstruction from the US is likely to be limited to this situation and should probably be dealt with as a separate and specific problem for the purpose of this article.[58] This is particularly true since the US has adopted a slightly more positive attitude towards the ICC.[59] As a result, the US may be less of an obstacle for the implementation of R2P coercive measures, including a referral to the ICC, except with regard to the situation in the Middle East and Palestine although this situation would equally fall under the scope of R2P. Consequently, a first step should be to identify what could influence the Russian Federation and China to support a resolution implementing R2P as a response to core international crimes.

It is important to note first that the Russian Federation and China are not opposed to the R2P concept per se.[60] They are both supportive of the concept if it is used as a preventive tool.[61] They agree that R2P may be a useful concept to strengthen the capacity of the State to tackle issues related to mass atrocities arising on its own territory. They would favour a domestic solution to the problem of mass crimes, including, if necessary, the support of the international community.[62] Russia and China would, therefore, support measures under the first and second pillars of R2P which do not undermine State sovereignty and are consistent with the principle of non-intervention in the internal affairs of a State.[63] Regrettably, experience has shown that they would still defend this position in a case where a State is unable or unwilling to respond to the commission of mass crimes, such as the situation in Syria for example. This can be explained, as mentioned in the introduction, by the fear of regime change which was aggravated by the situation in Libya.[64] The main problem here is that, in most cases, these two States prioritize their view of sovereignty and peace over justice and the protection of civilians.[65]

One of the issues that have often impeded a consensus on the implementation of R2P as a response to mass crimes is related to the impartiality of the entity collecting evidence. On several occasions, China and Russia, more particularly, criticized the methods used to collect evidence on the commission of the crimes and contested its authenticity.[66] Russia raised the issue during the Security Council's debates on general issues but it also put forward the same argument with regard to the evidence of core international crimes committed in Syria.[67] This was also a justification given to veto a draft resolution referring the situation to the ICC[68] because this would amount to acknowledging the commission of crimes against humanity in Syria. A possible consequence of acknowledging the commission of crimes against humanity would be the escalation to more coercive measures.[69] In a nutshell, even if one could rely on the universal consensus on condemning the commission of core international crimes to get support from Russia and China, it would still be necessary to overcome the different interpretations of the same events occurring on the ground.[70] This tends to show that more work needs to be done to ensure legitimacy in the assessment of early warnings preceding mass crimes under R2P and the impartiality of fact-finding missions, including UN Commissions of Inquiry[71] in order to address the concerns expressed by Russia. Redefining R2P as a response to international crimes may allow relying more heavily on clear criteria provided by the legal definitions of the crimes.

Another argument that is often put forward by Russia and China to justify their use of the veto power against coercive measures taken by the Security Council to respond to widespread violations of human rights is that it does not fall within the scope of the

Security Council's power.[72] The Russian Federation stressed that the Security Council should only be focused on matters of international peace and security whereas the Human Rights Council should deal with issues related to widespread violations of human rights.[73] However, even when the issue is dealt with by the Human Rights Council or the General Assembly, both Russia and China still vote against formally qualifying the acts committed on the ground as core international crimes or creating a Commission of Inquiry, at least with regard to the situation in Syria.[74] This may be used as a counter-argument against the idea of redefining R2P as a response to core international crimes rather than exclusively as threats to human life and peace and security. It is not certain that acknowledging the commission of atrocities would be powerful enough to overcome the political interests maintaining Bashar al-Assad in power. Russia and China have also argued on several occasions that the commission of core international crimes did not always amount to a threat to international peace and security and may not, therefore, require action from the Security Council.[75] This argument was used, for example, with regard to the situation in North Korea.[76] This argument relies on a textual reading of Article 24 of the UN Charter according to which the Security Council's primary responsibility is to maintain and restore international peace and security, not to ensure compliance with International Law.[77] Nevertheless, following this reasoning would result in excluding from the application of Chapter VII many occurrences of mass international crimes. The main weakness of this argument is that it ignores the common assumption that the commission of mass crimes left unanswered are more likely to become a threat to international peace and security.[78]

Shifting R2P focus: from threat to life and security to international crimes

Although similar arguments have been raised by China and the Russian Federation to justify their use of the veto power, one may identify different motivations behind their stance. This would tend to suggest that different approaches may be needed to obtain the support of China or Russia to respond to core international crimes. From the analysis of the statements given by the Russian Federation at the Security Council's meetings, it seems that Russia adopts a more nationalistic approach and strongly rejects any influence from Western powers.[79] It clearly wants to be distinguished from Western powers and wants to present itself as the representative of emerging powers.[80] This is an interesting position considering that China is often seen as the only non-Western permanent member.[81] In this sense, the motivations of Russia to use its veto may seem less rational than those of China. In order to address the concerns of Russia, it may be worth insisting on the fact that the prohibition of core international crimes is far from being limited to Western countries, as demonstrated by the existence of a universal consensus on the prohibition of core international crimes mentioned earlier in this article. On the contrary, the Chinese position seems to be more rational and legitimate, to some extent, although it may just be a façade. In the situation of Syria, the justifications of China to use its veto were relying on the necessity to carry on negotiations in order to reach a consensual solution.[82] China, therefore, advocates for more diplomacy and for finding a middle-ground, although, as mentioned earlier, these arguments may not be genuine. It could be argued here that the prohibition of core international crimes constitute, a common ground uniting the international community as a whole. Considering their different attitudes, it may be easier to convince China not to vote against the resolution or to abstain to vote than it would be for Russia.

This is particularly true since China is attached to having a positive image at the international level as an important economic actor in order to maintain its credibility.[83] This is further demonstrated by its preference for using abstentions rather than vetoes to express its disapproval.[84] This could be seen as a potential leverage that has already been proven successful in the situation of Sudan, for example.[85] In addition to this, pressure exercised by the civil society may also have an influence on China as well as informal consultations among the Security Council's members.[86] Unfortunately, such discussions are not disclosed to the public but it would be interesting to see whether the strong stance defended in formal meetings slightly varies from the position of these States behind closed doors. This could give an indication whether there would be a possible opening to explore by relying on the universal consensus to condemn core international crimes previously mentioned. The fact that China and Russia did not use their veto in the situation of Syria with regard to the issue of chemical weapons or humanitarian assistance may also be seen as a positive sign.

It is now widely accepted that the question, with which the international community is confronted, is no longer framed in terms of whether the commission of core international crimes should give rise to accountability but relates to how or what form the response to these crimes should take.[87] Consequently, R2P would benefit from being perceived as a response to core international crimes as such although this may not solve all the problems related to its implementation. Ensuring respect for the Rule of Law and ending impunity are objectives that are, at least in principle, accepted by a vast majority of the States, including Russia and China, as shown in various debates held at the UN.[88] Nevertheless, different States advocate different methods to reach the objective of ensuring accountability for mass crimes. R2P as a response to international crimes as such would allow relying on these statements made publicly by the States in order to encourage them to adopt a consistent behaviour and remain true to their position.[89] If a State has repeatedly expressed its position on the necessity to ensure accountability for mass crimes, it may be more difficult to rise against a response from the international community directly based on the prohibition of these crimes. This approach could certainly be criticized by realist scholars arguing that States would only act according to their own interests and not being true to their previous statements would have little influence on their decisions.[90] This counter-argument may be less powerful in the specific context of mass crimes.[91] Indeed, a few examples, including the situation in Darfur or Libya, have demonstrated that the specific nature of core international crimes may lead the States to take decisions not solely guided by their own national interests. Indeed, Russia and China did not vote in favour of the resolutions but abstained on the vote. In the situation in Sudan, one could argue that China actually acted against its own interests by allowing a referral to the ICC as it had close economic relations with Sudan.[92] Proposals from France and other States on reforming the veto power specifically in situations of mass crimes are another expression of this unique approach to core international crimes.[93]

The idea of redefining R2P as a response to core international crimes as crimes, in a legal sense, could also be assessed in light of the consensus that was reached at the Security Council on taking action with regard to the use of chemical weapons in Syria.[94] Both Russia and China strongly condemned the use of chemical weapons as 'inadmissible'.[95] The fact that the use of chemical weapons can never be tolerated may be compared to the consensus on condemning other core international crimes. Furthermore, it is important to note that the use of chemical weapons could indirectly fall under the scope of war crimes.[96] This raises the question: why this act potentially falling under war crimes had the power to trigger a response from the international community whereas other widespread crimes committed against civilians, such as the deliberate bombing of civilian areas by the Syrian security forces,[97] or other war crimes or crimes against humanity, do not have this effect? Other questions that should be explored in order to shed light on the potential of focusing R2P as a response to core international crimes are related to the fact that the use of chemical weapons was interpreted as if a threshold had been crossed. This is how the US explicitly expressed its concern about the use of chemical weapons in Syria.[98] It clearly stated that a 'red line' had been crossed which could be a trigger for military action.[99] Could the threat of military intervention explain the fact that Russia and China refrained from using their veto against a Security Council's resolution on chemical weapons in Syria? In the face of the threat of military intervention without the authorization of the Security Council, Russia and China may have preferred to agree on a middle-ground solution in order to have their say on this issue. In addition to this, it would be worth exploring further why evidence provided by the Organization for the Prohibition of Chemical Weapons was accepted as legitimate evidence by Russia and China.[100] This could be useful to determine what type of international entity would be able to provide legitimate evidence, accepted by China and Russia, with regard to the commission of other core international crimes. However, one should bear in mind that the issue of acceptable evidence for Russia and China may depend less on the legitimacy of the actual entity which gathers evidence than the particular geopolitical context in which the evidence is brought forward.

Conclusion

This article argued for a shift in the implementation of the R2P concept from a response to mass atrocities to a response to core international crimes as crimes, in a legal sense. As a result, R2P would not only be based on moral or political obligations but could also find legal bases which may be less subject to dispute. Relying on the universal consensus on prohibiting core international crimes may be helpful to obtain support from all the States to implement R2P as a response to crimes rather than solely a response to threat to human life although the two concepts overlap. The analysis of the positions of both China and the Russian Federation vetoing resolutions on more coercive measures with regard to the situation in Syria has demonstrated that many obstacles still need to be addressed. They include, inter alia, the question of the legality of the Security Council's decisions related to breaches of International Law or the contested validity of the evidence demonstrating the occurrence of crimes on the ground. Nevertheless, the study of the arguments put forward by Russia and China tend to show that an approach based on a response to core international crimes as such may facilitate a consensus or, at least, abstention on a vote at the Security Council. The hypothesis that focusing on core international crimes could have a potential positive impact on the implementation of R2P can only be confirmed or invalidated by practice. The fact that the Security Council's resolutions on condemning the use of chemical weapons in Syria and authorizing humanitarian access were adopted unanimously could be seen as positive signs towards adopting this approach.

Notes

1. Special Advisers on the Prevention of Genocide and the Responsibility to Protect, 'Statement by Adama Dieng, Special Adviser of the Secretary General on the Prevention of Genocide and Jennifer Welsh, Special Adviser of the Secretary General on the Responsibility to Protect on the Situation in Yarmouk, Syria' (United Nations, April 9, 2015).
2. Security Council, 'Resolution 2118 (2013)' (United Nations, September 27, 2013); Security Council, 'Resolution 2165 (2014)' (United Nations, July 14, 2014).
3. Security Council, '7216th Meeting on the Situation in the Middle East' (United Nations, July 14, 2014); General Assembly, '15th Plenary Meeting General Assembly' (United Nations, September 27, 2013).
4. International Commission on Intervention and State Sovereignty, 'The Responsibility to Protect: Report of the International Commission on Intervention and State Sovereignty' (Ottawa: Ottawa: International Development Research Centre, December 2001).
5. Security Council, '7155th Meeting on Prevention and fight against Genocide' (United Nations, April 16, 2014).
6. UN General Assembly, '2005 World Summit Outcome' (United Nations, October 24, 2005), para. 138–139.
7. International Commission on Intervention and State Sovereignty, 'The Responsibility to Protect: Report of the International Commission on Intervention and State Sovereignty.'
8. *Rome Statute of the International Criminal Court*, 1998.
9. Mahmood Mamdani, Responsibility to Protect or Right to Punish?', *Journal of Intervention and Statebuilding* 4, no. 1 (March 1, 2010): 53–67, doi:10.1080/17502970903541721.
10. Doudou Thiam, 'Twelfth Report on the Draft Code of Crimes against the Peace and Security of Mankind', Report from the Special Rapporteur (New York: United Nations, 1994), http://legal.un.org/ilc/documentation/english/a_cn4_460.pdf.
11. Doudou Thiam, 'Second Report on the Draft Code of Offences against the Peace and Security of Mankind', Report from the Special Rapporteur (New York: United Nations, 1984), http://legal.un.org/ilc/documentation/english/a_cn4_377.pdf.
12. Doudou Thiam, 'Draft Code of Crimes against the Peace and Security of Mankind (Part II) – Including the Draft Statute for an International Criminal Court', Report from the Special Rapporteur (New York: United Nations, 1983).
13. Preparatory Committee on the Establishment of an International Criminal Court, 'Report of the Preparatory Committee on the Establishment of an International Criminal Court (Volume II)', Compilation of delegations' proposals (New York: United Nations, 1996); Ad Hoc Committee on the Establishment of an International Criminal Court, 'Report of the Ad Hoc Committee on the Establishment of an International Criminal Court', General Assembly Official Records (New York: United Nations, September 6, 1995).
14. African Union, 'The Constitutive Act of the African Union' (African Union, 2001).
15. UN General Assembly, 'A/RES/60/1', para. 138–139.
16. Steven R. Ratner, *Accountability for Human Rights Atrocities in International Law: Beyond the Nuremberg Legacy*, 3rd ed (Oxford: Oxford University Press, 2009), 14.
17. Security Council, '7155th Meeting on Prevention and fight against Genocide'; Security Council, 'Open Meeting on the Promotion and Strengthening of the Rule of Law in the Maintenance of International Peace and Security', Open meeting (New York: United Nations, October 17, 2012).
18. Aidan Hehir, 'The Responsibility to Protect in International Political Discourse: Encouraging Statement of Intent or Illusory Platitudes?', *The International Journal of Human Rights* 15, no. 8 (2011): 1331–1348, doi:10.1080/13642987.2010.521128.
19. Andrea Birdsall, 'The Responsibility to Prosecute and the ICC: A Problematic Relationship?', *Criminal Law Forum*, March 1, 2015, 1–22, doi:10.1007/s10609-015-9244-5.
20. UN General Assembly, 'Resolution 66/253 Adopted by the General Assembly' (United Nations, August 7, 2012), 2536969; UN General Assembly, 'Resolution 69/189 Situation of Human Rights in the Syrian Arab Republic' (United Nations, December 18, 2014); Security

Council, '7180th Meeting on the Situation in the Middle East' (United Nations, May 22, 2014).

21. UN General Assembly, 'Resolution 66/253 Adopted by the General Assembly', 253.
22. UN General Assembly, 'UN General Assembly 124th Plenary Meeting' (United Nations, August 3, 2012).
23. General Assembly, '124th Plenary Meeting on the Prevention of Armed Conflicts' (United Nations, August 3, 2012).
24. Louis Charbonneau, 'U.N. Nations Condemn Syria; Russia, China Seen Isolated', *Reuters*, August 3, 2012, http://www.reuters.com/article/2012/08/03/us-syria-crisis-un-idUSBRE8720ZN20120803.
25. General Assembly, '15th Plenary Meeting General Assembly'; Security Council, '7180th Meeting on the Situation in the Middle East.'
26. Security Council, '7113th Meeting on the Promotion and Strengthening of the Rule of Law in the Maintenance of International Peace and Security' (United Nations, February 19, 2014); Security Council, 'Open Meeting on the Promotion and Strengthening of the Rule of Law in the Maintenance of International Peace and Security.'
27. General Assembly, '15th Plenary Meeting General Assembly.'
28. International Commission on Intervention and State Sovereignty, 'The Responsibility to Protect: Report of the International Commission on Intervention and State Sovereignty.'
29. Aidan Hehir and Anthony Lang, 'The Impact of the Security Council on the Efficacy of the International Criminal Court and the Responsibility to Protect', *Criminal Law Forum* March 1, 2015, 1–27, doi:10.1007/s10609-015-9245-4.
30. International Commission on Intervention and State Sovereignty, 'The Responsibility to Protect: Report of the International Commission on Intervention and State Sovereignty.'
31. High-level Panel on Threats, Challenges and Change, 'A More Secure World: Our Shared Responsibility', UN Secretary General Report (New York: United Nations, 2004).
32. African Union, 'The Constitutive Act of the African Union.'
33. Committee of the whole, 'Summary Record of the 6th Meeting' (Rome: United Nations, June 18, 1998), http://unbisnet.un.org:8080/ipac20/ipac.jsp?session=1383304CT4U50.20209&profile=bib&uri=link=3100006~!976266~!3100001~!3100040&aspect=alpha&menu=search&ri=3&source=~!horizon&term=A%2FCONF.183%2FC.1%2FSR.6&index=ZUNSYMA.
34. UN Secretary General, 'Responsibility to Protect: State Responsibility and Prevention' (New York: United Nations, July 9, 2013).
35. Carsten Stahn, *Opening Address*, Responsibility to Protect and Prosecute: The International Criminal Court after Libya, accessed February 16, 2015, http://iisr2p.leeds.ac.uk/current/responsibility-to-protect-and-prosecute/.
36. James Pattison, 'Is There a Duty to Intervene? Intervention and the Responsibility to Protect', *Philosophy Compass* 8, no. 6 (June 6, 2013): 570–579.
37. General Assembly, 'Verbatim Record: 85th Plenary Meeting', Verbatim record (New York: United Nations, April 6, 2005); General Assembly, 'Verbatim Record: 86th Plenary Meeting', Verbatim record (New York: United Nations, April 6, 2005); General Assembly, 'Verbatim Record: 87th Plenary Meeting', Verbatim record (New York: United Nations, April 7, 2005); General Assembly, 'Verbatim Record: 88th Plenary Meeting', Verbatim record (New York: United Nations, April 7, 2005); General Assembly, 'Verbatim Record: 89th Plenary Meeting', Verbatim record (New York: United Nations, April 7, 2005); General Assembly, 'Verbatim Record: 90th Plenary Meeting', Verbatim record (New York: United Nations, April 8, 2005).
38. Terry Nardin, 'From Right to Intervene to Duty to Protect: Michael Walzer on Humanitarian Intervention', *European Journal of International Law* 24, no. 1 (February 1, 2013): 67–82, doi:10.1093/ejil/chs085.
39. Ibid.
40. Ibid.
41. UN General Assembly, 'A/RES/60/1', para. 138–139.
42. *Charter of the United Nations and Statute of the International Court of Justice*, 1945.
43. Kirsten Ainley, 'The Responsibility to Protect and the International Criminal Court: Counteracting the Crisis', *International Affairs* 91, no. 1 (2015): 37–54, doi:10.1111/1468-2346.12185.

44. UN Secretary General, 'Early Warning, Assessment and the Responsibility to Protect', Report from the UN Secretary General (New York: United Nations, July 14, 2010); UN Secretary General, 'Responsibility to Protect: State Responsibility and Prevention.'
45. Jennifer Welsh, 'Civilian Protection in Libya: Putting Coercion and Controversy Back into RtoP', *Ethics & International Affairs* 25, no. 3 (2011): 255–262.
46. Gareth J. Evans, *The Responsibility to Protect Ending Mass Atrocity Crimes Once and for All* (Washington, DC: Brookings Institution Press, 2008), 149.
47. International Commission on Intervention and State Sovereignty, 'The Responsibility to Protect: Report of the International Commission on Intervention and State Sovereignty'; Carsten Stahn, 'Syria and the Semantics of Intervention, Aggression and Punishment On "Red Lines" and "Blurred Lines"', *Journal of International Criminal Justice* 11, no. 5 (December 1, 2013): 955–977, doi:10.1093/jicj/mqt066; Claire Garbett, 'The Concept of the Civilian: Legal Recognition, Adjudication and the Trials of International Criminal Justice', *International Journal of Law in Context* 8, no. 4 (December 2012): 469–486.
48. International Commission on Intervention and State Sovereignty, 'The Responsibility to Protect: Report of the International Commission on Intervention and State Sovereignty'; Ainley, 'The Responsibility to Protect and the International Criminal Court.'
49. Sheri Rosenberg, 'The Relationship between the International Criminal Court and the Prevention of Mass Atrocities', in *Genocide, Jerusalem, Israel* (Genocide, Jerusalem, Israel, 2012).
50. Darryl Robinson, 'Serving the Interests of Justice: Amnesties, Truth Commissions and the International Criminal Court', *European Journal of International Law* 14, no. 3 (June 1, 2003): 481–505, doi:10.1093/ejil/14.3.481.
51. International Commission on Intervention and State Sovereignty, 'The Responsibility to Protect: Report of the International Commission on Intervention and State Sovereignty.'
52. Permanent mission of France, 'Statement of France at the UN General Assembly Interactive Dialogue on R2P' (United Nations, September 8, 2014); UK Mission to the UN, 'Statement of UK to the UN General Assembly Interactive Dialogue on R2P' (United Nations, September 8, 2014); International Criminal Court, 'ICC at a Glance', *ICC CPI*, May 1, 2013.
53. Joëlle Sciboz, 'Security Council – Veto List', research starter, *Dag Hammarskjöld Library Research Guides*, accessed May 26, 2015, http://research.un.org/en/docs/sc/quick.
54. Ibid.
55. Security Council, '3475th Meeting on the Situation in the Republic of Bosnia and Herzegovina' (United Nations, December 2, 1994); Security Council, '5619th Meeting on the Situation in Myanmar' (United Nations, January 12, 2007); Security Council, '5933rd Meeting on Peace and Security in Africa' (United Nations, July 11, 2008); Security Council, '7180th Meeting on the Situation in the Middle East'; Security Council, '6810th Meeting on the Situation in the Middle East' (United Nations, July 19, 2012).
56. Ramesh Thakur, 'Law, Legitimacy and the United Nations', in *Legality and Legitimacy in Global Affairs*, eds. Richard A. Falk, Mark Juergensmeyer, and Vesselin Popovski (New York ; Oxford: Oxford University Press, 2012), 46–66.
57. Sciboz, 'Research Guides.'
58. Kurt Mills, 'R2P3: Protecting, Prosecuting, or Palliating in Mass Atrocity Situations?', *Journal of Human Rights* 12, no. 3 (July 1, 2013): 333–56, doi:10.1080/14754835.2013.812421.
59. Ibid.
60. Congyan Cai, 'New Great Powers and International Law in the 21st Century', *European Journal of International Law* 24, no. 3 (August 1, 2013): 755–795, doi:10.1093/ejil/cht050; Birdsall, 'The Responsibility to Prosecute and the ICC.'
61. Global Centre for the Responsibility to Protect, 'Summary of the 5th Informal Interactive Dialogue of the UN General Assembly on R2P' (New York: Global Centre for the Responsibility to Protect, October 22, 2013).
62. Security Council, '7180th Meeting on the Situation in the Middle East.'
63. Cai, 'New Great Powers and International Law in the 21st Century.'
64. Birdsall, 'The Responsibility to Prosecute and the ICC.'
65. Security Council, '7113th Meeting on the Promotion and Strengthening of the Rule of Law in the Maintenance of International Peace and Security.'
66. Security Council, '7155th Meeting on Prevention and fight against Genocide'; Security Council, '7180th Meeting on the Situation in the Middle East.'

67. Security Council, '7180th Meeting on the Situation in the Middle East.'
68. Security Council, 'Draft Resolution S/2014/348' (United Nations, May 22, 2014); Security Council, '7180th Meeting on the Situation in the Middle East.'
69. Kurt Mills, 'The Responsibility to Protect and the International Criminal Court: Complementary or Conflicting?', *R2P Ideas in Brief* 4, no. 2 (2014): 1–17.
70. Birdsall, 'The Responsibility to Prosecute and the ICC.'
71. Carsten Stahn and Catherine Harwood, 'Why Reports about the "Death of R2P" May Be Premature: Links between the Responsibility to Protect and Human Rights Fact-Finding', *European Society of International Law*, ESIL Reflections 3, no. 5 (May 22, 2014): 1–6.
72. Security Council, '7353rd Meeting on the Situation in the Democratic People's Republic of Korea' (United Nations, December 22, 2014).
73. Ibid.
74. Human Rights Council, 'Report of the Human Rights Council on Its Seventeenth Special Session' (Geneva: United Nations, October 18, 2011).
75. Security Council, '7353rd Meeting on the Situation in the Democratic People's Republic of Korea'; Phil C. W. Chan, 'A Keen Observer of the International Rule of Law? International Law in China's Voting Behaviour and Argumentation in the United Nations Security Council', *Leiden Journal of International Law* 26, no. 4 (December 2013): 875–907, doi:10.1017/S0922156513000459.
76. Security Council, '7353rd Meeting on the Situation in the Democratic People's Republic of Korea.'
77. *UN Charter* Article 24.
78. Security Council Report, 'Crafting Peace Mandates Offers Strategic Chance to Support National Rule-of-Law Priorities, Secretary General Tells Security Council Open Debate', Meetings coverage (New York: Security Council Report, February 19, 2014); Security Council, 'Security Council Working Methods', Open meeting (New York: United Nations, October 23, 2014); Security Council, 'Open Meeting on the Promotion and Strengthening of the Rule of Law in the Maintenance of International Peace and Security.'
79. Security Council, '7180th Meeting on the Situation in the Middle East'; Michael Contarino and Selena Lucent, 'Stopping the Killing: The International Criminal Court and Juridical Determination of the Responsibility to Protect', *Global Responsibility to Protect*, Martinus Nijhoff Publishers, 2009, no. 1 (July 8, 2009): 560–83.
80. Security Council, '6810th Meeting on the Situation in the Middle East.'
81. Chan, 'A Keen Observer of the International Rule of Law?'
82. Security Council, '7180th Meeting on the Situation in the Middle East.'
83. Contarino and Lucent, 'Stopping the Killing: The International Criminal Court and Juridical Determination of the Responsibility to Protect'; Cai, 'New Great Powers and International Law in the 21st Century.'
84. Chan, 'A Keen Observer of the International Rule of Law?'
85. Lawrence Moss, 'The UN Security Council and the International Criminal Court: Towards a More Principled Relationship', UN Security Council in Focus (Berlin, Germany: Friedrich-Ebert-Stiftung, March 2012).
86. Chan, 'A Keen Observer of the International Rule of Law?'
87. Birdsall, 'The Responsibility to Prosecute and the ICC.'
88. Security Council, 'Security Council Working Methods'; Security Council Report, 'Crafting Peace Mandates Offers Strategic Chance to Support National Rule-of-Law Priorities, Secretary General Tells Security Council Open Debate'; Security Council, 'Open Meeting on the Promotion and Strengthening of the Rule of Law in the Maintenance of International Peace and Security.'
89. Charbonneau, 'U.N. Nations Condemn Syria; Russia, China Seen Isolated.'
90. Olga A. Avdeyeva, 'Does Reputation Matter for States' Compliance with International Treaties? States Enforcement of Anti-trafficking Norms', *The International Journal of Human Rights* 16, no. 2 (February 1, 2012): 298–320, doi:10.1080/13642987.2010.540240.
91. Ibid.
92. Rosa Aloisi, 'A Tale of Two Institutions: The United Nations Security Council and the International Criminal Court', *International Criminal Law Review* 13, no. 1 (2013): 147–168.
93. Security Council, 'Security Council Working Methods.'

94.   Security Council, 'Resolution 2118 (2013)'; Security Council, 'Resolution 2209 (2015)' (United Nations, March 6, 2015).
95.   General Assembly, '15th Plenary Meeting General Assembly.'
96.   *Rome Statute of the International Criminal Court.*
97.   Independent International Commission of Inquiry on the Syrian Arab Republic, 'Report of the Independent International Commission of Inquiry on the Syrian Arab Republic' (United Nations, February 5, 2015).
98.   Spencer Zifcak, 'The Responsibility to Protect', in *International Law*, ed. Malcolm Evans (Oxford: Oxford University Press, 2014), 509–534.
99.   Glenn Kessler, 'President Obama and the "red Line" on Syria's Chemical Weapons', *The Washington Post*, September 6, 2013, http://www.washingtonpost.com/blogs/fact-checker/wp/2013/09/06/president-obama-and-the-red-line-on-syrias-chemical-weapons/.
100. United Nations Security Council, '7401st Meeting The Situation in the Middle East' (United Nations, March 6, 2015).

R2P, Global Governance, and the Syrian refugee crisis

Alise Coen

Political Science, University of Wisconsin-Sheboygan, USA

This article bridges Responsibility to Protect (R2P) with work on Global Governance (GG). Both are products of a normative shift away from state-centric conceptualizations of authority and towards collective efforts to address transnational problems where traditional (State) governance mechanisms are absent or have failed. By assessing the governance architecture of R2P and of refugee protection in the case of Syria, the article sheds light on how global structures of authority interact with national and local systems. The constraints on agents operating at multiple levels of authority and the inequalities inherent in these structures have important implications for the effectiveness of R2P outcomes. Given the power asymmetries associated with the governance architecture of R2P and the proxy war in Syria, the article argues that the use of coercive intervention under R2P's Pillar Three risks further de-legitimization of the concept itself. As an alternative, the article calls for greater emphasis on R2P as refugee protection, particularly in light of the largest refugee crisis in the post-World War II era. The international community can take immediate and important steps towards fulfilling R2P by responding to the millions displaced by mass atrocity crimes.

Introduction

The world is witnessing the greatest refugee crisis since World War II, with the UN Refugee Agency annual report indicating the total number of forcibly displaced persons for 2014 rose to a record high of 59.5 million. This figure includes over 38 million internally displaced persons (IDP) due to conflict, violence, and human rights violations. A primary cause of this displacement is the ongoing civil war in Syria. In 2014, Syria replaced Afghanistan as the world's largest source of refugees.[1] In this context, the burgeoning literature on Responsibility to Protect (R2P) has grappled with the status of the norm of human protection in the aftermath of much criticism and unresolved crisis following its 2011 application in Libya. Some have identified the Libyan intervention as a negative turning point in the evolution of R2P that facilitated inaction in Syria and reflected the failure of the concept.[2] Since the Libyan intervention, however, the UN Security Council has reaffirmed its commitment to R2P with resolution 2150 (2014) calling on states to recommit to fighting genocide and other serious crimes against humanity. The Security Council has also invoked R2P in South Sudan, Yemen, Mali, Somalia, the Central African Republic, and Syria to authorize UN forces or remind political authorities of their obligations to protect their populations from mass atrocity crimes.[3] Ten years after its global acceptance at the World Summit, R2P remains very much a work in progress, with its implementation heavily debated.

In light of ongoing failures by the international community to respond to the humanitarian catastrophe in Syria, R2P appears to be at a crossroads.[4] Given that these failures are particularly acute in the face of the largest refugee crisis since 1945, this article argues that a greater focus on R2P as refugee protection is needed. While much R2P scholarship has focused on the controversial Pillar Three component of the framework regarding coercive intervention, the international community can take immediate and important steps towards fulfilling R2P by responding to the millions displaced by mass atrocity crimes. Theoretically, this article bridges R2P scholarship with work on Global Governance (GG) to: locate R2P in an evolving international construction of *democratic sovereignty*; evaluate the *governance architecture* and diffusion of authority in R2P; and consider the implications of power asymmetries inherent in that dispersion of authority for the future legitimacy of R2P. Understanding the interaction between transnational and subnational forces and their attendant constraints is important for moving conceptualizations of both GG and R2P forward. The article focuses empirically on Syria, which has evolved into a protracted civil war and proxy war and the centre of the largest refugee crisis in the post-World War II era.

The article proceeds as follows: The first section explores connections between R2P and GG. This section locates the human protection norm within an evolving construction of *democratic sovereignty* that acknowledges the asymmetrical power advantages of states, while allowing non-state and civil society actors to play a significant role in shaping global visions of legitimate sovereignty practices. Next, the article evaluates the *governance architecture* of R2P that diffuses authority across overlapping webs of trans-state and sub-state actors, paying close attention to the dispersion of governance in the Syrian case. The article then assesses the role of power asymmetries in the global governance of R2P. Here, the Libyan intervention of 2011 and the power dynamics shaping the Syrian proxy war are considered with regard to the problems of coercive intervention under Pillar Three. The article argues that the interplay of power asymmetries and postcolonial historical legacies renders coercive interventions problematic such that they undermine the legitimacy of R2P. In this context the article argues for greater attention to refugee protections as non-coercive R2P policy tools.

Global governance and R2P

GG emerged within International Relations (IR) in the 1990s. With shifting patterns of authority at the end of the Cold War, interest in new approaches gave rise to diverse perspectives that typically shared a commitment to: moving beyond state-centric IR frameworks; recognizing the complexity of overlapping spheres of authority; and explicating the balance of universalistic and localized forces.[5] Despite critiques that the concept remains slippery,[6] Weiss and Wilkinson observe that 'global governance has become both widespread and useful for describing growing complexity in the way that the world is organized and authority exercised', but call for more efforts to 'identify and explain the structure of global authority' with regard to 'how regional, national, and local systems intersect with or push against that structure'.[7]

Amidst growing interest in global governance among both academics and policymakers, as well as concern about humanitarian failures and deficiencies, the 2001

International Commission on Intervention and State Sovereignty (ICISS) report argued that the changing international environment required a redefinition of state authority from sovereignty as 'control' to sovereignty as 'responsibility'.[8] While scholars of R2P observe that this represents a significant departure from preexisting legal conceptions of authority by grounding it in the capacity to provide effective protection to populations at risk,[9] it is important not to exaggerate the extent to which R2P undermines state sovereignty. Rather than wholly replacing state sovereignty with international authority, R2P 'reflects a negotiated global consensus on the appropriate balance between a basic minimum of human rights and other cherished principles of order [like] sovereignty [and] non-interference'.[10] The nature of this balance has important implications for understanding how global authority interacts with regional, national, and local systems. The degree to which R2P signifies a reconstitution of traditional approaches to state sovereignty also has important implications for the 'interregnum in global governance', which 'points to a state of accelerating transition away from the dominance of sovereignty ... to a potentially more pluralist (and hopefully more democratic) intellectual and practical ecosystem [and] to new structures of power'.[11] Echoing R2P's redefinition of sovereignty to encompass a state's responsibility to protect its citizens, GG scholars have argued for a more timely conceptualization of sovereignty that, drawing on Isaiah Berlin, reformulates state authority from an emphasis on 'sovereignty from external coercion' to 'sovereignty to the interests of one's citizens'.[12]

The shared contours of GG and R2P are not surprising given that both are products of a broader normative shift away from state-centric conceptualizations of authority and towards collective efforts to address transnational problems where traditional (State) governance mechanisms are absent or have failed. Serious violations of human rights manifesting in war crimes, ethnic cleansing, genocide, and crimes against humanity are viewed through GG and R2P prisms as transcending territorially-defined political boundaries via the heuristic of 'human security', which decentralizes security away from the State.[13] Thus, the literature on R2P can enhance our understanding of global governance, and GG concepts can contribute to better theorizing important dimensions of R2P. Insofar as R2P is a manifestation of global human rights governance, and the dynamics of global governance in turn shape patterns of authority and legitimacy in human protection, the two paradigms are intricately connected. To date, however, little work has explicitly bridged the two.[14] The following sections begin to address this gap by employing GG concepts to aid in the understanding of R2P's reconceptualization of sovereignty and diffusion of authority across multiple actors.

R2P and the paradox of democratic sovereignty

While GG scholars emphasize a move away from traditional conceptualizations of state sovereignty and towards increasingly complex spaces of what Rosenau termed 'disaggregated spheres of authority', it is recognized that ultimately states will need to implement the decisions made by global governance institutions and arrangements.[15] States remain prominent actors within human rights governance, though there has been an incremental delegating of authority from states to non-state actors.[16] Thakur notes that R2P is 'fundamentally about building state capacity'.[17] The first two of three pillars outlined in Ban Ki-moon's 2009 report on implementing R2P reiterate the responsibility and role of the State to protect its population from mass atrocity crimes. Rather than eroding state sovereignty, the application and lack of application of R2P works to uphold and reinforce aspects of sovereignty and the advantages of states in the international order. It is the opening for coercive intervention in Pillar Three that poses the greatest dilemma, particularly if a necessary condition of sovereignty is nonintervention.[18] However, coercive intervention is limited to situations in which the state has 'manifestly failed' to protect its population, authorization is granted by the UN Security Council, and other non-coercive measures have been exhausted. While imprecise, these qualifications indicate that R2P is not intended to extinguish traditional legal conceptions of state sovereignty.

Rather than R2P eroding state sovereignty, it is useful to apply Weinert's concept of evolving *democratic sovereignty* as 'a particular way of thinking about qualifications of supreme authority ... [in which] "democratic" refers to progressive processes, institutions, interventions, and actions designed to counter the misuse and abuse of authority'.[19] R2P does not, in this view, undermine the sovereign state; rather, it locates the state in a broader moral project and shared vision of a just political order. This vision evolves with changing perceptions, practices, and 'regulative principles of legitimacy' like R2P.[20] Viewed through the lens of *democratic sovereignty*, R2P represents an instance of both state and non-state agents reconstituting sovereignty on the basis of evolving ideas about acceptable sovereignty practices. As such, R2P embodies a form of negotiated and hybridized sovereignty wherein the authority of the State is reaffirmed by the international community up to a point, after which its abuses of authority – signified by its 'manifest failure' to protect its citizens from mass atrocities – may result in the forfeiture of its sovereignty rights.

In considering how global normative structures of authority interact with national systems, it is important to consider the complex relationship between democratic sovereignty at the international level and democratic governance at the domestic level. Many GG scholars presume the spread of liberal democracy will facilitate greater cooperation over transnational concerns like human rights and the prevention of mass atrocities, and studies have found a positive effect of the level of democracy on the likelihood and degree of access granted to transnational actors in issue areas like human rights.[21] However, others locate the current crisis in addressing global problems in the paralysis of democratic states: 'The democratic imperative may compound the difficulties associated with global governance' as 'democracy adds to the pressure for short-term and local preferences to be favoured over longer-term and global problem-solving'.[22] This failure to act effectively and cooperatively at the international level is linked to party politics and the role of special interests within democracies.

From this view, R2P appears trapped in a paradox in which democratic sovereignty at the international system level prioritizes the protection of populations from mass atrocities while democratic governance at the domestic level may simultaneously work against policy actions to further that normative order. In the United States (US), party polarization dynamics have hindered policy responses to mass atrocities in Syria, including the granting of asylum to Syrian refugees. Domestic politics dynamics have also blocked the US from supporting the International Criminal Court (ICC) as a response to mass atrocities and have worked against prioritizing human protection principles in the case of the Gaza War of 2014. Vaughn and Dunne note that leadership in the 2011 Libya intervention was politically risky for the Obama administration, as public opinion polls found that only 27% of Americans believed the US had 'a responsibility to do something' in response to the violence.[23] That voters have a 'national and often myopic view of international problems' poses a substantial challenge to the implementation of democratic sovereignty and the exercise of global authority regarding R2P.[24]

Assessing the governance architecture of R2P

Weiss and Wilkinson call on GG scholars to disaggregate global complexity by issue and context, to 'not only describe who the actors are and how they connect to one another, but also how a particular outcome has resulted and why and on what grounds authority is effectively or poorly exercised'.[25] While scholarship on global environmental governance has provided rich accounts of such complexity, the human rights arena is a salient domain for such inquiries given the overlapping webs of multilateral and transnational actors that comprise human rights regimes. GG scholarship has developed the concept of *governance architecture* to probe the diffusion of authority across these webs. Specifically, *governance architecture* analyzes the presence or absence of public and private institutions active in a given issue area, including regimes, structures, norms, and procedures, to assess the impact and interlinkages of these institutional complexes and their governance outcomes.[26] The framework acknowledges the role of power and interests, recognizing that both functional gaps and political motives interact to produce new institutions in global governance.[27]

With regard to human rights, emerging trans-state legal regimes governed by transnational courts and the norms legitimating them are of particular interest, as is the implementation of these norms by both domestic and trans-state actors.[28] In the case of R2P as an international norm in human protection, we see diffusion of authority across states, epistemic communities, the United Nations, regional intergovernmental organizations (IGOs), the ICC, and nongovernmental organizations (NGOs) like the International Committee of the Red Cross (ICRC), the International Crisis Group, and the Global Centre for the Responsibility to Protect – where members of the epistemic communities reside. The UN is prioritized as the most vital actor in this structure of R2P governance. Despite criticisms of institutional effectiveness, Gareth Evans argues that the UN is 'the only credible international institution' with the 'combination of legitimacy and authority' needed to respond to R2P situations.[29] In this way the governance architecture of R2P is arguably less 'fragmented' than the nature of authority in global environmental governance issues.[30] Pillar Three reiterates this top-down structure in scenarios of possible coercive intervention, which require authorization by the Security Council.

While the UN Security Council is central to the governance architecture of R2P, transnational actors like NGOs and epistemic communities contribute to knowledge construction, compliance monitoring, lobbying, and campaigning on the issue. Knowledge construction is particularly important given the lack of overarching legal authority, and for this reason global governance structures are arguably dependent on epistemic authority.[31] The ICRC has worked with over fifty human rights organizations to define human protection frameworks,[32] and the International Crisis Group produces a monthly *CrisisWatch* bulletin identifying and providing updates on potential R2P situations.[33] The Global Centre for the Responsibility to Protect engages in research, monitoring, and advocacy efforts aimed at promoting the universal acceptance and implementation of R2P, and sponsors annual meetings of the Global Network of R2P Focal Points, which includes the participation of 47 countries.[34]

R2P's call to respond and rebuild in mass atrocity situations necessitates that UN agencies work in collaboration with humanitarian NGOs, and advocacy by both national governments and civil society actors is crucial.[35] UN networks with such actors are important also to the preventive component of R2P, as studies have found that the domestic diffusion and implementation of international human rights norms depends on domestic-transnational advocacy networks that help to place norm-violating states on the international agenda, and challenge norm-violating governments from above and below by creating transnational pressure networks and mobilizing domestic opposition.[36] It is worth noting that high levels of repression in what the 2004 Arab Human Development Report and James Gelvin term 'Black Hole States' – in which control over domestic politics by the Executive Branch is so strong that it 'converts the surrounding social environment into a setting in which nothing moves and from which nothing escapes' – impeded civil society activism in Syria prior to the outbreak of violent conflict as well as in its earliest stages.[37] The repressive apparatus of the state, which included its military, *mukhabarat* (secret police/intelligence forces), and paramilitary groups, sought to 'crush' any resistance or pressure networks operating at the domestic level.[38] In considering the important preventive role played by domestic-transnational advocacy networks in the governance architecture of R2P, the Syrian case raises important questions as to how preventive mechanisms can operate in repressive environments and how civil society groups that are allowed to operate can be accountable to the constituencies they purport to serve.[39]

In the Syrian crisis, humanitarian NGOs like the ICRC, Syrian Arab Red Crescent (SARC), and the International Rescue Committee have played vital roles in response efforts. However, these organizations have been limited by the reluctance of the Syrian government to approve relief operations that go across borders and by rising levels of insecurity that have made parts of the country inaccessible.[40] Militant transnational actors like ISIS and Jabhat al-Nusra have additionally impeded access by humanitarian actors. While attacks on humanitarian personnel constitute a violation of international humanitarian law, such attacks in Syria and other conflict zones have escalated with an increasingly blurred line between politics and humanitarianism, in which humanitarian actors are viewed as targets and perceived to be associated with political and military actors.[41] For ISIS, targeting humanitarian workers in Syria facilitates its goals of instilling fear, controlling resources, and generating international media attention.

In theory the ICC should be a significant trans-state judicial actor in the governance architecture of R2P. The 2001 ICISS report includes the prosecution of perpetrators of crimes against humanity before the ICC as an example of the types of action needed to fulfill R2P,[42] and Pillar One of the R2P implementation strategy involves joining and strengthening relevant institutions.[43] In February of 2011, the Security Council passed resolution 1970, which, along with imposing an arms embargo, travel ban, and asset freeze against Libyan authorities, referred the situation to the ICC.[44] In May of 2014, 58 countries issued a statement calling on the Security Council to adopt a French-proposed resolution to refer the situation in Syria to the ICC. China and Russia ultimately vetoed the resolution.[45] The full potential of the ICC as an R2P actor is not yet realized in practice, and scholars have pointed to a lack of academic engagement with their complimentary goals.[46] That many states have yet to ratify the Rome Statute, hindering the Court's jurisdiction, poses a significant obstacle to its authority. In the MENA region, only Jordan and Tunisia are state parties to the ICC. As with global environmental governance, the institutionalization of global human rights governance and the internalization of R2P as a norm require that 'global standards [be] implemented and put into practice locally' since 'global norm-setting requires local decision making and implementation'.[47]

Regional IGOs are also pivotal actors in the R2P governance architecture. Condemnation of Gaddafi's actions and support for outside intervention in Libya by the Arab League, Gulf Cooperation Council (GCC), Organization of Islamic Cooperation (OIC), and African Union were crucial to facilitating the passing of resolution 1973.[48] With regard to the initial legitimacy of the intervention, support by the Arab League in calling for a no-fly zone prior to the passing of the resolution was vital to countering perceptions of 'another attack on an Arab State by the West'.[49] In the ongoing Syrian crisis, the Arab League has unequivocally condemned Assad's actions, suspended the membership of Syria, formulated a peace plan, worked with the UN in mediation efforts and in recommending the appointment of Kofi Annan as Special Envoy, deployed human rights monitors, and sponsored a resolution in the Security Council.[50] The Arab League has also imposed sanctions on Syria, including a travel ban for senior officers, a ban on transactions with Syria's central bank, and an end to commercial exchanges with the government.[51] In 2012, the OIC suspended Syria's membership, and the six-member GCC has repeatedly condemned the Assad regime. In May of 2015, GCC delegations met with President Obama to discuss efforts to resolve conflicts in Syria, Iraq, Yemen, and Libya; GCC leaders reiterated that Assad had lost all legitimacy, but emphasized that state sovereignty must be respected and that 'there is no military solution' to the civil conflicts in the region.[52]

While the dispersion of authority across regional IGOs in the governance architecture of R2P appears necessary for successful implementation of the norm, their participation does not automatically generate positive or effective governance outcomes. Regional IGOs like the Arab League, GCC, and OIC may become mired in the same political divisions tethered to geostrategic interests that have led to paralysis in the UN Security Council. In the Libyan case, divisions within the African Union intervened in the implementation of R2P, and the fact that NATO worked closely with the Sudanese military in coordinating the airstrikes raised questions about the ethical claims used to justify the intervention.[53] In the case of Sudan, both the Arab League and the OIC specifically objected to the adoption of R2P as a framework of analysis in the High Level Mission on Darfur's 2006 report, which shaped the Security Council's decision not to fully consider the report.[54] In considering the effectiveness of these regional actors, it is also worth noting that the Arab League's condemnations of the Assad regime have not been successful in overcoming Russian and Chinese vetoes within the Security Council, and the organization's decision in 2013 to transfer Syria's vacant seat to the representatives of the opposition was harshly criticized by Russia and was largely viewed as provocative.[55] This underscores the limitations of such organizations to effectively engage in conflict resolution and response when leaders and their allies perceive them negatively. Given the disproportionate power wielded by Saudi Arabia and Qatar in the organization, Bashar al-Assad has long viewed the Arab League with suspicion as an entity controlled by anti-Syrian states, and in early efforts to broker agreements to end the violence Assad claimed to perceive 'pernicious attempts through diplomacy to buy time for the opposition to regroup and rearm'.[56] The Arab League has also suffered a broader legitimacy crisis among its members due to its poor record in enforcing human rights protection and in solving previous conflicts.[57]

Power asymmetries and proxies

Just as the emergence of GG was criticized as a project to spread or impose a liberal world order, the emergence of R2P has been described as 'a strategy sustained by an underlying belief in both the moral rectitude of liberal states and progressive teleology'.[58] R2P is arguably a manifestation of a global cosmopolitan governance in which 'people have sought to reframe human activity and embed it in law, rights and responsibilities', affirming that 'human well-being is not defined by geographical or cultural locations'.[59] To this end, Weiss and Thakur argue that R2P provides hope for 'improved global governance' vis-à-vis the UN.[60] Critiques of an implicit liberal cosmopolitan bias notwithstanding, much of the GG literature is attentive to normative issues, manifesting in inquiries into the legitimacy, transparency, and fairness of new authority structures. A shift from 'formal rule-making to a more informal power domain of implementation' observed by GG scholars[61] is evident in the uneven application of R2P, which raises questions about attendant legitimacy and power asymmetry issues.

R2P lacks precise criteria and a standardized operationalization, and has been invoked on an ad hoc and selective basis depending on the political will of the great powers possessing veto rights on the Security Council. Pillar Three potentially allows for a scenario of 'governance without government' where the State manifestly fails to meet its obligations in protecting its population from mass atrocity crimes. In such situations, the traditional mode of authority (the State) may be transplanted by action from the international community as an alternate source of governance in the provision of protection to citizens. But who decides when the state is 'manifestly failing',[62] and when it has crossed the threshold for forfeiting its sovereignty rights? In light of the Libyan intervention, scholars also ask 'when, if ever, is it legitimate for the international community to enforce regime change?'[63]

The potential for inequalities to reassert themselves in the global governance of human protection has manifested in concerns that R2P serves as a justification for powerful states to serve their own interests by exploiting crises in weaker countries. These concerns extend back to humanitarian interventions in the 1990s, facilitated by 'selectivity and double standards in Security Council decisions about which conflicts warranted a response', and became further entrenched with *ex post facto* humanitarian justifications for the 2003 invasion of Iraq.[64] This concern has been prominent in the aftermath of the Libyan intervention. While some scholars pronounced the 2011 intervention an effective implementation of R2P, asking 'effective for whom' must remain central to any analysis of global governance efficacy.[65] As of 2015, the escalation of violence in Libya since the NATO intervention and death of Gaddafi has produced significant civilian casualties, led to the displacement of over 390,000 persons, and resulted in the destruction of public infrastructure and basic social services.[66] Human trafficking networks have taken advantage of the chaos in Libya to operate deadly smuggling regimes across the Mediterranean, the effects of which are discussed in the section below on refugees. Among R2P skeptics, the Libyan intervention 'stoked the embers of long-held suspicions over the trustworthiness of western powers with neo-imperial proclivities'.[67]

Given the power asymmetries associated with the governance architecture of R2P, and the reality that R2P scenarios typically emerge in weak states with a history of colonialism and outside intervention by self-interested and more powerful states, the use of coercive intervention under Pillar Three will likely be consistently mired in legitimacy crises that risk further de-legitimization of the concept itself. For this reason, Morris concludes that R2P's international standing would be better preserved 'through excision of its most coercive elements', as 'decisions over coercive military intervention [are] inevitably infused with considerations of strategic interest'.[68]

Additionally, coercive intervention is problematic in cases where alliances or proxies are perceived to benefit. Some might perceive Western-led intervention in Syria as providing a strategic advantage to Israel, though this is debatable.[69] The legitimacy of coercive intervention in Syria is further hindered by the evolution of the civil war into a proxy war, with Assad's Syrian Arab Army (SAA), the Free Syrian Army (FSA), and additional insurgent adversaries like ISIS, Jabhat al-Nusra, and Ahrar al-Sham reliant on support from external powers.[70] Regional powers backing their interests via support for various domestic actors in the Syrian conflict include Iran, Turkey, Qatar, and Saudi Arabia.[71] The conflict is also considered the site of a 'revived cold war' between Russia and Western powers.[72] Skepticism and suspicions regarding a coercive intervention in light of the proxy war are summarized by Nasser-Eddine: 'The great powers (US, Russia and China) are facing off in a context for a new Middle East ... they are happy for their proxies Iran and Syria on one side, and Turkey, Israel and Saudi Arabia on the other ... to risk protracted conflict with each other. These nations are competing for access to the region's resources'.[73] Thus, as Khashanah concludes regarding the Syrian crisis, 'the humanitarian intervention doctrine risks being viewed as a pretext for intervention to achieve neo-colonial or geopolitical objectives in a new world order'.[74]

Beyond the problem of power asymmetries and proxy wars, bad governance outcomes damage authority structures over time,[75] such that the United Nations and R2P will likely see diminished influence with future coercive interventions like Libya. As an alternative to Pillar Three interventions à la Libya, this article argues for a greater focus on refugee protection as a non-coercive R2P policy tool.

R2P and refugee protection

In probing what constitutes a 'manifest failing' for the purposes of R2P's Pillar Three, Gallagher observes that mass movements of IDPs and refugees 'help demonstrate that the government is failing in its internal responsibility to protect the safety and welfare of citizens'.[76] As of June 2015, the number of Syrian refugees approached four million, and as of December 2014 there were over 7.6 million Syrian IDPs. Facilitating asylum is a form of international protection that can prevent victimization and diminish the consequences of mass atrocities, yet access to asylum and other forms of refugee protection are largely overlooked in discussions of R2P.[77]

Refugee protection is an important form of human rights protection. In focusing on the protection of the human rights of others who are not nationals of the state, refugee protection operates within a more expansive conceptualization of the human rights responsibilities of states.[78] At the same time, international refugee law reaffirms important dimensions of state sovereignty, as states are not legally obligated to accept refugees and often implement policies aimed at reducing or preventing refugee flows from accessing their national borders.[79] While the 1951 Refugee Convention and its 1967 Protocol obligate states under the principle of *non-refoulement* not to send refugees back to the country from which they have fled, states have frequently violated this obligation or have utilized a strictly territorial reading in order to intercept refugees arriving by sea.[80] States have also frequently ignored the provision in Article 31 protecting refugees who are physically present in a receiving state to be free from punishment due to unlawful entry. In the Syrian case, both *refoulement* and the detention of Syrian asylum seekers has occurred in neighboring states like Egypt.[81]

GG scholars highlight a growing need for international cooperation on transnational movements of people, and such cooperation is particularly urgent in the realm of refugees, who have left their country of nationality due to a well-founded fear of persecution based on race, religion, nationality, or membership in a particular social group or political opinion. Like other global governance issues, refugee issues transcend established political boundaries and require some form of management 'articulated and operationalised at multiple scales of authority'.[82] The governance architecture in the case of Syrian refugee protection encompasses authority and support primarily by the UNHCR, which works with host governments, the International Organization for Migration (IOM), and humanitarian NGOs in constructing knowledge, coordinating donations, registering refugees, and providing cash assistance services. Local charities and political groups are also important; while little information exists about these groups, it appears that a great deal of their funding comes from overseas religious charities.[83] The International Rescue Committee has offered medical and emergency assistance to Syrians in IDP camps and via mobile clinics in the northern part of the country, and has established programs in Jordan, Lebanon, Iraq, and Turkey to provide humanitarian assistance to Syrian refugees.[84] Syria Bright Future, a local NGO started by two Syrian mental health professionals, originally worked to offer informal psychological treatment to Syrian refugees in Jordan. The group has grown into an international NGO called Bright Future for Mental Health, and as of March 2014 it provided health, educational, social, and psychological support to Syrian refugee children and families across Jordan.[85]

The layering of authority and humanitarian assistance in the governance architecture of refugee protection has in some cases produced significant protection gaps. Studies of Palestinian refugees impacted by the ongoing Syrian crisis demonstrate the inadequacy of existing refugee protection regimes structured by the UNHCR and the UNRWA. Territorial delineations of authority have impeded the fulfillment of the 1951 Refugee Convention principles due to the geographical mandate of the UNRWA. While the normative underpinnings of the Convention suggest Palestinian refugees fleeing mass atrocity scenarios like Iraq in 2003 and Syria since 2011 should be afforded equal protection, territorial borders have dictated their political objectification and limbo status as secondary forcibly displaced populations.[86]

Such protection gaps in the governance architecture of refugee protection notwithstanding, 'the historical record supports the conclusion that the grant of asylum is, or would be in many cases, the most practical, realistic and least controversial response to assisting victims of mass atrocities'.[87] Inadequate response to asylum-seekers fleeing mass atrocities has and continues to result in significant loss of life. Boats of Jewish refugees turned away by states during World War II often died in Nazi internment camps,[88] while boats of Syrian and other refugees fleeing Africa and the Middle East today too often die at sea. In the first four months of 2015 more than 1700 people were estimated to have perished attempting to cross by sea from North Africa and the Middle East into southern Europe.[89] The IOM links the increase in deaths from Mediterranean Sea crossings to a surge in the number of people fleeing conflict and persecution in the Middle East and Africa. In 2014, Eritreans and Syrians constituted the largest share of arrivals by sea crossing into Italy, and the deteriorating environment in Libya enabled it to become the launching point for the majority of human smuggling voyages.[90] In response to pressures from European electorates – who largely view refugees through the prism of 'migrants' – the search-and-rescue operation Mare Nostrum was dismantled in 2014 by the European Union and replaced with Operation Triton, which has been criticized as a border control operation prioritizing geographical restrictions over humanitarian response.[91]

The three principal forms of protection states can offer to refugees include *non-refoulement*, the granting of asylum, and the granting of temporary protection – a legal norm created to deal with mass influxes of refugees fleeing armed conflict or violence.[92] These actions warrant significant attention within the framework of R2P, particularly as the world faces the greatest refugee crisis since World War II. Inadequate response to the Mediterranean crossing crisis signifies an important failure of R2P, as does the fact that as of February 2015, UNHCR data indicated that less than eighty thousand places had been made available through resettlement or other forms of admission for 3.8 million registered Syrian refugees – approximately 2% – and this humanitarian resettlement has been disproportionately shouldered by relatively few states.[93] Millions remain in the strained infrastructure of refugee camps and communities in Turkey, Lebanon, Jordan, and Iraq, and the rise of ISIS in Iraq has further endangered Syrian refugees there.[94] Moreover, these neighboring states have grown averse to the absorption of additional refugees and have increasingly restricted entry, particularly to Syrians lacking proper documentation and to Syrian-Palestinians. Work on the status and treatment of Palestinian 'double refugees' in this context underscores the possibility that Syrian refugees could also eventually face unique discriminations as a Protracted Refugee Situation (PRS) population[95] if adequate resettlement and humanitarian protections are not granted and the conflict remains unresolved.

The securitization of refugees in a post-9/11 context complicates resettlement and *non-refoulement* as mechanisms of R2P. Under the 'security paradigm', the latest stage in the evolution of refugee protection, 'refugees are devalued to the point where providing asylum or intervening to provide source-country solutions are trumped by the desire to keep terrorists out'.[96] This paradigm is evident in the US, which admitted only 31 Syrian asylum-seekers in 2014.[97] In the spring of 2015, members of the House Homeland Security Committee issued a letter objecting to the Obama administration's plan to resettle thousands of Syrian refugees, and Republican Congressman Michael McCaul warned that the resettlement plan could become a 'jihadi pipeline' for radicalized Islamic militants.[98] Refugee response is complicated not only by short-term national interests and security concerns but by the persistence of negative attitudes towards migrants and refugees.[99] This is evident empirically in the growth of far-right anti-immigrant parties in Europe as well as in cross-national survey data on European attitudes towards migrants and minorities, particularly Muslims.[100] The social Othering of refugees presents its own distinct hurdle, which entails reconfiguring understandings of identity and alterity.[101]

While domestic politics and nativist challenges will continue to present an obstacle, R2P frameworks should encourage states to prioritize the protection needs of refugees fleeing mass atrocity situations and to enhance legal processes for determining the status of asylum-seekers.[102] This includes those attempting the dangerous journey across the Mediterranean. In accordance with international refugee law, these individuals should be treated with the assumption that they may be refugees and asylum-seekers until their status can be determined.[103] As refugee law scholars observe, there is also 'an evolving international consensus on *opinio juris* and state practice that refugees must receive asylum', making the right to asylum for refugees a norm within customary international law.[104]

Conclusion

This article has bridged R2P with work on Global Governance to further our understanding of both paradigms. Assessments of the governance architecture of R2P and of refugee protection in the case of Syria shed light on how global structures of authority interact with national and local systems. The constraints on agents operating at multiple levels of authority have important implications for the effectiveness of governance outcomes in these realms. Given the power asymmetries associated with the governance architecture of R2P and the proxy war in Syria, this article has argued that the use of coercive intervention under Pillar Three risks further de-legitimization of the concept itself. As an alternative, the article calls for greater emphasis on R2P as refugee protection.

In the aftermath of the intervention in Libya, Francis argued that 'the litmus test' for R2P would be 'the response of the European countries to the direct arrival of refugees, especially the burden-sharing extended by other European countries to the frontline states such as Malta and Italy'.[105] The 'goodwill' towards the sea-crossing refugees hoped for by Francis and others has fallen far short of fulfilling R2P, and the deficiencies in the international community's response to the Syrian refugee crisis indicate that the ethical remains unable to supersede the ontological, as R2P ethical principles are not yet prior to territorial sovereignty.[106] In order to move R2P forward as a legitimate norm in human protection, the international community should emphasize R2P as refugee protection and work to uphold *non-refoulement*, the grant of asylum, and the grant of temporary protections to the millions displaced by mass atrocity crimes.

Notes

1. Elias Groll, 'A Record Year in Misery: The World Has Never Seen a Refugee Crisis This Bad', *Foreignpolicy.com,* June 18, 2015, http://foreignpolicy.com/2015/06/18/a-record-year-in-misery-the-world-has-never-seen-a-refugee-crisis-this-bad/ (accessed June 18, 2015).
2. See Minerva Nasser-Eddine, 'How R2P Failed Syria', *Flinders Journal of History and Politics* 28 (2012), 16–30; Aidan Hehir and Robert Murray, eds., *Libya, the Responsibility to Protect and the Future of Humanitarian Intervention* (New York: Palgrave Macmillan, 2013).
3. Alex J. Bellamy, 'A Death Foretold? Human Rights, Responsibility to Protect and the Persistent Politics of Power', *Cooperation and Conflict* 50, no. 2 (2015), 286–293, 289.
4. Monica Serrano and Thomas G. Weiss, 'Introduction: Is R2P "Cascading"?' in *The International Politics of Human Rights: Rallying to the R2P Cause?* eds. Monica Serrano and Thomas G. Weiss (New York: Routledge, 2014), 1.
5. See Martin Hewson and Timothy J. Sinclair, eds., *Approaches to Global Governance Theory* (Albany, NY: SUNY Press, 1999); Steve Hughes and Rorden Wilkinson, eds., *Global Governance: Critical Perspectives* (London and New York: Routledge, 2002); Alice D. Ba and Matthew J. Hoffman, eds., *Contending Perspectives on Global Governance: Coherence, Contestation and World Order* (London and New York: Routledge, 2005); Michael Barnett and Raymond Duvall, eds., *Power in Global Governance* (Cambridge: Cambridge University Press, 2005).
6. For a detailed definitional discussion of Global Governance, see Matthias Hofferberth, 'Mapping the Meanings of Global Governance: A Conceptual Reconstruction of a Floating Signifier', *Millennium: Journal of International Studies* 43, no. 2 (2015): 598–617 and Timothy J. Sinclair, *Global Governance* (Cambridge and Malden: Polity Press, 2012).
7. Thomas G. Weiss and Rorden Wilkinson, 'Rethinking Global Governance? Complexity, Authority, Power, Change', *International Studies Quarterly* 58, no. 1 (2014), 207–215, 207.
8. Anne Orford, *International Authority and Responsibility to Protect* (Cambridge: Cambridge University Press, 2011), 15.
9. Orford, *International Authority,* 16.
10. Bellamy, 'A Death Foretold', 289.
11. Tom Pegram and Michele Acuto, 'Introduction: Global Governance in the Interregnum', *Millennium: Journal of International Studies* 43, no. 2 (2015), 584–597, 586.
12. Ian Goldin, *Divided Nations: Why Global Governance Is Failing, And What We Can Do About It* (Oxford: Oxford University Press, 2013), 112.
13. For an instructive discussion of the emergence of 'human security' and its applications, see Richard A. Matthew, Jon Barnett, Bryan McDonald, and Karen O'Brien, eds., *Global Environmental Change and Human Security* (Cambridge, MA and London: MIT Press, 2010).
14. See Thomas G. Weiss and Ramesh Thakur, *Global Governance and the UN: An Unfinished Journey* (Bloomington and Indianapolis, IN: Indiana University Press, 2010).
15. Goldin, *Divided Nations,* 94.
16. Tom Pegram, 'Governing Relationships: The New Architecture in Global Human Rights Governance', *Millennium: Journal of International Studies* 43, no. 2 (2015), 618–639, 622.
17. Ramesh Thakur, 'The Responsibility to Protect: Retrospect and Prospect' in *Responsibility to Protect and Sovereignty,* eds. Charles Sampford and Ramesh Thakur (Burlington, VT: Ashgate, 2013), Ch. 10, 209.
18. Martha Finnemore, *The Purpose of Intervention: Changing Beliefs about the Use of Force* (Ithaca, NY and London: Cornell University Press, 2003), 7.
19. Matthew S. Weinert, 'Democratic Sovereignty and The Responsibility to Protect', *Politics and Ethics Review* 2, no. 2 (2006), 139–158, 147.
20. Weinert, 'Democratic Sovereignty', 149–150.

21. See Jonas Tallberg, Thomas Sommerer, Theresa Squatrito, and Christer Jönsson, *The Opening Up of International Organizations: Transnational Access in Global Governance* (Cambridge: Cambridge University Press, 2013).
22. Goldin, *Divided Nations,* 57–58.
23. Jocelyn Vaughn and Tim Dunne, 'Leading From the Front: America, Libya and the Localisation of R2P', *Cooperation and Conflict* 50, no. 1 (2015), 29–49, 41.
24. Goldin, *Divided Nations*, 94.
25. Weiss and Wilkinson, 'Rethinking Global Governance', 211.
26. Pegram, 'Governing Relationships', 620.
27. Philipp Pattberg and Oscar Widerberg, 'Theorising Global Environmental Governance: Key Findings and Future Questions', *Millennium: Journal of International Studies* 43, no. 2 (2015), 684–705, 695–696.
28. Leslie F. Goldstein and Cornel Ban, 'The European Human-Rights Regime as a Case Study in the Emergence of Global Governance' in *Contending Perspectives,* eds. Ba and Hoffman, Ch. 9, 154.
29. Gareth Evans, *The Responsibility to Protect: Ending Mass Atrocity Crimes Once and For All* (Washington, DC: Brookings, 2008), 175–180.
30. Pattberg and Widerberg, 'Theorising Global Environmental Governance', 693–694.
31. Sinclair, *Global Governance,* 27.
32. Charles Sampford, 'Introduction', in *Responsibility to Protect and Sovereignty,* eds. Charles Sampford and Ramesh Thakur (Burlington: Ashgate, 2013), 3.
33. See http://www.crisisgroup.org/en/publication-type/crisiswatch.aspx (Accessed June 16, 2015).
34. See http://www.globalr2p.org/our_work/r2p_focal_points (Accessed June 16, 2015).
35. Thakur, *Responsibility to Protect*, 2013, 195–196.
36. See Thomas Risse, Stephen C. Ropp, and Kathryn Sikkink, eds., *The Power of Human Rights: International Norms and Domestic Change* (Cambridge: Cambridge University Press, 1999).
37. James Gelvin, *The Arab Uprisings: What Everyone Needs to Know* (Oxford: Oxford University Press, 2012), 5.
38. David W. Lesch, 'The Uprising That Wasn't Supposed to Happen: Syria and the Arab Spring', in *The Arab Spring: Change and Resistance in the Middle East,* eds. Mark L. Haas and David W. Lesch (Boulder, CO: Westview Press, 2013), Ch. 4, 83.
39. See Jan Aart Scholte, ed., *Building Global Democracy? Civil Society and Accountable Global Governance* (Cambridge: Cambridge University Press, 2011).
40. Brian Tisdall, 'The Challenge of Access in Syria', *Humanitarian Exchange Magazine* 59 (November 2013), http://www.odihpn.org/humanitarian-exchange-magazine/issue-59/the-challenge-of-access-in-syria (accessed June 16, 2015).
41. See Hikaru Yamashita, 'New Humanitarianism and Changing Logics of the Political in International Relations', *Millennium: Journal of International Studies* 43, no. 2 (2015), 411–428.
42. Orford, *International Responsibility,* 104.
43. Vaughn and Dunne, 'Leading From the Front', 33.
44. Hehir and Murray, *Libya,* 5.
45. 'Syria: 58 Countries Urge ICC Referral', *Human Rights Watch,* May 20, 2014, http://www.hrw.org/news/2014/05/20/syria-58-countries-urge-icc-referral (accessed June 16, 2015).
46. See Martin Mennecke, 'The International Criminal Court' in *The International Politics,* eds. Serrano and Weiss, Ch. 4.
47. Pattberg and Widerberg, 688.
48. See Justin Morris, 'Libya and Syria: R2P and the Spectre of the Swinging Pendulum', *International Affairs* 89, no. 5 (2013), 1265–1283, 1272 and Monica Serrano and Thomas G. Weiss, 'Introduction: Is R2P "Cascading"?', in *The International Politics,* eds. Serrano and Weiss, 6.
49. Alexandra dos Reis Stefanopoulos and George A. Lopez, 'From Coercive to Protective Tools: The Evolution of Targeted Sanctions', in *The International Politics,* eds. Serrano and Weiss, 55.
50. See Serrano and Weiss, *The International Politics,* 11–12 and Spencer Zifcak, 'Falls the Shadow: The Responsibility to Protect from Theory to Practice', in *The Responsibility to Protect,* eds. Sampford and Thakur, Ch. 2.
51. Zeynep Sahin Mencütek, 'The "Rebirth" of a Dead Organization? Questioning the Role of the Arab League in the "Arab Uprisings" Process', *Perceptions* 19, no. 2 (2014), 83–112, 98.

52. 'Annex to U.S.–Gulf Cooperation Council Camp David Joint Statement', *Whitehouse.gov,* May 14, 2015, https://www.whitehouse.gov/the-press-office/2015/05/14/annex-us-gulf-cooperation-council-camp-david-joint-statement (accessed June 16, 2015).
53. See Alex de Waal, 'My Fears, Alas, Were Not Unfounded: Africa's Responses to the Libya Conflict' and Theresa Reinold, 'Africa's Emerging Regional Security Culture and the Intervention in Libya' in Hehir and Murray, eds., *Libya,* Chs. 4 and 5.
54. Kevin Boreham, 'Sovereignty and R2P Ten Years after East Timor and Kosovo: A Failure to Protect: The UN Human Rights Council and Darfur' in *The Responsibility to Protect,* eds. Sampford and Thakur, Ch. 7, 132–133.
55. Mencütek, 'The Rebirth', 101.
56. Lesch, 'The Uprising', 94.
57. Mencütek, 'The Rebirth', 85.
58. Robert Murray, 'Humanitarians, Responsibility or Rationality? Evaluating Intervention as a State Strategy' in *Libya,* eds. Hehir and Murray, Ch. 2, 43.
59. David Held, 'Restructuring Global Governance: Cosmopolitanism, Democracy and the Global Order', *Millennium: Journal of International Studies* 37, no. 3 (2009), 535–547, 536–37.
60. Weiss and Thakur, *Global Governance,* 340.
61. Pegram and Acuto, 'Introduction', 591.
62. For a discussion of the ambiguity of the 'manifest failing' requirement see Adrian Gallagher, 'Syria and the Indicators of a "Manifest Failing"', *The International Journal of Human Rights* 18, no. 1 (2014), 1–19.
63. Nasser-Eddine, 'How R2P Failed', 22.
64. Thomas G. Weiss, 'Halting Genocide: Rhetoric versus Reality', *Genocide Studies and Prevention* 2, no. 1 (2007), 7–30, 18–19.
65. Martha Finnemore, 'Dynamics of Global Governance: Building on What We Know', *International Studies Quarterly* 58, no. 1 (2014), 221–224, 222.
66. 'Libya: Humanitarian Situation Report', *UNICEF,* March 2015, http://www.unicef.org/appeals/files/UNICEF_Libya_Sitrep_March_2015.pdf (Accessed June 16, 2015).
67. Morris, 'Libya and Syria', 1280.
68. Morris, 'Libya and Syria', 1266.
69. Zifcak, 'Falls the Shadow', 33.
70. See Geraint Alun Hughes, 'Syria and the Perils of Proxy Warfare', *Small Wars & Insurgencies* 25, no. 3 (2014), 522–538.
71. Khaldoun Khashanah, 'The Syrian Crisis: A Systemic Framework', *Contemporary Arab Affairs* 7, no. 1 (2014), 1–21.
72. Patrick Cockburn, *The Rise of the Islamic State: ISIS and the New Sunni Revolution* (London and New York: Verso, 2015), 94.
73. Nasser-Eddine, 'How R2P Failed', 17.
74. Khashanah, 'The Syrian Crisis', 18.
75. Finnemore, 'Dynamics', 222.
76. Gallagher, 'Syria and the Indicators', 9.
77. Brian Barbour and Brian Gorlick, 'Embracing the "Responsibility to Protect": A Repertoire of Measures Including Asylum for Potential Victims', *International Journal of Refugee Law* 20, no. 4 (2008), 533–566, 561.
78. Mark Gibney, *Global Refugee Crisis: A Reference Handbook* (Santa Barbara: ABC-CLIO, 2010), xv.
79. Gibney, *Global Refugee,* 51.
80. See Gibney, *Global Refugee,* 51–56.
81. Rochelle Davis, 'Syria's Refugee Crisis', *Great Decisions* (New York: Foreign Policy Association, 2015), 65–76, 75.
82. Pegram and Acuto, 'Introduction', 597.
83. Davis, 'Syria's Refugee Crisis', 71.
84. See http://www.rescue.org/crisis-syria (accessed July 28, 2015).
85. Mohammad Abo-Hilal and Omar Said Yousef, 'Beyond Survival: A Brief Description of Psychological Services for Syrian Refugees', *Peace and Conflict: Journal of Peace Psychology* 20, no. 3 (2014), 334–336.

86. See Noura Erakat, 'Palestinian Refugees and the Syrian Uprising: Filling the Protection Gap during Secondary Forced Displacement', *International Journal of Refugee Law* 26, no. 4 (2014), 581–621.
87. Barbour and Gorlick, 'Embracing', 562.
88. Barbour and Gorlick, 'Embracing', 563.
89. 'IOM Monitors Migrant Arrivals, Deaths in Mediterranean', *International Organization for Migration,* April 28, 2015, https://www.iom.int/news/iom-monitors-migrant-arrivals-deaths-mediterranean (accessed June 16, 2015).
90. Tara Brian and Frank Laczko, eds., 'Fatal Journeys: Tracking Lives Lost during Migration', *International Organization for Migration* (2014), 12, http://publications.iom.int/bookstore/free/FatalJourneys_CountingtheUncounted.pdf (accessed June 16, 2015).
91. 'Europe Response to Mediterranean Migrant and Refugee Tragedy Falls Short', *Oxfam International,* June 16, 2015, https://www.oxfam.org/en/pressroom/reactions/europe-response-mediterranean-migrant-and-refugee-tragedy-falls-short-oxfam (Accessed June 18, 2015).
92. Erakat, 'Palestinian Refugees', 610.
93. Germany, Canada, Australia, Norway, and Sweden have disproportionately provided resettlement pledges since 2013. 'Fact Sheet on Resettlement and Other Forms of Admission for Syrian Refugees', *UNHCR,* February 11, 2015, http://data.unhcr.org/syrianrefugees/asylum.php (Accessed June 16, 2015).
94. See Davis, 'Syria's Refugee Crisis', 70–75 and Cockburn, *The Rise of the Islamic State.*
95. See Erakat, 'Palestinian Refugees'.
96. Bill Frelick, 'Paradigm Shifts in the International Responses to Refugees' in *Fear of Persecution: Global Human Rights, International Law, and Human Well-Being,* eds. James Daniel White and Anthony J. Marsella (Lanham, MD and Plymouth: Lexington Books, 2007), Ch. 2, 47.
97. Davis, 'Syria's Refugee Crisis', 75. It is noteworthy that in 2014 the US government did renew the availability of Temporary Protected Status for Syrian passport holders and residents, allowing for the renewal of visas; thousands of Syrians were given visas to come to the US through family requests, but these were considered temporary and were not asylum cases.
98. Martin Matishak, 'Republican Fears US has Created "Federally Funded Jihadi Pipeline"', *The Hill,* February 11, 2015, http://thehill.com/policy/defense/232526-republican-fears-us-is-creating-federally-funded-jihadi-pipeline (accessed June 16, 2015).
99. Goldin, *Divided Nations,* 59.
100. Richard Wike, 'In Europe, Sentiment against Immigrants, Minorities Runs High', *Pew Research Center Fact Tank,* May 14, 2014, http://www.pewresearch.org/fact-tank/2014/05/14/in-europe-sentiment-against-immigrants-minorities-runs-high/ (accessed June 16, 2015).
101. Alain Toumayan, 'The Responsibility for the Other and The Responsibility to Protect', *Philosophy and Social Criticism* 40, no. 3 (2014), 269–288, 270.
102. Barbour and Gorlick, 'Embracing', 2008, 565.
103. Gibney, *Global Refugee,* 25.
104. William Thomas Worster, 'The Contemporary International Law Status of the Right to Receive Asylum', *International Journal of Refugee Law* 26, no. 4 (2014), 477–499, 478.
105. Angus Francis, 'Refugees and Military Intervention in the Name of Responsibility to Protect', in *The Responsibility to Protect,* eds. Sampford and Thakur, Ch. 3, 183.
106. Toumayan, 'The Responsibility', 278.

The responsibility to engage: cosmopolitan civic engagement and the spread of the Responsibility to Protect Doctrine

David William Gethings

International Conflict Management, Kennesaw State University, Kennesaw, USA

When the Responsibility to Protect (R2P) doctrine was widely adopted by the international community at the 2005 World Summit, it became the first such principle to advocate for the enforcement of international law and provide for both punishment and prevention of international human rights violations. While this created a shift away from the once sacrosanct norm of national sovereignty, another equally important change was occurring. The digital age has redefined the nature and scope of civic engagement. With increased communication and availability of information, citizenship has transcended national borders and expanded to engagement at the local, national, and international level. These new levels of engagement also change the nature of democracy through the inclusion of issues and opinions beyond the domestic constituency. Additionally, the methods of engagement have expanded through the use of social media and other digital platforms. The combination of the R2P doctrine and cosmopolitan civic engagement has created a vital nexus which gives human rights and international law a new form of accountability and enforcement. This article will explore the co-development of these norms and the implications for conflict prevention and resolution as well as democracy.

Introduction

The concepts of humanitarian intervention, democracy, citizenship, and cosmopolitanism have existed for centuries, but the digital age has created new possibilities for their realization, interaction, and implementation. Humanitarian intervention, as defined by the Responsibility to Protect (R2P) doctrine, has been widely adopted by the international community, as seen in the acceptance of the UN's 2005 World Summit Outcome Document. 'The R2P is a doctrine that challenges the long-established understanding that human rights are ultimately a profoundly national question, rather than an international matter'.[1] No longer can claims of sovereignty be used to justify the widespread and systematic abuse of human rights within a nation. Cosmopolitanism ideals have also expanded as territorial borders have diminished in significance. The once sacrosanct notion of sovereignty has had to adapt to these changing circumstances. With increased communication and availability of information, citizenship has transcended national borders and expanded to engagement at the local, national, and international level. These new levels of engagement also change the nature of democracy through the inclusion of issues and opinions beyond the domestic constituency. The combination of R2P and cosmopolitan civic engagement has created a vital nexus which gives human rights and international law a new form of accountability and enforcement. This article will explore the co-development of these norms and the implications for conflict prevention and resolution as well as democracy.

Humanitarian intervention, democracy, citizenship, and cosmopolitanism all share the common element of responsibility as a necessary condition. Without individual and collective responsibility, none of these concepts would have any true meaning. The R2P is perhaps the most obvious example of the importance of responsibility, but it also diffuses responsibility between the State, international community, and the individual. Democracy is a political system predicated on the belief that government can and ought to be administered by the people, by the citizenry, either directly or through elected representatives. James Kettner writes, 'Individual liberty and the security of the community as a whole could both be served – must both be served – by republican citizenship ... the individual alone would be responsible for making the choice between subjectship and citizenship.'[2] Without the active participation of citizens, democracy is not possible. Citizenship entails a responsibility for self-government and for involvement in the community. Finally, cosmopolitanism builds on the responsibility of citizenship by expanding it from the local to the global. As each of these concepts has developed with the interconnectedness of the digital age, the layers of responsibility begin to overlap, and it becomes clear that responsible democratic citizenship requires a commitment to protect and enforce human rights. Both the individual and the State have a duty to act on behalf of those who are suffering, regardless of geographic location. Cosmopolitan citizenship in the digital age must be characterized by a global awareness and a responsibility to engage.

The responsibility to protect

Although the concept of humanitarian intervention has existed for centuries,[3] the modern manifestation can, arguably, be traced to the post-World War II human rights development. In 1948, the *Universal Declaration of Human Rights* (UDHR) was presented to the General Assembly of the United Nations. For the first time in modern history, representatives from nations around the world met and agreed that all persons were entitled to certain rights, not because governments beneficently handed them to the people, but simply because 'people are born equal in dignity and rights' (Article 1, UDHR). The once sacrosanct idea of sovereignty as an absolute right for rulers to act towards their citizens as they wished was now beginning to erode. The UDHR made rights universal and explicitly stated that borders would no longer prevent all people from claiming these rights. However, the ideal did not mirror the reality. Between April and July of 1994, the world sat idly by while approximately 800,000 Rwandans were brutally murdered by their neighbours with government support. Ethnic cleansing in Yugoslavia, genocide in Timor-Leste and Cambodia, and the continuing targeted annihilation of the people of Darfur all exemplify why the international community can no longer ignore human suffering when governments claim it to be an internal matter simply because of sovereignty.

In response to the failures of the international community to prevent such atrocities, the International Commission on Intervention and State Sovereignty (ICISS) was established in September 2000 to examine how the world community ought to respond when governments are unwilling or unable to protect their own citizens. Their final report came to be known as the Responsibility to Protect doctrine, and it became enshrined as an international norm, although still contested, when it was included in the 2005 World Summit Outcome Document of the United Nations. It calls for prevention, protection, and reconstruction during the various phases of a conflict. The emphasis is always placed on prevention, but when that does not work, civilians may be in need of a humanitarian intervention. The ICISS explained the process as:

> The kind of intervention with which we are concerned in this report is action taken against a state or its leaders, without its or their consent, for purposes which are claimed to be humanitarian or protective. By far the most controversial form of such intervention is military, and a great part of our report necessarily focuses on that. But we are also very much concerned with alternatives to military action, including all forms of preventive measures, and coercive intervention measures – sanctions and criminal prosecutions – falling short of military intervention.[4]

While the burden of responsibility remains with the State, it is no longer the sole duty bearer for protection of the populous. According to the R2P principle, when a State fails in its responsibility, either due to inability or complicity, it becomes not only the right of the international community to take action, but its responsibility to do so.

Citizenship

The changing nature of State sovereignty has also had tremendous impacts on citizenship and civic responsibility. All of human history is the story of individuals coming together into a group and then rebelling against the responsibilities of communal living. Immanuel Kant addressed this dichotomy in what he called 'the unsocial sociability of human beings, that is, their tendency to enter into a society, a tendency connected, however, with a consistent resistance that continually threatens to break up this society'.[5] This contradictory nature has only been exacerbated in the 200+ years since Kant's writing. Globalization has diminished the importance of national sovereignty, and humanity's 'unsocial sociability' now not only includes the individual and society, but has enveloped the national and global community. Citizenship, which manifests the rights and responsibilities of the individual within a society, is now faced with the need for clarification in an age in which the nation and the cosmos both call for allegiance.

National citizenship is essential to the development of identity and the physically proximity to others on one's community confers certain moral obligations. Cosmopolitanism builds upon national citizenship by providing another set of moral obligations that levies certain requirements for how people act towards those in other countries. Living in a globally connected and interdependent world creates specific obligations that extend beyond borders. Humanity may still be characterized by its 'unsocial sociability', but by understanding the benefits that come from the responsibilities of citizenship, reason ought alleviate some of the existing tensions. If humanity is able to embrace the connections between national and cosmopolitan citizenship, then we may be able to move one step closer to Kant's *Perpetual Peace*, that undiscovered country, which may be closer than ever before.

At its most basic level, citizenship is a label assigned to an individual as a member of a political community. While this view of a citizen may have importance for migration and legal studies, it does little to contribute to what an individual is in relationship to the society. Kant points out time and time again that humanity thrives through reason only as a society, not as individuals (172 and this can also be seen in *Universal History*, proposition 2). It is for this reason that humans enter into a civil society with universal laws

(174 and proposition 5 in *Universal History*). His anthropological view is that humans have the physical ability to create (technical predisposition), the desire for personal gain through cooperation (pragmatic predisposition), and a cumulative nature that evolves through a better society (moral predisposition). It is these uniquely human predispositions which Kant believes will lead to societal evolution. If citizenship is understood to be an iterative process between the individual and society, then the nature of the rights and responsibilities can be examined. Citizenship thus evolves from a label to a process.

Many scholars, particularly from the field of political science, have examined citizenship as a function of participation within the community. Civic and political participation have often been treated as one in the same. While they are closely related, there are significant differences between the two. Verba, Schlozman and Brady define political participation as 'activity that has the intent or effect of influencing government action – either directly by affecting the making or implementation of public policy or indirectly by influencing the selection of people who make those choices'.[6] They acknowledge a difference between political and non-political participation, but the distinction is opaque at best Many authors have ascribed to this definition, or something very similar, to explain civic participation, including Fleming , Almond and Verba, Gaventa and Barrett, and others.[7] However, there is an important distinction between civic and political participation. Zukin et al. define civic participation as 'participation aimed at achieving a public good, but usually through direct hands-on work in cooperation with others'.[8] This distinction has also been noted by academics such as Bruch, Ferree and Soss, and Putnam, and others.[9] Civic participation has often been considered a subset of political participation, but the element of community rather than government must be given equal consideration. The important aspect of citizenship is the participatory nature rather than the passive attributes which are often assigned to it.

There are two flaws in the current *Oxford English Dictionary* definition of citizenship. The first is that 'citizen' and 'citizenship' are terms used to define the individual in relation to a particular geographic location.[10] If we accept the premise that randomness or 'luck' is responsible for the place and time into which an individual is born, then it must be true that the rights one inherits as a result of place of birth are equally random. If rights only exist within the relationship between the citizen and the State, then rights must be relative to the particular State. However customary international law and *jus cogens* law reflects universal consensus on certain fundamental human rights. This is not to say that there are no specific rights that are bestowed on the individual by the State, only that such a conception is incomplete at best. As Waldron[11] points out, nationality is just the most recent culmination of historical circumstances. There seems to be a logical inconsistency inherent within the concept of rights defined from nationality alone. Since boundaries are malleable, and culture continually changes and adapts, why should nationalism hold any special place in our hearts?

The second flaw is that these definitions omit any reference to responsibility. Rights and responsibilities are inseparable from one another, and without one, the other becomes hollow and meaningless. Etzioni examines the increasing attempt to bifurcate these terms, especially within the US. He warns that 'what is needed most is a change in the moral climate of the country, a greater willingness to share communitarian responsibilities, and a greater readiness to curb one's demands'.[12] The concept of citizenship as an entitlement devoid of individual responsibility is a grave threat, both to nations and to the world as a whole. Put another way, 'our rights are not merely rights *against* others; they are also rights *to* the positive aid of others – aid we need in order to develop our powers so that we may contribute to the common good'.[13] Although Etzioni uses the term 'responsibility' and Dagger uses the term 'right', both are correct because they are speaking of what is required of the individual. The problem with the term 'right' is that it is commonly understood to only be what the individual is entitled to, rather than what the responsibilities of the individual are. Citizenship must be understood as being part of something larger than one's self. No individual is capable of meeting all of his or her needs at all times and living within a community is meant to be a safeguard in times of hardship and a platform in times of prosperity.

With the new worldwide connections being fostered by globalization, peace requires a new conception of citizenship, one which goes beyond nationalism and embraces the universal. Benhabib argues that 'we are at a point in the political evolution of human communities when the unitary model of citizenship that bundled together residency on a single territory with subjection to a common bureaucratic administration representing a people perceived to be a more or less cohesive entity is at an end'.[14] As globalization continues to facilitate communication and increase interaction amongst people from various States, the State-centric view of citizenship loses importance. The world is bound together through commerce and telecommunications that provide for instantaneous flows of information and goods which cross political borders without consideration for traditional sovereignty. Yet within these changes looms the specter of new challenges to justice, freedom, and equality. The implications for democracy and citizenship created by these changing circumstances are stark. Decisions made by one society now impact people the world over. Even in 1795, Kant was aware that 'The growing prevalence of a (narrower or wider) community among the peoples of the earth has now reached a point at which the violation of right at any *one* place on the earth is felt in *all* places.'[15] It is only logical that such interconnectedness and interdependence must result in a shared concern for what happens not only within one's own borders but also in other States. In this shifting environment the role of a citizen becomes even more complex and important. Along with Benhabib, many scholars[16] have all concluded that as globalization brings the world closer together, the conception of citizenship must adapt to these changing conditions. Falk[17] contends that the traditional State-centric understanding of citizenship is in decline due to the growing irrelevance of State sovereignty and growing domination of economic forces. He also cautions that global citizenship may be on the rise, based not on one's connection to the State, but rather on shared values.

There still exists a tension between traditional conceptions of citizenship and cosmopolitan ideals of what a citizen ought to be. Heater[18] argues that a conflict can and often does exist between what is good for the State and what is good for the world. If national interests are given higher consideration than global interests, it would seem that State citizenship will outweigh cosmopolitan citizenship. However, this view is shortsighted. As environmental problems and terrorism have shown, what is good for one country in the short run may not be good for that country over time. Nations (and the people within them) must take the long view of what is really in their own best interests. Pallas cautions against a blind optimism in the power of global citizenship. He explains that proponents often claim that global citizenship will enhance the dignity and rights of all people, just as the State has done for its citizens. But they often fail to realize that 'within the state, equality of rights derives from a common pool of social and economic resources that does not exist at the global level'.[19] Again, this potential problem is resolved when cosmopolitan citizenship is viewed as having responsibilities that are fulfilled to the best of one's ability. This does not require the levelling of global wealth and resources, only the awareness of all humanity as equally entitled to basic rights. Bowden[20] takes criticism of cosmopolitanism one step further by arguing that it has a real danger in eliminating the safe guards provided to citizens by the State in which they reside. However, as will soon be shown, the State is often the one that provides the greatest threat to the safety of its inhabitants.

Even with the changing dynamics brought about by globalization, there is still an important role to be found for the State. One of the primary functions of the State is to provide the individual with a sense of cultural identity. The terms 'culture' and 'identity' have many meanings spanning many academic disciplines, but it will be sufficient to define cultural identity as 'patterns of thinking, feeling, and potential acting that were learned [through] the social environmental in which one grew up and collected one's life experiences'.[21] Cultural identity is necessary (but perhaps not sufficient) in answering the question 'who am I?' It provides the individual with an understanding of the self and of the community in which he or she lives. It is the foundation of the individual's understanding of the self.

The existence of the State allows for an existing network of institutions which can ensure the protection of cultural identity. Furthermore, political and civic participation also contribute to the establishment of identity as noted by Appiah, Falk, Heater, and Pallas.[22] Political and civic participation provide a sense of belonging and attachment to others in the community. For Kant, the State was an integral part of a cosmopolitan world. At first glance, it may seem odd that a cosmopolitan ideal is being put forth through a discussion of relations between States. Rather than attempting to justify a utopian ideal of a world government (which he also dismisses in the note on section 9 of *The Contest of Faculties*) Kant instead takes a pragmatic view of how the world ought to logically progress. The satire of perpetual peace being nothing more than a cemetery is meant partially to impart the difficulty of such a task. Kant does not offer perpetual peace as a guaranteed future State of existence, but rather as a hope for the continuing evolution of human relations. In *Perpetual Peace,* Kant shares his hope for a pacific federation of republican States which would maintain freedom and peace for all members (80).

Perhaps the most formidable challenge to reconciling State and global citizenship is the perceived tension between nationalism and cosmopolitanism. Cosmopolitanism's supporters and opponents have perpetuated the false notion that world citizenship is antithetical to nationalism and that they cannot compliment or even exist simultaneously. Baynes, and Thompson, and to a lesser extent, Habermas, and Held,[23] all discuss nationalism as a barrier or even threat to cosmopolitanism. The attachment an individual has with his or her State will only pose a threat to cosmopolitanism if he or she places a higher moral worth on those within the State. Just as sports fans may swear allegiance to a particular team, an individual can feel a special affinity to a certain geographical region or community group. The only danger is when that affinity turns into a belief in superiority. Tan attempts to show that liberal nationalism and cosmopolitan are not antithetical to one another and that, with proper understanding, they are actually compatible with one another. He argues that such a conflict is overstated, because 'moral cosmopolitanism' (as distinguished from institutional cosmopolitanism) is predicated on the belief that ' … the individual is the ultimate unit of moral worth … '..[24] He asserts that using moral cosmopolitanism can bridge the perceived gap between liberal nationalism and cosmopolitanism. While Tan offers the strongest defense of nationalism, Nussbaum also defends nationalism on the grounds that cosmopolitanism is often something to be added to nationalism rather than displacing it. Nussbaum suggests that cosmopolitan education is necessary, not only for developing an understanding of other cultures and values, but also for gaining a deeper understanding of our own culture.[25] Janowitz also reflects on the importance of civic education and frames it in terms of civic and political participation. He argues that ' … effective citizenship rests on a rigorous and viable system of civic education which informs the individual of his civic rights and obligations'.[26] Fleming[27] confirms Janowitz's conclusions by examining the impact on civic education on the likelihood of future participation and she finds a positive correlation between the two. Waldron challenges those who believe cosmopolitanism includes a levelling of culture and identity into one homogeneous 'cosmopolitan culture'.[28] He argues that 'cosmopolitan culture' is really about moving away from the differences within cultures and embracing the universal values that are found in them. He points out that even those who adhere to 'traditional culture' already have a multicultural aspect imbedded within that conception because no culture exists independently of outside influences. Finally, he stresses that 'cosmopolitan culture' is about embracing one's particular culture as the culmination of previous generation's work towards finding solutions, and that this should be applied to the common problems found throughout the world.

The foundation of cosmopolitan citizenship is the existence and value of universal human rights. Dagger writes 'By definition, a human right must be universal and equal, a right that all persons possess in equal measure; it must also entail a correlative duty that falls equally on all persons who are in a position to discharge it.'[29] Dagger is careful to note both the right and corresponding responsibility behind human rights. The UDHR (1948) opens with the profound statement that 'All human beings are born free and equal in dignity and rights. They are endowed with reason and conscience and should act towards one another in a spirit of brotherhood.' When the UDHR was written in the aftermath of World War II, it embodied the belief that there are values which are held by all people regardless of political borders. Written by Eleanor Roosevelt (US), John Humphrey (Canada), Rene Cassin (France), P.C. Chang (China), Charles Malik (Lebanon), and others, it represents one of the greatest accomplishments of world unity and cosmopolitanism. The UDHR is a prime example of how human rights form the basis of cosmopolitan citizenship, by recognizing the commonalities of all of humanity.

By accepting the premise offered by the UDHR, that all persons are in fact 'born equal in dignity and rights' it follows that these rights must be understood as universal. Since they apply to all people, the notion that the State is the responsible for the allocation and distribution of rights is no longer sufficient. One must be careful to distinguish between the State as the de facto enforcer of those rights and the State as the source of those rights. While the former is a historical fact, the latter is not. Young explains that 'Membership in a common political community, on the part of either the agent or the sufferers, is relevant only instrumentally as sometimes providing efficient means of discharging obligations and distributing particular tasks.'[30] Young rightly asserts that physical location is relevant only in the practical execution of responsibilities, not in the allocation of them. This is on par with Nussbaum's[31] idea of concentric circles of responsibility in which our responsibility radiates outward in tandem with our abilities. Nussbaum may be a bit more sympathetic to helping those closest to us, but Young shares the practicality of such responsibility.

With human rights as the basis for cosmopolitan citizenship, the question of how citizenship ought to exist in the modern globalized world can now be addressed. As Benhabib notes this follows ' … the Kantian tradition of thinking of cosmopolitanism as the emergence of norms that ought to govern relations among individuals in a global civil society'.[32] With all of humanity being equally endowed with rights (not ability), the cosmopolitan citizen must look past national boundaries and be willing to act towards all people, as the UDHR would say, 'in the spirit of brotherhood'. Parekh explain the cosmopolitan citizen thusly:

> As moral beings who have compelling reasons to acknowledge the equal intrinsic worth of all human beings, we have two fundamental duties, negative and positive. We have a duty not to inflict evils on others and damage their ability to pursue their well-being. ... Positively, we have a duty to alleviate their suffering and render them such help as they need and which we can provide within the limits of our abilities and resources.[33]

This mirrors the responsibilities of the citizen within a State, but expands those duties to all of humanity.

There are those who would challenge the need for the continued existence of State citizenship if cosmopolitan citizenship were to be achieved. Habermas[34] makes the case for the 'revised Kantian project' of a global cosmopolitan constitutionalism that would resolve many of the crises faced by modernity. Held's[35] work strongly builds on Habermas' and discusses the need for a cosmopolitan State or institution to address the global problems currently facing the world. Both Habermas and Held focus on the inconsistencies within the modern world system such as the free market which enables exploitation, the appeal to sovereignty when crimes against humanity are committed, and the failure to address global problems such as climate change, nuclear proliferation, and inequity. They both conclude that a cosmopolitan institution is necessary to rectify these deficiencies. Ypi is sympathetic to this reasoning and argues for a political context (which *could* be within the State system) which would allow for the political redress of rights claims. Ypi asserts that 'when enforcing political obligations, citizens can legitimately constrain the activities of fellow-members and act collectively to reform particular political institutions so as to align them cosmopolitan goals'.[36] Regardless of whether or not the State is relevant, it would seem that at least for this particular moment in time, the institutions with the ability to induce cosmopolitan change are at least partially at the State level.

If the premise that all people are both citizens of the State and citizens of the world is accepted, then the duties and responsibilities of cosmopolitan citizens must be considered.

Democracy

Democracy, when operating within the traditional State-centric paradigm, presents two interrelated problems for advancing the cause of the R2P. The first problem is that in an indirect democracy, elected officials are beholden to those they represent. The very foundation of a representative democracy is that voters show their preference by voting for the candidate they feel best represents their interest. The second problem is that elected officials are forced to be short sighted because their political lives are only as long as each election cycle. What is good for the short term is not always good for the long term. Emery Reves wrote, 'In every field of life, the method of conducting affairs which looks beyond the events that might happen in later years, we call wise and far-sighted. In public affairs, we call it "unrealistic" and "Utopian".'[37]

In the current system of democratic nation States, those who hold office are given that power by those they represent. Their constituency determines whether or not they retain power. Democratic office holders must be responsive to the concerns of those they represent. New sovereigntists[38] advocate that ' ... a constitutionally established, popularly sovereign state must make protecting and promoting its citizens' interests its top foreign policy priority ... '.[39] The R2P emphasizes State responsibility, but when that responsibility is neglected, it becomes the duty of the global community to act. However, when other States are considering action, those (democratic) States will only act if called to do so by the domestic population. During the Rwandan genocide, one of the few US senators to acknowledge a problem was Paul Simon. He was interviewed by National Public Radio (NPR) in July 1994 and explained the lack of a US response. He said 'If every member of the House and Senate had received 100 letters from the people back home saying we have to do something about Rwanda, when the crisis was first developing, then I think the response would have been different.'[40] The US did not act because of a lack of political will by the US citizenry. Since democratic power leaves leaders only responsible to those they represent, it must be the citizens of their own State who call for the protection of those outside their own political boundaries. In this sense, political leaders, when interested in re-election first and foremost, are actually constrained by democracy when their constituents insulate themselves from atrocities being committed in other States.

The other problem of traditional State-centric notions of democracy is the focus on the immediate future, at the expense of the long-term. '[Politicians] ... routinely confront *inter-temporal* dilemmas in making policy choices – trade-offs between the short-term impact and the long-run consequences of state action'.[41] Re-election is always one of the foremost thoughts on the mind of any office holder, and that limits the ability of a government to achieve certain goods, the benefits of which may not be seen during the politician's own tenure. The R2P must be universal policy and articulated international law rather than a principle applied to only some situations. Many of the worst atrocities happen in a relatively short time. During the Holocaust, 'In mid-March 1942 some 75–80 percent of all victims of the Holocaust were still alive, while 20 to 25 percent had perished. A mere eleven months later, in February 1943, the percentages were exactly the reverse'.[42] During the Rwandan genocide, over 800,000 people were murdered in only one hundred days.[43] The time to debate the merits of R2P is not when these widespread and systematic atrocities occur. United Nations Deputy Secretary General, Jan Eliasson recently explained, 'Too often, rhetoric has outpaced action when it comes to preventing atrocity crimes. How many times have we said "never again"? ... The lives of millions and the credibility of this Organ-ization hinge on our ability to do far better than we have done to date.'[44] In order to make the often heard credo of 'Never Again' a reality, R2P must be a doctrine that can be enforced when needed rather than debated while victims plead for help. This daunting task requires the willingness of States to see the long term necessity of instituting policy that will make the R2P a doctrine of action rather than debate.

Sovereignty has always been a foundational concern for political theorists and its sig-nificance has not been ignored within the debate surrounding the R2P. Advocates of R2P argue that sovereignty cannot claim rights without embracing the corresponding responsi-bilities. 'At its root, sovereignty as responsibility views sovereignty not simply as a grant of control over territory and people, but as an obligation to protect one's citizens from harm'.[45] Sovereignty entails certain rights, but only when the corresponding responsibilities are being fulfilled as well. The same conditions apply to citizens. Citizens are entitled to certain rights as long as they fulfilled their civic responsibilities. When someone breaks the law (neglects a civic responsibility) they forfeit their rights (aka, they go to jail). A State's claim to sovereign rights is only viable if their responsibilities are fulfilled. The ICISS recognized this element of sovereignty as responsibility when they proclaimed 'It is acknowledged that sovereignty implies a dual responsibility: externally – to respect the sovereignty of other states, and internally, to respect the dignity and basic rights of all people within the state.'[46] This dual role of the State, as right-holder and duty-bearer cannot be separated.

While fulfillment of sovereign responsibility is the most widely accepted dictate for intervention in another State to fulfill R2P obligations, sovereignty is often also beholden to democracy. Consent of the governed, a pillar of democracy, acts as a strong incentive for leaders. 'Mass behavior [consent of the governed] is relevant to elite choices because it determines part of elite incentives'.[47] History has provided numerous examples of elites (leaders) ignoring the will of the governed, but there is a cost to such inaction. In a democracy such leaders may be voted out of office, but in dictatorships, leaders may become the target of protests and forced removal such as in the cases of Tunisia, Libya, and Egypt during the Arab Spring. Consent is not a sufficient element to force leaders to embrace their role as duty bearer under their sovereign responsibility, but it is a necessary condition in the democratic political system.

Although democracy places limitations on the R2P when it is viewed in the traditional State-centric form, the core of democracy is built upon the need to strengthen and unite a community and those values are fully compatible with the R2P:

> Through democracy, members of a given public – a demos – take decisions that shape their own destiny jointly, with equal rights and opportunities of participation, and without arbitrarily imposed constraints on the debate. In one way or another, democratic governance is participatory, consultive, transparent, and publicly accountable.[48]

Additionally, civic duty *requires* a measure of protection for those who are unable to protect themselves. Democratic leaders are responsible for those they represent, but every person is responsible for ensuring the rights of those who are not fortunate enough to be born into a society which respects human rights. The rights of disadvantaged groups are especially critical in a pluralistic cosmopolitan democracy.

There are two ways to address the issue of representation as an impediment to R2P. The first is to acknowledge that people have a responsibility to others, including those beyond their own borders and that responsibility is transferred to their representatives who act on their behalf. Democracy is based upon the idea that people ought to have a say in the governance that impacts their lives. 'The theory of participatory democracy is built round the central assertion that individuals and their institutions cannot be considered in isolation from one another.'[49] Governments were established as a means to diffuse responsibility so that a better life could be had by all. Democracy in particular is recognition of the necessity of others and the protection of all.

The problem of representation is really a symptom of a deficiency of civic responsibility. Citizens who embrace responsibility and place demands upon their representatives would force government to act on their behalf. Citizenship must be understood in terms of both rights and responsibility. As previously discussed, authors such as Etzioni, and Dagger[50] have focused on the necessity of rights being understood when in relation to responsibilities. The second way to address the issue of representation as an impediment to R2P, which has already been alluded to, is to adopt a more cosmopolitan understanding of community. Democracy itself is based upon the idea of community. Doris Kearns Goodwin, an American historian, explained the view of Abraham Lincoln on democracy and community. She said, 'In fact to Lincoln's mind, the fundamental test of a democracy was its capacity, as he said, to elevate the condition of men, to lift all the artificial weight from all shoulders, to clear the path for laudable pursuit for all, to allow talent to rise to its natural level.'[51] Democracy is a collaborative effort in which a strong community allows all members to benefit, to 'elevate the condition of men'.

The expansion of a conception of community does not threaten the local concerns of representative government. Representative government can still focus on domestic issues without ignoring its responsibility to the rest of the world. On the eve of US' involvement in World War I, President Woodrow Wilson addressed the Senate with the hope of finding peace without American bloodshed. He asked, 'Is the present war a struggle for a just and secure peace, or only for a new balance of power? ... There must be, not a balance of power, but a community of power; not organized rivalries, but an organized common peace.'[52] Wilson recognized the cyclical nature of conflict that occurs when power is the primary aim. By challenging this power-centric paradigm, Wilson hoped the world would achieve a peace that would benefit all of humanity.

The digital age & increased capacity

Central to both of the ways to address the issue of representation is the increased capacity for communication and information. The twenty-first century has given birth to a generation that is more globally interconnected than any previous generation. The world is bound together through commerce and telecommunications that provide for instantaneous flows of information and goods which cross political borders without consideration for traditional sovereignty. The flow of information and access to means of communication continues to reach capacities never even dreamt of by previous generations. Both the speed and power of information sharing and communication increase at an exponential rate. Eric Schmidt and Jared Cohen summarize the momentous changes that have taken place:

> In the first decade of the twenty-first century, the number of people connected to the Internet worldwide increased from 350 million to more than 2 billion. In the same period, the number of mobile-phone subscribers rose from 750 million to well over 5 billion (it is now over 6 billion). ... By 2025, the majority of the world's population will, in one generation, have gone from having virtually no access to unfiltered information to accessing all of the world's information through a device that fits in the palm of the hand.[53]

Yet within these changes looms the specter of new challenges to justice, freedom, and equality. The implications for democracy and citizenship created by these changing circumstances are stark. From the social-media highlighted events of the 'Arab Spring' to the moral and legal battles of State secrecy with Wikileaks and similar organizations, the impacts of the digital age cannot be ignored. Decisions made by one society now very often impact people the world over. In this shifting environment the role of a citizen in a democracy becomes even more complex and important.

The digital age has created the ability for members of a community to engage with one another, even across great distances. 'Virtual communities [VCs] are extensions of real-world communities. VCs enable and support communication between people who are in different places and on different schedules.'[54] Furthermore, one concern of democracy is the ability to agree upon preferences in diverse communities. However, the dignity (or value) of the human person is a universal standard, as recognized in the UDHR and numerous other international treaties. Human rights are universal by nature, they are *human* rights that transcend physical borders and cultural differences. There are, of course, differences of opinion on the scope of these rights, but the right to life, the right to survival, is universally accepted. This is the mission of R2P.

Prior to the digital revolution, when human rights abuses or mass atrocities occurred, information would be transferred from officials in the field to the decision-makers at a headquarters. News coverage might generate public awareness, but it was still left to agents of the UN or other international or State organization to investigate, report on, and, if possible, resolve the situation. Evidence was often anecdotal, coming from reports of victims or witnesses. If a humanitarian intervention was to take place, it would be based on anecdotal information confirmed by officials in the field. The digital revolution has created a new paradigm in which evidence of human rights abuses and mass atrocities is vividly shared in real time through pictures, videos, and often, live transmissions:

> The revolution in information technology has made global communications instantaneous and provided unprecedented access to information worldwide. The result has been an enormously heightened awareness of conflicts wherever they may be occurring, combined with immediate and often very compelling visual images of the resultant suffering on television and in other mass media.'[55]

Instead of information travelling from officials in the field to headquarters, information travels directly from those experiencing the event to the entire world. Social media has created a platform in which information can be spread instantaneously across the globe. If a humanitarian intervention is to take place, it is now prompted by real time footage submitted by those affected. The world can no longer claim to be ignorant to the atrocities being committed against those in far off places. With the innovation provided by digital technology, ignorance of the action is no longer a plausible reason for lack of action. The digital age has enabled society to be informed, and that information calls out for action.

Conclusion

Citizenship, whether at the State level or cosmopolitan, requires the individual to fulfill certain responsibilities. Among those are the responsibility to work not only for one's self but for the community as a whole. When widespread and systematic abuses of human rights take place anywhere in the world, citizens must call upon their governments and the international community to fulfill the ideals of the R2P. It is not enough to proclaim these values, but they must be backed with consistent action. Both democracy and the R2P are the subject of great oratory, but they both will fail if those words are not matched with action. When Romeo Dallaire retired from the Canadian Parliament, he said:

> Today we point to the humanitarian aid dollars we've given, which are never enough, and proclaim we've done our part. Today we have more sabre-rattling and less credibility; more expressions of concern and less contingency planning; more endless consultation with allies, or so we are told, and less real action being taken; and more empty calls for respect for human rights and less actual engagement with the violators.[56]

Democracy is a community formed for the betterment of all. Democracy requires citizens to be informed and engaged. The R2P does not seek a levelling of society nor an equality of condition, it only seeks to ensure that when gross systematic violations of human rights occur, the world community is ready and willing to respond. When the world fails to respond, it tacitly condones the atrocities and neglects its own duty. 'If [the international community] stays disengaged, there is a risk of become complicit bystanders in massacre, ethnic cleansing, and even genocide.'[57] Society has the ability to live up to the promises of democratic community. By embracing the responsibilities that make those cherished rights possible, the world can, and must, embrace the R2P as a necessary element of democratic community.

Notes

1. Halil Rahman Basaran, 'Responsibility to Protect: An Explanation', *Houston Journal of International Law* 36, no. 3 (2014): 581–624, esp. 583.
2. James H. Kettner, *The Development of American Citizenship, 1608–1870* (Chapel Hill, NC: University of North Carolina Press, 1978), esp. 208.
3. For a detailed account of the historical development of humanitarian intervention, see Gary Bass' *Freedom's Battle: The Origin of Humanitarian Intervention* (2008).
4. International Commission on Intervention and Satte Sovereignty (ICISS), and International Development Research Centre. *The Responsibility to Protect: Report of the International Commission on Intervention and State Sovereignty*, Gareth J. Evans and Mohamed Sahnoun, eds. (Ottawa: International Development Research Centre, 2001), esp. 8.
5. Immanuel Kant, *Toward perpetual peace and other writings on politics, peace, and history* (New Haven: Yale University Press, [1784] 2006), esp. 6.
6. Sidney Verba, Kay Lehman Schlozman, and Henry E. Brady, *Voice and Equality: Civic Voluntarism in American Politics* (Cambridge, MA: Harvard University Press, 1995), 38.
7. Louise Conn Fleming, 'Civic participation: A curriculum for democracy', *American Secondary Education*, 40, no. 1 (2011): 39–50; Gabriel A. Almond and Sidney Verba, eds., *Civic Culture Revisited* (Newbury Park, CA: Sage Publications, 1989); John Gaventa and Gregory Barrett, 'Mapping the Outcomes of Citizen Engagement', *World Development* 40, no.12 (2012): 2399–2410.
8. Cliff Zukin, Scott Keeter, Krista Andolina, and Michael X. Delli Carpini, *A new engagement? Political participation, civic life, and the changing American citizen* (New York, NY: Oxford University Press, 2006), 51.
9. Sarah K. Bruch, Myra Marx Ferree, and Joe Soss, 'From Policy to Polity: Democracy, Paternalism, and the Incorporation of Disadvantaged Citizens', *American Sociological Review*, 75, no. 2 (2010): 205–226; Robert Putnam, *Bowling Alone: The Collapse and Revival of American Community* (New York: NY: Simon & Schuster, 2000); and others.
10. Oxford English Dictionary: *Citizen*: an inhabitant of a city or (often) of a town; especially one possessing civic rights and privileges, a burgess or freeman of a city; *Citizenship:* the position or status of being a citizen, with its rights and privileges.
11. Jeremy Waldron, *Dignity, Rank, and Rights* (Oxford: Oxford University Press, 2012).
12. Amitai Etzioni, 'Too Many Rights, Too Few Responsibilities', in *Toward a Global Civil Society,* Michael Walzer, ed. (Providence, RI: Berghahn Books, 1996), 99–106, esp. 101.
13. Richard Dagger, *Civic Virtues: Rights, Citizenship, and Republican Liberalism* (New York: Oxford University Press, 1997), esp. 21.
14. Seyla Benhabib, *Another Cosmopolitanism* (Oxford, New York: Oxford University Press, 2006), esp. 45.
15. Immanuel Kant, *Toward Perpetual Peace and Other Writings on Politics, Peace, and History* (New Haven, CT: Yale University Press, [1784] 2006), 84, 8:360.
16. Anthony Appiah, *Cosmopolitanism: Ethics in a World of Strangers* (New York: W.W. Norton & Co., 2006); Bhikhu Parekh, 'Cosmopolitanism and Global Citizenship', *Review of International Studies* 29, no. 1 (2003): 3–17; Kim Rubenstein, 'Citizenship in an Age of Globalisation: The Cosmopolitan citizen?', *Law in Context* 25, no. 1 (2007): 88–111; Kok-Chor Tan, 'Nationalism and Cosmopolitanism', in *The Cosmopolitan Reader,* Garrett Wallace Brown and David Held, eds. (Cambridge: Polity Press, 2012), 176–190.
17. Richard Falk, 'The Decline of Citizenship in an Era of Globalization', *Citizenship Studies* 4, no. 1 (2000): 5–17.
18. Derek Heater, *Citizenship: The Civic Ideal in World History, Politics, and Education* (Manchester: Manchester University Press, 2004).
19. Christopher Pallas, 'Identity, Individualism, and Activism Beyond the State: Examining the Impacts of Global Citizenship', *Global Society* 26, no. 2 (2012): 169–189.
20. Brett Bowden, 'The Perils of Global Citizenship', *Citizenship Studies* 7, no. 3 (2003): 349–362.

21. Geert Hofstede, Gert Jan Hofstede, and Michael Minkov, *Cultures and Organizations: Software of the Mind*, 3rd ed. (New York: McGraw Hill, 2010), 4–5.
22. Appiah, *Cosmopolitanism*; Falk, 'The Decline of Citizenship'; Heater, *Citizenship*; Pallas, 'Identity, Individualism, and Activism Beyond the State'.
23. Kenneth Baynes, 'Communitarian and cosmopolitan challenges to Kant's conception of world peace', in *Perpetual peace: Essays on Kant's cosmopolitan ideal*, James Bohman and Matthias Lutz-Bachmann, eds. (Cambridge, MA: The MIT Press, 1997), 219–234; Janna Thompson, 'Community identity and world citizenship', in *Re-imagining political community*, Daniele Archibugi, David Held, and Martin Kohler, eds. (Stanford, CA: Stanford University Press, 1998), 179–197; Jurgen Habermas, 'A political constitution for the pluralist world society?' in *The cosmopolitanism reader*, 267–288; David Held, 'Principles of a cosmopolitan order', in *The Cosmopolitanism Reader*, 229–247.
24. Kok-Chor Tan, *Nationalism and Cosmopolitanism*, esp. 182.
25. Ibid., 159.
26. Morris Janowitz, *The reconstruction of patriotism: Education for civic consciousness* (Chicago, IL: Chicago University Press, 1983), ix.
27. Fleming, 'Civic Participation'.
28. Jeremy Waldron, *Dignity, Rank, and Rights* (Oxford: Oxford University Press, 2012), esp. 167.
29. Dagger, *Civic Virtues*, esp. 42.
30. Iris Marion Young, *Responsibility for justice. Oxford Political Philosophy.* (Oxford, New York: Oxford University Press, 2011), 137.
31. Martha C. Nussbaum, 'Patriotism and cosmopolitanism', in *The Cosmopolitanism Reader*, 155–162.
32. Benhabib. *Another Cosmopolitanism*, esp. 20.
33. Parekh, 'Cosmopolitanism and Global Citizenship', esp. 6.
34. Habermas, 'A political constitution for the pluralist world society?'
35. Held, 'Principles of a cosmopolitan order'.
36. Lea L. Ypi, 'Statist cosmopolitanism', *Journal of Political Philosophy* 16, no. 1 (2008): 48–71.
37. Emery Reves, *A Democratic Manifesto* (New York: Random House, 1942), 11.
38. A term coined by Peter J. Spiro ('The New Sovereigntists: American Exceptionalism and Its False Prophets', *Foreign Affairs*, 79, no. 6 [2000]: 9–15) used by Goodhart and Taninchev ('The New Sovereigntist Challenge for Global Governance: Democracy Without Sovereignty' [2011]) to describe 'a group of American scholars, intellectuals, and policymakers who view the emerging international legal order and system of global governance with consternation' (p. 1047).
39. Michael Goodhart and Stacy Bondanella Taninchev, 'The New Sovereigntist Challenge for Global Governance: Democracy Without sovereignty', *International Studies Quarterly* 55, no. 4 (2011): 1047–1068, esp. 1047.
40. Cited in Samantha Power, *A Problem From Hell: America and the Age of Genocide* (New York: Perennial, 2003), esp. 177.
41. Alan M. Jacobs, *Governing for the Long Term: Democracy and the Politics of Investment* (Cambridge and New York: Cambridge University Press, 2011), esp. 7.
42. Christopher R. Browning, *Ordinary Men: Reserve Police Battalion 101 and the Final Solution in Poland* (New York: HarperCollins, 1992), esp. vx.
43. Gérard Prunier, *The Rwanda Crisis: History of a Genocide* (New York: Columbia University Press, 1995).
44. Jan Eliasson, Remarks delivered at the informal interactive dialogue on 'Fulfilling our collective responsibility: International assistance and the responsibility to protect', 8 September 2014, available at: http://www.un.org/News/Press/docs/2014/dsgsm793.doc.htm (accessed 15 June 2015).
45. Oona A. Hathaway, Julia Brower, Ryan Liss, Tina Thomas, and Jacob Victor, 'Consent-based Humanitarian Intervention: Giving Sovereign Responsibility Back to the Sovereign', *Cornell International Law Journal* 46, no. 3 (2013): 499–568, esp. 538.
46. International Commission on Intervention and State Sovereignty (ICISS) and International development Research Centre, *The Responsibility to Protect: Report of the International Commission on Intervention and State Sovereignty*, Gareth J. Evans and Mohamed Sahnoun eds. (Ottawa: International Development Research Centre, 2001), esp. 8.

47. Barry R. Weingast, 'The Political Foundations of Democracy and the Rule of Law' *The American Political Science Review* 91, no. 2 (1997): 245–263, esp. 261.

48. Jan Aart Scholte, 'Civil Society and Democracy in Global Governance', *Global Governance* 8, no. 3 (2002): 281–304, esp. 285.

49. Carole Pateman, 'Participation and Democratic Theory,' in *The Democracy Sourcebook,* José Antônio Cheibub, Ian Shapiro, and Robert Alan Dahl eds. (Cambridge, MA: MIT Press, 2003), 40–47, esp. 41.

50. Etzioni, 'Too Many Rights, Too Few Responsibilities'; Dagger, *Civic Virtues.*

51. National Constitution Center, *Doris Kearns Goodwin: 'Team of Rivals'.* Audio. We the People Podcasts, 2005.

52. Woodrow Wilson 'Peace Without Victory'. (Speech, Washington, DC, 22 January 1917), available at: http://www.firstworldwar.com/source/peacewithoutvictory.htm (accessed 21 May 2015).

53. Eric Schmidt, and Jared Cohen. *The New Digital Age: Reshaping the Future of People, Nations and Business* (New York: Alfred A. Knopf, 2013), esp. 4.

54. Cristian Maciel, Licínio Roque, and Ana Cristina Bicharra Garcia, 'Interaction and Communication Resources in Collaborative E-democratic Environments: The Democratic Citizenship Community', *Information Polity* 15, no. 1–2 (2010): 73–88, esp. 75.

55. International Commission on Intervention and State Sovereignty (ICISS) and International Development Research Centre, *The Responsibility to Protect*, esp. 6–7.

56. Romeo Dallaire, Speech delivered to the Senate. (Speech, Canada, 17 June 2014), available at: http://www.macleans.ca/politics/for-the-record-romeo-dallaires-last-speech-in-the-senate/ (accessed 1 June 2015).

57. International Commission on Intervention and State Sovereignty (ICISS) and International Development Research Centre, *The Responsibility to Protect*, esp. 5.

'To prevent future Kosovos and future Rwandas.'
A critical constructivist view of the Responsibility to Protect

Sassan Gholiagha

Department of Social Science, University of Hamburg, Hamburg, Germany

The 2005 World Summit led to the unanimous declaration that all states have a responsibility to protect (R2P) their own population from genocide, war crimes, crimes against humanities, and ethnic cleansing. Furthermore, it was agreed that, should a state manifestly fail, the international community would take over this responsibility. Despite this seemingly broad agreement of the R2P 10 years ago, more recent events in Libya and Syria have highlighted the ongoing contestation of R2P. Analysing the discourse within the UN Security Council on Libya and Syria between 2011 and early 2015, this article holds that the ongoing contestation is understandable through a critical constructivist framework, and that furthermore R2P, despite all criticism, can be credited with opening discursive spaces in which a politics of protection aimed at individual human beings, becomes possible.

1. Introduction

Following intense negotiations at the 2005 World Summit,[1] the UN member states agreed on a 'Responsibility to Protect' (R2P), stating that, '[E]ach individual state has the responsibility to protect its populations from genocide, war crimes, ethnic cleansing and crimes against humanity'.[2] The World Summit Outcome Document (WSOD) furthermore stated that the international community also had a responsibility to support states in this endeavour and should take over the responsibility should states manifestly fail in the protection of their populations.[3] This article is not so much interested in the history that led to this outcome document or the history of R2P. Nevertheless section 2 provides a short history of humanitarian interventions of the 1990s, the road to the WSOD, and the development and track record of R2P since 2005, to familiarize readers with the context in which this article is situated. This article is rather interested in adding to the ongoing debate about the actual impact and role of R2P today in preventing mass atrocities. The need for this endeavour becomes obvious in the ongoing conflicts in Iraq, Syria, Yemen, and elsewhere.

To this end, the article provides a theoretical framework to analyse and understand the ongoing contestation of R2P as visible in the debates about the right approach to the crises in Libya and Syria. The article argues that R2P as a 'complex norm'[4] opens discursive spaces in which a politics of protection can take place. This, the article claims, is the normative advancements R2P embodies. Ten years after the 2005 World Summit R2P has not always prevented 'future Kosovos and future Rwandas', as Alex J. Bellamy once aptly described R2P's aspirations.[5] This however should not be read as a complete failure or even 'death' of R2P, as some authors would have it.[6] The inconsistent application of R2P becomes understandable by understanding that R2P remains contested, even after a formal agreement.[7]

Following a history of humanitarian interventions and R2P in section 2, section 3 offers a theoretical framework based on critical constructivist literature. An interpretivist methodological framework and the method of positioning analysis as a specific approach to analyse discourse as data are presented in section 4. The theoretical and methodological framework are then combined to undertake a comparative analysis of the discourse[8] within the UN Security Council on Libya and Syria to shed light on the question how R2P played a role in these two discourses and to assess R2P's ability to prevent mass atrocities. The final section of this article, section 6, draws together the empirical insights from section 5 and the theoretical arguments provided in section 3, to draw some specific conclusions of R2Ps stand in current world politics and some general conclusions on what R2P means for our understanding of international relations.[9]

2. A short history of 'Humanitarian Interventions' and R2P

This section provides a short history of the so-called 'humanitarian interventions' of the 1990s, as well as of the developments toward R2P and its history since 2005. The illustrative character of the following part should be noted. By no means are the discussions of the events in Iraq, Somalia, Rwanda, and Bosnia exhaustive; the same is true for the discussion of the developments leading up to the 2005 World Summit and the overview of R2P's track record since then. The aim of this section is to set the ground for a more detailed analysis of the events in Libya and Syria provided in section 5.

Following the end of the cold war, the decision of the UN Security Council to authorize the use of force in an attempt to protect the Kurdish civilian population in northern Iraq,[10] has been seen as first event of the 1990s that turned away from the politics of non-interferences.[11] This development continued within the UN Security Council. In 1992 the Council passed Resolution 767,[12] which was the first resolution in which the Security Council avowed that ' … grave violations within a country or severe emergencies can be evaluated as a threat to peace or international security'.[13] That such a view also included the use of force via 'boots on the grounds' became clear in the operation *Restore Hope*/UNITAF in Somalia, which was authorized unanimously through UN Security Council Resolution 794.[14] This resolution meant that ' … humanitarian claims were being advanced and legitimated by members as justification for the use of force … '.[15] As is well known, the mission in Somalia ended in a disaster, leading to the death of hundreds of people, both amongst Somali civilians and US military personnel.[16]

When only a year later the conflict between *Hutu* and *Tutsi* escalated in Rwanda and 800,000 civilians (mostly *Tutsi*) were killed within a 100 days, the international community acted reluctantly, and very late. Part of the explanation for this was a lack of political will to get involved after the recent events in Somalia.[17] While today there is little doubt that swift and comprehensive military operations could have prevented the genocide that took place,[18] the two UN Security Council Resolutions 918[19] and 925[20] both passed in 1994, authorizing a the United Nations Assistance Mission in Rwanda II (UNAMIR II), provided 'too little, too late', as did the French *Operation Turquoise,* aimed at bridging the gap until the full deployment of UNAMIR II.[21] The other part for explaining the failure of the international community in Rwanda, was the reluctance of both the US and European states to call the events in Rwanda a genocide,[22] fearing legal obligations under the 1948 Genocide Convention.[23] A view later affirmed with reference to Bosnia by the International Court of Justice in its 2007 judgement on the application of the Genocide Convention.[24] A massacre during the war in Bosnia in 1995[25] shocked the conscience of the world again and showed how little the international community did at times to protect fellow individual human beings. In the beginning of July 1995 at least 7414 Bosnian men and boys were killed. All this happened under the eyes of a UN Mission and within an alleged 'safe haven' in the town of Srebrenica, a safe haven, which had been established through the UN Security Council Resolution 819[26] on the 16 April 1993.[27]

The 1990s thus were characterized by both successes and failures to protect individual human beings from mass atrocities and severe human rights violations. Four years after Rwanda and three years after Srebrenica, a conflict in the then-Serbian province of Kosovo escalated and reports of civilian casualties surfaced. As in the previously discussed conflicts, here as well an innerstate conflict, fuelled by ethnic rivalries, led to an outbreak of violence. In the Kosovo conflict the question rose again, ' ... to what extent and in which ways the international community has the right or even the obligation, to intervene in innerstate conflicts, in which grave human rights violations are looming or already being committed'.[28]

The question of intervention for humanitarian reasons by the international community had already come up in Iraq, Somalia, Rwanda, and Bosnia. The crucial difference in Kosovo was that this time there was no consensus whether to act or not to act, and despite a missing authorization by the UN Security Council, the North Atlantic Treaty Organisation (NATO), decided to act by conducting military air strikes in Kosovo and Serbia.[29] The conflict in Kosovo had escalated in early 1998. Estimations are that between February and September 1998 approximately 1000 civilians were killed.[30] The estimates for September 1998 to March 1999 are somewhat lower. At the same time, 400,000 people fled, about half of them into neighbouring countries.[31] The diplomatic negotiations with Serbia aiming to end the violence included the threat to resort to the use of force.[32]

In September of 1998 the UN Security Council condemned the events in Kosovo under Chapter VII of the Charter as a 'threat to peace and security in the region' in Resolution 1199.[33] The diplomatic means did not suffice to put an end to the violence, and NATO opted for military force. As Christine Gray notes, the arguments by NATO were political and moral[34] and there was no legal base, as the use of force was neither authorized by the UN Security Council nor an act of self-defence. However, a resolution condemning NATO for violations of international law only received three votes in favour by Russia, China, and Namibia, with the other 12 members of the Security Council voting against it.[35] In sum, the reaction towards the NATO operation was ambivalent,[36] with an international commission concluding that NATO's actions where illegal but legitimate.[37]

While Rwanda had been the result of lacking political will,[38] Kosovo shed light on a more general problem, which Lothar Brock has described fittingly as fracturing of the ' ... dualism of the current international legal order as a *law of states and human rights order* ... '.[39] The events of the 1990s showed that state sovereignty no longer was suitable to shield from all interference, no matter what happened within a state.[40] And while the interventions of the 1990s were not always successful and not always characterized by a consensus within the international community, human beings were identified independent of their location and their citizenship as worthy of protection.[41]

The political conflict over the intervention in Kosovo and the failures, especially in Rwanda, led to a growing debate within the United Nations about the right way forward in overcoming the tension between state sovereignty and human rights protection.[42]

A short piece, written by then-Secretary General Kofi Annan and published at the eve of the General Assembly meeting in the *Economist,* started the debate. It was titled *Two Concepts of Sovereignty.*[43] Annan criticized the lack of political will in Rwanda as well as the unauthorized action of NATO in Kosovo. However, he also wrote, with reference to Rwanda:

> Imagine for one moment that, in those dark days and hours leading up to the genocide, there had been a coalition of states ready and willing to act in defence of the Tutsi population, but the council had refused or delayed giving the green light. Should such a coalition then have stood idly by while the horror unfolded?[44]

Annan thus held that neither genocide nor actors circumventing the Security Council should occur. Bellamy has fittingly labelled these two aims as the prevention of 'future Rwandas' and 'future Kosovos'.[45] Annan, employing the term 'individual sovereignty'[46] suggested a complementarity between state sovereignty and individual human rights. Such an idea was already formulated in 1996 under the term of 'sovereignty as responsibility'[47] and a number of authors have also suggested such an understanding.[48] The debate of the 1990s about the tension between state sovereignty and human rights protection ended at the dawn of the twenty-first century with a call for complementarity.

This call was taken up by the Canadian sponsored International Commission on Intervention and State Sovereignty (ICISS).[49] And the ICISS answered this call with its suggestion of a R2P.[50] The ICISS began with the question, whether there was a 'right of humanitarian intervention',[51] put differently, whether military actions within another state with the aim of human rights protection was permissible.[52] The answer the commission provided was to move away from a 'right of intervention' to a R2P.[53]

Andreas von Arnauld highlights three key points, which distinguish R2P from humanitarian interventions; First, R2P takes the perspective of the person to be protected; humanitarian interventions are about the intervener. This claim is based on the understanding of humanitarian interventions as answering the question of 'doing something' and hence focusing on the intervener.[54] Second, the primary responsibility lies with the state; hence, R2P can be understood as strengthening sovereignty. Third, rebuilding and prevention constitute core aspects of R2P, neither of them can be found within humanitarian interventions.[55]

The ICISS report identified the UN Security Council as the body with the authority to decide whether a state failed that responsibility, in which case the international community should take over that responsibility.[56] It is noteworthy that the ICISS version of R2P and the version found in the WSOD[57] differ to certain extents. The 2005 version of R2P focuses primarily on the responsibility of each state to protect its own population from genocide, war crimes, crimes against humanity and ethnic cleansing. Only second to this, comes the responsibility of the international community.[58] Furthermore there is no list of criteria for possible military intervention[59] and the Security Council is supposed to act on a case-by-case basis.[60] Thus the 2005 version of R2P prima facie does not change much with regards on how the international community does act or does not act when facing grave violations of human rights in innerstate conflict. The 2005 version therefore seems not suitable to prevent 'future Rwandas' or 'future Kosovos' and has been consequently labelled by some advocates of R2P as 'R2P-lite'.[61] In this context some scholars have explored possibilities of circumventing the Security Council via actions based on the Uniting for Peace Resolution from 1950, especially following the inaction by the Security Council on

Syria.[62] Another important point is that while the ICISS report speaks of citizens, and thus limits itself to a very specific group within a state, the WSOD speaks of *populations*.[63] As one interviewee remarked, this was a very important distinction, as this broadened the range of those protected immensely.[64]

R2P was included relative quickly within Security Council resolutions 1674[65] and 1706[66] in 2006. However, it took another three years before in 2009 UN Secretary General Ban Ki-moon suggested a three pillar version in order to operationalize R2P within the UN system.[67] This suggestion was widely accepted during the debates of the 64th UN General Assembly,[68] even though it has been suggested that the substance of the agreement is not very strong.[69] R2P remained however heavily contested. As Bellamy notes, '[t]o further complicate matters, profound disagreements persist about the function, meaning, and proper use of RtoP, and the principle has been inconsistently applied'.[70] Bellamy evaluates the application of R2P (or RtoP) since 2005 critically, showing that:

> ... the RtoP has become a key part of the language used to debate and frame responses to humanitarian emergencies. However, there is little consistency in the way that RtoP is used. The inconsistencies seem to involve around two axes – scale and scope.[71]

Following 2005, a number of situations developed in which R2P was referenced.[72] These references however were not always universally accepted. This was for example the case when France attempted to frame the inability and unwillingness of the regime in Burma/Myanmar to help its population after cyclone Nargis in 2008 as a case for R2P.[73] Russia also did not find much support in its claim that the military conflict with Georgia was in fact a R2P situation, aiming at protecting Russian minorities in Georgia.[74] That R2P also could act as a preventive and work to assert diplomatic pressure became clear when Kofi Annan successfully negotiated a peace agreement between rivalling political parties in Kenya, following post-election violence after the elections in December 2007.[75] More recently conflicts in Mali, Cote d'Ivor, and the Central African Republic have been assessed under the label of R2P and actions have been taken accordingly, ranging from diplomatic efforts, to sanction, to military support in the form of UN Missions.[76] The situation in Libya (see section 5) is the first one where R2P was used within a Chapter VII resolution authorizing the use of force against the will of the state in question.[77] Having delivered an overview of the history of humanitarian interventions and R2P, the following section offers a theoretical framework addressing the ongoing contestation of R2P.

3. A theoretical framework for understanding R2P's ongoing contestation

Despite the large amount of research on R2P,[78] a number of blind spots remain, especially regarding the ongoing contestation of R2P. In this section I present a critical constructivist account that is able to shed light onto these blind spots. The section begins with a brief overview of constructivism and the development of critical constructivism, before applying this critical constructivist framework to R2P.

Constructivism emerged within IR Theory in the 1980s as an approach claiming to be able to recognize change within global politics much better than realist or liberal approaches to IR were capable of.[79] Early on constructivists focused on norms as an important building block of international relations, making the claim that they mattered. They were understood as ' ... collective expectations for the proper behaviour of actors with a given identity'.[80] This led to questions of how norms emerged and the well-known norm-life-cycle suggested by Martha Finnemore and Kathrin Sikkink seemed to provide a comprehensive answer to this question.[81]

The model however has received some criticism over the years, including a lack of acknowledging the co-constitutiveness of structure and agency,[82] too little focus on the actual process of how norms come into being,[83] and the analytical weakness of the linearity that the model inherits.[84] Such a linear notion and an understanding of norms as ontologized can also be found in approaches dealing with diffusion[85] and localization.[86] Constructivist of the 1980s, 1990s, and early 2000s thus did bring important insights into IR theory, but fell short of fully applying a constructivist ontology to the issue of norms research.

It is here where *critical* constructivism[87] makes an important contribution. Contrary to the linear model suggested by Finnemore and Sikkink, critical constructivist scholars claimed that norms remained contested even after prima facie agreement via treaties. In this context Antje Wiener notes that norms, ' ... and their meanings evolve through inter-action in context. They are therefore contested by default'.[88] Moreover, Antje Wiener and Uwe Puetter note, ' ... norms are what actors make of them; and we would add that they are as "good" [read: just, fair and legitimate] as what actors make them out to be'.[89] But critical constructivist not only point to the inherit contestedness of norms. They furthermore claim that contestation is a requirement for norms to work.[90] Wiener notes here that, '[c]ritical constructivists consider norms as constituted through practice'.[91] The majority of research on R2P, while making reference to norms research,[92] remains within the linear approaches criticized above.[93] They also keep language and practice separate,[94] something constructivists of any kind would claim not to be accurate, as in their understanding words are deeds.[95] Words of course only matter in the context of language and speaking.[96] I therefore argue that a critical constructivist understanding of the role of language and discourse[97] is furthermore necessary to overcome blind spots in research on R2P. The analysis provided below in section 5 will show this in detail; moreover, this has been illustrated in more recent literature.[98]

A critical constructivist perspective can also shed light on the ongoing discussion about what R2P exactly is. The question what R2P is may be irritating to some, given that the heads of states and governments agreed upon it nearly 10 years ago at the 2005 World Summit. But as a careful reading of the R2P literature reveals, the issue is far from settled and descriptions range from legal and political norms,[99] to concepts, ideas, and policies.[100]

Understanding R2P as a contested norm runs contrary to the often found assumption that there is a 'fixed meaning' of R2P.[101] Contestation is an ongoing process, and the meaning of norms as well as concepts depends on their use, what matters is its 'meaning-in-use'.[102] A critical constructivist perspective is better equipped to shed light on the development and application as well as non-application of R2P. From such a per-spective R2P is understood as a contested 'complex norm'.[103] Scholars studying the ongoing contestation can analytically grasp these processes of contestation by reference to the critical constructivist literature on norms as discussed in this section.

In a nutshell, the argument advanced here is that the ongoing debate about R2P after the prima facie agreement of the 2005 World Summit becomes understandable, when seen through a critical constructivist lens as outlined above. Hence the fact that there is still debate and contestation is firstly not surprising, and secondly it has been suggested that such ongoing contestation may lead to a further legitimization.[104] Having delivered the theoretical framework of this article and having illustrated its usefulness with reference to current research on R2P, the following section outlines the methodological framework necessary to engage with the study of the discourse on Libya and Syria within the UN Security Council.

4. Methodology and method

This section offers a methodology and a specific method in order to conduct the analysis of the discourse in the following section. This article applies a reconstructive methodology and undertakes interpretative research. That is research that ' … aims at understanding events by discovering the meanings human beings attribute to their behaviour and the external world'.[105] Interpretative research is also more open towards the material studied, in other words, the data is supposed to 'speak for itself'.[106]

A reconstructive methodology confines itself neither to a deductive testing of hypothesis, nor to an inductive approach of beginning with collected experiences and utterances of research objects and subjects.[107] Reconstruction aims at the creation of theory.[108] Flick *et al.* show why such a re-constructive approach befits the theoretical critical constructivist frameworks applied here. They argue that '[t]o grasp social reality/ies theoretically, first a re-construction and analysis of data gathered … '.[109] In such a framework, theory and literature can be understood as fulfilling a heuristic function.[110] How the discourse is analysed in detail is a question of method, which will be outlined in the following part.

4.1 *Positioning analysis*

Based on the interpretivist methodology outlined above, the article applies the method of positioning analysis in order to analyse the discourse within the UN Security Council on Libya and Syria. Positioning oneself and others within a discourse is understood here as a specific form of interaction and thus part of the social construction of reality.[111] Harré and van Langenhoven point to three basic features of interactions ' … i. the moral position of the participants and the rights and duties they have to say certain things, ii. the conversational history and the sequence of things already being said, iii. the actual saying with their power to shape certain aspects of the social world'.[112] As Gabriele Lucius-Hoene and Arnulf Deppermann explain, '[p]ositioning can be described as one of the most basic forms to construct and negotiate identities in social interactions'.[113] It can take place both ' … *directly and explicitly* or *indirectly and implicitly* … '.[114] Positioning always includes self-positioning and the positioning other undertake.[115] Within interviews, this takes place when interviewees position themselves in their stories against other actors.[116]

Furthermore positioning is always relational.[117] This reciprocal characteristic of positioning can be seen in line of the relational nature of the critical constructivist approach this article applies.[118] Positioning analysis was originally introduced in a work by Wendy Hollway on 'Gender difference and the production of subjectivity' in 1984.[119] Positioning analysis then is a specific method aiming at studying positioning. Korobov gives the following definition of positioning analysis. In his words it:

> … analyzes the different linguistic forms used to position oneself within different topics, during different interactive situations, and for the management of certain ideological tensions in the overall establishment of 'who I am' or 'who I am becoming'.[120]

A number of language elements indicate positioning; this includes perspectives and voices, as well as personal pronouns (I, you, we, they, etc.).[121] As will be shown in the following section, focusing on these aspects generates insights into the positions of relevant actors of the studied discourse. Having delivered an overview of the state of the art (section 2), the theoretical framework (section 3), and the methodological framework and method (section 4), section 5 now turns to the empirical analysis. As will become clear in the following empirical analysis, the position analysis of the discourse within the UN Security Council on Libya and Syria allows understanding the approaches taken in the two situations, as well as understanding the difference between the two approaches.

5.   R2P in Libya and Syria

The article uses so called 'monuments'[122] as a departure point for studying the discourse.[123] It then engages in a positioning analysis as a means of re-constructing the discourse. A number of texts have been selected for this, with most of them being UN Security Council Resolutions and the meeting records for the session in which the respective Resolution was made. In addition the analysis relies on newspaper reports, and on interviews conducted in New York in March and April of 2014. The first part of this section focuses on Libya, the second on Syria.

The analyses offered below do not aim at delivering a full account on the situations in these countries. Rather, the aim is show how R2P worked in these situations. The two situations share some common factors, such as time: both conflicts began in 2011; context: both conflicts emerged as part of the so-called 'Arab Spring'; and region: both countries are in the West Asia and North Africa (WANA) region. At the same time, the actions undertaken by the international community in both cases could not be more different. As the following analysis will reveal, this becomes understandable by focusing on the position of the individual human beings within the discourse.

5.1   *Libya*

Following the development of R2P since the 2005 Outcome document it took another six years until R2P was applied for the first time in a Chapter VII resolution authorizing the use of force.[124,125] The speed in which the international community acted is understandable in part, because the language of Gaddafi was so 'reminiscent of Rwanda',[126] as one interview partner remarked; a point made within the literature as well.[127]

Another reason for the swift action by the UN Security Council clearly lies in the support for action from regional actors. Statements in support of actions aiming at the protection of individual human beings in Libya were issued by the Organization Of The Islamic Conferences,[128] the African Union,[129] and the Arab League.[130] As Thomas Weiss noted, 'Libya was unusual: the legal, moral, and political/military dimensions all merged to create the perfect conditions for intervention under the Responsibility to Protect.'[131]

The Arab League was the first of the three regional actors to make a statement. A communique issued on 8 March 2011 states: 'The participants at the meeting extended their condolences to the families of the martyrs of the peaceful demonstrations and their sympathies to the wounded and expressed their regrets over the heavy loss of lives of the Libyan people ... '.[132] Here the killed and wounded individual human beings were the focal point of action. The meeting also called for an end to target civilians.[133]

Two days later, the African Union met in Addis Ababa on 10 March for the 265th Meeting of the Peace and Security Council. The council adopted a decision on Libya, pointing to the need of protecting Libyans as well as 'migrant workers'. Furthermore, the council ' ... conveys its condolence to the families of the victims and wishes early recovery to those who have been injured'.[134] Note the clear focus on individual human beings as victims, clearly positioning them as innocent and worthy of protection. This is also reinforced by stating that the armed rebellion began because of the targeting of 'pacifist demonstrations'.[135]

Only a day later the Arab League met in Cairo, supporting a no-fly zone and the establishment of safe areas.[136] It is noteworthy that in their council statement the protection ' ...

of the Libyan people and foreign nationals residing in Libya … '[137] is explicitly mentioned. This positions the individual human beings in Libya as worthy of protecting, regardless of nationality or citizenship.

Within this context,[138] the Security Council met on 17 March 2011 and adopted resolution 1973.[139] The resolution refers to its predecessor on the situation in Libya, Resolution 1970,[140] and begins by expressing 'grave concern' about the 'heavy civilian casualties', thus placing the wellbeing of individual human beings in Libya at the centre. This is followed by a reference to the responsibility of the Libyan government to protect its own population. Acting under chapter VII, the resolution: ' … demands the immediate establishment of a cease-fire and a complete end to violence and all attacks against, and abuses of, civilians',[141] and it makes direct reference to the Libyan people. A number of excellent analyses are available on the topic on how exactly these negotiations took place and how it was possible for the council to move forward so quickly.[142]

What we do see in this resolution is that the individual human beings in Libya are positioned by the members of the UN Security Council as beings in need and worthy of protection. The same positioning becomes visible in statements of council members. While it is little surprising that this is the case for those who voted in favour of the resolution, it is noteworthy that even those who abstained[143] had no doubt that individual human beings within Libya were in need of protection. Hence, the Council displayed an intersubjectively shared positioning of the individual human beings inside Libya. Illustrative for this positioning is Brazil's statement: "*Her delegation's vote today should in no way be interpreted* as condoning the behaviour of the Libyan authorities or *as disregard for the need to protect civilians and respect for their rights*'.[144] A similar statement was made by the German representative, who also abstained.[145]

The call to 'take all necessary measures' under Chapter VII[146] was taken up by some NATO states, who began to enforce the no-fly zone via air-strikes against military objects of the Libyan forces under control by Gaddafi. The intervention, even though without any ground forces, quickly turned the tide in the fight of Libyan revolutionary forces against Gaddafi. Without wanting to go into the details of the military campaign, the results deserve mentioning. As Jutta Brunnée and Stephen Toope aptly summarize, 'NATO not only established no-fly zones, but also provided general support to rebel forces, attacked Libyan military assets and ultimately precipitated regime change in the country.'[147] The air-support by NATO also led to Gaddafi's death,[148] naturally facilitating the process of regime change.

The way NATO interpreted Resolution 1973 and operationalized it, led to major criticism by permanent Security Council members, like Russia, and China, as well as non-permanent members like Brazil, India, and Germany. Criticism was also raised by the BRICS.[149] This criticism would make things difficult in the future, as the events in Syria showed.[150] The question arose whether regime change was on the agenda of NATO right from the beginning and whether this had to be part of any R2P endeavour.[151]

The analysis of Libya showed that the positioning of the individual human being in Libya as peaceful and worthy of protection allowed for an intersubjective agreement on politics of protection via R2P and military actions under Chapter VII of the UN Charter.[152] However, there are also critical voices regarding the success of NATO's operation 'Unified Protector'[153] Matteo Capasso notes the killing of Ghaddafi loyalists, who were not seen as civilians.[154] This is outlined in a report of the Human Rights Council from 8 March 2012.[155]

While this observation prima facie seems to counter the argument just made, a closer look reveals that these developments are in line with the argument made. The individual human beings who were not positioned by NATO as worthy of protection did not receive protection under R2P. This is not to say they should not have been protected, but rather, that the positioning has a direct and real-life effect on those positioned.

5.2 Syria

'Syria is not Libya'[156] or 'Syria is bigger than R2P'[157] are statements made when attempting to compare the situations in Libya and Syria. Indeed a completely different image becomes visible when juxtaposing the Libya and Syria cases.[158] Following uprisings in 2011, we have witnessed ' … four years of killing and mayhem … '.[159] This section does not aim to offer an analysis of the current situation in Syria. The analysis provided here focuses on the discourse within the UN Security Council on possible actions to protect individual human beings within Syria between 2011 and early 2015. It relies mostly on primary documents, i.e. resolution, resolution drafts, and meeting records. In addition secondary analyses of Security Council meetings provided by *Security Council Report*, a non-for-profit organization, are drawn upon.[160] Furthermore, interviews are again used as a secondary source, as in the Libya case study.

After protests against the government began in Syria on 26 January 2011 and grew steadily across the country, the security forces of the government began to react with violence against the protesters. Calls to end the violence were raised by the Human Rights Council and the UN Secretary General.[161] On 25 May 2011, the UK, France, Germany, and Portugal tabled a draft resolution, but as it included language that was criticized by some Council members, it was not put to a vote.[162] The Security Council issued a presidential statement on 3 August 2011 on the situation in Syria. In the statement the Council ' … expresses profound regret at the death of many hundreds of people', supports political reforms and asks to ensure humanitarian access.[163] A draft resolution was tabled on 4 October 2011 by France, Germany, Portugal, and the United Kingdom.[164] In the draft the ' … Syrian Government's primary responsibility to protect its population … ' was recalled and the human rights violations condemned.[165] The draft was vetoed by Russia and China.[166] This veto caused strong worded criticism by a number of council members.[167] The French representative Mr Araud, in a statement after the vote, described the veto as showing ' … disdain for the legitimate aspirations that have been so bravely expressed in Syria for the past five months. It is a rejection of this tremendous movement for freedom and democracy that is the Arab Spring'.[168] The resolution draft and the statement of France as well as others in support of the resolution not only condemned the violence against individual human beings in Syria. The representative of Portugal, Moraes Cabral, called on the Syrian Government, stating that its:

> … violent repression against its population and the ongoing violations of human rights and fundamental freedoms must cease immediately. We regret the huge loss of life and strongly condemn the widespread human rights violations.[169]

In these statements, the individual human beings within Syria are being positioned as suffering from human rights violations and violence. They are being depicted as innocent and in need of protection. In the view of the Portuguese representative the draft resolution aimed at preventing 'further bloodshed'.[170] The British representative Sir Mark Lyall Grant worded the view of his government in even stronger terms: 'The regime continues to brutally repress its people. It has killed almost three thousand civilians. It has used disproportionate force and has arbitrarily detained many thousands of people. Its actions may amount to crimes against humanity.'[171]

This positioning by the supporters of the resolution is in stark contrast to the positioning undertaken by Russia. The Russian representative Mr Churkin in his statement made clear, that the issue in Syria was one of terrorism:

> Recent events convincingly show that the radical opposition no longer hides its extremist bent and is relying on terrorist tactics, hoping for foreign sponsors and acting outside of the law. Armed groups supported by smuggling and other illegal activities are providing supplies, taking over land, and killing and perpetrating atrocities against people who comply with the law-enforcement authorities.[172]

The Syrian representative, Mr Ja'afari, who was present at the Council Meeting, expressed this positioning even clearer, when he stated that there was an:

> ... international campaign to intervene in Syria under the pretext of human rights and the protection of civilians. Those countries [who are part of this campaign] continue to reject the existence of the armed terrorist groups in Syria, for reasons that are known to all.[173]

These two distinct positioning of suffering civilians vs terrorist who needed to be fought remains present in the discourse on Syria to this day. A second draft resolution was tabled on 4 February 2012, this time the list of countries who tabled the draft resolution was much longer and included a number of regional actors[174] The draft expressed ' ... grave concern at the deterioration of the situation in Syria, and profound concern at the death of thousands of people ... '.[175] Furthermore the draft condemned:

> ... the continued widespread and gross violations of human rights and fundamental freedoms by the Syrian authorities, such as the use of force against civilians, arbitrary executions, killing and persecution of protestors and members of the media, arbitrary detention, enforced disappearances, interference with access to medical treatment, torture, sexual violence, and ill-treatment, including against children ... [176]

The resolution also condemned violence from all armed groups and called for holding accountable those responsible for human rights violations and violence.[177] The resolution gained nine votes and 4 abstentions but was vetoed by Russia and China. This time the statements of Council members were even more strongly worded. As Mr Araud, the French representative declared, '[t]his is a sad day for the Council; it is a sad day for the Syrians; and it is sad day for all the friends of democracy'.[178] Directed towards the Russian and Chinese representatives he said, 'I know the arguments that will be made by those who today opposed the Council's action. I have already heard them say that only a few more days would have sufficed for us to reach an agreement. How can one speak of a few more days when hundreds of Syrians are dying every day?'[179] (UNSC 2012, 3–4). Susan Rice, representative of the US, was even clearer in her opinion on the veto, calling it 'disgusting'.[180] Sir Mark Lyall Grant (UK) made clear what the situation in Syria is about in his government's view: 'It has been 10 months since the Syrian people bravely demanded their universal rights, and 10 months since the Syrian regime responded by violently repressing and killing its own people.'[181] As this positioning makes clear, those who are being killed are innocent individual human beings simply demanding what is theirs. Here again, the Russian statement showed an opposed positioning, focusing on terrorism as the real issue in Syria. Mr Churkin, while calling for an end of violence, also stated that:

> [t]he sponsors of the draft resolution did not take into account our proposed amendments to the draft resolution to the effect that the Syrian opposition must distance itself from extremist groups that are committing acts of violence, and calling on States and all those with any relevant opportunity to use their influence to stop those groups committing acts of violence.[182]

A chemical attack with sarin gas on 21 May 2013 in the Ghouta suburbs near Damascus led to the death of a large number of civilians with estimates between 281 and 1729 fatalities depending on the source of the information. While the Assad regime and the opposition blamed each other for the attack, it also raised the potential for military intervention again.[183] Following the attacks and the demands of the destruction of chemical weapons in Syria, Syria joined the Convention on Chemical Weapons in September of 2013.[184] Following negotiations,[185] the Security Council passed resolution 2118 demanding the destruction of all chemical weapons in Syria.[186]

The conflict between the two positions re-constructed above, is furthermore illustrated by the situation in Homs, a town that for a long time has been a central point or resistance against Assad. Following a deal made as part of Geneva talks on Syria, 1100 civilians were able to leave the city as part of a deal made at those talks.[187] When the 1100 civilians could leave the town, 300 boys and men were taken away for questioning by Syrian authorities with the UN Human Rights Commissioner expressing concern over this.[188] This can be understood as positioning these boys and men as possible combatants or 'terrorists', in which case they do not enjoy the kind of protection civilians enjoy under International Humanitarian Law (IHL). As Charli Carpenter has pointed out with reference to the notion of 'protection of civilians', this is often framed in a way ' ... that "women and children" (but not adult men) are "innocent" and "vulnerable".'[189] This then excludes female combatants and child soldiers as much as non-combatant males.[190]

This dichotomy between 'terrorists' and 'civilians' is also visible in a contribution on the International Red Cross blog by David Miliband when he writes,

'[t]he regime of Bashar al-Assad *talks about terrorism, while killing innocent civilians*'.[191] Furthermore a number of interview partners emphasized this distinction and its importance for understanding the situation in Syria[192] and as one interviewee remarked, in Syria a 'narrative of a war on terror ... superseded R2P ... '.[193]

Following three years of inaction by the Security Council (apart from the resolution on chemical weapons), the end of February 2014 saw the unanimous passing of UN Resolution 2139.[194] One of the reasons for the long inaction of the Council on Syria lies in the aftermath of resolution 1973 and NATO action against Gaddafi.[195] Despite the agreement, Russia's statement for example does not really move away from the 'anti-terrorist' position that had become visible in the debate about failed draft resolutions discussed above. As the Russian representative made clear in his statement explaining his vote:

> ... there was strong provision in the text calling on all parties to break with terrorists. It underscored the need for opposition groups to take on responsibilities, support the fight against terrorism, and pool efforts with the Government to solve that problem.[196]

The anti-terrorism position also becomes visible in the statement of Syria. Bashar Ja'Afari, speaking for the Syrian government made clear: 'Others, he said, had objected eight times to having the Council denounce terrorist acts that had taken the lives of innocent civilians. ... Terrorists, including those associated with Al-Qaida, were [the] main reason for Syrians' suffering'.[197] Contrary to this position, one can turn to the statement by the UK:

> It had been nearly three years since the Syrian people had stood up to demand their rights. Since then, Bashar Al-Assad had perpetuated one of the worst humanitarian situations the world had ever seen, including widespread violations of human rights.[198]

In the following month it became clear that nothing going further than calling for humanitarian aid would make it out of the Security Council, including a proposed referral of the situation in Syria to the ICC. A draft resolution referring the Syrian situation to the ICC, tabled on 22 May 2014 and co-sponsored by 65 countries[199] was vetoed by Russia and China.[200]

In the meantime reports on the implementation on resolution 2139 showed a clear lack of cooperation and difficulties actually delivering the humanitarian aid.[201] As a result of these difficulties, the Security Council passed resolution 2165,[202] authorizing the crossing of conflict lines for aid delivery and the need to only notify the Syrian authorities about these crossings.[203] Despite this resolution being solemnly about the delivery of humanitarian aid, Council members taking the floor after the unanimous vote, positioned the individual human beings in Syria either as innocent individual human beings in need of aid and protection or as terrorist.[204] More recent resolutions on Syria have dealt with the growing problem of terrorist attacks by so-called Islamic State.[205]

Advocates of R2P like Thomas Weiss have argued that ' ... Syria demonstrates that robust R2P rhetoric is automatic, even if actual responses are not'.[206] The prevailing analysis however revealed that the different positioning of those individual human beings in Syria as innocent civilians or as terrorists leads to situation in which a common ground for actions is difficult to find. In addition to the ongoing clashes of positioning over the last four years, current events and developments, especially the rise of so-called Islamic State have led to a situation where the 'fight against terrorism' seems to have overwritten anything else. As Jan Wilkens aptly writes, we have seen a development from the 'Arab Spring' to a 'civil war' to a 'war against terror' in Syria.[207] The final section of this article draws together the theoretical framework of section 3 with the empirical insights from section 5.

6. Conclusion

The article began with the observation of ongoing contestation of the R2P despite a formal agreement at the 2005 World Summit. Providing, in section 2, a history of humanitarian interventions, the development of R2P up to the 2005 World Summit, and R2Ps track record since then, the contestation of R2P came to the fore.

Offering a critical constructivist framework in section 3, the paper showed that such a framework is capable of providing a better understanding of R2P as a contested 'complex norm'. Furthermore, section 3 showed that such a framework was also able to shed light on a number of blind spots in current R2P research. A critical constructivist and post-positivist reading of R2P, as recently suggested in the literature as an avenue forward[208] allows solving the puzzle of ongoing contestation of R2P since 2005. Taking into account insights from critical constructivist norms research, these instances of contestation can be understood as part and parcel of how norms work in international relations. Norms remain inherently contested, but this does not mean the norm is weak or still 'emerging'.[209]

Section 4 offered an interpretivist and reconstructivist methodology and positioning analysis as a specific method to re-construct discourse. This methodology and method was then applied in Section 5, providing an analysis of two specific discourses within the UN Security Council on Libya and Syria. This analysis showed the usefulness of the critical constructivist framework for analysing the discourse on R2P. The analysis also applied positioning analysis to the two discourses, showing that the positioning of individual human beings as either worthy of protection or not worthy of protection within the discourse allows to understand the very different handling of the situations in Libya and Syria by the UN Security Council.

R2P came into being 15 years ago with the aim and aspiration to overcome tensions between human rights protection and state sovereignty, to overcome the divide within the UN Kosovo had caused, and to prevent further mass atrocities. The track record of

R2P, as this article has shown, is mixed. But not all hope is lost. As Thomas G. Weiss claimed, R2P has not been killed, even not through the gruesome and ongoing human rights violations in Syria.[210] R2P opens discursive spaces, in which a politics of protection becomes possible, even though not always enacted. Discursive spaces are understood as spaces in which a discourse becomes possible. This is in line with the understanding of discourse as ' ... the space where human beings make sense of the material world, where they attach meaning to the worlds and where representations of the world become manifest'.[211]

With regards to assessing R2Ps ability to prevent 'future Rwandas' and 'future Kosovos' the article suggests that R2P can be seen as the beginning of a debate about preventing and stopping mass atrocities and not as a the final result or solution. R2P thus opens discursive spaces in which the protection of human beings from mass atrocities can be discussed and feasible measures negotiated. This opening of discursive spaces can be as a particular normative advantage, R2P as a subject of ongoing contestation has produced. Individual human beings in the discourse on protection are no longer 'bodies' that need to be rescued[212], but beings with certain rights, carriers of 'individual sovereignty' as Kofi Annan worded it 15 years ago.[213] Within the discursive spaces opened by R2P, a politics of protection becomes possible. In this politics of protection, the focus shifts away from states, to the individual human being in need.[214]

Acknowledgements

I am grateful to my colleague Jan Wilkens for providing valuable feedback on an earlier version of this article. The article has also greatly profited from discussions at the ISA 2015 Workshop 'The Responsibility to Protect at Ten', organized by Phil Orchard and Jason Ralph. James Pattison, Jason Ralph, and Adrian Gallagher have also provided feedback on an earlier version of this article, for which I am grateful. I am also thankful for the discussions and comments from all participants at the ISA workshop. The responsibility for the article remains of course with me. The research on which this article is based is part of an ongoing PhD project at the University of Hamburg, entitled 'The individual human being in international relations: prosecution, protection, and killing.'

Notes

1. Alex J. Bellamy, 'Whither the Responsibility to Protect? Humanitarian Intervention and the 2005 World Summit', *Ethics & International Affairs* 20, no. 2 (2006): 143–169; Ekkehard Strauss, *The Emperor's New Clothes? The United Nations and the Implementation of the Responsibility to Protect* (Baden-Baden: Nomos Verlagsgesellschaft, 2009).
2. United Nations, 'Outcome Document of the 2005 World Summit' no. A/RES/60/1 (2005). http://daccess-dds-ny.un.org/doc/UNDOC/GEN/N05/487/60/PDF/N0548760.pdf (accessed August 19, 2010)
3. Ibid., §139.
4. Jennifer M. Welsh, 'Norm Contestation and the Responsibility to Protect', *Global Responsibility to Protect* 5, no. 4 (2013): 365–396, 384.
5. Bellamy, 'Whither the Responsibility to Protect', 143.
6. David Chandler, 'The R2P Is Dead, Long Live the R2P', *International Peacekeeping* 22, no. 1 (2015): 1–5.
7. Antje Wiener, *The Invisible Constitution of Politics. Contested Norms and International Encounters* (Cambridge: Cambridge University Press, 2008), 202; Antje Wiener and Uwe

Puetter, 'The Quality of Norms is What Actors Make of It: Constructivist Research on Norms', *Journal of International Law and International Relations* 5 no. 1 (2009), 6.

8. As part of this discourse I conducted interviews in March and April of 2014 in New York, with a range of actors from NGOs, diplomatic missions, and from within the UN. In accordance with agreements with those interviewed, all interviewees remain anonymous. The interviews are labelled as A1 through to A9. The audio recording and the transcripts of all interviews are on file with me. If a reference is made to a specific part of the interview, I use the line numbers within the transcript.

9. I follow the unwritten convention that 'international relations' refers to the field of studies, while International Relations or IR refers to the discipline within political science concerned with international relations.

10. UNSC, 'Resolution 688' (1991), United Nations. http://daccess-dds-ny.un.org/doc/RESOLUTION/GEN/NR0/596/24/IMG/NR059624.pdf (accessed 2 October 2014)

11. Nicholas J. Wheeler, *Saving Strangers – Humanitarian Intervention in International Society* (Oxford and New York: Oxford University Press, 2002), 139–171.

12. UNSC, 'Resolution 794' (1992), United Nations. http://daccess-dds-ny.un.org/doc/UNDOC/GEN/N92/772/11/PDF/N9277211.pdf (accessed October 2, 2014)

13. Christian Tomuschat, *Die Rechtmäßigkeit der Resolution 1973 (2011) des UN-Sicherheitsrates in Libyen: Missbrauch der Responsibility to Protect?*, ed. Gerhard Beestermöller (Baden-Baden: Nomos Verlagsgesellschaft, 2014), 17, my translation.

14. UNSC, 'Resolution 794' (1992)., United Nations. http://daccess-dds-ny.un.org/doc/UNDOC/GEN/N92/772/11/PDF/N9277211.pdf (accessed 2 October 2014).

15. Wheeler, *Saving Strangers*, 185.

16. Alex J. Bellamy *Global Politics and The Responsibility to Protect* (Oxford and New York: Routledge, 2011), 5; Karen E. Smith, *Genocide and the Europeans* (New York: Cambridge University Press, 2010), 140, 147; Wheeler, *Saving Strangers*, 188–200.

17. Brian Orend "Post-intervention", in *The Ethics of Armed Humanitarian Intervention*, ed. Don E. Scheid (Cambridge: Cambridge University Press, 2014), 224–242; Smith, *Genocide and the Europeans*, 179.

18. Wheeler, *Saving Strangers*, 202–219.

19. UNSC, 'Resolution 819' (1993), United Nations. http://daccess-dds-ny.un.org/doc/UNDOC/GEN/N93/221/90/IMG/N9322190.pdf. April 16, 1993 (accessed October 2, 2014)

20. UNSC, 'Resolution 925' (1994)., United Nations. http://daccess-dds-ny.un.org/doc/UNDOC/GEN/N94/244/54/PDF/N9424454.pdf. June 8, 1994 (accessed October 2, 2014)

21. Wheeler, *Saving Strangers*, 227–335; Smith, *Genocide and the Europeans*, 173–176.

22. Smith, *Genocide and the Europeans*, 154–167.

23. *Convention on the Prevention and Punishment of the Crime of Genocide* in *United Nations Treaty Series*, ed. United Nations.

24. *Case Concerning Application of the Convention on the Prevention and Punishment of the Crime of Genocide;* Anthony F. Lang Jr., 'Punishing Genocide: A Critical Reading of the International Court of Justice', in *Accountability for Collective Wrongdoing*, ed. Richard Vernon and Tracey Issacs (Cambridge: Cambridge University Press, 2011), 92–118.

25. Smith, *Genocide and the Europeans*, 105–141.

26. UNSC, 'Resolution 819' (1993), United Nations. http://daccess-dds-ny.un.org/doc/UNDOC/GEN/N93/221/90/IMG/N9322190.pdf. April 16, 1993 (accessed October 2, 2014)

27. Smith, *Genocide and the Europeans*, 123–129; Wheeler, *Saving Strangers*, 253–255.

28. Lothar Brock, 'Normative Integration und kollektive Handlungskompetenz auf internationaler Ebene', *Zeitschrift für Internationale Beziehungen* 6 no. 2 (1999): 323–347, 323, my translation.

29. NATO, 'NATO's role in relation to the conflict in Kosovo' (2015). http://www.nato.int/kosovo/history.htm. July 15, 1999 (accessed April 24, 2015).

30. It is contested, whether the acts of violence in Kosovo did amount to genocide (Smith, *Genocide and the Europeans*, 188–202; Anthony F. Lang Jr. 'Conflicting Rules: Global Constitutionalism and the Kosovo Intervention', *Journal of Intervention and State Building* 3, no.2 (2009): 185–204, 196.

31. Karen E. Smith, *Genocide and the Europeans*, 183–184.

32. Ibid., 184–186.

33. UNSC, 'Resolution 1199' (1998), United Nations. http://daccess-dds-ny.un.org/doc/UNDOC/GEN/N98/279/96/PDF/N9827996.pdf. 23.09.19984 (accessed 2 October 2014).

34. Christine Gray, *International Law and the Use of Force* (Oxford: Oxford University Press, 2008), 40.
35. Nicholas J. Wheeler, 'The Humanitarian Responsibility of Sovereignty: Explaining the Development of a New Norm of Military Intervention for Humanitarian Purposes in International Society', in *Humanitarian Intervention and International Relations*, ed. Jennifer M. Welsh (Oxford and New York: Oxford University Press, 2006) 29–52, 44.
36. T. J. Farer, *Humanitarian Intervention Before and After 9/11: Legality and Legitimacy* in *Humanitarian Intervention: Ethic, Legal and Political Dilemmas*, ed. J. L. Holzgrefe and Robert O. Keohane (Cambridge: Cambridge University Press, 2003), 53–89, 70; M. Byers and Simon Chesterman, 'Changing the Rules About the Rules? Unilateral Humanitarian Intervention and the Future of International Law', in ibid. 177–203, 184; Gray, *International Law and the Use of Force*, 35.
37. Farer, *Humanitarian Intervention Before and After 9/11*, 68.
38. Wheeler, 'The Humanitarian Responsibility of Sovereignty', 36.
39. Brock, 'Normative Integration und kollektive Handlungskompetenz', 323, emphasis in original, translation by author.
40. Andreas von Arnauld, 'Souveränität und responsibility to protect', *Die Friedenswarte: Journal of International Peace and Organization* 84 no. 1 (2009), 16.
41. Martha Finnemore, 'Constructing Norms of Humanitarian Intervention', in *The Culture of National Security. Norms and Identity in World Politics*, ed. Peter J. Katzenstein (New York: Columbia University Press, 1996): 153–185, 184; Wheeler, 'The Humanitarian Responsibility of Sovereignty', 48; Maja Zehfuß, 'Constructivism and Identity: A Dangerous Liaison', *European Journal of International Relations* 7 no. 3 (2001), 331.
42. This tension has been discussed in detail in the literature, Brock, 'Normative Integration und kollektive Handlungskompetenz'; Lothar Brock, 'Dilemmata des internationalen Schutzes von Menschen vor innerstaatlicher Gewalt. Ein Ausblick'; von Arnauld, 'Souveränität und responsibility to protect'; and Sassan Gholiagha 'Die Responsibility to Protect und Souveränität' in *Der Begriff der Souveränität in der transnationalen Konstellation*, ed. Christian Volk and Friederike Kuntz (Baden-Baden: Nomos Verlagsgesellschaft, 2014): 198–214.
43. Kofi Annan, 'Two Concepts of Sovereignty', *The Economist.*, September 18, 1999.
44. Ibid., 81.
45. Bellamy, 'Whither the Responsibility to Protect?', 143.
46. For a detailed analysis of the term 'individual sovereignty' and its analytical use today see Gholiagha 'Die Responsibility to Protect'.
47. F. M. Deng et al. *Sovereignty as Responsibility: Conflict Management in Africa* (Washington, DC: Brookings, 1996).
48. Alex J. Bellamy, *Responsibility to Protect – The Global Effort to End Mass Atrocities* (Cambridge: Polity Press, 2009), 14; Euan MacDonald and Philip Alston, 'Sovereignty, Human Rights, Security: Armed Intervention and the Foundational Problem of International Law', in *Human Rights, Intervention, and the Use of Force*, ed. Euan MacDonald and Philip Alston (Oxford: Oxford University Press, 2008): 1–31, 2; Anne Peters, 'Humanity as the A and of Sovereignty', *European Journal of International Law* 20, no. 3 (2009): 513–544.
49. Jutta Brunnée and Stephen J. Toope, 'The Responsibility to Protect and the Use of Force: Building Legality?', *Global Responsibility to Protect* 2, no. 3 (2010): 191–212, 194; ICISS, *The Responsibility to Protect* (Ottawa: International Development Research Centre, 2001); von Arnauld, 'Souveränität und responsibility to protect', 17.
50. ICISS, *The Responsibility to Protect* (Ottawa: International Development Research Centre, 2001).
51. Ibid., VII.
52. Ibid.
53. von Arnauld, 'Souveränität und responsibility to protect', 33.
54. Wheeler, *Saving Strangers*, 1
55. Ibid.
56. ICISS *The Responsibility to Protect* (Ottawa: International Development Research Centre, 2001), 13–14, 47–50.
57. United Nations, 'Outcome Document of the 2005 World Summit' no. A/RES/60/1 (2005). http://daccess-dds-ny.un.org/doc/UNDOC/GEN/N05/487/60/PDF/N0548760.pdf (accessed August 19, 2010)
58. Ibid., §138–§139.

59. Brunnée and Toope, 'The Responsibility to Protect and the Use of Force', 197; Nigel Rodley, 'Humanitarian Intervention' in *The Oxford Handbook of The Use of Force in International Law*, ed. Marc Weller (Oxford: Oxford University Press, 2015), 788–792.
60. United Nations, 'Outcome Document of the 2005 World Summit' no. A/RES/60/1 (2005). http://daccess-dds-ny.un.org/doc/UNDOC/GEN/N05/487/60/PDF/N0548760.pdf (accessed August 19, 2010).
61. Alex J. Bellamy, 'The Responsibility to Protect and the problem of military intervention', *International Affairs* 84, no. 4 (2008): 615–639, 616; Thomas G.Weiss, 'Military Humanitarianism: Syria Hasn't Killed It', The Washington Quarterly 37, no. 1 (2014): 7–20, 15.
62. Louise Arbour, 'Entmachtet die Großmächte', *Die ZEIT*; Adrian Gallagher and Jason Ralph, 'Syria: Can Legitimacy for Intervention be Found in a Uniting for Peace Resolution?' (2013), BSS Leeds. http://www.bss.leeds.ac.uk/2013/09/05/syria-can-legitimacy-for-intervention-be-found-in-a-uniting-for-peace-resolution/ (accessed March 15, 2014); Sassan Gholiagha, 'From Kosovo to Syria – Why R2P is of no use if the UN Security Council is unable to act together' (2013), Verfassungsblog. http://www.verfassungsblog.de/en/r2p-responsibility-to-protect-syrien-sicherheitsrat-voelkerrecht/ (accessed March 15, 2014); von Arnauld, 'Souveränität und responsibility to protect', 35.
63. United Nations, 'Outcome Document of the 2005 World Summit' no. A/RES/60/1 (2005). http://daccess-dds-ny.un.org/doc/UNDOC/GEN/N05/487/60/PDF/N0548760.pdf (accessed August 19, 2010).
64. Interview A2: 319-323.
65. UNSC, 'Resolution 1674' no. S/RES/1674 (2006). http://daccess-ods.un.org/access.nsf/Get?Open&DS=S/RES/1674%20(2006)&Lang=E&Area=UNDOC. April 28, 2006 (accessed April 30, 2006).
66. UNSC, 'Resolution 1706' no. S/RES/1706 (2006). http://daccess-ods.un.org/access.nsf/Get?Open&DS=S/RES/1706%20(2006)&Lang=E&Area=UNDOC. 31st of August 2006 (accessed 30th August 2010).
67. Ban Ki-Moon, *Implementing the Responsibility to Protect.*
68. ICRtoP, 'General Assembly Debate on the Responsibility to Protect and Informal Interactive Dialogue' (2009), International Coalition for the Responsibility to Protect. http://www.responsibilitytoprotect.org/index.php/component/content/article/35-r2pcs-topics/2493-general-assembly-debate-on-the-responsibility-to-protect-and-informal-interactive-dialogue- (accessed 30th August 2010).
69. Aidan Hehir, 'The Responsibility to Protect in International Political Discourse: Encouraging Statement of Intent or Illusory Platitudes?', *The International Journal of Human Rights* 15 no. 8 (2011):1331–1348.
70. Alex J. Bellamy, 'The Responsibility to Protect—Five Years On', *Ethics & International Affairs* 24 no. 2 (2010):143–169, 144.
71. Bellamy, *Global Politics and The Responsibility to Protect*, 68.
72. A full overview of all UN Security Council Resolutions which make references to R2P in a direct or indirect manner are available here: http://s156658.gridserver.com/media/files/unsc-resolutions-and-statements-with-r2p-table-as-of-march-2015-1.pdf (accessed 24 April 2015).
73. Marco Bünte, 'Myanmar und die Frage der externen Intervention: Von der "Responsibility to Protect" zum humanitären Dialog', *Die Friedenswarte: Journal of International Peace and Organization* 84, no. 1 (2009): 125–141; Jürgen Haacke, 'Myanmar, the Responsibility to Protect, and the Need for Practical Assistance', *Global Responsibility to Protect* 1, no. 2 (2009): 156–184; Andrew Selth, 'Even Paranoids Have Enemies: Cyclone Nargis and Myanmar's Fears of Invasion', *Contemporary Southeast Asia: A Journal of International and Strategic Affairs* 30, no. 3 (2008): 379–402.
74. Luke Glanville, 'Armed Humanitarian Intervention and the Problem of Abuse After Libya', in *The Ethics of Armed Humanitarian Intervention*, ed. Don E. Scheid (Cambridge: Cambridge University Press, 2014): 148–165, 156–157; Jerzey Kranz, 'Der Kampf um den Frieden und sein besonderer Facilitator – Anmerkungen zur Georgienkrise', *Archiv des Völkerrechts* 46, no. 4 (2008): 481–501; Otto Luchterhandt, 'Völkerrechtliche Aspekte des Georgien-Krieges', *Archiv des Völkerrechts* 46, no. 4 (2008): 435–480.
75. Elisabeth Lindenmayer and Josie L. Kaye, *A Choice for Peace? The Story of Forty-one Days of Mediation in Kenya* (New York: International Peace Institute, 2009); Monica K. Juma, 'African Mediation of the Kenyan Post-2007 Election Crisis', *Journal of Contemporary*

African Studies 27, no. 3 (2009): 407–430; Kirsten Ainley, 'The Responsibility to Protect and the International Criminal Court: Counteracting the Crisis', *International Affairs* 91 no. 1 (2015): 37–54, 52; African Union Assembly, 'Decision on the Situation in Kenya Following the Presidential Election of 27 December 2007' no. Assembly/AU/Dec.187(X) (2008), African Union. http://www.au.int/en/sites/default/files/ASSEMBLY_EN_31_JANUARY_2_ FEBRUARY_2008_AUC_TENTH_ORDINARY_SESSION_DECISIONS_AND_ DECLARATIONS.pdf. November 5, 2010 (accessed 11 April 2015).

76. UNSC, 'Resolution 2100' (2013), United Nations. http://www.un.org/en/peacekeeping/ missions/minusma/documents/mali%20_2100_E_.pdf 25 March 2013 (accessed 24 April 2014); UNSC, 'Resolution 2121' (2013), United Nations. http://www.un.org/en/ga/search/ view_doc.asp?symbol=S/RES/2121%282013%29. February 10, 2013 (accessed 24 April 2015); Ainley, 'The Responsibility to Protect and the International Criminal Court', 51.

77. UNSC, 'Resolution 1973' (2011), United Nations. http://daccess-dds-ny.un.org/doc/UNDOC/ GEN/N11/268/39/PDF/N1126839.pdf. March 17, 2011 (accessed 4 September 2014).

78. A review of the current state of R2P literature and research is provided by Sassan Gholiagha, 'The Responsibility to Protect: Words, Deeds, and Humanitarian Interventions', *International Political Theory* 10, no. 3 (2014): 361–370.

79. Stefano Guzzini, 'A Reconstruction of Constructivism in International Relations', *European Journal of International Relations* 6, no. 2 (2000): 147–182, 155; ibid.

80. Peter J. Katzenstein, 'Introduction: Alternative Perspectives on National Security' in *The Culture of National Security. Norms and Identity in World Politics*, ed. Peter J. Katzenstein (New York: Columbia University Press, 1996): 1–32, 5.

81. Martha Finnemore and Kathryn Sikkink, 'International Norm Dynamics and Political Change', *International Organization* 52, no. 4 (1998) 887–917.

82. Antje Wiener, 'Die Wende zum Dialog – Konstruktivistische Brueckenstationen und ihre Zukunft' in *Forschungsstand und Perspektiven der Internationalen Beziehungen in Deutschland*, ed. Gunther Hellmann, Klaus D. Wolf and Michael Zuern (Baden-Baden: Nomos Verlagsgesellschaft, 2003), 135.

83. Gregory Flynn and Henry Farrell, 'Piecing Together the Democratic Peace: The CSCE, Norms and the "Construction" of Security in Post-Cold War Europe', *International Organization* 53, no. 3 (1999): 505–535, 510–511.

84. Cornelia Ulbert, 'Vom Klang vieler Stimmen: Herausforderungen »kritischer« Normenforschung', *Zeitschrift für Internationale Beziehungen* 19, no. 2 (2012): 132, my translation

85. Thomas Risse, Stephen C. Ropp and Kathryn Sikkink, *The Power of Human Rights. International Norms and Domestic Change* (Cambridge: Cambridge University Press, 1999).

86. Amitav Acharya, 'How Ideas Spread: Whose Norms Matter? Norm Localization and Institutional Change in Asian Regionalism', *International Organization* 58, no. 2 (2004): 239–275; Amitav Acharya, 'Norm Subsidiarity and Regional Orders: Sovereignty, Regionalism, and Rule-Making in the Third World', *International Studies Quarterly* 55, no. 1 (2011): 95–123.

87. Karin Fierke has suggested to differentiate between 'inconsistent' and 'consistent' constructivism, arguing ' … that within international relations "constructivism" has come to be associated with an approach that identifies a causal relationship between ideas and material relations. in This position is criticized by poststructuralists because it is overly agentic, in so far as ideas are understood to be instrumentally employed by individual actors, with insufficient attention to how these actors are constrained by a social and historical context of interaction'. Karin M. Fierke *Critical Methodology and Constructivism* in *Constructing International Relations*, in ed. Karin M. Fierke and Knud E. Jorgensen (Armonk, New York and London: M.E. Sharpe, 2001), : 115–135, 121. In her view a 'consistent constructivism' would be able to overcome these weaknesses by placing itself between 'inconsistent constructivism' and post-structural approaches. ibid., 121–122.

88. Antje Wiener, *The Invisible Constitution of Politics. Contested Norms and International Encounters* (Cambridge: Cambridge University Press, 2008), 63.

89. Antje Wiener and Uwe Puetter, 'The Quality of Norms', 4.

90. Antje Wiener, *A Theory of Contestation* (Heidelberg and New York: Springer, 2014), 3.

91. Ibid., 21.

92. Cristina G. Badescu and Thomas G. Weiss, 'Misrepresenting R2P and Advancing Norms: An Alternative Spiral?', *International Studies Perspective* 11 no. 4 (2010); Nicole Deitelhoff, 'Scheitert die Norm der Schutzverantwortung?'; Grant Marlier and Neta C. Crawford,

'Incomplete and Imperfect Institutionalisation of Empathy and Altruism in the 'Responsibility to Protect' Doctrine', *Global Responsibility to Protect* 5 no. 4 (2013): 397–442, 408; Bellamy *Global Politics and The Responsibility to Protect*, 8.

93. Finnemore and Sikkink, 'International Norm Dynamics and Political Change'; Risse, Ropp and Sikkink, *The Power of Human Rights.*

94. Bellamy *Global Politics and the Responsibility to Protect*; Anne Orford, *International Authority and the Responsibility to Protect* (Cambridge: Cambridge University Press, 2011), 2–3, 10.

95. Nicholas G. Onuf, *World of our Making* (Columbia, SC: University of South Carolina Press, 1989), 59.

96. Anne Orford, *International Authority and the Responsibility to Project*, 138.

97. Jennifer Milliken, 'The Study of Discourse in International Relations', *European Journal of International Relations* 5, no. 2 (1999): 225–254; Jennifer Milliken 'Discourse Study: Bringing Rigor to Critical Theory', in *Constructing International Relations*, ed. Karin M. Fierke and Knud E. Jorgensen (Armonk, New York and London: M.E. Sharpe, 2001), 136–159; Anna Holzscheiter, 'Between Communicative Interaction and Structures of Signification: Discourse Theory and Analysis in International Relations', *International Studies Perspective* 15, no. 2 (2014): 142–162.

98. Nicole Deitelhoff and Lisbeth Zimmermann, 'Things We Lost in the Fire: How Different Types of Contestation Affect the Validity of International Norms' HSFK Working Papers no. 18 (2013); HSFK. http://www.hsfk.de/fileadmin/downloads/PRIF_WP_18.pdf (accessed 15 March 2014); Sassan Gholiagha and Antje Wiener, 'Responsibility to Protect' (2013). http://www.verfassungsblog.de/en/schutzverantwortung-ein-politikwissenschaftlicher-blick-auf-den-voelkerrechtsteil-des-koalitionsvertrags/. 9 December 2013 (accessed 20 February 2014); Welsh, 'Norm Contestation and the Responsibility to Protect'.

99. This often made distinction is from a critical constructivist viewpoint somewhat irrelevant as all norms are inherently contested, a legal ratification does not change this fact.

100. Anne Orford, *International Authority and the Responsibility to Protect* (Cambridge: Cambridge University Press, 2011), 106; Aidan Hehir *The Responsibility to Protect* (Houndsmill: Palgrave Macmillan, 2012), 29; Bellamy *Global Politics and The Responsibility to Protect*, 84–86.

101. Bellamy, *Global Politics and The Responsibility to Protect*, 162, emphasis in original.

102. Antje Wiener, 'Enacting Meaning-in-Use. Qualitative Research on Norms and International Relations', *Review of International Studies* 35, no. 1 (2009): 175–193, 180.

103. Welsh, 'Norm Contestation and the Responsibility to Protect'.

104. For a discussion of this with regards to R2P see: Gholiagha and Wiener, 'Responsibility to Protect'.

105. Donatella Della Porta and Michael Keating, 'How Many Approaches in the Social Sciences? An Epistemological Introduction' in *Approaches and Methodologies in the Social Sciences*, ed. Donatella Della Porta and Michael Keating (Cambridge: Cambridge University Press, 2008): 19–39, 26.

106. Joachim K. Blatter, Frank Janning and Claudius Wagemann, *Qualitative Politikfeldanalyse* (Wiesbaden: VS Verlag für Sozialwissenschaften, 2007), 4.

107. See Joan W. Scott, 'The Evidence of Experience', *Critical Inquiry* 17, no. 4 (1991): 773–797, 777 for a critical discussion of the term experience

108. Ulrich Franke and Ulrich Roos, 'Einleitung: Zu den Begriffen ‚Weltpolitik' und ‚Rekonstruktion' in *Rekonstruktive Methoden der Weltpolitikforschung*, ed. Ulrich Franke and Ulrich Roos (Baden-Baden: Nomos Verlagsgesellschaft, 2013): 7–29, 13.

109. Uwe Flick, Ernst von Kardorff, and Ines Steinke, Theorien Qualitativer Forschung' in *Qualitative Forschung*, ed. Uwe Flick, Ernst von Kardorff and Ines Steinke (Reinbek bei Hamburg: Rowohlt Taschenbuch Verlag GmbH, 2003): 106–109, 106, my translation.

110. Jan Kruse, *Einführung in die qualitative Interviewforschung* (unpublished manuscript, on file with author 2010), 305.

111. Peter Berger and Thomas Luckmann, *The Social Construction of Reality* (London: Penguin Books, 1991 [1966]).

112. Rom Harré and Luk van Langenhove, 'The Dynamics of Social Episodes', in *Positioning Theory: Moral Contexts of Intentional Action*, ed. R. Harré and L. van Langenhove (Malden, MA: Blackwell Publishing, 1999), 1–13, 6.

113. Gabriele Lucius-Hoene and Arnulf Deppermann, *Rekonstruktion narrativer Identität* (Wiesbaden: VS Verlag für Sozialwissenschaften, 2014), 196, my translation.

114. Ibid., 199, emphasis in original, my translation.

115. Jan Kruse, *Qualitative Interviewforschung* (Weinheim: Beltz Juventa, 2014), 511; Lucius-Hoene and Deppermann, *Rekonstruktion narrativer Identität*, 196.

116. Kruse, *Qualitative Interviewforschung*, 511.

117. Rom Harré, and Luk van Langenhoven 'The Dynamics of Social Episodes', 1; Gabriele Lucius-Hoene and Arnulf Deppermann *Rekonstruktion narrativer Identität* (Wiesbaden: VS Verlag für Sozialwissenschaften, 2014), 200.

118. I take this characterization from Patrick T. Jackson and Daniel H. Nexon, 'Relations Before States: Substance, Process and the Study of World Politics', *European Journal of International Relations* 5 no. 3 (1999): 293. They argue that, '[t]he majority of IR theories are substantialist – they presume that entities precede interaction, or that entities are already entities before they enter into social relations with other entities' (ibid.). Relational approaches on the contrary, do not presume this.

119. Wendy Hollway, 'Gender Difference and the Production of Subjectivity' in *Changing the Subject*, ed. Julian Henriques et al. (London, New York: Methuen, 1984); Luk van Langenhoven, and Rom Harré, 'Introducing Positioning Analysis', in *Positioning Theory: Moral Contexts of Intentional Action*, ed. Rom Harré and Luk van Langenhoven (Malden, MA: Blackwell Publishing, 1999): 14–31, 16.

120. Neill Korobov, 'Reconciling Theory with Method: From Conversation Analysis and Critical Discourse Analysis to Positioning Analysis', *Forum Qualitative Social Research* 2, no. 3 (2001): margin number 33.

121. Kruse, *Qualitative Interviewforschung*, 511.

122. This term is taken from Neumann: 'Some texts will show up as crossroads or anchor points, such as short government treaties outlining policies (called white papers in most English-speaking countries). These are called canonical texts or monuments. ... It is useful to select texts around these monuments, since monuments also contain reference to other texts ... ". Iver B. Neumann, 'Discourse Analysis', in *Qualitative Methods in International Relations*, ed. Audie Klotz and Deepa Prakash (Houndsmill: Palgrave Macmillan, 2008): 61–77, 67.

123. The term discourse is broadly used within political science as well as sociology and hence a number of understandings are discussed and presented in the literature: Milliken, 'The Study of Discourse in International Relations'; Milliken, 'Discourse Study: Bringing Rigor to Critical Theory'; Iver B. Neumann, 'Discourse Analysis', in *Qualitative Methods in International Relations*, ed. Audie Klotz and Deepa Prakash (Houndsmill: Palgrave Macmillan, 2008): 61–77; Reiner Keller, 'Analysing Discourse: An Approach From the Sociology of Knowledge', *Forum Qualitative Social Research* 6, no. 3 (2005); Reiner Keller, and Willy Viehöver 'Diskursanalyse', in *Methoden der Politikwissenschaft*, ed. Joachim Behnke et al. (Baden-Baden: Nomos Verlagsgesellschaft, 2006): 103–111 ; Norman Fairclough, and Ruth Wodak, 'Critical Discourse Analysis', in *Discourse as Social Interaction*, ed. van Dijk, Teujn Adrianus (London: SAGE Publications, 1997): 258–285. In this article I rely on the following definition by Anna Holzscheiter, who argues that ' ... discourse is the space where human beings make sense of the material world, where they attach meaning to the worlds and where representations of the world become manifest. The existence of a material world outside discourse is, thus, not denied – what is refuted is the assumption that we can relate to this material world without discourse. In its essence, discourse analysis is an engagement with meaning and the linguistic and communicative process through with social reality is constructed'. Holzscheiter, 'Between Communicative Interaction and Structures of Signification', 144.

124. As one interview partner remarked this somewhat refutes the argument that R2P was to serve as a Trojan horse for western imperialism (Interview A6: 180–182).

125. Roland Paris, 'The "Responsibility to Protect" and the Structural Problems of Preventive Humanitarian Intervention', *International Peacekeeping* 21 no. 5 (2014): 569–603, 580.

126. Interview A2: 200–202.

127. Paris, 'The "Responsibility to Protect" and the Structural Problems of Preventive Humanitarian Intervention', 586 ; Weiss, 'Military Humanitarianism', 13.

128. Organisation of Islamic Cooperation, 'Final Communique Issued By The Emergency Meeting Of The Committee Of Permanent Representatives To The Organization Of The Islamic Conference On The Alarming Developments In Libyan Jamahiriya' (2011). Organisation of Islamic Cooperation. March 8, 2011 (accessed October 16, 2014)

129. African Union Peace and Security Council, 'COMMUNIQUE OF THE 265th MEETING OF THE PEACE AND SECURITY COUNCIL' no. PSC/PR/COMM.2 (CCLXV) (2011). African Union. http://www.au.int/en/sites/default/files/COMMUNIQUE_EN_10_MARCH_2011_PSD_THE_265TH_MEETING_OF_THE_PEACE_AND_SECURITY_COUNCIL_ADOPTED_FOLLOWING_DECISION_SITUATION_LIBYA.pdf. March 10, 2011 (accessed 16 October 2014).

130. Arab League, 'The outcome of the Council of the League of Arab States meeting at the Ministerial level in its extraordinary session on the implications of the current events in Libya and the Arab position' (2011). League of Arab States. http://responsibilitytoprotect.org/Arab%20League%20Ministerial%20level%20statement%2012%20march%202011%20-%20english%281%29.pdf. October 12, 2014 (accessed 16 October 2014).

131. Weiss, 'Military Humanitarianism', 13.

132. Arab League, 'The Outcome of the Council of the League of Arab States Meeting at the Ministerial Level in its Extraordinary Session on the Implications of the Current Events in Libya and the Arab Position' (2011). League of Arab States. http://responsibilitytoprotect.org/Arab%20League%20Ministerial%20level%20statement%2012%20march%202011%20-%20english%281%29.pdf. October 12, 2014 (accessed 16 October 2014)

133. Ibid.

134. African Union Peace and Security Council, 'COMMUNIQUE OF THE 265th MEETING OF THE PEACE AND SECURITY COUNCIL' no. PSC/PR/COMM.2(CCLXV) (2011)., African Union. http://www.au.int/en/sites/default/files/COMMUNIQUE_EN_10_MARCH_2011_PSD_THE_265TH_MEETING_OF_THE_PEACE_AND_SECURITY_COUNCIL_ADOPTED_FOLLOWING_DECISION_SITUATION_LIBYA.pdf. March 10, 2011 (accessed 16 October 2014), emphasis removed.

135. Ibid.

136. Arab League, 'The outcome of the Council of the League of Arab States meeting at the Ministerial level in its extraordinary session on the implications of the current events in Libya and the Arab position' (2011)., League of Arab States. http://responsibilitytoprotect.org/Arab%20League%20Ministerial%20level%20statement%2012%20march%202011%20-%20english%281%29.pdf. October 12, 2014 (accessed 16 October 2014).

137. Ibid.

138. Resolution 1973 recalls and takes note of the statements of the regional actors.

139. UNSC, 'Resolution 1973' (2011). United Nations. http://daccess-dds-ny.un.org/doc/UNDOC/GEN/N11/268/39/PDF/N1126839.pdf. March 17, 2011 (accessed 4 September 2014).

140. UNSC, 'Resolution 1970' (2011). United Nations. http://www.un.org/en/ga/search/view_doc.asp?symbol=S/RES/1970%20%282011%29. February 26, 2011 (accessed 2 September 2014).

141. UNSC, 'Resolution 1973' (2011). United Nations. http://daccess-dds-ny.un.org/doc/UNDOC/GEN/N11/268/39/PDF/N1126839.pdf. March 17, 2011 (accessed 4 September 2014).

142. Jennifer M. Welsh, 'Civilian Protection in Libya: Putting Coercion and Controversy Back into RtoP', *Ethics & International Affairs* 25, no. 3 (2011): 255–262. Alex J. Bellamy, 'Libya and The Responsibility to Protect: The Exception and the Norm', *Ethics & International Affairs* 25, no. 3 (2011): 263–269. Wolfgang Seibel, 'Libyen, das Prinzip der Schutzverantwortung und Deutschlands Stimmenthaltung im UN-Sicherheitsrat bei der Abstimmung über Resolution 1973 am 17. März 2011' in *Internationale Schutzverantwortung. Normative Erwartungen und Politische Praxis*, ed. Christopher Daase and Julian Junk (Berlin: Berliner Wissenschafts-Verlag, 2013), 87–115; Rebecca Adler-Nissen and Vincent Pouliot, 'Power in Practice: Negotiating the International Intervention in Libya', *European Journal of International Relations* 20, no. 4 (2014): 889–911.

143. UN DPI, 'Security Council Approves 'No-Fly Zone' over Libya, Authorizing 'All Necessary Measures' to Protect Civilians, by Vote of 10 in Favour with 5 Abstentions' no. SC/10200 (2011). UN. https://www.un.org/News/Press/docs/2011/sc10200.doc.htm.

144. Ibid., emphasis added.

145. UN DPI, 'Security Council Approves "No-Fly Zone" over Libya, Authorizing "All Necessary Measures" to Protect Civilians, by Vote of 10 in Favour with 5 Abstentions' no. SC/10200 (2011). UN. https://www.un.org/News/Press/docs/2011/sc10200.doc.htm; UNSC, '6498th Meeting' (2011). United Nations. http://www.un.org/en/ga/search/view_doc.asp?symbol=S/PV.6498. March 17, 2011 (accessed 16 October 2014)

146. UNSC, 'Resolution 1973' (2011). United Nations. http://daccess-dds-ny.un.org/doc/UNDOC/GEN/N11/268/39/PDF/N1126839.pdf. March 17, 2011 (accessed 4 September 2014)

147. Jutta Brunnée and Stephen J. Toope, 'The Rule of Law in an Agnostic World: The Prohibition on the Use of Force and Humanitarian Exceptions' in *Koskenniemi and his Critics*, ed. Wouter Werner, Marieke de Hoon and Alexis Galan (Cambridge: Cambridge University Press, forthcoming); a version of this contribution is available at http://papers.ssrn.com/sol3/papers.cfm?abstract_id=2547022.

148. Paris, 'The "Responsibility to Protect" and the Structural Problems of Preventive Humanitarian Intervention', 582.

149. Rebecca Adler-Nissen and Vincent Pouliot, 'Power in Practice: Negotiating the International Intervention in Libya', *European Journal of International Relations* 20, no. 4 (2014): 889–911, 908 ; Brunnée and Toope, 'The Rule of Law in an Agnostic World', 15 ; Alex J. Bellamy, 'The Responsibility to Protect and the Problem of Regime Change' in *The Ethics of Armed Humanitarian Intervention*, ed. Don E. Scheid (Cambridge: Cambridge University Press, 2014), 166; Thomas G. Weiss, 'Military Humanitarianism', 8 ; Tzvetan Todorov, 'The Responsibility to Protect and the War in Libya' in *The Ethics of Armed Humanitarian Intervention*, ed. Don E. Scheid (Cambridge: Cambridge University Press, 2014) 46–58, 52.

150. Ainley, 'The Responsibility to Protect and the International Criminal Court', 40–41; Glanville, 'Armed Humanitarian Intervention', 153.

151. James Pattison, 'The Ethics of Humanitarian Intervention in Libya', *Ethics & International Affairs* 25, no. 3 (2011): 271–277, 273 ; Don E. Scheid, 'Introduction to Armed Humanitarian Intervention', in *The Ethics of Armed Humanitarian Intervention*, ed. Don E. Scheid (Cambridge: Cambridge University Press, 2014): 3–25, 23–24 ; Glanville, 'Armed Humanitarian Intervention', 162.

152. Adler-Nissen and Pouliot have a somewhat more strategic-based explanation for the agreement: 'In the struggle to look competent, other Council members could not counter P3 moves and resources. As one diplomat said, countries such as Russia were "skeptical at first, but they also didn't have sufficient information to say that [the P3 narrative] was a lie".' Rebecca Adler-Nissen and Vincent Pouliot, 'Power in practice: Negotiating the International Intervention in Libya', *European Journal of International Relations* 20, no. 4 (2014): 889–911, 901.

153. Paris, 'The "Responsibility to Protect" and the Structural Problems of Preventive Humanitarian Intervention', 585.

154. Matteo Capasso, 'The Libyan Drawers: "Stateless Society", "Humanitarian Intervention", "Logic of Exception" and "Traversing the Phantasy",', *Middle East Critique* 23, no. 4 (2014): 387–404, 393.

155. Human Rights Council. 'Report of the International Commission of Inquiry on Libya'. United Nations. http://www.ohchr.org/Documents/HRBodies/HRCouncil/RegularSession/Session19/A.HRC.19.68.pdf (accessed 24 June 2015).

156. Bruno Schoch, 'Die Libyen-Intervention: Warum Deutschlands Enthaltung im Sicherheitsrat falsch war' in *Libyen: Missbrauch der Responsibility to Protect?*, ed. Gerhard Beestermöller (Baden-Baden: Nomos Verlagsgesellschaft, 2014), 115–138, 132.

157. Interview A2: 241

158. Kathryn Kersavage, 'The "Responsibility to Protect" Our Answer to "Never again"?', *International Affairs Forum* 5, no. 1 (2014): 23–41, 33.

159. Bassam Haddad, 'Four Years On: Now Easy Answers in Syria (Part 1)' (2015). http://www.jadaliyya.com/pages/index/21117/four-years-on_no-easy-answers-in-syria-%28part-1%29. 18 March 2015 (accessed 24 April 2015).

160. Security Council Report, 'Syria: Chronology of Events' (2015). Security Council Report. http://www.securitycouncilreport.org/chronology/syria.php. 1 April 2015 (accessed 25 April 2015)

161. Ibid.

162. Ibid.

163. President of the Security Council, 'Statement by the President of the Security Council' no. S/PRST/2011/16 (2011). United Nations. http://www.securitycouncilreport.org/atf/cf/%7B65BFCF9B-6D27-4E9C-8CD3-CF6E4FF96FF9%7D/Syria%20%20SPRST%202011%2016.pdf. 3 August 2011 (accessed 25 April 2015).

164. France et al., 'Draft Resolution 04.10.2011' (2011). http://www.securitycouncilreport.org/atf/cf/%7B65BFCF9B-6D27-4E9C-8CD3-CF6E4FF96FF9%7D/Syria%20S2011%20612.pdf. 4 October 2011 (accessed 24 April 2015)

165. Ibid.
166. Security Council Report, 'Syria: Chronology of Events' (2015). Security Council Report. http://www.securitycouncilreport.org/chronology/syria.php. 1 April 2015 (accessed 25 April 2015)
167. UNSC, '6627th meeting' no. S/PV.6627 (2011). United Nations. http://www.un.org/en/ga/search/view_doc.asp?symbol=S/PV.6627. 4 October 2011 (accessed April 25, 2015)
168. Ibid., 3.
169. Ibid., 6.
170. Ibid.
171. Ibid., 7.
172. Ibid., 4.
173. Ibid., 12.
174. Bahrain, Colombia, Egypt, France, Germany, Jordan, Kuwait, Libya, Morocco, Oman, Portugal, Qatar, Saudi Arabia, Togo, Tunisia, Turkey, United Arab Emirates, United Kingdom, and the United States of America all co-sponsored the draft: Bahrain et al., 'Draft Resolution' no. S/2012/77 (2012). United Nations. http://www.securitycouncilreport.org/atf/cf/%7B65BFCF9B-6D27-4E9C-8CD3-CF6E4FF96FF9%7D/Syria%20S2012%2077.pdf. 4 February 2012 (accessed 25 April 2015).
175. Ibid.
176. Ibid.
177. Ibid.
178. UNSC, '6711th Meeting' no. S/PV.7611 (2012)., United Nations. http://www.securitycouncilreport.org/atf/cf/%7B65BFCF9B-6D27-4E9C-8CD3-CF6E4FF96FF9%7D/Syria%20SPV%206711.pdf. 4 February 2012 (accessed 27 April 2015)
179. Ibid., 3–4.
180. Ibid., 5.
181. Ibid., 6.
182. Ibid., 9.
183. BBC, 'Syria crisis: Russia and China step up warning over strike' (2013). http://www.bbc.com/news/world-us-canada-23845800. 27 August 2013 (accessed 26 April 2015).
184. OPCW, 'Member State – Syria' (2015). OPWC. https://www.opcw.org/about-opcw/member-states/member-states-by-region/asia/member-state-syria/ (accessed 26 April 2015)
185. Security Council Report, 'Syria: Chronology of Events' (2015)., Security Council Report. http://www.securitycouncilreport.org/chronology/syria.php. 1 April 2015 (accessed 25 April 2015).
186. UNSC, 'Resolution 2118' (2013). United Nations. http://www.securitycouncilreport.org/atf/cf/%7B65BFCF9B-6D27-4E9C-8CD3-CF6E4FF96FF9%7D/s_res_2118.pdf. 27 September 2013 (accessed 26 April 2015).
187. David Miliband, 'Syria May be Lost, But We Must Stand By its Victims' . http://www.rescue.org/blog/david-miliband-syria-may-be-lost-we-must-stand-its-victims-commentary. 10 February 2014 (accessed 19 February 2014).
188. What's in Blue, 'Draft Humanitarian Resolution on Syria and Briefing by Humanitarian Chief' (2014). http://www.whatsinblue.org/2014/02/draft-humanitarian-resolution-on-syria-and-briefing-by-humanitarian-chief.php?nomobile=1. 11 February 2014 (accessed 19 February 2014); BBC. 'Syria conflict: UN concerned over Homs detentions'. BBC. http://www.bbc.com/news/world-middle-east-26131742 (accessed 24 June 2015).
189. Charli Carpenter, '"Women, Children and Other Vulnerable Groups": Gender, Strategic Frames and the Protection of Civilians as a Transnational Issue"', *International Studies Quarterly* 49, no. 2 (2005): 295–334, 296.
190. Ibid.
191. Miliband, 'Syria May be Lost', emphasis added.
192. Interview A2: 251, 273; Interview A3: 196–197; Interview A4: 39–40, 42, 44–46; Interview A6: 344.
193. Interview A2: 251.
194. UN DPI, 'Security Council Unanimously Adopts Resolution 2139 (2014) to Ease Aid Delivery to Syrians, Provide Relief from "Chilling Darkness".' (2014). UN DPI. http://www.un.org/News/Press/docs/2014/sc11292.doc.htm.
195. Brunnée and Toope, 'The Rule of Law in an Agnostic World', 15 ; Paris, 'The "Responsibility to Protect" and the Structural Problems of Preventive Humanitarian Intervention', 587.

196. UN DPI, 'Security Council Unanimously Adopts Resolution 2139 (2014) to Ease Aid Delivery to Syrians, Provide Relief from 'Chilling Darkness'' (2014). UN DPI. http://www.un.org/News/Press/docs/2014/sc11292.doc.htm.
197. Ibid.
198. Ibid.
199. Albania et al., 'Draft Resolution' no. S/2014/348 (2014). United Nations. http://www.securitycouncilreport.org/atf/cf/%7B65BFCF9B-6D27-4E9C-8CD3-CF6E4FF96FF9%7D/s_2014_348.pdf. 22 May 2014 (accessed 25 April 2015).
200. UNSC, '7180th Meeting' no. S/PV.7180 (2014). United Nations. http://www.un.org/en/ga/search/view_doc.asp?symbol=S/PV.7180. 22 May 2014 (accessed 25 April 2015).
201. Secretary General, 'Implementation of Security Council resolution 2139 (2014)' no. S/2014/295 (2014). http://www.securitycouncilreport.org/atf/cf/%7B65BFCF9B-6D27-4E9C-8CD3-CF6E4FF96FF9%7D/s_2014_295.pdf. 23 April 2015 (accessed 26 April 2014).
202. UNSC, 'Resolution 2165' no. S/RES/2165 (2014) (2014). United Nations. http://www.un.org/en/ga/search/view_doc.asp?symbol=S/RES/2165%282014%29. 14 July 2015 (accessed 26 April 2015).
203. Ibid.
204. UNSC, '7216th meeting' (2014). United Nations. http://www.un.org/en/ga/search/view_doc.asp?symbol=S/PV.7216. 14 July 2014 (accessed 16 October 2014).
205. Security Council Report, 'Syria: Chronology of Events' (2015). Security Council Report. http://www.securitycouncilreport.org/chronology/syria.php. 1 April 2015 (accessed 25 April 2015).
206. Weiss, 'Military Humanitarianism', 18.
207. Jan Wilkens, 'Der "Islamische Staat" und die angebliche Alternativlosigkeit in Syrien' (2015). http://www.alsharq.de/2015/mashreq/syrien/der-islamische-staat-und-die-angebliche-alternativlosigkeit-in-syrien/. 21 March 2015 (accessed 23 March 2015).
208. Welsh, 'Norm Contestation and the Responsibility to Protect'.
209. For a critical view on the notion of R2P as an 'emerging norm' see Christopher Daase, 'Die Legalisierung der Legitmität – Zur Kritik der Schutzverantwortung als emerging norm'.
210. Weiss, 'Military Humanitarianism'.
211. Holzscheiter, 'Between Communicative Interaction and Structures of Signification', 144.
212. Frédéric Mégret, 'ICC, R2P, and the International Community's Evolving Interventionist Toolkit', *Finnish Yearbook of International Law* 21 (2010): 21–51, 49.
213. Annan, 'Two Concepts of Sovereignty', 81.
214. Peters, 'Humanity as the A and of Sovereignty', 535.

Responsibility to protect and inter-state crises: why and how R2P applies to the case of Gaza

Pinar Gözen Ercan

Hacettepe University, Faculty of Economic and Administrative Sciences, Department of International Relations, Beytepe/Ankara, Turkey

This article addresses a prominent question relating to the nature and scope of responsibility to protect (R2P), namely the situation in Gaza, and asks whether or not R2P can be implemented in 'inter-state' crises. Following a two-fold analysis in arguing why and how Gaza qualifies as an R2P case requiring the international community's attention, first the scope of R2P is discussed. Then, the crisis in Gaza is the focus, considering the two scenarios of Gaza as a territory of the independent state of Palestine, and as an occupied territory due to the effective control of Israel in and out of the territory.

Introduction

Since the international community unanimously adopted the responsibility to protect (R2P) under paragraphs 138 and 139 of the 2005 World Summit Outcome Document, it has reluctantly implemented its collective responsibility. Arguably, in March 2011 a turning point came with the international response to the situation in Libya, which Secretary General Ban Ki-moon considers to have affirmed 'clearly and unequivocally, the international community's determination to fulfil its responsibility to protect civilians from violence perpetrated upon them by their own Government'.

The international community's decisiveness to act swiftly first in Libya and immediately after in the Ivory Coast, led pro-R2P scholars into thinking that R2P was now being taken seriously, and that the much aspired change was finally taking place. Nevertheless, the excitement did not last long. First, the way the military operations were carried out both in Libya and in the Ivory Coast, and then, the international community's stand-by in the deteriorating situation in Syria allowed critics of R2P to question the norm's future as well as its ever-contested added value.

Despite all the downfalls in its institutionalization and implementation, my starting assumption is that R2P is still alive and still in evolution. As a norm that has not yet completed its life cycle, R2P is yet far from achieving its true potential and very distant from being internalized given its current limits and/or limitations. In its current state, I consider

R2P to have evolved into an international moral norm, which sets a standard of appropriate behaviour for individual states and the international community.[1] This eventually means that R2P lacks its own legally binding powers over states and the international community as well as mechanisms to ensure states' compliance. In this vein, states' individual failures put aside, since its unanimous adoption of the norm in 2005, the international community has been implementing its responsibility to protect selectively and interpreting it in a very narrow manner that is contrary to the main purpose of the norm.

In light of this, this article addresses a prominent question that relates to the nature and scope of R2P, that is the situation in Gaza, and asks whether or not R2P can be implemented in 'inter-state' crises. Accordingly, it discusses why and how this situation qualifies as an R2P case that requires the immediate attention of the international community. To this end, a two-fold analysis is presented. First, following a constructivist framework of analysis, the scope of R2P as established by the 2005 World Summit Outcome Document is discussed for understanding what R2P entails of and what its current limits are. Then, in the second part, the conflict in Gaza, which pertains to the larger question of the Israeli–Palestinian conflict, is placed under focus. In order to understand the nature of the conflict and the inherent R2P components in the crises, two main scenarios are analysed: Gaza as a territory of the independent state of Palestine; and Gaza as an occupied territory due to the effective control of Israel in and out of the territory. On this basis, it is discussed who has the R2P for the population of Gaza.

Norms' life cycle and their circulation

For the initial part of its analysis, this study adopts the norm life cycle model of Finnemore and Sikkink[2] to distinguish between stages of a norm's evolution. According to this model, Stage 1 comprises of 'norm emergence', in which norm entrepreneurs construct a new norm and introduce it to the international community. This is followed by persuasion efforts of norm entrepreneurs for the norm's adoption.[3] Nevertheless, in 'most cases, for an emergent norm to reach a threshold and advance to the second stage, it must become institutionalized in specific sets of international rules and organizations'.[4] It is the 'tipping point' that sets the borderline between Stages 1 and 2, and is attained when the norm is adopted by 'a critical mass of relevant state actors. … What happens at the tipping point is that enough states and enough critical states endorse the new norm to redefine appropriate behaviour for the identity called "state".'[5] Socialization is the key mechanism of Stage 2, 'norm cascade', and is carried out by norm leaders seeking to persuade others to adhere to the new norm.[6] A norm is accepted to have completed its life cycle, when it is internalized (Stage 3) that is, as Checkel[7] puts it, the end point 'where the community norms and rules become taken for granted' instead of being contested.

While the norm life cycle model places its emphasis on persuasion, for explaining and understanding R2P's current form and limits, additional factors need to be taken into consideration. In this context, two additional considerations, namely venue – which is 'the institutional setting in which an official diplomatic encounter occurs'[8] – and negotiation are included in the analysis. In structural terms, the responsibilities established by R2P pertain to two levels: the state-level reflecting the understanding of 'sovereignty as responsibility', and the international level reflecting the idea of a collective R2P. This two-level structure requires the adoption of the norm not only by states individually but also by the international community so that its institutionalization and implementation (at the levels of pillars two and three) become possible. In this vein, venue and negotiation help to explain the transformation of R2P in terms of its scope and density during the institutionalization process.

Lastly, to better understand the socialization of R2P, this analysis also benefits from the norm circulation framework of Amitav Acharya[9] in analysing the scope, limits and density of R2P in relation to its evolution, contestation and interpretation in the aftermath of the 2005 World Summit Outcome Document. Acharya's framework suggests a 'multiple-agency, two-way, multi-step process of norm diffusion, based on resistance, feedback and repatriation',[10] the end result of which can be universalization, which 'refers to the global diffusion of a purely locally constructed norm'.

Institutionalization of R2P and its new meaning

When the International Commission on Intervention and State Sovereignty (ICISS) introduced R2P to the international community in 2001, it followed the motto 'never again'. To this end, for preventing and/or halting mass atrocities against humanity, the Commission prescribed individual states and the international community the responsibilities to prevent, react and rebuild instead of recognizing a unilateral or collective 'right to intervene'. As its inception coincided with the 'war on terror', R2P was not embraced by a vast majority of states in its early years. It was the then Secretary General Kofi Annan who during his term of service carried R2P to the political discourse of the United Nations (UN) within a period of three years. As a locally-constructed norm, R2P's institutionalization began with the change of venue from the ICISS to the UN, that is to say from a small venue to a large one with global legitimacy.

Following the previous reports of the Secretary General endorsing R2P within the institutional framework of the UN, October 2005 became the watershed for R2P, as with paragraphs 138 and 139 of the World Summit Outcome Document state members of the General Assembly unanimously accepted their individual and collective responsibility to protect populations from genocide, war crimes, crimes against humanity and ethnic cleansing (hereinafter referred to as atrocity crimes). The two paragraphs, which Weiss[11] labels as 'R2P-lite', were the final product of negotiations within the UN and the compromises made from the original suggestions of the ICISS.

All in all, the change of venue not only enabled the vast recognition of R2P in four years time, but also led to a significant transformation of the norm regarding its content and the density. Considering the original idea behind the construction of the R2P norm, the changes imposed on R2P were not necessarily all positive. While based on states' feedback R2P became less ambiguous through the limitation of its scope to atrocity crimes, it also became undemanding as far as the responsibilities of the international community were concerned. To understand the current scope and content of R2P, it is important to focus on paragraphs 138 and 139 of the Outcome Document. As the main concern of this article is the crisis in Gaza in relation to the implementation of R2P, the analysis of R2P's process of institutionalization is kept limited to understanding the intersubjective meaning of R2P under the roof of the UN.

2005 World Summit Outcome Document and 'R2P-lite'

The World Summit Outcome Document[12] assigns all states, on an equal basis, 'the duty to promote and protect all human rights and fundamental freedoms' and acknowledges the individual responsibility of States 'to respect human rights and fundamental freedoms for all'. Building on such fundamental understanding of human rights, R2P is enshrined under a separate section entitled 'Responsibility to Protect Populations from Genocide, War Crimes, Ethnic Cleansing and Crimes Against Humanity', comprising of the three paragraphs of 138, 139 and 140. While the latter is a statement of support, the former two paragraphs are of significance in terms of what the norm entails of.

When read together, paragraphs 138 and 139 concisely refer to the 'responsibility to prevent' and the 'responsibility to react' aspects of R2P without touching upon the 'responsibility to rebuild'. While peace-building is separately considered through paragraphs 97 to 105 within the framework of the peace-building commission to be established as an advisory intergovernmental body by the General Assembly, it is not linked to R2P in a way to establish a responsibility to rebuild as it was originally suggested by the ICISS.

Paragraph 138 establishes that states individually have a responsibility for the protection of their populations from atrocity crimes. This responsibility not only covers the prevention of these crimes but also preventing their incitement. When we look at the wording of Paragraph 138, there is no explicit statement indicating that R2P applies solely to intra-state situations. Nevertheless, the responsibility is set out between the national authorities and the population living on that territory. As suggested with the 'sovereignty as responsibility' understanding, the authorities assuming control over a territory are accepted to bear the responsibility for the protection of the population within the boundaries of that state.

While making the Member States of the General Assembly pledge to act in accordance with their individual responsibility towards their populations, on the part of the international community, the paragraph also states that the 'international community should, as appropriate, encourage and help States to exercise this responsibility and support the UN in establishing an early warning capability'. Subsequently, Paragraph 139 defines the responsibility of the international community. To highlight the underlying ideas regarding what the global responsibility entails of, a sentence-by-sentence analysis of the paragraph helps:

> *The international community, through the United Nations, also has the responsibility* to use appropriate diplomatic, humanitarian and other peaceful means, in accordance with Chapters VI and VIII of the Charter, *to help to protect populations* from genocide, war crimes, ethnic cleansing and crimes against humanity. In this context, we are *prepared* to take *collective action*, in a timely and decisive manner, through the Security Council, in accordance with the Charter, including Chapter VII, on a *case-by-case basis* and in cooperation with relevant regional organizations as appropriate, *should peaceful means be inadequate and national authorities are manifestly failing to protect their populations* from genocide, war crimes, ethnic cleansing and crimes against humanity. We stress the need for the General Assembly to continue consideration of the responsibility to protect populations from genocide, war crimes, ethnic cleansing and crimes against humanity and its implications, bearing in mind the principles of the Charter and international law. *We also intend to commit ourselves, as necessary and appropriate, to helping States build capacity to protect their populations* from genocide, war crimes, ethnic cleansing and crimes against humanity *and to assisting those which are under stress before crises and conflicts break out* (emphasis added).

First and foremost, in the paragraph peaceful measures are prioritized over coercive ones while the international community is assigned the role of assisting in the protection of populations without making any specifications on whether these concern intra-state or inter-state situations. Secondly, member states indicate their preparedness to take collective action in severe cases where non-coercive measures have proven inadequate and national authorities are clearly failing to uphold their responsibility. The nature of the manifest failure is not clarified in the paragraph, but reference to the original suggestions of the ICISS helps to understand what is implied. In its report, the ICISS put forth 'the idea that sovereign states have a responsibility to protect their own citizens from avoidable catastrophe – from mass murder and rape, from starvation – but that when they are *unwilling* or *unable* to do so, that responsibility must be borne by the broader community of states' (emphasis added).[13] In this vein, in invoking the international community's R2P what is of significance is either the unwillingness or the inability of national authorities to protect their populations.

Furthermore, in determining the reaction of the international community, the Security Council is appointed as the appropriate authority, which can decide on the sanctioning of non-coercive as well as coercive measures, while the General Assembly is given the task of further consideration of R2P. Lastly, member states indicate their 'intention to commit' themselves in assisting states in capacity building and prevention. Evaluated as a whole, the undemanding language adopted throughout the paragraph avoids any legal commitments on the part of the international community. As the representative of India to the UN Mr. Puri states, the Outcome Document is practically 'a cautious go ahead' for the adoption and collective implementation of R2P.[14]

Nevertheless, there is a vital distinction between the responsibilities established by the two paragraphs. While both place special emphasis on preventive aspects of R2P, Paragraph 138 has a restrictive impact on the behaviour of states, since R2P as a norm is in conformity with the established standards of fundamental human rights as well as international criminal and humanitarian laws (such as the Convention on the Prevention and Punishment of the Crime of Genocide; International Covenant on Civil and Political Rights including the Second Optional Protocol; International Covenant on Social, Economic and Cultural Rights; Convention against Torture and Other Cruel, Inhuman or Degrading Treatment or Punishment; Convention on the Elimination of All Forms of Discrimination against Women; Convention on the Elimination of All Forms of Racial Discrimination; Convention relating to the Status of Refugees as well as the 1967 Protocol; Convention on the Rights of the Child; Rome Statute of the International Criminal Court; and Arms Trade Treaty). In this regard, it is possible to talk about previously established sanctioning mechanisms that can be enforced on states in cases of breaches of fundamental human rights through the machineries of the UN as well as the International Criminal Court (ICC).

Accordingly, it can be observed that states, at least signatories to the said conventions already have certain legal responsibilities that precede the construction of R2P. As the appropriate behaviour dictated by Paragraph 138 overlaps with these existing legal respon-sibilities, states' manifest failure to protect their populations can be sanctioned by the inter-national community if the international community prioritizes moral and/or legal considerations over political/self-interested motives in its responses to cases. In other words, the existing legal machinery can be mobilized for R2P if there is the will of the state members of the Security Council, especially the permanent members (P5) to do so. As both paragraphs suggest, prevention pertains not only to individual states but also to the international community. In this vein, the power to act on behalf of the international community is bestowed upon the Security Council. As far as reaction is concerned, action is fully dependent on the decision of the Security Council as well as being subject to evaluation on a case-by-case basis. This means not only that there is not one prescription to be applied to all situations uniformly, but also that due to the potential politicization of cases there are no guarantees that R2P will be implemented in all necessary cases.

Blurred lines: R2P and inter-state crises

In undertaking the task of further consideration of R2P, the Secretary General has so far published seven reports focusing solely on the different aspects as well as the implemen-tation of R2P. In the very first of these reports that was published in 2009, Ban Ki-moon notes: 'While the scope [of R2P] should be kept narrow, the response ought to be deep, employing the wide array of prevention and protection instruments available'.[15] In this vein, Ban clearly reaffirms that the scope of R2P which was limited to the four atrocity crimes in 2005 is to remain as such. Evaluated from this perspective, a first consideration is whether or not the situation in Gaza reaches the threshold of an R2P concern.

Of the four crimes that set the scope of R2P, the allegations of war crimes constitute the basis for the consideration of Gaza as an R2P situation. As Hehir[16]notes, there is in fact very little coverage on Gaza through the lens of R2P by non-governmental organizations that focus on R2P such as the Global Centre for R2P (GCR2P), the International Coalition for RtoP (ICRtoP) and the Asia Pacific Centre for R2P (APCR2P). Nevertheless, as indicated in the presidential statement of the Security Council, the increasing death toll and civilian casualties as a result of the retaliatory attacks by Israel in response to the rocket attacks by Hamas continue to create grave concern.[17] In this vein, in the case of Gaza, the question of responsibility is two-fold: who is to protect the Gazan population, and how are the authorities failing to uphold their responsibility? The subsequent section aims to tackle these questions on the basis of two scenarios: First, who has the responsibility if Gaza is considered as a territory of the independent state of Palestine? Second, who has the responsibility if Gaza is an occupied territory due to Israel's effective control in and out of the territory?

A question of protection of populations: who is to protect the people of Gaza?

The issue of Gaza pertains to the larger question of the Israeli–Palestinian conflict, which is in essence a political dispute requiring the political will of both the Israelis and the Palestinians to come to a peaceful solution. Nevertheless, compared to the situation in the West Bank, the conditions of the conflict are much different in Gaza regarding its impact on the population as this is a continuously violent conflict between the Israeli forces and those of Hamas, which is the authority assuming effective control inside the territory of Gaza. It is not only the number of displaced persons that is increasing fast, but also the death toll as a result of the effective retaliatory attacks by the Israeli forces. It is this violent nature of the ongoing conflict that makes Gaza a territory of interest from an R2P point of view, which requires the immediate attention of the international community.

In a nutshell, the situation in Gaza is an outcome of the armed attacks taking place between the Israeli Defense Forces (IDF) and Hamas. While the legitimate authority representing the State of Palestine is the Palestinian Authority (PA), Hamas is the de facto government exercising authority on the territory of Gaza since it won the Palestinian Parliamentary elections in 2006. Notwithstanding Israel's non-recognition of the Palestinian state, the UN has upgraded Palestine's status from an 'observer entity' to a 'non-member observer state' in November 2012, and currently there are 134 member states of the UN and international organizations such as the ICC that recognize Palestine as a state and the PA as its national representative. From an R2P point view, when Palestine is considered as an independent state governed by the PA, it is possible to argue that the national authorities are unable to protect their population living on the territory of Gaza due to their lack of control over the armed conflict between Israel and Hamas. Due to their inability to prevent the rocket attacks of Hamas on Israel from the Gaza Strip and Israel's retaliatory responses to these attacks, it can be argued that the PA is in need of international assistance in order to contain the situation.

Compared to this first scenario, the status of Gaza is much more complex since there is a triangle of control exerted over the Gazan territory. The PA being the representative of the

Palestinian State can be placed at the top of the triangle. The two actors in leading to the failure of the PA in protecting its population are Hamas and Israel. Though Israeli authorities consider Gazans as 'prisoners of Palestinian militant Islamist group Hamas',[18] Hamas assumes control inside the territory as an elected authority supported by the local population. As a Middle East expert, Dr Atmaca (personal communication, June 12, 2015) notes that as the living conditions of the world's largest open-air prison is becoming ever worse, the Gazan population is also becoming radicalized, which explains the favourable election results for Hamas in 2006.

In the meanwhile, even after withdrawing its civilian and military presence from Gaza in 2005, Israel remains a de facto occupying power thanks to the effective control it assumes in and out of the territory of Gaza. Notwithstanding its disengagement plan, after the election of Hamas, Israel has been applying an effective blockade over Gaza. Moreover, to counter the indiscriminate rocket attacks of Hamas, it has been undertaking military operations such as the 2008 Operation 'Hot Winter', 2008–2009 Gaza War, 2011 cross-border attack, March 2012 Operation 'Returning Echo', October 2012 Operation 'Pillar of Defense' or 2014 Operation 'Protective Edge', some of which have been at the centre of the allegations of war crimes. As the 2008 report of the UN Human Rights Commission asserts:

Israel's effective control is demonstrated by the following factors:

(a) Substantial control of Gaza's six land crossings [...];
(b) Control through military incursions, rocket attacks and sonic booms: sections of Gaza have been declared 'no-go' zones in which residents will be shot if they enter;
(c) Complete control of Gaza's airspace and territorial waters;
(d) Control of the Palestinian Population Registry: the definition of who is 'Palestinian' and who is a resident of Gaza and the West Bank is controlled by the Israeli military [...][19]

In this vein, the report concludes that 'The fact that Gaza remains occupied territory means that Israel's actions towards Gaza must be measured against the standards of international humanitarian law.'

Taking into consideration the big picture, arguably it is not only the PA, but also Hamas and Israel that have an R2P to the Gazan population due to the control they exercise over the territory. Furthermore, in this second scenario, it can be observed that both Hamas and Israel are unwilling to protect the Gazans given their behaviour since neither Hamas ceases its attacks against the Israeli territory and population, nor is the IDF successful in avoiding loss of civilian lives in Gaza in its retaliatory attacks. In this vein, a question to address is how to implement R2P in this specific crisis.

Devising a Three Pillar Strategy

In July 2014, during Israel's Operation Protective Edge, the death of over 2200 people in Gaza most of whom were Palestinian civilians was reported.[20] Following the collapse of the ceasefire, on 3 August 2014 Ban condemned the IDF's attack near a UN school in Rafah as a 'moral outrage and criminal act'. He further noted: '"United Nations shelters must be safe zones not combat zones" [...] the Israel Defense Forces (IDF) have been repeatedly informed of the location of these sites. "This attack, along with other breaches of international law, must be swiftly investigated and those responsible held accountable".'[21] Compared to the previous four instances where UN-protected shelters were hit, this was the first time that the Secretary General did not use a diplomatic/mild language and openly blamed Israel.[22] In response, the Israeli government stated that they have initiated investigations regarding the strike in Rafah and another strike in Jabalia on a shelter, which together led to the death of 40 civilians.[23] Furthermore, 'Israel claims it has taken numerous steps to avoid civilian casualties, such as leafletting areas that are about to be hit and telling the residents to leave. It places the responsibility for civilian casualties on Hamas, for firing rockets targeted at Israel from densely populated areas, using residents as human shields'.[24]

On their part, while Israeli military officials claim that they did not intentionally target the UN facility,[25] they also note that Hamas purposefully uses these protected areas to shield themselves and to store munitions, as well as 'to draw international condemnation of Israel if the IDF is forced to respond'.[26] Though, it has been confirmed by the UN that some of its facilities have been used by Hamas, these are referred to as vacant ones. The spokesman for the UN Relief and Works Agency, Chris Gunness states that the UN 'has found troves of rockets hidden in three of its schools since the conflict began', which he considers 'yet another flagrant violation of the neutrality of [the UN] premises'.[27] Nevertheless:

> Navi Pillay, the U.N. High Commissioner for Human Rights … pointed out that UN-run shelters are protected by the Geneva Conventions, and said that the IDF's repeated strikes on civilian targets amounted to 'deliberate defiance of obligations that international law imposes on Israel.' Pillay, who is South African, also condemned Hamas, saying that it, too, bore guilt. 'Locating rockets in schools and hospitals, or even launching these rockets from densely populated areas, are violations of international humanitarian law,' Pillay said. 'But it does not absolve the other party – that is, Israel – from not itself observing its obligations under international humanitarian law'.[28]

In this vein, it can be concluded that both Israel and Hamas have certain responsibilities in the situation regardless of the justifications they set forth for their actions.

While war crimes are traditionally included within the scope of international humanitarian law, the questions of investigation of breaches of international law and accountability also reminds of the international criminal law aspect of the crisis. In his 2009 report, Ban reminds that the crimes committed which lead to states' manifest failure can be referred to the ICC,[29] since of the four grave crimes that determine the scope of R2P, genocide, war crimes and crimes against humanity fall under the jurisdiction of the ICC. As suggested by his call for states to join 'the relevant international instruments on human rights, international humanitarian law and refugee law, as well as to the Rome Statute of the International Criminal Court',[30] Ban sees such involvement as an initial step in the full implementation of R2P, which in Acharya's words, can be seen as a step in strengthening the 'global diffusion of the norm'.

In general terms, the relationship between the ICC and R2P can be defined as a cyclical one in which the ICC provides the legal grounding whereas R2P provides the moral and political framework. While R2P's implementation at the international level requires the determination of an authority's failure to protect its population, in the next phase enforcement requires additional measures to be applied. In this regard, ICC processes can help not only to determine the manifest failure of an authority, but also its prosecutions may constitute part of R2P's enforcement measures.

On the basis of the Rome Statute, the Chief Prosecutor of the ICC 'can initiate an investigation on the basis of a referral from any State Party or from the UN Security Council. In addition, the Prosecutor can initiate investigations *proprio motu* on the basis of information on crimes within the jurisdiction of the Court received from individuals or organizations ("communications")'. In this vein, Palestine's admission to the ICC as of April 2015 as a state member and the Office of the Prosecutor's initiation of preliminary investigations into possible war crimes in the Palestinian territories are going to be a game changer in the conflict. While Israel is not a state party to the Rome Statute, with Palestine's membership in the Court, the actions of Israeli officials in the Palestinian territory and of Hamas can now be tried by the ICC where the facts support an ICC prosecution.

On the one hand, ICC proceedings may help attracting international attention to the case, on the other hand, it has agitated Israel and may lead to the escalation of the conflict. 'Prime Minister Benjamin Netanyahu vowed Sunday that Israeli soldiers would never be tried by the ICC and excoriated the court for giving "international cover to international terror" ... Israel promised to take retaliatory measures'.[31] Furthermore, Israel's most prominent ally, the US has criticized the decisions of the ICC to admit Palestine as a member and to initiate preliminary investigations against Israel. Summarizing the position of the US, State Department spokesman Jeff Rathke notes: 'As we have said repeatedly, we do not believe that Palestine is a state, and therefore we do not believe that it is eligible to join the ICC. ... It is a tragic irony that Israel, which has withstood thousands of terrorist rockets fired at its civilians and its neighborhoods, is now being scrutinized by the ICC.'[32]

Whether the involvement of the ICC in the situation has a positive or negative impact, it cannot provide a solution in the short-term. Considering that the crippled US brokered peace process has been further challenged by Hamas's ever strengthening position in Gaza, and the right-wing Likud leader Netanyahu's win in the Israeli elections, within the framework of R2P, the international community should be called upon to fulfil its responsibilities under pillars two and three.

In evaluating the situation in Gaza one needs to keep in mind the political and multinational aspects of the issue. In this vein, devising an R2P strategy based on the radical end of Pillar 3 is not necessarily an option. What is required is rather an international effort to persuade Israel and Hamas to cease their attacks whether through peaceful measures or through sanctions. As one of the very first resolutions reaffirming paragraphs 138 and 139 of the World Summit Outcome Document, Security Council Resolution 1674 (2006) '[r]ecalls that deliberately targeting civilians and other protected persons as such in situations of armed conflict is a flagrant violation of international humanitarian law, reiterates its condemnation in the strongest terms of such practices, and demands that all parties immediately put an end to such practices'. In this vein, given the gravity and imminence of the situation, it is no longer possible to turn a blind eye to the increasing civilian casualties by simply considering this as an inter-state crisis.

One prominent challenge in this regard is that R2P's implementation whether through pillar 2 or pillar 3, is dependent on the willingness of the members of the Security Council, especially that of the permanent members which wield the power of veto. In fulfilling the collective R2P, Secretary General touches upon particular responsibilities and duties, and urges the P5 'to refrain from employing or threatening to employ the veto in situations of manifest failure to meet obligations relating to R2P, as defined in paragraph 139 of the Summit Outcome, and to reach a mutual understanding to that effect'.[33] Nevertheless, currently there are no official restraints imposed upon the P5 to prevent them from blocking a decision in an R2P case. In this regard, considering that the US is clearly aligned with Israel, it is highly difficult to secure a decision that is against Israel's interests. A recent example is the resolution drafted by Jordan,[34] calling for the establishment of a Palestinian state and an end to the Israeli occupation, which was turned down with eight affirmative votes (by Argentina, Chad, Chile, China, France, Jordan, Luxembourg and Russia), five abstentions (Lithuania, Nigeria, Republic of Korea, Rwanda and the UK) and two negative votes (by the US and Australia) on 30 December 2014. All in all, though the moral framework provided by R2P sets the appropriate behaviour for states to follow in this specific conflict, R2P's implementation to prevent further civilian casualties fully rests on the political will of the international community as well as the parties involved in the conflict.

Conclusion: R2P as 'a core part of world's armour'?

From the broader point of the Israeli–Palestinian conflict, R2P is not 'the framework' to view the situation from. Nevertheless, in terms of avoiding losses of civilian lives in the ongoing conflict in Gaza, R2P provides an additional framework for developing an immediate international response to the violent situation. Since the crisis in Gaza is not a continuous situation of war and attacks take place from time to time, preventive measures of R2P can be implemented to avoid further losses of civilian lives. Secondly, considering the already existing state of failure of the involved actors in protecting the Gazan population, the international community may adopt reactionary measures under Pillar 3, without including the use of force among the options of enforcement measures.

The so-called inter-state aspect of the crisis, the tri-partite control over the territory, and the way the attacks take place as well as the involvement of other international actors such as the US, make this case unique in terms of the strategies to be followed. Whether we accept Gaza as an occupied territory or as part of the independent state of Palestine, authorities are clearly failing to protect the Gazan population. The stand by of the international community concerning the situation in Gaza is yet another showcase that highlights the urgent necessity for reform for enabling effective implementation of R2P. As in many other cases, the international community's failure to uphold its collective responsibility to prevent or react, or for that matter its recognition of such responsibility in this specific case, reminds us of the necessity to consider changes to the existing machinery of the UN or to R2P. Acharya posits that 'the initial norm goes through a period of contestation, leading to its localization or translation. This might create a feedback/repatriation effect which might travel back to the point of origin of the norm in the transnational space and lead to its modification or qualification'.[35] In this vein, the case of Gaza exemplifies the current failures of R2P while revealing its potential for contributing to the existing system, but which are not possible without modification of the norm.

When urging states to pursue 'an ambitious vision', the Secretary General defines R2P as 'a *principle* that has become a core part of the world's armour for protecting vulnerable populations from the most serious international crimes and violations'.[36] Based on international community's pillar two and pillar three practices of R2P in the last decade, it is possible to contest this definition. Considering that the reports of the Secretary General since 2009 has been addressing the issue of implementation of R2P at different levels as well as the necessity to turn 'words into deeds', it can hardly be claimed that R2P has already become 'a core part of world's armour' in practice. Embracing an idea, or assuming a (moral) responsibility and implementing it are two different things. R2P's unanimous adoption by the General Assembly has been an important first step in terms of the norm's inclusion in the machinery of the UN. Nevertheless, the compromises made throughout the institutionalization in order to achieve consensus also compromised the integrity and the potential impact of R2P in making a positive change in the existing system.

Limitations imposed on R2P, such as the emphasis on prevention, the move away from recognizing the importance of collective forceful action in cases of dire necessity, the dependence of R2P's sanctioning on the authority of the Security Council without any official restraint on the veto right of the P5, lack of legal obligations on the part of the international community in upholding its pillar 2 and pillar 3 responsibilities, and last but not least a very narrowly defined scope, can be considered as weak spots of the 'armour'. As displayed by the recent examples of standby in the cases of Syria and Gaza, it remains another question to what extent individual states and the international community have matured in terms of turning their acceptance of a moral responsibility into practice.

R2P's current utility is that it sets a moral standard of appropriate behaviour but this has a very limited impact in terms of constraining and/or changing the behaviour of states. While the internalization of Pillar 1 responsibilities is considered to be the ultimate goal, this is the far-fetched scenario. Considering that Pillar 1 responsibilities of states are already codified in international law, R2P's most genuine added value lies in the responsibilities defined for the international community. We cannot pursue a uniform strategy to respond to every R2P case. Each situation is unique and thus, each response needs to be tailored according to the specificities of each case. Nevertheless, the case-by-case evaluation should not be interpreted in a way to question whether to respond to a case or not. All R2P cases require a response when it is obvious that the state has failed to contain the situation. In this vein, a primary goal regarding the implementation of R2P should be to assure international attention. Currently, this power is vested in the Security Council. As Buchanan and Keohane summarize: 'The central problem with the Security Council is … not what it does, but what it fails to do'.[37] In this vein, R2P's dependency on the Security Council is arguably the greatest handicap before the effective global implementation of the norm. The Security Council suffers from bureaucratic inertia, the veto powers of the P5 hamper the processes of peace-making, it is an organ of the UN which falls short of representing the international community and delivering one voice in the face of international crises.

In his evaluation of the Cold War years, Gaddis notes that 'the United Nations could act only when its most powerful members agreed on the action, an arrangement that obscured the distinction between might and right. And the veto-empowered members of the Council were unlikely to reach such agreements'.[38] Though the conjuncture has changed, the end results have not changed much. For instance, in his speech on behalf of the Caribbean Community, Mr. Wolfe asks:

> How can we guarantee that the Security Council will refrain from the use of the veto and will not be stymied into inaction in future cases where crimes of genocide, ethnic cleansing, war crimes and crimes against humanity have occurred, are occurring or are on the brink of occurring? This is one area where urgent reform of the Security Council is required and around which virtual unanimity exists.[39]

As seen in the case of Gaza, draft resolutions are discussed in a venue which is not representative of the international community and can be blocked by any of the P5 depending on their alliances/alignments, and thus prevent the further discussion of peaceful resolutions to conflicts. Thus, in making R2P to realize its full potential without changing its scope, radical reforms in the machinery of the UN are necessary.

Ban Ki-moon notes: 'If the General Assembly is to play a leading role in shaping a United Nations response, then all 192 Member States should share the responsibility to make it an effective instrument for advancing the principles relating to R2P expressed so clearly in paragraphs 138 and 139 of the Summit Outcome'.[40] One of the important propositions of the ICISS in its report on R2P was the consideration of the General

Assembly as a 'right authority' that could replace the Security Council in cases of deadlock or inaction. This proposition was not taken up in the negotiations on the World Summit Outcome Document, so that paragraphs 138 and 139 did not empower the General Assembly with any explicit authority regarding implementation. In this vein, Ban's proposition reminds of a missing component, and leads to the question of to what extent the Assembly can play a genuine leading role if it cannot override the Security Council in cases of deadlock.

As observed in the case of the ongoing violence in Gaza and the increasing death toll, waiting on the political willingness of the involved parties and the Security Council should not be the only option. In order to make the system more efficient, a more representative organ of the UN needs to be enabled to speak for the world without any state having powers to block a decision. In this vein, the General Assembly should be empowered as the deciding authority with binding powers, while R2P cases should be referred to the Assembly by the Secretary General upon the independent or joint recommendations of the Human Rights Council and the Joint Office of the Special Advisers. Without carrying R2P to a higher level, that is beyond a moral norm, we cannot expect to break the cyclical patterns of failure.

At the completion of its very first decade following its unanimous adoption, R2P continues to be severely criticized and has already been pronounced dead. Hehir argues that R2P is 'sound and fury signifying nothing'.[41] Kersten posits: 'While it may have begun as an "R2P compliant" effort to protect civilians, NATO's intervention in Libya soon became an exercise in regime change. All roads to hell are indeed paved with good intentions, but the particular road named R2P has already proven to be especially and opulently well paved with them!'[42] While it is difficult to challenge the argument that R2P has yet proved to be of value, it can hardly be argued that R2P has moved beyond rhetoric in a way to be a tool of abuse in cases like Libya.

In conclusion, though R2P can be a favourable framework for protecting civilians in intra-state and unique cases of inter-state crises, with its current limitations it is far from making an impact. As Annan puts it: 'The current architecture of managing global affairs is broken and needs to be fixed. ... We cannot continue to run the world based on countries that won a war 60 years ago'.[43]

Acknowledgements

The author owes special thanks to Defne Günay and Ömür Atmaca for their valuable comments on this article.

Funding

An earlier version of this work was supported as a Scientific Research Project by Hacettepe University.

Notes

1. Gözen Ercan, Pınar. 'R2P: From Slogan to an International Ethical Norm.' *Uluslararasi Iliskiler* [*International Relations*] 43, no. 1 (2014): 35–52.
2. Finnemore, Martha and Sikkink, Kathryn, 'International Norm Dynamics and Political Change.' *International Organization* 52, no. 4 (2008): 887–917.
3. Ibid., 869.
4. Ibid., 900.
5. Ibid., 895, 902.
6. Ibid., 902.
7. Checkel, Jeffrey, 'Process Tracing.' *Qualitative Methods in International Relations: A Pluralist Guide*, edited by Audie Klotz and Deepa Prakash (New York: Palgrave Macmillan, 2008), esp. 117.
8. Coleman, Kathrina P., 'Locating Norm Diplomacy: Venue Change in International Norm Negotiations.' *European Journal of International Relations* 19, no. 1 (2013): 163–186, esp. 167.
9. Acharya, Amitav, 'The R2P and Norm Diffusion: Towards A Framework of Norm Circulation.' *Global Responsibility to Protect* 5, no. 4 (2013): 466–479.
10. Ibid., 471.
11. Weiss, Thomas G., 'Military Humanitarianism: Syria Hasn't Killed it.' *The Washington Quarterly* 37, no. 1 (2014): 7–20.
12. United Nations General Assembly. *2005 World Summit Outcome*. A/Res/60/1 (15 September, 2005), esp. 27–28.
13. International Commission of Intervention and State Sovereignty (ICISS), *The Responsibility to Protect* (Ottawa: International Development Research Centre, 2001), esp. viii.
14. United Nations General Assembly, 99th Preliminary Meeting, A/63/PV.99 (24 July 2009), esp. 25.
15. Ibid., 8.
16. Hehir, Aidan, 'Is Gaza in Israel? R2P and Inter-State Crises.' *Justice in Conflict.* (2014) Available at: http://justiceinconflict.org/2014/07/23/is-gaza-in-israel-r2p-and-inter-state-crises [accessed: 4 June 2015].
17. United Nations Security Council, *Statement by the President of the Security Council: Protection of Civilians in Armed Conflict,* S/PRST/2014/13 (12 February 2014).
18. BBC, *David Cameron Describes Blockaded Gaza as a 'Prison'.* (2010) Available at: http://www.bbc.com/news/world-middle-east-10778110 (accessed 26 May 2015).
19. United Nations General Assembly, *Human Rights Situation in Palestine and Other Occupied Arab Territories: Report of the Special Rapporteur on the Situation of Human Rights in the Palestinian Territories Occupied Since 1967,* John Dugard, A/HRC/7/17 (21 January 2008).
20. BBC, *Guide: Why are Israel and the Palestinians fighting Over Gaza?* (2015) Available at: http://www.bbc.co.uk/newsround/20436092) (accessed 26 May 2015).
21. United Nation News Centre, *Gaza: Ban Condemns Latest Deadly Attack Near UN School as 'Moral Outrage and Criminal Act'* (2014). Available at: http://www.un.org/apps/news/story.asp?NewsID=48396#.VZEY7GDldFI (accessed 25 May 2015).
22. Lynch, Colum, 'U.N. Chief: Israel Responsible for "Reprehensible" School Attack.' *Foreign Policy* (2014). Available at: http://foreignpolicy.com/2014/07/31/ u-n-chief-israel-responsible-for-reprehensible-school-attack/) (accessed 6 July 2015).
23. Cassidy, John, 'Israeli Pullback Won't Quell Questions About "War Crimes",' *The New Yorker* (2014). Available at: http://www.newyorker. com/news/john-cassidy/israeli-pullback-wont-quell-questions (accessed 6 July 2015).
24. Ibid.
25. Lynch, 2014.
26. McKoy, Terrence, 'Why Hamas Stores its Weapons Inside Hospitals, Mosques and Schools.' *Washington Post.* (2014). Available at: http://www.washingtonpost.com/news/morning-mix/wp/2014/07/31/why-hamas-stores-its-weapons-inside-hospitals-mosques-and-schools/ (accessed 6 July 2015).
27. McKoy, 2014.
28. Cassidy, 2014.
29. United Nations General Assembly, *Implementing the Responsibility to Protect*, A/63/677 (2009), esp. 23.
30. Ibid., 11.

31. Booth, William and Eglash, Ruth. 'Palestinian Move at International Criminal Court Signals a Volatile New Stage.' *Washington Post.* (2015). Available at: http://www.washingtonpost.com/world/middle_east/palestinian-move-at-international-criminal-court-signals-a-volatile-new-stage/2015/01/18/15336c6e-9ed5-11e4-86a3-1b56f64925f6_story.html (accessed 18 June 2015).
32. Booth and Eglash, 2015.
33. United Nations General Assembly, *Implementing the Responsibility to Protect*, A/63/677 (2009), esp. 26–27.
34. United National General Assembly – Security Council, *Fulfilling Our Collective Responsibility: International Assistance and the Responsibility to Protect*, A/68/947 – S/2014/449 11 July 2014.
35. Acharya, Amitav. 'The R2P and Norm Diffusion: Towards A Framework of Norm Circulation.' *Global Responsibility to Protect*, 5, 466-479 (2013), esp. 471.
36. United Nations General Assembly – Security Council, *Fulfilling Our Collective Responsibility: International Assistance and the Responsibility to Protect*, A/68/947 – S/2014/449 11 July 2014.
37. Buchanan, Allen and Keohane, Robert, 'Precommitment Regimes for Intervention: Supplementing the Security Council.' *Ethics and International Affairs* 25, no. 1 (2011): 41–63, esp. 51.
38. Gaddis, John Lewis, *The Cold War: A New History* (New York: The Penguin Press, 2005), esp. 159.
39. United Nations General Assembly, 100th Preliminary Meeting, A/63/PV.100 (28 July 2009), esp. 6.
40. United Nations General Assembly, *Implementing the Responsibility to Protect*, A/63/677 (2009), esp. 27.
41. Hehir, 2010.
42. Kersten, Mark, 'R2P isn't a Useful Framework for Gaza – Or Anything.' *Justice in Conflict* (2014). Available at: http://justiceinconflict.org/2014/07/25/r2p-isnt-a-useful-framework-for-gaza-or-anything/#more-5512 (accessed 16 June 2015).
43. Hooper, Simon, Annan: 'World Faces "Crisis of Governance".' *CNN* (2009). Available at: http://edition.cnn.com/2009/BUSINESS/01/28/davos.wef.annan/index.html?eref=rss_ (accessed 2 June 2015).

R2P and the Syrian crisis: when semantics becomes a matter of life or death

Sonja Grover

Lakehead University, Faculty of Education, Ontario, Canada

The proposition advanced here is that the failure of the international community to implement R2P respecting the Syrian situation is itself an 'act of aggression' against the sovereignty of the Syrian State which derives from the sovereignty of the people and does not reside in the Assad regime or any particular Syrian regime. The framing of the responsibility to protect (R2P) and its potential implementation in any particular context, such as Syria, is tragically most often reduced to a semantic game version of Roulette with life or death consequences, with the latter more probable the longer the members of the UN Security Council with veto power play the game and stall on action by force where no peaceful options can end the mass atrocities. Hence human rights advocates must play the semantic game more deftly if they are to be positioned to contribute to saving civilian lives. Here follows then a tentative, but perhaps in some ways audacious attempt at just such semantic gamesmanship in support of R2P as not only a viable principle; but one which goes to the heart of the international rule of law, the intent and meaning of the UN Charter and the very credibility of the UN as a mechanism for the promotion of human rights and the achievement of international peace and security.

The semantics of defining the act of aggression

The proposition here is that the use of force to prevent or end genocide, war crimes, ethnic cleansing and crimes against humanity (the crimes which trigger responsibility to protect [R2P]) does not constitute the State 'act of aggression'[1] or the 'crime of aggression regarding the conduct of individuals;'[2] the latter as defined under the Rome Statute[3] where all other options have failed even when not authorized by the UNSC. Rather, on the view here, the situation is quite the converse: resistance by member States of the UN Security Council (hereafter referred to as the 'resistant State members') to implementation of R2P (where, for instance, a particular regime continues to subject its peoples to the grave mass atrocity crimes designated as covered by R2P) itself constitutes the State act of aggression and potentially then the crime of aggression with regard to those persons most responsible.[4] This, in that the failure to act to implement R2P by force where all else fails, renders the 'resistant State members' complicit against the sovereignty *of the people* upon which

State sovereignty is grounded under the UN Charter as implicitly if not explicitly reflected in the following excerpt, among possible others, from the Charter proper:

> Article 1
> The Purposes of the United Nations are:
>
> 2. To develop *friendly relations among nations based on respect for the principle of equal rights and self-determination of peoples*, and to take other appropriate measures to strengthen universal peace.
>
> 3. To achieve international cooperation in … promoting and encouraging *respect for human rights and for fundamental freedoms for all …*
>
> 4. To be a center for harmonizing the actions of nations in the attainment of *these common ends.* (emphasis added)[5]

The UN Charter explicitly refers to friendly relations between States being preconditioned on 'equal rights and self-determination *of peoples*' hence re-affirming that State sovereignty is a derivative of the inalienable human right of the people in any particular jurisdiction to chart their own destiny. There is no doubt that totalitarian regimes do not then have legitimacy but the international community has chosen to look the other way in part given the logistical, political and strategic realities of a nuclear world. However we are discussing here implementation of R2P in a State such as Syria where such action *is* yet feasible. In this regard recall that the UN Charter does *not*, in principle at least, provide unfettered freedom to the member States to do as they might in regards to treatment of their peoples based on a claim of State sovereignty:

> Article 2.
> All Members,[6] in order to ensure to all of them the rights and benefits resulting from membership, shall fulfil in good faith the obligations assumed by them in accordance with the present Charter.[7]

Clearly the launch of chemical attacks on one's own people – as has been alleged occurred in Syria at the behest of the Assad regime in some, if not most, of the instances – is not consistent with the responsibility of UN member States in respect of the State's peoples.[8] It has been said that:

> The ICISS [International Commission on Intervention and State Sovereignty] report[9] turned humanitarian intervention on its head – shifting the focus from the rights of states (rights to intervene vs rights to territorial integrity) *to* the rights of individuals and the responsibility of states and, ultimately, the international community to protect those rights. *Rather than the subject having to demonstrate fidelity to his sovereign, the state had to justify itself to its Citizens.* (emphasis added)[10]

Respectfully the current author would suggest, in contrast to the above proposition, that in fact the ICISS report returned States back to consideration of the original intent and meaning of the UN Charter. The ICISS report then, on the analysis here, rights the turning on its head of that treaty resulting from repeated *jus cogens* violations becoming the 'new normal'[11] and being falsely appropriated by States as allegedly within their prerogative under exercise of sovereign power of the State. The preamble to the UN Charter, while not binding law, nonetheless gives guidance as to the proper interpretation of the treaty. The preamble makes it clear that international peace and security is to be founded on respect for human rights and is not separate and apart from that matter. Even more significant is perhaps that the UN Charter is written from the perspective *of the peoples* of the UN and hence relies on the sovereignty of the people, what has been referred to as 'popular sovereignty':[12]

WE THE PEOPLES OF THE UNITED NATIONS
DETERMINED

to save succeeding generations from the scourge of war, which twice in our lifetime has brought untold sorrow to mankind, and

to *reaffirm faith in fundamental human rights, in the dignity and worth of the human person, in the equal rights* of men and women and of nations large and small, and

to establish conditions under which *justice and respect for the obligations arising from treaties and other sources of international law* can be maintained, and
to promote social progress and better standards of life in larger freedom. (emphasis added)[13]

The preamble is in essence a version of the more modern colloquial expression 'no justice no peace' which can be interpreted also to mean that the status quo and stability is not equivalent to peace and security where there is no justice; justice requiring as a precondition respect for the fundamental human rights of every human being. The UN Charter preamble in fact makes it clear that resort to war is potentially a necessary and legitimate option in certain circumstances:

... to ensure, by the acceptance of principles and the institution of methods, that *armed force shall not be used, save in the common interest.* (emphasis added)[14]

The issue of implementing R2P in Syria by force if necessary has been largely debated in the UN Security Council in terms of: (1) whether war can be/is ever a legitimate option when implementing R2P; and (2) whether use of such force violates, for instance, article 2(4) of the UN Charter. However, the issue of using force to implement R2P where all else fails, it is here suggested, is to be properly decided first and foremost upon: (1) the fact that the nature of the threat to the basic human rights of a certain people (here, for instance, wherever established, the threat to the Syrian people by the Assad regime) triggers the pre-existing 'common interest' (explicitly referenced in the UN Charter purpose) to preserve and protect those human rights; and (2) the fact that Article 2(4) requires, by implication, that any threat or use of force be consistent with the UN Charter purpose and principles which in fact includes protection of *jus cogens* norms including those related to fundamental human rights. The preamble to the UN Charter makes it clear that the fundamental human rights and right of self determination of all peoples are central to and a significant part of the pre-existing axiomatic 'common interest' referred to in that preamble. Furthermore, Article 2(4) makes it clear that it is a violation of the UN Charter to use force or the threat of force in a manner that is 'inconsistent with the Purposes of the United Nations':

CHAPTER I
PURPOSES AND PRINCIPLES

Article 2

4. All Members shall refrain in their international relations from the threat or use of force against the territorial integrity or political independence *of any state,*[15] or *in any other manner inconsistent with the Purposes of the United Nations.* (emphasis added)[16]

Clearly, the protection of the fundamental human rights and human dignity of all peoples as foundational to international peace and security is *not* inconsistent with the purposes of the UN and is in fact articulated in the UN Charter as a core purpose ('common interest')[17] of the UN both in the preamble and at Article One. Yet; through various semantic games that 'common interest' has been equated to discretionary 'humanitarian intervention' which is not clearly grounded on the R2P obligations of the UN Security Council under the UN Charter. At what point those human rights violations (threatened or actual) are egregious enough to warrant UN Security Council involvement via the use of authorized threats of or use of force to prevent and/or end such international atrocity crimes is of course very much coloured by political and strategic State interests. Hence, as we all know, the international community has since World War II tolerated many mass atrocities of varying scales in diverse States on more than one continent. That particular aspect of disingenuousness, however, is not the focus of this discussion. Rather we concern ourselves here as to whether the UN Charter prohibits UN Security Council action to implement R2P in Syria by threat of the use of force or use of force if and when necessary as the last available option. In considering then any actual or perceived UN Charter admonitions regarding UN Security Council authorized use of force in a circumstance such as the Syrian situation recall also the following guidance from the Vienna Law of Treaties:

Article 31, GENERAL RULE OF INTERPRETATION 1. *A treaty shall be interpreted* in good faith in accordance with the ordinary meaning to be given to the terms of the treaty in their context and *in the light of its object and purpose.* 2. *The context for the purpose of the interpretation of a treaty shall comprise, in addition to the text, including its preamble* and annexes ... (c) Any relevant rules of international law applicable in the relations between the parties. ... Article 32. SUPPLEMENTARY MEANS OF INTERPRETATION Recourse may be had to supplementary means of interpretation, including the preparatory work of the treaty and the circumstances of its conclusion, in order to confirm the meaning resulting from the application of article 31, or to determine the meaning when the interpretation according to article 31: (a) Leaves the meaning ambiguous or obscure; or (b) *Leads to a result which is manifestly absurd or unreasonable.* (emphasis added)[18]

It has been pointed out here previously that the preamble of the UN Charter, as well as Article 2(4), are grounded on respect for human rights as a key precondition for international peace and security i.e. UN Charter Article 2(4) is not to be read out of context separate and apart from Article 1(2) for instance. Hence, it is suggested that interpreting Article 2(4) of the UN Charter to allow for the threat of force or use of force where a State is shown to have committed atrocities and declines to cease and desist from committing mass atrocity of the gravest kind upon its people is consistent with the rules of interpretation as set out at Article 31 of the Vienna Law of Treaties.[19] Further to suggest that Article 2(4) *precludes* the use of force or threat of force in a situation where, for instance, a regime may be shown to have used chemical weapons on its people and to have committed other atrocities, is to reach a manifestly absurd and unreasonable conclusion inconsistent with customary and *jus cogens* law prohibiting all forms of torture as well as with international law such as the Chemical Weapons Convention.[20] Since crimes against humanity under the Rome Statute are considered manifestly unlawful[21] insofar as the Assad regime and other parties within Syria are responsible for such crimes; on this basis it is also patently unreasonable to suggest that Article 2(4) of the UN Charter prohibits the threat of force or use of force when all else fails to stop such international crimes. Further, to consider, where politically expedient, the crimes listed under R2P as simply a matter of internal domestic affairs is: (1) to deny the nature and character of those international crimes, including their manifest unlawfulness; (2) to undermine and significantly erode the moral legitimacy and effectiveness of the rule of international law and to shirk State member responsibility under the UN Charter to fulfil their obligations under the Charter which includes respecting and protecting the human rights of their peoples and all peoples (see UN Charter Articles 1 [2] and 2[2]);[22] and (3) to treat certain States (those committing the grave crimes that should trigger the implementation of R2P) *as above* the rule of international law rather than to treat them as equal in their *rights and responsibilities* as per the UN Charter Article 2(1).[23] To implement R2P in the case of Syria through the threat of or actual use of force as and when necessary is, on the contention here, neither a breach of the UN Charter nor an act of aggression nor reducible to an alleged 'punishment' of a regime contrary (as this author understands it) to the suggestions of some scholars as shown in the following statements:

> ... the idea of 'punishing' a regime for unlawful action under jus in bello through resort to the threat or use of force without a collective security mandate, is flawed. ... This reasoning disregards that there are other competing, and at least as important, 'red lines' that require respect, i. e. Articles 2(1) and (4) of the UN Charter which constitutes a prohibition of aggression and a viable collective security system.[24]

Stahn alleges that in the discourse on Syria:

> Humanitarianism was invoked as entitlement to justify action that is 'punitive' in nature, outside the realm of self-defence or collective security.[25]

In contrast to Stahn's contention, as explained here, the proposition of the current author is that implementing R2P by force if and as necessary in Syria is consistent with Article 2(1) (2) and 2(4) of the UN Charter since the use of force is *not ipso facto* equivalent to an act of aggression nor intervention as an attack on the sovereignty of the State. Rather implementing R2P by force *if necessary* is permissible under the means permissible per the UN Charter Article 2(4) as it serves the purposes set out at Article 1 (2) and (3) relating to safeguarding the rights and freedoms of the peoples of a State which underpins the sovereignty of that State.[26] Instead it is the failure to act and implement R2P by all means necessary in fact that constitutes a breach of Articles 1 (2) and (3) of the UN Charter and renders the 'resistant member States' of the UN Security Council arguably, to some extent at least, complicit in attacking the sovereignty of the peoples at risk. This in that the resistant member States of the UN Security Council (those which veto implementation of R2P by force where there is no other option and where the mass atrocity crimes covered by R2P are, on objective evidence, occurring), it is argued, act beyond their jurisdiction under the UN Charter. That is; they through their veto at the UNSC violate their obligations under Article 2 (2) of the UN Charter in respect of Article 1 (2) (3) (4) in declining to implement R2P using the last resort where necessary (where all peaceful means have failed); that is where the offending State considered for R2P action continues or is at imminent risk of perpetrating the international mass atrocity crimes that trigger the applicability of R2P (those acts being other than a matter of the State in question's sovereign prerogative under Article 2(7) of the UN Charter).

Article 2(4) permits then, on the analysis here: (1) the threat of the use or actual use of force where *consistent* with the UN Charter purpose of the need to foster friendly international relations between States, and international peace and security[27] *based on* the rule of international law, justice, respect for fundamental human rights and the freedoms of all the peoples of the member States (which would hence include also the Syrian civilians opposed to the Assad regime); and (2) the threat of or actual use of force without a UN Security Council mandate where some or all of the UN Security Council permanent members with veto power decline to implement R2P by the means necessary.[28] The current author then (based on the above analysis of the meaning of UN Charter Articles 2 [4] and 2 [7]; and the purposes of the UN Charter) challenges the notion that R2P, implemented by threat of or use of force where required, even where a UN Security Council vote of authorization was not achievable, undermines the concept of R2P. On this point then let us consider the following statements which express a contrary view:

> It is partly a relief that R2P has not been applied to justify military intervention in the absence of a Security Council mandate. Any attempt to interpret the concept in this direction would have presented a further attack on the damaged credibility of the concept. The very rationale of punishing the violation of a taboo ('red line') through unilateral military action appears to be incompatible with the underlying foundations of the R2P doctrine. R2P is not a punitive concept. It is centred on the idea of protecting civilian populations, rather than sanctioning moral outrage, horror and fear caused by the use of a specific category of weapons, such as chemical weapons. Its development into a punitive tool – a 'responsibility to punish' state action or inaction – stands partly in contrast to its humanitarian rationale and would increase fears of instrumentalization that have haunted the concept since its inception.[29]

> On the other hand the elements of a so called timely and decisive response are far more problematic. Articles 2.4 and 2.7 of the Charter prohibit the use of force. Article 24 confers on the UN Security Council responsibility to maintain peace and Article 39 to determine any threat, breach of peace or aggression and measures to restore peace. Article 41 spells out breaking diplomatic relations, sanctions, and embargoes. If these fail Article 42 empowers force. None of these would cover responsibility to protect unless the situation is a threat to international peace and security. *The Security Council's powers are not directed even against violations of international legal obligations but against an immediate threat to international peace and security.* (emphasis added)[30]

It is here argued that immediate threats to international peace and security are very often sparked by the violation of *jus cogens* and of international customary norms regarding the proper treatment of civilians and the State population in general. Furthermore, as discussed previously, the UN Charter Article 1 obligation of the UN Security Council in regards to dealing with immediate threats to peace is linked to international peace and security grounded on justice and respect for human rights. Hence it is, respectfully, on the view here, misdirected to suggest that: 'The Security Council's powers are not directed even against violations of international legal obligations but against an immediate threat to international peace and security.' [31] Rather the responsibilities and conduct of the UN Security Council, consistent with the principles set out in the UN Charter, are to be understood in terms of international legal obligation including those in respect of populations at risk. Indeed the rise of ISIS is instructive on the very point that ignoring, where established, gross violations of human rights perpetrated by a State on its own people and sometimes also on neighbouring peoples erodes international law and order generally and leaves a vacuum that can and commonly is filled by extremists who significantly threaten international peace and security.

In brief, on the view here, the obligation of UN State members to implement R2P thus honouring their R2P (i.e. using the threat of force or force as a last resort) supersede where there is an *extra jurisdictional failure* of certain of the permanent members of the UN Security Council (through a veto) to meet their R2P responsibilities (the latter being clearly implicated in the purposes of the UN organization as set out in particular at Article 1 and in the preamble).[32] It is to be emphasized that the absence of a UN Security Council mandate for the threat of or use of force in implementing R2P where all else has failed is *not* tantamount to an absence of a 'collective common interest' (the latter referring to that common interest defined under the UN Charter with reference to the purposes of the UN Charter and the legitimate means available to meet R2P obligations under the UN Charter). Paragraph 139 of the World Summit Outcome Document on R2P contemplates the UN being able to take collective action through the UN Security Council *in accordance with the Charter* to meet its R2P obligations:

> The international community, through the UN, also has the responsibility to use appropriate diplomatic, humanitarian and other peaceful means, in accordance with Chapters VI and VII of the Charter, to help protect populations from genocide, war crimes, ethnic cleansing and crimes against humanity. In this context, we are prepared to take collective action, in a timely and decisive manner, through the Security Council, in accordance with the Charter ... should peaceful means be inadequate and national authorities manifestly fail to protect their populations from genocide, war crimes, ethnic cleansing and crimes against humanity.[33]

In other words, the outcome document contemplates the UN Security Council providing a remedy 'should peaceful means be inadequate and national authorities manifestly fail to protect their populations from genocide, war crimes, ethnic cleansing and crimes against humanity' which UNSC remedy could include the threat of or use of force if necessary. There is no basis in international law, however, it is here contended, to suggest that should the UN Security Council fail to meet its obligation under the UN Charter to provide a remedy for a State's failure to protect its population from the international crimes covered by R2P that something less than collective action vetted by the Security Council is, as a result, legally inconsistent with the UN Charter. The converse is in fact, on the analysis here, the case; namely that such action, even without the UN Security Council's blessing/authorization (where the latter was not achievable), meets the solemn responsibility of member States so taking action to implement R2P (a responsibility under the stated express Purposes of the UN Charter (which by implication evoke R 2P at Article 1[2] [3]) to prevent and end manifestly unlawful mass atrocity crimes constituting genocide, war crimes, ethnic cleansing and crimes against humanity). Put differently, to say that the exercise of threat or use of force through 'collective action'[34] in the implementation of R2P would be 'through the Security Council, *in accordance with the Charter*'[35] is implicitly to assume that the UN Security Council at all times is obligated to act and *will act* in accord with the UN Charter. Where the latter is not the case and the UN Security Council instead, *through its inaction*, is in fact complicit in perpetuating the crimes of genocide, war crimes, ethnic cleansing and/or crimes against humanity in a particular jurisdiction; R2P may be lawfully implemented, it is here contended, by threat of or use of force where the only option even without UNSC authorization. Hence para. 139 of the World Summit Outcome Document, it is here suggested, releases the member States to take action on their own under R2P to prevent or end the aforementioned mass atrocity international crimes where the UNSC does not meet its R2P obligations. That is, it is the UN Charter that guides the actions of member States and hence the UN Security Council does not have authority (through vetoes by UNSC permanent members or through the actions of any of its members) to subvert the requirements of the UN Charter and to preserve the status quo where that, in the particular circumstance, is *not* equivalent to preserving international peace and security based on principles of justice and respect for the equality of human rights and right to self-determination of all peoples as per Article one of the UN Charter.[36] Respectfully, it is on the view here, misguided for the President of the UN General Assembly as spokesperson to appear to lay the groundwork for justification of UN Security Council inaction where such occurs in the face of the mass atrocity crimes that should trigger the R2P by threat of or use of force if required:

> Colonialism and interventionism used responsibility to protect arguments. National Sovereignty in developing countries is a necessary condition for stable access to political, social and economic rights and it took enormous sacrifices to recover this sovereignty and ensure these rights for their populations.[37]

'Colonialists' and 'interventionists', in the sense referred to in the preceding quote, act upon their own agendas and not those of the victims of mass atrocity crimes who are pleading for the international community's help and protection as is the case according to independent NGO reports with, for instance, the Syrian civilian opponents of the Assad regime in Syria.[38] There is, given the circumstance, no 'sovereignty' barrier to R2P implementation in Syria by the means necessary including threat of or use of force should that be the case. While UN documents on R2P refer to the fact that "The people have inalienable rights and are sovereign"[39] nevertheless these documents; such as the concept note on R2P, too often rely on claims to sovereignty *to fail to implement* R2P that are in fact *not* grounded on the will of the majority of the suffering population:

> It [R2P] should not become a 'jemmy in the door of national sovereignty'.
> The concept of responsibility to protect is a sovereign's obligation and, if it is exercised by an external agency, sovereignty passes from the people of the target country to it. The people to be protected are transformed from bearers of rights to wards of this agency.[40]

The current author would dispute the notion that sovereignty *ever* 'passes from the people'. Rather the regime in power is but a steward of that sovereignty belonging to the people and is not imbued with the jurisdiction to oppress its own people (i.e. through the international crimes of genocide, war crimes, ethnic cleansing and/or crimes against humanity) on the pretence of necessary means in the exercise of sovereignty. It is the responsibility of the international community to ensure that *sovereignty remains with the people* at all times; neither usurped by the regime in power and the international community's inaction and unwillingness to implement R2P in the face of mass atrocities nor by an 'external agency' with false pretence under *the guise* of implementing R2P. The quote above, on the current analysis, inadvertently sets up *a false* 'catch 22' wherein the R2P becomes a 'responsibility to *inaction*' notwithstanding the suffering of a people at the hands of their 'sovereign' (the ruling regime). This on the erroneous claim that implementing R2P (which in fact is designed to acknowledge the sovereignty of the people and restore *their* power) somehow routinely transforms the no longer victimized into 'wards' of those who have restored the people's power. While it is valid to point out that the concept of R2P can be abused in its implementation; the remedy is to work to prevent this through means other than an abandonment of the international community's R2P where the State is unwilling and/or unable to do so for its own people. The UN concept note on R2P furthermore suggests that:

... it is the preventive aspects of responsibility to protect that are both important and practicable but these need both precise understanding and political will.[41]

While it is no doubt correct that 'the preventive aspects of responsibility to protect ... are both important and practicable', at the same time the reality is that sometimes only threat of or use of force will 'prevent' the next round of mass atrocities in a cycle of violence targeting the population (especially the civilian opposition) for mass atrocity international crimes. The President of the General Assembly in addition states in his concept note on R2P:

> Collective security is a specialized instrument for dealing with threats to international peace and security and not an enforcement mechanism for international human rights law and international humanitarian law. The discretion given to the Security Council to decide a threat to international peace and security implies a variable commitment totally different from the consistent alleviation of suffering embodied in the responsibility to protect. The Security Council has not been willing to relinquish to the International Criminal Court its power to determine crimes of aggression.[42]

The UN General Assembly President's statement 'collective security is a specialized instrument for dealing with threats to international peace and security and not an enforcement mechanism for international human rights law and international humanitarian law', respectfully, on the view here, largely ignores the fact that *jus ad bellum* and *jus in bello* are arguably, in many instances, intricately intertwined. The blocking by a State such as Syria of humanitarian aid to civilians under the Assad regime[43] coupled with, where established, mass atrocities in part by the regime committed against the Syrian peoples (i.e. against any Syrian government-perceived Syrian civilian opposition) as alleged by Amnesty International and Human Rights Watch amongst other independent parties[44] (conduct contrary to the rules of *jus in bello*) arguably gives rise to the legitimate use of threat of or use of force under *jus ad bellum*. Were this not the correct reading then 'international peace and security' would *de facto be defined essentially as maintaining the status quo* and, even when that status quo is achieved through grave violations of human rights and humanitarian law by infliction of mass atrocity crimes upon the peoples of certain of the member State(s) of the UN by their own State regimes, it would have to be considered acceptable under the UN Charter; the latter then clearly *not* an interpretation consistent with the purposes of the UN Charter.

Let us next consider the President of the UN General Assembly's suggestion that to implement R2P by force to prevent or end mass atrocity crimes without UNSC endorsement, notwithstanding whether force in the circumstance may have been the only option, would be contrary to the ILCO draft Article 50 on R2P:

> In case peremptory norms are breached, the International Law Commission's draft Articles on State Responsibility specify two sets of consequences: (1) a positive obligation of States 'to cooperate to bring the serious breach to an end through lawful means' [Article 41 (i)]; and (2) not to recognize as lawful a situation created by the breach and not to render aid in maintaining that situation [Article 41 (ii)]. *The use of military force is expressly excluded from the realm of possible counter measures. Article 50 (i) (a) categorically says that counter-measures shall not affect 'the obligation to refrain from the threat or use of force as embodied in the Charter of the United Nations'.* (emphasis added)[45]

Let us examine the ILC Article 50 below therefore more closely:

Article 50. Obligations not affected by countermeasures
1. Countermeasures shall not affect:

(*a*) the obligation to refrain from the threat or use of force *as embodied in the Charter of the United Nations*;

(*b*) obligations for the protection of fundamental human rights;

(*c*) obligations of a humanitarian character prohibiting reprisals;

(*d*) other obligations under peremptory norms of general international law. (emphasis added)[46]

The obligation under ILC Draft Article 50(1)(a) on State Responsibility to 'refrain from the threat or use of force' *as embodied in the Charter of the United Nation*s is to be understood as an admonition that comes with a qualifier. This in that the UN Charter Article 2(4), which is implicitly relied on in the ILC Draft Article 50(1)(a); refers to not using the threat of force or force 'against the territorial integrity or political independence of any state, or *in any other manner inconsistent with the Purposes of the United Nations'*.[47] Article 2 (4) of the *Charter* does *not* require that so-called 'friendly relations' be achieved by ignoring a State's violation of peremptory norms when all peaceful means by other States to prevent and/or end them occurring in the impugned State have failed. The argument here has been then that the implementation of R2P by threat of or use of force, where the only option left to prevent and/or end mass atrocity crimes that trigger R2P,[48] does *not* constitute the threat or use of force as an act of aggression – it is *not* 'inconsistent with the Purposes of the United Nations' but rather precisely the converse. Hence Article 50 1(a) of the Draft ILC articles on the Responsibility of States for Internationally Wrongful Acts in fact does *not*, on the analysis here, in the proper circumstance preclude the threat of or use of force in implementing R2P. Rather it only precludes the threat of or use of force as an act of State aggression or in some other manner inconsistent with the purposes and principles of the UN Charter (i.e. as an act of aggression such as an attack on the territorial integrity or political independence of the State to which such threat of force or force is applied). Further, Article 50 1(a) of the Draft ILC articles is not to be read in isolation from the rest of Article 50 that refers to State obligations to protect fundamental human rights, humanitarian law and "other obligations under peremptory norms of general international law." While the Draft ILC Article 50 (b)(c)(d) refer to these latter obligations in terms of their necessary observance in the manner of implementation of countermeasures of an injured State party; it is implicit in this that such *protection obligations* exist and may therefore also trigger R2P. Taken together it is clear then that the threat of force or the use of force may be used consistent with the purposes and principles of the UN Charter to protect the sovereignty of a people whose fundamental human rights, humane treatment and/or rights under *jus cogens* and other customary international law have been violated by their own and/or proxy States.

The threat or use of force as a last option must be implemented in a manner so as to alleviate the suffering of a people at imminent risk of or enduring the grave crimes that trigger R2P. Tragically inadvertent mistakes costing innocent lives may occur on occasion in the implementation of R2P by force given the realities of the frontline and the particularly brutal tactics of certain extremist groups which commonly use human shields, mix with civilians and otherwise exploit the vulnerabilities of civilians. However, such events need always to be thoroughly investigated and assessed, and where there are human rights violations, those responsible should be held to account through an impartial and independent domestic and/or international judicial process.

The obligation is non-derogable of the States under Article 50 of the Draft ILC articles on State Responsibility to act at all times (even when engaged in counter-measures as an injured party): (1) in a manner consistent with the Purposes of the UN Charter; and (2) so as to honour human rights, humanitarian and *jus cogens* international law. It follows logically then that this obligation must also trigger R2P where necessary and also on occasion where threat of or use of force is the only option available for implementing R2P. To do so is not a violation of the equal sovereignty of all UN member States as articulated in Article 2(1) of the UN Charter but rather the reverse – a manifestation of the fact that all States are *equally obligated* to exercise State sovereignty in a manner that respects the equal human rights of all the peoples of the UN Member States and their right to self-determination.

Further it should be understood that the implementation of R2P by force where necessary is *not a reprisal* for the violation of international peremptory and other norms as referred to by the ILC in Draft Article 50.[49] R2P is not about reprisal; it is in part about taking all reasonable and feasible measures necessary and sufficient to protect a population at imminent risk of and/or enduring genocide, crimes against humanity, war crimes and/or ethnic cleansing. It should also be appreciated that the implementation by threat of or use of force, where necessary, of R2P is not a 'counter-measure' (if properly so characterized) *used as an act of aggression* (by a particular injured State[50] against the State responsible for wrongful acts) and due to the latter element thus inconsistent with the UN Charter. R2P is rather the international community attempting to restore the 'common interest' in peace and security *built on* the international rule of law and justice and *equality of all peoples* consistent with the principles and purpose espoused in the UN Charter by preventing and/or ending the mass atrocity crimes triggering R2P.

Note that the crime of aggression as defined under the amendments to the Rome Statute requires a manifest infringement of the UN Charter ('The act of aggression, by its character, gravity and scale, constituted a manifest violation of the Charter of the United Nations').[51] Recall at the same time that Article 33 of the Rome Statute sets out that ' … orders to commit genocide or crimes against humanity are manifestly unlawful'. It follows that attempts to prevent or stop such international crimes as genocide, crimes against humanity and the crimes, carried out on a systemic and widespread scale of ethnic cleansing and war crimes, can neither be considered as acts of aggression nor as manifestly unlawful.[52] The preamble of the UN Charter contemplates the use of force where necessary to uphold the purposes and principles espoused in the Charter where all else fails and when the international system of justice and friendly relations built on respect for *jus cogens* law and other foundational international law is in jeopardy. The 'common interest' as referred to in the UN Charter is technically *not* defined by the number of UNSC members that have endorsed or blocked the threat or use of force to implement R2P where no other option exists but rather by the purposes and principles of the UN Charter itself. These UN Charter purposes and principles do *not* countenance achieving a superficial and tenuous international peace and security for the many through the sacrifice of the human dignity and lives of those left at the mercy of their own State and/or proxies inflicting upon them the crimes of genocide, ethnic cleansing, war crimes and/or crimes against humanity.

The threat of or actual use of armed force by a State to protect the population of another State from such mass atrocities as trigger R2P (where all other R2P options have been exhausted and failed) is in fact an act to ensure and restore the *sovereignty of the people*. As is well known, but constantly needs reminding, the sovereignty of the State is not separate and distinct from the sovereignty of the people but rather derives from it. It is a fundamental premise of the international rule of law and *jus cogens* law both that: (1) mass atrocity inflicted upon a population is beyond the jurisdiction of the State engaging in such conduct and hence that; and (2) such State conduct is *not* an exercise of the sovereignty of the State regardless the political organization of that State – democratic or totalitarian. Such gross violations of international law trigger obligations under the UN Charter on the part of the international community relating to the 'common interest' in peace and security *founded on* justice and the rule of international law including respect for fundamental human rights (in other words R2P obligations). That the UN Security Council has too often not taken action to prevent or stop mass atrocities does not substantiate the erroneous inference that the impugned State's involvement in mass atrocity is consistent with the exercise of that State's sovereignty. The all too frequent apoplexy of the member States of the UN Security Council in their failure to implement R2P cannot then find justification in any alleged arguments grounded on sovereignty of the impugned State. The sovereignty of a State is best ensured via protection of the human rights of all its peoples – in part since preservation of the sovereignty of the people is most likely to ensure the State maintaining its territorial integrity and political independence in the longer term.

This author would argue that R2P is furthermore not reducible to humanitarian 'intervention' though humanitarian assistance is one consequence of its implementation. R2P is rather fundamentally premised on the notion that the *jus cogens* rights of the population must be respected if legitimacy is to be accorded to a State claiming both membership in the international community and to be acting in all respects within its sovereign jurisdiction. This view is consistent it is suggested with that of the ICJ:

> *Every State, by virtue of its membership in the international community, has a legal interest in the protection of certain basic rights and the fulfilment of certain essential obligations.* Among these the Court [International Court of Justice] instanced 'the outlawing of acts of aggression, and of genocide, as also ... the principles and rules concerning the basic rights of the human person, including protection from slavery and racial discrimination ... ' (emphasis added) [53]

It has been argued here that R2P implementation by threat or use of force where there is no other option to prevent and/or end the manifestly unlawful international crimes of genocide, systematic mass war crimes, crimes against humanity and mass systematic ethnic cleansing is consistent with the purposes of the UN Charter. In fact it is the failure to implement R2P by threat or use of force where all peaceful means have failed and where such was feasible but not employed, due to UNSC veto for instance, that is manifestly inconsistent with the purposes and principles of the UN Charter. It has been here argued further that permanent UNSC State members that veto the threat or use of force where that is the only option to stop the aforementioned mass atrocity crimes are in fact complicit in an act of aggression on the sovereignty of that State which the vetoing members claim is inviolate regardless its brutalization of its own people.[54] This is the case in that the sovereignty of the State resides wholly with the people of that State who are under siege by their own regime and/or other state or non-state groups or forces. On the legal evaluation here then the failure of the UNSC to endorse the effective implementation of R2P in Syria by the means necessary to end the ongoing mass atrocities is in itself: (1) an act of State aggression by the vetoing States[55] against the sovereignty of Syria (a sovereignty that resides fundamentally with the people of Syria and not the regime whichever that may be); and (2) an act that is manifestly inconsistent with the purposes of the UN Charter and the 'common interest' articulated in the Charter to protect fundamental human rights and humanitarian interests and to ground friendly inter-State relations upon respect for international human rights and *jus cogens* norms.

Notes

1.   Where a regime is the perpetrator of or complicit in mass atrocity through action or non-action in international crimes that trigger R2P, on the analysis here, it has no moral or legal legitimacy under international law.

2.   See Resolution RC/Res.6 http://www.icc-cpi.int/iccdocs/asp_docs/Resolutions/RC-Res.6-ENG.pdf (Crime of Aggression: Amendment to the Rome Statute) (accessed 13 May 2015).

3.   Rome Statute entered into force 1 July, 2002 http://www.icc-cpi.int/nr/rdonlyres/ea9aeff7-5752-4f84-be94-0a655eb30e16/0/rome_statute_english.pdf (accessed 13 May 2015).

4.   This paper does *not* address any potential liability of any sort under international law for delegates of the State (individuals) who serve on the UNSC as agents of their respective States and who on behalf of their State have vetoed necessary life saving R2P implementation measures in the face of incontrovertible evidence of the mass atrocity crimes which are covered by R2P and where peaceful means to end the atrocities have all failed.

5.   UN Charter signed in San Francisco, California, on 26 June 1945 (Article 1) https://treaties.un.org/doc/publication/ctc/uncharter.pdf (accessed 13 May 2015).

6.   'UN Member States Egypt and Syria were original members of the United Nations from 24 October, 1945. Following a plebiscite on 21 February, 1958, The United Arab Republic was established by a union of Egypt and Syria and continued as a single Member. On 13 October, 1961, Syria having resumed its status as an independent State, resumed its separate membership in the United Nations. On 2 September, 1971, the United Arab Republic changed its name to the Arab Republic of Egypt.' (UN listing of member States of the United Nations) http://www.un.org/en/members / (accessed 13 May 2015).

7.   UN Charter signed in San Francisco, California, on 26 June 1945 (Article 2[2]) https://treaties.un.org/doc/publication/ctc/uncharter.pdf (accessed 13 May, 2015).

8.   See UN to examine Syria chemical weapons attacks (BBC News August 2015) http://www.bbc.com/news/world-middle-east-33825861 (accessed 7 August, 2015); UN Security Council Resolution 2118 (2013) http://www.securitycouncilreport.org/atf/cf/%7B65BFCF9B-6D27-4E9C-8CD3-CF6E4FF96FF9%7D/s_res_2118.pdf (accessed 24 May 2015). Also see Resolution 2209 (2015) *"The Security Council, Expresses* deep concern that toxic chemicals have been used as a weapon in the Syrian Arab Republic as concluded with a high degree of confidence by the OPCW Fact-Finding Mission and *notes* that such use of toxic chemicals as a weapon would constitute a violation of resolution 2118 and of the CWC." Adopted by the Security Council at its 7401st meeting, on 6 March 2015 (regarding the use of chlorine; reports are that the Assad regime is using barrel bombs to deliver chlorine as a chemical weapon against his Syrian civilian opposition in violation of international law). See Resolution 2209 (2015) Adopting Resolution 2209 (2015), Security Council Condemns Use of Chlorine Gas as Weapon in Syria (UN Press Release 6 March, 2015) http://www.un.org/press/en/2015/sc11810.doc.htm (accessed 24 May 2015).The claim that the Assad regime is the party responsible cannot be ruled out as improbable given the past chemical attacks in Eastern Ghouta and Mo'damiya areas of Syria attributed to the Assad regime by the international community based in part on evidence collected by independent NGOs such as Amnesty International (see Amnesty International (2015) Syria: Evidence of a fresh war crime as chlorine gas attack kills entire family (17 March 2015); https://www.amnesty.org/en/articles/news/2015/03/syria-war-crime-chlorine-gas-attack/ (accessed 24 May 2015).

9.   International Commission on Intervention and State Sovereignty (2001) The Responsibility to Protect Published by the International Development Research Centre http://responsibilitytoprotect.org/ICISS %20Report.pdf (accessed 25 May, 2015), The current author is in accord with the view expressed in the ICISS aforementioned 2001 report that 'The Security Council should take into account in all its

deliberations that, if it fails to discharge its responsibility to protect in conscience-shocking situations crying out for action, concerned states may not rule out other means to meet the gravity and urgency of that situation – and that the stature and credibility of the UnitedNations may suffer thereby' (viii). Further, this author holds that such actions by States is lawful and consistent with the purposes and principles of the UN Charter where the UNSC does not meet its obligation to implement R2P by proportionate use of military action where all else has failed.

10. Francis, A., Popovski, V., and Sampford, C. eds., *Norms of Protection: Responsibility to Protect, Protection of Civilians and Their Interaction.* (New York: United Nations University Press, 2012,) 4.

11. Since the international crimes that trigger R2P are arguably all *jus cogens* violations (see for example Badescu, C.G., *Humanitarian Intervention and the Responsibility to Protect: Security and Human Rights* [New York: Routledge, 2011], 133); members States of the UN are, on that basis, conferred universal jurisdiction to act to prevent and/or end such grave international mass atrocity crimes where the State that would normally have jurisdiction is unable and/or unwilling to do so even though ostensibly the crimes may be occurring extra-territorially relative to the State implementing R2P

12. "Should popular sovereignty be subjected to attack, the integrity of other rights identified in the UDHR will also be subject to attack" cited from Araujo, R., "Sovereignty, Human Rights, and Self-Determination: The Meaning of International Law", *Fordham international Law Journal* 24, no. 5 (2000): 1477–1532, especially 1480.

13. UN Charter (preamble) signed in San Francisco, California, on 26 June 1945 https://treaties.un.org/doc/publication/ctc/uncharter.pdf (accessed 13 May 2015).

14. UN Charter (preamble) signed in San Francisco, California, on 26 June 1945 https://treaties.un.org/doc/publication/ctc/uncharter.pdf (accessed 13 May 2015).

15. Although R2P is not directed to regime change; the latter may be the by-product of the implementation of R2P in certain instances where force has been the only option remaining to protect the people of that State from its own government or other ruling entity. The political independence of the State is not to be equated with the necessary preservation of any particular regime in power in that State especially when that regime systematically and consistently violates *jus cogens* international law. A state that engages in the crimes covered under R2P is acting beyond its sovereign jurisdiction and hence to stop it doing so is not an attack on territorial integrity or political independence (it is not an attack on State sovereignty)

16. UN Charter (preamble) signed in San Francisco, California, on June 26,1945 (Article 2(4) https://treaties.un.org/doc/publication/ctc/uncharter.pdf (accessed 13 May 2015).

17. UN Charter (preamble) signed in San Francisco, California, on June 26,1945 (Article 2(4) https://treaties.un.org/doc/publication/ctc/uncharter.pdf (accessed 13 May 2015).

18. Vienna Law of Treaties (entered into force 27 January, 1980) (Article 31, 32) https://treaties.un.org/doc/Publication/UNTS/Volume%201155/volume-1155-I-18232-English.pdf (accessed 13 May 2015).

19. Vienna Law of Treaties (entered into force 27 January, 1980) (Article 31) https://treaties.un.org/doc/Publication/UNTS/Volume%201155/volume-1155-I-18232-English.pdf (accessed 13 May 2015).

20. Chemical Weapons Convention (Convention on the Prohibition of the Development, Production, Stockpiling and Use of Chemical Weapons and on their Destruction) (entry into force 1997) http://www.opcw.org/chemical-weapons-convention/ (accessed 13 May 2015).

21. Rome Statute Article 33(2) "Superior orders and prescription of law: For the purposes of this article, orders to commit genocide or crimes against humanity are manifestly unlawful." (Rome Statute Elements of the Crime (Official Records of the Review Conference of the Rome Statute of the International Criminal Court, Kampala, 31 May -11 June 2010, International Criminal Court publication, RC/11) http://www.icc-cpi.int/NR/rdonlyres/336923D8-A6AD-40EC-AD7B-45BF9DE73D56/0/ElementsOfCrimesEng.pdf [accessed 13 May 2015]).

22. UN Charter (preamble) signed in San Francisco, California, on 26 June 1945 (Article 1(2)and 2 (2) https://treaties.un.org/doc/publication/ctc/uncharter.pdf (accessed 13 May 2015).

23. UN Charter (1945): Article 2(1): "'1. The Organization is based on the principle of the sovereign equality of all its Members."

24. Stahn, C., "Syria and the Semantics of Intervention: Aggression and Punishment: On Red Lines and Blurred Lines", *Journal of International Criminal Justice* 11(5) (2013): 955–977, especially 958.

THE RESPONSIBILITY TO PROTECT

25. Stahn, C., "Syria and the Semantics of Intervention: Aggression and Punishment: On Red Lines and Blurred Lines", *Journal of International Criminal Justice* 11(5) (2013): 955–977, especially 960.

26. Implementation of R2P by all means necessary is: (1) the operationalization of the *ergo omnes* obligation of States and simultaneously; (2) an act by the R2P -implementing State or States to prevent the erosion of respect for the rule of international law *based on justice and respect for fundamental human rights* which erosion undermines international peace and security and is inevitable when grave systematic mass atrocity crimes are left to be committed by a State or States unfettered (Contrast the view of Johnson, L.D. *AJIL Unbound* (American Society for International Law) 'United for Peace: Does it Still Serve a Useful Purpose?'(July 15, 2014) 'The difficulty arises with regard to … stopping a genocidal state from murdering parts of its own population. Here, outside the self-defense context and absent a Security Council Chapter VII use of force authorization, it is difficult to see how an Assembly recommendation that States use force squares with the norm reflected in Article 2(4) … ' http://www.asil.org/blogs/%E2%80%9Cuniting-peace%E2%80%9D-does-it-still-serve-any-useful-purpose (accessed 3 July 2015.

27. Recall, for instance, Security Council Resolution 2118 (2013) that 'the use of chemical weapons anywhere constitutes a threat to international peace and security' hence the use of force to prevent such occurrences where no other options are available is *not* inconsistent with Article 2(4) of the UN Charter. At the time of writing there are grounded concerns that the Assad regime likely is continuing the use of chemical weapons against its own people.

28. Recall that Article 24 of the UN Charter (Chapter V) granting the Security Council primary responsibility for upholding international peace and security provides at Article 24(2) that in meeting this obligation the Security Council shall act in accordance with the Purposes and Principles of the United Nations. The latter, it is here argued, necessarily includes in part: (1) maintaining international peace and security grounded on respect for human rights as per Article 1(2) and (2) authorizing the threat or use of force where the aforementioned purpose of the United Nations is sufficiently at risk or compromised and all other options have been exhausted and were unsuccessful.

29. Stahn, C., "Syria and the Semantics of Intervention: Aggression and Punishment: On Red Lines and Blurred Lines", *Journal of International Criminal Justice* 11(5) (2013): 955–977, especially 964.

30. Office of the President of the UN General Assembly Concept note on responsibility to protect populations from genocide, war crimes, ethnic cleansing and crimes against humanity, at p. 2. http://www.un.org/ga/president/63/interactive/protect/conceptnote.pdf (accessed 18 May 2015).

31. Office of the President of the General Assembly Concept note on responsibility to protect populations from genocide, war crimes, ethnic cleansing and crimes against humanity at p. 2. http://www.un.org/ga/president/63/interactive/protect/conceptnote.pdf (accessed 18 May 2015).

32. The suggestion here then is that a veto by a UNSC permanent member cannot block the lawful use of force in the implementation of R2P where failure to implement would violate the purposes and principles of the UN Charter -such a veto is extra jurisdictional under the UN Charter in that context . It is here contended that the operation of the UNSC is as an extra checkpoint for the judicial use of force not as an entity with power that can thwart State action required under the UN Charter purposes and principles.

33. World Summit Outcome Document (September, 2005), para 139 (World Summit Outcome Document: International Coalition for the Responsibility to Protect (Outcome Document of the High-level Plenary Meeting of the General Assembly, September 2005). http://responsibilitytoprotect.org/index.php/component/content/article/35-r2pcs-topics/398-general-assembly-r2p-excerpt-from-outcome-document (accessed 13 May, 2015).

34. World Summit Outcome Document (September, 2005), para 139 id.

35. World Summit Outcome Document (September, 2005), para 139 id.

36. UN Charter (1945). Hence, on the analysis here, it is *not* a necessary block to the use of force in implementing R2P, where force is the only option, that such action is vetoed at the UNSC nor that "Neither do the Council's procedures have any provision for due process of law nor are its decisions subject to judicial review."(compare Office of the President of the UN General Assembly at p. 2). Recall on this point the "Uniting for Peace Resolution" UN General Assembly Resolution 377 (V) A (1950) 3 November, 1950 regarding the United Nations' and member State

responsibility to uphold UN Charter principles and objectives which obligation is not obviated by the UNSC failure to fulfil its mandate of maintaining international peace and security and in doing so with due regard to international law and respect for human rights as required under the purposes and principles expressly stated in the UN Charter:

> Conscious that failure of the Security Council to discharge its responsibilities on behalf of all the Member States ... does not relieve Member States of their obligations or the United Nations of its responsibility under the Charter to maintain international peace and security [nor]deprive the General Assembly of its rights or relieve it of its responsibilities under the Charter in regard to the maintenance of international peace and security (http://www.un. org/en/sc/repertoire/otherdocs/GAres377A(v).pdf [accessed 2 July 2015]).

37. Office of the President of the General Assembly Concept note on responsibility to protect populations from genocide, war crimes, ethnic cleansing and crimes against humanity at p. 1 http://www.un.org/ga/president/63/interactive/protect/conceptnote.pdf (accessed 18 May 2015).
38. Human Rights Watch World Report 2015 Syria https://www.hrw.org/world-report/2015/country-chapters/syria Grave abuses of human rights were committed and continue to be committed by government and non-government forces in Syria.
39. Office of the President of the General Assembly Concept note on responsibility to protect populations from genocide, war crimes, ethnic cleansing and crimes against humanity at p. 2 http://www.un.org/ga/president/63/interactive/protect/conceptnote.pdf (accessed 18 May 2015).
40. Office of the President of the General Assembly Concept note on responsibility to protect populations from genocide, war crimes, ethnic cleansing and crimes against humanity at p. 2 http://www.un.org/ga/president/63/interactive/protect/conceptnote.pdf (accessed 18 May, 2015)
41. Office of the President of the General Assembly Concept note on responsibility to protect populations from genocide, war crimes, ethnic cleansing and crimes against humanity at p. 2 http://www.un.org/ga/president/63/interactive/protect/conceptnote.pdf (accessed 18 May 2015).
42. Office of the President of the General Assembly Concept note on responsibility to protect populations from genocide, war crimes, ethnic cleansing and crimes against humanity at p. 2 http://www.un.org/ga/president/63/interactive/protect/conceptnote.pdf (accessed 18 May 2015).
43. Syria: UN urged to defy Assad on aid or risk lives of hundreds of thousands http://www.theguardian.com/world/2014/apr/28/legal-experts-urge-united-nations-ignore-assad-ban-aid-syria-rebels
44. Amnesty International: Syria http://www.amnestyusa.org/our-work/countries/middle-east-and-north-africa/syria (accessed 7 August 2015); See also, for instance, Human Rights Watch, *Death From the Skies: Deliberate and Indiscriminate Air Strikes on Civilians* (2013) https://www.hrw.org/report/2013/04/10/death-skies/deliberate-and-indiscriminate-air-strikes-civilians (accessed 7 August 2015); Amnesty International, *Torture Archipelago: Arbitrary Arrests, Torture, and Enforced Disappearances in Syria's Underground Prisons Since March 2011* (2012) http://www.hrw.org/reports/2012/07/03/torture-archipelago-0 (accessed 7 August 2015); Amnesty International, *By All Means Necessary: Individual and Command Responsibility for Crimes Against Humanity in Syria* (2011) http://www.hrw.org/sites/default/files/reports/syria1211webwcover_0.pdf (accessed 7 August 2015).
45. Office of the President of the General Assembly Concept note on responsibility to protect populations from genocide, war crimes, ethnic cleansing and crimes against humanity at p. 3 http://www.un.org/ga/president/63/interactive/protect/conceptnote.pdf (accessed 18 May 2015).
46. International Law Commission (2001) Draft Articles on the Responsibility of States for Internationally Wrongful Acts, with commentaries (Article 50) http://legal.un.org/ilc/texts/instruments/english/commentaries/9_6_2001.pdf (accessed 24 May 2015).
47. UN Charter (1945) signed in San Francisco, California, on 26 June 1945 (Article 1[4]) https://treaties.un.org/doc/publication/ctc/uncharter.pdf (accessed 13 May 2015).
48. Referring here to instances in which the State that controls the territory upon which these grave international crimes are occurring is unwilling or unable to prevent these mass atrocity crimes and force is the only option left available.
49. International Law Commission (2001) Draft Articles on the Responsibility of States for Internationally Wrongful Acts, with commentaries (Article 50) http://legal.un.org/ilc/texts/instruments/english/commentaries/9_6_2001.pdf (accessed 24 May 2015).

50. Note that implementation of countermeasures also are in the Draft Principles grounded on the recognition of respecting fundamental human rights first and foremost as reflected in the following for example: 'First, for some obligations, for example those concerning the protection of human rights, reciprocal countermeasures are inconceivable.' International Law Commission (2001) Draft Articles on the Responsibility of States for Internationally Wrongful Acts, with commentaries (Chapter II Countermeasures Commentary [item 5]) http://legal.un.org/ilc/texts/instruments/english/commentaries/9_6_2001.pdf (accessed 8 August 2015).

51. Amendments to the Rome Statute of the International Criminal Court on the Crime of Aggression http://www.icc-cpi.int/iccdocs/asp_docs/RC2010/AMENDMENTS/CN.651.2010-ENG-CoA.pdf.

52. The Rome Statute amendments regarding a State act of aggression and the crime of aggression committed by individuals of that State makes reference to the United Nations General Assembly resolution 3314 (XXIX) of 14 December 1974: http://crimeofaggression.info/documents/6/General_Assembly_%20Resolution_%203314.pdf. That resolution it should be noted: (1) does not preclude the use of lawful force. ... Nothing in this Definition shall be construed as in any way enlarging or diminishing the scope of the Charter, including its provisions concerning cases in which the use of force is lawful' (Article 6); (2) stipulates that the acts listed at Article 3 (reproduced in the amendments to the Rome Statute regarding the crime of aggression) as qualifying as acts of aggression are so designated provided there is no "relevant circumstance" that would *disqualify* them as such as per Article 2 of the Resolution (Arguably the imminent threat of and/ or occurrence of mass atrocity crimes triggering R2P is such a 'relevant circumstance' where all peaceful means to end the atrocities have been exhausted and failed and hence would preclude referral by the UNSC to the ICC); and (3) specifies at Article 7 that 'Nothing in the Definition [of Aggression], and in particular Article 3 [which lists acts of aggression], could in any way prejudice the right to self-determination, freedom and independence, as derived from the Charter, *of peoples* forcibly deprived of that right ... nor *the right of these peoples* to struggle to that end *and to seek and receive support in accordance with the principles of the Charter* and the above-mentioned declaration' [2625 (XXV) Principles of International Law concerning Friendly Relations and Co-operation among States in accordance with the Charter of the United Nations http://www.un-documents.net/a25r2625.htm]. Note that the latter Declaration stipulates amongst other things that: 'Every State has the duty to promote through joint and separate action universal respect for and observance of human rights and fundamental freedoms in accordance with the Charter' and not to interfere with States that are 'conducting themselves in compliance with the principle of equal rights and self-determination of peoples ... and thus [are States] possessed of a government representing the whole people belonging to the territory ... '

53. Cited from Crawford, J., *Law Commissions Articles on State Responsibility: Introduction, Text and Commentaries* (Cambridge: Cambridge University Press, 2002), 79.

54. The Legality of Military Action in Syria: Humanitarian Intervention and Responsibility to Protect'The UN Charter provides 2 clear exceptions to the prohibition of the use of force: self defence and authorization by the UN Security Council http://www.ejiltalk.org/humanitarian-intervention-responsibility-to-protect-and-the-legality-of-military-action-in-syria/ Blog of the European Journal of International Law (Dapo Akande August 28, 2013, Accessed 24 May, 2015).' On the analysis of the current author arguably the implementation of R2P by force where the only option is a self-defence of the integrity of the international system grounded on certain basic law such as *jus cogens* law and simultaneously defence on behalf of the people (a protection of their sovereignty) which is under siege by their own government and sometimes also that government's proxies through means that include genocide, war crimes, ethnic cleansing and or crimes against humanity.

55. Hossain, K., "The Concept of Jus Cogens and the Obligation Under The U.N. Charter", *Santa Clara Journal of International Law* 3, no. 1 (2005): 71–98: 'the Charter of the United Nations reflects the norm of *jus cogens* as its fundamental principle' (abstract); 'The role of the Security Council is also to safeguard the hierarchical norms of international law. ... In this sense, the Security Council itself is also under an obligation to follow such legal principles ... ' (97).

Bahrain: an R2P blind spot?

Aidan Hehir

Security and International Relations Programme, University of Westminster, London, UK

The 'Arab Spring' has catalysed an intense debate about the efficacy of the Responsibility to Protect (R2P). These debates have primarily focused on Libya and Syria; in this article I argue that the international community's engagement with Bahrain, though generally overlooked, also has major implications for assessments of the contemporary efficacy of R2P. This article provides a brief overview of the 2011 uprising in Bahrain and events since before assessing whether Bahrain constitutes an 'R2P situation'. Having concluded that Bahrain does meet the 'R2P situation' criteria I detail how key actors integral to the implementation of R2P have engaged with Bahrain. In analysing this engagement I argue that Bahrain demonstrates that the permanent five members of the Security Council continue to prioritise national interests over the protection of human rights; that NGOs specifically focused on R2P apply the concept selectively; that R2P has not become a 'lens' through which intra-state humanitarian crises are viewed; and that states can avoid international censure by undertaking certain policies which enable them to violate R2P's principles without incurring significant costs.

Introduction

While the responsibility to protect (R2P) has been described as having 'begun to change the world'[1] the post-intervention turmoil in Libya and the crisis in Syria have cast a shadow over its efficacy.[2] In this article I argue that the international community's engagement with Bahrain, though generally overlooked, also has a number of implications for assessments of the contemporary efficacy of R2P.

The article starts with a brief overview of the uprising in Bahrain in 2011 and events since. It then argues that Bahrain constitutes an 'R2P situation', before examining how key actors integral to the implementation of R2P have engaged with crisis. In the final section this engagement is analysed and four implications are advanced. The article argues that the international engagement with Bahrain demonstrates that the United States (US) and the United Kingdom (UK), as two of the permanent five members of the Security Council (P5), continue to prioritise national interests over the protection of human rights; that R2P is applied selectively by non-governmental organisations (NGOs) specifically focused on the concept; that R2P has not become a 'lens' through which intra-state humanitarian crises are viewed; and that states can avoid international censure by undertaking certain policies which enable them to violate R2P's principles without incurring significant costs.

The crisis in Bahrain 2011–2015

Details on the 2011 uprising and the situation since are contested; to minimise bias, the following narrative is based on the analysis provided by international NGOs, United Nations (UN) agencies and, in particular, the Bahrain Independent Commission of Inquiry (BICI) report.[3]

The 2011 uprising

In early 2011 a Facebook page called 'February 14th Revolution in Bahrain' called for mass protests on the 14 February. Despite the deployment of the Bahraini police, protests were held across the country; BICI noted they focused on 'political grievances and ... socio-economic demands' and involved 'a large degree of popular support that crossed religious, sectarian and ethnic lines'.[4] By 16 February some 12,000 people had gathered at the Pearl Roundabout in the capital Manama in a 'festive' mood.[5] In the early hours of 17 February over 1000 armed police cleared protesters from the roundabout; three people were killed by the police as some resisted. This sparked an escalation in tension as opposition parties – the most vocal being Al Wefaq – and civil society organisations condemned the security service's heavy-handed tactics and called for more popular participation. The funerals of those killed became rallies for the opposition and by 19 February the protestors had regained control of the Pearl Roundabout, where some 15,000 protestors gathered in 'celebratory' mood.[6] At this stage the crown prince accepted that the protestors constituted 'a very significant proportion of our society'.[7]

On 20 February some 80–85% of employees in Bahrain took part in a nation-wide strike.[8] By 26 February the demands of the protestors – which now included large numbers of university students and staff – had hardened and the monarchy's offers of reform were rejected in favour of the chant, 'The people demand the removal of the regime', which had become the rallying cry of protestors across the region. BICI found that this change in demands was not accompanied, however, by a change in tactics and 'the protestors remained peaceful'.[9] The main opposition group Al Wefaq repeatedly called for the protests to remain non-sectarian and peaceful.[10] In early March negotiations between protesters and the government faltered on the issue of the role of the monarchy. During this period various armed groups – described as 'vigilantes' by the US Ambassador to Bahrain[11] – began to target both Sunni and Shia's and sectarian tensions rose.

On the evening of 14 March the Gulf Cooperation Council (GCC) Jazeera Shield Forces entered Bahrain. According to the force commander the aim was, ' ... to help the government to bring goodness, peace, and love to Bahrain'.[12] The decision was also justified on the grounds that Bahrain needed support against 'external threats', meaning Iran, but fears about Bahrain precipitating a 'snowballing effect from Bahrain into other GCC members' were also to the fore.[13] UN Secretary General Ban Ki-Moon stated that he viewed the intervention 'with concern'.[14] Following the arrival of the GCC Jazeera Shield Forces, Al Wefaq issued a statement describing the intervention as, ' ... a sign that the governing authority of Bahrain considers itself to have lost all legitimacy'.[15] On 15 March King Hamad passed Royal Decree No. 18 which declared a 'State of National Safety' for three months. According to BICI this, 'opened the door for the perpetration of grave violations of human rights, including the arbitrary deprivation of life, torture and arbitrary detention'.[16]

On 16 March the government sent 5000 personnel to clear protestors from the Pearl Roundabout; according to BICI the force used was 'unnecessary and disproportionate'[17] and the security services engaged in 'terror-inspiring behaviour and unnecessary damage to property'.[18] The International Crisis Group (ICG) described the government's response as 'brutal repression'.[19]

Later that day a curfew was declared and all demonstrations were banned. Described by BICI as often undertaken in a purposely 'terrorising manner',[20] 17 March witnessed mass arrests. Checkpoints were established throughout Bahrain at which Shia were often 'verbally abused because of their religious and sectarian beliefs'.[21] From 1 March to the end of April Shia religious buildings, including 28 mosques, were demolished. According to BICI this was viewed by the Shia community as 'a collective punishment' that served to 'inflame the tension between the GoB and the Shia population'.[22] Likewise the ICG described the government's repression as sectarian[23] and a report in the *New York Times* accused state-owned media of stoking anti-Shia sentiments.[24]

Following the crack-down, the National Security Agency and Ministry of the Interior engaged in 'a systematic practice of physical and psychological mistreatment, which in many cases amounted to torture'.[25] According to BICI, detainees ' … were subjected to various forms of mistreatment, including beatings, kicking, lashing with rubber hoses and verbal insults'.[26] BICI noted, 'these measures fall within the meaning of torture as defined in the Convention Against Torture'.[27] BICI found that between 14 February and 14 April 35 people died; five were tortured to death.[28] The report noted that torture had long been central to the Bahrain security apparatus and stated that it was 'a systemic problem'.[29] The European Centre for Constitutional and Human Rights also argued that the torture perpetrated by the Bahraini authorities constituted 'an overall pattern of crimes that might constitute crimes against humanity'.[30] The manner in which the Bahrain government and security forces responded was ultimately summarised by BICI as 'unnecessary, disproportionate, and indiscriminate'.[31]

Post-2011 reform?

The situation became less volatile after April 2011; BICI was established by the king in June 2011 and released its report in November that year which, in addition to providing a comprehensive narrative of the crisis, advanced recommendations on political and judicial reform.[32] In the intervening period, however, progress on implementing the recommendations has been slow and systemic human rights abuses continue. Indicatively the UK's Foreign Affairs Committee (FAC) wrote, 'In our view the Bahrain Independent Commission of Inquiry made sensible recommendations and the Bahrain government's failure to implement them fully is inexplicable'.[33] The FAC report also expressed concerns about 'a number of regressive policies' implemented since 2011 such as the banning of street protests, revoking the nationality of opposition activists, banning opposition groups from meeting foreign officials without the government's permission and a member of the government present, the lack of judicial independence, and 'serious concerns about due process'.[34]

Since the 2011 uprising many human rights organisations, think tanks, UN bodies and government bodies and Ministries have issued highly critical statements and reports on the Bahraini government's continued violation of basic human rights and systemic use of torture. In August 2012, 44 international NGOs signed a letter condemning Bahrain's suppression of political opposition and the curtailment of human rights.[35] In January 2013 the UN Human Rights Council condemned 'the continued harassment and imprisonment of persons exercising their rights to freedom of opinion and expression in Bahrain'.[36] A report by Human Rights Watch (HRW) in February 2013 declared that there had been 'no progress on key reform promises', stating that the government's promises on reform 'mean nothing'.[37] The UK FAC 2013 Annual Report on Human Rights and Democracy likewise concluded 'we see little or no evidence that Bahrain has made enough progress in implementing political reform and safeguarding human rights'.[38] In April 2013 the Bahrain government cancelled a visit by the UN Special Rapporteur on Torture, the second time that the Rapporteur had been denied entry since 2011. In February 2014 the International Federation for Human Rights stated, 'Bahraini authorities continue to fail in their promises of implementing the BICI recommendations'.[39] In July 2014 Tom Malinowski, US Assistant Secretary of State for Democracy, Human Rights and Labor, was expelled from the country after he met with leaders of the opposition.[40] The UN Human Rights Council's Working Group on Arbitrary Detention ruled 'Bahrain in violation of its international human rights obligations' in July 2014.[41] In June 2014, 47 countries issued a joint statement at the UN Human Rights Council's 26th Session which described the human rights situation in Bahrain as 'an issue of serious concern', noting 'the lack of guarantee of fair trial', 'the repression of demonstrations', 'the continued harassment and imprisonment of persons exercising their rights to freedom of opinion' and 'ill-treatment and torture in detention facilities'.[42] An article in *Foreign Policy* in March 2015 affirmed that violations were still occurring, noting 'allegations of the use of torture, sexual abuse and forced confessions were again commonplace'.[43]

HRW's 2013 country report on Bahrain noted 'the government failed to fully implement the commission's core recommendations', and that the 'Security forces used excessive force in 2012 to disperse anti-government protests'.[44] Its 2014 report stated 'Bahrain's human rights record regressed further', highlighted, 'Continuing reports of torture and ill-treatment in detention' and again condemned 'The government's failure to implement key recommendations of the BICI'.[45] HRW's 2015 report likewise listed a series of indictments of the Monarchy noting, ' ... the justice system has failed to hold members of the security forces accountable for serious rights violations, including in cases where their use of excessive and unlawful force proved fatal' and the ' ... failure to address the security forces use of lethal and apparently disproportionate force'. The report also notes that the Bahraini government has jailed opposition leaders on 'vague terrorism charges', curtailed freedom of expression, facilitated the 'physical abuse and forced labour' of migrant workers, and passed a new law giving the Interior Ministry the power to revoke the citizenship of any Bahraini who 'causes harm to the interests of the Kingdom or acts in a way that contravenes his duty of loyalty to it'.[46]

A March 2015 report by Reporters Without Borders condemned the ' ... systematic persecution of journalists and human right defenders and the renewed deterioration in the climate for freedom of information in Bahrain'.[47] A 2015 review of press freedom globally found Bahrain to be 163rd out of 180.[48] Freedom House's 2015 report likewise recorded a sharp decline in freedom within Bahrain since 2011, giving the country a score of 6.5 (7 being the lowest possible).[49] In 2013 the Genocide Prevention Advisory Network ranked Bahrain second in the list of 'Countries with High Risks of Genocide and Politicide if they Should Have Major Conflicts or State Failures' noting a 'sharp increase after 2010' in the column 'Recent Changes and Hazards'.[50] The organisation's most recent 'Countries at Risk of Genocide, Politicide, or Mass Atrocities' also listed Bahrain.[51] In 2014 Cherif Bassouni, Chair of BICI, noted the Bahraini government's implementation of his recommendations had been 'piecemeal' and warned that people 'who do not have the hope of seeing themselves as equal citizens' eventually 'explode'. He stated that unrest is 'bound to continue to increase unless we address the social and economic reasons'.[52]

Amnesty International's 2014–2015 country report on Bahrain notes, 'The security forces regularly used excessive force' listing various methods employed including, 'severe beating, punching, electric shocks, suspension by the limbs, rape and threats of rape, and deliberate exposure to extreme cold'.[53] This echoes two other reports published by Amnesty International in 2015; the first condemns ' … the rampant abuses including torture, arbitrary detentions and excessive use of force against peaceful activists and government critics, which continue to take place in Bahrain four years after the uprisings', and with respect to the BICI recommendation states 'most of these measures have had little impact in practice'.[54] The second report published in April 2015 is more ominous; it finds 'Bahrain, today, continues to go through a political and human rights crisis', hopes for reform have 'all but evaporated', 'tension within the Kingdom remains critically high' and 'Bahrain is more deeply divided than ever'.[55]

An R2P situation?

R2P is about much more than coercive military intervention; such action is invariably presented as an option of last resort within R2P.[56] In his 2009 report, UN Secretary General Ban Ki-Moon outlined three 'Pillars' of R2P; Pillar I: ' … the enduring responsibility of the State to protect its populations'; Pilar II: ' … the commitment of the international community to assist States in meeting those obligations'; Pillar III: ' … the responsibility of Member States to respond collectively in a timely and decisive manner when a State is manifestly failing to provide such protection'.[57] Thus, the applicability of R2P – and the means by which it can be operationalised – extends far beyond just reacting, through non-consensual military intervention, to actual cases where the 'four crimes' are occurring.

R2P advocates have, indeed, continually sought to distance the concept from coercive military intervention and present it as primarily a means to prevent the occurrence of the 'four crimes' by working with the state in question through Pillar I and Pillar II.[58] UN Secretary General Ban Ki-Moon argued that the 'the ultimate purpose of the responsibility to protect [is] to save lives by preventing the most egregious mass violations of human rights'.[59] Likewise Alex Bellamy, Director of the Asia Pacific Centre on R2P, stated, 'R2P has real value precisely because it has the potential to improve the prevention of mass atrocities and protection of vulnerable populations'.[60] The 2014 crisis in Gaza led to a debate about R2P's applicability; in response to claims that R2P did not apply in Gaza, Bellamy stated,

> There should be no question about whether R2P 'applies' or not. In fact, posing that very question mistakes what states agreed about R2P in 2005. R2P is not conditional. It does not arise or evaporate with circumstance. It is universal and enduring; it applies everywhere, all the time.[61]

An 'R2P situation' does not, therefore, only mean one that meets a threshold for military intervention or even a case where one or more of the four crimes has occurred.

This applicability beyond reacting to actual cases of the 'four crimes is reflected in the wording of paragraphs 138 and 139 of the 2005 World Summit Outcome Document; paragraph 138 reads, 'This responsibility entails the prevention of such crimes, including their incitement, through appropriate and necessary means', while paragraph 139 commits the international community, 'to helping States build capacity to protect their populations from genocide, war crimes, ethnic cleansing and crimes against humanity and to assisting those which are under stress before crises and conflicts break out'. Within the remit of prevention there are myriad issues deemed to be within R2P's purview on the basis that they are potential catalysts for the outbreak of one or more of the four crimes.[62] Ban Ki-Moon's prescriptions on the responsibility to prevent in 2013 focused on the need to 'build societies that are resilient to atrocity crimes' by leveraging R2P long before atrocities are committed; he stated,

> Building resilience implies developing appropriate legal frameworks and building State struc-tures and institutions that are legitimate, respect international human rights law and the rule of law in general, and that have the capacity to address and defuse sources of tension before they escalate. It means building a society which accepts and values diversity and in which different communities coexist peacefully.[63]

In 2014 The Joint Office of the Special Adviser on the Prevention of Genocide and the Responsibility to Protect (OSAPGR2P) published the 'Framework of Analysis for Atrocity Crimes: A Tool for Prevention'. This was described by the UN Secretary General as 'a guide for assessing the risk of genocide, crimes against humanity and war crimes' which places, 'the prevention of atrocity crimes at the centre of our work'.[64] The report notes, 'Atrocity crimes tend to occur in countries with some level of instability or crisis' and advises states to use this framework to address the root causes of tension and conflict.[65]

Does Bahrain warrant attention?

The number of fatalities during the 2011 uprising was not very high in relative terms,[66] but this excuse was explicitly rejected by HRW; criticising the international community for 'averting their eyes' during the government crack-down, they stated that the number of people killed in less than two months in 2011 was 'substantial and greater than the casual-ties resulting from five years of protracted unrest in the 1990s'.[67] Thus, while the number of the fatalities was certainly less than other crises, this overlooks the sudden spike in fatalities and Bahrain's small population.

Looking at the crises specifically with respect to R2P's '4 crimes', again the evidence suggests that, in relative terms, the 2011 uprising and its aftermath were not characterised by the egregious commission of these crimes. There is no evidence of genocide having been either planned or undertaken in Bahrain; if one adopts a circumscribed definition of 'war crimes' as being reserved for criminal acts undertaken during international armed conflict then again this is not applicable to Bahrain[68]; while the government's response to the upris-ing has been marked by sectarianism, heavy-handed tactics against predominantly Shia vil-lages and the destruction of Shia mosques, it is difficult to argue that ethnic cleansing has been evident. Crimes against humanity, however, appear to have been perpetrated both during and since the uprising. Article 7 of the Rome Statute lists torture as a crime against humanity, a point made by the OSAPGR2P in its framework for analysis.[69] In addition to systemic torture, there has also been evidence of 'murder', 'deprivation of phys-ical liberty in violation of fundamental rules of international law', 'persecution against any identifiable group' and 'intentionally causing great suffering or serious injury to body or to mental or physical health', which are all covered under Article 7 of the Rome Statute if 'committed as part of a widespread or systematic attack directed against any civilian popu-lation, with knowledge of the attack'. BICI did find that torture, at least, was indeed 'systemic'.[70]

Even if it is the case that crimes against humanity have not been committed – which contradicts the evidence supplied by reputable human rights NGOs like Amnesty Inter-national, HRW and the ICG – or were committed on a relatively small scale, this does not mean Bahrain is not an 'R2P situation'. As detailed in previous sections, it is incontrovertible that systemic state-sponsored human rights violations occurred during the March 2011 uprising and since; that Bahrain is experiencing sectarian tension exacerbated by what some have alleged to be state-orchestrated persecution of Shias[71]; that the political and judicial system do not conform to normative standards; and, most worryingly that the situation at present is deteriorating, described by some as a 'crisis' with tensions 'critically high'[72] that threaten to 'explode'.[73]

The OSAPGR2P's 2014 report – described by Ban Ki-Moon as a means through which to implement the preventative element of R2P[74] – lists 14 'risk factors' which are presented as a means to 'guide an assessment of whether a particular State faces the kind of stress that could generate an environment conducive to atrocity crimes'.[75] Of the 14 'Risk Factors' listed, eight appear, on the basis of the evidence detailed earlier, to be manifest in Bahrain either during the 2011 uprising or in the period since; these are, 'Situations of armed conflict or other forms of instability'; 'Record of serious violations of international human rights and humanitarian law'; 'Motives or incentives'; 'Capacity to commit atrocity crimes'; 'Intergroup tensions or patterns of discrimination against protected groups'; 'Signs of an intent to destroy in whole or in part a protected group'; 'Signs of a widespread or systematic attack against any civilian population'; and 'Serious threats to those protected under international humanitarian law'.[76] Collectively, this constitutes definitive grounds for deeming Bahrain, both in 2011 and since, to be a definite 'R2P situation', especially when taken in tandem with the various ominous warnings about the situation deteriorating of late.

Where is R2P?

Since 2011 Bahrain has witnessed 'brutal repression'[77] by the government against pro-democracy protestors, 'systemic torture',[78] external military intervention, state-sponsored sectarianism,[79] and institutionalised corruption within the judiciary[80]; in the past four years the situation has steadily deteriorated to the point where many have issued warnings that the situation could soon explode into open conflict again; indicatively, the ICG warned that the government's tactics were 'Laying the groundwork for a potential future uprising. In this tense atmosphere, any further provocation or violent action could trigger an explosion.'[81]

Yet, despite the evidence presented by various human rights NGOs, states, UN bodies and BICI, the application of R2P to Bahrain has been minimal. The following sub-sections assess the manner in which three actors/groups central to the operationalisation of R2P have responded to the crisis in Bahrain.

The Security Council's response

The Security Council was established long before R2P but it is central to the application of the concept; the efficacy of R2P is, to a large extent, dependent on the Security Council's willingness to invoke and act upon the concept.[82] Some have argued that as R2P has not initiated, or called for, structural reforms of the UN, it has facilitated the perpetuation of the Security Council's, and specifically the P5's, powers which has meant that narrow national interests continue to impede the enforcement of human rights.[83] In response, however, many R2P advocates have argued that the Security Council's disposition towards R2P has improved dramatically in the past five years. This has been manifest, supporters claim, in the upsurge in Security Council resolutions which mention R2P, the use of R2P and associated terms in Security Council debates, the unwillingness of any Security

Council member to disavow R2P, and most emphatically, Security Council Resolution 1973 which sanctioned the use of force against Gadhafi's Libya in March 2011.[84]

Yet, while expressions of optimism about the Security Council's recent ostensible embrace of R2P, and the principles it embodies, are increasingly common, the Security Council's response to Bahrain has been negligible; no Security Council resolution or presidential statement has ever mentioned Bahrain since the crisis began.

The secretary general's response

UN Secretary General Ban Ki-Moon has been a particularly vocal proponent of R2P which he described as 'a core part of the world's armour for protecting vulnerable populations from the most serious international crimes and violations'.[85] In his 2012 report on R2P Ban Ki-Moon reaffirmed the need to see R2P as a means to prevent atrocity crimes by tackling root-cause issues such as 'discrimination, marginalization, exclusion, stigmatization, dehumanization and denial of fundamental human rights'.[86] Each of these have been evident in Bahrain since 2011.

Since the crisis in Bahrain began Ban Ki-Moon has issued 15 statements specifically on Bahrain.[87] The statements have consistently reiterated certain themes, namely, the need for a peaceful resolution of the crisis,[88] calls for the full implementation of the BICI recommendations,[89] the right to protest,[90] judicial independence,[91] and adherence to international humanitarian law.[92] In none of these statements on Bahrain, however, did the secretary general mention R2P. Additionally, since 2009 he has issued six annual reports on R2P, none of which refer to Bahrain.[93]

The Office of the Special Advisers on the Prevention of Genocide and the Responsibility to Protect

In October 2014 OSAPGR2P published the 'Framework of Analysis for Atrocity Crimes' which emphasised the need for proactive preventative action to mitigate the deleterious effects of societal tension which could lead to the commission of atrocity crimes. The report outlined 18 'Risk Factors' each with a set of on average eight 'Indicators'; the evidence presented suggests that the situation in Bahrain meets at least eight of these 'Risk Factors' and many more of their associated 'Indicators'. In particular the report warns that atrocity crimes invariably stem from discriminatory practices and societal fissures; given the reports of 'systematic sectarian discrimination'[94] and 'sectarian turmoil'[95] within Bahrain, and the fact that violence already broke out in 2011, the situation appears to be an archetypal situation of concern.

Despite this, to date OSAPGR2P has not engaged with Bahrain. The Special Advisers have not visited the country; their website lists all the 42 official statements made by both special advisers to date, none of which mention Bahrain; the website also lists nine 'Country Situations' but Bahrain is not listed.[96]

The NGO response

The role of NGOs is central to the promotion of R2P, and indeed a key part of the strategy underpinning its normative role.[97] The following analysis focuses on the three most prominent NGOs singularly focused on R2P, namely the Global Centre for R2P (GCR2P), the International Coalition for RtoP (ICRtoP) and the Asia Pacific Centre for R2P (APCR2P). Building on the presumption that 'global civil society' has an influence on state behaviour, these R2P-orientated NGOs seek to promote the concept and highlight the plight of people across the globe at risk from, or suffering, one or more of the four crimes.[98]

Asked about the GCR2P's engagement with Bahrain, Ryan D'Souza – GCR2P's advocacy officer – responded, 'We don't have any publications on Bahrain but we did carefully monitor the situation at the time of the instability in Bahrain.'[99] Since January 2012 GCR2P has published the 'R2P Monitor' bi-monthly, describing it as 'applying an R2P lens to situations where populations are at risk of, or are currently facing, mass atrocity crimes'.[100] None of the 21 editions published have mentioned Bahrain. The GCR2P's website also hosts a 'Populations at Risk' section with the countries listed divided into groups: 'Current Crises', 'Imminent Risk', 'Serious Concern' and 'Previously Studied Situations'. Bahrain is not one of the 23 countries listed.[101] The GCR2P publishes an 'Occasional Paper Series' which has focused on a number of intra-state conflicts, but never Bahrain.[102] There is additionally no record of the GCR2P having ever issued a statement on Bahrain. The GCR2P has never published their own tweet or Facebook post on the situation. The GCR2P also retweets/reposts links from other NGOs and the international media on a wide variety of issues; since the uprising in Bahrain began, the GCR2P has mentioned Bahrain in just one tweet[103] and two Facebook posts.[104]

Bahrain is not listed by the ICRtoP on its 'Crises' page. When asked about its coverage of Bahrain, ICRtoP responded 'We have not published anything directly on Bahrain ... we have not tweeted or posted on Bahrain'.[105] The ICRtoP has actually published one tweet[106] on Bahrain and one Facebook post,[107] both of which referred to reports by others.

Since 2011 the APCR2P has published 'R2P Ideas in Brief', short articles on 'important issues of R2P concern'.[108] None of the 28 articles focus on Bahrain, nor do any of the Centre's nine 'Newsletters' published to date.[109] The centre's list of its staff's publications since 2011 does not include anything on Bahrain[110] and its academic journal *Global Responsibility to Protect* has never published an article on Bahrain.[111] The APCR2P has never mentioned Bahrain on twitter but it has published seven Facebook posts.[112]

Other less prominent R2P-orientated organisations evidence similar trends. The Canadian Centre for R2P, the Montreal Institute for Genocide Prevention and the Will to Intervene Project have never published anything on Bahrain; collectively they have published two tweets.[113]

Collectively, since 2011, the GCR2P, the ICRtoP, the APCR2P, the Canadian Centre for R2P, the Montreal Institute for Genocide Prevention and the Will to Intervene Project have published three tweets and eight Facebook posts about Bahrain. Since the GCR2P joined twitter in September 2011 it has issued a total of 8600 tweets, an average of over 200 per month; since the ICRtoP joined twitter in April 2011 it has issued 12,500 tweets, an average of 250 a month. Thousands of these tweets constitute the organisation retweeting reports and statements from other NGOs on a huge array of issues; from April to June 2015 alone, the GCR2P and the ICRtoP have retweeted on issues such as the destruction of UNESCO World Heritage Sites,[114] the rehabilitation of child soldiers,[115] resolutions on the small arms trade,[116] the election campaign for a new UN secretary general,[117] a conference on women's role in peacebuilding,[118] 'Earth Day',[119] and North Korea's non-compliance with the Nuclear Proliferation Treaty.[120] Given that combined they have issued over 21,000 tweets since April 2011 on an eclectic array of issues, it is remarkable that they have only mentioned Bahrain once. The APCR2P is primarily focuses on a region which does not include Bahrain, yet, it has published tweets on a number of issues related to areas outside this region such as policing in Sudan,[121] the crisis in Burundi[122] and the conflict in Syria.[123]

While Bahrain has not been at the very top of the international political agenda, and the crisis is certainly not as grave as elsewhere, it has been regularly commented on by high-profile human rights NGOs such as HRW and Amnesty International, as well as newspapers such as *The New York Times*, *The Guardian*, *Le Monde* and many others; to have consistently neglected to even refer to these reports and articles via twitter and Facebook is clearly noteworthy.

Assessing the Bahrain blind spot

The situation in Bahrain both during the 2011 uprising and since appears to clearly warrant more attention than it has achieved, particularly from those closely connected with promoting and implementing R2P. The demonstrably paltry coverage outlined above has four implications for assessments of the contemporary efficacy of R2P.

Security Council mendacity

In looking for explanations for the complete absence of any references to Bahrain at the Security Council since 2011 it is perhaps obvious that geopolitics has played a significant role; both the US and the UK are allies of Bahrain. In 1995 the US chose Bahrain as the base for its Naval Fifth Fleet and in 2002 the US declared Bahrain to be 'a major non-NATO ally'.[124] Since the 2011 uprising the US has continued to sell millions of dollars' worth of arms to the monarchy; though it initially put restrictions on the sale of certain weapons, it has begun to repeal these and recently increased the size of its naval fleet based there.[125] Justifying the resumption of arms sales to Bahrain, the US State Department acknowledged that the human rights situation in Bahrain was not 'adequate' but spokesman John Kirby argued, 'Bahrain is an important and longstanding ally'.[126] The UK–Bahrain relationship was described by the Royal United Services Institute as 'crucial to the UK's pursuit of its national strategic aims',[127] and the UK FAC noted that 'Bahrain provides an immensely valuable home in the Gulf for UK naval assets which would be difficult to find elsewhere'.[128] To this end, the UK announced in 2014 that it was starting construction on a new £15 million naval base in Bahrain.[129]

Given their close ties, the US and UK are perhaps understandably reluctant to publicly rebuke Bahrain through either a Security Council resolution or a presidential statement. This has obviously troubling implications for R2P; the manner in which both countries have shielded their ally from censure,[130] and indeed continued to provide the monarchy with arms and investment, suggests that these democracies, both of whom have historically been rhetorically supportive of R2P, continue to pursue foreign policy strategies which at times relegate human rights to a secondary position behind narrowly conceived national interests. Given that R2P is, to a great extent, dependent on the P5's support for its practical application, the persistence of this disposition will naturally inhibit the realisation of R2P across all three pillars and lead to its politicised application.

The selective application of R2P

R2P ostensibly 'applies everywhere, all the time'[131]; the coverage of Bahrain by R2P-orientated NGOs, however, appears to contradict this as these NGOs have been virtually silent on Bahrain. It is impossible to believe that these organisations were ignorant of the situation in Bahrain or indeed the myriad reports by NGOs on this situation; indeed both HRW and the ICG are members of the ICRtoP. It is potentially conceivable that these organisations did not recognise the applicability of R2P to Bahrain. While this strains credulity, even if

this was the case, it contradicts the 'R2P applies everywhere' narrative; if these organisations specifically focused on R2P do not recognise an 'R2P situation' then what hope is
there that other actors, especially states, will?

The final, more troubling explanation relates to a long-standing critique of R2P, and
indeed human rights-orientated NGOs generally, namely that both serve 'Western' interests.[132] There is an obvious link between Western state interests – especially from the
UK and the US – and the monarchy in Bahrain, and indeed its major ally Saudi Arabia.
It could conceivably be argued, therefore, that the R2P NGOs have not focused on
Bahrain because they have, covertly or otherwise, been encouraged to refrain from embar-
rassing a Western ally; this charge has been made previously with respect to the lack of R2P
coverage of Israel by these NGOs.[133] The APCR2P is primarily funded by the Australian
government, while the ICRtoP and the GCR2P are both based in New York. The GCR2P
lists those who have provided it with 'generous financial support'; there are 15 governments, only two of which are not European or North American (Mexico and Rwanda),
seven foundations, all of which are US-based, and three individuals, all of whom are
US-based. This does not necessarily mean this organisation is controlled by Western interests of course, but in tandem with the selective application of its 'R2P lens', could be interpreted as supporting the charge that R2P is applied frequently in accord with Western
interests and perspectives. Whether this is true or not, such perceptions naturally inhibit
the efficacy both of R2P and these NGOs. R2P was lauded as a value-neutral substitute
for 'humanitarian intervention' which was deemed to be too closely associated with
Western interests[134]; the selective application of R2P, particularly with respect to an
obvious ally of the West, will naturally undermine the concept's popularity.

The 'R2P lens'

A key element of the strategy underpinning R2P is to develop an 'R2P lens' through which
intra-state unrest is viewed.[135] In his 2010 report on prevention and R2P, Ban Ki-Moon advocated this, stating, 'the existing mechanisms for gathering and analysing information for the
purpose of early warning do not view that information through the lens of the responsibility
to protect'.[136] The 'R2P lens' appears to have been ineffective in the course of the crisis in
Bahrain; since 2011 R2P-orientated NGOs and the OSAPGR2P have, essentially ignored
the situation, and additionally, those organisations that have sought to highlight both the
ongoing systemic human rights abuses and the potential for the situation to explode into
mass conflict, have not employed R2P in so doing. Those that *have* focused on Bahrain,
such as the ICG, Amnesty International, HRW and indeed the UN secretary general, have
never mentioned R2P in any of their reports or statements. Illustrative of the absence of a
link between the humanitarian crisis and R2P is the fact that only one human rights organisation has ever mentioned R2P and Bahrain in the same tweet.[137] This suggests that R2P has not
become a 'lens' through which human rights violations are viewed.

How to oppress with impunity?

The Bahrain Centre for Human Rights claimed that the lack of any international condemnation of the 16 March 2011 crackdown emboldened the Khalifa monarchy to commit further
atrocities. In the years since, they note, 'the authorities in Bahrain, due to the lack of international consequences, have no incentive to stop the human rights violations'.[138] Thus,
Bahrain potentially provides insight into how governments can engage in, and get away
with, oppression against their own people in the post-R2P era.

The government has managed to avoid international censure of the type meted out to other oppressive regimes such as Libya, Syria, Myanmar and Burundi through a combination of factors. First, as noted earlier, Bahrain has cultivated a series of alliances with key international actors, most notably Saudi Arabia,[139] the UK and the US. These states have shielded Bahrain from international censure at important international fora – such as the Security Council – and raised the political costs for others tempted to criticise them. Second, Bahrain has engaged with the international community in ways which have made condemnation of its internal policies unattractive to those with important investments – political, economic and reputational – in the country, a point openly acknowledged by the UK FAC report.[140] Bahrain is a key venue for international investments, an important oil exporter and has major investments in the US and the UK; a report by *The Financial Times* found that Premier Group, an investment firm run by the monarchy, has investments worth £900 million in the UK alone.[141] The monarchy, though religiously conservative, has also sought to open the country up to tourism and international sport; illustratively, the 'Bahrain Grand Prix' has taken place annually since 2004. As a result, a number of non-political international figures have a vested interest in cultivating a benign image of Bahrain; Formula 1 chief executive Bernie Ecclestone, for example, has resisted calls to boycott the country due to the human rights violations, describing protestors as simply 'lot of kids having a go at the police'.[142] Third, the monarchy established BICI which enabled it to do two things; first, present itself as progressive and open, and second, advance a narrative since that it was instituting reforms.[143] This later point, indeed, has been a common refrain issued when criticism has flared and has often been echoed by both the US and UK when justifying their continued support for the monarchy.[144] Yet, this has been rejected by others as disingenuous; indicatively Kenneth Roth stated that those who argue that Bahrain's human rights record has improved are living 'in a dream world'.[145]

Finally, the monarchy has expressed its fulsome support for R2P, thereby sidestepping any criticism for antipathy to the concept, such as has been directed at Venezuela, Nicaragua, Sudan and Cuba.[146] In September 2012, describing itself as 'a country responsive to its international responsibilities', the Bahraini ambassador stated in the General Assembly:

> Our organisation must therefore shoulder its responsibilities for the protection of unarmed civilians and must not allow the procedures for the United Nations to impede its ability to prevent crimes against humanity. It must put aside the narrow geopolitical interests and proceed to the attainment of the supreme goal which is the responsibility to protect civilians in armed conflicts.[147]

This recognition that 'the responsibility to protect civilians in armed conflicts' is 'the supreme goal' contrasts sharply with the myriad reports published since 2011 discussed above which charge Bahrain with systemic human rights abuses, the use of excessive force and violent sectarianism. It is also potentially significant that at the 2009 General Assembly debate on R2P Bahrain was one of the few states not to issue a statement on R2P; it was only after the 2011 uprising that Bahrain expressed its support for the concept. To derive benefits from rhetorically supporting R2P whilst systemically acting against its ethos clearly has ominous implications for the utility of R2P.

Conclusion

The 2011 response by the Bahrain government was described by HRW as a 'systematic and comprehensive crackdown to punish and intimidate government critics and to end dissent root and branch'.[148] Yet, the international response – from the Security Council, the OSAPGR2P and R2P-orientated NGOs – at the time was negligible.[149]

Since 2011 Bahrain has witnessed repeated systemic human rights violations and exhibited numerous signs of looming calamity; given the sectarian nature of the conflict, the persistent simmering violence, the government's repressive tactics, the failure to implement the BICI reforms and the fact that external forces have already militarily intervened – the GCC force in 2011 – and others – most notably Iran – are alleged to be stoking internal dissent, Bahrain exhibits many obvious warning signs. Yet, whilst this has been regularly highlighted by the international media and reputable human rights organisations, the response from those most closely associated with R2P has continued to be paltry.

R2P is presented as a framework for preventing conflicts by helping states to address sources of tension domestically – as well as a reactive means to halt the occurrence of one or more of the 'four crimes'. According to Bellamy, 'R2P provides a commonly understood political framework which actors and institutions of all shapes and sizes, ranging from individuals to global organizations and superpower states can utilise, individually or collectively'.[150] In the case of Bahrain, this normative role for R2P has not materialised and this has troubling implications for the future efficacy of R2P.

Disclosure statement

No potential conflict of interest was reported by the author.

Notes

1. Alex Bellamy, *The Responsibility to Protect: A Defence* (Oxford: Oxford University Press, 2015), 111.
2. Aidan Hehir, 'From Human Security to the Responsibility to Protect: The Co-Option of Dissent?', *Michigan State International Law Review* 23, no. 3 (2015): 675–99; Justin Morris, 'Libya and Syria: R2P and the Spectre of the Swinging Pendulum', *International Affairs* 89, no. 5 (2013): 1265–83.
3. A number of NGOs specifically focused on Bahrain have released reports outlining the continued repression and lack of reform post-2011. These include the Bahrain Institute for Rights and Democracy, the Bahrain Center for Human Rights, the Bahrain Youth Society for Human Rights, and Americans for Democracy and Human Rights in Bahrain. Their analysis is not included here, nor is that of the Bahraini government.

4. Bahrain Independent Commission of Inquiry, 'Report of the Bahrain Independent Commission of Inquiry', 23 November 2015, 68 and 162, http://www.bici.org.bh/BICIreportEN.pdf (accessed 26 June 2015).
5. Ibid., 72.
6. Ibid., 82.
7. Ibid., 83.
8. Ibid., 83.
9. Ibid., 164.
10. Ibid., 98.
11. Ibid., 142.
12. Asharq Al-Awsat, 'A Talk with Peninsula Shield Force Commander Mutlaq Bin Salem al-Azima', Asharq Al-Awsat, 28 March 2011, http://www.aawsat.net/2011/03/article55247010/a-talk-with-peninsula-shield-force-commander-mutlaq-bin-salem-al-azima (accessed 26 June 2015).
13. Silvia Colombo, 'The GCC Countries and the Arab Spring', in *The Arab Spring and the Arab Thaw*, ed. John Davies (Surrey: Ashgate, 2013), 169.
14. Ban Ki-Moon, 'Statement Attributable to the Spokesperson for the Secretary-General on Bahrain', New York, 14 March 2011, http://www.un.org/sg/statements/index.asp?nid=5137 (accessed 26 June 2015).
15. Bahrain Independent Commission of Inquiry, 'Report of the Bahrain Independent Commission of Inquiry', 134.
16. Ibid., 419.
17. Ibid., 166.
18. Ibid., 416.
19. ICG, 'Bahrain's Rocky Road to Reform', *Middle East/North Africa Report* No. 111, 28 July 2011, 1.
20. Bahrain Independent Commission of Inquiry, 'Report of the Bahrain Independent Commission of Inquiry', 148.
21. Ibid., 159.
22. Ibid., 329.
23. International Crisis Group, 'Bahrain's Rocky Road to Reform', 4.
24. Anthony Shadid, 'Bahrain Boils Under the Lid of Repression', *New York Times*, 15 September, http://www.nytimes.com/2011/09/16/world/middleeast/repression-tears-apart-bahrains-social-fabric.html?pagewanted=1&_r=2 (accessed 26 June 2015).
25. Bahrain Independent Commission of Inquiry, 'Report of the Bahrain Independent Commission of Inquiry', 298.
26. Ibid., 152.
27. Ibid., 417.
28. Ibid., 219–25.
29. Ibid., 300.
30. The European Centre for Constitutional and Human Rights, 'Submission to Bahrain Independent Commission of Inquiry: Re. Specific Incidents of Violence Against Peaceful Protestors in the Kingdom of Bahrain and Their Widespread and Systemic Character', 9 September 2011, 2.
31. Bahrain Independent Commission of Inquiry, 'Report of the Bahrain Independent Commission of Inquiry', 268.
32. Ibid., 422.
33. House of Commons Foreign Affairs Committee, 'The UK's Relationship with Saudi Arabia and Bahrain: Volume I', 11.
34. Ibid., 89.
35. '44 International NGOs: Release Bahraini Human Rights Activist NOW', http://www.bahrainrights.org/en/node/5388 (accessed 26 June 2015).
36. Bill Law, 'Bahrain Urged to Free Jailed Activists to End Unrest', *BBC News*, 19 March 2013, http://www.bbc.co.uk/news/world-middle-east-21845329 (accessed 26 June 2015).
37. Human Rights Watch, 'Bahrain: No Progress on Reform', 28 February, 2013, http://www.hrw.org/news/2013/02/28/bahrain-no-progress-reform (accessed 26 June 2015).
38. Foreign Commonwealth Office, 'Annual Report on Human Rights and Democracy 2013', http://www.publications.parliament.uk/pa/cm201415/cmselect/cmfaff/551/55106.htm#a9 (accessed 26 June 2015).

39. FIDH, 'Failed Promises in Bahrain', 13 February 2014, https://www.fidh.org/International-Federation-for-Human-Rights/north-africa-middle-east/bahrain/14659-failed-promises-in-bahrain-human-rights-violations-linger-on (accessed 26 June 2015).
40. BBC, 'Expelled US Diplomat Tom Malinowski Condemns Bahrain', 8 July 2014, http://www.bbc.co.uk/news/world-us-canada-28221189 (accessed 26 June 2015).
41. Human Rights Council Working Group on Arbitrary Detention, 'Opinions Adopted by the Working Group at its Sixty-ninth Session: No. 1/2014 (Bahrain)', 21 July 2014, 4, http://adhrb.org/wp-content/uploads/2014/11/Tagi-al-Maidan-WGAD-Decision.pdf, (accessed 26 June 2015).
42. 'Joint Statement on the OHCHR and the Human Rights Situation in Bahrain', 26th Session of the Human Rights Council, Item 2, 10 June 2014, https://www.scribd.com/fullscreen/231408541?access_key=key-LRbCUldbORWFRmxvCMHI&allow_share=true&escape=false&view_mode=scroll (accessed 26 June 2015).
43. Emanuel Stoakes, 'Whatever Happened to Bahrain's Torture Reforms?', *Foreign Policy*, 30 March 2015, http://foreignpolicy.com/2015/03/30/bahrain-reforms-torture/ (accessed 26 June 2015).
44. Human Rights Watch, 'World Report 2013: Bahrain', http://www.hrw.org/world-report/2013/country-chapters/bahrain (accessed 26 June 2015).
45. Human Rights Watch, 'World Report 2014: Bahrain', http://www.hrw.org/world-report/2014/country-chapters/bahrain?page=2 (accessed 26 June 2015).
46. Human Rights Watch, 'World Report 2015: Bahrain', https://www.hrw.org/world-report/2015/country-chapters/bahrain?page=1 (accessed 26 June 2015).
47. Reporters Without Borders, 'Media Freedom Still Under Attack in Bahrain', 11 March 2015, http://en.rsf.org/bahrain-media-freedom-still-under-attack-11-03-2015,47675.html (accessed 26 June 2015).
48. Reporters Without Borders, 'World Press Freedom Index 2015', http://index.rsf.org/#!/index-details (accessed 26 June 2015).
49. Freedom House, 'Freedom in the World 2015', https://freedomhouse.org/report/freedom-world/freedom-world-2015#.VXhP-s9Viko (accessed 26 June 2015).
50. Genocide Prevention Advisory Network, 'Risk of New Onsets of Genocide and Politicide in 2013', http://www.gpanet.org/content/risks-new-onsets-genocide-and-politicide-2013 (accessed 26 June 2015).
51. Genocide Prevention Advisory Network, 'Countries at Risk of Genocide, Politicide or Mass Atrocities', http://www.gpanet.org/content/countries-risk-genocide-politicide-or-mass-atrocities-2012 (accessed 26 June 2015).
52. Antoun Issa, 'Bassiouni: Bahrain's Progress Limited by "Piecemeal" Approach to Reforms', *Al-Monitor*, 13 June 2014, http://www.al-monitor.com/pulse/originals/2014/06/cherif-bassiouni-bici-bahrain-uprising-violations.html# (accessed 26 June 2015).
53. Amnesty International, 'Amnesty International Report 2014/15: Kingdom of Bahrain', 2015, https://www.amnesty.org/en/countries/middle-east-and-north-africa/bahrain/report-bahrain/ (accessed 26 June 2015).
54. Amnesty International, 'Bahrain: Hopes of Reform Crushed Amid Chilling Crackdown on Dissent, 15 April 2015. https://www.amnesty.org/en/articles/news/2015/04/bahrain-hopes-of-reform-crushed-amid-chilling-crackdown-on-dissent/ (accessed 26 June 2015).
55. Amnesty International, *Behind the Rhetoric* (Amnesty International: London, 2015), 6 and 9.
56. Gareth Evans, *The Responsibility to Protect: Ending Mass Atrocity Crimes Once and For All* (Washington, DC: Brookings Institution Press, 2008), 56–8.
57. Ban Ki-Moon, 'Implementing the Responsibility to Protect', UN General Assembly A/63/677, 12 January 2009, 8–9.
58. Gareth Evans, 'From an Idea to an International Norm', *Responsibility to Protect*, ed. Richard H. Cooper and Juliette V. Kohler (Hampshire and New York: Palgrave Macmillan 2009), 79; Jennifer Welsh, 'What Next for R2P?', Hague Institute for Global Justice, 27 October 2014, http://www.thehagueinstituteforglobaljustice.org/index.php?page=News-News_Articles-Recent_News-Whats_Next_for_R2P_Dr_Jennifer_Welsh_on_the_Responsibility_to_Protect&pid=138&id=303 (accessed 26 June 2015).
59. Ban Ki-Moon, 'Implementing the Responsibility to Protect', 28.
60. Bellamy, *The Responsibility to Protect*, 56.

61. Alex Bellamy, 'The Responsibility to Protect and the 2014 Conflict in Gaza', *E-International Relations*, July 22 2014, http://www.e-ir.info/2014/07/22/the-responsibility-to-protect-and-the-2014-conflict-in-gaza/ (accessed 26 June 2015).
62. See, Office of the Special Adviser on the Prevention of Genocide, 'Framework of Analysis for Atrocity Crimes: A Tool for Prevention', 2014, http://www.un.org/en/preventgenocide/adviser/pdf/framework%20of%20analysis%20for%20atrocity%20crimes_en.pdf (accessed 26 June 2015).
63. Ban Ki-Moon, 'Responsibility to Protect: State Responsibility and Prevention', A/67/929, 9 July 2013, 2.
64. Office of the Special Adviser on the Prevention of Genocide, 'Framework of Analysis for Atrocity Crimes', iii.
65. Ibid., 2.
66. The BICI report found that 35 people had died during the 2011 unrest; Bahrain Independent Commission of Inquiry, 'Report of the Bahrain Independent Commission of Inquiry', 219.
67. Human Rights Watch, 'Bahrain's Human Rights Crisis', *News*, 5 July 2011, http://www.hrw.org/news/2011/07/05/bahrains-human-rights-crisis (accessed 26 June 2015).
68. This restricted understanding of war crimes is arguably no longer tenable, however, since the ICTY (International Criminal Tribunal for the former Yugoslavia) ruling during the 1995 'Tadic Case'; see, Antonio Cassese, *International Law* (Oxford: Oxford University Press, 2005), 437. Nonetheless, 'war crimes' have not been alleged in the context of Bahrain by any of the international NGOs discussed above.
69. Office of the Special Adviser on the Prevention of Genocide, 'Framework of Analysis for Atrocity Crimes', 3.
70. Bahrain Independent Commission of Inquiry, 'Report of the Bahrain Independent Commission of Inquiry', 300.
71. Freedom House, 'Freedom in the World 2014: Bahrain', https://freedomhouse.org/report/freedom-world/2014/bahrain#.VXhQVs9Viko (accessed 26 June 2015).
72. Amnesty International, *Behind the Rhetoric*, 6.
73. Issa, 'Bassiouni: Bahrain's Progress Limited by "Piecemeal" Approach to Reforms'.
74. Office of the Special Adviser on the Prevention of Genocide, 'Framework of Analysis for Atrocity Crimes', iii.
75. Ibid., 6.
76. A case could be made for the other six, and would no doubt be made by NGOs specifically focused on Bahrain. The eight chosen are derived from the evidence presented by international NGOs and the BICI Report.
77. International Crisis Group, 'Bahrain's Rocky Road to Reform', 1.
78. Bahrain Independent Commission of Inquiry, 'Report of the Bahrain Independent Commission of Inquiry', 300.
79. Freedom House, 'Freedom in the World 2014: Bahrain'.
80. House of Commons Foreign Affairs Committee, 'The UK's Relationship with Saudi Arabia and Bahrain: Volume I', 89.
81. International Crisis Group, 'Bahrain's Rocky Road to Reform', ii.
82. Evans, *The Responsibility to Protect*, 137; Bellamy, *The Responsibility to Protect*, 11; Ban Ki-Moon, 'Implementing the Responsibility to Protect', 25.
83. Aidan Hehir, 'The Permanence of Inconsistency: Libya, The Security Council and the Responsibility to Protect', *International Security* 38, no. 1 (2013): 137–59; Theresa Reinold, 'The Responsibility to Protect: Much Ado About Nothing?', *Review of International Studies* 36, no. S1 (2010): 55–78.
84. Thomas Weiss, 'Military Humanitarianism: Syria Hasn't Killed It', *The Washington Quarterly* 37, no. 1 (2014): 7–20; Ed Luck, 'The Responsibility to Protect at Ten: The Challenges Ahead', Stanley Foundation Policy Analysis Brief, May 2015, http://www.stanleyfoundation.org/publications/pab/LuckPAB515.pdf (accessed 26 June 2015); Alex Bellamy and Paul Williams, 'The New Politics of Protection? Cote d'Ivoire, Libya and the Responsibility to Protect', *International Affairs* 82, no. 7 (2011): 825–50.
85. Ban Ki-Moon, 'Fulfilling our Collective: International Assistance and the Responsibility to Protect', A/68/947, 11 July 2014, 20.
86. Ban Ki-Moon, 'Responsibility to Protect: Timely and Decisive Response: Report of the Secretary-General', A/66/874, 25 July 2012, 2.

87. Full list of statements available at, http://www.un.org/sg/statements/sgstatssearchFull.asp (accessed 26 June 2015).
88. Ban Ki-Moon, 'Concerned at Violence in Bahrain, Ban Calls for Restraint and Dialogue', UN News Centre, 13 April 2011, http://www.un.org/apps/news/story.asp?NewsID=38105&Cr=bahrain&Cr1=#.VXbhIs9Vikp (accessed 26 June 2015).
89. Ban Ki-Moon, 'Statement Attributable to the Spokesperson for the Secretary-General on the Bahrain Independent Commission of Inquiry', New York, 24 November 2011, http://www.un.org/sg/statements/index.asp?nid=5708 (accessed 26 June 2015).
90. Ban Ki-Moon, 'Statement Attributable to the Spokesperson for the Secretary-General on Bahrain', New York, 1 November 2012, http://www.un.org/sg/statements/?nid=6395 (accessed 26 June 2015).
91. Ban Ki-Moon, 'Statement Attributable to the Spokesperson for the Secretary-General on Bahrain', New York, 8 January 2013, http://www.un.org/sg/statements/index.asp?nid=6541 (accessed 26 June 2015).
92. Ban Ki-Moon, 'Statement Attributable to the Spokesperson for the Secretary-General on Bahrain', New York, 3 March 2014, http://www.un.org/sg/statements/index.asp?nid=7500 (accessed 26 June 2015).
93. All six reports can be accessed via http://www.responsibilitytoprotect.org/index.php/about-rtop/core-rtop-documents (accessed 26 June 2015).
94. Freedom House, 'Freedom in the World 2014: Bahrain'.
95. Geneive Abdo and Lulwa Rizkallah, 'Falling Dominoes', *National Interest*, 31 December 2014, http://nationalinterest.org/feature/falling-dominos-bahrains-sectarian-turmoil-11945 (accessed 26 June 2015).
96. The countries are, Syria, Sudan, South Sudan, Libya, Cote D'Ivorie, Guinea, Kyrgyzstan, Sri Lanka and the DRC. See, http://www.un.org/en/preventgenocide/adviser/ (accessed 26 June 2015).
97. Evans, 'From an Idea to an International Norm', 16; Samantha Power, 'Foreword', in *Responsibility to Protect*, ed. Richard H. Cooper and Juliette V. Kohler (Hampshire and New York: Palgrave Macmillan 2009), x; Anne-Marie Slaughter, 'A Day to Celebrate But Hard Work Ahead', *Foreign Policy*, 18 March 2011.
98. The aims and strategy of each organisation can be found on their websites; GCR2P, http://www.globalr2p.org/about_us#history; ICRtoP, http://responsibilitytoprotect.org/index.php/about-coalition/founding-purposes; APCR2P, http://www.r2pasiapacific.org/about (accessed 26 June 2015).
99. Ryan D'Souza, email message to author, 9 June 2015.
100. GCR2P, 'R2P Monitor', http://www.globalr2p.org/our_work/r2p_monitor (accessed 26 June 2015).
101. GCR2P, 'Populations at Risk', http://www.globalr2p.org/regions/ (accessed 26 June 2015).
102. GCR2P, 'Publications', http://www.globalr2p.org/publications/ (accessed 26 June 2015).
103. On 25 January 2012 the GCR2P published a tweet about a speech given by Navi Pillay in which she discussed the uprisings across the Middle East, including Bahrain.
104. Ibid.; on 3 March 2012 GCR2P published a Facebook post about a speech given by Navi Pillay about uprisings across the Middle East, including Bahrain.
105. Twitter correspondence with author, 5 June 2015.
106. On 13 April 2012 the ICRtoP retweeted an Amnesty International report.
107. On 9 May 2012 the ICRtoP posted a link to an ICG report on Bahrain.
108. APCR2P, 'Ideas in Brief', http://www.r2pasiapacific.org/index.html?page=187568 (accessed 26 June 2015).
109. APCR2P, 'Newsletters', http://www.r2pasiapacific.org/index.html?page=189076 (accessed 26 June 2015).
110. APCR2P, 'Publications', http://www.r2pasiapacific.org/index.html?page=187762 (accessed 26 June 2015).
111. Global Responsibility to Protect, http://www.brill.com/cn/global-responsibility-protect (accessed 26 June 2015).
112. The seven are: 22 November 2011, on the release of the BICI report; 16 April 2012, a link to an ICG report; 28 September 2012, posted Bahrain's call at the General Assembly for action on Syria; 8 January 2013, posted a link on the jailing of Bahraini dissidents; 24 April 2013, posted a link to a *New York Times* article on the cancellation of the UN special rapporteur's visit to Bahrain; 28

December 2014, posted a link on women protestors in Middle East including in Bahrain; 30 December 2014, posted a photo from UN Human Rights on freedom of expression in Bahrain.

113. The Montreal Institute for Genocide Prevention published a tweet on 25 January 2012 about a speech by Navi Pillay in which she mentioned Bahrain; the Will to Intervene Project published a tweet on 22 February 2012 with a link to an article in the *Ottawa Citizen* on Bahrain.

114. GCR2P, retweeted from reported.ly, 12 June 2015.

115. ICRtoP, retweeted from Child Soldiers Int., 31 March 2015.

116. GCR2P, retweeted from NZ Mission to the UN, 22 May 2015.

117. ICRtoP, retweeted from 1 for 7 Billion, 27 April 2015.

118. GCR2P, retweeted from UK_UN New York, 21 May 2015.

119. ICRtoP, retweeted from CoalitionfortheICC, 22 April 2015.

120. GCR2P, retweeted from RaMurmokaite, 30 April 2015.

121. APCR2P, Twitter, 18 June 2015.

122. APCR2P, Twitter, 29 April 2015.

123. APCR2P, Twitter, 21 April 2015.

124. House of Commons Foreign Affairs Committee, 'The UK's Relationship with Saudi Arabia and Bahrain: Volume I', 84.

125. Eliot Abrams, 'How Obama Caved on Bahrain', *Foreign Policy*, 27 February 2015, https://foreignpolicy.com/2015/02/27/how-obama-caved-on-bahrain-manama-human-rights/ (accessed 26 June 2015).

126. Michael Gordon, 'U.S. Lifts Ban on Bahrain Aid', *The New York Times*, 29 June 2015, http://www.nytimes.com/2015/06/30/world/middleeast/us-lifts-ban-on-bahrain-aid.html?ref=topics (accessed 10 July 2015).

127. House of Commons Foreign Affairs Committee, 'The UK's Relationship with Saudi Arabia and Bahrain: Volume I', 85.

128. Ibid., 5.

129. BBC, 'UK to Establish £15 Permanent Middle East Military Base', *BBC News*, 6 December 2014, http://www.bbc.co.uk/news/uk-30355953 (accessed 26 June 2015).

130. Both states have issued some public rebukes to the monarchy, though not through the Security Council.

131. Bellamy, 'The Responsibility to Protect and the 2014 Conflict in Gaza'.

132. Jonathan Graubart, 'NGOs and the Security Council', in *The UN Security Council and the Politics of International Authority*, ed. Bruce Cronin and Ian Hurd (London: Routledge, 2008), 154–72.Chase Madar, 'Hawks for Humanity', *Al Jazeera*, January 21, 2014, http://america.aljazeera.com/opinions/2014/1/hawks-for-humanity.html (accessed 26 June 2015)

133. Aidan Hehir, 'A Propensity to Ignore?', *E-International Relations*, 15 July 2014, http://www.e-ir.info/2014/07/15/a-propensity-to-ignore-r2p-advocacy-and-the-crisis-in-gaza/ (accessed 26 June 2015).

134. Evans, *The Responsibility to Protect*, 33.

135. Thomas Weiss, *Thinking about Global Governance* (London: Routledge, 2011), 120; David Hollenbach, *Driven From Home* (Washington, DC: Georgetown University Press, 2010), 221; Abiodun Williams and Jonas Claes, 'Leadership and the Responsibility to Protect', in *The Routledge Handbook of the Responsibility to Protect* ed. Andy Knight and Frazer Egerton (London: Routledge, 2012), 130.

136. Ban Ki-Moon, 'Early Warning, Assessment and the Responsibility to Protect', A/64/864, 14 July 2010, 4.

137. The Auschwitz Institute published a tweet on 19 July 2012 linking to an article in *E-International Relations*; and another on 31 October 2012 linking to a report by the Bahrain Centre for Human Rights.

138. Bahrain Centre for Human Rights, 'No Progress, No Peace', 20 September 2012, 7, http://www.bahrainrights.org/en/node/5422 (accessed 26 June 2015).

139. Indicatively, the ICG described Bahrain as 'an existential issue' for Saudi Arabia. International Crisis Group, 'Bahrain's Rocky Road to Reform', 21.

140. House of Commons Foreign Affairs Committee, 'The UK's Relationship with Saudi Arabia and Bahrain: Volume I', 11–12.

141. Cynthia O'Murchu and Simon Kerr, 'Bahrain Land Deals Highlight Alchemy of Making Money from Sand', *Financial Times*, 10 December 2014.

142. Paul Weaver, 'Why This Year's Bahrain Grand Prix Should Not be Taking Place', *The Guardian*, 16 February 2012, http://www.theguardian.com/sport/blog/2012/feb/16/bahrain-grand-prix-bernie-ecclestone (accessed 26 June 2015).

143. 'Statement of the Kingdom of Bahrain at the Sixty-Seventh Session of the UN General Assembly', 27 September 2012, 3, http://gadebate.un.org/sites/default/files/gastatements/67/BH_en.pdf (accessed 26 June 2015); Editorial Board, 'Bahrain's Rulers Now Flout the US Openly', *Washington Post*, 22 June 2015, http://www.washingtonpost.com/opinions/bahrains-rulers-now-flout-the-us-openly/2015/06/19/049c3356-1516-11e5-89f3-61410da94eb1_story.html (accessed 26 June 2015).

144. Abrams, 'How Obama Caved on Bahrain'; Editorial Board, 'Bahrain's Rulers Now Flout the US Openly'.

145. Tweet from @kenRoth, 21 January 2015.

146. Gareth Evans, 'The Responsibility to Protect in Action', *Courier*, 24 June 2015, http://www.stanleyfoundation.org/resources.cfm?id=721&article=1 (accessed 26 June 2015).

147. 'Statement of the Kingdom of Bahrain at the Sixty-Seventh Session of the UN General Assembly', 4.

148. Human Rights Watch, 'Bahrain's Human Rights Crisis'.

149. International Crisis Group, 'Bahrain's Rocky Road to Reform', 21.

150. Bellamy, *The Responsibility to Protect: A Defence*, 89.

The responsibility to protect, the use of force and a permanent United Nations peace service

Annie Herro

Centre for Peace and Conflict Studies, University of Sydney, Australia

The United Nations Emergency Peace Service (UNEPS) is a civil society-led idea to establish a permanent service that would improve United Nations peace operations and operationalise the emerging norm, the 'responsibility to protect'. The idea, however, has encountered multiple obstacles, especially in relation to its proposed capacity to use of force. This article argues that when the right conditions have been met, there may be cases where force could be applied by the proposed UNEPS. Support for a UNEPS might also be found if its deployments were conditional on UN Security Council authorisation and backed by the consent of the host country.

Introduction

The United Nations (UN) has come a long way in a short space of time towards notionally affirming its commitment to civilians caught up in humanitarian crises. In 2005 the responsibility to protect (R2P) doctrine was unanimously endorsed by member states at the World Summit hosted by the UN. World leaders agreed that all states had the responsibility to protect their populations from genocide, war crimes, ethnic cleansing and crimes against humanity, and committed to take 'timely and decisive action' in cases where governments 'manifestly failed to protect their populations' from such atrocities.[1]

Despite this political head-nodding, the UN still struggles to operationalise these commitments or turn 'words into deeds', especially in the context of UN peace operations. The world body has all too often either deployed peacekeeping forces 'too little, too late' in response to crises, or not at all. Preventative deployments are rare and it takes an average of 46 days for missions to deploy after they have received the green light from the UN Security Council (UNSC).[2] This is partly because each operation must be formed 'from scratch'.[3] And when peacekeepers are deployed, peace operations often suffer from a lack of adequate numbers of well-trained and equipped peacekeepers and supplies needed to fulfil the mandates of missions.[4]

In his 2009 report on R2P, UN Secretary-General Ban Ki-moon stated that 'there are substantial gaps in capacity, imagination and will across the whole spectrum of prevention and protection measures relating to the responsibility to protect'. 'Nowhere is that gap more pronounced or more damaging than in the realm of forceful and timely response to the most flagrant crimes and violations relating to the responsibility to protect', he wrote.[5] During the UN General Assembly (UNGA) debate on R2P this same year, South Korea and New Zealand called for the creation of a rapid reaction force.[6] Despite this recognition of a gap in the potential implementation of R2P, the UNSG noted that the UN 'is still far from developing the kind of rapid-response military capacity most needed to handle the sort of rapidly unfolding atrocity crimes'.[7]

In response to these problems and in an attempt to provide the UN with the tools to enable it to respond 'timely and decisively' to situations where civilians are under threat as a result of mass atrocities, a transnational advocacy network dedicated to researching and promoting the idea of a UN Emergency Peace Service (UNEPS) was formed. UNEPS is an ambitious reform proposal for a UN standing capacity comprising well-trained and well-equipped troops, police and civilians who would be able to deploy at short notice 'to prevent genocide and crimes against humanity'.[8] According to UNEPS' promoters, the establishment of a UNEPS would be a valuable addition to the UN's toolbox in operationalising R2P.[9]

There are, however, multiple obstacles confronting the implementation of the UNEPS proposal, not the least a reluctance to support a new UN entity with the means to use force. Therefore, responses to specific questions about the appropriate course of action when a state is unable or unwilling to protect its population from atrocities, or when the state itself becomes the perpetrator of violence against its own people, are intrinsically linked to attitudes towards the UNEPS proposal. Indeed, answers to these questions become all the more significant when the mechanism of intervention is a permanent UN capacity.

In general, the subject of a standing UN force or service is strikingly under-researched. Recent studies have analysed some of the practical and political obstacles confronting a UNEPS, yet these examinations are limited to issues such as the size of the proposed service, the lack of perceived legitimacy of, and political will within, its authorising body[10] – the UN – and its short-term deployment philosophy.[11] Moreover, Kinloch-Pichat and Roberts have both independently identified some objections to a UN standing force such as a fear of its supra-national dimension[12] and doubts the appropriateness of the UNSC as a military authorisation body.[13] Neither study, however, considers ways to overcome the obstacles they identify, nor do they present an in-depth exploration of the intersection between attitudes towards the use of force and proposals for a standing UN military force. Unlike previous research and based on interviews with individuals across different regions of the world who have a stake in peace and security issues, this article examines attitudes towards aspects of the UNEPS proposal that relate to the use of force in the face of atrocities. It also considers the implications of these attitudes for increasing support for the proposal.

This article next introduces the UNEPS proposal. It then presents the sources of information used in this article, after which it presents two perspectives on a UNEPS that would have the capacity to use force: (1) a cautious response and (2) a cautious but interested response – and explores some of the norms used to justify these positions. It ends with a discussion on what this examination could tell us about increasing support for a proposed UNEPS.

The United Nations Emergency Peace Service proposal

UNEPS is the latest in a long line of proposals for a permanent service that would be directly recruited, trained, equipped and controlled by the UN. The roots of the idea stretch back to the inter-war years when the impressive fighting record of the French

Foreign Legion in World War I inspired a model for an international police force. Since then, proposals for a standing peacekeeping capacity have periodically resurfaced and have been championed by a range of individuals, organisations and states.

Peter Langille can be credited as the catalyst for the global initiative for a UNEPS. He developed the concept, case, model and initial plans for a UNEPS in 2002 and has devoted much of the last decade to its promotion and to further research.[14] In December 2003, Langille presented his idea in a consolidated form at a symposium called 'Genocide and Crimes Against Humanity: The Challenge of Prevention and Enforcement' in Santa Barbara, California.[15] Participants at the conference included activists and academics, and many of them have continued to meet each subsequent year partly through the coordination of the New York-based non-governmental organisation (NGO) Global Action to Prevent War (GAPW) to increase awareness of the need for UN-based rapid reaction capabilities. The UNEPS network receives support from numerous civil society organisations in diverse global regions, former politicians and current and former UN officials. The following is a truncated summary of the proposal.

UNEPS would be a permanent service comprising citizens of member nations acting in their individual capacity. It would have the ability to respond preventively to crises, operating with a 'first-in, first-out' deployment philosophy, and would have a maximum deployment of six months. It would thus close the gap between the approved UNSC resolution authoring an operation and action. Having UNEPS readily available might also assist in obtaining UNSC authorisation for the use of force and reduce unilateral interventions. Second, since UNEPS would be self-contained with readily available personnel (around 15,000–18,000 civilians, police and military), equipment and supplies at the disposal of the UN, it could overcome governments' unwillingness to expose their citizens and resources to security threats in countries perceived to be of little geopolitical significance. Such a rationale partly explains why so many UN peace operations are under-resourced and unable to fulfil their mandate.[16]

The UNSC would be the preferred mode of authorisation for a UNEPS but, according to its proponents, it could also be authorised by the UNGA through the 'Uniting for Peace' Resolution. The proposed UNEPS would comprise personnel from diverse cultural, religious, social and geographical backgrounds and be based at UN-designated sites, including field headquarters, functioning under a unified UN command. This is intended to both facilitate better interaction with host communities and remove some of the neo-colonial stigma that is often associated with interventions. Personnel would be carefully screened and have a range of professional and language skills covering these areas: human rights, gender, police, military service, humanitarian assistance, judicial proceedings and penal matters, conflict transformation and environmental protection, and would operate within and enforce international humanitarian and human rights law. UNEPS would complement – not replace – other protection actors, including the host governments, UN protection agencies and NGOs, and it would need to be replaced by more robust, longer-term peacekeeping after it withdraws.[17]

Despite the apparent contribution of a UNEPS in providing the UN with a tool to operationalise R2P, persuading governments of the merits of the proposal is not without its challenges. This article unpacks some of the reasons for this. But before it does so, I briefly present those sources of information on which I base my argument.

Source of information

This article is based on interviews conducted between 2007 and 2013 with political, military and non-state actors concerned with international peace and security issues. Two, often intersecting, types of people were consulted. The first comprises decision-makers, such as members of the government, senior members of government bureaucracies or senior UN officials in relevant departments. They were in positions of power and consequently were able to advise what it would take for the proposed UNEPS to receive support in their respective domains – a key step towards the establishment of a UNEPS. The second group of people both reflect and influence the views of these kinds of decision-makers. This group can be divided into two sub-groups: those who were previously in powerful positions within government, the UN, military or regional organisations (specifically the Association of Southeast Asian Nations) but had recently retired; and those unofficial observers such as those working for, or closely affiliated with, NGOs, media organisations, universities or influential think tanks who (try to) influence governments through their advocacy and reporting on UNEPS-related issues. Through their knowledge of, and experience in, fields related to the proposed UNEPS, they were able to shed further light on the types of obstacles that the proposal might meet and strategies that might shift a decision-maker who is unsupportive to a more supportive posture. I triangulate the interviews with other primary as well as secondary sources of information, including transcripts and reports from conferences and reports on R2P and the proposed UNEPS and literature on previous proposals for a permanent UN force, to sharpen and elaborate responses from the key informants mentioned above. I also consulted institutional data that were publically available in government statements and UN reports, and the media reports and scholarly analyses of issues related to the central features of the UNEPS proposal.

A cautious approach towards the use of force

To understand why the UNEPS proposal as it stands is rejected or challenged, we must understand the norms (or ideas shared among an identity group about what is appropriate) that underlie the respondents' antipathy. This section explores three types of cautious responses to the proposal.

1. *Non-intervention and territorial integrity: 'many countries ... will not be comfortable giving the UN an independent force that they fear may be used against them!'*

Non-intervention and territorial integrity are perhaps the most obvious obstacles confronting the proposal. They are often referred to as the doctrine of Westphalian sovereignty (based on the 1648 Peace of Westphalia, even though this took place over a hundred years *before* non-intervention was first clearly articulated). Krasner makes the point that the norms associated with sovereignty have always been violated, through both coercive and non-coercive means.[18] This suggests that Westphalian principles are something of a myth and that the so-called inviolability status of sovereignty is possibly overstated given how countries have behaved in the international sphere.

Despite such contradictions, the norms of Westphalian sovereignty are still constitutively powerful and clearly play a role in shaping respondents' interests and, by extension, their views on UNEPS. A former Indonesian ambassador, who is an influential member of a prominent Jakarta-based think tank, was opposed to peace enforcement operations – that is, international peacekeepers using force, for whatever reason – within a sovereign's territory. He said, 'a peacekeeping force is ... not a war fighting machine ... ' He further stated that 'when we were fighting the Dutch, there were only military observers'.[19] He is expressing his support for traditional peacekeeping missions that are deployed at the point between a ceasefire and a political settlement. Such missions do not propose or enforce solutions between states but rather try to build confidence between belligerents in an attempt to facilitate political dialogue. The ambassador's response is both a testimony to the strength of non-intervention and a reflection of his expectations of the UN's role in managing international conflict. This is the system that Beck calls 'schizophrenic' because it is mandated to function as an impartial as well as a partisan organisation.[20]

Non-intervention is also central to the political culture of Southeast Asia of which Indonesia is a part. The Association of Southeast Asian Nations (ASEAN) embodies a set of regional principles put forward in the 1990s by former Prime Ministers Lee Kuan Yew of Singapore and Mahathir bin Mohamad of Malaysia. At heart they advocate non-interference in the domestic affairs of other states and promote a consensus-based style of decision-making. Since the organisation's birth, during the conflict between Indonesia and Malaysia from 1962 to 1966 and many other civil wars in Southeast Asia, it has renounced the threat or use of force to settle international disputes. Indeed, the ASEAN Charter calls for 'respect for the independence, sovereignty, equality, territorial integrity and national identity of all ASEAN member states'.[21]

Having said this, UN peace operations were in fact deployed in Cambodia in the early 1990s and East Timor from 1999. These interventions had tenuous consent from the host states though they violated the norms of both Westphalian sovereignty and the ASEAN Way. Some have argued that the ASEAN Way has evolved its thinking since Lee and Mahathir held sway. The so-called post-Westphalian ideas, which put human rights at the centre of the agenda, have resulted in – among other things – the creation of the ASEAN Intergovernmental Commission on Human Rights. So while the views of the Indonesian ambassador might reflect the 'old' ASEAN and the traditional narrative of Westphalian sovereignty, others also share his views.[22]

Non-intervention as a guiding tenet is guarded for a variety of reasons. It tends to be the view taken up by states that are conscious of their own frailty and have experienced colonisation in their history. It is often espoused by tyrants who seek cover for human rights violations and also by people with humane values unwilling to create opportunities for oppression.[23] But what reasons did respondents cite? A representative of the Permanent Mission of Australia to the UN who also sits on the UN Special Committee on Peacekeeping Operations said in relation to UNEPS that many countries in the UNGA would not be comfortable giving the UN 'an independent force that they fear may be used against them!'[24] As an Indonesian scholar candidly noted: 'That's why the idea isn't going to fly. Because it is against the sovereignty of the state. While everyone agrees that we don't want Rwanda to happen, but what happens to you [the "intervened"] can happen to us!'[25] She is recognising that despite the moral imperative to prevent and respond to atrocities, she would be reluctant to permit an intervention force like UNEPS into her country if such crimes took place there because it would violate their territorial integrity, and domestic authority and control. In the lead up to the 2005 World Summit, ministers of the so-called Non-Aligned Movement – traditionally strong advocates of non-intervention, sovereignty and mutual non-aggression – were of the same view. They requested clarification on how these norms would be reconciled with R2P.[26]

In sum, the views of those in this category suggest that the fear of being the target of a UNEPS intervention is a significant obstacle to the proposed UNEPS receiving support. On the one hand, this fixation with the norms of Westphalia may be the usual antipathy to establishing any kind of supra-national arrangement. Indeed, nurturing strong states is the bedrock of R2P because it guards against imperialism among other positive qualities. On the other hand, it invites UNEPS advocates to consider what safeguards might be built into the idea to placate such fears. These ideas are explored further below.

2. *Patriotic norms: 'how can the troops be independent if the money comes from states?'*

Some respondents were cautious about a permanent, supra-national UN service that would have the capacity to use force because they insisted, as realists do, that states are at the centre of the international system and that the pursuit of morality in the international sphere will never be possible because states are driven by power. All politics, wrote the classical realist Hans Morgenthau, is a struggle for power.[27] Some respondents hold such views because they believe that states *do* behave like this, while others think that states *should* behave like this. Because of these beliefs, respondents could not accept that a mechanism like UNEPS would ever be created for purely cosmopolitan reasons – that it would have its own *esprit de corps* and be independent of states' narrowly defined interests. As a senior representative of the Australian Department of Foreign Affairs and Trade put it: 'with a UN mission [like UNEPS] ... Who do you serve? Not national interests ... Australians fight for national interest'.[28] Like Kenneth Waltz, for this respondent national interests were viewed in fairly limited terms such as increasing military power, economic growth and security.[29]

Echoing classical realist arguments, other respondents claimed that the legitimacy of interventions will always be questionable because the powerful set the agenda. Morgenthau writes that, whenever possible, people and states attempt to convince those who must submit to their will that they are acting in their interests or those of the wider community.[30] He insists that 'universal moral principles cannot be applied to the actions of states'.[31] Respondents' concerns specifically related to the funding of the proposed UNEPS and the potential for it to be manipulated by Western states. A representative at the Permanent Mission of Croatia to the UN, who had experience working with Security Council members during Croatia's tenure on the council, said 'money is a big question – whoever gives the money wants to have control – how can the troops be independent if the money comes from states?'[32] Despite being a supporter of R2P capacities such as UNEPS, he went on to comment that 'if UNEPS is influenced by the "white" states how will it not be perceived as imperial?' He is arguing that all interventions have an imperialist agenda even though the aim of UNEPS is to maintain a degree of autonomy from member states. As Noam Chomsky has argued, throughout history the most violent and destructive interventions, including Japan's attack on Manchuria, Mussolini's invasion of Abyssinia (Ethiopia) and Hitler's occupation of parts of Czechoslovakia (Czech Republic), have been justified in the name of a humanitarian imperative.[33] More recently we see the language of civilian protection used by Russian President Vladimir Putin to justify intervention in the Crimea. Putin announced that Russia had 'the right to use all available means' to protect the Russian-speaking population in the eastern and southern regions of Ukraine.[34]

Patriotic norms are also apparent in the response of an influential Indonesian journalist who worked closely with a former Indonesia president.[35] She claimed that interveners 'always end up taking sides' and implied that UNEPS could only be trusted if it were neutral, which, she also argued, is impossible. She goes on to say that:

> It all comes down to interest ... in the end, we are all nationalistic ... Someone is going to pay the bulk of the fees for UNEPS and the country that does will end up calling the shots and that will cause problems.

The Indonesian ambassador (cited above) supported this view, saying: 'In the end, we are all nationalistic. Maybe when there is an attack from Mars then we will become more united.'[36] Similar concerns were raised in 1948 when a small committee was set up to debate Lie's proposal for a permanent UN Guard. The representative from South Africa questioned whether it would be possible for the UN Guard to be impartial and neutral.[37] The same issues were raised a decade later when Georg Schwarzenberger, the Rapporteur of the Committee on the Charter of the UN, argued for a study to investigate a proposal to establish a permanent Peace Force of between two and ten thousand personnel to assist the organisation in maintaining international peace and security. Concerns about military capability and interference by the powerful in states' affairs proved, again, to be a stumbling block. The representatives from the USSR, Ceylon (Sri Lanka) and Poland argued that they were cautious about the idea because, among other reasons, they feared the force might be used to interfere with state sovereignty or used by a group or bloc of states to advance their own interests rather than the interests of the UN.[38]

3. *More harm than good*

One respondent – a former Secretary-General of ASEAN – opposed the idea of a UNEPS that would have the capacity to use force based on the view that military interventions cause more harm than good.[39] He gives the example of 2009 when many in the international community accused the leader of Myanmar, General Than Shwe, and his military junta of committing crimes against humanity when they resisted relief efforts for the millions affected by Cyclone Nargis. Coercive measures would have made 'the situation worse', he says. While he is mounting a practical argument on the negative consequences of intervention, his views are undoubtedly informed by the widespread suspicions in the ASEAN community which were mentioned earlier. Nevertheless, there are valid practical concerns about the disadvantages of a UNEPS-type capacity. In 1963, Brian Urquhart, who is now a strong advocate of a permanent UN force, argued that a 'permanent international police force ... might, by its very existence or through precipitate and inappropriate use, complicate the very situation it was designed to solve'.[40]

Alan Kuperman has mounted a similar argument with regard to NATO's 2011 humanitarian military intervention in Libya. He writes that the intervention extended the war's duration about six-fold; increased its death toll approximately seven to ten-fold; and exacerbated human rights abuses, humanitarian suffering, Islamic radicalism and weapons proliferation in Libya and its neighbours.[41] He has also argued with regard to Libya and Kosovo that R2P military intervention, even if mounted for the 'right' reasons, can exacerbate a conflict because of what he labels 'the moral hazard of humanitarian intervention'. He believes that some groups (for example the Kosovo Liberation Army) were encouraged by the possibility of humanitarian intervention 'to launch armed challenges against the state, provoking genocidal retaliations'.[42] Notwithstanding Bellamy's convincing argument that claims made by Kuperman and others about moral hazard and R2P have no empirical basis, such perceptions are worth taking seriously as they are an obstacle to UNEPS' creation.[43] Similar concerns were identified – but not resolved – by participants at the conference on UNEPS in 2005, with the rapporteur noting that it is 'important to have developed and publicised ways to discourage people from instigating violence deliberately in the hope of triggering UNEPS intervention'.[44] This issue is further discussed later in this article.

Interested but with reservations

Respondents in this category comprised those who were interested in the proposed military capability of UNEPS but had certain reservations relating to its mandate and modes of authorisation.

Cosmopolitanism v. non-intervention and sovereignty

Those in this category can be seen weighing up the validity of R2P and other cosmopolitanism norms against the strength of Westphalian norms like non-intervention and sovereignty. I explore how these norms might be reconciled through a recalibration of the UNEPS proposal. On the one hand, a respondent who was a scholar from an Indonesian political science think tank and had once served the government of Indonesia in the area of foreign affairs was cautious about the supranational dimension of UNEPS and worried that it would circumvent the collective will of states by intervening in countries without the UNSC's agreement to do so.[45] She said:

> What stops countries from intervening in a country like Myanmar is the fear of fallout in countries concerned. China or India don't want the economic fallouts of intervention, Myanmar might leak too heavily. A standing UNEPS would not have this fear because they are not [reliant on contributions from] member states – there is less hesitancy to upset countries … So you are going to see a more proactive UN and one that will be more intrusive into the affairs of Member States. If there is a need for rapid deployment, New York can say we will send troops to Aceh and it doesn't matter what Indonesia has to say about it.

She is concerned that a proposed UNEPS might compromise the material benefits states gain from bilateral relationships with countries that could be the target of a UNEPS intervention (even if such governments are illegitimate). Some have argued that a principal reason that Russia failed to support a UNSC resolution authorising the use of force against the Assad regime in Syria is because it is the main supplier of arms to Syria, accounting for approximately 10% of Russia's arms sales. In the wake of the significant financial losses in cancelled arms sales after the UN imposed an arms embargo on Libya, a further loss could be damaging to the Russian economy.[46] The respondent is also concerned that if a UNEPS were established there would be more coercive interventions, which would erode the norms of Westphalia, including a state's territorial integrity. Therefore, unlike those in the cautious group above, her reluctance to support a truly cosmopolitan peacekeeping service is not because of a concern about certain states controlling UNEPS but rather because of a concern that states connected to the intervened *will not have enough* control. On the other hand, this same respondent was also prepared to accept that, in some instances, there is a moral imperative to use force to protect civilians from mass violence. She said:

> You are not neutral in term of the crimes. You don't accept atrocities … You have to bring certain values [to an intervention] … there are often clear victims and perpetrators of a crime … in Kosovo you had Serbs killing Muslims.[47]

She seems to be expressing her support for the 1999 NATO-led airstrikes over Kosovo, ostensibly conducted to stop Serbian ethnic cleansing in Kosovo.[48] While most states opposed this intervention, Malaysia – a predominately Muslim state and Indonesia's neighbour – supported it, stating that it 'was necessary to prevent genocide in Kosovo'.[49] Indeed, many in the Arab and Islamic world were in 'two minds' about the intervention. Some supported it out of an emotional solidarity with other Muslims, but from a political view-point it was seen to set a dangerous precedent.[50] In sum, this respondent is showing some interest in applying R2P norms in certain circumstances but falls short of expressing support for a permanent UN standing capacity.

Increasing support for the UNEPS proposal

What opportunities to increase support for the proposed UNEPS can be gleaned from this analysis of the use of force? First, there is a strong belief that any kind of permanent UN force could be misappropriated by the most powerful states and a suspicion that such a cosmopolitan *esprit de corps* would be an impossible goal. These two beliefs may come to be insurmountable hurdles in building a viable UNEPS proposal. Such concerns are real – we have seen the effects of domestic politics interfering with the funding of a UN body when the US government cut off tens of millions of dollars in annual funding to the UN Educational, Scientific and Cultural Organisation after it voted to admit Palestine as a full member.[51]

Yet these fears also point to a possible solution: the creation of an alternative funding structure that does not (solely) rely on contributions from member states. The task of making a standing UN force financially independent is an old debate. The essence of the argument is that a fund would be established from sources such as arms, air travel or taking a portion of national defence budgets so that a UNEPS would not be held hostage to the interests of individual donor states. Others suggest the UN could control the right to exploit resources from the oceans.[52] Similar initiatives have been proposed to overcome traditional impasses in UN budgets and to increase its limited resources. One such initiative is a proposed tax on international currency transactions – the so-called Tobin tax – which would provide the UN with independent revenues to alleviate the organisation's reliance on member states' contributions.[53] But while such solutions could provide a standing force with a degree of autonomy, it could not make it fully independent as it would still need capabilities such as transport and 'projection capability' (the ability to intimidate and implement policy by threatening or using force in a distant area).[54]

Second, the issue of a coercive UNEPS intervention causing more harm than good is important to address both in the context of increasing support for the proposal and in light of the practical and ethical considerations of a UNEPS deployment. The report of the International Commission on Intervention and State Sovereignty (ICISS) provides some suggestions on how to respond to such concerns. The report adopts the principle, based on the Just War doctrine, that military action can only be justified if it is likely to halt or avert the atrocities that triggered the intervention in the first place.[55] In other words, military intervention is unjustified if actual protection cannot be achieved, or if the consequences of an intervention are likely to be worse than if there is no action at all. UNEPS' supporters have also adopted this same precautionary principle.[56] The question, of course, is how do you know if coercive action is likely to do more harm than good?

Kuperman has provided two suggestions on preventing interventions from doing more harm than good that pertain to a proposed UNEPS and might respond to concerns about the ability of such a service to achieve its ends: to alleviate suffering and save lives. The first is that the potential interveners should be aware of misinformation – resulting from inaccurate reporting or their own biased perceptions – and disinformation from concerted propaganda campaigns.[57] Pattison also highlights the importance of having the correct information to allow interveners to make a reasonable judgment about the long-term consequences of any intervention. His focus, however, is on whether the interveners are capable of, and have a clear strategy to carry out, their mission as well as having sufficient local and global support for an intervention.[58] While this list is far from exhaustive, it identifies some principles for UNEPS' advocates to consider in response to accusations that the proposed service would make an already volatile situation worse. This discussion also highlights the value of other criteria identified in the ICISS report (and in the UNEPS literature) that guide decision-makers on whether or not to take robust action in the face of extreme violence against civilians.

Third, what can we make of the tension between, on the one hand, cosmopolitan norms such as those pertaining to R2P and the supra-national dimension of UNEPS with, on the other hand, commitments to Westphalian norms? Given that a major concern was the ability of a permanent service to intervene in situations where vital national interests are at stake, the UNEPS proposal could contain clearer safeguards indicating that it would only be able to deploy with UNSC authorisation with the consent of the state in question. Indeed, the veto ensures that the UN will not identify a global interest that is inconsistent with the national interests of the permanent five members of the Security Council (P5). Among those expressing a preference for a UNSC authorisation was an influential European scholar in genocide studies who said:

> Going outside the UNSC would not be productive – it is dangerous to move outside the UNSC regarding the use of force. The danger of relaxing the rules is worse than the benefits – ultimately [it means] letting any country intervene when they feel like it, using R2P as justification.[59]

This discussion highlights one of the paradoxes of a recalibrated UNEPS proposal. The logic behind UNEPS is to create a service that would not be held hostage to the interests of member states; however, in order for UNEPS to achieve support, it might need to be contingent on UNSC authorisation. A similar process occurred when the R2P doctrine was transitioning from the ICISS report to the World Summit Outcome Document. The ICISS report's suggestion – that a military intervention to protect civilians might be deployed under a UNGA 'Uniting for Peace Resolution'– was omitted from the Outcome Document and the final wording on the authority placed R2P's coercive components firmly within the ambit of the UNSC.[60]

The creation of an independent funding structure for the proposed UNEPS to increase the autonomy of such a service is not necessarily incommensurable with adding safeguards, such as UNSC authorisation. The former may address concerns about the domination of one state, while the latter might provide comfort to those who fear that a UNEPS intervention could compromise the strategic and economic interests of states that are connected to the intervened. This might exclude situations where the state is the perpetrator of the atrocities; however, as the deployment of the International Force for East Timor (INTERFET) (discussed further below) suggests, a peace enforcement operation can still be deployed with the consent of the host even when an arm of the state – the Indonesian military in this case – is committing the atrocities.

Another safeguard is obtaining the consent of the host state into whose territory UNEPS would intervene. This is cited by, among others, a representative of the Jakarta office of a prominent international NGO that deals with preventing and resolving violent conflict (who was formerly a British diplomat). He said:

> The more you flag this as a force that could get sent in regardless of the wishes of the local government, the harder I'd imagine it would be in more benign circumstances to invite them

in. The UN is normally careful to badge its interventions in the most un-confrontational way possible because that maximises the chances of them being invited in.[61]

In fact, with the exception of the 2011 peace enforcement operation in Libya, full-scale military interventions to protect civilians have only been undertaken with host country consent or when there is no functioning government to consult such as in Somalia and Rwanda.[62] Furthermore, the modest British-led intervention force in Sierra Leone (2000) and the European Union-led Operation Artemis in the Democratic Republic of the Congo (2003) are just two examples that illustrate the potential value of the consent-based, short-term deployment of an international military presence to help prevent the esca-lation of armed conflict.[63] Consent, however, is not always static, and can also be the result of coercion. For example, former Indonesian President B.J. Habibie, and his minister for defence and security (and commander-in-chief of the Indonesian armed forces or TNI), General Wiranto, agreed to the peace enforcement operation, INTERFET, partly because of pressure from the international community. But even nominal consent of the host state can serve as a safeguard against attacks on the interveners. Scholars have argued that the cooperation of the TNI with INTERFET was a major reason behind the very low number of casualties of Australian and other foreign forces.[64]

The importance of obtaining consent from the host state and securing the UNSC as the sole authorising body imply that support might be found in a UNEPS that would operatio-nalise R2P Pillar Two. According to UN Secretary-General Ban, Pillar Two refers to the international community's responsibility to assist states in preventing atrocities from break-ing out.[65] It includes preventative deployments or an international military presence to help prevent the escalation of armed conflict. Breakey coined the term R2P Pillar Two mission to refer to the goals and tasks of a mission designed to implement this norm and it is a useful concept to frame a possible mode of operation for UNEPS. In R2P situations, there is the threat of atrocity crimes, meaning that violence against civilians is not peripheral to the armed conflict or symptoms of the conflict. Rather, the threat against civilians posed by one or both sides is large-scale, deliberate and systematic, and might take place in times of war or peace. A systematic strategy and the robust use of force under Chapter VII are essential for such R2P Pillar Two operations. Host state consent (even begrudgingly given) is needed for logistical and political reasons, and the perception of the mission's neu-trality is helpful but not essential. Thus, in contrast to Pillar Three Missions, which engage in war-fighting to constrain or neutralise the regime's capacity to commit atrocities against its population and perhaps even defeats the regime (e.g. Libya), a Pillar Two UNEPS inter-vention would deploy with the consent of the host state and try to foster perceptions of neu-trality towards its missions.[66]

Conclusion

This article has examined attitudes towards the norms constituting the UNEPS proposal that relate to the use of force. It reports respondents and other actors citing multiple norms that, on the one hand, were potentially incompatible with the UNEPS proposal but, on the other, provided an opportunity to recalibrate it. First, a commitment to the norm of non-interven-tion can explain respondents' cautious approach to UNEPS. This was partly because of the concern (or an awareness of the concerns of others) that their country might be the recipient of a UNEPS intervention and a belief that such a permanent force might compromise econ-omic relations between the state intervened upon and those with which it has bilateral relationships. A cautious approach to UNEPS was also informed by respondents' scepticism that the cosmopolitan nature of the intervention was false and that, indeed, funding would rely on member states with an agenda. Finally, a cautious response to the UNEPS proposal was taken based on the belief that such interventions would do more harm than good. Despite these objections, some respondents expressed an interest in cosmopolitan values, including R2P, acknowledging the moral imperative to use force to prevent and respond to mass atrocities where there are clear victims and perpetrators Of course identifying the victims and perpetrators in such situations is inherently political which implies that such a permanent service will always be vulnerable to a certain degree of politicking.

How can we respond to misgivings about R2P but still edge towards the creation of a supra-national capacity like UNEPS, while responding to respondents' misgivings about the proposal? I argue that creating an alternative funding structure could partly reduce the reliance on member states' contributions and, by proxy, their influence. This might go some way towards placating fears that UNEPS would be used for purposes other than those professed. I further argue that the development of certain principles would demonstrate that a UNEPS intervention would not cause more harm than good. I suggest other changes to increase support for the idea, including that the proposed service would only deploy with UNSC authorisation and the consent of the host state which, taken together, suggest that UNEPS could help the UN operationalise R2P Pillar Two.

Acknowledgements

Parts of this article are based on sections of the author's book *UN Emergency Peace Service and the Responsibility to Protect* (Abingdon, UK: Routledge, 2015), 4–8, 43–4, 75–81, 83–6, 129. They are reproduced with the permission of Routledge.

Disclosure statement

No potential conflict of interest was reported by the author.

Notes

1. UN General Assembly, 'Resolution Adopted by the General Assembly: 60/1. 2005 World Summit Outcome', A/RES/60/1 of 24 October 2005, paras 138–9.
2. Kavitha Suthanthiraraj, 'United Nations Peacekeeping Missions: Enhancing Capacity for Rapid and Effective Troop Deployment', *Global Action To Prevent War*, 2008, http://www. globalactionpw.org/wp/wp-content/uploads/troop-deployment-paper.pdf.
3. United Nations Department of Peacekeeping Operations and Department of Field Support, *United Nations Peacekeeping Operations Principles and Guidelines* (New York: United Nations, 2008), 63.
4. UN General Assembly, 'Report of the Panel on United Nations Peace Operations', A/55/305 of 21 August 2000.
5. UN General Assembly, 'Implementing the Responsibility to Protect: Report of the Secretary-General', A/63/677 of 12 January 2009, para. 60.

6. Aidan Hehir, *The Responsibility to Protect: Rhetoric, Reality and the Future of Humanitarian Intervention* (Basingstoke: Palgrave Macmillan, 2012), 247.
7. UN General Assembly, 'Implementing the Responsibility to Protect'.
8. Robert C. Johansen, ed., *A United Nations Emergency Peace Service: To Prevent Genocide and Crimes against Humanity* (New York: World Federalist Movement – Institute for Global Policy, 2006).
9. World Federalist Movement – Canada and Global Action to Prevent War, 'Support for UNEPS at UN GA Interactive Dialogue on R2P', https://www.worldfederalistscanada.org/0611%20UNEPS%20&%20R2P%20sign-on%20Ltr%20%20(1).pdf.
10. James Pattison, 'Humanitarian Intervention and a Cosmopolitan UN Force', *Journal of International Political Theory* 4, no. 1 (2008): 126–45.
11. Jonathan Gilmore, 'Protecting Strangers: Reflections on a Cosmopolitan Peacekeeping Capacity', in *Perspectives on Peacekeeping and Atrocity Prevention: Expanding Stakeholders and Regional Arrangements*, ed. Trudy Fraser (New York: Springer, forthcoming). A notable exception is the report by Suthanthiraraj and Quinn which identifies some of the challenges the UNEPS proposal faces vis-à-vis the use of force. The data used in their report overlaps to some degree with those used in this article. In their analysis, however, the subject of the use of force was more narrowly conceived than how it is dealt with in this article (for example they did not specifically address perceptions of the R2P doctrine and the affect they have on attitudes towards the UNEPS proposal) and consequently their conclusions on generating support for the UNEPS proposal were quite different to those in this study. Kavitha Suthanthiraraj and Mariah Quinn, *Standing for Change in Peacekeeping Operations: Project for a United Nations Emergency Peace Service (UNEPS)* (New York: Global Action to Prevent War, 2009).
12. Stephen Kinloch-Pichat, *A UN 'Legion': Between Utopia and Reality* (Abingdon: Routledge, 2012), 203–18.
13. Adam Roberts, 'Proposals for UN Standing Forces: A Critical History', in *The United Nations Security Council and War: The Evolution of Thought and Practice since 1945*, ed. Vaughan Lowe, Adam Roberts, Jennifer Welsh and Dominik Zaum (New York: Oxford University Press, 2008), 99–130.
14. H. Peter Langille, 'Bridging the Commitment-Capacity Gap: A Review of Existing Arrangements and Options for Enhancing UN Rapid Deployment' (Center for UN Reform Education, 2002).
15. Justine Wang, 'A Symposium on Genocide and Crimes against Humanity: The Challenge of Prevention and Enforcement' (paper presented, Convened by the Nuclear Age Peace Foundation and Simons Centre for Peace and Disarmament Studies, University of Santa Barbara, California, 5–6 December 2003).
16. William J. Durch, 'Paying the Tab: Financial Crises', in *The Evolution of UN peacekeeping*, ed. William J. Durch (New York: St. Martin's Press, 1993), 39–58, 50.
17. Summarised from Robert C. Johansen, 'Expert Discussion of the United Nations Emergency Peace Service: Cuenca Report', in *A United Nations Emergency Peace Service*, ed. Robert C. Johansen, 43–74. It also incorporates other literature on UNEPS.
18. Stephen Krasner, *Sovereignty: Organized Hypocrisy* (Princeton, NJ: Princeton University Press, 1999), 20.
19. Interview by author, 7 May 2008, Jakarta, Indonesia.
20. Cited in Kinloch-Pichat, *A UN 'Legion'*, 225.
21. ASEAN Secretariat, 'The ASEAN Charter' (Jakarta: ASEAN Secretariat, 2008).
22. Global Action to Prevent War, Centre for Peace and Conflict Studies and Centre for Strategic and International Studies, 'Peacekeeping and Civilian Protection: Asia-Pacific Perspectives', 11 June 2009, Convened by Global Action to Prevent War, Centre for Peace and Conflict Studies, Centre for Strategic and International Studies, http://www.globalactionpw.org/wp/wp-content/uploads/jakarta-full-reportv6.pdf.
23. Alex Bellamy, *Responsibility to Protect: The Global Effort to End Mass Atrocities* (Cambridge: Polity, 2009), 16, 8–9.
24. Interview by Kavitha Suthanthiraraj, 30 June 2010, New York.
25. Interview by author, 8 May 2008, Jakarta, Indonesia.
26. Bellamy, *Responsibility to Protect*, 88.
27. Hans J. Morgenthau, *Politics among Nations: The Struggle for Power and Peace*, 4th edition (New York: Knopf, 1948).

28. Interview by author, 11 July 2007, Canberra, Australia.
29. Kenneth Waltz, *Theory of International Relations* (Reading, MA: Addison-Webley, 1979).
30. Hans J. Morgenthau, *The Decline of Domestic Politics* (Chicago: University of Chicago Press, 1958), 59.
31. Morgenthau, *Politics among Nations*, 10.
32. Interview by Kavitha Suthanthiraraj, 25 June 2010, New York.
33. Noam Chomsky, 'Statement by Professor Noam Chomsky to the United Nations General Assembly Thematic Dialogue on the Responsibility to Protect' (United Nations, 2009), http://www.un.org/ga/president/63/interactive/protect/noam.pdf.
34. Kathy Lally and Will Englund, 'Putin Defends Ukraine Stance, Cites Lawlessness', *Washington Post*, 4 March 2014, http://www.washingtonpost.com/world/putin-reserves-the-right-to-use-force-in-ukraine/2014/03/04/92d4ca70-a389-11e3-a5fa-55f0c77bf39c_story.html.
35. Interview by author, 30 April 2008, Jakarta, Indonesia.
36. Interview by author, 7 May 2008, Jakarta, Indonesia.
37. Stephen M. Schwebel, *Justice in International Law* (Cambridge: Cambridge University Press, 1994), 313.
38. D.W. Bowett, *United Nations Forces: A Legal Study* (New York: Praeger, 1964), 326.
39. Interview by author, 16 June 2009, Singapore.
40. Brian E. Urquhart, 'United Nations Peace Forces and the Changing United Nations', *International Organization* 17, no. 2 (1963): 351.
41. Alan J. Kuperman, 'A Model Humanitarian Intervention? Reassessing NATO's Libya Campaign', *International Security* 38, no. 1 (2013): 105–36.
42. Alan J. Kuperman, 'Humanitarian Hazard: Revisiting Doctrines of Intervention', *Harvard International Review* 26, no. 1 (2004): 64–9, 66.
43. Alex Bellamy, *Global Politics and the Responsibility to Protect: From Words to Deeds* (London: Routledge, 2011), 71–80.
44. Johansen, 'Cuenca Report', 54.
45. Interview by author, 8 May 2008, Jakarta, Indonesia.
46. Jess Gifkins, 'The UN Security Council Divided: Syria in Crisis', *Global Responsibility to Protect* 4, no. 3 (2012): 377–93, 391.
47. Interview by author, 8 May 2008, Jakarta, Indonesia.
48. Nicholas J. Wheeler, *Saving Strangers* (Oxford: Oxford University Press, 2000), 259.
49. BBC News, 'World: Europe Mixed Asian Reaction to NATO Strikes', *BBC News*, 25 March 1999, http://news.bbc.co.uk/2/hi/europe/303671.stm.
50. Richard H. Curtiss, 'Kosovo Tragedy Contains Hard Lessons', *The Daily Star*, 30 May 1999, http://www.dailystar.com.lb/Opinion/Commentary/1999/Apr-30/108392-kosovo-tragedy-contains-hard-lessons.ashx#axzz2zQ1YG0Ek.
51. Gregg Carlstrom, 'US Condemns UNESCO Over Palestine Vote', *Al Jazeera*, 1 November 2011, http://www.aljazeera.com/news/middleeast/2011/10/2011103172551498181.html.
52. Kinloch-Pichat, *A UN 'Legion'*, 209–10.
53. Thomas G Weiss, *What's Wrong With the United Nations and How to Fix it* (Chichester: John Wiley & Sons, 2013), 196–7.
54. Stephen P. Kinloch, 'Utopian or Pragmatic? A UN Permanent Military Volunteer Force', *International Peacekeeping* 3, no. 4 (1996): 166–90, 177.
55. International Commission on Intervention and State Sovereignty, *The Responsibility to Protect* (Ottawa: International Development Research Centre, 2001), 37.
56. Robert C. Johansen, 'Proposal for a United Nations Emergency Peace Service to Prevent Genocide and Crimes against Humanity', in *A United Nations Emergency Peace Service*, ed. Robert C. Johansen, 23–42, 29.
57. Kuperman, 'A Model Humanitarian Intervention?'.
58. James Pattison, 'The Ethics of Humanitarian Intervention in Libya', *Ethics & International Affairs* 25, no. 3 (2011): 271–7.
59. Interview by Kavitha Suthanthiraraj, 30 September 2008, unknown location.
60. ICISS, *The Responsibility to Protect*, xiii, UN General Assembly.
61. Interview by author, 9 May 2008, Jakarta, Indonesia.
62. Alex Bellamy, 'We Can't Dodge the Hard Part Stabilising Libya', *The Australian*, 21 March 2011, http://www.theaustralian.com.au/news/opinion/we-cant-dodge-the-hard-part-stabilising-libya/story-e6frg6zo-1226025034896.

63. UN General Assembly, 'Implementing the Responsibility to Protect', para. 42.
64. Nicholas J. Wheeler and Tim Dunne, 'East Timor and the New Humanitarian Interventionism', *International Affairs* 77, no. 4 (2001): 805–27, 818–20, 25.
65. UN General Assembly, 'Implementing the Responsibility to Protect'. For a full discussion of the intersection between Pillar Two and UNEPS see Chapter 3 of Annie Herro, *UN Emergency Peace Service and the Responsibility to Protect* (Abingdon, UK: Routledge, 2015).
66. Hugh Breakey, 'The Responsibility to Protect and the Protection of Civilians in Armed Conflict: Overlap and Contrast', in *Norms of Protection: Responsibility to Protect, Protection of Civilians and Their Interaction*, ed. Angus Francis, Vesselin Popovski and Charles Sampford (Tokyo: United Nations University Press, 2012), 62–81, 77. Although there is considerable overlap between Pillar Two and Pillar Three missions.

Protecting the world's most persecuted: the responsibility to protect and Burma's Rohingya minority

Lindsey N. Kingston

Department of History, Politics, and International Relations, Webster University – Saint Louis, Missouri, USA

The Rohingya in Burma have been called 'the world's most persecuted minority' and subjected to pervasive human rights violations, including ethnic cleansing, statelessness and possibly genocide. Despite the international community's commitment to the responsibility to protect (R2P), which includes violence prevention, the plight of vulnerable populations such as the Rohingya has been relatively ignored. This article encourages dialogue about the R2P's potential for preventing direct and structural violence, building on its foundation of sovereignty as responsibility. While preventative action to assist the Rohingya comes with an array of challenges, the normative foundations of R2P – including connections to combatting internal displacement and 'unbundling' protection to challenge structural inequalities – provide a toolkit of responses apart from military force. It is imperative that scholars and practitioners alike critically consider the practical value of R2P, as well as re-examine glaring and overlooked cases of widespread human rights abuse. In addition to thwarting mass atrocities and preventing future violence, further consideration of ongoing structural violence is also necessary for protecting basic human rights.

The Rohingya have been called 'the world's most persecuted minority' by the United Nations (UN) and human rights advocates, with living conditions in internally displaced persons (IDP) camps described as those 'worse than animals'.[1] The Muslim ethnic minority group lives in northern Arakan/Rakhine State in Western Burma,[2] where they have suffered government oppression for decades. In November 2014, US President Barack Obama strongly urged the Burmese government to end its persecution of the Rohingya minority, noting that legitimate government was based on 'the recognition that all people are equal under the law'.[3] The acknowledgement sparked brief international interest in an ongoing human rights crisis that remains relatively absent from discussions of rights, development and peacebuilding in Southeast Asia. In Rohingya villages, as well as in IDP and refugee camps, members of the ethnic group lament the lack of human rights protections available to them: 'Rohingya people who are living in [Burma] don't have rights. Even a bird has rights. A bird can build a nest, give birth, bring food to their children and raise them

165

until they are ready to fly. We don't have basic rights like this.'[4] Indeed, the suffering of Burma's Rohingya has been linked to widespread direct and structural violence – including ethnic cleansing and genocide.

The concept of the 'responsibility to protect' (R2P), coined in a 2001 report by the International Commission on Intervention and State Sovereignty (ICISS), was meant to tackle the kinds of pervasive human rights violations that face Burma's Rohingya. Building on the idea of sovereignty as responsibility, the ICISS argued that sovereignty must yield to egregious violations of humanitarian and international law. The report stressed prevention as 'the single most important dimension' of R2P and identified military intervention as a 'last resort' option in the face of large-scale loss of life and/or ethnic cleansing.[5] The 2005 World Summit Outcome helped codify R2P within the international community by including the concept in paragraphs 138 and 139; among other things, the UN General Assembly asserted that world governments have a responsibility to protect civilians from the mass atrocity crimes of genocide, war crimes, crimes against humanity and ethnic cleansing.[6] Ten years after this affirmation, however, R2P's potential for preventing conflict and rights violations remains limited and oft-ignored. In the case of Burma's Rohingya minority, indicators of mass atrocity crimes – already occurring and impending – have been similarly overlooked.

In an attempt to spur dialogue about R2P's potential for preventing direct and structural violence, this article focuses on the Rohingya in Burma as a case study for considering R2P's potential and challenges. Although R2P is often (wrongly) equated with military intervention, its normative foundations related to sovereignty as responsibility and violence prevention provide valuable starting points for thwarting mass atrocity crimes. The Rohingya, who face instances of direct violence (including rape, torture and murder) as well as structural violence (including widespread denial of legal nationality, or statelessness), are just one of the world's minority groups facing deeply-rooted human rights abuse at the hands of the state. While preventative action to assist the Rohingya comes with an array of challenges, the normative foundations of R2P – including connections to combatting internal displacement and 'unbundling' protection to challenge structural inequalities – provide a toolkit of responses apart from military force. It is imperative that scholars and practitioners alike critically consider the practical value of R2P, as well as re-examine glaring and overlooked cases of widespread human rights abuse. From the Rohingya in Burma to ongoing violations in countries such as Sudan and Syria, deliberate and genuine discussion of global responsibility is sorely needed.

The responsibility to prevent

Serious discussion of the responsibility to prevent is made possible by a growing acceptance of expanded international obligations, which moves beyond traditional conceptions of state sovereignty and non-intervention. These incremental changes include three different but related concepts: global responsibility, sovereignty as responsibility and R2P. First, 'global responsibility' is a broad foundational concept that refers to emerging international responsibility to protect and assist vulnerable people within their own countries. Such responsibilities must be reconciled, however, with the cardinal principles of non-interference that are central to the UN Charter.[7] Second, 'sovereignty as responsibility' expands global possibilities by recasting sovereignty in terms of obligations. Effective and legitimate sovereignty 'implies a system of law and order that is responsive to the needs of the national population for justice and general welfare'.[8] From this perspective, sovereignty cannot be disassociated from responsibility; a state should not be able to claim the rights of sovereignty unless it carries out internationally recognised obligations to its citizens. Third, R2P is a new norm that addresses the international community's failure to prevent and halt the four mass atrocity crimes of genocide, war crimes, ethnic cleansing and crimes against humanity. R2P signals a normative shift towards greater global responsibility and re-frames the debate by no longer speaking of a right of outsiders to intervene, but rather of a responsibility of all states to meet the needs of individuals.[9] In this sense, R2P is a 'linking concept' that 'bridges the divide between the international community and the sovereign state'.[10] Although scholars have increasingly argued that R2P does not create obligations for states or the UN to take action, the responsibility further empowers actors to take action in the face of mass atrocities. 'The vocabulary of "responsibility" works here as a language for imposing authority and allocating powers rather than as a language for imposing binding obligations and commanding obedience', writes Anne Orford.[11]

Unfortunately, scholars and practitioners alike tend to equate R2P with military intervention and rarely consider the concept's original foundation as a tool for violence prevention. In reality, filling the gap between the international community's rhetorical support for prevention and its level of tangible commitment to achieving it was a fundamental aim of the ICISS's work on R2P. In its 2001 report, the ICISS called for the UN Security Council to play a leading role in preventative activities, and identified four key dimensions of root cause prevention: (1) political – governance, rights and confidence building, (2) economic – poverty, inequality and economic opportunity, (3) legal – rule of law and accountability, and (4) military – disarmament, reintegration and sectoral reform.[12] That culture of prevention was jettisoned by a UN High-Level Panel in 2003, however, and R2P's focus on prevention was weakened by the time it reached the World Summit in 2005. The panel put forth nine discrete proposals, yet not all were overtly connected to conflict prevention or the prevention of mass atrocity crimes, and they all pointed to work already being undertaken. Assessment of the panel's recommendations finds that 'there is no call for states to assume a responsibility to prevent; the focus of the ICISS on centralization was eschewed; and the thorny question of bridging the gap between early warning, practical commitment, and the generation of consensus was overlooked entirely'.[13] This weakening of preventive culture was furthered by some states wanting to focus R2P on an even narrower set of issues, or to remove conflict prevention altogether. Although a handful of states dissented from these efforts – Canada, New Zealand, Japan, Sweden, Mexico and Rwanda argued that conflict prevention should be given a central place in any World Summit statement concerning R2P – their alternative proposals attracted only a modest degree of attention and support.[14]

At least three factors contribute to the relative neglect of the responsibility to prevent: 'the inherent difficulty of translating a commitment to prevention into coherent policy, the impact of the place of prevention in the war on terrorism, and the question of authority and agency'.[15] First, R2P faces the 'dilemma of comprehensiveness' because violent conflict is caused by a wide range of structural and direct causes that require similarly varied responses. Conflict prevention thus commands significant costs before violence erupts, making it difficult for political leaders to prove that a commitment of such resources is necessary or effective. There is also no agreement about how comprehensive the responsibility to prevent should be; the ICISS attempted to remedy this problem by outlining four areas of root causes, but this approach was replaced by the High-Level Panel's wider definition of 'international threat' which emphasised security and economic development. Second, the post-9/11 'War on Terror' has skewed Western attention away from preventing mass atrocity crimes and towards the prevention of terrorism. Additionally, the strategies of preemption and prevention adopted by the United States (US) and its allies make other states more reluctant to endorse measures that could assist powerful states' interference with domestic affairs. Third, it is simply not clear where the responsibility to prevent lies. For instance, does responsibility lie with the UN, state governments, or other organisations? Resolving these questions of authority and agency is difficult because they 'go the heart of what states are entitled to do within their own borders', as well as the nature of international authority and culture.[16] This final trial is shared by other elements of R2P and creates serious challenges for effective implementation of preventive actions. Thomas G. Weiss further warns that it is 'preposterous to argue that to prevent is *the* single most important priority' out of R2P's three temporal phases of prevention, reaction and rebuilding. He contends that 'the most urgent priority is to react better', and notes that reframing sovereignty as responsibility provides a way to 'navigate around the shoals of state sovereignty' for humanitarian causes.[17]

With these challenges in mind, the responsibility to prevent nevertheless offers opportunities for thwarting mass atrocities that should not be ignored. Lawrence Woocher writes that the responsibility to prevent is preferable to reaction: It is *morally* superior because it prevents the destruction and loss of life that mass atrocities wreak, rather than responding to humanitarian crises after the fact; it is *politically* preferable because it avoids the fundamental concerns about violations of sovereignty associated with military intervention and helps preserve regional and global stability by averting conflict; and is *financially* superior because preventive action is relatively inexpensive compared to the large investments required to rebuild after major episodes of violence.[18] In a 2009 report, UN Secretary General Ban Ki-Moon stressed that the scope of R2P should be kept narrow, but the response 'ought to be deep, employing the wide array of prevention and protection instruments available [to the international community]', including early warning and assessment for genocide.[19] A follow-up report in 2013 focused specifically on state responsibility and prevention, outlining risk factors for mass atrocity crimes and encouraging partnerships and targeted measures to prevent the escalation of violence.[20] (Notably, the report outlined risk factors for genocide, including identity-based discrimination, exclusionary ideologies, and deliberate exclusion of minority groups[21]; these factors are all present in the case of Burma's Rohingya, as discussed below.) Woocher contends that 'direct or operational prevention' measures can dissuade specific actors from committing mass atrocity crimes or reduce their ability to commit such crimes, while 'structural or root cause prevention' measures are designed to impact the underlying factors that make mass atrocities more likely in a given state.[22]

For instance, the creation of a genocide early warning system is a tool that could facilitate both direct and structural prevention of mass atrocities. In 1977, Israeli social scientists Israel Charny and Chanan Rapaport proposed the creation of a central information centre that could receive, categorise and investigate reports of trouble, before issuing warnings. A similar proposal was made in a UN study in 1985, and in December 1998 US President Bill Clinton proposed a genocide early warning system (GEWS) at the 50th anniversary of the Genocide Convention.[23] In 2008, a US task force declared genocide prevention an 'achievable goal' and recommended the creation of an inter-agency task force to analyse threats, work with other countries, and coordinate action in places like Darfur. Former US Secretary of State Madeleine Albright noted that military intervention was just one possible option, and the report emphasised early detection and diplomacy to avoid crises. 'We need to have a choice between doing nothing and sending in the Marines', she explained.[24] The creation of the UN Joint Office of the Special Adviser on the Prevention of Genocide and on the Responsibility to Protect provides new possibilities for genocide prevention, including an early warning system aimed at forecasting genocide (or at least genocidal trouble) several months or years in advance. Such an emphasis on prevention of mass violence requires extensive coordination and advance planning in order to be effective. Daniel Chirot and Clark McCauley explain:

> By the time Hitler had control of Germany, had conquered most of Europe, and had decided to exterminate Jews, it was too late to do much about it other than to defeat him and destroy his military power. The time to take preventive action would have been years before Hitler came to power, perhaps even decades earlier. The same holds true for other major tragedies of this sort. The final, most terrible steps may develop quickly and in unforeseeable ways, but the conditions that make them possible do not develop overnight. Knowing how they happen can lead to awareness of the coming danger.[25]

Despite its challenges, R2P's potential for preventing mass atrocity crimes is an important starting point for protecting human rights and thwarting regional conflict in places such as Burma. As the next section illustrates, the Rohingya minority group suffers from direct and structural violence that has already been linked to the mass atrocities of ethnic cleansing and genocide. While this may not be a case for military intervention based on R2P principles, nevertheless this situation highlights a human rights crisis in dire need of preventative action. R2P's normative foundations related to responsibility and prevention provide important tools for the international community to consider.

The Rohingya in Burma

The Rohingya face human rights violations stemming from structural and direct violence in Burma. Structural violence – the systematic ways in which a social institution or structure kills people slowly by preventing them access to basic necessities – are social harms resulting from the pervasive and persistent impact of economic, political and cultural violence in societies.[26] In the case of direct violence, there is a specific event – physical damage to the human body occurring in a distinct time-bound incident, with individual victims and perpetrators. Direct violence shows immediate outcomes while structural violence is part of a more slow and steady process.[27] In Burma, the Rohingya face structural violence as a result of state-sanction marginalisation, including statelessness as a result of discriminatory nationality laws. As a stateless minority group, the Rohingya are denied a range of human rights protections available to citizens, including economic, social and cultural rights (ESCR) such as the rights to a basic education and employment. Direct violence, including murders and rape, have been equated with ethnic cleansing and crimes against humanity by human rights observers; some contend that the violence, which targets members of the Muslim minority, is a warning of impending genocide. Violence by Buddhist mobs and some state actors has left approximately 280 dead and displaced another 140,000 since 2012, leaving the Rohingya to live under 'apartheid-like conditions' in camps and restricted villages in Rakhine state.[28]

State-sanctioned discrimination against the Rohingya is entrenched in the country's 1982 Citizenship Law, which fails to recognise the ethnic group as a 'national race' worthy of legal nationality and creates the condition of statelessness. (The eight primary 'races' in Burma are Arakanese, Burman, Chin, Kachin, Karen, Karenni, Mon and Shan, as well as ancestors of those who settled in Burma before it was colonised by Britain in 1823.) The law designates three categories of citizens – full citizens, associate citizens and naturalised citizens – and issues colour-coded citizenship security cards accordingly. In most cases, the Rohingya hold white 'temporary registration' cards that are not associated with citizenship rights or legal status. Rather, the cards simply contain ethnic and religious biographical data that facilitate discrimination by local officials. Although the 1982 law allows so-called 'foreigners' to become naturalised citizens, they must either have one parent who already holds Burmese citizenship or they must provide conclusive evidence that they or their parents entered and resided in Burma prior to independence in 1948. (This requirement prevents children born to non-citizens from obtaining citizenship, perpetuating the denial of citizenship and extending the condition of statelessness across generations.) Those seeking to become naturalised citizens must be at least 18 years old, able to speak one of the national languages (the Rohingya language is not recognised as such), and be of good character and sound mind. Only full and naturalised citizens are entitled to enjoy citizen rights under Burmese law, and such citizenship may be revoked by the state. Since most Rohingya families lack formal documentation, even those who have lived in Burma for generations are unable to provide conclusive evidence of lineage prior to 1823 or 1948. Such difficulties were exacerbated in June 2012, when many Rohingya lost possessions – including whatever documents were available to them – due to arson attacks and thefts targeting the minority group.[29]

In response to widespread killings and violence against Rohingya in 2012, the Burmese government created a plan that has been heavily criticised by human rights advocates. Following April 2013 recommendations of the Rakhine Investigative Commission, which was established by President Thein Sein, the Burmese government's Rakhine State Action Plan is touted by government officials as a path towards development and post-conflict reconstruction, including the relocation and encampment of more than 133,000 Rohingya from IDP camps in the city of Sittwe and other townships. The plan also outlines steps for citizenship assessment using the 1982 Citizenship Law as its guide, which refuses to recognise the Rohingya as a group and would instead categorise these individuals as 'Bengali'. The recorded population would be divided into three categories: Those previously recorded or registered, the unrecorded who are willing to go through the assessment process according to existing Burmese laws, and those who refuse to be categorised as 'Bengali'; the third category would be denied the right to be considered for citizenship.[30] Phil Robertson, Deputy Asia Director for Human Rights Watch, argues that the plan 'expands and solidifies' government discrimination by forcing Rohingya to repudiate their ethnic identity in order to apply for citizenship. Noting that the plan is a 'blueprint for permanent segregation and statelessness', Robertson warns that those who agree to be called 'Bengali' are basically admitting to being undocumented immigrants (despite their long history within the country) and could later be denied naturalised citizenship and face deportation. Others will face 'years of life in locked down camps' if they refuse to participate in the proposed plan.[31] (Notably, the UN General Assembly approved a non-binding resolution in December 2014 urging Burma to provide 'full citizenship' to the Rohingya and to guarantee free movement.[32])

Such ongoing discrimination against the Rohingya, combined with attacks of direct violence against the minority group, has prompted leading humanitarians such as Roméo Dallaire to warn of the 'very real prospect of genocide in Burma'.[33] Since the 1990s, UN special rapporteurs have identified international crimes against the Rohingya – including forced population transfers and deportations – and characterised such activities as 'widespread', 'systematic', and resulting from state policy.[34] Violence committed against Rohingya and Kaman Muslim communities in Rakhine State beginning in June 2012 has provided new evidence of such crimes, and Human Rights Watch argues that recent violence constitutes the mass atrocities of crimes against humanity and ethnic cleansing. Evidence suggests that political and religious leaders 'planned, organized, and incited attacks against the Rohingya and other Muslims with the intent to drive them from the state or at least relocate them from areas in which they had been residing – particularly from areas shared with the majority Buddhist population'.[35] As part of this programme of ethnic cleansing, local authorities have blocked the Rohingya from conducting ordinary day-to-day activities, denying Muslims their rights to freedom of movement, the ability to earn a living, and access to markets and humanitarian aid in a coercive effort to drive Muslim populations from the area. At the same time, crimes against humanity include killings, forcible population transfers and deportation, persecution, rape, and other forms of direct violence that are systematic and targeted at the Muslim minority population.[36] Burmese government involvement has been both direct and indirect; although much violence has been carried out by armed mobs, various branches of state security forces have witnessed attacks and refused to offer protection to Rohingya. In some cases, government agents – including local police, Lon Thein riot police, the inter-agency border control called Nasaka, the army, and the navy – have participated in the atrocities directly. Human Rights Watch reported that no indications suggested that the Burmese government had seriously investigated or taken legal action against those responsible for planning or carrying out violence since June 2012. Instead, state forces have impeded investigations by ordering the digging of mass graves or digging graves themselves; in June 2012, a government truck dumped 18 bodies near a Rohingya IDP camp outside of Sittwe for local Rohingya to bury in mass graves.[37]

Direct violence targeting Rohingya since June 2012 has forced tens of thousands of Rohingya to seek safety outside of Burma, undertaking treacherous journeys and risking human trafficking in the process. In 2012 alone, approximately 140,000 people were internally displaced within Burma and almost 86,000 sought safety in neighbouring countries.[38] Some smugglers transport Rohingya down the Bay of Bengal, over Thailand's southern coast, and (for those who can afford the smugglers' fees) into Malaysia. The displaced face a myriad of threats, including chronic malnutrition and physical abuse by unscrupulous smugglers known for killing or abandoning charges who cannot pay their steep fees; more than 2,000 are presumed drowned. Those caught by the Thai government face so-called 'soft' deportation, when they are moved out of detention cells and put on wooden boats headed towards the Andaman Sea. There, they are often picked up again by smugglers who, some human rights groups argue, are in league with Thai officials; those who cannot pay ransom for passage to Malaysia are often forced into indentured servitude on Thai farms and fishing vessels.[39] Rohingya who endure such human trafficking may be sold for 5,000 to 50,000 baht each, or US$155 to US$1,550. Speaking with Reuters journalists, a Rohingya man named Ismail said that Thai immigration officials sold him to human traffickers in 2013: 'It seemed so official at first', he said. 'They took our photographs. They took our fingerprints. And then once in the boats, about 20 minutes out at sea, we were told we had been sold.'[40]

Limitations of and opportunities for R2P in Burma

The Rohingya in Burma suffer from direct violence that has been connected to mass atrocity crimes, as well as structural violence that marginalises the minority group and creates vulnerabilities for future harms. Although human rights advocates contend that their suffering constitutes crimes against humanity and ethnic cleansing – and the group has been identified as under threat for genocide – this case has not yet been actively considered under the auspices of R2P. Rather, the international community has relied on incremental improvements to Burma's human rights record as a promise that the Rohingya's situation will improve. In addition to widely publicised developments such as the release of pro-democracy leader Aung San Suu Kyi from house arrest in 2010, the government has garnered Western praise for actions such as the 2014 conditional release of Rohingya rights activist U Kyaw Hla Aung.[41] Amid ongoing political and legal reforms, human rights non-governmental organisations such as Amnesty International warn that the international community should not let its guard down against rights abuse in Burma; the government continues to engage in a range of violations including unlawful killings, excessive use of force, arbitrary arrest, torture and other ill-treatment, and unlawful confiscation or destruction of property, as well as providing impunity for past crimes, including crimes against humanity.[42]

Burma has been at the centre of international debate in the past, but calls for action have been unsuccessful and have rarely included discussion of the Rohingya. In response to widespread rights violations and severe government repression, the US and the United Kingdom drafted a peaceful UN Security Council resolution in January 2007. The resolution encouraged the Burmese government to allow humanitarian access to its citizens, uphold international norms related to human rights, make progress towards democratisation, and release political prisoners. The Russian Federation and the People's Republic of China both voted against the resolution (along with South Africa), using their veto power in the Security Council to end the discussion.[43] More sustained consideration of R2P implementation in Burma followed landfall of the deadly Cyclone Nargis on 2 May 2008. According to official figures, 84,500 people were killed and 53,800 went missing across the south of the country. The UN estimates that as many as 2.4 million people were affected, including those who were left homeless in the aftermath of the storm.[44] When the Burmese government initially blocked outside organisations from providing desperately needed food, clean drinking water, shelter and medical care, the concept of R2P entered international discussions as a justification for humanitarian intervention. Although 'crimes against humanity' could arguably apply to the government's blocking of outside aid, R2P was not invoked in this case – partly because natural and environmental disasters had been intentionally left out of R2P formulations, and partly because military intervention would have most likely made the situation for civilians worse. 'To attempt to introduce [interventions for natural disasters] by the back door would strengthen suspicion of Western motivations and reinforce cynicism of Western tactics', writes Ramesh Thakur, who noted that fighting to get into Burma in order to provide aid would be 'ludicrous'.[45] Instead, the Association of Southeast Asian Nations (ASEAN) eventually persuaded the Burmese government to grant humanitarian access and helped coordinate an international relief and rehabilitation effort. Critics contend that ASEAN's response was 'painfully slow, uncoordinated and ad hoc' and that it highlighted the association's institutional incapacity, but that ASEAN also illustrated its gradual accommodation between R2P and the principle of non-interference by pressuring Burma to act.[46]

It is unlikely that political will currently exists to spur any sort of military intervention in response to direct, physical violence against the Rohingya in Burma – particularly given Western optimism about government reforms and the fact that both China and Russia have blocked intervention in the past. In the spirit of R2P's supposed dedication to the prevention of mass atrocity crimes, however, it is imperative that the international community monitors the situation and makes good use of available resources to respond to rights abuse. Human Rights Watch recommends that concerned governments – including Australia, Canada, Japan, the US and EU member states – encourage the creation of a UN special rapporteur on Burma to conduct independent human rights investigations, as well as use diplomatic pressure to monitor ongoing violations and to press the government to end discriminatory policies such as the 1982 Citizenship Law. UN agencies and the donor community are encouraged to provide sufficient funds for humanitarian aid, to urge the Burmese government to ensure humanitarian access (particularly to northern Rakhine State, where assistance was suspended in June 2012), and ensure that a national census includes members of the Rohingya minority. The World Bank, the Asian Development Bank, and other donors can potentially influence the situation by explicitly conditioning development projects on non-discrimination in the provision of assistance.[47] While it seems unreasonable to expect military intervention to protect the Rohingya, the international community's growing acceptance of R2P reflects increasing respect for 'civilian immunity' and 'a web of rules and institutions aimed at preventing mass killing ... '[48] States, regional organisations, and international institutions 'have increasingly demonstrated that they recognize that they bear an obligation to either respond in a meaningful way to mass atrocities and humanitarian crises or to provide a reasonable justification for inaction'.[49] In short, the international community must utilise its complete toolkit for violence prevention, which includes a variety of measures in addition to possible military intervention.

The normative foundations underpinning R2P also provide groundwork for combatting persistent human rights violations such as internal forced displacement, which impacts Rohingya fleeing state-sanctioned violence. The 1998 Guiding Principles on Internal Displacement reaffirm the rights of IDPs and emphasise state responsibility in the face of human rights violations, including the four mass atrocity crimes outlined by R2P. For many, growing acceptance of R2P has been seen as logically following from consensus on IDP protection. 'When R2P was adopted by the UN General Assembly in 2005, it was generally expected that the concept would enhance security for IDPs since the concept of sovereignty as responsibility was recognized as its antecedent, and IDPs were so often the victims of R2P related crimes', writes Roberta Cohen, who played a central role in developing the concept of 'sovereignty as responsibility' in her own work on forced displacement.[50] Yet R2P's application to IDP situations has proven problematic for a variety of reasons, including the limited application of the responsibility to protect and the narrowness of its scope. R2P interventions (such as actions responding to post-election violence in Kenya in 2008) focus on halting direct violence but do not adequately deal with the aftermath of conflict, including displacement. The exclusion of disaster IDPs from R2P discussions, as well as the unfortunate tendency to equate R2P with military action, has also served to sideline IDP protection from an R2P perspective.[51] Yet it is important to note that protection gaps for IDPs and those facing mass atrocities are not due to lack of legal standards, but rather implementation. 'The R2P doctrine breathes new life into these long-standing obligations by bolstering accountability among states, both individually and collectively, to fulfil their commitments to protect populations from these serious crimes', writes Erin Mooney, noting that mass atrocity crimes 'almost invariably will result in mass displacement'.[52] In order to better operationalise R2P to protect IDPs, special protection of the displaced must be integrated into response strategies and the meaning of 'IDP protection' should be defined from the start. Moving beyond the emergency phase, IDP protection must be included in plans related to protection and capacity building. That includes reinforcement of nationality responsibility towards IDPs and the promotion of the Guiding Principles as part of any R2P strategy.[53]

Although R2P is intended for cases of mass atrocity crimes, the norm's underlying principles may be 'unbundled' to apply to a broader range of challenges, including instances of extreme structural violence such as the pervasive statelessness faced by Burma's Rohingya. Lloyd Axworthy and Allan Rock contend that three principles of R2P are of particular importance in this respect: the continued recognition of the state as 'first responder', the international community's duty to support states in their responsibilities, and the international community's refusal to accept a state's failure or refusal to act.[54] Ultimately, the central theme of global responsibility and R2P is that world actors should protect and assist vulnerable people if their governments cannot or will not uphold their responsibilities. Mass violations of human rights are not limited to acts of direct violence; structural violence is also a cause of large-scale suffering and serves as the root cause of further violations, including mass atrocities such as ethnic cleansing. With the 'unbundled' approach to global sovereignty in mind, structural violence targeting the Rohingya – including pervasive statelessness due to government discrimination – are issues worthy of international concern. 'The aim is not to weaken global responsibility by spreading its range of issues too thin, but rather to expand the available tools necessary for effective rights protection', writes Lindsey Kingston and Saheli Datta.[55] Norms of global responsibility therefore 'offer opportunities to remedy existing deficiencies and ensure that the problem of statelessness is adequately understood and prioritized'.[56] In the case of the Rohingya in Burma, increased international attention and action aimed and eliminating statelessness may help combat the direct violence (including ethnic cleansing) that is currently supported by state discrimination, as well as help prevent mass atrocities such as genocide from happening in the future.[57]

Ultimately, human rights violations targeting Burma's Rohingya minority highlight the challenges for R2P prevention, as well as the opportunities that the norm provides. The government of Burma has ignored its responsibilities by sanctioning direct violence against members of the ethnic minority, as well as perpetuating structural inequality and statelessness through discriminatory citizenship regulations. The international community's tendency to equate R2P with military intervention neglects the norm's potential for violence prevention, which could help to stop mass atrocities in progress and future rights violations against the Rohingya. R2P's alignment with IDP protection and its emphasis on 'sovereignty as responsibility', for instance, provide vital foundations for responding to forced displacement and statelessness. While military intervention is not a realistic solution to this particular problem, it is imperative that the international community engage in serious discussion and problem-solving to help protect the rights of Burma's ethnic minorities. In this case – and in other areas where minorities face the threat of mass atrocity crimes – growing recognition of global responsibility must translate into sustained dialogue and preventative action.

Disclosure statement

No potential conflict of interest was reported by the author.

Notes

1. Peter Popham, 'No End in Sight to the Sufferings of "the World's Most Persecuted Minority" – Burma's Rohingya Muslims', *The Independent*, 8 October 2012, http://www.independent.co.uk/news/world/asia/no-end-in-sight-to-the-sufferings-of-the-worlds-most-persecuted-minority–burmas-rohingya-muslims-8202784.html (accessed 21 January 2015).

2. The country's military-led government officially changed the state's name from 'Burma' to 'Myanmar' in 1989, but the author continues to use the term 'Burma' in solidarity with Burmese human rights advocates and the country's pro-democracy movement.

3. Jared Ferrie, 'Obama Calls on Myanmar to Protect Rohingya; Suu Kyi Urges Harmony', *Reuters*, 14 November 2014, http://www.reuters.com/article/2014/11/14/us-myanmar-usa-rohingya-idUSKCN0IY0VN20141114 (accessed 21 January 2015).

4. Greg Constantine, *Exiled to Nowhere: Burma's Rohingya* (Nowhere People, 2012).

5. International Commission on Intervention and State Sovereignty, *The Responsibility to Protect* (December 2001), http://responsibilitytoprotect.org/ICISS%20Report-1.pdf (accessed 31 January 2015), xi–xii.

6. United Nations General Assembly, '2005 World Summit Outcome', 15 September 2005, http://responsibilitytoprotect.org/world%20summit%20outcome%20doc%202005%281%29.pdf (accessed 31 January 2015).

7. Roberta Cohen, 'Humanitarian Imperatives are Transforming Sovereignty', *Northwestern Journal of International Affairs* (Winter 2008), http://www.brookings.edu/research/articles/2008/01/winter-humanitarian-cohen (accessed 17 January 2015).

8. Roberta Cohen and Francis M. Deng, *Masses in Flight: The Global Crisis of Internal Displacement* (Washington, DC: Brookings Institution Press, 1998), 275–6.

9. Gareth Evans, *The Responsibility to Protect: Ending Mass Atrocity Crimes Once and For All* (Washington, DC: Brookings Institution Press, 2008).

10. Ramesh Thakur, *The United Nations, Peace and Security: From Collective Security to the Responsibility to Protect* (Cambridge: Cambridge University Press, 2006), 251.

11. Anne Orford, *International Authority and the Responsibility to Protect* (Cambridge: Cambridge University Press, 2011), 26.

12. ICSS, *The Responsibility to Protect*.

13. Alex J. Bellamy, 'Conflict Prevention and the Responsibility to Protect', *Global Governance* 13 (2008): 135–56, at 139–40.

14. Ibid.

15. Ibid., 142.

16. Ibid., 147.

17. Thomas G. Weiss, *Humanitarian Intervention: Ideas in Action, Second Edition* (Cambridge and Malden: Polity Press, 2012), 113, 103.

18. Lawrence Woocher, 'The Responsibility to Prevent: Toward a Strategy', in *The Routledge Handbook of the Responsibility to Protect*, ed. W. Andy Knight and Frazer Egerton (London and New York: Routledge, 2012), 22–35, 22.

19. United Nations General Assembly, 'Implementing the Responsibility to Protect: Report of the Secretary-General', 12 January 2009, http://responsibilitytoprotect.org/implementing%20the%20rtop.pdf (accessed 17 January 2015), 8.

20. United Nations General Assembly and Security Council, 'Responsibility to Protect: State Responsibility and Prevention, Report of the Secretary-General', 9 July 2013, http://www.un.org/en/ga/search/view_doc.asp?symbol=A/67/929 (accessed 17 January 2015).

21. Ibid., 4–5.

22. Woocher, 'The Responsibility to Prevent', 28–30.

23. John G. Heidenrich, *How to Prevent Genocide: A Guide for Policymakers, Scholars, and the Concerned Citizen* (Westport: Praeger, 2001).

24. Brian Knowlton, 'Panel Urges Creation of Genocide Alert System', *The New York Times*, 8 November 2008, http://www.nytimes.com/2008/12/08/world/americas/08iht-genocide.4.18497285.html (accessed 17 January 2015).

25. Ibid., 9.

26. Johan Galtung and Tord Höivik, 'Structural and Direct Violence: A Note on Operationalization', *Journal of Peace Research* 8, no. 1 (1971): 73–6, at 73.

27. George Kent, 'Children as Victims of Structural Violence', *Societies Without Borders* 1 (2006): 53–67, at 55.

28. *Al Jazeera*, 'UN Calls for "Full Rohingya Citizenship"', 30 December 2014, http://www.aljazeera.com/news/americas/2014/12/un-calls-full-rohingya-citizenship-myanmar-monks-rakhin-2014123044246726211.html (accessed 17 January 2015).

29. Human Rights Watch, *'All You Can Do is Pray': Crimes against Humanity and Ethnic Cleansing of Rohingya Muslims in Burma's Arakan State* (2013), http://www.hrw.org/sites/default/files/reports/burma0413webwcover_0.pdf (accessed 15 January 2015), 109–13.
30. Human Rights Watch, 'Burma: Government Plan Would Segregate Rohingya', 2 October 2014, http://www.hrw.org/news/2014/10/03/burma-government-plan-would-segregate-rohingya (accessed 16 January 2015).
31. Human Rights Watch, 'Burma's Rohingya Plan is a "Blueprint for Segregation"', 5 October 2014, http://www.hrw.org/news/2014/10/05/burmas-rohingya-plan-blueprint-segregation (accessed 16 January 2015).
32. *Al Jazeera*, 'UN Calls for 'Full Rohingya Citizenship'''.
33. Roméo Dallaire, 'The Very Real Prospect of Genocide in Burma', *Global Brief*, 24 March 2014, http://globalbrief.ca/romeo-dallaire/2014/03/24/the-very-real-prospect-of-genocide-in-burma/ (accessed 16 January 2015).
34. Human Rights Watch, *'All You Can Do is Pray'*, 11.
35. Ibid., 12.
36. Ibid.
37. Ibid., 15.
38. Amie Hamling, 'Rohingya: The Most Persecuted Refugees in the World', *Amnesty International Australia*, 13 August 2014, http://www.amnesty.org.au/refugees/comments/35290/ (accessed 17 January 2015).
39. Jane Perlez, 'For Myanmar Muslim Minority, No Escape from Brutality', *The New York Times*, 14 March 2014, http://www.nytimes.com/2014/03/15/world/asia/trapped-between-home-and-refuge-burmese-muslims-are-brutalized.html?_r=0 (accessed 17 January 2015).
40. Jason Szep and Andrew R.C. Marshall, 'Special Report: Thailand Secretly Dumps Myanmar Refugees into Trafficking Rings', *Reuters*, 5 December 2013, http://uk.reuters.com/article/2013/12/05/uk-thailand-rohingya-special-report-idUKBRE9B400920131205 (accessed 17 January 2015).
41. Amnesty International, 'Urgent Action: Rohingya Activist Conditionally Released', 8 October 2014, http://www.amnesty.org/en/library/asset/ASA16/024/2014/en/0d227d34-033e-4949-ae11-2fbd774e10df/asa160242014en.pdf (accessed 19 January 2015).
42. Amnesty International, 'Annual Report 2013: Myanmar', http://www.amnesty.org/en/region/myanmar/report-2013 (accessed 19 January 2015).
43. International Coalition for the Responsibility to Protect, 'Burma Resolution in Security Council, Vetoed by Russia and China: Implications for RtoP', http://www.responsibilitytoprotect.org/index.php/crises/128-the-crisis-in-burma/793-burma-resolution-in-security-council-vetoed-by-russia-and-china-implications-for-r2p (accessed 31 January 2015).
44. International Federation of Red Cross and Red Crescent Societies, 'Myanmar: Cyclone Nargis 2008 Facts and figures', 3 May 2011, http://www.ifrc.org/en/news-and-media/news-stories/asia-pacific/myanmar/myanmar-cyclone-nargis-2008-facts-and-figures/ (accessed 19 January 2015).
45. Ramesh Thakur, *The Responsibility to Protect: Norms, Laws and the Use of Force in International Politics* (London and New York: Routledge, 2011), 152–3.
46. Alex J. Bellamy and Catherine Drummond, 'Southeast Asia: Between Non-interference and Sovereignty as Responsibility', in *The Routledge Handbook of the Responsibility to Protect*, ed. W. Andy Knight and Frazer Egerton (London and New York: Routledge, 2012), 245–56, at 252.
47. Human Rights Watch, *'All You Can Do is Pray'*, 132–5.
48. Alex J. Bellamy, *Massacres and Morality: Mass Atrocities in an Age of Civilian Immunity* (Oxford: Oxford University Press, 2012), 3.
49. Luke Glanville, 'The International Community's Responsibility to Protect', in *Protecting the Displaced: Deepening the Responsibility to Protect*, ed. Sara E. Davies and Luke Glanville (Leiden and Boston, MA: Martinus Nijhoff Publishers, 2010), 185–204, at 204.
50. Roberta Cohen, 'Reconciling R2P with IDP Protection', in *Protecting the Displaced: Deepening the Responsibility to Protect*, ed. Sara E. Davies and Luke Glanville (Leiden and Boston, MA: Martinus Nijhoff Publishers, 2010), 35–57, at 40–1.
51. Ibid., 41–9.
52. Erin D. Mooney, 'Something Old, Something New, Something Borrowed … Something Blue? The Protection Potential of a Marriage of Concepts between R2P and IDP Protection', in

Protecting the Displaced: Deepening the Responsibility to Protect, ed. Sara E. Davies and Luke Glanville (Leiden and Boston, MA: Martinus Nijhoff Publishers, 2010), 59–84, 68–9, 64.

53. Cohen, 'Reconciling R2P with IDP Protection', 51–2.
54. Lloyd Axworthy and Allan Rock, 'R2P: A New and Unfinished Agenda', *Global Responsibility to Protect* 1 (2009): 54–69, 64–65.
55. Lindsey N. Kingston and Saheli Datta, 'Strengthening the Norm of Global Responsibility: Structural Violence in Relation to Internal Displacement and Statelessness', *Global Responsibility to Protect* 4 (2012): 475–504, at 484.
56. Ibid., 496.
57. It is important to note that genocide occurs in cases of mass-scale killing, as well as instances where the number of deaths is relatively low. Rather than using body counts as a litmus test for identifying acts of genocide, Article 2 of the UN Genocide Convention defines genocide as acts committed 'with the intent to destroy, in whole or in part, a national, ethnical, racial or religious group'. This includes acts such as: killing members of the group, causing serious bodily or mental harm to members of the group, deliberately inflicting conditions calculated to bring about physical destruction of the group in whole or in part, imposing measures intended to prevent births, and forcibly transferring children of the group to another group. See: United Nations General Assembly, 'Convention on the Prevention and Punishment of the Crime of Genocide', 9 December 1948, https://treaties.un.org/doc/Publication/UNTS/Volume%2078/volume-78-I-1021-English.pdf (accessed 11 February 2015).

Will R2P be ready when disaster strikes? – The rationale of the Responsibility to Protect in an environmental context

Konstantin Kleine

Graduate Institute of International and Development Studies, Geneva, Switzerland

This article answers the question whether the rationale behind the Responsibility to Protect can be applied or should be applicable in an environmental context. While the original report by the International Commission on Intervention and State Sovereignty, which developed the Responsibility to Protect, allowed for such application, the discussion remained mainly centred on the protection from atrocity crimes. To this end, the article first assesses the two main rationales behind the Responsibility to Protect which are implied in the present discourse about the Responsibility to Protect and then applies the more favourable rationale to three scenarios within an environmental context.

Introduction

Even though the debate about the Responsibility to Protect (R2P) is soon going into its 15th year, it is still a hot candidate for the next international Supernorm.[1] But will it be ready when disaster strikes again?

Unfortunately, it might not be. The debate about R2P focuses on protection from man-made mass atrocities. If those would represent the full scope of R2P, the concept might indeed not be ready to react to all kinds of disasters that might occur and deeply affect human lives.

To assess the readiness of R2P, this article will in the first part probe into the rationale behind R2P – is it meant to protect from genocide, crimes against humanity, war crimes and ethnic cleansing,[2] or is its focus on the protection from human suffering irrespective of whether the cause for the suffering is man-made.

The second part of the article will apply the rationale and prevailing concepts from the discourse on R2P to three scenarios with an environmental scope. Scenario one is the deliberate destruction of the natural basis of the livelihood of a defined group of people. Scenario two is a natural disaster, not man-made, which leads to mass human suffering and death. Scenario three is a deliberate act by a state, which has no direct effect on human life, but on the environment, which likely leads in a long-term perspective to a partial destruction of the basis for human life on earth.

The focus of this article is on the rationale of R2P. The main question is in which cases coercive, potentially military, action should be allowed. Reference to the other elements of the R2P concept is only made when it takes the discourse forward.

The rationale behind the Responsibility to Protect

What is R2P?

After an almost two-century-long struggle to reconcile the principles of state sovereignty and the interest to intervene, also with military force, to protect human life and limb, the concept of R2P is an attempt to solve this riddle by redefining state sovereignty. In line with this approach, the notion of sovereignty has shifted. Sovereignty is no longer exclusively preoccupied with total discretion in internal affairs of the respective state and the principle of non-interference with the domestic internal affairs of other states, but includes a component of responsibility,[3] the responsibility to protect its own citizens.[4] This responsibility is not conflicting with state sovereignty, but an integral part of the new concept of sovereignty.[5] As the R2P is an inherent part of state sovereignty, the primary responsibility is on the state which exercises sovereignty. Only if a state is unable or unwilling to fulfil its responsibility, is the responsibility of the international community, the other states, entailed.[6] Following the approach of the International Commission on Intervention and State Sovereignty (ICISS), R2P consists of three pillars: the responsibility to prevent, the responsibility to react, and the responsibility to rebuild.[7]

The origins and present status of R2P

The doctrine of R2P is not a solitary development in international law, but the latest incarnation of the discourse about sovereignty and humanitarian intervention. In this discourse, reference is made to philosophical concepts as far back as two millennia ago. The concept of just war, *bellum iustum*, for a just cause is seen as the remote forefather of R2P.[8] The full-fledged dichotomy between intervention and sovereignty evolved subsequent to the development of the concept of sovereignty as a predominantly absolute right of control and exclusion, which assumes disentangled spheres of control, power and loyalty.[9] This concept of sovereignty was, and arguably still is, at the core of international law and international relations,[10] named the Westphalian system or, more critically, Westphalian myth. The Greek War of Independence between 1821 and 1830 is often regarded as the first test case for the doctrine of humanitarian intervention.[11] While the actual term was coined later,[12] the humanitarian cause for intervention was acknowledged as one reason for the intervention.[13] Subsequently, the term humanitarian intervention stayed, but the contours of the concept behind the name shifted.

The two most audacious atrocities in the twentieth century before the founding of the United Nations, the Armenian genocide and the holocaust committed by Germany, did not lead to an intervention.[14] The establishment of the United Nations under the still immediate impression of the atrocities committed during World War II did not solve the conflict between intervention and sovereignty. While the preamble and article 1(3) of the United Nations Charter include human rights and humanitarian cooperation as fundamental principles, the principle of state sovereignty is equally enshrined in the Charter in Article 2. This established human rights as a matter of the international community, no longer a purely internal issue, a development which was supported by the subsequent establishment of the international human rights covenants and conventions. But the prevailing interpretation of Article 2 of the United Nations Charter left no room for unilateral interventions for humanitarian reasons, and the emergence of the Cold War made the question of multilateral interventions with United Nations Security Council backing, under Chapter VII of the Charter, a mostly academic exercise for almost 40 years.[15]

The matter started evolving again after the collapse of the iron curtain and the end of the Cold War. The Security Council allowed intervention of different degrees in Iraq,[16] Somalia[17] and Haiti,[18] in all cases with a humanitarian purpose.[19] But the cases which burned themselves into the common memory are those where the reaction of the international community was absent or wholly insufficient: the genocide in Rwanda in 1994 and the massacre in Srebrenica in 1995. The multilateral intervention in Kosovo in 1999 failed to attain explicit authorisation by the United Nations Security Council; the consensus between the veto powers from the early 1990s had already vanished. Also, there was no international consensus which would allow humanitarian interventions without Security Council authorisation. The prevailing opinion considered such attempts as sacrificing the basic principle of international law – state sovereignty – on the altar of human compassion.[20]

But the issue became topical, and Kofi Annan made it part of his agenda as United Nations Secretary General. He famously asked the supporters of absolute sovereignty in his report 'We the People' which alternatives they would like to see to react to atrocities such as those that occurred in Srebrenica and Rwanda:

> But to the critics I would pose this question: if humanitarian intervention is, indeed, an unacceptable assault on sovereignty, how should we respond to a Rwanda, to a Srebrenica – to gross and systematic violations of human rights that offend every precept of our common humanity? […] We confront a real dilemma. Few would disagree that both the defence of humanity and the defence of sovereignty are principles that must be supported. Alas, that does not tell us which principle should prevail when they are in conflict.[21]

Kofi Annan did not conceal his own answer to the question – state sovereignty should not be a shield for crimes against humanity and the United Nations Security Council should be the right authority to act in such cases.[22] In reaction to this question, the Canadian government established the ICISS,[23] whose report[24] shaped the concept of R2P and overcame the stark dichotomy between sovereignty and humanitarian intervention by defining sovereignty as responsibility. Conscious of the often negative connotations the term humanitarian intervention had inherited in its discourse history, the ICISS decided to no longer use the term and distinguish R2P from humanitarian intervention.[25] Nevertheless, the 'Ghosts of Humanitarian Intervention'[26] are still present in the current debate and useful to fully understand the origins and concepts of the R2P. It should also be noted that the understanding of sovereignty in R2P does not represent a sudden shift of the notion, and it was in this understanding the ICISS could build upon the ideas of predecessors, dating back to Hugo Grotius[27] and including, non-exhaustively, John Locke,[28] the Island of Palmas Arbitration,[29] the dissenting opinion of Alvarez Alejandro Álvarez in the Corfu Channel Case[30] and United Nations Secretary-Generals Javier Pérez de Cuéllar and Boutros Boutros-Ghali.[31] The ICISS brought as novelties the connection to the concept of human security,[32] the perspective of potential victims, and an overall cohesive approach to R2P.

It might be too early, and beyond the scope of this article, to fully assess whether the R2P has become a new paradigm in international law. In the wider picture, the concept of sovereignty as responsibility seems to find broad support among states.[33] But the controversy whether coercive action by foreign states is permitted, unilaterally or multilaterally, is by no means finished[34] and the question whether foreign states would not only be permitted, but also obliged to act on their responsibility is far from being consensually solved.[35]

For the present article it is worthwhile in this context to assess the outcome document of the World Summit 2005, since it has implications on the scope of R2P.[36] The concept of R2P is addressed in paragraphs 138 and 139 of the outcome document. Both paragraphs limit the application of R2P to protection 'from genocide, war crimes, ethnic cleansing and crimes against humanity'.[37] This is a significant departure from the ICISS proposal and limits the scope of R2P considerably compared to the wider 'just cause threshold'[38] for military protection developed by the ICISS, which requires 'large scale loss of life' or 'large scale "ethnic cleansing"',[39] but not the occurrence of one of the already defined international crimes.[40] This limitation was a conscious decision of the states present at the World Summit 2005.[41] It made the acceptance of the core concept of sovereignty as responsibility possible, as it makes the application more predictable.[42] In addition, for state parties to the Genocide Convention[43] and the Geneva Conventions on humanitarian law,[44] the outcome document mostly re-states their already existing obligation to prevent and not commit the respective crimes.[45] This marks a return to an approach focused on state obligations and rights.

The limitation at the World Summit 2005 to the four international crimes was no accident, but confirmed by states in later discussions, namely in relation to the secretary-general's report on the implementation of R2P in 2009.[46] Almost as if they were surprised by their own courage to accept the concept of sovereignty as responsibility in 2005, the states organised in the Non-Aligned Movement and individual states such as China expressly opposed any expansion of the scope beyond the four international crimes.[47] The scope of R2P, which found unanimous acceptance by states, is therefore limited to genocide, war crimes, ethnic cleansing and crimes against humanity.

The rationale behind R2P

To answer the question whether this scope of protection from genocide, war crimes, ethnic cleansing and crimes against humanity (hereinafter also the four international crimes or with David Scheffer atrocity crimes[48]) reflects the full desirable scope of R2P, the rationale behind R2P will be assessed. Has the R2P been devised to protect only from these four atrocities?

This assessment has three phases. First, the text of the ICISS report will be analysed, both the text directly relating to the just threshold criterion for military interventions and implications from the other parts of the concept as developed by the ICISS. Second, the rationale focusing on atrocity crimes as reflected in the contemporary political and academic discourse is analysed and assessed whether it presents a viable approach to delimit the scope. Third, the implications of a potential proximity between a R2P limited to genocide, war crimes, ethnic cleansing and crimes against humanity and international criminal law will be evaluated.

ICISS report

The ICISS was created to answer the question posed by Kofi Annan about how to 'respond to a Rwanda, to a Srebrenica'.[49] The question was verbatim taken up in the foreword of the report,[50] indicating a focus on protection from genocide, war crimes and crimes against humanity, as these were at the core of the atrocities committed in Rwanda and Srebrenica.

But the ICISS ultimately took a different approach and developed its own distinct definition of a just cause threshold.[51] While this definition only applies to military interventions, as coercive measures are both the scope of this article and the core of the discourse about interventions and R2P, the analysis will focus on the just cause threshold. The just cause threshold permits coercive measures if irreparable harm to human beings is occurring or likely to immediately commence occurring.[52] The level of harm has to meet a certain threshold:

A. large scale loss of life, actual or apprehended, with genocidal intent or not, which is the product either of deliberate state action, or state neglect or inability to act, or a failed state situation; or

B. large scale 'ethnic cleansing', actual or apprehended, whether carried out by killing, forced expulsion, acts of terror or rape.[53]

This threshold defines the scope of R2P as both partly narrower as well as wider than the four international crimes accepted at the World Summit 2005. The definition is narrower with respect to war crimes. A single killing or a single act of torture can constitute a war crime, if it took place in the context of an international armed conflict.[54] But a single act would not fulfil the ICISS threshold of large-scale loss of life or ethnic cleansing. In other aspects the ICISS scope is significantly broader than only encompassing the four international crimes.

The crucial point is the renunciation of the element of intent by the state. It shall neither matter whether the large-scale loss of life is caused by state-action or 'deliberate inaction' nor whether the actor creating the risk is a state.[55] Consequentially, the word 'crime', which would have implied the requirement of *mens rea*, is absent in the threshold definition. This opens the definition up to embrace cases of failing states, which lead to mass starvation, civil war and thereby indirectly to the risk of large-scale loss of life, as well as natural disasters, where the concerned state is 'unwilling or unable' to provide disaster relief or facilitate the provision of disaster relief by foreigners.[56]

To ensure coercive action remains the exception and therefore only applies in the most extreme, conscience-shocking cases,[57] the ICISS's scope is primarily limited by the requirement of a large-scale atrocity or disaster,[58] and, arguably, by a relative brevity of the timeframe in which the loss of life occurs or would potentially occur. A large-scale loss of life stretched over many years is not necessarily conscience-shocking, but accepted as a common contingency of life.

Ensuring reaction to conscience-shocking events would also have a structural function in international law apart from limiting the scope of R2P. The reaction to the conscience-shocking events serves to re-state the basic values of the international community.[59]

The text of the just cause threshold, the ICISS 'take' on the scope of R2P, indicates that the rationale behind R2P has to be different from the protection against the four international crimes. But the ICISS has also addressed its perception of the rationale more directly in the context of shifting the terminology from humanitarian intervention to R2P. The new terminology was not only adopted because of the perception of humanitarian intervention as a failed endeavour and the negative subtext of the term, but also to signify a shift of the focus of the debate from intervention to protection.[60] For the ICISS, protection implies an assessment from the perspective of potential victims.[61] In other words, the ICISS aimed to design the concept of R2P to fit its rationale: protection for (potential) victims of large-scale atrocities or disasters. The wide scope assessed before is one way to adopt this rationale.

The assessment of the rationale followed by the ICISS is of particular value for the present article. Even though some of the members of the ICISS might have brought a political approach to the discussion,[62] and governments had their say in the roundtables and consultations held by the ICISS,[63] the outcome was still mostly unaltered by Realpolitik. The ICISS tried to create a document which would achieve its rationale also after it had gone through the mills of the political grind, which led to self-imposed limits of the scope of its proposals, but these limits did, arguably, not affect its understanding of the rationale of the project. The ICISS report can therefore serve as evidence as to what the global academic community predominantly perceived to be the rationale behind R2P 15 years ago: ensuring protection for (potential) victims of large-scale atrocities or disasters, irrespective of whether the disaster is man-made or the result of a state decision.

R2P to end atrocity crimes

Nevertheless, the present debate on R2P has not encompassed this understanding by the ICISS, but remains focused on R2P as a reaction to or prevention of the four international crimes. This reflects the outcome of the World Summit 2005 as outlined above. Exemplary for this discourse is the essay 'Atrocity Crimes Framing the Responsibility to Protect', by David Scheffer, which already in the title illustrates the focus of the debate on atrocity crimes and later formulates the hope of R2P diminishing or even ending atrocity crimes.[64] There are several potential reasons for this focus.

First, the development of R2P was strongly connected to the eradication of atrocity crimes. Kofi Annan asked in the report 'We the People', which triggered the creation of the ICISS, explicitly for answers on how to react to atrocities as committed in Rwanda or Srebrenica.[65] The leading figures pushing forward on the development of R2P, Kofi Annan, who gave the impulse with said report, and the ICISS co-chairs Gareth Evans and Mohamed Sahnoun, also had personal motives which might explain their engagement especially to end atrocity crimes. Gareth Evans explained that for himself R2P represents a way to fulfil the promise of 'never again', given after the Holocaust and repeated since, with devastatingly little influence on the genocides which followed.[66] The promise of 'never again' also has a special meaning for Kofi Annan after his involvement in the failure to prevent the Rwandan Genocide.[67] Mohamed Sahnoun had analysed the failure of the United Nations in Somalia, where he was the Special Representative of the Secretary-General of the United Nations in 1992, and made a plea for reforms in the United Nations system to allow for effective reaction to such atrocities in his book *Somalia: The Missed Opportunities*.[68] These motives might have, at least subconsciously, influenced their work on the development of the concept and in later implementation attempts.

Second, the 'Ghosts of Humanitarian Intervention'[69] become particularly evident here. Humanitarian intervention is perceived as a reaction to gross human rights violations and as part of a framework to prevent crimes against humanity and genocide,[70] in contrast to R2P, which originally was preoccupied with the protection of individuals regardless of the reason for their vulnerability.[71] As outlined above, the development of R2P was an attempt to overcome the stalemate between sovereignty and protection by intervention in the debate surrounding humanitarian intervention. Nevertheless, many of the arguments from the 'old' debate made their way into the discourse about R2P, leading again to a discourse mainly focused on gross human rights violations and atrocity crimes.

Third, defining the rationale of R2P as protecting (potential) victims of genocide, crimes against humanity, ethnic cleansing and war crimes seems to be the most, maybe even the only, acceptable solution for states. It matches the outcome of the World Summit 2005 and, considering the already existing conventions on genocide and war crimes, as well as the Rome Statute, mostly reflects obligations states are already subjected to, making it easy to accept it. As an acceptance of the concept of R2P by states even with restricted rationale, compared to the original conception, can still be seen as a step forward – states recognise their responsibility to protect and the possibility of interventions – preserving state consent for the concept as a whole could be a reason for restricting the rationale.

In conclusion, this approach to a rationale of 'never again' is protection for (potential) victims of genocide, crimes against humanity, ethnic cleansing and war crimes.

International criminal law

The third consideration relating to scope and rationale is the implication of similarities between an approach to R2P focusing on protection from genocide, war crimes and crimes against humanity and the application of liability under international criminal law. This approach to R2P is so closely related to international criminal law and specifically the Rome Statute,[72] that the Rome Statute is used to define certain elements relating to the scope of R2P.[73]

This leads to a delicate situation. States have mainly refused the notion of themselves as international criminals. This became especially evident in the tedious process in the International Law Commission, which struggled for almost 50 years with the topic of state responsibility. A key decision was to dismiss the 'utopian project' of criminalising state conduct.[74] Now applying the principles and laws from international criminal law directly to states under the umbrella of R2P would potentially introduce the state as international criminal through the backdoor. Coercive action, especially military intervention, although only permissible with Security Council approval, is likely to be perceived as punishment, especially when the reasons for such action make explicit reference to state conduct as the decisive element. Therefore, if the scope of R2P is to be based on a rationale which closely mirrors international crimes, this might erode state consensus for R2P as a whole.

Conclusion on the rationale

Concerning the rationale of R2P, the assessment in this section has revealed two main approaches: the rationale which shaped the work of the ICISS on R2P – ensuring protection for (potential) victims of large-scale atrocities or disasters, irrespective of whether the disaster is man-made or the result of state decision – and the rationale focusing on atrocity crimes and the promise of 'never again' – of protection for (potential) victims of genocide, crimes against humanity and war crimes.

It should first be noted that the ICISS approach also encompasses – with the exception of war crimes with small numbers of victims – protection for all potential victims whose protection is also the rationale of the approach focusing on the four international crimes. The ICISS approach is coherent with the structure of the R2P as developed by the ICISS, but it might face obstacles on the path to full acceptance by state consensus.

Here lies the strength of the approach focused on the four international crimes, which seems to be reflected in the present consensus amongst states on R2P. But this approach turns, with its strong focus on state consent, to some extent, the wheel of development back to 1999. The focus is again on state obligations and a potential right to intervene, not the protection of potential victims. Essentially, R2P would become only a new word for humanitarian intervention.

Crucially, the 'never again' approach fails to provide a coherent explanation why suffering and death should be treated differently depending on whether they are caused by a natural disaster or state action. Morally, the gravity is the same.[75] Sovereignty as responsibility of the state to protect its population does not stop at the state constraining itself from committing acts of atrocity, but extends to everything happening under its sovereignty. The only reason given for the distinction and the thereby implied requirement of state intent is Realpolitik – states would simply not accept the wider ICISS rationale. The short discourse into the relationship between R2P and international criminal law weakens this policy argument, states might indeed also refuse the absolute requirement of state intent to dispel the notion of states as criminals.

Therefore, the rationale, which was the foundation for the coherent structure of R2P developed by the ICISS, is favourable. The rationale of R2P should be to ensure protection for (potential) victims of large-scale atrocities or disasters, irrespective of whether the disaster is man-made or the result of state decision.

The scope of the implementation of R2P should be adapted to ensure full realisation of the rationale behind R2P. The implementation in the World Summit outcome document is insufficient to this end, but represents the present state consensus.

Three scenarios

Three scenarios will be analysed to assess the implications of the ICISS rationale for the application of R2P to environmental disasters.

Scenario one – deprivation of livelihood

Scenario one covers the deliberate destruction of the natural basis of the livelihood of a defined group of people. This could mean the deforestation of a forest which is the habitat of a group of indigenous people, who depend on the forest both for nourishment and shelter, or the damming, diversion or poisoning of a river which constitutes the sole source of potable water for a community, thereby endangering the pure survival of the affected groups.

Following the findings in the previous section, R2P is meant to protect (potential) victims of large-scale atrocities or disasters, irrespective of whether the disaster is man-made or the result of state decision. The deliberate deprivation of livelihood would affect the survival of the whole group and, assuming the group is of considerable size, also fulfil the large-scale criterion. But does it also constitute an atrocity, a conscience-shocking event?

The deliberate deprivation of livelihood brings this scenario close to the crime against humanity of extermination, defined as killing by intentionally inflicting conditions of life calculated to bring about the destruction of part of a population.[76] Extermination includes cases where a part of the population is killed by inter alia the deprivation of access to food or medicine.[77] Destroying the natural basis of the livelihood directly leads to a deprivation of access to food and water. It is submitted that acts which fulfil the criteria of extinction as a crime against humanity, in this case the crime of extermination, are indeed atrocious acts which should not be left unanswered by the international community, not least to restate its basic values. The inclusion of the crime of extermination in crimes against humanity also indicates that it should not matter how people are dying, from gunfire or induced starvation. In addition, if the conditions of life are inflicted on a group as defined in article 6 of the Rome Statute, the state conduct could also constitute genocide. In any case, they should be protected by the principles of R2P.

It should be noted that in such cases where state conduct amounts to the crime of extermination or genocide, the case would also fall within the rationale of R2P, following the approach focusing on the four international crimes. The state is deliberately acting and the crime of extermination or potentially genocide is part of the international crimes from which (potential) victims should also be protected in this approach.

The exact outline of the rationale behind R2P becomes crucial if the scenario is modified in one respect – what if the destruction of the natural basis of the livelihood occurs non-deliberate, but is still man-made? The deprivation of livelihood would still affect the survival of the group and, assuming the group is of considerable size, still fulfil the large-scale criterion. But the assessment of the atrocity would have to follow a different path. The lack of intent does not allow for direct or analogue application of criminal law. The previously addressed idea of brevity gains importance. While gradual deterioration of livelihood might be despicable, it is part of the common contingencies of life that not all environmental circumstances will always remain the same. The complete destruction of livelihood in one instant exceeds the notion of common contingencies and can be conscience-shocking, the latter the more likely the larger the affected group is. But only a rationale which is focused on the protection of all potential victims and not limited to the scope of the four international crimes could extend protection to victims in this modified scenario.

Scenario one has particular importance in the context of indigenous people and other groups culturally living in direct dependence on their natural environment, groups who source their food and their water directly from natural resources. In contrast, the destruction of the complete livelihood of a metropolis in one instant is difficult to imagine. The ICISS rationale behind R2P allows for protection of these indigenous groups and other culturally nature-dependant groups from such instant destruction of their livelihood.

Scenario two – natural disaster

Scenario two contains a natural disaster, not man-made, which leads to mass human suffering and death. Examples would be large-scale earthquakes, tropical storms, floods and tsunamis. It goes without saying that such scenarios invoke the responsibility of the respective state to protect its population. The scenario becomes one of international responsibility and potential coercive measures when the respective state is unable or unwilling to protect its population and unwilling to accept help to do so from the outside.

This scenario is arguably the most extensively discussed, both in particular in reaction to the disaster in Myanmar following Cyclone Nargis and in a more academic context by the International Law Commission under the heading 'Protection of Persons in the Event of Disasters'.[78]

The aftermath of Cyclone Nargis in Myanmar (2008) was an almost stereotypical example for scenario two. The storm had caused flooding and together the storm and flood killed more than 130,000 people immediately and put an even larger number at imminent risk of death.[79] The government, a military dictatorship, initially refused to accept any disaster relief from outside.[80] At the time the government finally accepted external help, the debate whether this should be a case of R2P had already commenced.[81] As the Myanmar disaster took place after the World Summit 2005 had laid down a narrow interpretation of R2P as state consensus, which would exclude the application of R2P to natural disasters, the debate centred on the question whether the omission to accept foreign disaster relief by the Burmese government could be construed as a crime against humanity.[82] It was held that a military intervention in this case, with or without approval by the United Nations Security Council, would endanger the whole state consensus on R2P and the option of intervention should be left for cases 'where it is really needed'.[83] The ICISS rationale would have extended protection to the victims of this natural disaster, as it is not preoccupied with a quasi-criminal law approach but focuses on the scale of the disaster. The idea that Myanmar was, ex-ante, allegedly a case where protection and help, also by coercive action, was not really needed seems cynical considering the sheer dimension of human suffering. Whether slavishly following the World Summit 2005 take on R2P could actually ensure persistent state consensus has already been critically assessed.

The idea of R2P applying in the context of disaster was almost rejected outright by the International Law Commission in its debate on the second report on the protection of persons in the event of disasters. The members of the International Law Commission followed the state consensus of R2P only applying to the four international crimes, excluding outside circumstances triggered in the first instance by natural disasters.[84] The draft articles on the protection of persons in the event of disaster, which are at the moment in the consultation process with governments and international organisations,[85] include in the same line in Article 14(1) regarding the requirement of state consent for any external assistance.[86] It should be noted that the duty to reduce the risk of disasters in Article 11 is strongly reminiscent of the responsibility to prevent facet of R2P.[87]

On a more abstract level, the ICISS rationale would be applicable in the scenario of natural disasters which bring (potential) large-scale life loss, as it does not distinguish between the causes for death and suffering, but is aimed at protecting all potential victims.

Scenario three – making earth uninhabitable

Scenario three is a deliberate act by a state which has no direct effect on human life, but on the environment, which likely leads in a long-term perspective to a partial destruction of the basis for human life on earth. This could include a broad range of acts, ranging from, for example, unsafe deposition of nuclear waste to excessive emissions of greenhouse gases to abuse of antibiotics which leads to epidemics of MRSA. All of these represent grave concerns and endanger in a long-term perspective not only large groups of people but the survival of humanity on earth. But, as addressed before, gradual deterioration of livelihood remains part of the common contingencies of life that not all environmental circumstances will always remain the same. In the context of long-term perspectives this notion is also supported by the inherently uncertain future. R2P was not devised to prohibit any and all endeavours with uncertain or unpredictable outcomes.

Apart from the fact that scenario three is not in the same sense conscience-shocking – given the time component – as it was the basis for the ICISS rationale, this scenario also points to the question of whether R2P should be applicable to cases where the primary and predominant damage is done to the environment. Both rationales discussed are grounded on the protection of humans, they are straightforwardly anthropocentric.[88]

Conclusion

The rationale identified as best representing the concept of R2P – sovereignty as responsibility – is the rationale of protecting (potential) victims of large-scale atrocities or disasters, irrespective of whether the disaster is man-made or the result of state decision. This rationale was developed by the ICISS. Sovereignty as responsibility is more than self-restraint not to commit atrocity crimes, it entails the protection from serious harm of anyone subject to this sovereignty. The rationale focusing on atrocity crimes and the promise of never again – protection for (potential) victims of genocide, crimes against humanity, ethnic cleansing and war crimes – falls short in this respect and is in addition unable to explain why suffering and death should be treated differently depending on its cause.

Unfortunately, the state consensus on R2P, represented in the World Summit 2005 outcome document, is based on this second, narrower, rationale. As the analysis of three scenarios has shown, applying R2P only to implement the rationale based on genocide, crimes against humanity, war crimes and ethnic cleansing, would indeed mean that R2P is not ready when disaster, especially natural disaster, strikes.

Therefore, bringing forward the ICISS rationale, directly based on the concept of sovereignty as responsibility, would have distinct advantages: it is more coherent, best represents the paradigm shift envisioned by the ICISS and, most importantly, extends the protection to more cases. R2P would thereby not necessarily become an unfocused concept with interminable application, as long as the assessment of what represents a conscience-shocking atrocity is diligently undertaken.

Last, on the issue of political acceptance:

> If the mission of diplomats and politicians is to find an acceptable solution to a problem, the mission of academics and experts is to find the best solution.[89]

This article takes an academic perspective. It seeks to find the best solution, not the most politically acceptable one. And the best solution allowing for more potential victims of human suffering to be protected would be to apply the ICISS rationale. Then, finally, R2P would be ready when disaster strikes.

Acknowledgements

This article was written as part of the author's LL.M. in International Law at the Graduate Institute of International and Development Studies. The topic was self-conceived. The author would like to thank Professor Andrea Bianchi for his supervision.

Disclosure statement

No potential conflict of interest was reported by the author.

Notes

1. The term Supernorm is borrowed from Anthony D'Amato, 'It's a Bird, It's a Plane, It's Jus Cogens!', *Connecticut Journal of International Law* 6 (1990): 1; for the impact of R2P see

Spencer Zifcak, 'Falls the Shadow: The Responsibility to Protect from Theory to Practice', in *Responsibility to Protect and Sovereignty*, ed. Charles Sampford and Ramesh Thakur (Farnham: Ashgate, 2013), 11; Peter Hilpold, 'Von der Humanitären Intervention zur Schutzverantwortung', in *Die Schutzverantwortung (R2P): Ein Paradigmenwechsel in der Entwicklung des Internationalen Rechts*, ed. Peter Hilpold (Leiden: Martinus Nijhoff Publishers, 2013), 2–4.

2. Gareth Evans, *The Responsibility to Protect: Ending Mass Atrocity Crimes Once and For All* (Washington, DC: Brookings Institution Press, 2008), 11.

3. International Commission on Intervention and State Sovereignty (ICISS), *The Responsibility to Protect: Report of the International Commission on Intervention and State Sovereignty* (Ottawa: IDRC Books, 2001), 13.

4. ICISS, *The Responsibility to Protect*, viii.

5. Hilpold, 'Schutzverantwortung', 9.

6. ICISS, *The Responsibility to Protect*, 17.

7. Ibid.

8. Peter Hilpold, 'Schutzverantwortung und Humanitäre Intervention in Historischer Perspektive', in *Die Schutzverantwortung (R2P): Ein Paradigmenwechsel in der Entwicklung des Internationalen Rechts*, ed. Peter Hilpold (Leiden: Martinus Nijhoff Publishers, 2013), 64–6.

9. Hilpold, 'Historische Perspektive', 79.

10. Andreas Osiander, 'Sovereignty, International Relations, and the Westphalian Myth', *International Organizations* 55 (2001): 251.

11. Hilpold, 'Historische Perspektive', 89, 92.

12. Ibid., 61.

13. Ibid., 92.

14. Ibid., 108

15. Ibid., 111.

16. UNSC, Res. 688 (5 April 1991), UN Doc. S/RES/688.

17. UNSC, Res. 794 (2 December 1992), UN Doc. S/RES/794.

18. UNSC, Res. 940 (31 July 1994), UN Doc. S/RES/940.

19. 'Deeply disturbed by the magnitude of the human suffering involved', UNSC, Res. 688 (5 April 1991), UN Doc. S/RES/688; 'Gravely alarmed by the deterioration of the humanitarian situation in Somalia and underlining the urgent need for the quick delivery of humanitarian assistance', UNSC, Res. 794 (2 December 1992), UN Doc. S/RES/794; 'Gravely concerned by the significant further deterioration of the humanitarian situation in Haiti', UNSC, Res. 940 (31 July 1994), UN Doc. S/RES/940.

20. Bruno Simma, 'NATO, the UN and the Use of Force: Legal Aspects', *European Journal of International Law* 10 (1999): 14.

21. United Nations General Assembly (UNGA), 'We the Peoples: The Role of the United Nations in the Twenty-first Century: Report of the Secretary-General' (27 March 2000), UN Doc. A/54/2000, paras 217–18.

22. Ibid., para. 219.

23. ICISS, *The Responsibility to Protect*, vii.

24. ICISS, *The Responsibility to Protect*.

25. Ibid., 16; Carsten Stahn, 'Responsibility to Protect: Political Rhetoric or Emerging Legal Norm?', *American Journal of International Law* 101 (2007): 102–3; Jonah Eaton, 'An Emerging Norm? Determining the Meaning and Legal Status of the Responsibility to Protect', *Michigan Journal of International Law* 32 (2011): 774.

26. Eaton, 'An Emerging Norm?', 770.

27. Hilpold, 'Historische Perspektive', 84; Stahn, 'Responsibility to Protect', 111.

28. Stahn, 'Responsibility to Protect', 111.

29. Ibid., 112.

30. Hilpold, 'Schutzverantwortung', 5.

31. Ibid., 7; Stahn, 'Responsibility to Protect', 114.

32. Stahn, 'Responsibility to Protect', 115.

33. Ibid., 118; Michael W. Doyle, 'Law, Ethics, and the Responsibility to Protect', in *The Ethics of Armed Humanitarian Intervention*, ed. Don E. Scheid (Cambridge: Cambridge University Press, 2014), 188–9.

34. Stahn, 'Responsibility to Protect', 117, 119.

35. Ibid., 120.

36. UNGA, Res. 60/1 '2005 World Summit Outcome' (24 October 2005), UN Doc. A/RES/60/1.
37. Ibid., paras 138–9.
38. ICISS, *The Responsibility to Protect*, XII.
39. Ibid.
40. See for international crimes: International Criminal Court, *Elements of Crime* (2011); for the ICISS scope see also ICISS, *The Responsibility to Protect*, 33.
41. Eaton, 'An Emerging Norm?', 779–80.
42. Ibid., 779–80.
43. Convention on the Prevention and Punishment of the Crime of Genocide, 9 December 1948, 78 U.N.T.S. 277.
44. Geneva Convention for the Amelioration of the Condition of the Wounded and Sick in Armed Forces in the Field, 12 August 1949, 75 U.N.T.S. 31; Geneva Convention for the Amelioration of the Condition of Wounded, Sick and Shipwrecked Members of Armed Forces at Sea, 12 August 1949, 75 U.N.T.S. 85; Geneva Convention Relative to the Treatment of Prisoners of War, 12 August 1949, 75 U.N.T.S. 135; Geneva Convention Relative to the Protection of Civilian Persons in Time of War, 12 August 1949, 75 U.N.T.S. 287.
45. For the lack of such convention on crimes against humanity see International Law Commission, 'First Report on Crimes against Humanity' (17 February 2015), UN Doc. A/CN.4/680, paras 10–15.
46. UNGA, 'Implementing the Responsibility to Protect: Report of the Secretary-General' (12 January 2009), UN Doc. A/63/677.
47. Doyle, 'Law, Ethics, and the Responsibility to Protect', 205–6.
48. David Scheffer, 'Atrocity Crimes Framing the Responsibility to Protect', *Case Western Reserve Journal of International Law* 40 (2007): 117.
49. UNGA, 'We the Peoples', para. 217.
50. ICISS, *The Responsibility to Protect*, vii.
51. Ibid., xii.
52. Ibid.
53. Ibid.
54. International Criminal Court, *Elements of Crime* (2011), 13–14.
55. ICISS, *The Responsibility to Protect*, 33.
56. Ibid., 33.
57. Ibid., 31.
58. Ibid., 34.
59. Kenneth Veitch, 'Social Solidarity and the Power of Contract', *Journal of Law and Society* 38 (2011): 189, 204.
60. ICISS, *The Responsibility to Protect*, 17–18.
61. Ibid., 17–18.
62. Gareth Evans names himself and Lee Hamilton as the (former) politicians in the ICISS: Evans, *Responsibility to Protect*, 5.
63. ICISS, *The Responsibility to Protect*, 83.
64. Scheffer, 'Atrocity Crimes Framing the Responsibility to Protect', 117, 135.
65. UNGA, 'We the Peoples', paras 217–18.
66. Evans, *Responsibility to Protect*, 2–3.
67. Jason A. Edwards, 'The Mission of Healing: Kofi Annan's Failed Apology', *Atlantic Journal of Communication* 16 (2008): 92–4.
68. Mohamed Sahnoun, *Somalia: The Missed Opportunities* (Washington, DC: United States Institute of Peace, 1994).
69. Eaton, 'An Emerging Norm?', 770.
70. Paul R. Williams and Meghan E. Stewart, 'Humanitarian Intervention: The New Missing Link in the fight to Prevent Crimes Against Humanity and Genocide?', *Case Western Reserve Journal of International Law* 40 (2007): 97.
71. Gareth Evans, 'The Responsibility to Protect: Rethinking Humanitarian Intervention', *ASIL Proceedings* 98 (2004): 83.
72. Rome Statute of the International Criminal Court (adopted 17 July 1998, entered into force 1 July 2002, last amended 2010).
73. Gareth Evans, 'The Responsibility to Protect in Environmental Emergencies', *ASIL Proceedings* 103 (2009): 29.

74. International Law Commission, *Yearbook of the International Law Commission 1998* (Volume II (Part Two)), UN Doc. A/CN.4/SER.A/1998/Add.l (Part 2), paras 322–30.

75. Ramesh Thakur, 'The Responsibility to Protect: Retrospect and Prospect', in *Responsibility to Protect and Sovereignty*, ed. Charles Sampford and Ramesh Thakur (Farnham: Ashgate, 2013), 200.

76. International Criminal Court, *Elements of Crime* (2011), 6; see also Scheffer, 'Atrocity Crimes Framing the Responsibility to Protect', 114; and Linda A. Malone, 'Green Helmets: Eco-Intervention in the Twenty-First Century – Unilateral and Multilateral Intervention', *ASIL Proceedings* 103 (2009): 24.

77. International Criminal Court, *Elements of Crime* (2011), n. 9.

78. International Law Commission, 'Protection of Persons in the Event of Disasters', UN Doc. A/61/10 Annex C.

79. Evans, *Responsibility to Protect*, 65.

80. Thakur, 'Retrospect and Prospect', 200.

81. Ibid., 201.

82. Evans, *Responsibility to Protect*, 66–7; Thakur, 'Retrospect and Prospect', 200.

83. Evans, *Responsibility to Protect*, 69; Thakur, 'Retrospect and Prospect', 200.

84. International Law Commission, 'Provisional Summary Record of the 3018th Meeting on 9th July 2009' (27 August 2010), UN Doc. A/CN.4/SR.3018, 4, 6, 7, 11, 14, 15, 16, 18.

85. International Law Commission, 'Report on the Work of its Sixty-sixth Session' (5 May to 6 June and 7 July to 8 August 2014), UN Doc. A/69/10, 86.

86. Ibid., 88.

87. Ibid., 88.

88. Malone, 'Green Helmets', 26.

89. Ibid., 25.

The responsibility to protect and the lack of intervention in Syria: between the protection of human rights and geopolitical strategies

Gabriele Lombardo

Department of Political Science, University Sapienza, Rome, Italy

Non-intervention in Syria highlights how the theory of the responsibility to protect (R2P) is flexible and depends on the strategic position and geopolitics of the state which violates human rights. Indeed the Security Council's several attempts to adopt a resolution have been blocked by the threat of Russia and China to veto. Accepting a Kofi Annan proposal, the only, but unsuccessful, resolution adopted was 2042/2012 which provided for sending a team of observers to verify the maintenance of the ceasefire. Subsequently, the United States proposed a resolution condemning Syria for the failure to authorise the sending of aid to the people but to no avail as this resolution also did not result in any action based on R2P.

1. Responsibility to protect

The concept emerged for the first time in the report *The Responsibility to Protect*, drafted in 2001 by the International Commission on Intervention and State Sovereignty of States (ICISS) established by Canada, following UN Secretary-General Kofi Annan's *The Millennium Report of 2000* written in 1999 after the war in the Balkans to address in part the need to prevent humanitarian crises requiring intervention. The report of the Secretary-General entitled *We The Peoples: The Role of the United Nations in the 21st Century* explores the issue of humanitarian intervention, asking the international community ' … if humanitarian intervention is, indeed, an unacceptable assault on sovereignty, how should we respond to a Rwanda, to a Srebrenica – to gross and systematic violations of human rights that affect every precept of our common humanity?',[1] when intervention breaches the second article, paragraph 4, of the Charter of the United Nations (UN)[2] and also paragraph 7 establishing non-intervention by the UN in the internal affairs of the state.[3] The novelty introduced by the report lies in suggesting assessment by the international community of any possible action in case the state is *unab*le or *unwilling*[4] to adopt measures in order to protect and safeguard its population and everybody who is in that territory at that moment. The report also points out how the concept of sovereignty should be revised and *modernised*, making the state the main party responsible for protection and safeguarding of its population.[5] The ICISS also outlined in the report three types of responsibility: to prevent, to react and to rebuild, and it is around these three aspects that there exists the problem of humanitarian intervention. Only when the state is *unable* or *unwilling* to act is the international community able to intervene under R2P through, for instance, mechanisms of *early warning*, which may include everything from sanctions to military intervention. The international community, however, under R2P must also assist the state in meeting its responsibility to rebuild post intervention.[6] The report points out that any military intervention must be authorised in advance by the Security Council, respecting the idea of *competent authority*. The Security Council, after examining the situation, may decide to implement measures included in Chapter VI of the UN Charter and if they are unsuccessful the Security Council may carry out the measures provided for in Chapter VII against any state that violates human rights, considering that this breach could threaten international peace and security. The Security Council could also decide not to intervene if the situation does not represent a threat to peace and international security, or even be compelled not to adopt a resolution because of a real or simply threatened veto by one of the permanent members, as in the case of Syria. Other essential elements for implementing an intervention by the international community that are set out in the report are: (i) *the just cause* that applies in the case of loss of life on a large scale, with the intent or less to commit, or in cases of real or perceived, genocide, or actual or perceived ethnic cleansing; (ii) *the right intention* in wanting to put an end to human rights violations; (iii) *the last resort* – military intervention should be a last resort, occurring only when peaceful policy options have not succeeded; (iv) *proportional measures* – military intervention should be the minimum necessary to ensure the protection and defence of human rights; and (v) the final element to be considered is *the reasonable prospect*, referring to the real possibility of successful intervention without this aggravating the situation of the population.[7]

Further references to the concept of R2P can be found in the 2004 report *A More Secure World: Our Shared Responsibility del High Level Panel on Threats*[8]; and in the 2005 report *In Larger Freedom: Towards Development, Security and Human Rights for All*.[9] These reports aim to improve the tools and procedures of the Security Council so that it can intervene on a more objective basis and have more transparent decision-making in cases of violations of human rights.[10] R2P is also discussed at paragraphs 138 and 139 of the 2005 *World Summit Outcome*[11] document: para. 138 gives each state the responsibility to protect its population from *genocide, war crimes, ethnic cleansing* and *crimes against humanity*, and to prevent these crimes, while para. 139 emphasises how the international community has to implement all the necessary tools to intervene and help to protect populations from *gross violation* but, in accord with Chapters VI and VII of the UN Charter, only if the state is unable or unwilling to do so.[12] Only in paragraphs 138 and 139 is there a specific reference to the R2P as a tool for early warning and risk assessment in cases of genocide, war crimes and crimes against humanity. States have pledged to increase and implement all the instruments of *rapid intervention*.[13] The only regional instrument referring to the R2P is the African Union Constitutive Act, article 4, para. H, which also provides for a possible action by the international community to protect a population only when the African Union has been proved to be unable or unwilling.[14]

The theory of the R2P was applied both in the crisis in Kenya and in the crisis in Libya, two opposing situations. In the case of the post-election crisis in Kenya in 2007, the success of Mwai Kibaki, re-elected for the second time, prompted protests from the defeated candidate, Raila Odinga, who complained of electoral fraud. The situation deteriorated and in the months following the crisis there were about 1,200 Kenyans killed and an estimated 500,000 had suffered violence, marking the beginning of a civil war between opposing political factions. The notion of R2P was applied in Kenya without any military intervention by the international community thanks to the role of the former UN Secretary-General Kofi

Annan who has always considered it essential to come to a peaceful resolution to a crisis. The Secretary-General arrived on 28 February 2008 for the signing of an Agreement of National Unity for reconciliation.[15] Kofi Annan considers the resolution of the crisis in Kenya a success of the R2P,[16] led by Great Britain and France. Libya is a more controversial case in respect of R2P. The Security Council has adopted two resolutions on the crisis in Libya, the first, resolution 1970/2011, adopted 26 February 2011, condemned the systematic violations of human rights by the Libyan government – and the incitement of violence against civilians as reported by international organisations. On that basis, the Security Council decided to adopt the measures provided for in article 41 of the UN Charter, and also referred the situation in Libya to the Prosecutor of the International Criminal Court.[17] The referral addressed the internal situation in Libya, indicating it could be a risk to peace and international security, and rebuking the Libyan government's failure to intervene in order to protect the population 'recalling the Libyan Authorities responsibility to protect ITS population'.[18] The Security Council moreover imposed sanctions such as the ban on the import/export of weapons and the freezing of Gaddafi family goods. Resolution 1973/2011 had greater effects, giving the green light to states to every *necessary measure*[19] to protect the civilians from conflict, referring to the 2005 outcome document, paragraph 139, requiring compliance with the no-fly zone and the checking of embargoed arms against Libya.[20] This example shows that the international community may decide to intervene in specific areas and not in others, so that in some countries *gross violations* of human rights could be committed and the international community will not take a position to intervene in defence of these populations. Both resolutions recall the R2P, even if they do not always conform to the instruments that provide for the R2P.[21]

2. The Syrian crisis and the failure to implement the R2P

The Syrian situation is very different, even if the matrix is similar to the Libyan one, Syrian rebels called on the government of al-Assad to step down and in the wake of the Arab Spring, demanded a radical change and democratisation. The civil war has produced many victims in the civilian population as evidenced by the report of the UN.[22] A large number of children have been killed (as we can see in UNICEF's report *Humanitarian Action for Children 2012*[23]) due largely to the violent crackdown by the Syrian government against rebels. Indeed, despite the serious human rights violations carried out by the Syrian government and to some degree by rebel forces, as evidenced by the report of the Commission of Inquiry of the Human Rights Council of the United Nations,[24] the UN has not been able to intervene, nor has the international community adopted a position or taken steps to put an end to the revolt and the serious violations being committed. The Security Council is paralysed in adopting a resolution because Russia and China threaten to veto any resolution.[25]

The difference in the position adopted by Russia and China can be understood with reference to Syria's geographical position, which is strategically important in the Middle East. Syrian allies are against intervention and take the position that the main elements of the R2P are respect for sovereignty, respect for territorial integrity and independence of the state where the intervention is set. They are concerned that the situation in Kosovo could be repeated, that the intervention of the international community in Syria to stabilise the country will lead to an infringement of sovereignty. In fact, the territory of Kosovo today is overseen and regulated by both UNMIK (United Nations Interim Administration Mission in Kosovo) and EULEX (The European Union Rule of Law Mission in Kosovo). Despite this, the situation in Kosovo is still not stabilised. In addition

Serbia does not recognise the unilaterally declared independence of Kosovo of 2008 nor that the NATO intervention was justified. Instead, Serbia claims serious and persistent violations of its sovereignty. There have been numerous criticisms of any potential intervention in Syria by some states who fear that their sovereignty could be violated as a result of intervention by the international community to protect human rights as justified by former UN Secretary-General Kofi Annan under the R2P. Moreover, they argue that an intervention by the international community can be achieved only if a state is *unable* or *unwilling* to protect its own population, but that during a civil war it is difficult to assess these elements, always bearing in mind the principle of *self-determination* and the right of the state to defend itself from internal revolts designed to destabilise it. Only two resolutions have been adopted by the Security Council: resolution 2042/2012, authorised sending a group of observers, with the approval of the Syrian government, aiming to monitor a ceasefire, maintain territorial integrity, sovereignty and independence and to urge the Syrian government to follow up on the commitments of 25 March 2012 respecting the six points[26] proposed by the Joint Special Envoy of the United Nations and the Arab States, Kofi Annan, and of the subsequent communication of 1 April 2012.[27] The Syrian government made a commitment to: (i) prohibit armed troops entering towns; (ii) prohibit the use of heavy weapons within these populated centres; and (iii) begin the withdrawal of troops currently stationed in and around the towns, which withdrawal was to be completed by 10 April 2012. The hope was that the rebels and the government would maintain the agreement. Resolution 2043/2012[28] established the United Nations Supervision Mission in Syria (UNSMIS) – a group of unarmed military observers under the command of a Chief Military Observer with the aim of monitoring the ceasefire and facilitating respect of the accepted six points. In addition, the Security Council called on the Syrian government to ensure that the population could have access to international assistance as is required under international humanitarian law (para. 11). The resolutions were adopted because they do not consider military intervention on Syrian territory, given the threat of veto by China and Russia, the latter trying to regain its sphere of influence on Syria. In fact, in 2005, Putin reduced Syrian debt to 70%; also, the Russian fleet was allowed to anchor at the port of Tartous, showing that Syria is geopolitically strategic for Russia.[29] In contrast, Russia abstained during the voting on resolutions 1970 and 1973 on Libya. This demonstrates how the R2P is a theory that is flexible and dependent on geopolitical and strategic elements.

Given the fact that (in compliance with the UN Charter) any intervention without UN Security Council permission is considered illegal under international law,[30] states try to prevent the Security Council adopting a resolution for intervention. Nevertheless 'humanitarian interventions', such as in Kosovo, have been addressed through subsequent resolutions ad hoc, so that humanitarian interventions have often been perceived or considered by some states that have been subject to them as an action interfering with that state's internal affairs and as a pretext for the allocation of troops on its territory.

The UN's non-intervention in Syria highlights that the institution of the R2P has no well-defined practice and that it is influenced by the geopolitical and strategic issues of the state which violates said human rights or does not oppose such violations. Nevertheless, the unilateral action by a coalition of states attempting to protect the interests of the population is often perceived as an act of interference in violation of Article 2, para. 7[31] of the UN Charter, and for this reason it is consequently perceived as an act of force against states which do not benefit from both strong allies and a stretch of the Statute. The non-intervention in Syria shows once again that the UN system for protection of human rights and the protection of the people from gross human rights violations is often ineffective and that action is still tied to decisional issues of the Security Council,[32] which is often unable to adopt a resolution.

3.   Non-intervention in Syria and the lack of protection of human rights by the international community and comparison with the Libyan crisis

Regarding Syria, the non-intervention has highlighted that actions to protect human rights are at the discretion of the international community through the Security Council; only two resolutions have been adopted and they only required that a group of observers had to be sent. Another example of the flexibility of the R2P could be the failure of the Security Council to define its position about continuing human rights violations suffered by the Palestinian and Tibetan peoples. Possible intervention by the international community in these situations has not been considered, although there are many elements supporting intervention in compliance with the R2P.

Comparing the Libyan and the Syrian crises it is possible to distinguish two different kinds of intervention during the crisis in Libya, a 'coalition of the willing' under the auspices of the UN, which immediately defined its position against the Libyan leader Gaddafi,[33] and Security Council resolution 1970/2011,[34] which imposed on Libya an arms embargo and individual sanctions on the family of the Rais. The resolution officially launched *Operation Odyssey Dawn* and the main promoters of the resolution were Britain, France and the United States; other states the joined the United States. The situation in Libya worsened due to the lack of efficacy of resolution 1970. This resulted in the Security Council adopting resolution 1973/2011, since the crisis was so serious that it threatened international peace and security. The Security Council allowed a coalition of states to act under Chapter VII of the UN Charter, a resolution that has been adopted with the abstention of Russia, China, Brazil, India and Germany. Operations were transferred to NATO[35] without any reference to a possible deployment of ground troops; the resolution actually provided for an immediate ceasefire and for the end of the involvement of the civilian population (para. 1), for the invitation to find by all means a peaceful resolution of the crisis (para. 2) and for the Libyan government's compliance with international law, international humanitarian law and human rights (para. 3).

The lack of intervention in Syria by the UN or by a coalition of *the willing states* is mainly due to geopolitical and strategic reasons. In fact, the human rights violations suffered by the Syrian people are the same as those suffered by the Libyan population. Also in this case, the international community would have to intervene in defence of the Syrian people through humanitarian means, without the prior authorisation of the Security Council, as was the case for Kosovo. However, differently from Libya, which was immediately isolated from its allies and the international community, Syria did not lose the support of its allies. In fact, as well as Russia and China, Iran also continues to support al-Assad's regime, making any intervention quite impossible. This is well demonstrated by the only two resolutions adopted by the Security Council: 2042 and 2043.

4.   Conclusion

Considering that the R2P has been established as a tool for the prevention of genocide, it could be an effective tool for a rapid intervention in cases of *gross human rights violations* suffered by a population, whether this violation is committed by the population's own state or by rebel forces during a civil conflict. The central element of R2P is the role of the state, which is to employ every measure to prevent infringements. The political value the involved state has in the international arena is crucial in regard to implementation or non-implementation of R2P, as evidenced by the intervention of the international community in Libya by a coalition of willing states. Those states acting under the name of R2P immediately bombed government forces, thus supporting the rebels against Gaddafi. Unfortunately the bombings did not help to stop the violence, in fact, the rebels and the army loyalists continue to fight in the south of Libya, while the northern area, near the country's oil wells, seem to be somewhat pacified.

Despite the dramatic and severe nature of the Syrian crisis and civil society being involved in the fighting between government forces and the rebels, the international community has not applied the theory of the R2P, nor has the Security Council adopted a resolution. There is the threat that Russia and China would veto, since any intervention would likely be delegated to the United States and NATO. Some states argue this would be to apply the 'Libyan model' to Syria, with the result of expanding the conflict to destabilise the entire region.

The only resolutions adopted have merely been an invitation to the Syrian government to respect human rights and to prevent the involvement of the civilian population in the clashes, since the UN hopes for a peaceful resolution of the crisis, as supported by China. Once again we can see that the international community's actions are dictated primarily by very specific interests which prevail over respect for human rights and this is the reason why even the R2P is not a uniform practice in its application. R2P is considered by some states as a form of humanitarian imperialism by those affected by the intervention as intervention is often undertaken against some states, especially those which have a significant geopolitical position and which are not backed by powerful allies, as clearly demonstrated by the cases of Syria and Libya. In those cases the violations of human rights were the same; however the international community intervened in Libya but not in Syria.

Disclosure statement

No potential conflict of interest was reported by the author.

Notes

1. *We The Peoples: The Role of the United Nations in the 21st Century*, UN Doc. A/54/2000, 48; United Nations General Assembly, Resolution 55/2, 18 September 2000, UN Doc. A/RES/55/2.
2. Charter of United Nations, article 2, para. 4: 'All Members shall refrain in their international relations from the threat or use of force against the territorial integrity or political independence of any state, or in any other manner inconsistent with the Purposes of the United Nations.'
3. Ibid., para. 7: 'Nothing contained in the present Charter shall authorize the United Nations to intervene in matters which are essentially within the domestic jurisdiction of any state or shall require the Members to submit such matters to settlement under the present Charter; but this principle shall not prejudice the application of enforcement measures under Chapter Vll.'
4. Report ICISS, *The Responsibility to Protect*, cap. 4, para. 4.1: 'The responsibility to protect implies above all else a responsibility to react to situations of compelling need for human protection. When preventive measures fail to resolve or contain the situation and when a state is unable or unwilling to redress the situation, then interventionary measures by other members

of the broader community of states may be required. These coercive measures may include political, economic or judicial measures, and in extreme cases – but only extreme cases – they may also include military action. As a matter of first principles, in the case of reaction just as with prevention, less intrusive and coercive measures should always be considered before more coercive and intrusive ones are applied.'

5.   Ibid., Synopsis Basic Principles: 'A. State sovereignty implies responsibility, and the primary responsibility for the protection of its people lies with the state itself. B. Where a population is suffering serious harm, as a result of internal war, insurgency, repression or state failure, and the state in question is unwilling or unable to halt or avert it, the principle of non-intervention yields to the international responsibility to protect.'

6.   C. Focarelli, 'La dottrina della "Responsabilità di Proteggere" e l'intervento umanitario', *Rivista di diritto internazionale* 2 (2008): 323–4.

7.   Report ICISS, *The Responsibility to Protect*: 'The Just Cause Threshold Military intervention for human protection purposes is an exceptional and extraordinary measure. To be warranted, there must be serious and irreparable harm occurring to human beings, or imminently likely to occur, of the following kind: A. large scale loss of life, actual or apprehended, with genocidal intent or not, which is the product either of deliberate state action, or state neglect or inability to act, or a failed state situation; or B. large scale "ethnic cleansing", actual or apprehended, whether carried out by killing, forced expulsion, acts of terror or rape. The Precautionary Principles A. Right intention: The primary purpose of the intervention, whatever other motives intervening states may have, must be to halt or avert human suffering. Right intention is better assured with multilateral operations, clearly supported by regional opinion and the victims concerned. B. Last resort: Military intervention can only be justified when every non-military option for the prevention or peaceful resolution of the crisis has been explored, with reasonable grounds for believing lesser measures would not have succeeded. C Proportional means: The scale, duration and intensity of the planned military intervention should be the minimum necessary to secure the defined human protection objective. D. Reasonable prospects: There must be a reasonable chance of success in halting or averting the suffering which has justified the intervention, with the consequences of action not likely to be worse than the consequences of inaction', Focarelli, 'La dottrina della "Responsabilità di Proteggere" e l'intervento umanitario', 324–5.

8.   United Nations, General Assembly Resolution A/59/565, 2 December 2004.

9.   United Nations, General Assembly Resolution A/Res/60/1, 24 October 2005.

10.   P. Hilpold, 'The Responsibility to Protect', in *The Responsibility to Protect (R2P), a New Paradigm of International Law?*, ed. Peter Hilpold (Leiden: Brill Nijhoff, 2015), 1–38, at 13.

11.   United Nations, General Assembly Resolution A/59/2005, 21 March 2005.

12.   World Summit Outcome Document, paras 138–9: 138. 'Each individual State has the responsibility to protect its populations from genocide, war crimes, ethnic cleansing and crimes against humanity. This responsibility entails the prevention of such crimes, including their incitement, through appropriate and necessary means. We accept that responsibility and will act in accordance with it. The international community should, as appropriate, encourage and help States to exercise this responsibility and support the United Nations in establishing an early warning capability'; 139: 'The international community, through the United Nations, also has the responsibility to use appropriate diplomatic, humanitarian and other peaceful means, in accordance with Chapters VI and VIII of the Charter, to help protect populations from genocide, war crimes, ethnic cleansing and crimes against humanity. In this context, we are prepared to take collective action, in a timely and decisive manner, through the Security Council, in accordance with the Charter, including Chapter VII, on a case-by-case basis and in cooperation with relevant regional organizations as appropriate, should peaceful means be inadequate and national authorities manifestly fail to protect their populations from genocide, war crimes, ethnic cleansing and crimes against humanity. We stress the need for the General Assembly to continue consideration of the responsibility to protect populations from genocide, war crimes, ethnic cleansing and crimes against humanity and its implications, bearing in mind the principles of the Charter and international law. We also intend to commit ourselves, as necessary and appropriate, to helping States build capacity to protect their populations from genocide, war crimes, ethnic cleansing and crimes against humanity and to assisting those which are under stress before crises and conflicts break out.'

13. L. Panella, 'La responsabilità di proteggere: un'ulteriore possibilità di tutelare i diritti umani o un diritto d'ingerenza?', in *Studi in Onore di Augusto Sinagra*, ed. P. Bargiacchi (Roma: Aracne Editrice, 2013), 468; Focarelli, 'La dottrina della "Responsabilità di Proteggere" e l'intervento umanitario', 328.

14. African Union Constitutive Act, article 4, para. H: 'the right of the Union to intervene in a Member State pursuant to a decision of the Assembly in respect of grave Circumstances, namely: war crimes, genocide and crimes against humanity'.

15. S.K. Sharma., 'The 2007–08 Post-election Crisis in Kenya, A Success Story for the Responsibility to Protect?, in *Responsibility to Protect from Principle to Practice*, ed. J. Hoffmann and A. Nolkaemper (Amsterdam: Pallas Publications/Amsterdam University Press, 2012), 27–35.

16. R. Cohen, 'How Kofi Annan Rescued Kenya', *The New York Review of Books*, 14 August 2008.

17. Panella, 'La responsabilità di proteggere', 477.

18. T. Ballarino, 'RtoP/Responsability to Protect', *scritti in memoria di Maria Rita Saulle, edizione scientifiche*, 23–48.

19. U. Villani, *Dalla dichiarazione universale alla Convenzione europea dei diritti dell'uomo* (Bari: Cacucci Editore, 2012), 60.

20. Cf. *Rivista di diritto internazionale* 2 (2011): 630.

21. U. Villani, 'L'intervento militare in Libia: responsibility to protect o ... responsabilità per aggressione?', in *I diritti dell'uomo. Cronache e battaglie* 2 (2011): 53–9.

22. Human Rights Council, *The Independent International Commission of Inquiry on the Syrian Arab Republic*, 22 August 2011, S-17/1, http://www.ohchr.org/Documents/HRBodies/HRCouncil/CoISyria/ResS17_1.pdf.

23. United Nations Children's Fund (UNICEF), January 2012, http://www.unicef.it/Allegati/HAC2012_LOW_WEB_Final.pdf.

24. Human Rights Council, *The Independent International Commission of Inquiry on the Syrian Arab Republic*, 16 August 2012, A/HRC/21/50, http://www.ohchr.org/Documents/HRBodies/HRCouncil/RegularSession/Session21/A-HCR-21-50_en.pdf.

25. *Siria, una crisi senza fine*, http://ispinews.ispionline.it/?p=2766.

26. United Nations General Assembly, Resolution 2042, 14 April 2012, UN Doc. S/RES/2042 Annex Six-Point Proposal of the Joint Special Envoy of the United Nations and the League of Arab States '(1) commit to work with the Envoy in an inclusive Syrian-led political process to address the legitimate aspirations and concerns of the Syrian people, and, to this end, commit to appoint an empowered interlocutor when invited to do so by the Envoy; (2) commit to stop the fighting and achieve urgently an effective United Nations supervised cessation of armed violence in all its forms by all parties to protect civilians and stabilize the country; To this end, the Syrian government should immediately cease troop movements towards, and end the use of heavy weapons in, population centres, and begin pullback of military concentrations in and around population centres; As these actions are being taken on the ground, the Syrian government should work with the Envoy to bring about a sustained cessation of armed violence in all its forms by all parties with an effective United Nations supervision mechanism. Similar commitments would be sought by the Envoy from the opposition and all relevant elements to stop the fighting and work with him to bring about a sustained cessation of armed violence in all its forms by all parties with an effective United Nations supervision mechanism; (3) ensure timely provision of humanitarian assistance to all areas affected by the fighting, and to this end, as immediate steps, to accept and implement a daily two hour humanitarian pause and to coordinate exact time and modalities of the daily pause through an efficient mechanism, including at local level; (4) intensify the pace and scale of release of arbitrarily detained persons, including especially vulnerable categories of persons, and persons involved in peaceful political activities, provide without delay through appropriate channels a list of all places in which such persons are being detained, immediately begin organizing access to such locations and through appropriate channels respond promptly to all written requests for information, access or release regarding such persons; (5) ensure freedom of movement throughout the country for journalists and a non-discriminatory visa policy for them; (6) respect freedom of association and the right to demonstrate peacefully as legally guaranteed.'

27. United Nations Security Council Resolution S/RES/2042 adopted on 14 April 2012.

28. United Nations Security Council Resolution S/RES/2043 adopted on 21 April 2012.

29. *Siria: il ruolo chiave della Russia*, 28 May 2012, http://it.euronews.com.

30. *Syria Insta-Symposium: André Nollkaemper – Intervention in Syria and International Law: Inside or Out?,* 1 September 2013, http://www.opiniojuris.org.
31. Charter of United Nations, article 2, para. 7.
32. *Syria Insta-Symposium: André Nollkaemper.*
33. V. Risuglia, *Ripensare l'ONU. La Risoluzione 1973 e la guerra in Libia,* http://magna-carta.it/content/ripensare-nazioni-unite-risoluzione-1973-e-lintervento-libia.
34. United Nations Security Council Resolution S/RES/1970 adopted on 26 February 2011.
35. Ibid.

Genocide, obligations *erga omnes*, and the responsibility to protect: remarks on a complex convergence

Marco Longobardo

School of Law, University of Rome 'Sapienza', Italy

In 2007, the International Court of Justice declared that states have a duty to prevent genocide from occurring in another state since the prevention and punishment of genocide is a concern of every state and of the international community as a whole. The doctrine of the responsibility to protect will be analysed in the light of the *erga omnes* and *erga omnes partes* character of the rules embodied in the Convention on the Prevention and Punishment of the Crime of Genocide. It is argued that, even though there are differences between the court's decisions about genocide and the applicable regime regarding the consequences of serious violations of *erga omnes* obligations, they are both consonant with the doctrine of the responsibility to protect since they are both inspired by the need to guarantee the protection of fundamental legal values.

1. Introduction

Genocide is considered one of the most heinous international crimes; consequently, the whole international community has an interest both in punishing and preventing it. This responsibility lies primarily within every single state that has the duty not to commit genocide. One of the most serious problems is that states have limited means to prevent the occurrence of genocide in another country due to international law constraints that protect state sovereignty. However, it is indisputable that the commission of genocide violates legal interests that concern every state and respect for which is considered a fundamental value for the international community. The doctrine of the responsibility to protect emphasises the collective dimension of the duties to prevent and punish genocide; the International Court of Justice (ICJ) in the 2007 *Bosnia and Herzegovina* v. *Serbia and Montenegro* case (*Bosnian Genocide* case) has also asserted this collective dimension.[1]

Even if genocide is not so frequent an occurrence as some believe, the problematic nature of reactions to genocide is not an obsolete academic issue: for instance, the United Nations (UN) acknowledged that in the ongoing crisis in the Middle East the self-proclaimed Islamic State likely committed genocide against religious minorities.[2] Therefore, even in order to build a more efficient strategy against the Islamic State, an analysis of the relations between the duties to prevent and punish genocide and the doctrine of the responsibility to protect in light of the law on obligations *erga omnes* can be useful.

2.   A brief overview on the ICJ case law

Two separate and autonomous duties to prevent and punish genocide

The *Bosnian Genocide* case clarified the normative content of Article 1 of the Convention on the Prevention and Punishment of the Crime of Genocide (Genocide Convention), according to which 'The Contracting Parties confirm that genocide, whether committed in time of peace or in time of war, is a crime under international law which they undertake to prevent and to punish.'[3] The ICJ has been involved in this 'fascinating judicial saga'[4] arising from the Genocide Convention on a number of occasions. In 1951, the ICJ rendered a famous advisory opinion on *Reservations to Genocide Convention* stressing the importance of the humanitarian and civilising purposes of the Convention.[5] Then in 1993, it also passed two orders of provisional measures[6] followed by a judgment on preliminary objections in 1996.[7] More recently, the ICJ passed another judgment on the application of the convention in 2015.[8]

Many international lawyers have commented on the *Bosnian Genocide* case as it presents several interesting legal aspects.[9] However, for the purposes of the present article, the ICJ's decision is most relevant when it declares and explains the content of the duty to prevent genocide as independent from the duty to punish it.

Duties to prevent wrongful acts are not new in international law,[10] but this case represents the first time that the ICJ made a clear distinction between the duty to punish and the duty to prevent genocide based on Article 1 of the Genocide Convention. The ICJ affirmed that this provision includes two separate but connected obligations, the duty to punish and the duty to prevent genocide[11]; accordingly, Article 1 comprises three elements: the qualification of genocide as an international crime both in times of peace and of war, the duty to prevent genocide, and the duty to punish it should prevention fail.[12] Punishment naturally implies a failure of the convention, given that a genocide occurred and a number of people lost their lives or suffered some other consequence due to perpetrator genocidal intent; consequently, preventing genocide is extremely more satisfactory than punishing the perpetrators.[13]

According to the ICJ, the duty to prevent is an obligation of conduct and not a duty of result.[14] States must do everything they can – including modifications to their own domestic laws – in order to prevent the commission of genocide. In case of failure, states will not be held automatically responsible for lack of prevention, but will be provided the opportunity to demonstrate that they had used the due diligence required by the convention.[15]

In one of the most challenging parts of its decision,[16] the ICJ affirmed that the obligation to prevent genocide is territorially unlimited, and therefore a state must prevent genocide also in relation to acts committed outside its borders,[17] that is affirming that states have a duty to interfere in the sovereign sphere of another state that is about to commit genocide or to tolerate genocide taking place in its territory.

Extraterritorial application of certain treaties is not something new in the international law discourse. Although normally conventions bind states only for actions that occur within a particular state's borders, treaties bind states extraterritorially where a member state exercises its own jurisdiction outside its borders.[18] Often treaties embody jurisdictional clauses that explain when and where a state party is bound by the provision of the convention. Similar clauses are based on the concept of state jurisdiction over individuals or territory and can be found for instance in Article 2 of the International Covenant on Civil and Political Rights and in Article 1 of the European Convention on Human Rights. By contrast, there is no such clause in the Genocide Convention; however, absence of such a clause is not a hindrance for its extraterritorial application since the ICJ's jurisprudence admits that even conventions without jurisdictional clauses can be applied extraterritorially following the state party's jurisdiction.[19]

The ICJ's conclusion on the extraterritorial application of the duty to prevent genocide is a novelty, however, since the obligations that arise from the Genocide Convention are not triggered by the existence of a state's extraterritorial jurisdiction, but rather by the state's 'capacity to influence' the genocidal intent and course of action,[20] a totally new criterion.[21] Because it is not easy to grasp the precise legal meaning of influence, a standard which is characterised by a clear factual nature that changes in relation to different circumstances, the possible behaviours of states cannot be identified once and for all,[22] but rather should be asserted case-by-case on the basis of their 'capacity to influence effectively the action of persons likely to commit, or already committing, genocide'.[23]

The capacity to influence the perpetrators of genocide is the result of several qualitative and quantitative elements; with scant regard to accuracy,[24] the ICJ mentions the spatial proximity and geopolitical links as relevant factors, but the meaning of this statement is actually 'rather obscure'.[25] The result of this decision is that different states equally bound by the Genocide Convention are subject to the duty to prevent genocide in different ways, according to the principle that the more a state can do, the more it is expected to do. The ICJ thus broadened the scope of the duty to prevent genocide in relation to acts that occurred in another state's territory, while at the same time narrowing it by stressing that the duty to prevent does not have the same intensity for all the member states in order to avoid giving the impression that powerful states are always responsible for lack of prevention (since the Great Powers have sufficient military force to influence events in every corner of the world).[26]

The erga omnes/erga omnes partes *nature of the duties embodied in the convention*

On a number of occasions, the ICJ has remarked on the normative structure of the duties arising from the Genocide Convention. In the *Reservations* advisory opinion, it affirmed that the prevention and repression of genocide – the pivotal legal interests at the basis of the convention – are not merely a concern of single contracting states, but rather affect the entire group of member states simultaneously.[27] This dictum was later used in the famous 1970 *Barcelona Traction* case when, for the first time, the ICJ mentioned the existence of the obligations *erga omnes*, including among them the duty to outlaw genocide.[28] Two and a half decades later, in 1996, the ICJ clearly stated that all the duties arising from Article 1 of the Genocide Convention are obligations *erga omnes*,[29] a conclusion that has been reiterated in the 2006 *Case concerning Armed Activities on the Territory of the Congo (New Application)*.[30] In the *Bosnian Genocide* case, the ICJ acknowledged that *the applicant* considered the duties of the convention to be obligations *erga omnes*[31] and, by not challenging this opinion, appeared itself to consider *erga omnes* the duties to prevent and punish genocide, in accordance with its past jurisprudence. More recently, dealing with the problem of the nature of the obligations arising from the 1984 Convention against Torture and Other Cruel, Inhuman or Degrading Treatment or Punishment, the ICJ stated that the obligations contained in the Genocide Convention are *erga omnes partes*.[32] Finally, in 2015 the ICJ re-stated that the obligations embodied in the Genocide Convention are *erga omnes*.[33]

Albeit these hints in the ICJ's case law are not perfectly cohesive, they are fundamental in order to understand which acts are permitted to contracting states when another state breaches its obligation under the Genocide Convention. Because the ICJ is the body institutionally devoted to the interpretation and application of the convention when disputes arise pursuant to Article 9, its role in this process should not be underestimated. Slightly different is the situation in relation of the duty to prevent genocide *qua* international customary law, where the ICJ does not have the monopoly of the interpretation and application of the law but rather a highly regarded opinion.

According to the ICJ's dictum in the *Barcelona Traction* case, obligations *erga omnes* are 'obligations of a State towards the international community as a whole', and are 'the concern of all States'; consequently, '[i]n view of the importance of the rights involved, all States can be held to have a legal interest in their protection'.[34] Therefore, it is incorrect to say that obligations *erga omnes* are simply binding on all states irrespective of their express will – because this is the characteristic of all customary norms.[35] The key feature of obligations *erga omnes* is that all states have a legal interest in the respect of these obligations and can put forward a claim in the event of violations; in other words, the norms *erga omnes* protect legal interests that are so relevant for the whole international community that every state is to a certain extent affected by their violation and is concerned with their implementation.[36] In the past, a violation of this kind of obligation formed the basis of the so-called international crimes of states envisaged by the International Law Commission in Article 19 of the 1976 Draft of Articles on the Responsibility of States for International Wrongful Acts (DARSIWA). More recently, the final 2001 Draft Articles, adopted under the direction of Professor James Crawford, centred the special regime of international responsibility on the serious breaches of peremptory norms, shifting from obligations *erga omnes* to the *jus cogens* category that was traditionally envisaged as a limit to states' treaty-making power.[37] Obligations *erga omnes* and *jus cogens* norms are not completely overlapping categories[38]; significantly, the DARSIWA still mentions *erga omnes* obligations in Article 48(1)(b), according to which 'obligation[s] [...] owed to the international community as a whole' are relevant for the new regime of aggravated international responsibility.[39]

Obligations *erga omnes partes* are quite different. This category is formed by norms enshrined in multilateral conventions that promote pivotal interests at the basis of the agreement and are not of a synallagmatic nature but, rather, are due to the group of states parties to the convention indifferently.[40] According to the International Law Commission, an *erga omnes partes* obligation is 'owed to a group of States' and is 'established for the protection of a collective interest of the group' at the basis of the decision to conclude a specific agreement.[41] Even in this case, the emphasis is on the legal interests protected by the norms that are not confined to the position of individual states but are the concern of an entire group.

After this brief overview, one must verify whether the duty to prevent a genocide that is about to be committed or is occurring in the territory of another state is an obligation *erga omnes*, *erga omnes partes*, or both. Even though the ICJ lacked precision in its use of these categories, on the basis of a comparison between the normative structure of the Genocide Convention and the Convention against Torture, there is room to argue that all the duties enshrined in Article 1 of the Genocide Convention are obligations *erga omnes partes*. However, this is not an obstacle to asserting as well their *erga omnes* nature in the framework of general international law. The duties to prevent and punish genocide are also customary obligations,[42] and their structure is obviously that of obligations *erga omnes* since they protect interests that are pertinent to every state of the international community.

As a matter of treaty law, these duties are obligations *erga omnes partes*. As a matter of customary law, they are obligations *erga omnes*. After all, it is well established in international law that the same obligation can be part of both treaty and customary law, even with the coexistence of two different normative regimes.[43]

3. Obligations *erga omnes/erga omnes partes* regarding genocide and the responsibility to protect

Preliminary observations

In the aftermath of the *Bosnian Genocide* case decision, some legal scholars have stressed that the extraterritorial duty to prevent genocide should be considered the legal basis for asserting the binding character of the responsibility to protect doctrine, for some of them even as a legal tool to justify the use of force with the purpose of saving civilians from mass atrocities.[44]

In brief, the responsibility to protect is a doctrine based on the idea that sovereignty consists principally in the state duty to protect its own population; consequently, if a state does not want or cannot protect them, the responsibility for their protection falls upon the international community, institutionally through the UN or upon every state in the case of UN inactivity. For some supporters of this doctrine, in the case of mass atrocities (such as genocide, war crimes, crimes against humanity and ethnic cleansing), if the Security Council does not authorise the use of the force to protect civilians, other universal or regional organisations (and, finally, even singular states) could attack the perpetrators and end the atrocities.[45]

Actually, the dream of the responsibility to protect as the legal basis to use the force beyond the limits of the UN Charter when the Security Council is blocked by vetoes is not realistic. There is no new international rule related to *jus ad bellum* and humanitarian intervention; and accordingly, in 2005, the General Assembly endorsed the responsibility to protect only through the use of 'appropriate diplomatic, humanitarian and other *peaceful means, in accordance with Chapters VI and VIII of the Charter*',[46] excluding the emergence of a new customary rule regarding the use of force. State practice confirmed this conclusion in the case of Syria when, in 2013, a number of states willing to attack were renounced due to the lack of a Security Council authorisation.[47] Even the fact that the 2011 Libyan war was authorised by a Security Council resolution expressly mentioning the responsibility to protect did not prove useful for the promotion of this doctrine, given that several states disapproved of the attack because it did not merely protect civilians but led to the overthrow of the Libyan government. The responsibility to protect concept gained such a bad reputation in the aftermath of the 2011 Libyan war[48] that it has not been invoked in order to justify a military intervention since then,[49] except in situations clearly illegal such us the Russian annexation of Crimea.[50]

With regard to the possibility that states use force as a means of implementing the duty to prevent a genocide, it is fundamental to stress that the ICJ clearly affirmed that '[t]he State's capacity to influence must also be assessed by legal criteria, since it is clear that every State may only act *within the limits permitted by international law*'[51] and that states have to 'take such action as they can to prevent genocide from occurring, *while respecting the United Nations Charter and any decisions that may have been taken by its competent organs*'.[52] The ICJ openly excluded the legality of humanitarian intervention based on the duty to prevent genocide pursuant to the ban on the use of force contained in the United Nations Charter.[53] Since the ICJ is the ultimate authority on the interpretation of the Genocide Convention and except for unexpected and unlikely changes in its jurisprudence, the duties enshrined in the convention cannot be interpreted such that states can use force outside the framework of the UN Charter.

Changing perspectives will prove useful in order to address the problem of the interferences that states have to or can undertake against another state that is committing or is about to commit genocide.

The erga omnes *character of the Genocide Convention duties and countermeasures*

Acknowledging the fact that the Genocide Convention embodies obligations *erga omnes partes* that are also correspondent to customary obligations *erga omnes* could shed some light on the measures available for states willing to stop or prevent a genocide that is occurring in the territory of another state.

Among legal scholars, the possibility of states taking countermeasures in order to react to serious violation of an obligation *erga omnes* has been greatly debated. In 2001, the International Law Commission seemed to exclude this possibility given that only the state directly injured can take countermeasures, whilst other states can only invoke responsibility and, pursuant to Article 54 of the DARSIWA, 'take lawful measures [...] to ensure cessation of the breaches and reparation in the interest of the injured State'. According to the commentary on Article 54, State practice in favour of countermeasures from states other than the injured is 'embryonic' and therefore not decisive.[54]

The authoritative commentary should be analysed alongside the actual practice of states and it is necessary to face some issues arising from the drafting of the relevant provisions. First, it has been suggested that the 'legal measures' of Article 54 are countermeasures; in this context, the adjective 'legal' does not refer to acts *per se* licit, but rather to measures that would be illicit except for the fact that they are adopted as countermeasures against a wrongful act.[55] The opposite interpretation, according to which Article 54 refers only to acts that are *per se* legal, would render the provision superfluous because it would only restate the proposition that international law allows states to adopt allowed behaviours.[56]

Second, the practice of countermeasures unilaterally taken in the collective interest, far from being nascent, is well-established with regard to peaceful countermeasures. According to state practice analysed by several authors, states adopt such countermeasures when a serious breach of an obligation *erga omnes* occurs and consider their response to be legal.[57] As a recent example, one could consider the international sanctions unilaterally levied against Russia after its annexation of Crimea. In the absence of a centralised decision by the Security Council, many Western countries decided to freeze assets and limit commerce in violation of previous international agreements and general international law as a reaction to the Russian violation of Ukrainian territorial integrity and sovereignty, even if the only directly affected state was Ukraine; these Western states adopted these measures on the basis of the belief that Russia's actions violated legal interests that are not merely conferred to Ukraine, but that are also pertinent to the international community as a whole.[58] Consequently, the position according to which states can adopt specific countermeasures against violations of obligations *erga omnes* appears well-grounded.[59] This same regime should apply equally to the case of the preparation or commission of genocide; all the states have an interest in preventing the genocide from being committed, and, therefore, they should be able to take every peaceful measure available, even if such measures might otherwise violate other international law rules.

However, this conclusion is only partially in line with the ICJ's findings since it concerns not a duty but a faculty of taking actual measures in order to prevent genocide. There is therefore room to argue that the duty to prevent genocide encompasses only lawful measures but that, at the same time, states can – and not must – take countermeasures pursuant to the *erga omnes* character of the customary duty to prevent genocide.

The matter is far more complex with regard to measures involving the use of force. Due to the general ban on the use of force in both conventional and customary international law, several commentators argue that states cannot adopt coercive countermeasures in order to put an end to the atrocities without a Security Council authorisation, even in the case of a serious breach of obligations *erga omnes*, such as those embodied in the Genocide Convention.[60] However, the paralysis of the Security Council has hindered states' ability to respond to atrocities in the past. For instance, the Security Council's failure to pass a resolution in response to mass atrocities committed in Kosovo in 1999 brought some states to respond by attacking Serbia in operations conducted without UN authorisation. After this crucial episode, Professor Antonio Cassese affirmed that

> [T]his particular instance of breach of international law may gradually lead to the crystalliza-tion of a general rule of international law authorizing armed countermeasures for the exclusive purpose of putting an end to large-scale atrocities amounting to crimes against humanity and constituting a threat to the peace […] It would amount to an exception similar to that laid down in Article 51 of the Charter (self-defence).[61]

Professor Cassese was focused on a *de jure condendo* trend rather than clearly affirming the state of the law, but there is room for a broader debate.

Professor Paolo Picone, who has studied this issue in depth, believes that Article 51 codifies a forcible countermeasure against the specific violation of the ban on aggression that is an obligation *erga omnes*, the only breach of an obligation *erga omnes* that was clearly addressed when the UN Charter was adopted. Countermeasures in response to gen-ocide and other mass atrocities were not mentioned in the UN Charter simply because, at that time, states did not agree to formally acknowledge that violations of these fundamental norms would affect the legal interests of every state and of the international community as a whole so as to legitimise countermeasures including force. However, according to Professor Picone, state practice has evolved and relevant events (culminating with the attack in Kosovo) tend to show that, in the case of paralysis of the Security Council and when inter-national customary law allows such responses, as a last resort against a serious breach of obligations *erga omnes*, states can adopt forcible countermeasures. Following Picone's reasoning, this use of force, although untied to the UN Charter, rather finds its legitimisation in general international law[62] and fits into the definition of legal measures provided by Article 54 of the DARWISA.[63] However, the possibility of taking forcible countermeasures against a serious breach of an obligation *erga omnes* is constrained by several factors that should safeguard against abuses: the force employed should be necessary and proportion-ate, the action should respect international humanitarian law, and the action should end when the Security Council proves itself willing and capable of dealing with the situation.[64] This solution is particularly fit for cases in which there is not a state directly injured in the sense of the DARSIWA because the author of the atrocities is the government that should react as the injured state according to the same articles.[65] Accordingly, the recent interven-tion of a coalition of Western states in Syria against the Islamic State, which is not based on any request of the Syrian government, can be considered as the collective response to the violation of many *erga omnes* obligations perpetrated by the jihadists.[66] It should be noted, however, that also the Assad regime violated some obligations *erga omnes*, such as those governing the protection of civilians during armed conflicts.

This fascinating theoretical construction has the value to envisage a response to mass atrocities that is based on legal argumentation and not on the moral evaluations at the basis of the traditional humanitarian intervention.[67] However, there are some elements of the practice and *opinio juris* that are not consistent, for instance, the large consensus on the definition of aggression adopted in 2010 in Kampala during the Review Conference of the Rome Statute of the International Criminal Court, which appears to be a manifestation of the international community's belief that, even in the most tragic situations, force can be used only in ways allowed by the UN Charter.[68] Consequently, the issue of forcible measures deserves further analysis beyond the scope of this article. Regarding the specific breach of the obligations *erga omnes* related to genocide, though, state practice is thin and insufficient to definitively conclude that general international law allows forcible countermeasures in this specific case.

In conclusion, the *erga omnes* character of the duty to prevent genocide clearly allows states to adopt peaceful countermeasures in order to prevent or effectively repress at an early stage a genocide occurring in another state's territory, in accordance with the doctrine of responsibility to protect. By contrast, state practice related to the possibility of adopting forcible countermeasures for the prevention of genocide is still uncertain and it is highly doubtful whether force can be used beyond the limits of the UN Charter in this specific case.

Procedural consequences of the erga omnes/erga omnes partes *qualification*

The *erga omnes*/*erga omnes partes* character of the duty to prevent genocide also has relevant procedural consequences that will be examined here very briefly.[69]

The ICJ, on the basis of the *erga omnes partes* character of the obligations embodied in the Convention against Torture, affirmed the *jus standi* of all the states members to the treaty when a serious violation occurs, irrespective of any special position as affected states.[70] In addition, the Marshall Islands claim their *jus standi* in a number of recent cases pending before the ICJ on the *erga omnes partes* character of the obligations embodied in Article 6 of the 1968 Non-Proliferation of Nuclear Weapons Treaty and in the *erga omnes* character of the alleged corresponding customary norm[71]; the cases are still pending and in due time the ICJ might rule on these issues, if it finds that it has jurisdiction on these cases.[72]

The acknowledgement of the *jus standi* is something less relevant than the opportunity to take countermeasures because a controversy on genocide can only be triggered after the breach of one of the duties enlisted in Article 3 of the Genocide Convention.[73] However, the *erga omnes partes* qualification of the duty to prevent genocide could be useful in the future for assessing the admissibility of a claim brought by any member state to the Genocide Convention before the ICJ pursuant to Article 9. It could be argued that all contracting states can be considered parties to any dispute arising from the convention thanks to the *erga omnes partes* nature of its provisions despite the unlikelihood of the ICJ recognising *jus standi* of every state when an *erga omnes* obligation has been breached.

4. Concluding remarks

After having briefly discussed the *Bosnian Genocide* case, the differences between obligations *erga omnes* and *erga omnes partes* and the issue of countermeasures as an effective response to mass atrocities, there is room to argue here that there is a strong interplay between the doctrine of the responsibility to protect and of the obligations *erga omnes* regime in relation to the duties embodied in the Genocide Convention.

Apart from vainly attempting to create new rules on *jus ad bello*, the doctrine of the responsibility to protect aims to change the way in which states think of their sovereignty and attribute to the international community an effective role in the protection of the human rights of individuals seriously persecuted by their own state. In this respect, obligations *erga omnes* allow states to intervene at least with peaceful countermeasures against a state that is responsible for mass atrocities against its citizens. The consonance between the regime of obligations *erga omnes* and the responsibility to protect is particularly clear in the case of the commission of a genocide, the crime of crimes, since the conventional obligations arising from the Genocide Convention are *erga omnes partes* and they allow states not directly affected to complain against gross violations before competent international courts and tribunals, a goal consistent with the doctrine of the responsibility to protect, which aims to monitor the exercise of state sovereignty at an international level.

The convergence between responsibility to protect, treaty obligations and obligations *erga omnes* may be relevant in situations like the current fight against the Islamic State, not only in relation to genocide but also with regard to different atrocities. Other obligations *erga omnes* are at the basis of the responsibility to protect and, at the same time, embodied in conventions that compel states to ensure respect of the treaty provisions; this is the case of international humanitarian law rules, which have been constantly and brutally violated in Syria and Iraq.[74]

Disclosure statement

No potential conflict of interest was reported by the author.

Notes

1. *Application of the Convention on the Prevention and Punishment of the Crime of Genocide (Bosnia and Herzegovina v. Serbia and Montenegro)*, Judgment, 26 February 2007 (*Bosnian Genocide* case).
2. See Human Rights Council, *Report of the Office of the United Nations High Commissioner for Human Rights on the Human Rights Situation in Iraq in the Light of Abuses Committed by the So-called Islamic State in Iraq and the Levant and Associated Groups* (A/HRC/28/18, 13 March 2015).
3. On the Genocide Convention, see John Quigley, *The Genocide Convention, An International Law Analysis* (Aldershot: Ashgate, 2006); Paola Gaeta, ed., *The UN Genocide Convention: A Commentary* (Oxford: Oxford University Press, 2009); William A. Schabas, *Genocide in International Law, The Crime of Crimes*, 2nd edition (Cambridge: Cambridge University Press, 2009); Christian Tams, Lars Berster, and Björn Schiffbauer, eds, *Convention on the Prevention and Punishment of the Crime of Genocide. A Commentary* (Munchen/Oxford/Baden Baden: Beck/Hart/Nomos, 2014).
4. Orna Ben-Naftali, 'The Obligation to Prevent and Punish Genocide', in *The UN Genocide Convention*, 27–57, 35.
5. *Reservations to the Genocide Convention*, Advisory Opinion, 28 May 1951, para. 23.
6. *Application on the Convention on the Prevention and Punishment of the Crime of Genocide, (Bosnia and Herzegovina v. Serbia and Montenegro)*, Order, 8 April 1993; *Application on the Convention on the Prevention and Punishment of the Crime of Genocide, (Bosnia and Herzegovina v. Serbia and Montenegro)*, Order, 13 September 1993.
7. *Application of the Convention on the Prevention and Punishment of the Crime of Genocide (Bosnia and Herzegovina v. Serbia and Montenegro)*, Judgment, 11 July 1996 (*Preliminary Objections*).
8. *Application of the Convention on the Prevention and Punishment of the Crime of Genocide (Croatia v. Serbia)*, Judgment, 3 February 2015 (*Croatian Genocide* case).

9. See, *ex plurimis*, Olivier Corten, 'L'arrêt rendu par la CIJ dans l'affaire du crime de génocide (Bosnie-Herzégovine c. Serbie): vers un assouplissements des conditions permettant d'engager la responsabilité' d'une État pour génocide, *Annuaire français de droit international* 53 (2007): 249–90; Andrea Gattini, 'Breach of the Obligation to Prevent and Reparation Thereof in the ICJ's Genocide Judgment', *European Journal of International Law* 18 (2007): 695–713; Bruno Simma, 'Genocide and International Court of Justice', in *The Genocide Convention Sixty Years after its Adoption*, ed. Christoph Safferling and Eckart Conze (The Hague: T.M. C. Asser Press, 2010), 259–72.

10. See, generally, Mirko Sossai, *La prevenzione del terrorismo nel diritto internazionale* (Torino: Giappichelli, 2012); Emmanuel Decaux and Sébastien Touze, ed., *La prévention des violations des droits de l'Homme* (Paris: Pedone 2015).

11. *Bosnian Genocide* case, para. 425.

12. Ben-Naftali, 'The Obligation to Prevent and Punish Genocide', 28.

13. Ibid., 30. On the temporal scope of the duty to prevent genocide and its relationship with the duty to punish it, see Etienne Ruvebana and Marcel Brus, 'Before It's Too Late: Preventing Genocide by Holding the Territorial State Responsible for Not Taking Preventive Action', *Netherlands International Law Review* 62 (2015): 25–47, 28–33.

14. *Bosnian Genocide* case, para. 430.

15. Sheri P. Rosenberg, 'Responsibility to Protect: A Framework for Prevention', *Global Responsibility to Protect* 1 (2009): 444–477, 467.

16. '[A] significant new development' according to Simma, 'Genocide and International Court of Justice', 262.

17. On the territorial scope of the Genocide Convention, see Marko Milanovic, 'Territorial Application of the Convention and State Succession', in *The UN Genocide Convention*, 473–493.

18. For an overview, see Pasquale De Sena, *La nozione di giurisdizione statale nei trattati sui diritti dell'uomo* (Torino: Giappichelli, 2002); Marko Milanovic, *Extraterritorial Application of Human Rights Treaties: Law, Principles, and Policy* (Oxford: Oxford University Press, 2011); Karen da Costa, *The Extraterritorial Application of Selected Human Rights Treaties* (Leiden: Brill, 2013).

19. *Legal Consequences of the Construction of a Wall in the Occupied Palestinian Territory*, Advisory Opinion, 9 July 2004, para. 112; *Application of the International Convention on the Elimination of all Forms of Racial Discrimination (Georgia v. Russia)*, Order, 15 October 2008, para. 109.

20. *Bosnian Genocide* case, para. 430.

21. Gattini, 'Breach of the Obligation to Prevent', 699–700.

22. Serena Forlati, 'The Legal Obligation to Prevent Genocide: Bosnia v Serbia and Beyond', *Polish Yearbook of International Law* 31 (2011): 189–205, 201.

23. *Bosnian Genocide* case, para. 430.

24. Anne Peters, 'The Security Council's Responsibility to Protect', *International Organizations Law Review* 8 (2011): 1–40, 11.

25. Gattini, 'Breach of the Obligation to Prevent', 701.

26. Simma, 'Genocide and International Court of Justice', 262.

27. *Reservations to the Genocide Convention*, 23: 'In such a convention the contracting States do not have any interests of their own; they merely have, one and all, a common interest, namely, the accomplishment of those high purposes which are the *raison d'être* of the convention'.

28. *Barcelona Traction, Light and Power Company, Limited*, Judgment, 5 February 1970, para. 34. For some remarks on the relationship between this decision and the 1951 advisory opinion, see Maurizio Ragazzi, *The Concept of International Obligations Erga Omnes* (Oxford: Oxford University Press, 1997), 92–4.

29. *Preliminary Objections*, para. 31.

30. *Case Concerning Armed Activities on the Territory of the Congo (New Application: 2002) (DRC v. Uganda)*, Judgment, 26 February 2006 (*Armed Activities* case), para. 64.

31. *Bosnian Genocide* case, paras 147 and 185.

32. *Questions Relating to the Obligation to Prosecute or Extradite (Belgium v. Senegal)*, Judgment, 20 July 2012 (*Belgium v. Senegal* case), para. 68.

33. *Croatian Genocide* case, para. 87.

34. *Barcelona Traction, Light and Power Company, Limited*, para. 33.

35. Roberto Ago, 'Obligation *Erga Omnes* and the International Community', in *International Crimes of State: A Critical Analysis of the ILC's Draft Article 19 on State Responsibility*, ed. Joseph H.H. Weiler, Antonio Cassese, and Marina Spinedi (Berlin: Walter de Gruyter, 1988), 237–9.

36. According to the Institut de Droit international 'an obligation erga omnes is: (a) an obligation under general international law that a State owes in any given case to the international community, in view of its common values and its concern for compliance, so that a breach of that obligation enables all States to take action' (Institut de Droit international, Krakow Session, Resolution of 27 August 2005, Article 1(a), http://www.idi-iil.org/idiE/resolutionsE/2005_kra_01_en.pdf (accessed 17 June 2015)). See also Paolo Picone, 'The Distinction between *Jus Cogens* and Obligations *Erga Omnes*', in *The Law of Treaties beyond the Vienna Convention*, ed. Enzo Cannizzaro (Oxford: Oxford University Press, 2011), 411–24, 414–16.

37. Vienna Convention on the Law of Treaties, Vienna, 23 May 1969, Article 53.

38. On the distinction between peremptory norms and obligations *erga omnes*, see Linos-Alexander Sicilianos, 'The Classification of Obligations and the Multilateral Dimension of the Relations of International Responsibility', *European Journal of International Law* 13 (2002): 1127–45, 1136–7; Picone, 'The Distinction between *Jus Cogens* and Obligations *Erga Omnes*', 411–24.

39. On the International Law Commission's shift from peremptory norms to obligation *erga omnes*, see Paolo Picone, 'Obblighi *erga omnes* e codificazione della responsabilità degli Stati', *Rivista di diritto internazionale* 88 (2005): 893–954.

40. Sicilianos, 'The Classification of Obligations', 1134–6; Paolo Picone, 'Le reazioni collettive ad un illecito *erga omnes* in assenza di uno stato individualmente leso', *Rivista di diritto internazionale* 96 (2013), 5–47, 21.

41. DARSIWA, Article 48(1)(a). See also the definition of the Institut de Droit international, Krakow Session, Resolution of 27 August 2005, Article 1(b).

42. Ben-Naftali, 'The Obligation to Prevent and Punish Genocide', 43–4; Giorgio Gaja, 'The Role of the United Nations in Preventing and Suppressing Genocide', in *The UN Genocide Convention*, 397–406, 405.

43. *Military and Paramilitary Activities in and against Nicaragua (Nicaragua v. United States of America)*, Judgment, 26 November 1984, para. 73.

44. See, for an overview of the different opinion, Sarah Mazzocchi, 'Humanitarian Intervention in a Post-Iraq, Post-Darfur World: Is There now a Duty to Prevent Genocide Even Without Security Council Approval?', *Annual Survey of International and Comparative Law* 17 (2011): 111–28; Luke Glanville, 'The Responsibility to Protect Beyond Borders', *Human Rights Law Review* 12 (2012): 1–32, 15–28; Very significantly, Bruno Simma, who served as a judge during the trial, patently affirmed about his contribution to the decision: 'I would call it my court's specific contribution to the development (and continued vitality) of the "responsibility to protect"' (Simma, 'Genocide and International Court of Justice', 264).

45. For the early theorisation of this doctrine, see International Commission on Intervention and State Sovereignty, 'The Responsibility to Protect', December 2001, responsibilitytoprotect.org/ICISS%20Report.pdf (accessed 17 June 2015). Some references can be found in the Security Council resolutions 1873 (S/RES/183, 17 March 2011), 1975 (S/RES/1075, 30 March 2011), 2085 (S/RES/2085, 20 December 2012). See, among others, Carlo Focarelli, 'Ahead to the Past? Responsibility to Protect and the Global System', *Groningen Journal of International Law* 1 (2012): 1–10; *Responsibility to Protect: From Principle to Practice*, ed. Julia Hoffmann and André Nollkaemper (Amsterdam: Pallas, 2012); Peter Hilpold, ed., *Responsibility to Protect (R2P): A New Paradigm of International Law?* (Leiden/Boston: Brill/Nijhoff, 2015).

46. General Assembly, *2005 World Summit Outcome Document* (A/RES/60/1, 24 October 2005), para. 139 (emphasis added).

47. On the possibility to intervene in Syria without authorisation from the Security Council, see Saira Mohamed, 'The U.N. Security Council and the Crisis in Syria', *ASIL Insights* 16, no. 11 (2012), http://www.asil.org/insights/volume/16/issue/11/un-security-council-and-crisis-syria (accessed 17 June 2015); Dapo Akande, 'Self Determination and the Syrian Conflict – Recognition of Syrian Opposition as Sole Legitimate Representative of the Syrian People: What Does this Mean and What Implications Does it Have?', *EJIL: Talk!*, 6 December 2012, http://www.ejiltalk.org/self-determination-and-the-syrian-conflict-recognition-of-syrian-opposition-as-sole-legitimate-representative-of-the-syrian-people-what-does-this-mean-and-what-implications-does-it-have/ (accessed 17 June 2015); Carsten Stahn, 'Syria and the

Semantics of Intervention, Aggression and Punishment. On "Red Lines" and "Blurred Lines"', *Journal of International Criminal Justice* 11 (2013): 955–77.

48. Enzo Cannizzaro, 'Responsabilità di proteggere e intervento delle Nazioni Unite in Libia', *Rivista di diritto internazionale* 94 (2011): 821–4, 823–4; Bruno Pommier, 'The Use of Force to Protect Civilians and Humanitarian Action: The Case of Libya and Beyond', *International Review of the Red Cross* 93 (2011): 1063–83, 1079; Jeremy Sarkin, 'Is the Responsibility to Protect an Accepted Norm of International Law in the post-Libya Era? How its Third Pillar Ought to be Applied', *Groningen Journal of International Law* 1 (2012): 11–48, 21 and 23.

49. The responsibility to protect is not mentioned in the UK governmental statement *Chemical Weapon Use by Syrian Regime – UK Government Legal Position*, 29 August 2013, http://www.gov.uk/government/publications/chemical-weapon-use-by-syrian-regime-uk-government-legal-position (accessed 17 June 2015).

50. Meg Sullivan, 'Justifying Crimea: President Putin Invokes R2P', *Brown Political Review*, 11 April 2014, http://www.brownpoliticalreview.org/2014/04/justifying-crimea-president-putin-invokes-r2p/ (accessed 17 June 2015).

51. *Bosnian Genocide* case, para. 430.

52. Ibid., para. 427.

53. Simma, 'Genocide and International Court of Justice', 262; William A. Schabas, *Unimaginable Atrocities* (Oxford: Oxford University Press, 2012), 116–18; Marco Longobardo, 'L'obbligo di prevenzione del genocidio al di fuori del proprio territorio come base della responsabilità di proteggere. Rilievi critici', in *Un Diritto senza terra? Funzioni e limiti del principio di territorialità nel diritto internazionale e dell'Unione europea/A LackLand Law? Territory, Effectiveness and Jurisdiction in International and EU Law*, ed. Adriana Di Stefano (Torino: Giappichelli, 2015) 493–517.

54. See commentary on DARSIWA, Article 54, in James Crawford, *Report of the International Law Commission on its Fifty-third Session*, 137, para. 3.

55. A countermeasure is 'the act of non-compliance, by a State, with its obligations owed to another State, decided upon in response to a prior breach of international law by that other State and aimed at inducing it to respect its obligation' (Christian J. Tams, *Enforcing Obligations Erga Omnes in International Law* (Cambridge: Cambridge University Press, 2005), 20). See, generally, Carlo Focarelli, *Le contromisure nel diritto internazionale* (Milano: Giuffrè, 1994).

56. On this point, see Sicilianos, 'The Classification of Obligations', 1143; Giorgio Gaja, 'In tema di reazioni alle violazioni di obblighi *erga omnes*', in *Ordine internazionale e valori etici*, ed. Nerina Boschiero (Napoli: Editoriale Scientifica, 2004), 43–6, 45.

57. For the practice on countermeasures in case of violation of obligations *erga omnes*, see Linos-Alexander Sicilianos, *Les réactions décentralisées à l'illicite: des contre-mesures à la légitime défense* (Paris: LGDJ, 1990), 155–74; Tams, *Enforcing Obligations Erga Omnes in International Law*, 207–49.

58. Emanuele Cimiotta, 'Le reazioni alla "sottrazione" della Crimea all'Ucraina. Quali garanzie del diritto internazionale di fronte a gravi illeciti imputati a grandi potenze?', *Diritti umani e diritto internazionale* 8 (2014): 491–504.

59. Institut de Droit international, Krakow Session, Resolution of 27 August 2005, Article 5(c). See also Luigi Condorelli and Laurence Boisson De Chazournes, 'Quelques remarques à propos de l'obligation des États de "respecter et faire respecter" le droit international humanitaire "en toutes circonstances"', in *Études et essais sur le droit international humanitaire et sur les principes de la Coix-Rouge en l'honneur de Jean Pictet*, ed. Christophe Swinarski (Genève/Dordrecht: Comité International de la Croix-Rouge/Martinus Nijhoff Publishers, 1984), 17–35, 31–2; Giorgio Gaja, 'Obligations *Erga Omnes*, International Crimes and *Jus Cogens*: A Tentative Analysis of Three Related Concept', in *International Crimes of State*, 150–60, 155–6; Karel Wellens, 'General Observations', in *Public Interest Rules of International Law: Towards Effective Implementation*, ed. Teruo Komori and Karel Wellens (Farnham: Ashgate, 2009), 15–51, 43; Christian J. Tams, 'Individual States as Guardians of Community Interests', in *From Bilateralism to Community Interests. Essays in Honour of Judge Bruno Simma*, ed. Ulrich Fastenrath et al. (Oxford: Oxford Universty Press, 2011), 379–405, 389–392.

60. Gaja, 'In tema di reazioni alle violazioni di obblighi *erga omnes*', 46; Tams, 'Individual States as Guardians of Community Interests', 388. With regard to genocide prevention, see Andreas

Zimmerman, 'The Obligation to Prevent Genocide: Towards a General Responsibility to Protect?', in *From Bilateralism to Community Interests*, 629–45, 637.

61. Antonio Cassese, '*Ex iniuria ius oritur*: Are We Moving towards International Legitimation of Forcible Humanitarian Countermeasures in the World Community?', *European Journal of International Law* 10 (1999): 23–30, 29. See also Francesco Francioni, 'Balancing the Prohibition of Force with the Need to Protect Human Rights: A Methodological Approach', in *Customary International Law on the Use of Force: A Methodological Approach*, ed. Enzo Cannizzaro and Paolo Palchetti (Leiden: Brill, 2005), 269–92, 277–8.

62. This theory was principally developed by Paolo Picone and this article is not the proper place to analyse it in depth. Among many works, see 'La "guerra del Kosovo" e il diritto internazionale generale', *Rivista di diritto internazionale* 83 (2000): 326–60; 'La guerra contro l'Iraq e le degenerazioni dell'unilateralismo', *Rivista di diritto internazionale* 86 (2003): 337–93; 'L'évolution du droit international coutumier sur l'emploi de la force entre obligations "erga omnes" et autorisations du Conseil de Sécurité', in *Customary International Law on the Use of Force: A Methodological Approach*, 305–19; 'Le reazioni collettive ad un illecito *erga omnes*', 5–47.

63. Paolo Picone, 'Il ruolo dello Stato leso nelle reazioni collettive alla violazioni di obblighi *erga omnes*', *Rivista di diritto internazionale* 95 (2012): 957–87, 972–4.

64. Picone, 'La "guerra del Kosovo" e il diritto internazionale generale', 344–5; Cassese, '*Ex iniuria ius oritur*', 27; Francioni, 'Balancing the Prohibition of Force with the Need to Protect Human Rights', 285–7.

65. For example, the situation in Syria where there is not an injured state regarding the violations committed by the government against its own civilians (Picone, 'Le reazioni collettive ad un illecito *erga omnes*', 9).

66. Paolo Picone, 'Unilateralismo e guerra contro l'ISIS', *Rivista di diritto internazionale* 98 (2015): 5–27.

67. According to Francesco Francioni and Christine Bakker, 'Responsibility to Protect, Humanitarian Intervention and Human Rights: Lessons from Libya to Mali', *Transworld* (2013): 1–19, 4: 'The difference between the second [i.e. traditional humanitarian intervention] and the third doctrinal strands [i.e. admissibility of forcible countermeasures] is that the second relies on a moral-political theory justification, while the third is based on a legal argument.'

68. William A. Schabas, 'Attacking Syria? This Is the Crime of Aggression', *PhD Studies in Human Rights*, 30 August 2013, humanrightsdoctorate.blogspot.co.uk/2013/08/attacking-syria-this-is-crime-of.html (accessed 17 June 2015).

69. On the relevance of obligations *erga omnes* on the ICJ's jurisdiction, see Paolo Picone and Maria Irene Papa, 'La giurisdizione della Corte internazionale di giustizia e obblighi *erga omnes*', in *Comunità internazionale e obblighi "erga omnes"*, ed. Paolo Picone, 3rd edition (Napoli: Jovene, 2013), 675–721.

70. *Belgium* v. *Senegal* case, paras 68–70. For some interesting remarks, see Maria Irene Papa, 'Interesse ad agire davanti alla Corte internazionale di giustizia e tutela dei valori collettivi nella sentenza sul caso *Belgio c. Senegal*', *Diritti umani e diritto internazionale* 7 (2013): 79–104.

71. *Obligations concerning Negotiations relating to Cessation of the Nuclear Arms Race and to Nuclear Disarmament (Marshall Islands v. Pakistan)*, Application instituting proceedings against Pakistan, 24 April 2014, paras 35–6; *Obligations concerning Negotiations relating to Cessation of the Nuclear Arms Race and to Nuclear Disarmament (Marshall Islands v. India)*, Application instituting proceedings against the Republic of India, 24 April 2014, paras 40–1; *Obligations concerning Negotiations relating to Cessation of the Nuclear Arms Race and to Nuclear Disarmament (Marshall Islands v. U.K.)*, Application instituting proceedings against the United Kingdom of Great Britain and Northern Ireland, 24 April 2014, paras 85–6.

72. Many scholars are sceptical about the chance that these cases reach the merit phase due to an alleged lack of the ICJ's jurisdiction. See Marco Roscini, 'The Cases Against the Nuclear Weapons States', *ASIL Insights* 19, no. 10 (2015), http://www.asil.org/insights/volume/19/issue/10/cases-against-nuclear-weapons-states (accessed 17 June 2015); Katherine Maddox Davis, 'Hurting More than Helping: How the Marshall Islands' Seeming Bravery Against Major Powers Only Stands to Maim the Legitimacy of the World Court', 11 March 2015, papers.ssrn.com/sol3/papers.cfm?abstract_id=2577111 (accessed 17 June 2015).

73. Professor James Crawford, who is against the admissibility of countermeasures, frankly wrote: 'Better to give States standing to the Court to protect what they perceive as global values than to leave them only with non-judicial means of dispute settlement, whether in the guise of counter-measures or under the rubric of "responsibility to protect"' (James Crawford, 'Responsibility for Breaches of Communitarian Norms: An Appraisal of Article 48 of the ILC Articles on Responsibility of States for International Wrongful Acts', in *From Bilateralism to Community Interests*, 224–40, 225).

74. According to Article 1 common to the four 1949 Geneva Conventions, states parties must respect and ensure respect of the conventions. For the relationship between this provision and the responsibility to protect, see Laurence Boisson de Chazournes and Luigi Condorelli, 'De la responsabilité de protéger, ou d'une nouvelle parure pour une notion déjà bien établie, *Revue Générale de Droit International Public* 110 (2006): 11–18. For the *erga omnes* character of some international humanitarian law norms, see *Legal Consequences of the Construction of a Wall in the Occupied Palestinian Territory*, paras 155 and 157.

The 'deterrent argument' and the responsibility to protect

Conall Mallory[a] and Stuart Wallace[b]

[a]School of Law, Northumbria University, Newcastle-upon-Tyne, UK; [b]Human Rights Law Centre, School of Law, University of Nottingham, Nottingham, UK

States have presented a range of arguments against the expansion of human rights law into the extra-territorial military sphere. This article focuses on one argument in particular – the 'deterrent argument'. This is the idea that if states are expected to uphold human rights obligations during extra-territorial military operations, it will deter them from contributing troops to United Nations (UN) peace support missions, which would naturally include those sanctioned under the responsibility to protect (R2P) doctrine. This article considers how the European Court of Human Rights' jurisprudence could actually apply to such military operations in practice and whether states should logically be deterred from participating in such missions. We argue that the involvement of the UN and the types of missions undertaken under R2P should not deter states from participation, but rather that UN involvement neutralises or mitigates many of the negative issues states fear in this area, reducing the likelihood of human rights liability for states.

Section 1: introduction

International human rights law (IHRL) was once conceived as a law for times of peace, an internal law, bound to the institutions of the state and its systems of governance.[1] That anachronistic view has been discarded in recent years as the application of IHRL has shifted from the domestic sphere to the extra-territorial and from peace to conflict. While traces of this shift have been evident for many years,[2] its full force is only now being felt. The past decades have seen the European Court of Human Rights (ECtHR) apply the European Convention on Human Rights (ECHR) to a variety of military operations, including international armed conflicts,[3] foreign belligerent occupations,[4] peace-support operations,[5] domestic counter-insurgency operations,[6] and non-international armed conflicts.[7] It is particularly notable that the ECtHR's jurisdiction has extended to extra-territorial military operations with increasing frequency.

The subject has drawn a great deal of academic scrutiny.[8] Indeed despite the increasing prevalence of this phenomenon, academics continue to argue over what can be considered theoretical and preliminary issues, such as whether human rights law applies extra-territorially and whether it should be superseded by international humanitarian law or United Nations Security Council Resolutions (UNSCRs).[9] While there is some continued merit to these discussions, the reality is that the ECHR is currently being applied to extra-territorial military operations and there is a need to shift focus towards considering the practicalities of this new paradigm and its implications for states. In the words of one academic, it is time to 'stop debating the theory and start defining the pragmatic'.[10]

One implication of this new paradigm is clear – states are very concerned about the expansion of human rights law into the extra-territorial military sphere. States have vehemently opposed the extension of human rights law to this field in many cases brought before the ECtHR and have deployed a range of arguments against it. These arguments typically revolve around the degree of control exercised by the state in the circumstances,[11] the role of other parties in causing the alleged violation,[12] and arguments over circumstances that existed *de jure* and *de facto* at the time of the alleged violation.[13] In this article we wish to focus on one state argument in particular – the deterrent argument. The deterrent argument is the contention that if states are obliged to uphold human rights obligations during extra-territorial military operations, it will deter them from contributing troops to UN peace support missions, which would naturally include those sanctioned under the R2P doctrine.

Contracting states to the convention have repeatedly raised this argument, claiming that if the court were to impose liability upon them, there would be 'serious repercussions' and a 'real risk' that states would be deterred from participating in future missions.[14] Thus, as IHRL, and the ECHR in particular, is increasingly applied to extra-territorial military operations, it may generate a significant risk to state participation in R2P missions, in particular because these missions are voluntary and undertaken for ostensibly altruistic purposes.

As a policy argument, it should not, in principle at least, influence the ECtHR's decisions. This point has been recognised by at least one judge at the court who has described the argument as being 'insubstantial from a legal perspective'.[15] Nevertheless we must recognise that it is within the purview of states to withdraw such support and attempt to assuage the fears they have over this expanding area of law in order to avoid any reduction in support for R2P missions. This article therefore considers how the ECtHR's jurisprudence could actually apply to R2P missions in practice and whether states should logically be deterred from participating in such missions. It does so by making particular reference to recent military operations sanctioned under the R2P, most notably the 2011 intervention in Libya. We argue that the involvement of the UN and the types of missions undertaken under R2P should not lead states to be deterred from participation, rather the involvement of the UN neutralises or mitigates many of the negative issues states fear in this area, reducing the likelihood of human rights liability for contracting states. The article is divided into four sections. Section 2 examines the origins of the deterrent argument before the ECtHR and contextualises the discussion. Section 3 reflects on how the ECtHR's jurisprudence on extra-territorial human rights obligations could apply in the context of R2P missions and discusses the ECtHR's jurisprudence on attribution and state responsibility in relation to R2P missions, while section 4 concludes.

Section 2: the 'deterrent argument'

The deterrent argument arose from European states trying to avoid accountability for human rights violations when acting collectively on military and peacekeeping operations. The first invocation of the argument was in the case of *Banković and Ors* v. *Belgium and Ors*. In this case, North Atlantic Treaty Organisation (NATO) forces conducted an aerial bombardment of the offices of Radio-Television Serbia during the Balkan conflict. The broadcaster had been identified as part of Serbia's military command, control and communications network. The attack killed 16 people and seriously injured another 16, prompting an allegation that the respective contracting parties had violated the victims' right to life under Article 2 of the convention. In their submissions before the court, the respondent states contended that if the ECtHR were to hold that they owed extra-territorial human rights obligations during the attack, there would be 'serious consequences for international military collective action', which would 'risk undermining significantly the States' participation in such missions'.[16]

The argument was raised again shortly afterwards in *Behrami and Saramati v. France and Ors*,[17] another case involving the NATO-led humanitarian intervention operation in the Balkans. In *Behrami*, one child died and a group of his friends were severely injured by an unexploded cluster bomb in Kosovo. The parents of the children alleged that their right to life under Article 2 ECHR was violated as the military forces there should have removed the ordnance. In *Saramati*, the applicant was subject to extrajudicial detention for a period of six months under orders from the NATO-led international peacekeeping force in Kosovo (KFOR). This led him to complain that his rights to liberty and security under Article 5 and his right to a fair trial under Article 6 had been infringed. When the case came before the Grand Chamber of the ECtHR, European states again posited that there would be 'serious repercussions' and even a 'devastating effect' on such actions[18] if the ECtHR's jurisdiction extended to UN-authorised peacekeeping missions.[19]

The argument was most recently recited by the UK as an intervening third party in the case of *Jaloud v. the Netherlands*.[20] This application arose from the death of a 29-year-old Iraqi man who had been shot by a Dutch soldier deployed as part of the Stabilisation Force in southern Iraq pursuant to UNSCR 1483. The applicant, the victim's father, complained under the procedural limb of Article 2 that there had been an ineffective investigation into his son's death. At the hearing in Strasbourg, British officials argued that the imposition of extra-territorial obligations created a real risk that states might in future be:

> deterred from answering the call of the United Nations Security Council to contribute troops to United Nations mandated forces, to the detriment of the United Nations Security Council's mission to secure international peace and security.[21]

This argument presents two problems for the R2P doctrine. First, if the warning from states translates into actual action and withdrawals of support, it represents a clear and present danger to the entire R2P enterprise, which is predicated on the economic, political and military support of the global community. Second, the argument itself may give rise to accusations of double standards and pose a credibility threat to the R2P doctrine if it is used as a defence. The premise of the assertion arguably contradicts the reasons why states undertake R2P military operations, namely humanitarian concerns and concerns over respect for human rights. It would be hypocritical for a state, supposedly motivated by humanitarian intentions when participating in an R2P mission, to cultivate a climate of impunity among its own forces. Such a position could damage the credibility of the R2P doctrine as a whole as states appear to assume a 'do as I say, not as I do' attitude.

These dangers give rise to the possibility that either states refuse to provide military support to R2P missions, or, they contribute forces and when called to account argue that imposing human rights liability upon them would only deter further support in similar operations. The detrimental impact of either of these outcomes on the content, operation and reputation of the R2P is concerning, particularly given the almost inevitability that one day a case involving actions undertaken under an R2P mandate will be brought before the ECtHR.

To date the ECtHR has never refrained from considering an application purely on the basis that it concerned violations arising during an armed conflict. Instead the court has recognised the application of the convention to a range of different military activities.[22] Most commonly these actions have been unilateral in nature; however the court has also recognised the convention's applicability to military operations which are undertaken for ostensibly humanitarian purposes. The court's unwillingness to distinguish between operations conducted for states' self-interests, and those purportedly undertaken in the interests of others, suggests that cases involving the R2P are equally as likely to arrive before the court.

Armed conflict of any nature gives rise to the danger that civilians will be injured or killed, or individuals will face other human rights abuses, which may result in claims that convention rights have been breached. The experience of the Libyan R2P operation is an example of this. Despite generally being heralded as a success, the NATO-led intervention in 2011 gave rise to a number of civilian casualties. The UN Human Rights Council Commission of Inquiry into the Libyan conflict recommended that NATO undertake further investigations into a small number of the targeted operations.[23] In one instance in particular, in the town of Majer, NATO forces are alleged to have killed 16 civilians in an airstrike, before returning and killing a further 18 rescuers in a second strike.[24] There are strong similarities between events like this and previous applications brought before the Strasbourg Court.[25] Thus there is no reason from a procedural or substantive perspective why R2P claims will not be brought before and decided by the ECtHR.

Although we do not intend to address the legitimacy of the deterrent argument in this article, we take the position that it is highly unlikely that a concern for human rights obligations alone will influence the decision of whether a state contributes forces to a UN-mandated operation like an R2P mission. Certainly the rise in litigation regarding extra-territorial human rights violations will concern states. The UK in particular has faced a high financial cost to meet the investigative and compensation obligations arising from its activities in Iraq.[26] The reality, however, is that states participate and refuse to participate in extra-territorial military actions, including those authorised under the R2P, for a variety of complex reasons and increased liability for human rights violations in and of itself should not be a sufficient deterrent to outweigh the other motivations which compel state participation in such actions.[27] Zifcak notes that self-interest, political alliances and strategic regional importance all play influential roles in the consideration of whether a nation will endorse, or block, intervention.[28] Gramyk cites the motivations of expanding global influence and exercising power in the humanitarian sphere as two reasons why states would engage in military interventions, with the primary reason for non-participation being a lack of political will domestically.[29] Moreover, historical precedent shows that human rights liability has not been sufficient to deter other extra-territorial military actions. Despite being aware of the potential for human rights liability for over four decades, European states have freely embarked on various extra-territorial military operations, including unilateral 'wars of choice' like the invasion of Iraq. Thus, although we accept that potential human rights liability may be a relevant consideration, it is just one of a myriad of different factors states consider and it is unlikely to be the determining factor as, if it were, states would have refused to undertake other military operations on these grounds.

Section 3: human rights accountability and the R2P

Military action under the R2P doctrine depends upon Security Council authorisation. The text of the 2005 World Summit, which formally introduced the doctrine to the international community, allowed for 'collective action, in a timely and decisive manner, *through the*

Security Council.[30] This authorisation, referred to by some as the 'legalization' of the R2P doctrine,[31] has been read as a mandatory requirement for the use of force under the R2P.[32] The result of this is that the UNSC will play an important role in defining the manner in which military action should be conducted in accordance with the R2P mandate. The military parameters of such action will therefore be restricted by economic and political factors, as well as the willingness for states to contribute their own forces to any such action. Conversely when a state, or group of states, act without UNSC authorisation they have greater flexibility to define their own parameters of military engagement. Thus, in order to meet their military objectives in Iraq, the United States (US), the UK and their allies followed an aerial bombardment with a wide-scale ground offensive and occupation.

As a mechanism, this requirement for any R2P action to be authorised by the UNSC arguably restricts the likelihood that a state will be held accountable for any human rights violation arising during the course of an R2P operation. It does so in two ways: first, by restricting the parameters of military action in accordance with what the Security Council can collectively agree to take, and second, by arguably reducing the possibility that states will be held solely responsible for human rights violations while they act under UN authorisation. Thus, our argument is that if we accept that states will participate in extra-territorial military operations, the involvement of the UN and the existence of an R2P mandate should, far from deterring them, neutralise, or at the very least mitigate, many of the perceived negative consequences of their participation, as without the involvement of the UN and an R2P mandate, states will shoulder the full burden of human rights liability themselves.

Extra-territorial human rights obligations on R2P-sanctioned military operations

The deterrent argument presupposes that a state will be deterred from contributing to missions of a humanitarian nature due to the possibility that it may be held accountable for any resulting breach of human rights obligations during the course of such activities. In order for a state to owe human rights obligations, however, it must first exercise jurisdiction over a person or place. The requirement for the UNSC to sanction any military action under the R2P doctrine limits the military parameters of any R2P operation to that which can be agreed upon within the UNSC. This in turn limits the scope of the state's jurisdiction over people and places, meaning that the involvement of the UNSC, in effect, limits the extent or in some instances even likelihood of human rights obligations being established in the first place.

This is particularly the case after the NATO-led intervention in Libya. The military action was authorised by UNSCR 1973 with a mandate 'to protect civilians and civilian populated areas under threat of attack in the Libyan Arab Jamahiriya'.[33] It has been suggested that the military campaign grossly exceeded this mandate as military operations were not only conducted to protect civilians, but also to overthrow the Qaddafi administration. Ulfstein and Christiansen have argued that the operations, which went beyond civilian protection and effected regime change, including support for Libyan rebels, were an illegal use of force.[34] Moreover, they have suggested that the abuse of the UNSCR in the Libyan conflict may have caused permanent, even terminal, damage to any support for the R2P doctrine in the future.[35] A key legacy of the Libyan conflict is therefore that where any future military operation is authorised under the R2P doctrine it will most likely be restrictively defined by the UNSC to prevent further 'mission creep'.[36]

The restriction of the military parameters of any R2P operation will have a consequential restriction on the extent to which states exercise jurisdiction over people and places affected by the military engagement. The extra-territorial human rights obligations of states are derived by interpreting the convention's jurisdiction clause in Article 1, which stipulates that states shall secure to everyone 'within their jurisdiction' the rights and freedoms set out in the convention. Thus, for a state to owe an extra-territorial obligation to someone, and for that person to be entitled to the protection of convention rights, they must first be within the jurisdiction of a contracting party at the time of any alleged action. This small phrase has been regarded as 'one of the most problematic' in the convention.[37] In recent years, the court has made an effort to clarify the understanding of jurisdiction in Article 1, particularly in cases involving the use of force by states, however the concept remains fluid.

Broadly speaking, the ECtHR accepts two forms of jurisdiction: when authority and control is exercised over an area – spatial jurisdiction – and when it is exercised over a person – personal jurisdiction. The approach of the UNSC to implementing the R2P, and the ECtHR's jurisprudence on jurisdiction, ultimately may make it unlikely that such jurisdiction would arise in an R2P-sanctioned operation.

Spatial jurisdiction arises when a state exercises effective control over an area outside of its own borders. The test for spatial jurisdiction is whether *de facto* control has been exercised over the relevant territory, either by a contracting state or through a subordinate local administration.[38] Once established, the state exercising jurisdiction is obligated to uphold all of the rights and responsibilities in the convention and any additional relevant protocols.[39] The difficulty with establishing a jurisdictional link on the spatial basis is that it involves some form of 'boots on the ground', which the UN Security Council may be unlikely to sanction. This is particularly the case given that the purpose of military action under the R2P is 'to help lay the foundation for the State to reassure its responsibility and for assisting or persuading national authorities to meet their responsibilities'.[40] It is difficult to see how taking effective control of an area of that state's territory would be seen as supporting them in this pursuit. Moreover, members of the UNSC have already illustrated an unwillingness to sanction occupying forces under the mandate of the doctrine. UNSCR 1973 explicitly excluded 'a foreign occupation force of any form on any part of Libyan territory'.[41] After the Libyan conflict, it is arguably even less likely that a military operation which aims to take effective control of another state's territory would be authorised.

Even if the UNSC were to sanction the use of force to take control of another state's territory, the ECtHR has been reluctant to establish jurisdiction in this manner. For an R2P operation to give rise to spatial jurisdiction, the participating states would have to contribute enough forces to effectively secure an area of another state's territory, and to stay in that area for a prolonged period of time. The degree of permanence, in particular, has been influential in the court's approach to spatial jurisdiction.[42] The ECtHR have held that Turkey was exercising spatial jurisdiction during its long-term *de facto* annexation of northern Cyprus,[43] and the same for the Russian forces in the Transdniestrian region of Moldova,[44] but the ECtHR has been less willing to even consider whether the UK's shorter-term military occupation of southern Iraq was an exercise of spatial jurisdiction.[45] Furthermore, taking effective control of an area for a prolonged period of time would clearly be incompatible with the intention of the R2P of assisting the forum state in meeting its own obligations.

The court's unwillingness to directly address the relationship between belligerent occupation and spatial jurisdiction, despite being presented with an opportunity to do so in several cases,[46] renders this area of the law uncertain. The court has only provided indications for the position it may take. For instance, in the recent *Sargsyan* v. *Azerbaijan* case, the court indicated that it could not foresee occupation arising without 'boots on the ground', stating actual authority and effective control required 'such elements as presence of foreign troops, which are in a position to exercise effective control without the consent of the sovereign'.[47] Elsewhere it has indicated that when belligerent occupiers are tackling armed insurgency, the possibility of finding effective control will be diminished.[48]

The ECtHR's approach to personal jurisdiction is broader than its approach to spatial jurisdiction. When established, the state is not required to fulfil all rights within the convention, but only those which are relevant to the individual in the particular situation.[49] One manner in which personal jurisdiction may arise during the course of an R2P operation is when a state exercises public powers normally exercised by the forum state:

> the exercise of extra-territorial jurisdiction by a Contracting State when, through the consent, invitation or acquiescence of the Government of that territory, it exercises all or some of the public powers normally to be exercised by that Government.[50]

In *Al-Skeini and Others* v. *United Kingdom*, six civilians died in occupied Basrah in the context of UK military operations there. The court held that because the UK was responsible for security in the region, it was exercising public powers and the deceased individuals fell within UK jurisdiction at the time of their deaths.[51] This model could support a finding of jurisdiction in the R2P context because R2P missions should, wherever possible, be constituted with the consent and compliance of the domestic state. The primary responsibility in the R2P doctrine lies with the territorial state, which would give consent to the exercise of security powers by an intervening force. Although this clearly was not possible in the Libyan case and would have been equally as unlikely in relation to the Rwandan genocide, which is so often cited as the catalyst for the R2P movement, it was attempted in the establishment of a peacekeeping force during the Darfur crisis where the relevant UNSCR invited the consent of the Government of National Unity for the deployment of forces.[52] It was also present in the Solomon Islands in 2003 where the government invited the deployment of the Regional Assistance Mission to the Solomon Islands to provide 'comprehensive military, civilian and peace support to national authorities'.[53]

Along with the exercise of public powers, personal jurisdiction has also been found to arise when state forces exercise authority and control at checkpoints,[54] and when they take an individual into their custody.[55] The court has been less willing to address the more sensitive situation of whether a jurisdictional link will arise when an individual is shot and killed by a state agent, although there are some cases which envisage this possibility.[56] In any event, similar to the spatial basis for jurisdiction, these instances of extra-territorial jurisdiction are all incumbent on some level of 'boots on the ground' authorisation, which may not be forthcoming from the UNSC.

It would be more likely therefore that the UNSC authorises shorter-term and more carefully defined military operations under the R2P heading. Zifcak suggests that the relative success of the NATO-led 'no fly zone' in Libya may hold an important lesson for any future interventions that the UNSC may contemplate.[57] This type of military engagement would still be unlikely to result in human rights obligations being owed to anyone injured or killed during bombing raids. In the case of *Banković* discussed above, the court held that there was no jurisdictional link between contracting parties and the victims of the NATO air strike in Belgrade during the Balkan conflict.[58] Instead it stated that this 'cause and effect' notion of jurisdiction was unsustainable.[59] Although this principle has been challenged on numerous occasions since, it has yet to be contradicted by any more recent judgment and for that reason, although controversial, it remains 'good law'.

State responsibility and attribution

We have already noted that in light of the Libyan intervention any R2P missions in the near future are, generally speaking, unlikely to involve a deployment of troops and the situations where R2P missions generate jurisdictional links should as a result be fairly limited. Yet, even with these caveats, the above analysis illustrates that there remains the possibility that the ECtHR could find jurisdictional links to a contracting state during an R2P mission, particularly with the deployment of a peacekeeping force, but jurisdiction is only one half of the equation. A jurisdictional link on its own is not sufficient to trigger liability under the convention. The ECtHR must also determine that the alleged rights violation was attributable to the state for state responsibility to arise. Yet, here again, the involvement of the United Nations and a state's participation in an R2P mission can offer states tangible benefits when it comes to determining the attribution of wrongful conduct and any potential state responsibility for extra-territorial human rights violations.

In order to explain this point we must first make a distinction between state jurisdiction and state responsibility and a further distinction between the attribution of conduct and attribution of responsibility. The distinction between jurisdiction and state responsibility can easily be seen in the Articles on State Responsibility (ASR) drafted by the International Law Commission (ILC), which determine the legal consequences of a failure to fulfil international obligations, e.g. treaty obligations. For state responsibility to arise, two criteria must be met. The conduct consisting of an action or omission must be (a) attributable to the state under international law and (b) it must constitute a breach of the state's international obligations.[60] Before a state can breach an obligation, the obligation must first be owed.[61] In the context of the convention, this means that the applicant must, generally speaking, be within the state's jurisdiction before attribution is determined and state responsibility held to arise.[62] State responsibility may not arise for every act/omission that occurs within a state's jurisdiction. In addition it may be necessary to further differentiate between the attribution of conduct and the attribution of responsibility. Thus, it does not necessarily follow in all circumstances that once conduct is considered attributable to either a state or international organisation that they automatically bear responsibility for it under international law. As Bell points out, conduct may be attributable to one entity, e.g. a state, and yet both entities, the state and the international organisation, may be responsible for the wrongful nature of the act. Thus attribution of conduct to an international organisation or state on its own does not rule out the possibility of attribution of responsibility to both the international organisation and the state.[63]

In the cases of *Behrami and Saramati* v. *France and Ors* (discussed above), the presence of a UN-mandated force effectively shielded the contracting states from responsibility under the ECHR. When the ECtHR examined the cases it did not focus on extra-territorial jurisdiction.[64] Instead, the court examined the *ratione personae* question, i.e. to whom the acts and omissions giving rise to the complaints should be attributed. The ECtHR considered that the arrest and detention of Saramati came within the mandate of KFOR, while supervision of de-mining activities fell within the mandate of the UN Interim Administration Mission in Kosovo (UNMIK).[65] The key issue for the court was whether 'the Security Council retained ultimate authority and control so that operational command only was delegated'.[66] The ECtHR held that the UN had exercised 'ultimate authority and control' over the mission because they authorised it.[67] Thus, the KFOR troops' actions in detaining Saramati and UNMIK's failure to de-mine were both deemed attributable to the UN and not their contributing countries.

We do not want to dwell on the veracity of the ECtHR's ruling, as many academics have already criticised the outcome extensively.[68] Instead we want to highlight that in this situation where troops had been present in a country under a UN mandate, that UN mandate had shielded the sending state from its international obligation to uphold the ECHR rights within that territory. Indeed this prompted one academic to conclude that the ECHR is unlikely to be an effective remedy for local individuals alleging human rights violations by European states participating in peace support operations abroad in the future.[69] While another remarked that the court has created a loophole in which contracting states acting under UN authority are not held accountable for their convention obligations.[70]

We have already noted above that states are losing ground in the fight to curtail the circumstances in which extra-territorial jurisdiction arises. While we do not wish to encourage states to avoid their human rights obligations during conflict, the fact remains that the UN's involvement in a military operation offers states an outlet through which they can avoid full responsibility by claiming that any actions that violated human rights committed by their soldiers were undertaken in the name of the UN and that they were not attributable to the sending state. Thus, the expansion in extra-territorial jurisdiction should, if anything, encourage rather than deter calculating states to participate more readily in UN operations, rather than conducting military action unilaterally.

Admittedly there are doubts about whether *Behrami* remains good law in Strasbourg. After all, the ECtHR failed to consider the possibility that both the state and the international organisation could bear responsibility for wrongful acts perpetrated against the applicants.[71] As Nollkaemper notes, if governance is distributed across multiple interacting layers, accountability should logically also straddle those layers.[72] There is a distinct possibility that the ECtHR will start to find that states and international organisations are concurrently responsible for human rights violations that occur in the context of UN-sanctioned military operations.[73] The possibility of such simultaneous responsibility is expressly envisaged in both the Articles on Responsibility of International Organisations (ARIO),[74] and the ASR.[75] The ILC's commentary on the Articles states:

> Although it may not frequently occur in practice, dual or even multiple attribution of conduct cannot be excluded. Thus, attribution of a certain conduct to an international organization does not imply that the same conduct cannot be attributed to a State; nor does attribution of conduct to a State rule out attribution of the same conduct to an international organization.[76]

A key development in multiple attribution occurred in the case of *Al-Jedda* v. *United Kingdom*.[77] There the UK's military forces in Iraq interned persons pursuant to authority granted in UNSCR 1546 and the letter annexed to that UNSCR by US Secretary of State Colin Powell.[78] They detained the applicant in this case from October 2004 to December 2007 as he was suspected of assisting insurgents in Iraq. He sought judicial review of his detention before the British courts and the ECtHR. On the subject of attribution, the UK accepted that the applicant was within UK jurisdiction, but argued that because the applicant was detained under a UNSCR, his detention was attributable to the UN and was, as a result, outside the scope of the convention. Thus, the UK raised a similar argument to that which was brought before the court in *Behrami*. At the House of Lords, the domestic judges rejected this claim and distinguished the case of *Behrami* on the facts, stating that the position of the UK forces in Iraq could not be considered analogous to that of UNMIK in Kosovo because 'the multinational force in Iraq was not established at the behest of the UN, was not mandated to operate under UN auspices and was not a subsidiary organ of the

UN'.[79] The ECtHR followed the domestic judges' reasoning. They analysed the UNSC resolutions authorising the multinational force in Iraq and concluded that the UN Security Council did not have ultimate authority and control over the acts and omissions of the troops participating in the multinational force.[80] The ECtHR stated:

> The Court does not consider that, as a result of the authorisation contained in Resolution 1511, the acts of soldiers within the Multi-National Force became attributable to the United Nations or – more importantly, for the purposes of this case – ceased to be attributable to the troop-contributing nations.[81]

The latter statement is seen by many as a crucial detail because it indicates that the ECtHR accepts the possibility of dual or multiple attribution of the same conduct to the UN and to a state, and also the possibility of concurrent responsibility, which it did not do in *Behrami*.[82] It may be that the judgment in *Al-Jedda* is foreshadowing a move away from the position in *Behrami* and towards a realignment of ECtHR jurisprudence with the ILC's interpretation of multiple attribution in ARIO and ASR.[83] So where does this leave *Behrami* and the argument that states will be shielded from responsibility by the UN? First, there remains little state practice on this issue,[84] and international law at its present stage of development offers little guidance as to how responsibility should be shared between multiple actors, making this idea difficult to operationalise.[85] Indeed, the ECtHR itself did not ultimately determine in *Al-Jedda* that the impugned conduct was attributable to both the UK and the UN. Thus, the idea of multiple attribution of conduct remains, at least for the time being, theoretical in the ECtHR's jurisprudence. Second, and perhaps related to the former point, it has been argued that neither the UK House of Lords, nor the ECtHR itself, has expressly overruled the decision in *Behrami*.[86] While such shifts in jurisprudence are rarely openly acknowledged by the ECtHR, and pride perhaps plays a role in this, the absence of an express departure could mean that *Behrami* is still good law, especially in the domestic sphere where national courts may be loath to go against an established ECtHR precedent without a clearer indication of departure.[87] Indeed, even if the ECtHR starts to attribute conduct to states and international organisations in the context of R2P missions, it should still not deter states from participating in them because the participation of the UN will offer the state another party to share the burden of responsibility with, which they would not otherwise have. Thus, it should always be preferable from the standpoint of attribution of responsibility for states to participate in a UN-sanctioned R2P mission as the alternative is for the state to face full responsibility on its own.

Section 4: conclusion

Although states are increasingly being obliged to uphold human rights obligations during extra-territorial military operations, we have argued throughout this article that this should not have a significant deterrent effect on states' participation in any UN-sanctioned military operation, particularly those which are authorised under the R2P doctrine. The prospect of human rights liability, in and of itself, does not appear to have been a significant deterrent to military operations thus far and states have continued to embark upon such missions despite the possibility of such liability. However, even if it were a significant factor, we have demonstrated that the particular nature of R2P missions should not deter participation. The types of operations that are likely to be agreed by the Security Council and pursued under the R2P, namely operations where the state does not deploy troops on the ground and where states establish no-fly zones, are unlikely to give rise to extra-territorial jurisdiction under the European Convention on Human Rights. Equally, from the standpoint of state responsibility, the involvement of the UN would mean that any prospective human rights liability would either be placed directly and solely upon the UN, or at the very least shared between the state and the UN, rather than leaving the human rights burden to be shouldered by the state alone. It is hoped that this article will go some way towards assuaging the fears of states in this developing area of law by illustrating some of the legitimate benefits states gain from participation in R2P missions and safeguarding state participation in this noble and altruistic endeavour.

Disclosure statement

No potential conflict of interest was reported by the authors.

Notes

1. Guglielmo Verdirame, 'Human Rights in Wartime: A Framework for Analysis', *European Human Rights Law Review* (2008): 689–90.
2. Cases on the extra-territorial application of the convention arise at the European Court and Commission of Human Rights (ECtHR) from the 1960s: *X* v. *Federal Republic of Germany* (App. No. 1611/62) EComHR 25 September 1965. The crossover between human rights law and armed conflict begins in the 1950s – Cordula Droege, 'The Interplay between International Humanitarian Law and International Human Rights Law in Situations of Armed Conflict', *Israel Law Review* 40 (2007): 310, 312–17.
3. *Cyprus* v. *Turkey* (1982) 4 EHRR 482; *Georgia* v. *Russia (II)* (2012) 54 EHRR SE10.
4. The occupation of Iraq in *Al-Skeini and Others* v. *United Kingdom* (2011) 53 EHRR 18 (hereinafter *Al-Skeini*).
5. Kosovo in *Behrami* v. *France* (2007) 45 EHRR SE10.
6. Counter-insurgency in South-East Turkey in *Ergi* v. *Turkey* (2001) 32 EHRR 18.
7. Russian operations in Chechnya in *Isayeva* v. *Russia* (2005) 41 EHRR 38 (hereinafter *Isayeva*).
8. Antoine Buyse, ed., *Margins of Conflict: The ECHR and Transitions to and from Armed Conflict* (Antwerp: Intersentia, 2011); Andrea Gioia, 'The Role of the European Court of Human Rights in Monitoring Compliance with Humanitarian Law in Armed Conflict', in *International Humanitarian Law and International Human Rights Law*, ed. Orna Ben-Naftali (Oxford: Oxford University Press, 2012), 201; William Abresch, 'A Human Rights Law of Internal Armed Conflict: The European Court of Human Rights in Chechnya', *European Journal of International Law* 16, no. 4 (2005): 741.
9. Barbara Miltner, 'Revisiting Extraterritoriality after Al-Skeini: The ECHR and Its Lessons', *Michigan Journal of International Law* 33 (2012): 693–748; Natasha Balendra, 'Defining Armed Conflict', *Cardozo Law Review* 29, no. 6 (2008): 2482–5; Michelle Hansen, 'Preventing

the Emasculation of Warfare: Halting the Expansion of Human Rights into Armed Conflict', *Military Law Review* 194 (2007): 1; Michael Dennis, 'Application of Human Rights Treaties Extraterritorially to Detention of Combatants and Security Internees: Fuzzy Thinking All Around?', *ILSA Journal of International & Comparative Law* 12 (2006): 474; William Hays Parks, 'Part IX of the ICRC "Direct Participation in Hostilities" Study: No Mandate, No Expertise, and Legally Incorrect', *International Law and Politics* 42 (2010): 797–9.

10. Geoffrey Corn, 'Mixing Apples and Hand Grenades the Logical Limits of Applying Human Rights Norms to Armed Conflict', *International Humanitarian Legal Studies* 1 (2010). 52, 90.

11. See, for example, *Banković and Others* v. *Belgium and Others* (2007) 44 EHRR SE5 (hereinafter *Banković*), para. 44.

12. See, for example, the attempts by the United Kingdom (UK) to shift blame onto the administrators of occupied Iraq and the UN in *Al-Skeini*, paras 113 and 97.

13. See, for example, arguments about the *de facto* and *de jure* control over prisoners in *Al-Saadoon and Mufdhi* v. *United Kingdom* (Admissibility) (2009) 49 EHRR SE11 (hereinafter *Al-Saadoon*), para. 79; See also the same argument made in reverse in *Hassan* v. *United Kingdom* (App. No. 29750/09) 16 September 2014, (hereinafter *Hassan*), para. 72.

14. See references to 'serious repercussions' made by Norway and France in *Behrami and Saramati* v. *France et al.* (App. No. 71412/01) 2 May 2007 (hereinafter *Behrami*), paras 108–9; See also reference to a 'real risk' in *Jaloud* v. *the Netherlands* (App. No. 47708/08) 20 November 2014 (hereinafter *Jaloud*), para. 126.

15. *Jaloud*, concurring opinion of Judge Motoc, para. 7.

16. *Banković*, para. 43.

17. *Behrami*.

18. See Polish argument in *Behrami*, para. 112; See also Dannenbaum, who argues that the resulting deficit in the supply of peacekeepers for UN missions means that such a scenario cannot be taken lightly – Tom Dannenbaum, 'Translating the Standard of Effective Control into a System of Effective Accountability: How Liability Should be Apportioned for Violations of Human Rights by Member State Troop Contingents Serving as United Nations Peacekeepers', *Harvard International Law Journal* 51, no. 1 (2010): 184; See also Caitlin Bell, 'Reassessing Multiple Attribution: The International Law Commission and The Behrami and Saramati Decision', *New York University Journal of International Law and Politics* 42 (2010): 504.

19. *Behrami*, paras 108–9.

20. *Jaloud*.

21. *Jaloud*, para. 126.

22. See notes 3–7 and discussion in Abresch, 'A Human Rights Law of Internal Armed Conflict'.

23. UN, Human Rights Council, Report of the International Commission of Inquiry on Libya, A/HRC/19/38, para. 122.

24. Ibid., para. 87.

25. See inter alia, *Banković* and *Isayeva*.

26. For instance, the Baha Mousa Inquiry cost the UK government £25 million, the Al-Sweady Inquiry £31 million.

27. Dannenbaum, 'Translating the Standard', 184–7.

28. Spencer Zifcak, 'The Responsibility to Protect after Libya and Syria', *Melbourne Journal of International Law* 13 (2012): 89–90.

29. Eva Gramyk, 'Increased Franco-British Military Cooperation: The Impetus, Its Results, and the Impact on International Humanitarian Interventions', *San Diego Journal of International Law* 15 (2013): 379, 423.

30. UNGA, 60/1. 2005 World Summit Outcome, 24 October 2005, A/Res/60/1: para. 139. Emphasis added by author.

31. Jonathan Graubart, 'R2P and Pragmatic Liberal Interventionism: Values in the Service of Interests', *Human Rights Quarterly* 35 (2013): 76.

32. Alex Belamy, *Global Politics and the Responsibility to Protect: From Words to Deeds*, (London: Routledge, 2011), 163; Terry Gill, 'The Security Council', in *An Institutional Approach to the Responsibility to Protect*, ed. Gentian Zyberi (Cambridge: Cambridge University Press, 2013), 95; Gary Wilson, 'Applying the *Responsibility to Protect* to the "Arab Spring"', *Liverpool Law Review* 35 (2014): 160. Others see it as an emerging right to unilateral intervention – Alicia Bannon, 'The Responsibility to Protect: The UN World Summit and the

Question of Unilateralism', *Yale Law Journal* 115 (2006): 1158; Stephen John Stedman, 'UN Transformation in an Era of Soft Balancing', *International Affairs* 83 (2007): 938.

33. United Nations Security Council Resolution 1973, 17 March 2011, S/RES/1973 (2011), para. 4.
34. Geir Ulfstein and Hege Fosund Christiansen, 'The Legality of the NATO Bombing in Libya', *International & Comparative Law Quarterly* 62, no.1 (2013): 159, 162.
35. Ulfstein and Christiansen, 'The Legality of the NATO Bombing in Libya', 171.
36. Spencer Zifcak, 'The Responsibility to Protect at the United Nations', in *Rethinking International Law and Justice*, ed. Charles Sampford, Derya Aydin Okur, and Spencer Zifcak (Aldershot: Ashgate, 2015), 267–73.
37. See *Jaloud*, concurring opinion of Judge Motoc, para. 2.
38. Al-Skeini, para. 138.
39. Ibid.
40. UNGA, 'Responsibility to Protect: Timely and Decisive Response', 25 July 2012, A/66/874–S/2012/578, para. 14.
41. UNSCR 1973, 17 March 2011, S/RES/1973 (2011), para. 4.
42. In one judgment, the court appeared willing to consider that temporary effective control over an area was sufficient to establish jurisdiction, however this was not found on the facts and the approach has not been considered in other cases. See *Issa and Others* v. *Turkey* (2005) 41 EHRR 567.
43. *Loizidou* v. *Turkey* (Preliminary Objections) (1995) 20 EHRR 99.
44. *Ilaşcu and Others* v. *Moldova and Russia* (2004) 40 EHRR 46.
45. *Al-Skeini*.
46. See for instance *Al-Skeini*; *Al-Jedda* v. *United Kingdom* (2011) 53 EHRR 23 (hereinafter *Al-Jedda*); *Hussein* v. *Albania et al.* (App. No. 23276/04) 14 March 2006; *Al-Saadoon* and *Jaloud*.
47. *Sargsyan* v. *Azerbaijan* (App. No. 40167/06) 16 June 2015, para. 144.
48. The court in *Hassan* appeared willing to take the position that the UK was 'far from being in effective control of the south-eastern area which it occupied' in the earlier *Al-Skeini* case – *Hassan*, para. 75.
49. This concept was introduced by the ECtHR in the *Al-Skeini* case in 2011 and has not yet been fully articulated.
50. *Al-Skeini*, para. 135.
51. *Al-Skeini*, paras 143–50.
52. Nonetheless, the Sudanese government refused to participate in the UNSC session. UNSCR 1706, 31 August 2006, S/RES/1706 (2006), para. 1.
53. UNGA, 'Fulfilling Our Collective Responsibility: International Assistance and the Responsibility to Protect', A/68/947–S/2014/449, 11 July 2014, para. 67.
54. *Jaloud*.
55. See inter alia *Medvedyev* v. *France* (2010) 51 EHRR 39; Al-*Saadoon* and *Ocalan* v. *Turkey (Merits)* (2005) 41 EHRR 45.
56. See inter alia *Issa*, *Andreou* v. *Turkey* (App. No. 45653/99) ECtHR 27 October 2009 and *Pad* v. *Turkey* (App. No. 60167/00) ECtHR 28 June 2007.
57. Zifcak, 'The Responsibility to Protect after Libya and Syria', 69.
58. *Banković*, para. 82.
59. Ibid., para. 75.
60. James Crawford, 'Draft Articles on Responsibility of States for Internationally Wrongful Acts, With Commentaries', *Yearbook of the International Law Commission* 2 (2001): 34.
61. Samantha Besson, 'The Extraterritoriality of the European Convention on Human Rights: Why Human Rights Depend on Jurisdiction and What Jurisdiction Amounts to', *Leiden Journal of International Law* 25 (2012): 867; Michael O'Boyle, 'The European Convention on Human Rights and Extraterritorial Jurisdiction: A Comment on "Life After Bankovic"', in *Extraterritorial Application of Human Rights Treaties*, ed. Fons Coomans and Menno Kamminga (Antwerp: Intersentia, 2004), 130.
62. Crawford, 'Draft Articles', 35; Occasionally the court may be required to determine whether the acts of particular soldiers are attributable to the state first, before considering the issue of control, see Marko Milanovic and Tatjana Papic, 'As Bad As It Gets: The European Court of Human Rights's Behrami and Saramati Decision and General International Law', *International and Comparative Law Quarterly* 58 (2009): 273. The ECtHR has also failed to draw clear lines between these issues in some of its cases, see for example, Stefan Talmon, 'The Responsibility

of Outside Powers for Acts of Secessionist Entities', *International and Comparative Law Quarterly* 58 (2009): 493, 508–17.

63. Bell, 'Reassessing Multiple Attribution', 517; Aurel Sari, 'Jurisdiction and International Responsibility in Peace Support Operations: The Behrami and Saramati Cases', *Human Rights Law Review* 8 (2008): 159.

64. *Behrami*, para. 71.

65. Ibid., para. 127.

66. Ibid., para. 123.

67. Ibid., para. 134.

68. Sari, 'Jurisdiction and International Responsibility', 151; Milanovic and Papic, 'As Bad As It Gets', 267; Kjetil Mujezinovic Larsen, 'Attribution of Conduct in Peace Operations: The "Ultimate Authority and Control" Test', *European Journal of International Law* 19 (2008): 509; Alexander Breitegger, 'Sacrificing the Effectiveness of the European Convention on Human Rights on the Altar of the Effective Functioning of Peace Support Operations: A Critique of Behrami & Saramati and Al Jedda', *International Community Law Review* 11 (2009): 155.

69. Breitegger, 'Sacrificing the Effectiveness', 157. Breitegger also notes at 181 that national courts dealing with similar issues will be very slow to go against the ruling in *Behrami* unless the ECtHR expressly disavows the judgment, which in turn means that states may be able to continue to pass responsibility on to the UN.

70. Bell, 'Reassessing Multiple Attribution', 533.

71. See also *Beric and Ors* v. *Bosnia and Herzegovina* (App. No. 36357/04), 16 October 2007; Marko Milanovic, 'Al-Skeini and Al-Jedda in Strasbourg', *European Journal of International Law* 23 (2012): 134; Sari, 'Jurisdiction and International Responsibility', 159 and 167.

72. André Nollkaemper, 'Multilevel Accountability in International Law: A Case Study of the Aftermath of Srebrenica', in *The Shifting Allocation of Authority in International Law: Considering Sovereignty, Supremacy, and Subsidiarity*, ed. Yuval Shanay and Tomer Broude (Oxford: Hart Publishing 2008), 354.

73. The decisions of the Dutch courts, which have openly accepted the possibility of dual attribution of responsibility, could be influential here, prompting the court to be more open about accepting dual and multiple attribution scenarios – see André Nollkaemper, 'Dual Attribution: Liability of the Netherlands for Conduct of Dutchbat in Srebrenica', *Journal of International Criminal Justice* 9 (2011): 1143–57. These Dutch decisions have since been openly referenced by the ECtHR in the case of *Jaloud*.

74. See generally International Law Commission, *Draft Articles on the Responsibility of International Organizations, with Commentaries*, August 2011, Supplement No. 10 (A/66/10 and Add.1), Chapter 2 and Article 48(1).

75. Crawford, 'Draft Articles', Articles 6 and 47; Bell, 'Reassessing Multiple Attribution', 520–3.

76. International Law Commission, *Draft Articles on the Responsibility of International Organizations, with Commentaries*, 16.

77. *Al-Jedda*.

78. UNSC Res. 1546 (8 June 2004) UN Doc. S/RES/1546, annexed letter from Secretary of State Colin L. Powell.

79. *R. (Al-Jedda)* v. *Secretary of State for Defence* [2007] UKHL 58, para. 24.

80. *Al-Jedda*, para. 84.

81. Ibid., para. 80.

82. Sari, 'Jurisdiction and International Responsibility', 167–9; Milanovic, 'Al-Skeini and Al-Jedda', 136; Francesco Messineo, 'Things Could Only Get Better: Al-Jedda beyond Behrami', *Military Law and the Law of War Review* 50 (2011): 337–40.

83. In this regard it is interesting to note that the ECtHR cited the passages where the Dutch Supreme Court accepted the possibility of multiple attribution of conduct extensively in *Jaloud*, paras 70–4.

84. Paolo Palchetti, 'The Allocation of Responsibility for Internationally Wrongful Acts Committed in the Course of Multinational Operations', *International Review of the Red Cross* 95 (2013): 740.

85. Sari, 'Untangling Extra-territorial Jurisdiction', 11; There are also discrepancies between the ASR and ARIO as to how to test shared responsibility – Bell, 'Reassessing Multiple Attribution', 522–4.

86. Messineo, 'Things Could Only Get Better', 339–40.

87. Breitegger, 'Sacrificing the Effectiveness', 157.

State collapse, peace enforcement and the responsibility to protect in Somalia

Oscar Gakuo Mwangi

Department of Political and Administrative Studies, National University of Lesotho, Roma, Lesotho

Somalia is a collapsed state, hence the responsibility to protect has shifted to the peace enforcement African Union Mission in Somalia (AMISOM). This article examines the relationship between state collapse, peace enforcement and the responsibility to protect in Somalia. It focuses on the military component of AMISOM and argues that under conditions of state collapse, coupled with the missions' structural and operational limitations, AMISOM lacks the functional capacity to enforce peace, and extend and restore state authority in Somalia. The structural and operational weaknesses emanating from its mandate have adversely affected its concept of operations and rules of engagement, resulting in human rights violations. It is unable to effectively protect civilians in the country. AMISOM is, therefore, an impediment to the responsibility to protect in Somalia. Under state collapse, shifting the responsibility to protect to the international community can produce unintended detrimental consequences.

Introduction

Somalia is a collapsed state and has had no functional government since the end of Siad Barre's rule in 1991 despite several attempts to establish one. The responsibility to protect in Somalia has therefore shifted to the international community – the United Nations (UN)-sanctioned African Union Mission in Somalia (AMISOM). This article examines the relationship between state collapse, peace enforcement and the responsibility to protect in Somalia and demonstrates that under conditions of state collapse AMISOM is itself a hindrance to the implementation of the responsibility to protect due to its structural and operational weaknesses. The article is divided into three sections. The first section outlines the conceptual issues surrounding the responsibility to protect so as to provide a framework of analysis. The second section provides a brief and general historical background of AMISOM. The third section examines the relationship between AMISOM's structural and operational weaknesses and the responsibility to protect in Somalia.

Responsibility to protect

The central view of the responsibility to protect is that sovereignty involves responsibility. Each state has a responsibility to protect its citizens. If a state is unable or lacks the political will to carry out that function, the state rescinds its sovereignty, hence the right, and the responsibility, to fix the situation shifts to the international community. The responsibility to protect adopts a comprehensive approach to humanitarian crises that outlines intervention as ranging from diplomatic and economic sanctions through to military intervention as a last resort. Moreover, it includes 'responsibility to prevent' and 'responsibility to rebuild' as vital elements on either side of intervention.[1] The responsibility to protect requires a state to protect its population from mass atrocity crimes. The term 'atrocity crimes' refers to three legally-defined international crimes: genocide, crimes against humanity and war crimes. The term now includes ethnic cleansing. Atrocity crimes are the most serious crimes against humankind. They affect the basic human dignity of the most vulnerable persons who should be protected by states, both in times of peace and in times of war.[2]

The implementation of the responsibility to protect involves a three-pillar approach. Pillar one focuses on the protection responsibilities of the state, pillar two deals with international assistance and capacity building, while pillar three pays attention to timely and decisive response. Pillar one emphasises the continuing responsibility of the state to protect its populations from atrocity crimes, and from their incitement, the latter of which, is critical to effective and timely prevention strategies. The responsibility stems both from the nature of state sovereignty and from the previous and current legal obligations of states. Pillar two is the pledge of the international community to assist states in achieving those obligations. It seeks to solicit the cooperation of member states, regional and subregional arrangements, civil society, the private sector, and the UN system. Pillar two is critical to forging policies, procedures and practices that can be regularly applied and broadly supported. Prevention, building on pillars one and two, is a key ingredient for a successful strategy for the responsibility to protect. Pillar three focuses on the responsibility of member states to respond collectively in a timely and decisive manner when a state clearly fails to provide such protection. A decisive and timely response may involve any of the comprehensive assortment of tools available to the UN and its partners. These include appeasing measures under Chapter VI of the UN Charter, coercive measures under Chapter VII and/or collaboration with regional and sub-regional arrangements under Chapter VIII. The process of determining the best course of action must adhere to the provisions, principles and purposes of the UN Charter. According to the UN Charter, measures under Chapter VII must be authorised by the UN Security Council. All three pillars must be equipped so as to be utilised concurrently at any point, as there is no set sequence for moving from one to another.[3]

The responsibility to protect that entails military intervention to protect civilians in harm's way should be used when peaceful means have failed. Protection is the central organising aim under the responsibility to protect. In peacekeeping operations, protection is one task among others within a mission with broader goals. Peacekeepers may aim to protect civilians in harm's way, yet this is hardly the primary goal. UN peacekeeping operations to protect civilians refer to protecting civilians 'under imminent threat', 'within capabilities' and 'within areas of responsibility'.[4] Principles that must be satisfied before a military intervention takes place include: just cause; right intention; proportional means; last resort; reasonable prospects; and right authority.[5] This article pays attention to crimes against humanity as an atrocity crime. Crimes against humanity encompass acts that are part of a widespread or systematic attack directed against any civilian population.[6]

In the context of the foregoing arguments, this article examines the relationship between state collapse, peace enforcement and the responsibility to protect in Somalia. Somalia is a collapsed state, hence the responsibility to protect has been shifted, partly to the UN-mandated AMISOM. The AMISOM can be termed a peace enforcement operation. This article examines the military component of AMISOM and argues that under conditions of state collapse, AMISOM lacks the functional capacity, due to its structural and operational weakness, to enforce peace, as well as to extend and restore state authority, in Somalia. These structural and operational weaknesses, compounded by conditions of state collapse, emanate from its initial mandate that has adversely affected its strategic concept of operations (CONOPS) and rules of engagement (ROE). Its ROE have resulted in human rights violations rendering it unable to effectively protect civilians in the country. The UN-sanctioned AMISOM is, therefore, in itself an impediment to the second pillar of the strategy for the implementation of the responsibility to protect, namely international assistance and capacity building. In other words, AMISOM has adversely affected the responsibility to protect in Somalia.

AMISOM's background

AMISOM is an active, regional peacekeeping mission operated by the African Union (AU) with the approval of the UN. It was created by the AU's Peace and Security Council on 19 January 2007 with an initial six-month mandate. AMISOM replaced and incorporated the Inter-Governmental Authority on Development (IGAD) Peace Support Mission to Somalia or IGASOM. This was a proposed IGAD protection and training mission in Somalia approved by the AU in September 2006. IGASOM was also approved by the UN Security Council.[7]

The IGASOM was initially proposed for implementation in March 2005 to provide peacekeeping forces for the Somali conflict, when the Union of Islamic Courts (UIC) had not yet taken control of Mogadishu, and when most hopes for national unity lay with the Transitional Federal Government (TFG). By June 2006, however, the UIC had established control of the capital. Nonetheless, plans for IGASOM continued despite opposition from the UIC which perceived it as a United States-backed initiative meant to curb the growth of the Islamic movement. Until December 2006, the UN Security Council had imposed an arms embargo on the UIC, but the embargo was partially lifted and a mandate for IGASOM issued in December 2006.[8]

On 20 February 2007, the UN Security Council authorised the AU to deploy a peacekeeping mission with a mandate of six months, adopting resolution 1744(2007). The aim of the peacekeeping mission was to support a national reconciliation congress and the UN requested a report within 60 days on a possible UN peacekeeping mission. In October 2014, the Security Council (Resolution 2182 (2014) authorised the AU to continue its mission in Somalia until 30 November 2015. The Security Council also authorised AMISOM to take all measures, as appropriate, to carry out support for dialogue and reconciliation by assisting with free movement, safe passage and protection of all those stakeholders involved in a national reconciliation congress, including political leaders, clan leaders, religious leaders and representatives of civil society.[9]

The AMISOM comprises different components. This article pays attention to the military component. The military component is the biggest of AMISOM's components. It is mandated to conduct peace support operations in Somalia. It seeks to stabilise the situation in the country, create the enabling environment for the conduct of humanitarian activities and an eventual handover of the mission to a UN peacekeeping operation. The component also provides protection to the country's federal institutions while discharging their functions and helps secure Somalia's key infrastructure, including its airports and seaports.[10] Currently, the military component is composed of troops drawn from Uganda, Burundi,

Djibouti, Sierra Leone, Kenya and Ethiopia. These are deployed in six sectors covering south and central Somalia. Ugandan troops are deployed in Sector 1, which comprises the Banadir and Lower Shabelle regions. Kenyan forces are responsible for Sector 2, comprising Lower and Middle Jubba. Sector 3, comprising Bay and Bakool as well as Gedo (Sub Sector 3) is under Ethiopian command. Troops from Djibouti are in charge of Sector 4, which covers Hiiraan and Galgaduud. Burundian forces are in charge of Sector 5, which covers the Middle Shabelle region. Additionally, Sierra Leone forces are in charge of Sector Kismayo, covering the port city and its environs.[11] The AMISOM military component, which was first deployed in March 2007, has been instrumental in helping Somali National Security Forces (SNSF) push *Al-Shabaab* out of much of southern Somalia, including most major towns and cities.[12]

AMISOM's structural and operational weaknesses and responsibility to protect

The UN Capstone Doctrine of 2008 outlines the nature, scope and core business of UN peacekeeping operations and explains the basic principles that guide their planning and conduct.[13] According to the doctrine, multi-dimensional peacekeeping operations aim at supporting the restoration and extension of state authority so that the state can generate and provide basic political and socio-economic goods to its population. The peacekeeping operations do so by creating an enabling security environment, providing political leadership, operational support to state institutions, and coordinating the efforts of other international actors.[14] The Capstone Doctrine points out that for the military component of the peacekeeping operation, the activities of troop contributing countries (TCCs) should be guided by the tasks set out by the mission's UN-authorised mandate, CONOPS and the accompanying mission ROE.[15]

In as far as the role of peacekeeping operations in implementing the responsibility to protect is concerned, pillar two points out that prevention efforts are either structural or operational. Structural prevention, which is long-term and difficult to assess, aims to change the unstable structural conditions under state fragility or collapse to those that can facilitate the restoration and extension of state authority. Operation prevention is short-term and seeks to deter the imminent threat of an atrocity. In doing so, atrocity prevention concerns must be reconciled simultaneously with conflict prevention concerns. The deployment of peacekeeping operations under Chapter VI or of combat forces under Chapter VII of the UN Charter can be considered under the second pillar.[16] Given AMISOM's mandate and that it is a peace enforcement mission, this article lays more emphasis on operational prevention. It is in this context that this section examines the way in which AMISOM's structural, hence operational, weaknesses emanating from its mandate, CONOPS and ROE adversely affect its responsibility to protect in Somalia.

AMISOM's mandate

AMISOM's structural and operational weaknesses that impede its functional capacity are, arguably, attributed to the rationale behind its deployment, hence, and more importantly, its initial and subsequent mandates. The rationale behind its deployment was based on the lack of viable alternatives rather than the preference for an African peacekeeping operation in Somalia. Under conditions of state collapse, the prevailing complex security situation in the country coupled with the lack of a peace agreement prompted the UN Security Council to regard a UN peacekeeping operation unsuitable.[17] More importantly, however, are its structural weaknesses due to its initial mandate that consequently affected its operational capabilities, particularly its CONOPS and ROE. AMISOM lacks the financial, human and military sources needed to effectively implement its mandate due to its structural, hence operational, limitations.

AMISOM currently suffers from structural limitations due to the nature of its initial mandate, which is focused on supporting the transitional federal institutions rather than peace-building. The implication here is that AMISOM is an authorised extension of the Federal Government of Somalia (FGS) and its SNSF.[18] However, in reality, international military assistance to Somalia has paid more attention to mechanisms of building the capacity of AMISOM and its TCCs than building that of the SNSF.[19] As such, this provides the AMISOM and its TCCs the leeway to pursue their strategic interests rather than the mission's mandate, hence compromising the responsibility to protect.

The initial 2006–2007 mandate of AMISOM was aimed at conducting peace support operations in Somalia, as well as stabilising the situation in the country in order to create conditions for the conduct of humanitarian activities and an immediate takeover by the UN. Its tasks included (1) supporting dialogue and reconciliation in Somalia by working with all stakeholders; (2) providing protection to transitional federal institutions (TFIs) and key infrastructure to enable them carry out their functions; (3) assisting in the implementation of the National Security Stabilization Programme (NSSP); (4) providing technical assistance and other support to the disarmament and stabilisation efforts in the country; (5) monitoring the security situation in areas of operation; (6) facilitating humanitarian operations including repatriation of refugees and internally displaced persons (IDPs); and (7) protecting AMISOM personnel, installations and equipment, including self-defence.[20]

The current mandate tasks AMISOM to: (1) take all necessary measures, as appropriate, and in coordination with the Somalia national defence and public safety institutions, to reduce the threat posed by *Al-Shabaab* and other armed opposition groups, (2) assist in consolidating and expanding the control of the FGS over its national territory, (3) assist the FGS in establishing conditions for effective and legitimate governance across Somalia, through appropriate support in the areas of security as well as the protection of Somali institutions and key infrastructure, governance, rule of law and delivery of basic services, (4) provide, as appropriate and within its capabilities, technical and other support for the enhancement of the capacity of the Somalia state institutions, particularly the national defence, public safety and public service institutions, (5) support the FGS in establishing the required institutions and conducive conditions for the conduct of free, fair and transparent elections by 2016, in accordance with the provisional constitution, (6) liaise with humanitarian actors and facilitate, as may be required and within its capabilities, humanitarian assistance in Somalia, as well as the resettlement of IDPs and the return of refugees, (7) facilitate coordinated support by relevant AU institutions and structures towards the stabilisation and reconstruction of Somalia, and (8) provide protection to AU and UN personnel, installations and equipment, including the right of self-defence.[21]

As already noted, AMISOM TCCs have the leeway to pursue their strategic interests in Somalia at the expense of the mission's mandate. This is precisely what is happening; the Kenya Defence Forces (KDF) component of AMISOM based in Sector 2 is pursuing its strategic interests rather than the mission's mandate and compromising the responsibility to protect. The KDF has disregarded the tasks outlined in the mandate by taking a partisan role in local-level governance, abetting corruption and depriving the FGS of revenue, compromising dialogue and reconciliation efforts by exacerbating rather than mitigating clan rivalry and tensions, and interfering with the smooth implementation of Somali national security plans.[22]

A key task of AMISOM is to provide security governance so as to reduce the security threats posed by violent armed opposition groups. In particular, it is meant to take all essential measures, as suitable, and in harmonisation with the Somalia national defence and public safety institutions, to diminish the threat posed by *Al-Shabaab* and other violent armed non-state actors. The aim is to establish an enabling political and security environment for effective and legitimate governance in Somalia. The KDF component of AMISOM that is based in Sector 2 is mandated to carry out this task as part of UN resolutions. The KDF in Kismayo has, however, been accused of not coordinating particularly with the Somali National Army in reducing the threat of violent non-state armed actors, but has instead collaborated with Ras Kamboni, a violent militia group opposed to the FGS in local-level governance.[23] By empowering Ras Kamboni, as opposed to the FGS, the KDF has been partisan in its operations by obstructing the establishment of an environment conducive for effective and legitimate governance in the region and therefore compromising the peace-building and governance processes. *Al-Shabaab* has taken advantage of this compromise to be part of the local-level governance process in Somalia thereby enhancing its legitimacy at the grass-roots level.[24] Security governance processes are also adversely affected, given that AMISOM is also partisan in its approach.

AMISOM is also mandated to support the FGS in creating conditions for effective and legitimate governance across Somalia, through provision, as applicable, in the areas of security, as well as the protection of Somali institutions and key infrastructure, governance, rule of law and delivery of basic services. The KDF, as part of AMISOM, has also been accused of flouting this task. It has been alleged that KDF has not been providing the required protection to FGS officials to enable them to discharge their duties or provide security for key infrastructure.[25] The KDF has been blamed for being an impediment to the government's ability to discharge its function of managing key infrastructure, particularly the seaport and airport in Kismayo. While discharging its task as mandated, the KDF, in collaboration with Ras Kamboni militia, has been blamed for abetting corruption and in the process depriving the FGS of revenue generated from the Kismayo airport and seaport.[26]

With regard to good governance and the rule of law, AMISOM's mandated task of supporting dialogue and reconciliation in Somalia by facilitating the free movement, safe passage and protection of all individuals and groups involved in peace-making efforts is important given the often adverse nature and effects of clan politics in the country. Key political actors in the country emphasise that this task has been compromised by KDF's partisan role in the local administration of Jubaland, especially its support of the Ogaden clan. The KDF is accused of pursuing parochial interests by enhancing existing clan tensions, therefore hindering clan reconciliation efforts in Somalia.[27] The FGS has criticised the KDF for exacerbating clan rivalry and tensions in Kismayo, thus hindering efforts by its security forces to establish peace and stability in the region. Kenya's actions in Jubaland, and by association AMISOM and the Ras Kamboni militia, risk fostering detrimental Somali clan politics.[28] The Rahaweyn, Bantu, Dir and Hawiye clans who are particularly apprehensive of Kenya's attempts to enhance the dominance of the Ogaden in Jubaland purportedly shifted their allegiance to *Al-Shabaab* since the group was seen as impartial in the region's clan politics.[29] The KDF has also been accused of hindering reconciliation efforts by denying protection and safe passage for senior FGS officials to enable them to meet warring clans as part of the reconciliation process.[30]

The AMISOM is also meant to provide, within its means and as applicable, technical and other support for the development of the capacity of Somalia's state institutions, especially the national defence, public safety and public service institutions. This is meant to be achieved, in part, by facilitating the implementation of the Somali national security plans. The KDF has been adversely portrayed in its operations with regard to this facilitation. The refusal of the KDF-supported Ras Kamboni militia to integrate into official Somali security institutions is perceived by the FGS as a deliberate attempt to operate outside the limits of the national constitution, hence constituting a threat to peace and security.[31] Though the KDF is involved in the training of security personnel in the country as part of its responsibilities, the implication here is that, by not facilitating the integration of Ras Kamboni, it is partly hindering the implementation of the security plans.[32] The refusal of the KDF-supported Ras Kamboni militia to integrate into official Somali security institutions deprives the Somali National Army (SNA) of human resources, in particular, the military personnel required for it to perform its duties effectively.

AMISOM is also required to create conducive conditions to allow UN personnel to carry out functions mandated by the UN Security Council. The UN points out that the KDF has been unwilling to perform this task in Kismayo. The UN emphasises that its Monitoring Group on Somalia has been unable to carry out its work in Kismayo effectively partly due to the lack of cooperation from the KDF. The UN Monitoring Group indicates that the KDF, to some degree, has been unwilling to clarify its operational status and allegiance within AMISOM and that as of February 2012, the operational presence was more theoretical than practical.[33] The KDF is a major actor in the political economy of Jubaland that has significantly impacted the capacity of the FGS to enhance state autonomy and effectively perform its basic functions. The KDF's operations have opened up opportunities for corruption, which has deprived the FGS of the financial resources and military personnel required to extend and restore state authority.

AMISOM's strategic concept of operations

AMISON'S CONOPS has also to a large extent been adversely affected by its structural and operational limitations. The original AMISON's CONOPS was revised and endorsed in 2012. Given the prevailing hostile political and security situation in Somalia, AU and UN planners jointly developed a strategic concept for future AMISOM operations in the country. The concept aimed at combining all ongoing separate military operations in Somalia into a coordinated and coherent effort against *Al-Shabaab* so as to extend the authority of the TFG beyond Mogadishu and to create an enabling environment for the effective implementation of AMISOM's mandate. The AU Peace and Security Council endorsed the strategic concept on 5 January 2012.[34] The revised CONOPS provided for three phases. Phase I was to be devoted to the reinforcement of AMISOM troops to the UN-approved strength to meet threats in Mogadishu and its environs as well as create an enabling environment for political dialogue and reconciliation. Phase II entailed the expansion of AMISOM's operations beyond Mogadishu into south and central Somalia. Phase III aimed to create enabling conditions for the deployment of a UN peacekeeping operation to take over from AMISOM and, in the long-term, enhance reconstruction and stabilisation efforts in Somalia. The revised CONOPS was premised on the availability of a number of military capabilities such as air and maritime capabilities and other force enablers.[35]

The AMISOM original and revised CONOPS have, however, been adversely hindered by the mission's lack of adequate financial, human and military resources, thereby rendering it ineffective in its mandated operations. AMISOM is financially supported by the UN, the European Union (EU), as well as bilateral partners. These financial contributions, however, only cover specified areas and periods. Funding for AMISOM, therefore, remains unpredictable and unreliable. Though AMISOM's military component has had considerable operational success, with current force strength, but without critical multipliers and enablers such as a guard force and air assets, it is constrained in its functional capacity to expand its area of operations. AMISOM does not have the operational capacity to recover and extend state authority until such a time that the SNSF has developed the necessary capacity to take over responsibility for the security of the recovered areas. Multipliers and enablers are therefore necessary for AMISOM to complete its mandate, particularly for targeting *Al-Shabaab*'s strategic resources, provide air cover for supply convoys, and help it reach areas where it currently has little or no presence.[36] As of October 2014, the strength of AMISOM's uniformed personnel deployed across the six sectors stood at 22,056 out of an authorised strength of 22,126. The difference arises from rotations of the various contingents. Field troops comprised 6,220 Ugandan soldiers; 5,338 Burundian soldiers; 4,395 Ethiopian soldiers; 3,664 Kenyan soldiers; 1,000 Djiboutian soldiers; 850 Sierra Leone soldiers, There are also 75 staff officers in the force headquarters.[37]

As a peace enforcement operation, AMISOM's stability operations involve the use of force, especially when dealing with *Al-Shabaab*. Under conditions of state collapse, stability operations can be described as counterinsurgency operations. However, for stability operations, as an integral component for counterinsurgency to be successful, this means building credibility in the early stages of the operation. This requires the conducting of meticulous planning before any military incursion begins.[38] A number of indicators suggest that in the early stages AMISOM neither planned nor implemented an effective counterinsurgency strategy. It does not appear to have a long-term counterinsurgency strategy.[39] The lack of an effective counterinsurgency strategy by AMISOM is evident whereby few of its troops actually employ counterinsurgency tactics after having displaced *Al-Shabaab* from its strongholds. This reduces the chances of such measures achieving their intended longer-term outcomes of peace-building and enhancing good governance.[40] AMISOM also appears not to have conceptualised what it considers a victory, indicating that it did not engage in critical long-range planning that would include an exit strategy.[41] According to the UN Capstone Doctrine, the success of a peacekeeping mission in achieving its mandate is determined to a large extent by its entry and subsequent exit strategies. The doctrine points out that experience indicates that 'a domestic peace is truly sustainable when the warring parties are able to move their struggles from the battlefield and into an institutional framework where disputes can be settled peacefully'.[42] *Al-Shabaab* is institutionalised, making it difficult to defeat it militarily or psychologically as it penetrates all spheres of socio-political and economic life.[43] Hence AMISOM requires an effective counterinsurgency strategy that will prevent *Al-Shabaab* waging a successful asymmetrical campaign which is devastating for the population psychologically and physically as well as detrimental to peace-building and governance processes.[44]

AMISOM's rules of engagement

An integral element of the normative framework for UN peacekeeping operations is international human rights law. Peacekeeping operations should be conducted in respect of human rights as outlined in the UN Declaration for Human Rights, and meaningfully advance human rights through the implementation of their missions' mandates. Peacekeeping personnel are not supposed to be perpetrators of human rights abuses and when they are, they should be held accountable. In particular, international humanitarian law (IHL), also known as 'the law of war' or 'the law of armed conflict', as contained in the Geneva and other protocols, constrains the methods of armed conflicts, and is designed to protect non-participants in hostilities. It maintains the fundamental rights of civilians, victims and non-combatants in an armed conflict. UN peacekeepers must fully understand the tenets of IHL and apply them positively in conflict and post-conflict situations. The UN Secretary-General's Bulletin on the Observance by UN Forces of International Humanitarian Law of 6 August 1999 outlines the fundamental principles and rules of international law that apply to UN peacekeepers.[45]

The Capstone Doctrine outlines the importance of a peacekeeping operation's ROE. It points out that the mission-wide ROE for the military component of a UN peacekeeping operation clarifies the different levels of force that can be used in various circumstances, how each level of force should be used, and any authorisations that must be obtained by commanders. In the conflict and post-conflict environments in which contemporary peace-keeping operations are often deployed, these ROE should be adequately robust to ensure that a peacekeeping operation retains its credibility and autonomy to implement its mandate. The mission leadership should ensure that these ROE are fully comprehended by all relevant personnel in the mission and are applied uniformly.[46] AMISOM's ROE have, however, been adversely affected due to the mission's structural and operational limit-ations, thereby compromising it fulfilling its tasks regarding the responsibility to protect. AMISOM has committed human rights violations, in particular by inflicting harm and death on civilians as well as its soldiers engaging in sexual exploitation and abuse women and girls in Somalia.[47]

AMISOM's ROE are key to ensuring that military operations are conducted in compli-ance with IHL obligations in Somali's socio-political context. Though the ROE were revised in 2012 to ensure that they are in conformity with the operational realities of the mission, AMISOM continues to operate in extremely volatile conditions created by state collapse, whereby *Al-Shabaab*'s asymmetrical warfare targets civilians within populated areas. This includes *Al-Shabaab* bombarding areas populated by civilians, the use of impro-vised explosive devices, the use of civilians as human shields, and masquerading as civi-lians when conducting attacks against AMISOM and the Somali authorities. This prevalent situation makes it extremely difficult for AMISOM to ensure civilian protection in the conduct of its operations and to apply the mission's ROE in a consistent manner at all times.[48]

Ensuring the protection of civilians while applying its ROE is a key challenge facing AMISOM. The protection of civilians has created a fundamental dilemma for AMISOM. AMISOM's mandate was to protect very important persons involved in the political recon-ciliation process, fight off *Al-Shabaab* and other violent armed non-state actors, and provide basic services and humanitarian assistance to significant numbers of Mogadishu's suffering civilians in the absence of humanitarian actors on the ground. AMISOM personnel, on the other hand, have been portrayed as supporting the ruthless occupying Ethiopian National Defense Force in Mogadishu.[49] AMISOM's military operations have harmed civilians both directly through their indiscriminate fire policies and targeting of civilians and indirectly through failing to protect others from *Al-Shabaab* attacks.[50] These problems have been aggravated by several factors: (1) AMISOM's delayed adoption of an explicit protection-of-civilians mandate in May 2013; (2) the immense difficulty of accurately ver-ifying the nature and perpetrators of civilian harm under conditions of state collapse; (3) *Al-Shabaab's* adoption of asymmetrical warfare tactics deliberately designed to increase the harm to civilians; and (4) repeated allegations that AMISOM had violated IHL and was unable to protect civilians.[51] The Somali populace has not mainly judged AMISOM on the number of *Al-Shabaab* fighters it has killed but on whether it implemented its mandate while minimising civilian casualties. Though the exact figures are impossible to generate, large numbers of civilians have been killed or injured as a direct result of

AMISOM's deployment.[52] AMISOM has stated that the ROE it employs are designed to minimise harm to civilians but civilians continue to report incidences of harm to civilians. Many cases of indiscriminate and disproportionate shelling by AMISOM have been documented by HRW. AMISOM has admitted responsibility for a limited number of unlawful attacks on civilians and responsibility for civilian deaths. Though AMISOM operates under conditions of state collapse, *Al-Shabaab*'s asymmetrical tactics do not relieve AMISOM from its obligation under the IHL to prevent indiscriminate attacks that cause disproportionate civilian casualties and loss of property.[53]

Despite causing harm to civilians, and being aware of its obligations under IHL, and relevant AU policies and guidelines, AMISOM continues to make considerable efforts to ensure that its operations are conducted in compliance with IHL notwithstanding conditions of state collapse. These efforts include directing all its sector commanders to follow strictly the UN Secretary-General's Human Rights Due Diligence Policy (HRDDP) in the conduct of its operations and making recommendations on further measures to ensure better compliance with the HRDDP.[54] Others include the establishment of a Civilian Casualty Tracking Analysis and Response Cell (CCTARC) that was approved by the UN Security Council in resolution 2036 (February 2012).[55] A mission-wide protection of civilians strategy for AMISOM was approved, as indicated earlier in the article, in May 2012. The strategy provides a comprehensive mission-wide approach towards mainstreaming protection considerations in all aspects of AMISOM.[56] As a core component of its protection strategy, AMISOM began moving towards the establishment of a CCTARC as outlined in various Security Council resolutions. A framework for the establishment of a robust mechanism in AMISOM was developed that focusses on three key functions of the cell: (1) assessing civilian harm occurring within AMISOM areas of responsibility; (2) assisting with operational effectiveness and prevention of civilian harm by informing force decision-making; and (3) responding to any harm caused.[57] The CCTARC, which has begun its operations, is augmented by the development of a civilian casualty matrix.[58]

AMISOM troops have also been accused of violating human rights in Somalia by committing sexual and gender-based violence against Somali women and girls, particularly the displaced.[59] Some AMISOM soldiers, deployed to Somalia since 2007 to help restore stability in Mogadishu, have abused their positions of power to prey on the city's most vulnerable women and girls. The soldiers have committed acts of rape and other forms of sexual abuse, as well as sexual exploitation. Sexual exploitation involves the abuse of a position of vulnerability, differential power, or trust, for sexual purposes. The UN Secretary-General's 2003 Bulletin on Special Measures for Protection from Sexual Exploitation and Sexual Abuse is a policy document that augments a variety of policy statements on sexual exploitation and abuse in UN peacekeeping missions. It clearly prohibits peacekeepers from exchanging any money, goods or services for sex. Its definition of exploitation includes situations where women and girls are vulnerable and a differential power relationship exists. This definition means that whether a woman has consented to engage in sex for money is irrelevant in the peacekeeping context. The AU Commission's Reviewed Code of Conduct (AUC Code of Conduct), with which AMISOM TCCs must comply, prohibits sexual exploitation and abuse. As in international peacekeeping operations, all AMISOM personnel, including locally recruited Somalis, are immune from local legal processes in the country of deployment for any criminal acts they commit while deployed. The TCCs have exclusive jurisdiction over their personnel for any criminal offenses they commit. They are, however, bound both by memorandums of understanding signed with the AU prior to deployment and by their international human rights and humanitarian obligations to investigate and prosecute serious allegations of misconduct and crimes.[60]

In order to deal with sexual exploitation and abuses which are grave violations of human rights, AMISOM TCCs, to varying degrees, have established procedures to deal with their forces' misconduct. These include forces receiving pre-deployment trainings on the AUC Code of Conduct, and deploying legal advisors and military investigators to Somalia to follow up on allegations of misconduct. AMISOM initially denied allegations of sexual abuse, but its leadership has started to take some measures to tackle the problem. In particular, AMISOM developed a draft policy on prevention and response to sexual exploitation and abuse (PSEA policy) in 2013. It has also begun to put in place structures to follow up on sexual exploitation and abuse.[61]

Conclusion

AMISOM is itself to some extent an impediment to the implementation of the responsibility to protect, especially under pillar two which focuses on international assistance and capacity building. Given the political context within which it operates under conditions of state collapse, and due to its structural and operational limitations, AMISOM has been less than effective in adequately protecting civilians. In fact, AMISOM has, in addition, also committed certain human rights violations. Instead of preventing atrocity crimes, AMISOM is by both political default and due to its design, too often part and parcel of the problem of harm coming to civilians. Implementing pillar one as a strategy for the implementation of the responsibility to protect in Somalia is not apt since it is a collapsed state, nor is it appropriate to place too much emphasis on the third pillar that deals with a timely and decisive response since AMISOM's deployment in the country was done rather belatedly. This demonstrates that under conditions of state collapse, where there is no functional government or state authority, shifting the responsibility to protect to the international community can produce unintended detrimental consequences.

There is a critical need for proper oversight of AMISOM peace operations by the AU and for addressing the structural weaknesses of AMISOM to ensure its compliance with protecting the fundamental rights of civilians, victims and non-combatants in violent conflict. In addition, the use of civil society organisations is a critical component of peace initiatives. Civil society organisations in Somalia, particularly community and faith-based organisations, can play a crucial role with regard to the responsibility to protect. Such organisations can coordinate with fundamental Somali socio-political structures such as clans and clan leaders that have the capacity to use informal process-oriented means not only to protect civilians from harm, but also to play a key role in providing local-level security governance and in peacebuilding efforts. Hence the responsibility to protect will become socially acceptable and legitimate at the local level and gradually at the national level.

Disclosure statement

No potential conflict of interest was reported by the author.

Notes

1. Rebbeca J. Hamilton, 'The Responsibility to Protect: From Document to Doctrine – But What of Implementation?', *Harvard Human Rights Journal* 19 (2006): 289–90.
2. UN, *Framework of Analysis for Atrocity Crimes: A Tool for Prevention* (New York: United Nations, 2014), 1.
3. UN, Implementing the Responsibility to Protect, General Assembly, 12 January 2009, A/63/677, 8–9.
4. Victoria Holt, 'The Military and Civilian Protection: Developing Roles and Capabilities', Humanitarian Policy Group (HPG) Research Briefing, No. 22, March 2006, 1–2.
5. Hamilton, 'The Responsibility to Protect', 290–1.
6. UN, *Framework of Analysis for Atrocity Crimes*, 1.
7. AMISOM, 'AMISOM Background', 2015, http://amisom-au.org/amisom-backround.
8. Ibid.
9. Ibid.
10. AMISOM, 'AMISOM Military Component', 2015, http://amisom-au.org/mission-profile/military-component.
11. Ibid.
12. Ibid.
13. UN, *United Nations Peacekeeping Operations: Principles and Guidelines* (New York: United Nations, 2008), 8–9.
14. Ibid., 27–35.
15. Ibid., 14.
16. UN, 'The Role of Regional and Sub-regional Arrangements in Implementing the Responsibility to Protect', Report of the Secretary-General, General Assembly, 27 June 2011, A/65/877-S/2011/393, 7–9.
17. Cecilia Hill Wiklund, 'AMISOM – A Model for a Peace Operation in Mali, Peace Operations Project and Security in African Security', March 2013, FOI Swedish Defence Research Agency, Memo 4393, 2.
18. Andrews Atta-Asamoah and Neus Ramis Segui, 'Somalia: fighting the Odds in the Search for Peace after the Transition', Institute for Security Studies (ISS) Situation Report, March 2014, 5–6.
19. Paul D. Williams, 'AMISOM in Transition: The Future of the Africa Union Mission in Somalia', Rift Valley Institute (RVI) Briefing Paper, 13 February 2013, 5.
20. AMISOM, 'AMISOM Mandate', 2015, http://amisom-au.org/amisom-mandate.
21. Ibid.
22. United Nations Security Council (UNSC), Report of the Monitoring Group on Somalia and Eritrea Pursuant to Security Council Resolution 2060 (2012), 12 July 2013, S/2013/413, 120.
23. International Crisis Group (ICG), 'Somalia: Al-Shabaab – It Will Be a Long War', Policy Briefing, Africa Briefing No. 99, Nairobi/Brussels, 26 June 2014, 3.
24. Ibid., 3.
25. UNSC, Report of the Monitoring Group on Somalia and Eritrea, 120.
26. Ibid., 120.
27. Graham Turbiville, Josh Meservey, and James Forest, *Countering the al-Shabaab Insurgency in Somalia: Lessons for U.S Special Operations Forces, JSOU Report 14–1, February 2014* (Tampa Point Boulevard: JSOU, 2014), 80.
28. Ibid., 80.
29. Ibid., 80.
30. UNSC, Report of the Monitoring Group on Somalia and Eritrea, 3–4.

31. Federal Government of Somalia and Interim Jubba Administration (FGS/IJA), Agreement Between the Federal Government of Somalia and Jubba Delegation, 27 August 2013, Addis Ababa, Ethiopia, 3–4; UNSC, Report of the Monitoring Group on Somalia and Eritrea, 120.
32. UNSC, Report of the Monitoring Group on Somalia and Eritrea, 120.
33. FGS/IJA, Agreement Between the Federal Government of Somalia and Jubba Delegation, 3–4; UNSC, Report of the Monitoring Group on Somalia and Eritrea, 120.
34. UN, Special Report of the Secretary-General on Somalia, Security Council, 31 January 2012, S/2012/74, 3–5.
35. AU, Report of the Chairperson of the Commission on the Situation in Somalia, Peace and Security Council 293rd Meeting, Addis Ababa, Ethiopia, 13 September 2011, PSC/PR/2 (CCXCIII), 11–13.
36. AU, Report of the African Union Commission on the Strategic Review of the African Union Mission in Somalia (AMISOM), Peace and Security Council 356th Meeting, Addis Ababa, Ethiopia, 27 February 2013, PSC/PR/2 (CCCLVI), 4–11.
37. AU, Report of the Chairperson of the Commission on the Situation in Somalia, Peace and Security Council 462nd Meeting, Addis Ababa, Ethiopia, 16 October 2014, PSC/PR/2 (CDLXIII) 4.
38. Heather S. Gregg, 'Beyond Population Engagement: Understanding Counterinsurgency', *Parameters*, Autumn (2009): 19–20.
39. Graham Turbiville and James Forest, 'Al-Shabaab', Joint Special Operations University (JSOU) Report 14-1, December 2013 (Tampa Point Boulevard: JSOU), 66.
40. Ibid., 66–9.
41. Ibid., 66.
42. UN, *United Nations Peacekeeping Operations*, 87.
43. ICG, 'Somalia: Al-Shabaab – It Will Be a Long War', 12.
44. Matt Bryden, 'The Reinvention of Al-Shabaab: A Strategy of Choice or Necessity?', A Report of the CSIS Africa Program, February 2014 (Washington, DC: Center for Strategic & International Studies, 2014), 2.
45. UN, *United Nations Peacekeeping Operations*, 15.
46. Ibid., 35.
47. Human Rights Watch (HRW), *'You Don't Know Who to Blame': War Crimes in Somalia* (New York: Human Rights Watch, 2011), 16–17; HRW, *'The Power These Men Have Over US': Sexual Exploitation and Abuse by African Union Forces in Somalia* (New York: Human Rights Watch, 2014), 1–4.
48. AU, Report of the Workshop on Mainstreaming Protection of Civilian Considerations into the Operations of the African Union Mission in Somalia (AMISOM), Nairobi, Kenya, 21–22 June 2012, 10–11.
49. Paul D. Williams, 'The African Union Mission in Somalia and Civilian Protection Challenges', *Stability: International Journal of Security & Development* 2, no. 2 (2013): 2–3.
50. HRW, *'You Don't Know Who to Blame'*, 16–17.
51. Williams, 'The African Union Mission in Somalia', 2–3.
52. Ibid., 8.
53. HRW, *'You Don't Know Who to Blame'*, 16–17; HRW, *Hostages of the Gatekeeper: Abuses against the Internally Displaced in Mogadishu, Somalia* (New York: Human Rights Watch, 2013), 15.
54. AU, Report of the Chairperson of the Commission on the Situation in Somalia, 8.
55. Ibid., 4.
56. UN, Report of the Chairperson of the African Union Commission on the Implementation of the Mandate of the African Union Mission in Somalia, submitted pursuant to paragraph 8 of Security Council resolution 2093 (2013), Annex, 24 June 2013, S/2013/371, 3.
57. Ibid., 13–14.
58. AU, Report of the Chairperson of the Commission on the Situation in Somalia, 8.
59. HRW, *'The Power These Men Have Over US'*, 1.
60. Ibid., 1–4.
61. Ibid., 4.

Government failure, atrocity crimes and the role of the International Criminal Court: why not Syria, but Libya

Hovhannes Nikoghosyan

American University of Armenia, Yerevan, Armenia

The Chapter VII resolutions on Libya by the United Nations Security Council (2011) and the UNSC-approved French-led intervention in Mali (2013) and the absence of a consensus on Syria ever since the popular uprising have reminded us of the 'why-not-Rwanda-but-Kosovo' type of a challenge used to identify the objective determinants for the trans-boundary use of force to stop mass atrocity crimes. I adopt a legalistic approach in finding ways to pursue consensus on R2P Pillar Three operations; and through the available state practice and body of international law in general, I illustrate the normative progress to argue that a sound foundation has emerged to suggest that genocide, crimes against humanity, war crimes and ethnic cleansings are of *erga omnes* character wherever they happen; whereas the International Criminal Court has been emerging as a capable and legitimate institution for bringing the most odious perpetrators to justice and providing legal background for the use of force against 'manifestly failed' governments.

The doctrine of the 'responsibility to protect', or R2P, authored by the International Commission on Intervention and State Sovereignty (ICISS) in 2001,[1] proposed 'a reorientation of the international debate'[2] and resulted in *reconsideration* of the existing framework of international law and politics applicable to the prevention, punishment and prosecution for internationally wrongful, *erga omnes* crimes, such as genocide, crimes against humanity, war crimes and ethnic cleansing (hereinafter – 'R2P crimes').[3] Indeed, the R2P did not emerge as a binding legal norm (and it never may become),[4] but a *'political concept*, albeit based on well-established legal principles and norms' (emphasis added).[5] The R2P doctrine has been acknowledged by the heads of states in the 2005 UN World Summit Outcome Document, giving important political weight to it, whereas the UNSC unanimously confirmed it in Res. 1674 (2006). The United Nations General Assembly (UNGA) yet again evaluated the doctrine in resolution 63/308 in 2009, by consensus.[6] The language of the concept,[7] with or without quoting Res. 1674 (2006), has been reaffirmed in relevant resolutions on intra-state conflicts ever since, such as UNSC Res. 1706 (2006) on Darfur/Sudan, Res. 1807 (2008) on Democratic Republic of Congo (DRC), Res. 1970 and 1973 (2011) on Libya, Res. 1975 (2011) on post-election violence in Ivory Coast, Res. 2014 (2011) on civilian unrests in Yemen, Res. 2085 (2012) on Mali, etc.

Paragraphs 138–9 of the 2005 UN Outcome Document fell short of recognising any common patterns of individual governments' 'manifest failure' to protect their populations from four types of international crimes, and maintained that the UNSC will tackle those violations on a *case-by-case basis* and in cooperation with relevant regional organizations *as appropriate*' (emphasis added). Paragraph 139 of the document only declared that the international community shall be prepared ' … to take collective action, in a timely and decisive manner, through the Security Council [when] national authorities are *manifestly failing to protect their populations* from genocide, war crimes, ethnic cleansing and crimes against humanity' (emphasis added). Altogether, this led to two acknowledgements: (1) any common pattern to serve as an indicia of 'manifest failure' of a government, notwithstanding such calamities as in Rwanda, Srebrenica and DRC, has not been acknowledged; and (2) states will continue to act selectively, case by case.[8]

In order to prevent open-ended abuse by usual power politics the R2P concept embraced certain precautionary principles – the *manifest failure* of the incumbent regime through 'unable or unwilling' test. This was endorsed by the ICISS report and later packed by the UN Secretary-General into the three-pillar-approach.[9] This *cascade* of triggering factors has been equally recognised by the applicable UNSC practice and the International Criminal Court (ICC) on various occasions. However, the lack of established international consensus on the matter, due to often mutually exclusive national interests of the great powers, did not amend the selective approach of the international community in identical situations such as Libya and Syria. This was once again evidenced in the UNSC open debate in February 2013, when member states voiced diverging opinions about the role and capacities of the incumbent Syrian regime in unleashing atrocity crimes against its civilian population.[10] Nevertheless, the R2P concept was once more confirmed in the UNSC Presidential Statement in February 2013 to ensure it remains the appropriate 'reading-rule' for the international community to prevent and/or stop mass-atrocity crimes wherever they happen.[11]

This article outlines the frameworks of 'manifest failure' of local government in atrocity prevention and protection of civilian populations – in times of peace and war – in order to arrive at generic conclusions of thresholds that may create R2P obligations for the international community as a whole. This author does not intend to get back to the discussions of the 1990s about the 'right cases' in which to intervene,[12] even though until now some scholars have continued seeking the threshold of last resort consistent with the 'just war tradition'.[13] Rather what is discussed is the issue of 'sufficient gravity' and local government failure as legitimate warrants for lawful international engagement under the R2P doctrine, including with coercive measures, where the UNSC shall exercise its obligations of the maintenance of international peace and security. To that end, it will be argued that there are *erga omnes* obligations of states established by a framework of treaties of international humanitarian and human rights law which generally outlines the internationally recognised human rights standards, while the ICC's Rome Statute elaborates on what exceeds the universally recognised patterns of behaviour and what should be punished criminally. It is useful to recall that the statutes of the International Criminal Tribunal for the Former Yugoslavia (ICTY) and the International Criminal Tribunal for Rwanda (ICTR) also embraced the same crimes as listed in ICC Rome Statute Art. 5, which shows that there is *opinio juris* on the need for prosecution for those heinous crimes in the UNSC and beyond it. In sum, this study is built on the normative observation that R2P rests on *erga omnes* obligations of states to protect populations from genocide and other mass atrocity crimes, and guarantee universal criminal prosecution of responsible individuals for its failures[14];

whereas the appropriate and legitimate chamber for the prosecution is the ICC, which still needs to expand its territorial jurisdiction.

Erga omnes crimes and R2P obligations of states

The idea of universal jurisdiction for certain types of crimes – initially only slavery, piracy and the like – appeared when states decided to prosecute and punish those offences in *terra nullius,* 'where no State could exercise territorial jurisdiction'.[15] The ICJ confirmed this approach in the *Barcelona Traction* ruling.[16]

The UN Secretary-General has elaborated in the 'Implementing the Responsibility to Protect' report (2009) that ' ... only four specified crimes and violations: genocide, war crimes, ethnic cleansing and crimes against humanity'[17] shall be the crimes to trigger R2P obligations.[18] Apart from the crime of ethnic cleansing (the initial term 'pogrom' – from the Russian 'devastation' – emerged in 1988–1990 for the state policies against Armenians in Soviet Azerbaijan[19] and was then coined as 'ethnic cleansing' during the conflict in Bosnia in the 1990s) these are the same crimes for international prosecution under the mandate of the ICC, which stands in The Hague.[20] The Rome Statute of the ICC is very clear and detailed in Articles 5–8, as well as in the section Elements of Crimes, detailing the descriptions of crimes it would prosecute.

Often called a 'theoretical forerunner' to R2P,[21] the Inter-American Court of Human Rights ruled in the *Velásquez Rodríguez* case (1988) that even if a state does not commit the violation of international human rights in question through its agents or organs, it has a duty of *'due diligence to prevent the violation or to respond to it'*, otherwise '[it] can lead to *international* responsibility of the State' (emphasis added).[22] Under the R2P doctrine and the existing international order and the law, whenever an intra-state conflict erupts, its government is the first to react on it as a matter 'essentially within the domestic jurisdiction of any state' (Art. 2(4) of the UN Charter), and employ all *lawful* measures to crack down on the systematic violation to civilian peace, employing its inherent right of monopoly on legitimate use of force, set forward in its constitution and applicable laws, in conformity with the international law. Having the exclusive legitimacy of lawful use of force (Weberian approach), governments hold this obligation not only before their own people, but also before the international community as a whole, given that those universal values of humankind are enshrined in different instruments of international law in the form of multilateral treaties.[23] International law has established individual criminal prosecution for those violators, and therefore the two-way traffic between the implementation of the R2P doctrine and the operation of the ICC is crucial to maintain, as the court furthers the experience of Nuremberg, Tokyo and other ad hoc tribunals, enabling individual criminal prosecution for the most egregious crimes against humankind – and it is important to underline – both in times of peace and war. As the ICTY Appeals Chamber ruled in the *Tadic* case, ' ... it is by now a settled rule of customary international law that crimes against humanity do not require a connection to international armed conflict. Indeed, as the prosecutor points out, customary international law may not require a connection between crimes against humanity and any conflict at all'.[24] With a view to the unfolding crisis in Syria, it is to be acknowledged that the lawfulness of all measures, e.g. the Syrian incumbent government's fight against rebels, is dependent upon the domestic laws of the state concerned (rebellions, uprisings or mass protests are governed by the domestic laws and constitution)[25] unless the gravity of the crisis reaches an international dimension involving crimes listed in ICC Rome Statute Arts 5–8, which shall then trigger the international obligations of a state as party to the international treaties it had *voluntarily* acceded to (*Lotus* case).[26]

There are two mutually reinforcing avenues that local governments shall equally follow: first, to bring the *erga omnes* human rights violations to a speedy end, and second, to re-establish the peace and rule of law by bringing the alleged perpetrators to justice. In the frameworks of the R2P concept, the governments shall either pursue these goals themselves, or shall seek international cooperation to this end (Pillars One and Two). Should the local government disregard either of these, the international community shall act on meeting its own obligations for civilian protection and prevention of atrocity crimes, as established by relevant rulings of international courts (Pillar Three).

In this regard, it is very relevant to investigate the applicability of the 1948 Genocide Convention Art. 1 with reference to the ICJ landmark *Bosnia v. Serbia* (2007) decision, where the court outlined certain responsibilities of the international community of states. The ICJ concluded that even though Serbia or its agents did not commit genocide in Bosnia (para. 471(2, 3)), it 'violated the obligation to prevent genocide'[27] (para. 471(5)), thus broadening the scope of Genocide Convention Art. 1, and extending the obligation of genocide prevention to *inter-state* relations, rather than leaving it solely in the intra-state domain as a unique responsibility of a local government.[28]

The international obligation of governments to prosecute *erga omnes* crimes was once again recognised by the ICJ in *Belgium v. Senegal* (July 2012) regarding the 'obligation to prosecute or extradite' ex-President of Chad Hissène Habré, 'accused of thousands of political killings and systematic torture during his presidency',[29] who had enjoyed political asylum and de facto immunity in Senegal for 22 years.[30] The ICJ unanimously held that Senegal ' ... must, without further delay, submit the case of Mr. Hissène Habré to its competent authorities for the purpose of prosecution, if it does not extradite him [to Belgium]',[31] thus confirming the obligation of state parties to the Convention against Torture 'to take effective measures to prevent torture and hold accountable those who engage in torture'.[32]

In the follow up developments, Senegal amended its constitution to provide for an exception to the principle of non-retroactivity of its criminal laws and provided that absence of references to *erga omnes* crimes in national legislation ' ... shall not prejudice the prosecution, trial and punishment of any person for any act or omission which, at the time when it was committed, was defined as criminal *under the rules of international law* concerning acts of genocide, crimes against humanity and war crimes[33] (para. 31) (emphasis added). In early February 2013, the Senegalese authorities inaugurated a special court to handle the case.[34]

However, the most important contribution of the ICJ ruling in this case was the confirmation that breaches to peremptory norms of international law[35] are of *erga omnes* character, that is, against the fundamental interests of the international community as a whole, and therefore states shall prosecute those crimes regardless of where they were committed and the claimed immunities of the people accused. Translated into the R2P concept, the failure of the national justice system, in this case the Senegalese, may become another avenue to prove that local government is 'unwilling or unable genuinely to carry out the investigation or prosecution' (Rome Statute Art. 17), and in those cases an ICC or other alien court referral (or extradition of the suspect) shall become one of the tools at the hands of the international community to fight impunity for *erga omnes* crimes.

Thus, what the R2P doctrine truly established is that after a certain gravity of violence has been reached in the face of local government failure to restore law and order, amounting to any of the R2P crimes, the matter would cease remaining merely under the sovereignty of the given state – due to the violence and human rights violations becoming a threat to international peace and security.

Assembling the facts on the ground

In order to establish manifest breaches to the *erga omnes* obligations of governments in respect to human rights, the international practice has so far suggested several avenues: media or human rights watchdog reports from the ground – as supporting materials, as well as UN (including UN Human Rights Council (HRC)) or regional arrangements' fact-finding mission reports dispatched to the region concerned.[36] Without depreciating the huge service done by the media,[37] human rights and other advocacy groups may some-times, to an extent, present somewhat biased information impacted by their aims and mission. Though those reports are essential in raising public awareness,[38] governments and courts refer to those dispatches quite rarely. Therefore, the most credible sources of information remain the accounts collected by observer and fact-finding missions dispatched by the UN or other regional arrangements and organisations, put forward at UNSC debates. As such, for example, the affirmative stance towards enforcement action held by the Arab League and the African Union (AU) appeared to be a major factor to secure the concurring votes of Russia and China in UNSC Res. 1973.

So, what then should the fact-finding missions pay attention to?

First and foremost, although the Genocide Convention of 1948, for instance, may consider the killing of even one member of a protected/identifiable group as genocide, there are other important contextual aspects, such as: the criminal (a person acting on his own behalf, or on behalf of the government) shall have intent to destroy the group in whole or in part (ICTY, *Prosecutor* v. *Jelisic*),[39] though a plan is not a required element of the crime of genocide, but a 'state policy' is, as Schabas argued.[40] Other authors[41] and, most notably, the Judge Hans-Peter Kaul challenged[42] the view of the ICC Pre-Trial Chamber II that an *organis-ation* different from the central government may commit crimes against humanity, thus sup-porting the previously available experience and practice of prescribing the commission of Rome Statute Art. 7 crimes to governments and affiliated agents only, as, for example, the ICTY held in its proceedings. Nevertheless, when referring to the 'state policy', Pre-Trial Chamber III concluded in the *Côte d'Ivoire situation*, that crimes against humanity shall not necessarily be conceived 'at the highest level of the State machinery, [but] a policy adopted by regional or even local organs of the State could satisfy the requirement of a State policy'[43] (para. 45). The most important contextual parameter of the crimes against human-ity henceforth remains the *adopted policy* at a level that enables its execution in a systematic and/or widespread manner. Thus, unless there are facts that indicate the target state's gov-ernment or any other organised group (with or without central government's consent and order) conspires, incites or actually starts or is prepared to start massive killings of civilians, there shall be no sufficient grounds to claim that the gravity of acts reach to the level of *erga omnes*, that is, crimes against the international community as a whole. To give rise to an R2P situation requiring an urgent prevention measure, from the legal point of view, ICC Pre-Trial Chamber II adopted the approach of looking at the 'situation as a whole' in author-ising the prosecutor's application to investigate the 'Kenya situation' against possible charges of crimes against humanity.[44] After all, in many cases the ICC Pre-Trial Chambers have followed 'the lowest evidential standard' pursuant to Article 53(l)(a) of the Statute, that is, on the grounds of 'reasonable basis to believe', in authorising the investigations of alleged crimes.[45]

The public statements and policy directives by local government officials may reveal an 'actual or apprehended' plan of mass atrocity crimes against the civilian population,[46] that is, a plan for a use of force or threat thereof, banned by international law. All this explains why the statements of then-Libyan leader Muammar Qadhafi to 'cleanse Libya house by house' until the 'cockroaches' (that is, the protesters)[47] surrender for many, including the UNSC member states, meant an obvious plan of masterminding atrocity crimes, making it easier for the proponents of R2P to argue a 'just cause threshold had been reached'.[48] Therefore, the UNSC adopted Res. 1970 to remind the Libyan authorities of their respon- sibility to protect their own people, also referring the situation to the ICC. It was due to the unwillingness of the Qadhafi regime to abide by international rules and norms of civilian protection, that a month later the UNSC affirmed the Libyan government's manifest failure and ruled on the use of force under Chapter VII to protect the Libyan people from apparent state crimes against humanity (UNSC Res. 1973).

As noted above, the independent international fact-finding missions undertake a tre- mendously important job in ringing the alarm bell of R2P crimes.

In both the Libyan and Syrian cases, the UN HRC has established ad hoc commissions to investigate vioaltions of *internationally recognised human rights*,[49] and 'to identify those responsible' for those violations.[50] Both commissions had been issuing reports on a rolling basis, where they argued war crimes and crimes against humanity had been perpetrated against civilian populations in both countries, whereas the respective regimes were either unable or unwilling to stop atrocities and bring those responsible to justice.[51] In the Libyan situation, this led to UNSC Res. 1973, authorising peace enforcement under Chapter VII for the protection of civilians. Both the African Union[52] and the League of Arab States[53] served as pivotal regional organisations assembling international efforts against atrocity crimes in Libya. The ICC had also undertaken speedy investigation and issued arrest warrants for Colonel Qadhafi and other prominent figures of his regime.[54] The HRC ad hoc commission also urged the UNSC to refer the situation in Syria to the ICC,[55] but those calls remained unheard, unlike in the Libyan case. The gravity of the humanitarian situation in Syria did not result in the UNSC raising concerns about Syria's violation of R2P obligations. Furthermore, the P5 states did not adopt a Chapter VII resol- ution since some member states suggested the Syrian government was able and willing to ensure R2P obligations were met for its population. By December 2012 three P5 states – the United States (US), the United Kingdom (UK) and France – recognised the Syrian National Coalition as the sole and 'legitimate representative of the Syrian people in opposition to the Assad regime', that is, a de facto government, and officially extended 'non-lethal' support to them.[56] Before that tipping point, China and Russia twice employed their veto power on tabled resolutions at the UNSC, in February and July 2012.[57] All this effectively caused deadlock in the council. For the most part, the Sino-Russian position so far has been resting on 'Westphalian sovereignty' (most often quoted through UN Charter Art. 2(4)) and 'no more Libya'[58] objections.[59]

The UNSC Res. 1973, that authorised use of 'all necessary means' in Libya, refrained from citing the R2P Pillar Three motives of the forthcoming operation. Jennifer Welsh observed that mentioning only 'responsibility of the Libyan authorities to protect the Libyan population' without also underlining the relevant responsibilities of the inter- national community following the manifest failure of an incumbent regime 'suggest[ed] that the latter notion was still contested by some members of the Security Council as an appropriate rationale for military action'.[60] The vote explanations and Sino-Russian absten- tion on Res. 1973 are self-explanatory in this regard.[61] And the voting record shows that Russia (and China – more mildly), blaming the North Atlantic Treaty Organization (NATO) forces for abusing the UNSC Res. 1973 in Libya and in fact engaging in a 'regime change' operation through supporting the rebel forces, adopted a policy of blank rejection to any similar scenario in Syria, a long-standing ally, and where the Russian Mediterranean fleet is harboured. Perhaps it was the alleged abuse of Res. 1973 that led the group of BRIC (Brazil, Russia, Indian and China) countries to reconsider their flexible position with the Euro-Atlantic group on the crisis in Syria. After a second veto to a more robust draft resolution in July 2012, the Russian Ambassador Vitaliy Churkin hinted that it was purportedly the Libyan 'lesson' that prevented an affirmative stance on collective measures with regard to Syria.[62] China aligned to this view of Russia, and the Chinese ambassador condemned the drafters of the resolution for allegedly 'put[ting] pressure on only one party'.[63]

To conclude, the uprisings in Libya and Syria emerged into identical situations within the meaning of the R2P doctrine: the local regimes proved to be unable or unwilling to stop the sufferings of their civilian population, and according to the UN HRC reports, engaged in the commission of and providing impunity for *erga omnes* crimes.

The issue of 'sufficient gravity'

In a *realpolitik* calculus, even though a targeted killing of a single member of an identifiable group may be part of a mass atrocity plot, the international community, indeed, lacks the necessary capacities to engage to address all isolated acts.[64] In any case, that is under the sovereign obligation of an individual state. The ICC Rome Statute introduced the 'sufficient gravity' (embodied in Art. 17(1)(d)) threshold for the court's admissibility of situations in which sovereign governments had been 'unwilling or unable' to prevent or prosecute. In essence, this is also the threshold that the international community employs in addressing R2P situations, whether ongoing or apprehended.

Still in the Preamble of the Rome Statute the governments agreed to prosecute *not only* those 'most serious crimes of concern to the international community as a whole', but the most prominent leaders and perpetrators of those crimes. The *Prosecutor v. Dyilo* case is the only one so far where the ICC has elaborated on the 'sufficient gravity' issue of Art. 17(1)(d), arguing that the sole fact of an *erga omnes* crime having taken place 'is not sufficient for it to be admissible before the Court'[65] (para. 41). In the authorisation to investigate the situation in Kenya, the Pre-Trial Chamber II footnotes *Prosecutor* v. *Dyilo* to argue that the sufficient gravity test appears as an '*additional safeguard* [to] prevent the Court from investigating, prosecuting and trying peripheral cases[66] (emphasis added), given its limited capacities. In the same *Prosecutor v. Dyilo* case the Pre-Trial Chamber I stipulated three important determinants of 'sufficient gravity': the 'systematic' pattern of incidents, and the 'large scale' of the crimes as well as 'the social alarm [that] such [criminal] conduct may have caused in the international community'.[67] In a rare case when the prosecutor has applied his/her powers to initiate a *proprio motu* investigation – the post-electoral situation in Kenya – Pre-Trial Chamber II paid attention to two interconnected characteristics for admissibility ' ... by way of reference to ... (i) the groups of *persons*; and (ii) the *crimes* within the jurisdiction of the Court allegedly committed during the incidents[68] (emphasis added). The Pre-Trial Chamber also tackled the issue of gravity, arguing it would follow both qualitative and quantitative approaches to select appropriate cases, following not the number of victims ' ... but rather the existence of some aggravating or qualitative factors attached to the commission of crimes', such as:

1. The scale of the alleged crimes (including assessment of geographical and temporal intensity);

2. The nature of the unlawful behaviour or of the crimes allegedly committed;
3. The employed means for the execution of the crimes (i.e., the manner of their commission); and
4. The impact of the crimes and the harm caused to victims and their families. In this respect, the victims' representations will be of significant guidance for the Chamber's assessment.[69]

Generally, none of the R2P crimes is a result of a single act. The practice of the ICTR and ICTY suggests that, for example, the crime of genocide results after continuous repetition over time of the policy of crimes against humanity, ethnic cleansings and arbitrary persecutions of targeted groups (e.g. *Prosecutor* v. *Ratko Mladic*, ICTY). As for the crimes against humanity, as well as relying on Art. 7(1) of the Rome Statute, the ICC has chosen to emphasise that the attack against civilians shall be 'either widespread or systematic'[70] in order to be admissible to the court. This clarification has obviously been made to exclude 'isolated or random acts'[71] from the consideration of the court, in order to pursue its original goal of prosecuting only the most outrageous perpetrators. For any violence to be claimed as *systematic* there must be enough evidence to show continuity of 'identical or analogous breaches, which are *sufficiently numerous* and inter-connected to amount not merely to isolated incidents or exceptions, but to a pattern or system' (emphasis added), as the ECHR ruled in *Ireland* v. *the United Kingdom* in 1978.[72]

The threshold of 'sufficient gravity', of course, does not imply a quantitative approach towards the casualties, as that would be both highly cynical and exclude preventive measures.[73] Any single violation of the *jus cogens* norms, regardless of the scale, is a serious breach to the interests of the international community as a whole, as all of those norms are fundamental to international peace and stability. On the conceptual level this threshold of 'sufficient gravity' appears in recognition of sovereign rights (and equality) of states, provided that sitting governments bear primary responsibility for protection of their populations, and only their failure – leading to even more egregious crimes – will require an international response. Both the ICTR and ICTY ruled that an important component of 'widespread or systematic' crimes is the 'common policy' or 'a political objective or plan' involving a 'large-scale or continuous commission of crimes which are linked'.[74] In the authorisation of the investigation into the Kenyan situation, ICC Pre-Trial Chamber II found a 'state or organizational policy', as an element consistent with Article 7(2)(a) of the Rome Statute, in the post-electoral developments in the country which qualified the situation sufficiently grave for the court's consideration.[75]

Henceforth, as far as we speak of 'multiple acts', they should amount to a certain gravity in order to trigger the 'R2P obligations' of the domestic government, which is different than the constitutional obligation to prosecute a single or few criminal acts that remain in the domain of the domestic criminal code, and do not show patterns of international crimes. Art. 15 of the International Law Commission's (ILC) Draft Articles on State Responsibility (DASR) sheds light on this debate about 'a series of actions or omissions defined in aggregate as wrongful'. The ILC concluded that such 'composite acts' are those like genocide, crimes against humanity or war crimes, which represent repetitive breaches of the same laws in a given period of time.[76]

Of course, in any country across the political map of the globe there may erupt certain ' … isolated acts'[77] constituting offences, such as extra-judicial executions or other common crimes punishable under municipal law.'[78] The government in whose territory the R2P crime has occurred or continues to unfold, irrespective of the violator's identity (for example, the *Velasquez* case, 1988) should show resolve and willingness to prosecute the crime in the domestic judicial system and restore law and legitimate order (as noted above), otherwise the conduct ' ... [may] be considered an act of that State under international law ... to the extent that the State acknowledges and adopts the conduct in question as its own', according to Article 11 of DASR.[79] In the latter case, even though there may be straightforward official statements of the state that it 'adopts the conduct in question as its own' (which hardly ever happens), the state may also acknowledge the act by the means of indirect actions, such as refusal or hesitation to prosecute alleged criminals.[80] Alternatively, the state may willingly or unwillingly establish and guarantee an environment of impunity, endorsing specific types of crimes, for example, against an identified community.[81] Likewise the state may show its culpability when the domestic government fails to surrender beyond reasonable time limits, or otherwise grants immunity to alleged criminals that are wanted by foreign governments (*Belgium* v. *Senegal*, 2012), an ad hoc tribunal or the ICC by an arrest warrant. To this end, once a situation is referred to the ICC, and even more, when arrest warrants are issued to those allegedly responsible for R2P crimes, granting amnesty or immunity to those people by the domestic government would mean not only jeopardising the authority of the court, but may constitute an act against the international community as such, stemming from the *erga omnes* nature of the crimes. So a deferral may only be made by the UNSC (by its powers under Rome Statute Art. 16) in acknowledgement of its primary role in the maintenance of international peace and security; and in no other ways.[82]

The 'rogue' governments also have the tendency of minimising or bluntly rejecting that atrocities have been committed. In the absence of fact-finding missions on the ground, it is even harder, if possible at all, to gather evidence of the 'sufficient gravity' threshold in the case of ongoing calamities. One rarely can determine whether the crimes already committed are just the beginning of a wider practice, or an end in itself, since the perpetrators hardly ever follow rational or predictable logic. Therefore, as soon as sufficient elements of either R2P crimes, or the threat thereof, are established, the international community shall become alarmed of the situation and speed up R2P endeavours. Past experiences of unhindered genocides and crimes against humanity are enough to learn the lesson of the need for early prevention of grave calamities and make the 'Never again!' promise a policy. Even after the crime has taken place, the perpetrators always tend to either minimise the gravity of atrocities, or treat them with blanket denial. For instance, the government of Turkey denies the Armenian Genocide of 1915–1923[83] a century later and threatens the affirmative and condemnatory voices of some of its own nationals with imprisonment,[84] whereas the government of Rwanda ascribed the atrocities to tribal enmity and 'spontaneous' uprising,[85] which was an interpretation rejected by ICTR proceedings shortly thereafter. Similar to this was the case of Drazan Erdemovic in ICTY proceedings.

Re-introducing the 'unable or unwilling' test

The issue of local government's role in mass atrocity crimes has long been in the inherently political and even ideological embrace. The relevant discussions in the UNSC of atrocious situations around the world, including, but not limited to, Libya and Syria, and the political determinants of declaring a foreign government as 'unable or unwilling' lies in the political domain rather than legal. The latter issue is being hotly debated through the prism of P5 states' national interests (for example, in Syria). In a nutshell, the 'unwilling or unable' test is set to determine the role of the local government in an ongoing intra-state crisis, its scale and gravity, as well as its capacity to end the violence with legitimate means in cases where it is not a direct side to the crisis. The 'failure' concerns both the inability to stop violence and the obligation to prosecute the individuals engaged in that violence, which failure may lead to aggravating the situation. For instance, ICC Pre-Trial Chamber II established that the Kenyan authorities failed to arrange criminal prosecution of those allegedly guilty for crimes against humanity during the post-electoral violence of 2008–2009,[86] contrary to the Kenyan government's initial promises and the main recommendations of the Commission of Inquiry into Post Election Violence (Waki Commission)[87]; and the government thus created an environment of impunity for those *erga omnes* crimes.

The verbatim records of respectively the Libyan and Syrian situation discussions in the UNSC suggest that political and normative disagreements among P5 nations are paramount on the matter of the role of respective governments in intra-state violence.

In an affirmative vote explanation before the Council on Resolution 1970, Russia held the view that ' ... a settlement of the situation in Libya is possible only through political means',[88] implying that the sitting regime of Colonel Qadhafi was capable of negotiating peace with political opposition factions. The French ambassador advocated for the R2P to be exercised in the Libyan situation, by arguing that Resolution 1970 (adopted unanimously) ' ... recalls the responsibility of each State to protect its own population and *of the international community to intervene when States fail in their duty*' (emphasis added). While the UK, France and the US pushed for strong measures to stop apparent atrocity crimes, the non-formal group of BRIC countries (South Africa voted in favour of resolution) united in a view that the situation in Libya might and should be resolved through 'diplomacy and dialogue', as expressed in Brazil's position.[89] Eventually this group abstained on the more robust Resolution 1973 (2011).

Russia (and China – more mildly), blaming the NATO forces for allegedly abusing the UNSC Res. 1973 in Libya and engaging in a 'regime change' operation through supporting the rebel forces, adopted a policy of blank rejection to any similar scenario in Syria, a longstanding ally, where the Russian Mediterranean fleet is harboured. As of April 2013, the Sino-Russian position on a resolution of the Syrian crisis firmly rests on the belief that the incumbent regime of President Bashar Assad is willing and capable of engaging in political resolution of the conflict with the unarmed opposition factions. As it was in the Libya situation, the widespread and systematic nature of civilian casualties in Syria *per se* does not cause disagreements in the UNSC. The differences among P5 states concern instead the role of the respective governments in perpetrating, or complicity in, those atrocity crimes and their ability and willingness to stop those crimes. Under these circumstances, the referral of the Syrian situation to the ICC through a UNSC Chapter VII resolution, also providing for a complete arms embargo to the country, would mark international cooperation on a matter of international peace and security that engages more than individual state self-interest.

Conclusions

Summarising the issue of the gravity of local government failure, it should be noted that the two key issues for evoking the R2P doctrine in the protection of civilians in intra-state conflicts are 'why' (are the *triggering factors* proven and *primary* aims legitimate enough?) and 'when' (is the gravity and state failure 'sufficient'?) to keep the intervention largely legitimate. As has here been discussed, the judgments and rulings of ad hoc tribunals serve as a visible illustration of what, when and why certain acts shall be considered as *erga omnes* crimes against the international community as a whole. This leads to a conclusion, that the eventual indictments by the ICC in given situations are an objective illustration of the gravity of the widespread and systematic human rights abuses that triggered international concern. The statutes and indictments of already established ad hoc tribunals for the former Yugoslavia, Rwanda and Sierra Leone represent existing *opinio juris*, whereas criminal prosecution of the 'most wanted' perpetrators may become a customary law basis or *ex post-facto legalisation* for Pillar Three operations in years to come – with a first ever permanent criminal court in force since 2002, operating in times of peace and war.

Even though the R2P doctrine has not yet created any definite new rule or norm in international affairs or the law (it may never do so), it nevertheless has become the 'reading rule' for the well-established international humanitarian and human rights laws, resulting in incorporation of the doctrine by the UNSC in a number of relevant resolutions regarding intra-state violence dealing with atrocity crimes. Referring to the role of the UNSC, the normative progress of the R2P doctrine shall already provide for 'soft law' obligations upon the council to refer a grave humanitarian situation to the ICC through 'constructive abstention' of member states whenever core national interests prevent more robust peace enforcement under Chapter VII.[90]

During the development of the R2P Doctrine, inevitably, it may face abuses by States wishing to return to power politics, or, to what the developing nations have long been accused of; namely neo-colonialism. In order to further minimize the trans-boundary use of force undertaken either by pivotal states or ad hoc coalitions following an *arbitrary* assessment of grave situations in third countries, *the ICC should gain the right to issue Advisory Opinions on breaches to the R2P obligations (by commission of crimes listed in Rome Statute) by local governments.* To make this process legitimate; ICC Advisory Opinions would need to be either requested by the UN HRC or be *proprio motu* by the ICC Prosecutor's Office, though both avenues would require further development of the Rome Statute in subsequent Review Conferences. Eventual investigation by the ICC will serve as an objective assessment of allegations of R2P crimes. Moreover, the confirmation of *erga omnes* crimes and indictments of those responsible will empower the UNSC to find the common ground among the P5 on enforcement actions, thus facilitating cooperation among the P5 States. Should this option remain unlikely in the coming decade, the regional organizations will inevitably become more willing to provide relief to their own Member-States whenever necessary (e.g. African Union Charter Art 4(h)), since they are the only legitimate power beyond the UNSC with the authority to override the sacrosanct principle of state sovereignty. The latter approach would further erode the role of the P5 members to find collective solutions in the present world order.

The R2P Doctrine and the ICC should go hand in hand, whenever *ad hoc* coalitions of states consider intervention to stop mass atrocity crimes in the name of the international community. When the peace enforcement operation under Chapter VII is under threat of veto, political negotiations with the perpetrator regimes (which practically never end in different avenues) about stepping down and establishing transitional governments, on one hand; and a referral of the situation to the ICC by the UNSC (if that is a non-signatory power) or *proprio motu* investigation by ICC prosecutor, on the other hand, may become the two mutually reinforcing measures to end mass scale atrocities. The threat of criminal prosecution hanging as the *sword of Damocles* over those feeding the violence may also be a critical measure available that would be acceptable to both advocates of state sovereignty and the R2P Pillar Three.

Acknowledgements

This article has been part of a wider research project, generously supported with a scholarship funded by Magdalena Yesil at the Sanford School of Public Policy, Duke University, between August 2012 and June 2013. The author is thankful to Professor Judith Kelley and Professor Bruce Jentleson for their numerous feedback and advisorship, without which this research would not have seen the light. The project has also hugely benefitted from the unwavering support of the (former) Dean, Professor Bruce Kuniholm and enriched by discussions with the faculty at the Sanford School of Public Policy – Professors Peter Feaver, Francis Lethem, Natalia Mirovitskaya, Catherine Admay, Francis Webb and others contributing to all stages of my research, all of whom I am fully indebted to.

Disclosure statement

No potential conflict of interest was reported by the author.

Notes

1. International Commission on Intervention and State Sovereignty (ICISS), *The Responsibility to Protect. Report of the International Commission on Intervention and State Sovereignty* (Ottawa: International Development Research Center, 2001), http://responsibilitytoprotect.org/ICISS%20Report.pdf (accessed 5 August 2014).
2. Don Hubert, 'The Responsibility to Protect: Preventing and Halting Crimes against Humanity', in *Mass Atrocity Crimes: Preventing Future Outrages*, ed. Robert I. Rotberg (Washington, DC: Brookings Institution Press, 2010), 89–108.
3. Note: As observed by Jennifer Welsh, the UN World Summit Outcome Document of 2005, in fact, established the list of 'R2P crimes', whereas the original ICISS report was making the case solely for crimes incurring 'large scale loss of life'. Jennifer Welsh, 'Civilian Protection in Libya: Putting Coercion and Controversy Back into RtoP', *Ethics & International Affairs* 25 (2011): 255–262, doi:10.1017/S0892679411000207.
4. Note: The International Court of Justice (ICJ) acknowledged in *Bosnia* v. *Serbia* that obligations of genocide or atrocity prevention cannot be imposed as 'binding obligation' on states. Case Concerning Application of the Convention on the Prevention and Punishment of the Crime of Genocide (*Bosnia and Herzegovina v. Serbia and Montenegro*); Judgment of 26 February 2007. [para. 430] http://www.icj-cij.org/docket/files/91/13685.pdf
5. Edward C. Luck, 'Building a Norm: The Responsibility to Protect Experience', in *Mass Atrocity Crimes: Preventing Future Outrages*, ed. Robert I. Rotberg, 108–28 (Washington, DC: Brookings Institution Press, 2010).
6. UN General Assembly Resolution 63/308 (14 September 2009), UN Doc. A/RES/63/308.
7. Note: The terms 'doctrine' and 'concept' with reference to the responsibility to protect are used interchangeably and as synonyms in the text.
8. Nicholas J. Wheeler and Tim Dunne, 'Operationalizing Protective Interventions: Alternative Models of Authorization', in *The Routledge Handbook of the Responsibility to Protect*, ed. Andy W. Knight and Frazer Egerton (London: Routledge, 2012), 87–103, at 99.
9. 'In Larger Freedom: Towards Development, Security and Human Rights For All'. Report of the Secretary-General, 2005. UN Doc. A/59/2005.
10. UN Security Council 6917th Meeting, Press Release, UN Doc SC/10913, 12 February 2013, http://www.un.org/News/Press/docs//2013/sc10913.doc.htm (accessed 5 August 2014).
11. Statement by the President of the Security Council, adopted 12 February 2013. UN Doc. S/PRST/2013/2.

12. Note: For instance, the United States National Security Strategy in 1994 singled out four necessary preconditions to 'guide decisions on when to use force'; those were: (1) considerations of national interests; (2) commitments to allies and their security; (3) support of public opinion and political consensus; (4) 'reasonable cost and feasibility thresholds'. None of them was suitable for Rwanda, as the permanent five (P5) states voted to reduce the capabilities of UNAMIR (United Nations Assistance Mission for Rwanda) in Rwanda (S/RES/912 (1994), 21 April 1994), as genocide was unfolding before the eyes of the international community, that left no other available means for General Romeo Dellaire than to 'shake hand with the devil'. Romeo Dellaire, *Shake Hands with the Devil: The Failure of Humanity in Rwanda* (Boston, MA: Da Capo Press, 2004).

13. For example, Daniel Brunstetter and Megan Braun, 'From Jus ad Bellum to Jus ad Vim: Recalibrating Our Understanding of the Moral Use of Force', *Ethics & International Affairs* 27 (2013): 87–106. doi:10.1017/S0892679412000792.

14. Jennifer M. Welsh and Maria Banda, 'International Law and the Responsibility to Protect: Clarifying or Expanding States' Responsibilities?', in *The Responsibility To Protect and International Law*, ed. Alex Bellamy, Sara Davies, and Luke Granville (Leiden: Martinus Nijhoff Publishers, 2011), 119–39.

15. William A. Schabas, *An Introduction to the International Criminal Court* (Cambridge: Cambridge University Press, 2007), 60.

16. Note: In the *Barcelona Traction* case (*Belgium* v. *Spain*, 1970) the ICJ ruled that beyond genocide, certain other crimes, such as piracy, apartheid, racial discrimination and slavery are also unlawful assaults against the international community as a whole. *Barcelona Traction, Light and Power Company, Limited* (*Belgium* v. *Spain*) (New Application: 1962), http://www.icj-cij.org/docket/files/50/5387.pdf.

17. 'Implementing the Responsibility to Protect', Report of the UN Secretary-General, 12 January 2009; UN doc. A/63/677, para. 9d, http://globalr2p.org/pdf/SGR2PEng.pdf. Note: The UNSG also urged in his report not to extend the R2P cover to 'other calamities, such as HIV/AIDS, climate change or the response to natural disasters', which would eventually lead to renegotiation of '2005 consensus'. This research will align with the same position.

18. Note: A general international consensus emerged in 2008 after Cyclone Nargis hit Myanmar that natural disasters do not give rise to R2P obligations of the international community, despite France fiercely advocating for that.

19. Thomas De Waal, *Black Garden: Armenia and Azerbaijan Through Peace and War* (New York: New York University Press, 2003), 32–7.

20. Note: The Report of the UN Secretary-General about the situation in Yugoslavia equated the policy of ethnic cleansing to crimes against humanity. *Report of the Secretary General Pursuant to Paragraph 2 of the Security Council Resolution 808 (1993)*, UN Doc. S/25704, 3 May 1993, para. 48. Note: Although the UNGA resolution on the former Yugoslavia (A/Res/47/121 – http://www.un.org/documents/ga/res/47/a47r121.htm) on a political level claimed that 'ethnic cleansing ... is a form of genocide', the legalistic approach dictates that there is a difference between these two, particularly with regard to the gravity and intentions of perpetrators. For the difference between the gravity of 'ethnic cleansing' and genocide, see the European Court of Human Rights (ECHR) case of *Jorgic* v. *Germany* (12 July 2007), http://www.icty.org/x/file/Legal%20Library/Statute/statute_re808_1993_en.pdf.

21. For more discussion of the *Velásquez Rodríguez* case, see: Tessa Davis, 'Taking International Law at its Word and its Spirit: Re-envisioning Responsibility to Protect as a Binding Principle of International Law', *Florida State University Law Review* 38, no. 4 (2011), http://www.law.fsu.edu/journals/lawreview/downloads/384/Davis.pdf (accessed 5 August 2014).

22. Para. 172 of the court's ruling stated: 'Thus, in principle, any violation of rights recognized by the Convention [American Convention on Human Rights – H.N.] carried out by an act of public authority or by persons who use their position of authority is imputable to the State. However, this does not define all the circumstances in which a State is obligated to prevent, investigate and punish human rights violations, nor all the cases in which the State might be found responsible for an infringement of those rights. *An illegal act which violates human rights and which is initially not directly imputable to a State (for example, because it is the act of a private person or because the person responsible has not been identified) can lead to international responsibility of the State, not because of the act itself, but because of the lack of due diligence to prevent the violation or to respond to it as required by the Convention'. Velásquez Rodríguez*

case, Judgment of 29 July 1988, Inter-Am.Ct.H.R. (Ser. C) No. 4 (1988), http://www1.umn.edu/humanrts/iachr/b_11_12d.htm

23. Antonio Cassese, 'The Status of Rebels under the 1977 Geneva Protocol on Non-International Armed Conflicts', *The International and Comparative Law Quarterly* 30, no. 2 (1981): 416–39, http://www.jstor.org/stable/759535.

24. *Prosecutor* v. *Tadic*, No. IT-94-1, ICTY Appeals Chamber. Decision on the Defense Motion for Interlocutory Appeal on Jurisdiction, 2 October 1995, para. 141, http://www.un.org/icty/ind-e.htm. Note: This quote also appears in: George J. Andreopoulos, 'Violations of Human Rights and Humanitarian Law and Threats to International Peace and Security', in *From Sovereign Impunity to International Accountability: The Search for Justice in a World of States*, ed. Ramesh Thakur and Peter Malcontent (Tokyo, New York: United Nations University Press, 2004), 80–100.

25. Cassese, 'The Status of Rebels under the 1977 Geneva Protocol on Non-International Armed Conflicts'.

26. The Permanent Court of International Justice concluded in the *Lotus* case (*France* v. *Turkey*) that 'International law governs relations between independent sovereign States. The rules of law binding upon States emanate from their own *free will* as expressed in conventions or by usages generally accepted as expressing principles of law … .' (emphasis added), http://www.icj-cij.org/pcij/serie_A/A_10/30_Lotus_Arret.pdf. However, for example, Libya did not join the ICC Rome Statute, but the case of mass atrocity crimes was referred to the court by the UNSC, in fact, in violation of the 'free will' principle. This is exactly the example that shows that the sovereignty issue is now amended by emerging R2P doctrine, placing 'R2P crimes' above the sovereignty issue.

27. *The Application of the Convention on the Prevention and Punishment of the Crime of Genocide (Bosnia and Herzegovina v. Serbia and Montenegro)* [2007] Judgment, ICJ General List No. 91, http://www.icj-cij.org/docket/files/91/13685.pdf.

28. Note: It is remarkable, that Judge Skotnikov – himself a Russian national – dissented the ruling of the ICJ by arguing that 'there is no such a thing as State criminal responsibility' as long as states are 'organized entities' where individuals act on behalf of the state, and not the state 'as such', and states only have duties to prevent genocide if it is 'committed within the territory where it exercises its jurisdiction or which is under its control'. Judges Shi and Koroma also issued a joint declaration, where they questioned the judgment and called it 'inconsistent with the object and purpose of the Convention', that 'State[s] can be held directly to have committed the crime of genocide'. Declaration of Judge Skotnikov, http://www.icj-cij.org/docket/files/91/13705.pdf. Joint Declaration of Judges Shi and Koroma, http://www.icj-cij.org/docket/files/91/13695.pdf.

29. 'Senegal: Hissène Habré Court Opens', Human Rights Watch, 8 February 2013, http://www.hrw.org/news/2013/02/08/senegal-hissene-habre-court-opens.

30. Note: The ICC Rome Statute considers 'torture' as a crime against humanity or war crime, depending on the background of the alleged violation (Art. 7(1), 8(2)).

31. Questions Concerning the Obligation to Prosecute or Extradite (*Belg.* v. *Sen.*), Judgment (20 July 2012)], http://www.icj-cij.org/docket/files/144/17064.pdf (accessed 5 August 2014).

32. http://www.asil.org/insights120911.cfm.

33. Questions Concerning the Obligation to Prosecute or Extradite (*Belg.* v. *Sen.*) .

34. http://www.hrw.org/news/2013/02/08/senegal-hissene-habre-court-opens.

35. Note: The ICJ confirmed in *Belgium* v. *Senegal* (2012) that the prohibition of torture had become a *jus cogens* norm in customary international law (Judgement, para. 99). Questions Concerning the Obligation to Prosecute or Extradite (*Belg.* v. *Sen.*) .

36. Note: Allan Kuperman suggests that the emerging doctrine of R2P, at least, has a negative side-effect of provoking retaliation from the government against any rebellion, which 'causes some genocidal violence that otherwise would not occur'. Alan J. Kuperman, 'The Moral Hazard of Humanitarian Intervention: Lessons from the Balkans', *International Studies Quarterly* 52, no. 1 (2008): 49–80, http://www.jstor.org/stable/29734224.

37. Note: The ICC prosecutor partly relied on the 'publicly-available sources (international organisations, non-governmental organisations and the media)' information when suggesting the arrest of then-incumbent president of Côte d'Ivoire on charges of crimes against humanity before the ICC Pre-Trial Chamber III. Situation in the Republic of Côte d'Ivoire, *Decision Pursuant to Article 15 of the Rome Statute on the Authorisation of an Investigation into the*

Situation in the Republic of Côte d'Ivoire, ICC-02/11, 15 November 2011. (Corrigendum) http://www.icc-cpi.int/iccdocs/doc/doc1268605.pdf. Note: The UNSC Res. 2042 (2012), which suggested the six-point-plan for political transition in Syria, included the restoration of the right of journalists to freedom of movement as a basic and important point in the nego-tiations with the incumbent regime, which meant yet another credit to the work of the media in voicing atrocities elsewhere. For the full text see: http://www.un.org/en/peacekeeping/documents/six_point_proposal.pdf (accessed 5 August 2014).

38. For example, the Syrian Observatory for Human Rights is a prominent campaign hub, based in London, UK, that provides daily casualty figures in Syria for the international media, and is actively quoted by leading media companies, such as the BBC. However, as the *New York Times* revealed, 'despite its central role in the savage civil war, the grandly named Syrian Obser-vatory for Human Rights is virtually a one-man band', http://www.nytimes.com/2013/04/10/world/middleeast/the-man-behind-the-casualty-figures-in-syria.html. Olivia Lang, 'Profile: Syrian Observatory for Human Rights', *BBC News*, 28 December 2011, http://www.bbc.co.uk/news/world-middle-east-15896636 (accessed 5 August 2014).

39. *Prosecutor v. Jelisic*, Case No. IT-95-10-, International Criminal Tribunal for Former Yugosla-via, Appeals Chamber Judgment (2001), para. 46, http://www.icty.org/x/cases/jelisic/acjug/en/jel-aj010705.pdf.

40. William Schabas, 'State Policy as an Element of International Crimes', *Journal of Criminal Law & Criminology* 98, no. 3 (2008): 953–82.

41. Claus Kress, 'On the Outer Limits of Crimes against Humanity: The Concept of Organization within the Policy Requirement: Some Reflections on the March 2010 ICC Kenya Decision', *Leiden Journal of International Law* 23 (2010): 855–73, doi:10.1017/S0922156510000415 (accessed 5 August 2014).

42. *Situation in the Republic of Kenya*, Decision Pursuant to Article 15 of the Rome Statute on the Authorization of an Investigation into the Situation in the Republic of Kenya, ICC-01/09, 31 March 2010, http://www.icc-cpi.int/iccdocs/doc/doc854287.pdf.

43. Situation in the Republic of Côte d'Ivoire, Decision Pursuant to Article 15 of the Rome Statute on the Authorisation of an Investigation into the Situation in the Republic of Côte d'Ivoire, ICC-02/11, 15 November 2011. (Corrigendum) http://www.icc-cpi.int/iccdocs/doc/doc1268605.pdf.

44. Situation in the Republic of Kenya, paras 135, 188–90.

45. Situation in the Republic of Côte d'Ivoire, paras 23–5.

46. The 'actual or apprehended' dimension of atrocity crimes, particularly of genocide, has been suggested by the ICJ in *Bosnia v. Serbia*, 2007.

47. 'Libya Protests: Defiant Gaddafi Refuses to Quit', *BBC News*, 22 February 2011, last updated at 18:03 Eastern Time (ET), http://www.bbc.co.uk/news/world-middle-east-12544624 (accessed 5 August 2014).

48. Wheeler and Dunne, 'Operationalizing protective interventions', 87–103.

49. Note: The term 'internationally recognised human rights' was first introduced by Professor Sean D. Murphy of George Washington University, who effectively argued that the human rights concept may vary from state to state, whereas all states have certain international obligations in part to relevant international treaties of humanitarian law, and altogether those are 'interna-tionally recognised human rights', and not just 'human rights', which in some cases may mislead. For more, see: Sean Murphy, *Humanitarian Intervention: The United Nations in an Evolving World Order* (Philadelphia: University of Pennsylvania Press, 1996).

50. 'Report of the Independent International Commission of Inquiry on the Syrian Arab Republic', UN Human Rights Council, 23 November 2011. UN Doc. A/HRC/S-17/2/Add.1, paras 5–6, http://www2.ohchr.org/english/bodies/hrcouncil/specialsession/17/docs/A-HRC-S-17-2-Add1.pdf (accessed 5 August 2014).

51. UN Human Rights Commission Doc. A/HRC/19/68; 'Report of the Independent International Commission of Inquiry on the Syrian Arab Republic'.

52. Communique of the 261th Meeting of the Peace and Security Council of the African Union, 23 February 2011, http://ps.au.int/en/sites/default/files/2011_feb_23_psc_261stmeeting_libya_communique_en.pdf (accessed 5 August 2014).

53. 'Arab League: Violence Against Protesters Must Come to an End', *Voice of America*, 21 Feb-ruary 2011, http://www.voanews.com/content/libyas-gadhafi-vows-to-not-to-leave-116663264/135426.html (accessed 5 August 2014).

54. Note: Though the UNSCR 1970 referred the situation in Libya to the ICC, suspecting crimes against humanity being perpetrated during the civil war, and subsequent arrest warrants to prominent leaders of the regime, including Qadhafi himself (case terminated after his death), the ICC prosecutors still have to find hard and sufficient evidence that *erga omnes* crimes had been committed.

55. Statement delivered on behalf of all special procedures mandate-holders of the United Nations Human Rights Council at the Nineteenth Special Session of the Human Rights Council on the Situation of Human Rights in the Syrian Arab Republic Geneva, 1 June 2012, http://www.ohchr.org/EN/NewsEvents/Pages/DisplayNews.aspx?NewsID=12211&LangID=E (accessed 5 August 2014).

56. Jill Dougherty, 'Obama Recognizes Syrian Opposition Coalition', *CNN world*, 12 December 2012, http://www.cnn.com/2012/12/11/world/us-syria-opposition (accessed 5 August 2014).

57. Rick Gladstone, 'Friction at the U.N. as Russia and China Veto Another Resolution on Syria Sanctions', *New York Times*, 19 July 2012, http://www.nytimes.com/2012/07/20/world/middleeast/russia-and-china-veto-un-sanctions-against-syria.html (accessed 5 August 2014); Michelle Nichols, 'Russia, China Veto U.N. Security Council Resolution on Syria', *Reuters*, 19 July 2012, http://www.reuters.com/article/2012/07/19/us-syria-crisis-un-idUSBRE86I0UD20120719 (accessed 5 August 2014).

58. '"Syria is not Libya" – Lavrov', *Russia Today*, 5 December 2012, http://rt.com/politics/syria-russia-chemical-weapons-nato-lavrov-314/ (accessed 5 August 2014).

59. Jennifer Welsh's explanation of Sino-Russian abstention on UNSCR 1973 seems to be rather close to the reality; Welsh, 'Civilian Protection in Libya', 255–62.

60. Ibid.

61. UN Doc. S/PV.6498.

62. Note: 'We simply cannot accept a document … that would open the path for the pressure of sanctions and further to external military involvement in Syrian domestic affairs', explained Ambassador Churkin to the Council. Quoted by: http://www.reuters.com/article/2012/07/19/us-syria-crisis-un-idUSBRE86I0UD20120719 (accessed 19 July 2012).

63. Zhang Yuwei and Li Lianxing, 'Beijing Against Sanctions on Syria', *China Daily*, 2 February 2012, http://www.chinadaily.com.cn/china/2012-02/02/content_14521923.htm.

64. Note: The ICC Prosecutor Moreno-Ocampo declined calls to start prosecution of British soldiers in Iraq in February 2006, who had allegedly committed war crimes, on the basis of the lack of 'sufficient gravity', comparing the situation in Iraq with Northern Uganda, DRC and Darfur. Above legal opinions, this has also shown the political limitations of the court. The Office of the Prosecutor, The Hague, 9 February 2006, http://www.icc-cpi.int/iccdocs/asp_docs/library/organs/otp/OTP_letter_to_senders_re_Iraq_9_February_2006.pdf.

65. *The Prosecutor* v. *Thomas Lubanga Dyilo*, Case No. ICC-01/04-01/06, Decision Concerning Pre-Trial Chamber I's Decision of 10 February 2006 and the Incorporation of Documents into the Record of the Case against Mr Thomas Lubanga Dyilo (24 February 2006), ¶¶ 41–54, full text available at http://www.icc-cpi.int/iccdocs/doc/doc236260.PDF (accessed 5 August 2014) (hereinafter *Prosecutor v. Dyilo*).

66. *Situation in the Republic of Kenya*, para. 56.

67. SáCouto, Susana and Katherine A. Cleary, 'The Gravity Threshold of the International Criminal Court', *American Journal of International Law* 23, no. 5 (2008): 807–54.

68. Situation in the Republic of Kenya, paras 59–60.

69. Ibid., para. 62.

70. Ibid., para. 94.

71. Ibid., para. 94.

72. *Ireland* v. *the United Kingdom* (1978), European Court of Human Rights, http://hudoc.echr.coe.int/sites/eng/pages/search.aspx?i=001-57506.

73. Note: The death toll alone is not the most objective indication of the situation on the ground, as some interventions happen in anticipation of greater atrocities. For example, in Libya the ICC estimate of civilian deaths for February 2011 is between 500 and 700 civilians; but on top of likely plans of further atrocity crimes, that was 'sufficiently' grave to warrant ICC referral by the UNSC and international engagement in March 2011. Marlise Simons and Neil MacFarquhar, 'Hague Court Seeks Warrants for Libyan Officials', *New York Times*, 4 May 2011, http://www.nytimes.com/2011/05/05/world/africa/05nations.html (accessed 5 August 2014).

74. ICTR, *Prosecutor* v. *Akayesu*, Case No. ICTR-96-4-T, Judgment, 2 September 1998, para. 580; ICTY, *Prosecutor* v. *Blaskic*, Case No. IT-95-14-T, Judgment, 3 March 2000, para. 203.
75. Situation in the Republic of Kenya, paras 117–28.
76. Draft Articles on Responsibility of States for Internationally Wrongful Acts, with commentaries. *Yearbook of the International Law Commission* (2001), vol. II, Part Two, http://untreaty.un.org/ilc/texts/instruments/english/commentaries/9_6_2001.pdf.
77. Note: DASR Art. 15 also foresees state responsibility in cases when the isolated acts, over time, would show a continuing pattern and transform into a composite act, punishable under international law.
78. Report of the Commission of Experts on breaches to Geneva Conventions in the territory of the former Yugoslavia: UN Doc. S/1994/674, 27 May 1994, para. 52.
79. Draft articles on Responsibility of States for Internationally Wrongful Acts, with commentaries.
80. For example: *The United States Diplomatic and Consular Staff in Tehran (United States v. Iran)*, International Court of Justice (1980), para. 74, http://www.icj-cij.org/docket/files/64/6291.pdf.
81. *Velasquez Rodriguez*, Inter-American Court of Human Rights (1988), paras 174–6, http://www1.umn.edu/humanrts/iachr/b_11_12d.htm.
82. Note: The Special Court for Sierra Leone had gone a step further to establish in its statute that amnesty to those 'falling within the jurisdiction' of the court 'shall not be a bar to prosecution' (Art. 10), thus warranting itself from political manipulations and guaranteeing effective punishment for the alleged criminals. Statute of the Special Court for Sierra Leone, http://www.sc-sl.org/LinkClick.aspx?fileticket=uClnd1MJeEw%3d&tabid=176 (accessed 5 August 2014).
83. Ministry of Culture of the Republic of Turkey, Armenian Issue – Allegations/Facts, http://www.kultur.gov.tr/EN,32379/chronolgy.html (accessed 5 August 2014).
84. 'Orhan Pamuk's Victory', *Slate Magazine*, 12 October 2006, http://www.slate.com/articles/news_and_politics/recycled/2006/10/orhan_pamuks_victory.html (accessed 5 August 2014); 'Publisher and PEN Member Ragip Zarakolu Released in Turkey Pending Trial', *Pen America*, 10 April 2012, http://www.pen.org/press-release/2012/04/10/publisher-and-pen-member-ragip-zarakolu-released-turkey-pending-trial (accessed 5 August 2014).
85. Richard Goldstone, 'The Role of the International Criminal Court', in *Mass Atrocity Crimes: Preventing Future Outrages*, ed. Robert I. Rotberg (Washington, DC, Brookings Institution Press, 2010), 55–69.
86. Situation in the Republic of Kenya, paras 183–4.
87. Donald Kipkorir, 'Waki Report Breaks New Ground, But Will it be Implemented?', *Daily Nation*, 17 October 2008, http://www.nation.co.ke/oped/Opinion/-/440808/481268/-/3mepxg/-/index.html (accessed 5 August 2014).
88. UN Doc. S/PV.6491 (26 February 2011).
89. UN Doc. S/PV.6498 (17 March 2011).
90. Note: Though the ICC seems to be the legitimate avenue that the P5 nations have employed on various occasions, it shall not be forgotten that out of all other institutions of global order, the ICC represents normative and value-based conflict among the P5 nations, at best. Among those states, only France and the UK joined the court and ratified the Rome Statute, whereas Russia and the US are among the most vocal critics of the court, questioning its measures and legal competence at all. 'Russia against Handing "Syrian dossier" to ICC', *Voice of Russia*, 19 January 2013, http://english.ruvr.ru/2013_01_19/Russia-against-handing-Syrian-dossier-to-ICC/; Bakhtiyar Tuzmukhamedov, 'The ICC and Russian Constitutional Problems', *Journal of International Criminal Justice* 3, no. 3 (2005): 621–6, doi:10.1093/jicj/mqi048; Curtis A. Bradley, 'U.S. Announces Intent Not to Ratify International Criminal Court Treaty', *American Society of International Law* (May 2002), http://www.asil.org/insigh87.cfm; Ruth Wedgwood, Anne-Marie Slaughter, John Bolton, and Kenneth Roth. 'Toward an International Criminal Court?', Council on Foreign Relations, July 1999, http://www.cfr.org/international-criminal-courts-and-tribunals/toward-international-criminal-court/p3202.

Responsibility to protect: dead, dying, or thriving?

Maggie Powers

Columbia Global Policy Initiative, Columbia University, New York, USA

An intense backlash against the norm of responsibility to protect (R2P) emerged following the 2011 United Nations (UN)-authorised intervention in Libya. This research assesses empirically how significantly the post-Libya backlash affected the normative acceptance of R2P and offers insight into where in the lifecycle of acceptance or rejection R2P currently falls. Through the collection and analysis of UN Security Council and Human Rights Council documents, this research creates an empirical picture of how often, when, and by whom R2P terminology has been referenced over time at the UN. The analysis reveals that post-Libya debate on R2P has not resulted in a decrease in rhetorical acceptance of the norm or a decrease in authorization of R2P framed policies. Instead, R2P has become further internalised and is increasingly utilised in the Security Council and Human Rights Council.

Mass atrocities have ravaged Syria for more than four years while the international community has been unwilling or unable to act. More than 200,000 have died, millions have been displaced, and the country now faces the extreme threat of the Islamic State. Clearly the United Nations Security Council, the guardians of international peace and security, has failed to adequately address the horrors in Syria. But does this also mean the doctrine of the responsibility to protect (R2P), intended as a political and policy tool to halt mass atrocities, has also failed?

Following the failures in Rwanda and Srebrenica, an obligation to respond to mass atrocity crimes developed from the concepts of 'sovereignty as responsibility',[1] the 'right to intervene'[2] and 'two sovereignties: a sovereignty of peoples and a sovereignty of states'[3]; and finally what we now term R2P. The concept of R2P was first coined by the International Commission on Intervention and State Sovereignty in 2001. It shifted the conception of sovereignty from an absolute and sacrosanct right of states to an acknowledgement that with sovereignty comes responsibility to the people of a state. The three pillars of R2P assert that each state has the primary responsibility to prevent or halt atrocities, other states and the international community have a duty to assist in this effort, and should a state fail to prevent or halt mass atrocities, the international community has a responsibility to act collectively, including with force if necessary. Quickly breaking into the international framework, the responsibility to protect was included in the secretary-general's 2004 report *A*

More Secure World, Our Shared Responsibility, adopted by consensus in the General Assembly in the 2005 World Summit Outcome Document (WSOD), and reaffirmed unanimously by the Security Council in Resolution 1674 in 2006.

Most strikingly, Security Council (UNSC) Resolution 1973 (2011) used R2P to justify the coercive use of military force in Libya for the protection of civilians from imminent atrocities. This marked a watershed moment for the new norm – consensus that actually resulted in implementation. For the first time since the failures of Rwanda and Srebrenica, the UNSC was meeting its commitment to peace and security and actively addressing a rapidly deteriorating crisis. But the consensus, if it was that, was short lived. Intense backlash and 'buyer's remorse' to the Libya intervention and R2P emerged, leading David Rieff to ponder 'R2P, RIP' in *The New York Times*.[4] Since then, R2P has faced another, seemingly insurmountable, challenge with the crisis in Syria calling into question how much R2P really has been accepted and internalised.

All of this leaves one question that scholars have been forced to ask – how much did the Libya backlash really affect the acceptance of R2P? And – if not dead, as most contend it is not – where in the lifecycle of acceptance or rejection does R2P currently fall?

An analysis of UN records reveals that, far from dying with Libya or Syria, R2P continues to be invoked and implemented by the UNSC. Empirical text analysis of all UNSC resolutions, presidential statements and open meeting records from 14 September 2005 through 28 February 2014 and Human Rights Council (HRC) resolutions from 2006 through 2013 reveals four key trends in the frequency of R2P use, all of which point to the norm's continued utilisation and entrenchment. First, despite the backlash surrounding Libya, references to R2P in Security Council documents have significantly increased since Resolution 1973. Second, the volume of member state affirmations of R2P has increased while the number of member state rejectionist has decreased. Third, and unsurprisingly, pillar one primary R2P is now widely internalised. Finally, fourth, the UNSC has also once again authorised the use of force to address mass atrocities in the Central African Republic – an expression of R2P's most controversial aspect (albeit with the nominal consent of the transitional government).

Methodology

NVivo text analysis software was utilised to create an empirical picture of how often, when, and by whom R2P and related terminology have been referenced over time at the UN. NVivo is a qualitative data analysis software system capable of examining large quantities of data and PDF files to determine trends. All UNSC resolutions, presidential statements (PRSTs) and open meeting records from 14 September 2005[5] until 28 February 2014 were collected; all HRC resolutions from 2006 through 2013 were collected. In total 3,159 documents were collected and analysed using NVivo.

The UNSC and HRC were selected for analysis because of the relation of their important and distinct mandates to R2P. As the primary body responsible for international peace and security and the intergovernmental body with the legal mandate to authorise coercive measures (including military intervention) against a sovereign state, the UNSC is one of the most influential bodies by which to gauge acceptance and operationalisation of R2P. Although it is a political body of five permanent and 10 rotating member states that does not establish legislation, its resolutions when passed under Chapter VII of the UN Charter are legally binding on every member state and carry significant political and legal weight. As the main intergovernmental body delegated to deal specifically with human rights abuses, analysis of HRC resolutions contextualises the UNSC data and reveals how other global, intergovernmental bodies interact with R2P. Only operational since 2006, the HRC has played a far less active role on R2P. Its resolutions are non-binding recommendations, but as a body of 47 elected member states, HRC resolutions require a more diverse constituency of member state support.

To reveal what, if any, influence the 2011 Libya intervention had on R2P's normative trajectory, the UNSC and HRC documents collected were divided into two data sets for analysis:

(1) 14 September 2005 (the end of negotiations on the WSOD) through 17 March 2011 (the adoption of UNSC Resolution 1973);
(2) 22 March 2011 (first post-Libya meeting) through 28 February 2014.

Word frequency queries were developed to extract and code explicit references to R2P (e.g. the exact phrase 'responsibility to protect' or 'responsibility of the government to protect' and similar variants) in each of the data sets.

Frequency queries were also developed to extract explicit references to six other terms related to R2P – protection of civilians (PoC), mass atrocities, war crimes, genocide, crimes against humanity, and ethnic cleansing. Each of these terms – particularly PoC – has a separate and unique framework that should not be conflated or confused with R2P. However, their frequency trajectories serve as a frame of reference to contextualise the data on R2P and may also reveal deeper internalisation of these interconnected and tangential concepts.

Recognising that mere frequency of use does not reveal member states' intentions or determine a norm's acceptance, all explicit R2P references at open meetings of the UNSC were also coded by the following criteria:

- *Topic* (designated topic of the meeting and/or country-specific topic (e.g. if speaker referenced R2P for a specific country situation during a thematic debate on PoC);
- *Speaker*;
- *Date* (month and year);
- *Attribute* (affirmation, neutral, negative, mixed/other);
- *Pillar of R2P referenced* (primary R2P, shared/international R2P, duty to assist in R2P, Security Council R2P);
- *References to a failure to uphold R2P*;
- *Reference to a specific country's R2P*.

Four attribute categories were developed to assess R2P references from member states at the UNSC open meetings. Although ascribing an attribute to each R2P reference is an inherently subjective act, the author established criteria for each category and worked to apply each criterion as objectively as possible.

Affirmation:

- Explicit assertion of support for R2P as a principle or R2P's use in a certain case context;
- Affirmation that states have a primary responsibility to protect, that the UNSC has a responsibility to protect, that there exists a shared or collective responsibility to protect;
- Assertion that a state or party has failed its responsibility to protect.

Neutral:

- Mention of R2P in the WSOD (or similar official document) but not containing an affirmation of the document or R2P's inclusion;
- Mention of R2P in the title of the Special Adviser on the Responsibility to Protect but not containing an affirmation;
- Calls for the General Assembly to discuss R2P (note: if statement indicates the UNSC should not be discussing R2P then statement would be classified as negative);
- Statement that aspects of R2P require further consideration though not objecting to the principles underlying R2P (e.g. 'there are still many aspects of the responsibility to protect civilians in armed conflicts that require further and careful elaboration')[6];
- Assertion that there exists a clear distinction between R2P and protection of civilians.

Negative:

- Outwardly negative statements towards the principle of R2P (e.g. 'the current propagation of the so-called "responsibility to protect"')[7];
- References to the lack of consensus surrounding R2P or multiple interpretations of R2P (e.g. 'it is to be expected that the responsibility to protect has not yet become a reality today specifically because in its present form it does not enjoy sufficiently broad support from Member States').[8]

Mixed/other:

- This category was used when it was not clear what the statement's intent was;
- If R2P terminology was used to address circumstances that do not fall within one of the four R2P crime categories (e.g. if R2P was used to reference the challenges of climate change or the Russian intervention in Georgia in 2008).

From these data we are able to determine empirically how often the UNSC and member states have positively and negatively referenced R2P before and after the Libya intervention. If the number of affirmative references to R2P has remained consistent or increased, it would certainly suggest that acceptance of R2P has continued despite the backlash. The data extrapolated from this analysis are potentially very telling about how deeply (or superficially) R2P has been embraced at the UN.

There, of course, remain limitations to the significance of this data. As a body of only 15 member states, the UNSC does not reflect the views of all member states or all regions equally. It favours the permanent five members (P5) as their frequency trajectory of R2P statements are the only ones that can truly represent a complete historical view at the council (since no other states have attended every meeting or voted on every resolution). This, however, is the political reality of the current international system and cannot be ignored.

Initial data on R2P: from 2005's World Summit to Libya watershed

Just one week after the adoption of the WSOD, Argentina and the United Kingdom highlighted the importance of R2P in statements at the UNSC, beginning R2P's normative development at the Council.[9] Despite the strong WSOD, 'there was no overall agreement over R2P' and it 'was considered "toxic"' at this time.[10]

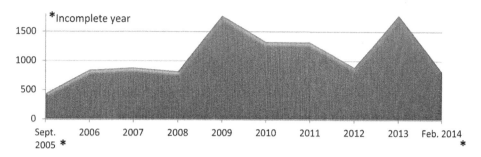

Figure 1.   All references at the UNSC per year (14 September 2005–28 February 2014). Source: M. Powers.

Figures 1 and 2 reveal the collective trajectory of R2P and six related terms over time in UNSC resolutions, PRSTs and open meeting records. Figure 3 presents the disaggregated trajectories of each of the seven terms. These graphs track individual references to each term (e.g. countries may have three references to R2P in one statement; these are all counted individually) by month and year respectively.

Although PoC and the other terms analysed are not referenced exclusively in the context of R2P, their frequency trajectories contextualize data on R2P. PoC is of course a distinct – although connected – concept. It obliges parties to armed conflict to protect civilians as required under international humanitarian, human rights and refugee law. R2P, on the other hand, only applies to the prevention and protection of the four atrocity crimes, which (with the exception of war crimes) may be committed outside of an armed conflict. PoC language is widely accepted and used. Its frequency trajectory serves as an example of a highly internalised (at least rhetorically) norm.

Figures 1 and 2 reveal over 700 references at the February 2014 UNSC thematic debate on the PoC. The majority of these are references to PoC (almost 500 in February 2014), and, notably, each major uptick in Figures 2, 3, 4 and 5 (references per month) correlates with the thematic debates on the PoC at the UNSC. Explicit R2P language has been used much more sparingly, with a maximum of 64 references in February 2013, though also most commonly at the thematic PoC debates. These small numbers make each reference to R2P more significant as an expression of continued acceptance of the norm. Figures 6 and 4 reveal the individual trajectory of explicit R2P references at the UNSC (per month and per year) while Figures 7 and 8 display the frequency of the terminology in HRC resolutions.

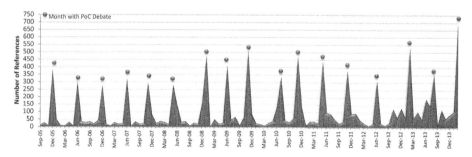

Figure 2.   All references at the UNSC per month (14 September 2005–28 February 2014). Source: M. Powers.

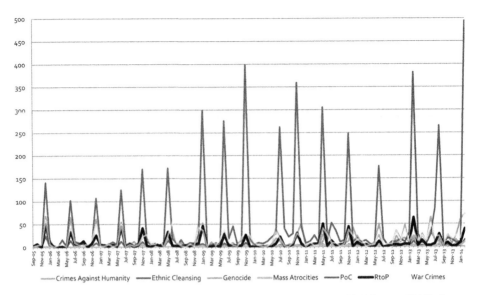

Figure 3. Each reference at the UNSC per month (14 September 2005–28 February 2014). Source: Author's own.

2005 – an introduction to R2P at the UNSC

The first major use of R2P at the UNSC was on 9 December 2005 at the thematic PoC debate. At this debate, R2P was referenced 50 times, a high watermark not reached again until February 2013. These 50 references came from 26 different member states: 21 countries made a combined 40 affirmative R2P references,[11] and five countries made a combined seven neutral references.[12] Only three references were explicitly negative, coming from the governments of Egypt, Russia and Algeria. Both Egypt and Russia argued that the UNSC should not take up the issue since the General Assembly had not yet held consultations on R2P, as mandated by the WSOD.[13] Algeria went one step further, stating that, while discussion at the General Assembly was needed, there was 'still no unanimity within the international community' on what R2P meant.[14] Of those countries that referenced R2P neutrally, Brazil noted that R2P 'does merit an adequate

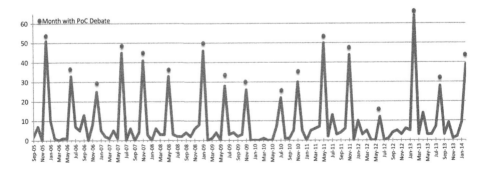

Figure 4. Explicit R2P references at the UNSC per month (14 September 2005–28 February 2014). Source: M. Powers.

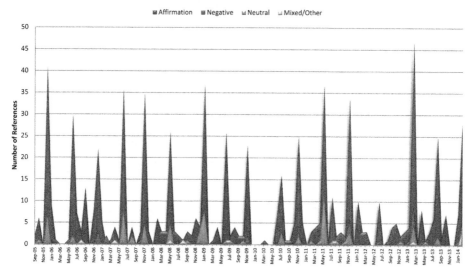

Figure 5. Explicit R2P references at UNSC open meetings by attribute (14 September 2005–28 February 2014). Source: M. Powers.

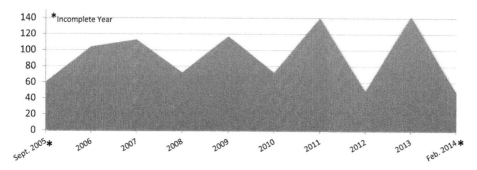

Figure 6. Explicit R2P references at the UNSC per year (14 September 2005–28 February 2014). Source: M. Powers.

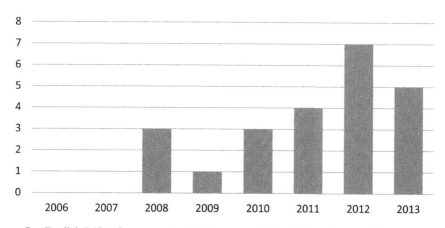

Figure 7. Explicit R2P references at the HRC per year (2006–2013). Source: M. Powers.

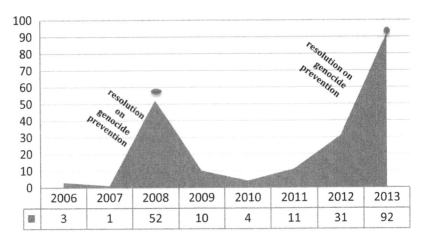

Figure 8.   All references at the HRC per year (2006–2013). Source: M. Powers.

place in our system' but all peaceful means of conflict settlement must be exhausted first. They went on to say, 'the United Nations was not created to disseminate the notion that order should be imposed by force', revealing an acceptance of the principle in theory but a more wary position towards implementation of the use of force under R2P.[15]

Thus, at the beginning of R2P's normative life in the UNSC many states affirmed the concept, several states were generally positive on the underlying principles but concerned about implementation, and only a few countries explicitly opposed the use of R2P language at the UNSC. Many of these same trends are true today.

2006 – from statements to documents

Another watershed moment for R2P's normative life was its first inclusion in a UNSC resolution. While inclusion in the WSOD was a significant step forward it was not legally binding and carried little, if any, practical implementation. Inclusion in a UNSC resolution, on the other hand, is more legally significant and moves R2P from a theoretical aspiration to a policy tool for implementation.

R2P was first referenced in Resolution 1653 on the situation in the Great Lakes region of Africa, specifically the Democratic Republic of the Congo and Burundi, adopted unanimously on 27 January 2006. This resolution not only referenced R2P but took R2P from an abstract concept to the specifics of a conflict and attributed responsibility to specific actors in the conflict. In the meeting adopting Resolution 1653, R2P was referenced affirmatively by the governments of Canada, Denmark, Norway and Slovakia. No neutral or negative references were made.[16]

R2P was then reaffirmed again in Resolution 1674 on the protection of civilians, unanimously adopted by the UNSC on 28 April 2006. Resolution 1674: *'Reaffirms* the provisions of paragraphs 138 and 139 of the 2005 World Summit Outcome Document regarding the responsibility to protect populations from genocide, war crimes, ethnic cleansing and crimes against humanity'.[17] This marked the first time the UNSC recognised the R2P paragraphs of the WSOD. It is arguably a very strong R2P affirmation as it recognises not only the state's primary responsibility but its own commitment to act 'in a timely and decisive manner' to protect civilians from mass atrocities crimes and their incitement.[18]

Human Rights Council data 2006–2011

The HRC has also taken up R2P language in its country specific and thematic resolutions. From 2006 through 17 March 2011 the HRC used R2P language eight times. This number seems quite significant given the HRC only first took up R2P language in 2008. These references included three resolutions on Sudan and resolutions on the prevention of genocide and the situations in Guinea, Kyrgyzstan, Afghanistan and Libya. All eight are pillar one primary R2P references and seven were adopted by consensus.[19] These data reveal R2P is slowly beginning to diffuse and mainstream beyond being discussed exclusively in the UNSC or General Assembly.

Overall analysis of R2P frequency 2005–2011

In total from 14 September 2005 to 17 March 2011 the UNSC adopted six resolutions that reference R2P. Of those six documents, four are on country specific situations[20] and two are on the protection of civilians.[21] There is only one explicit reference to primary R2P[22] (although others cite government responsibility) and three reaffirmations of paragraphs 138 and 139 of the WSOD.[23] As evident from Figure 6, there were a significant number of references to R2P in the UNSC in 2006 (the year of two resolutions citing R2P) and 2009 (the year of the first report of the secretary-general on R2P).

In total during this first data set there were 549 references to R2P made in UNSC open meetings and documents. Coded by attribute, the 541 references made in open meetings were overwhelmingly affirmative of R2P principles (see Figure 9). Only 25 of 541 references coded (5%) qualify as explicitly negative. These negative statements came from seven countries: Sudan (6), Venezuela (6), China (5), Egypt (3), Russia (3), Algeria (1) and Qatar (1). While this is not a significant number of countries compared to the number using affirmative language, Russia and China's use of negative language reveals a lack of consensus within the P5 on R2P. As permanent members of the UNSC, China and Russia have the power to block any R2P language or policies from adoption, as has become painfully apparent with the crisis in Syria.

Fifty-two neutral R2P references were made – 41 by 19 different member states[24] and 11 by UN representatives or regional organisations.[25] China made a notably high number of neutral references (nine), most of which underlined that R2P was important but still lacked consensus and needed to be discussed further.

Four references qualified in the mixed/other category, revealing a lack of common understanding of the scope of R2P following the 2005 WSOD. These references either use R2P language for situations clearly falling outside of the four mass atrocity crimes

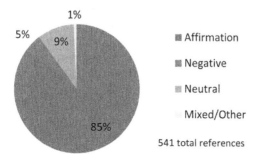

Figure 9.   Explicit R2P references in UNSC open meetings by attribute (2005–Libya 2011). Source: M. Powers.

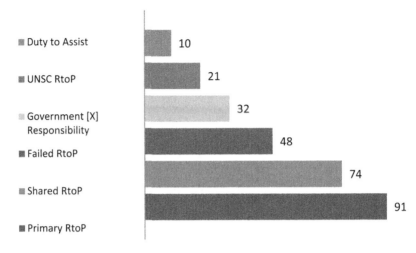

Figure 10. Explicit R2P references at UNSC and HRC by pillar (14 September 2005–17 March 2011). Source: M. Powers.

or use R2P in a way that was widely condemned internationally as a misuse of R2P and humanitarian language. First, Israel used R2P language in August 2006 speaking on the issue of Lebanon and its military action against Hezbollah.[26] Second, in 2007 Papua New Guinea referenced R2P in the context of climate change and its impact on small island states.[27] Third, France referenced R2P in an effort to push for international action following destruction by Cyclone Nargis in Burma in 2008.[28] Finally, in 2008 Russia recalled R2P in reference to its military action in Georgia.[29]

Primary R2P and shared responsibility to protect were both referenced regularly in the UNSC and HRC (see Figure 10). In UNSC open meetings, primary responsibility to protect was referenced by 35 member states and three UN agencies a combined 75 times.[30] This included four references each from China, France, Russia, and the UK, revealing, unsurprisingly, a strong acceptance of pillar one of R2P among critical states. A shared, international, or UN responsibility to protect was referenced by 32 countries and three UN/regional agencies a combined 74 times.[31]

Nigeria made the most references to a shared R2P with six. France, India, the UK and the US all made references to a shared R2P, but notably China, Brazil and Russia did not. Sixteen states and one UN agency made specific reference to the UNSC's responsibility to protect.[32] This included references from France, the UK, the US, South Africa and Turkey. This does not represent widespread state usage explicitly recognising a UNSC responsibility to protect, which can be equated to a recognition of pillar three, but it does clearly show a base of acceptance within the P5 and regional powers.

Critical states in the UNSC for R2P's normative internalisation (the P5 and BRICS countries – Brazil, Russia, India, China, and South Africa) were generally affirmative of R2P. Figure 11 portrays the top 15 affirmative member states on R2P and P5 and BRICS countries during this time period. Of the P5 and BRICS only China and Russia used negative statements, although both also had shallow affirmative language on the underlying principles of primary R2P. Thus, prior to the backlash surrounding the intervention in Libya, R2P was increasingly being used in the UNSC and HRC. Many critical states voiced their support for R2P, paving the way for increased normative legitimacy and internalisation. Their support, however, was quickly tested with the case of Libya.

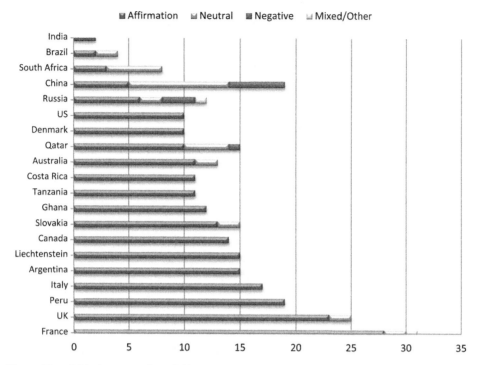

Figure 11.   Critical states and top R2P users at UNSC (September 2005–Libya 2011). Source: M. Powers.

The case of Libya: R2P over sovereignty?

The NATO no-fly zone in Libya authorised by UNSC Resolution 1973 (2011) was the first time R2P was used to morally legitimise coercive military intervention for humanitarian purposes. The moment was heralded by advocates as the first time the UNSC moved beyond the rhetoric of 'never again' to actively respond to an imminent threat of mass atrocities.

Part of the widespread and spontaneous outburst of protests around the Arab world in 2011, the Libyan crisis began on 15 February when Colonel Muammar Gaddafi's forces attacked peaceful protesters in Benghazi.[33] By 22 February, Gaddafi's ambassador to the UN had resigned 'calling [Gaddafi] a genocidal war criminal'[34]; and Gaddafi himself promised he would 'cleanse Libya house by house'.[35] The UNSC responded with the unanimous adoption of Resolution 1970 on 26 February 2011. This resolution, passed under Chapter VII, 'recall[ed] the Libyan authorities' responsibility to protect its population', referred the situation to the International Criminal Court, and established an arms embargo, travel ban and asset freeze on Libya.[36] After this resolution failed to deter Gaddafi, the Gulf Cooperation Council, Organization of Islamic Cooperation and Arab League called on the UNSC to authorise a no-fly zone. Together these regional calls for action, especially by the Arab League, convinced the UNSC to respond.

The UNSC authorised the use of 'all necessary measures … to protect civilians and civilian populated areas under threat of attack' with Resolution 1973.[37] This resolution under Chapter VII once again used R2P language, stating in a preambular clause: 'Reiterating the responsibility of the Libyan authorities to protect the Libyan population and reaffirming that parties to armed conflicts bear the primary responsibility to take all feasible steps to ensure

269

the protection of civilians.'[38] It authorised the implementation of a no-fly zone, use of all means necessary short of occupation to protect civilians, strengthened the arms embargo and asset freeze, and imposed travel restrictions on several members of the regime. This marked the first time the UNSC authorised the use of force against a government under the framework of R2P. Resolution 1973 was, however, much more contentious than Resolution 1970 and five member states (Brazil, China, Germany, India and Russia) abstained from the vote.

The explicit use of R2P in Resolutions 1970 and 1973 under Chapter VII shows a more robust use of R2P than in past UNSC resolutions. However, as Aidan Hehir and Jennifer Welsh note, these resolutions only reference the government's responsibility to protect. They do not reference the more robust and controversial pillar three responsibility of the international community or the UNSC to protect.[39] At meetings on 25 and 26 February for Resolution 1970, only four direct references to R2P were made. The secretary-general made three references and the Portuguese ambassador to the UN made one.[40] At the meeting adopting Resolution 1973 on 17 March 2011, only France referenced R2P – hardly a diverse or meaningful representation of the norm.[41]

Libya is both a watershed moment of acceptance of R2P and the impetus for significant re-evaluation of the normative framework of R2P. Following Resolution 1973, there was a swift backlash against R2P due to the perception that NATO exceeded its mandate and sanctioned regime change. The Arab League condemned the 'broad scope' of NATO action,[42] and India's Ambassador to the UN, Hardeep Singh Puri, negatively called NATO the 'armed wing' of the UN.[43] Ultimately, the negative reactions of the Arab League, African Union and key emerging regional powers to the NATO intervention led to discussions reconsidering the legitimacy of any Western military operation in the Global South. It revealed continued scepticism in the Global South 'over *how* and *who* will do *what* in the implementation' of R2P, as well as 'a serious concern over the *unintended consequences* of using force in each particular case'.[44] This concern led to new conceptual developments on how to improve the R2P framework. Brazil formulated the concept of 'Responsibility While Protecting' in an effort to ensure greater accountability for the implementation of intervention,[45] while Ruan Zongze, the Vice President of the China Institute of International Studies, formulated the concept of 'Responsible Protection' focused on government responsibility and 'strictly limited' defined protection efforts.[46] Contrary to some opinions at the time, the debates following Libya did not undermine the normative development of R2P. Instead, focus shifted to the practical realities and challenges of implementing R2P well – moving the norm from rhetoric into reality.

R2P and Syria: the absent norm – the death of R2P?

While there has clearly not been an adequate response from the UNSC to the glaring human needs and devastation in Syria, the UN has still applied R2P language to the crisis in its efforts for accountability and protection. As Gareth Evans notes, 'for all of the lamentable inadequacy of the Security Council's response to the situation in Syria, no one has seriously argued that it is not an R2P case'.[47] Although Russia and China vetoed multiple resolutions on Syria, which they arguably would have done without fear of the Libyan precedent, they have still allowed the UNSC to apply R2P language. Since 2011, the UNSC has referenced the primary responsibility of the Syrian government to protect civilians in two presidential statements (S/PRST/2013/15 adopted 2 October 2013 and S/PRST/2015/15 adopted 17 August 2015) and Resolution 2139, adopted unanimously in 2014. These documents authorised cross-border access for humanitarian aid and expressed support for the UN Special

Envoy to Syria. These references do not mean the UNSC has done nearly enough to meet its obligation, but they do reveal that Russia is not strongly opposed to R2P language in and of itself. In open meetings of the council, there have also been 24 affirmations of R2P on the topic of Syria from 13 member states, the secretary-general, the European Union (EU) and the Organization of Islamic Cooperation.[48] Only Syria and Russia have made negative R2P references regarding the conflict in Syria.

The HRC has also actively engaged with the situation in Syria. From 2011 to 2013, the HRC adopted six resolutions 'urging', 'calling upon' and 'demanding' that the Syrian authorities meet their primary R2P.[49] The General Assembly has adopted four resolutions 'expressing grave concern' or 'grave alarm' at 'the failure of the Government of the Syrian Arab Republic to protect its population'.[50] If anything, the sheer devastation of Syria may have further entrenched and broadened the commitment of supportive states to R2P. Unfortunately, 'Syria demonstrates, if there was any doubt, that a robust R2P response is never automatic', but what it does not demonstrate is a lack of member state willingness to invoke R2P language in their efforts to advocate for change.[51]

Current data on R2P: from Libya to February 2014

Despite the rhetoric that NATO stretched its mandate to the brink and irrevocably damaged any consensus surrounding R2P, the UNSC has continued to use R2P language in both negotiated resolutions and open meetings. Primary responsibility to protect, the least political of the three pillars, is now common language in UNSC resolutions. The rate at which R2P is referenced in the UNSC is increasing and the use of military force to address mass atrocities has once again been authorised under the R2P framework – this time in the Central African Republic. Many R2P scholars and advocates claim that the focus of member state negotiations is now around implementation while the principles that underlie R2P are commonly accepted. This assertion is fully supported by an empirical analysis of the UNSC documents and meeting records.

Post-Libya discontent

This is not to suggest that the Libya backlash had no impact on the acceptance and use of R2P. Looking at Figure 6, 2011 marked a highpoint for R2P usage with 133 references in UNSC documents and open meetings. Only 11 of those references came between 1 January and 17 March 2011. Concern about the Libya intervention was not publically raised in the UNSC until the 10 May 2011 PoC thematic debate. During that meeting, Russia, China, India and Brazil all raised concerns about the implementation of Resolution 1973 and the actions of NATO. India insightfully commented, 'I cannot but ask the question: *Quis custodiet ipsos custodies*? Who watches the guardians?'[52]

Despite this concern, the day after Gaddafi's assassination the UNSC passed a resolution on the situation in Yemen, recalling the government's primary R2P (S/RES/2014). What becomes apparent then is that Russia's concern over R2P was directed mainly towards the situation in Syria. In other country situations where no Russian national interests were involved, R2P's inclusion did not appear to be a point of contention.

2012 – a year of lows and highs

What is also apparent in Figure 6 is a significant decrease in R2P references in 2012. Only 49 references to R2P were made at the UNSC over the entire year. Looking at Figure 4, 41 of those references were affirmations while only one was negative (from Russia[53]). However, China, India and South Africa still expressed some support for pillars one and two of R2P, while noting that implementation needs to be monitored. China expressed support for pillar one but was concerned about the selectivity of application and cautioned 'military intervention adds fuel to the fire and exacerbates humanitarian crises'.[54] India expressed support for pillar two stating, 'to enable States to fulfil their responsibility to protect their populations' national capacities need to be strengthened, where needed, without political or extraneous motives'.[55] South Africa, a vocal opponent of NATO's actions in Libya, expressed strong support for R2P and accountability mechanisms, stating:

> We wish to underline that it remains the primary responsibility of States to protect civilians within their borders. Armed opposition groups also bear responsibility for ensuring that unarmed civilians are protected, and the failure by both State and non-State actors to uphold that principle should not go unpunished. Accountability must first and foremost be sought at the national level. Failing that, the international community has a collective responsibility to act, using mechanisms at its disposal, including independent fact-finding commissions, commissions of enquiry and the International Criminal Court.[56]

The lack of references to R2P in open meetings may suggest a concern on the part of member states that R2P was 'toxic' at the time or too politically charged to be helpful in achieving their policy goals.

However, despite conventional wisdom, the UNSC continued to use R2P language in PRSTs and resolutions that year. Two PRSTs and three resolutions[57] used R2P language that year, revealing a disconnect between the rhetoric in open debates and the willingness to insert R2P language into negotiated documents. The resolutions passed included Resolution 2040 on the situation in Libya, which referenced the Libyan government's primary R2P in an operative paragraph[58]; and Resolution 2085 on Mali, which included a pillar one reference to the Malian government's R2P and a pillar two reference authorising a peacekeeping mission explicitly 'to support the Malian authorities in their primary responsibility to protect the population' among other tasks.[59]

These resolutions show a more holistic implementation of R2P language than in previous resolutions. Thus, 2012 was both a year of challenge to the rhetorical level of acceptance of R2P and of continued and expanding implementation of R2P frameworks. Discontent over the intervention in Libya seemed to forestall talking about R2P but not implementing R2P policies.

2013 and 2014 – a new watershed

A new highpoint for R2P references was marked in 2013. One hundred and forty-two references to R2P were made in the UNSC, the highest of any year in this study: 125 of these references were made in open meetings; 104 were affirmations, 12 negative, 8 neutral, and 1 mixed/other. The 12 negative statements were made by the following governments: Nicaragua (4),[60] Sudan (4),[61] Syria (2),[62] Russia (1)[63] and Venezuela (1).[64] With the exception of Russia, none of the states were on the UNSC at the time but were speaking at open PoC debates or debates concerning their countries. Syria and Sudan of course both face charges of war crimes and crimes against humanity because of their abhorrent human rights records. Russia's negative statement expressed concern about the 'arbitrary interpretation of norms of international humanitarian law' including R2P.[65] Eight neutral statements were made by the following governments: Pakistan (2)[66]; Argentina (1)[67]; Ecuador (1)[68]; Portugal (1)[69]; Nicaragua (1)[70]; Rwanda (1)[71], and Sudan (1).[72]

In 2013, R2P language was also included in seven resolutions[73] and five PRSTs,[74] more than any other year. As of 28 February 2014, R2P had already been referenced 48 times – nearly equal to the entire year of 2012. Of those 48 references, 36 were affirmations, 5 were neutral, 1 was negative, and 3 were mixed/other. The one negative reference came from Venezuela,[75] while the three mixed references came from the governments of Syria and Sudan.[76] R2P references appeared in one PRST on the protection of civilians and two country specific resolutions in the 2014 sample.[77] What remains to be seen is if that positive trend of support will transcend the current membership of the UNSC and continue in years to come.

Human Rights Council data 2011–2014

Since the Libya intervention, the HRC has continued and increased the rate at which it applies R2P language (see Figure 7). From 23 March 2011 through 2013 the HRC used R2P language 14 times, nearly double its use from 2006 to March 2011. These references included eight resolutions on Syria and various resolutions on Guinea, the prevention of genocide, internally displaced persons, Afghanistan and Libya. Particularly in the face of UNSC deadlock on Syria, the HRC took up the mantel of strong R2P language, condemning those responsible for mass atrocities. R2P language has, thus, been increasingly mainstreamed in Geneva by the HRC, and this positive trend reveals further internalisation of R2P by member states across intergovernmental bodies.

Overall analysis of R2P post-Libya 2011–February 2014

Comparing the 2005–Libya 2011 data set to the post-Libya–February 2014 data set, several conclusions can be reached. First, the overall trajectory of R2P language at the UNSC from 2005 to 2014 has shown a slight increase. Time and continued usage will tell how significant this trajectory is but, for now, R2P language is frequently (and increasingly) used at the UNSC. Several aspects of R2P appear relatively uncontroversial now, especially and unsurprisingly pillar one R2P. No governments, even R2P detractors, make negative comments towards the primary R2P of each state – revealing strong internalisation of pillar one, potentially reaching the level of a 'taken for granted' quality.[78] In 2014, the government of Sudan (a frequent R2P rejectionist) even used positive primary R2P language while denying the validity of R2P in the same paragraph.[79]

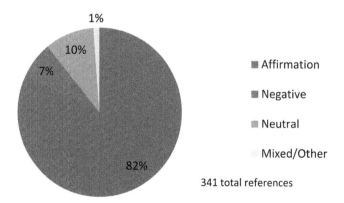

341 total references

Figure 12.   Explicit R2P references in UNSC open meetings by attribute (post-Libya 2011–February 2014). Source: M. Powers.

Second, comparing Figures 9 and 12, the percentage of affirmations of R2P at the UN open meetings has fallen slightly in the post-Libya–February 2014 data set (from 85% in the 2005–Libya 2011 data to 82%) while the percentage of negative statements slightly increased (from 5% in the 2005–Libya 2011 data to 7%). The slight increase in percentage of negative references, however, appears to be the result of an increased number of negative statements from traditional R2P rejectionists rather than an increase in the number of member states making negative comments. Seven countries used negative R2P language in the UNSC from 2005–Libya 2011. Only five countries made explicit negative statements on R2P from post-Libya 2011–February 2014: Sudan (6); Nicaragua (5); Syria (5); Venezuela (5); and Russia (2). Two of these states stand accused of war crimes and crimes against humanity and two have been R2P rejectionists since the concept's introduction.

Third, primary R2P was referenced more frequently in the UNSC and HRC (see Figure 13), while references to shared R2P decreased in frequency slightly. In UNSC open meetings, 45 member states and four UN/regional organisations referenced primary R2P a combined 85 times.[80] This includes at least one reference from all of the P5 and BRICS states, revealing deep internalisation of pillar one. Twenty-six member states and three the UN/regional organisations referenced a shared, international or UN responsibility to protect a combined 42 times.[81] And 11 member states and one regional organisation referenced a UNSC responsibility to protect a combined total of 18 times.[82]

Generally the critical states for normative acceptance (P5 and BRICS) continued to use R2P and use it affirmatively, with the notable outlier of Russia (see Figure 14). Russia significantly decreased use of R2P language from post-Libya 2011 to February 2014. When they did use R2P language, Russia focused only on pillar one or expressed negative remarks. This lack of engagement from such a key player in the UNSC is troubling for R2P's normative internalisation. However, the Russian Foreign Ministry also welcomed Special Adviser on the Responsibility to Protect, Jennifer Welsh, and Simon Adams, Director of the Global Centre for the Responsibility to Protect to participate in a panel discussion on R2P in autumn 2013, suggesting that they remain open to engagement and discussion of the issues and are not outright R2P rejectionists.

Fourth, the rate at which R2P language is being used has increased over time. R2P was referenced six times in UNSC resolutions, eight times in HRC resolutions, and 512 times

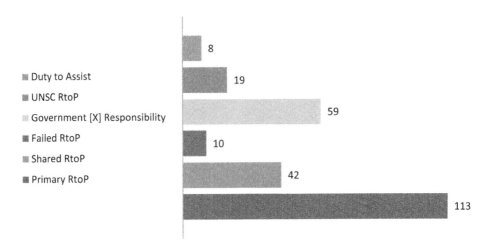

Figure 13.   Explicit R2P references by pillar at UNSC and HRC (18 March 2011–28 February 2014). Source: M. Powers.

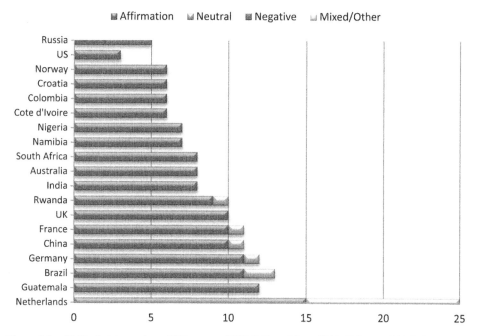

Figure 14.   Critical states and top R2P users at UNSC (Post-Libya 2011–February 2014). Source: M. Powers.

affirmatively and neutrally in UNSC open meetings over the course of more than six years from 14 September 2005 to 17 March 2011. In the three years since – from 18 March 2011 to 28 February 2014 – R2P was referenced 33 times in UNSC resolutions and presidential statements, 14 times in HRC resolutions, and 312 times affirmatively and neutrally in UNSC open meetings. Comparing the two data sets, there are over five times more references to R2P in UNSC resolutions and PRSTs after Libya than before. This increase in rate is despite the significant decrease in usage of R2P in 2012. Some would suggest that this is merely a reflection of the ongoing situations of mass atrocities – namely Syria. While Syria's importance may skew the data, that statement assumes that another situation of mass atrocities would equally propel an increase in R2P references, strengthening internalisation of the norm.

Finally, there is also an apparent increase in the frequency of R2P references in PRSTs and resolutions, displaying a willingness of states to continue to use and implement R2P frameworks and revealing that states wary of R2P (namely Russia and China) have not held up documents that include R2P references. Most notably, in February 2014 a resolution on Syria even included a reference to the government's primary responsibility to protect its people. That may be a very shallow reference to only pillar one of R2P, but it does show a willingness to say the R2P framework applies to that crisis and Russia did not make R2P's inclusion a point of contention in the negotiations.

Conclusion

R2P is not dead and, if anything, the debates and concern following the intervention in Libya and the shock to our common humanity from the ongoing crisis in Syria have deepened and expanded the normative internalisation of the responsibility to protect. It is now commonplace for the UNSC to utilise R2P language in its resolutions and authorise peace-keeping missions under the framework of R2P. It is now even common for R2P detractors to co-opt the language of R2P in support of their own political agenda – revealing the moral and political currency captured by the R2P framework. What remains is moving that rhetorical commitment from words to deeds and using the moral and political legitimacy of R2P to implement smart, effective policies to prevent and protect against mass atrocities and their devastating impact on civilians.

Acknowledgements

My deepest gratitude to Professor Michael W. Doyle, Director of the Columbia Global Policy Initiative for his guidance and support and to Alicia Evangelides, Assistant Director of the Columbia Global Policy Initiative. The research detailed in this article was also summarised on the openGlobal Rights blog of openDemocracy: Maggie Powers, 'The Responsibility to Protect after Libya – Dead, Dying or Thriving?', *openDemocracy*, 24 June 2014, https://www.opendemocracy.net/openglobalrights-blog/maggie-powers/responsibility-to-protect-after-libya-%E2%80%93-dead-dying-or-thriving.

Disclosure statement

No potential conflict of interest was reported by the author.

Notes

1. Francis M. Deng et al., eds, *Sovereignty as Responsibility: Conflict Management in Africa* (Washington, DC: The Brookings Institution, 1996).
2. Bernard Kouchner, 'The Right to Intervention: Codified in Kosovo', *New Perspectives Quarterly* 16, no. 4 (1999): 4–7, doi:10.1111/j.1540-5842.1999.tb00057.x.
3. Michael Barnett, *Empire of Humanity: A History of Humanitarianism* (Ithaca, NY: Cornell University Press, 2011), 166.
4. David Rieff, 'R2P, R.I.P.', *The New York Times*, 7 November 2011, sec. Opinion, http://www.nytimes.com/2011/11/08/opinion/r2p-rip.html.
5. Data collection begins on 14 September 2005 as this is the first UNSC meeting to occur after the negotiation of the WSOD adopted at the UN General Assembly session held 14–16 September 2005.
6. Turkish statement to the UN Security Council, *S/PV.6066: Protection of Civilians in Armed Conflict*, 14 January 2009, http://www.un.org/en/ga/search/view_doc.asp?symbol=S/PV.6066.
7. Sudanese statement to the UN Security Council, *S/PV.6216 (Resumption 1): Protection of Civilians in Armed Conflict*, 11 November 2009, http://www.un.org/en/ga/search/view_doc.asp?symbol=S/PV.6216(Resumption1).
8. Russian statement to the UN Security Council, *S/PV.5577 (Resumption 1): Protection of Civilians in Armed Conflict*, 4 December 2006, http://www.un.org/en/ga/search/view_doc.asp?symbol=S/PV.5577(Resumption1).
9. UN Security Council, *S/PV.5264: The Role of Civil Society in Conflict Prevention and the Pacific Settlement of Disputes*, 20 September 2005, 16, 20, http://www.un.org/en/ga/search/view_doc.asp?symbol=S/PV.5264.

10. Cristina Gabriela Badescu, *Humanitarian Intervention and the Responsibility to Protect: security and human rights* (London: Routledge, 2010), 109.
11. Affirmative references from: Peru (5), Tanzania (4), Liechtenstein (3), Norway (3), Slovakia (3), South Korea (3), Canada (2), Denmark (2), Nepal (2), the UK (2), Argentina (1), Benin (1), China (1), France (1), Germany (1), Greece (1), Italy (1), Japan (1), Rwanda (1), Spain (1), Switzerland (1).
12. Neutral references from: Brazil (2), China (2), France (1), Russia (1), South Africa (1).
13. Russian statement at UN Security Council, *S/PV.5319: The Protection of Civilians in Armed Conflict*, 9 December 2005, 19, http://www.un.org/en/ga/search/view_doc.asp?symbol=S/PV.5319. Egyptian statement at UN Security Council, *S/PV.5319 (Resumption 1): Protection of Civilians in Armed Conflict*, 9 December 2005, 6, http://www.un.org/en/ga/search/view_doc.asp?symbol=S/PV.5319(Resumption1).
14. UN Security Council, *S/PV.5319 (Resumption 1): Protection of Civilians in Armed Conflict*, 3.
15. UN Security Council, *S/PV.5319: The Protection of Civilians in Armed Conflict*, 10.
16. UN Security Council, *S/PV.5359: The Situation in the Great Lakes Region*, 27 January 2006, http://www.un.org/en/ga/search/view_doc.asp?symbol=S/PV.5359; UN Security Council, *S/PV.5359 (Resumption 1): The Situation in the Great Lakes Region*, 27 January 2006, http://www.un.org/en/ga/search/view_doc.asp?symbol=S/PV.5359(Resumption1).
17. UN Security Council, *Resolution 1674 (2006): Protection of Civilians in Armed Conflict*, 28 April 2006 2, http://www.un.org/en/ga/search/view_doc.asp?symbol=S/RES/1674(2006).
18. UN General Assembly, *2005 World Summit Outcome: Resolution Adopted by the General Assembly*, 24 October 2005, http://www.refworld.org/docid/44168a910.html.
19. Only one resolution on Sudan (A/HRC/RES/11/10) was not adopted by consensus.
20. UN Security Council, *Resolution 1653 (2006): The Great Lakes Region*; UN Security Council, *Resolution 1706 (2006): Sudan*, 31 August 2006, http://www.un.org/en/ga/search/view_doc.asp?symbol=S/RES/1706(2006); UN Security Council, *Resolution 1970 (2011): Peace and Security in Africa*, 26 February 2011, http://www.un.org/en/ga/search/view_doc.asp?symbol=S/RES/1970(2011); UN Security Council, *Resolution 1973 (2011): Libya*, 17 March 2011, http://www.un.org/en/ga/search/view_doc.asp?symbol=S/RES/1973(2011).
21. UN Security Council, *Resolution 1674 (2006): Protection of Civilians in Armed Conflict*; UN Security Council, *Resolution 1894 (2009): Protection of Civilians in Armed Conflict*, 11 November 2009, http://www.un.org/en/ga/search/view_doc.asp?symbol=S/RES/1894 (2009).
22. UN Security Council, *Resolution 1653 (2006): The Great Lakes Region*.
23. UN Security Council, *Resolution 1674 (2006): Protection of Civilians in Armed Conflict*; UN Security Council, *Resolution 1706 (2006): Sudan*; UN Security Council, *Resolution 1894 (2009): Protection of Civilians in Armed Conflict*.
24. List of neutral references by country: China (9), South Africa (5), Qatar (4), Australia (2), Brazil (2), France (2), Russia (2), Slovakia (2), Turkey (2), the UK (2), Benin (1), Colombia (1), Japan (1), Libya (1), Mexico (1), Palestine (1), Papua New Guinea (1), Sudan (1), Uruguay (1).
25. List of neutral references by organisations: UN Under Secretary-General for Humanitarian Affairs (5), UN High Commissioner for Refugees (3), Commonwealth Secretary (1), European Union (1), UN Secretary-General (1).
26. UN Security Council, *S/PV.5508: The Situation in the Middle East*, 8 August 2006, 5, http://www.un.org/en/ga/search/view_doc.asp?symbol=S/PV.5508.
27. UN Security Council, *S/PV.5663: Climate Change*, 17 April 2007, 28, http://www.un.org/en/ga/search/view_doc.asp?symbol=S/PV.5663.
28. UN Security Council, *S/PV.5898: Protection of Civilians in Armed Conflict*, 27 May 2008, 18, http://www.un.org/en/ga/search/view_doc.asp?symbol=S/PV.5898.
29. UN Security Council, *S/PV.5952: The Situation in Georgia*, 8 August 2008, 5, http://www.un.org/en/ga/search/view_doc.asp?symbol=S/PV.5952.
30. References to primary R2P: Qatar (5); China (4); France (4); Russia (4); the UK (4); Austria (3); Burkina Faso (3); UN DPKO (3); Portugal (3); Sri Lanka (3); Denmark (2); Chile (2); Colombia (2); Costa Rica (2); Guatemala (2); Liechtenstein (2); Morocco (2); Nigeria (2); UN OCHA (2); Slovakia (2); Vietnam (2); Argentina (1); Belgium (1); Brazil (1); Congo-Brazzaville (1); Croatia (1); Egypt (1); Germany (1); Ghana (1); Iceland (1); Kenya (1); Norway (1); Peru (1); Rwanda (1); South Africa (1); South Korea (1); Spain (1); and SRSG on Sexual Violence in Armed Conflict (1).

31. References to shared R2P: Nigeria (6); France (5); Australia (4); Liechtenstein (4); Peru (4); the UK (4); the US (4); Panama (3); Slovakia (3); Turkey (3); Belgium (2); Denmark (2); Croatia (2); Guatemala (2); Iceland (2); Slovenia (2); South Korea (2); Tanzania (2); UN OCHA (2); Argentina (1); Benin (1); Congo-Brazzaville (1); Commonwealth Secretariat (1); Costa Rica (1); Ghana (1) Greece (1); India (1); Libya (1); Mexico (1); Norway (1); Portugal (1); Qatar (1); Rwanda (1); Spain (1); and UN Secretary-General (1).

32. Argentina (2); Canada (2); Costa Rica (2); Libya (2); Denmark (1); Croatia (1); France (1); Guatemala (1); Lebanon (1); Mexico (1); Palestine (1); Somalia (1); South Africa (1); Turkey (1); the UK (1); the US (1); and UN OCHA (1).

33. 'Libyan Protesters Clash with Police in Benghazi', *The Guardian*, 16 February 2011, http://www.guardian.co.uk/world/2011/feb/16/libyan-protesters-clash-with-police.

34. Colin Moynihan, 'Libya's U.N. Diplomats Break With Qaddafi', *The New York Times*, 21 February 2011, sec. World/Africa, http://www.nytimes.com/2011/02/22/world/africa/22nations.html.

35. 'Gaddafi Vows to Crush Protesters', accessed 14 December 2012, http://www.aljazeera.com/news/africa/2011/02/2011225165641323716.html.

36. UN Security Council, *Resolution 1970 (2011): Peace and Security in Africa*.

37. UN Security Council, *Resolution 1973 (2011): Libya*, 3.

38. UN Security Council, *Resolution 1973 (2011): Libya*.

39. Jennifer M. Welsh, 'Norm Contestation and the Responsibility to Protect', *Global Responsibility to Protect* 5, no. 4 (January 1, 2013): 365–96, doi:10.1163/1875984X-00504002; Aidan Hehir, 'The permanence of inconsistency: Libya, the Security Council, and the Responsibility to Protect', *International Security* 38, no.1 (2013): 137–159.

40. UN Security Council, *S/PV.6490: Peace and Security in Africa*, 25 February 2011, 2, http://www.un.org/en/ga/search/view_doc.asp?symbol=S/PV.6490; UN Security Council, *S/PV.6491: Peace and Security in Africa*, 26 February 2011, 5, http://www.un.org/en/ga/search/view_doc.asp?symbol=S/PV.6491.

41. UN Security Council, *S/PV.6498: The Situation in Libya*, 2.

42. 'Arab League Condemns Broad Western Bombing Campaign in Libya', *Washington Post*, http://articles.washingtonpost.com/2011-03-20/world/35260239_1_arab-league-amr-moussa-libyan-ground-forces (accessed 14 December 2012).

43. Barbara Plett, 'UN Security Council Middle Powers' Arab Spring Dilemma', *BBC*, 8 November 2011, sec. Middle East, http://www.bbc.co.uk/news/world-middle-east-15628006.

44. W. Andy Knight and Frazer Egerton, eds, *The Routledge Handbook of the Responsibility to Protect* (London: Routledge, 2012), 266.

45. Permanent Representative of Brazil to the United Nations, *Responsibility While Protecting: Elements for the Development and Promotion of a Concept*, 9 November 2011, http://www.un.int/brazil/speech/Concept-Paper-%20RwP.pdf.

46. Ruan Zongze, 'Responsible Protection: Building a Safer World', *China Institute of International Studies*, 15 June 2012, http://www.ciis.org.cn/english/2012-06/15/content_5090912.htm.

47. Gareth J. Evans, 'The Responsibility to Protect Comes of Age', *Project Syndicate*, 26 October 2011, http://www.project-syndicate.org/commentary/the-responsibility-to-protect-comes-of-age/english.

48. From the UK (3); Colombia (2); France (2); Guatemala (2); Organization of Islamic Cooperation (2); Rwanda (2); Turkey (2); Argentina (1); Brazil (1); Estonia (1); European Union (1); Germany (1); Lithuania (1); Qatar (1); Secretary-General (1); and Togo (1).

49. A/HRC/RES/S-18/1 adopted 5 December 2011; A/HRC/RES/19/22 adopted 23 March 2012; A/HRC/RES/S-19/1 adopted 1 June 2012; A/HRC/RES/20/22 adopted 6 July 2012; A/HRC/RES/21/26 adopted 28 September 2012; A/HRC/RES/22/24 adopted 22 March 2013; A/HRC/RES/23/1 adopted 29 May 2013; and A/HRC/RES/23/26 adopted 14 June 2013.

50. A/RES/66/253 B adopted 7 August 2012; A/C.3/67/L.52* adopted by the General Assembly Third Committee, 9 November 2012; A/67/L.63 adopted 8 May 2013; A/C.3/68/L.42/Rev.1 adopted 19 November 2013.

51. Thomas G. Weiss, 'After Syria, Whither R2P?'. *Into the Eleventh Hour* (2014): 36.

52. UN Security Council, S/PV.6531: *Protection of Civilians in Armed Conflict*, May 10, 2011, 10, http://www.un.org/en/ga/search/view_doc.asp?symbol=S/PV.6531.

53. UN Security Council, *S/PV.6790: Protection of Civilians in Armed Conflict*, 25 June 2012, 21, http://www.un.org/en/ga/search/view_doc.asp?symbol=S/PV.6790.

54. Ibid., 29.
55. UN Security Council, S/PV.6790: Protection of Civilians in Armed Conflict, June 25, 2012, 25, http://www.un.org/en/ga/search/view_doc.asp?symbol=S/PV.6790.
56. Ibid., 28.
57. S/PRST/2012/18 and S/PRST/2012/28 on the LRA-affected region of Central Africa.
58. S/RES/2040 on Libya, S/RES/2085 on Mali, and S/RES/2093 on Somalia.
59. Resolutions 1970 and 1973 only included R2P references in the preamble so this may even be a stronger R2P reference.
60. S/RES/2085.
61. UN Security Council, *S/PV.6917: Protection of Civilians in Armed Conflict*, 12 February 2013, 53–4, http://www.un.org/en/ga/search/view_doc.asp?symbol=S/PV.6917.
62. Ibid., 66; UN Security Council, *S/PV.7019: Protection of Civilians in Armed Conflict*, 19 August 2013, 71, http://www.un.org/en/ga/search/view_doc.asp?symbol=S/PV.7019.
63. UN Security Council, *S/PV.6917: Protection of Civilians in Armed Conflict*, 19; UN Security Council, *S/PV.6949: The Situation in the Middle East*, 18 April 2013, 10, http://www.un.org/en/ga/search/view_doc.asp?symbol=S/PV.6949.
64. UN Security Council, *S/PV.6903: United Nations Peacekeeping Operations*, 21 January 2013, 17, http://www.un.org/en/ga/search/view_doc.asp?symbol=S/PV.6903.
65. UN Security Council, *S/PV.6917 (Resumption 1): Protection of Civilians in Armed Conflict*, 12 February 2013, 45, http://www.un.org/en/ga/search/view_doc.asp?symbol=S/PV.6917 (Resumption1).
66. UN Security Council, *S/PV.6903: United Nations Peacekeeping Operations*, 17.
67. UN Security Council, *S/PV.6917: Protection of Civilians in Armed Conflict*, 16; UN Security Council, *S/PV.7019: Protection of Civilians in Armed Conflict*, 19.
68. UN Security Council, *S/PV.6917: Protection of Civilians in Armed Conflict*, 27.
69. UN Security Council, *S/PV.6917 (Resumption 1): Protection of Civilians in Armed Conflict*, 57.
70. Ibid., 14.
71. Ibid., 53.
72. UN Security Council, *S/PV.6962: The Situation in Libya*, 8 May 2013, 8, http://www.un.org/en/ga/search/view_doc.asp?symbol=S/PV.6962.
73. UN Security Council, *S/PV.7019: Protection of Civilians in Armed Conflict*, 18.
74. Resolutions 2093 on Somalia, 2095 on Libya, 2100 on Mali, 2109 on South Sudan, 2117 on Small Arms, and 2121 and 2127 on the Central African Republic.
75. S/PRST/2013/2 on the protection of civilians; S/PRST/2013/4 on peace and security in Africa; S/PRST/2013/15 on Syria; and S/PRST/2013/6 and S/PRST/2013/18 on the LRA-affected region of Central Africa.
76. UN Security Council, *S/PV.7105: Maintenance of International Peace and Security*, 29 January 2014, 60, http://www.un.org/en/ga/search/view_doc.asp?symbol=S/PV.7105.
77. UN Security Council, *S/PV.7109: Protection of Civilians in Armed Conflict*, 12 February 2014, http://www.un.org/en/ga/search/view_doc.asp?symbol=S/PV.7109.
78. S/PRST/2014/3 on the protection of civilians, S/RES/2134 on the Central African Republic, and S/RES/2139 on Syria.
79. In interviews conducted by the author all interviewees noted the highly accepted nature of primary responsibility of states and several interviewees commented that primary R2P language has become so commonplace in UNSC resolutions that it does not come up as an issue in negotiations.
80. Sudan said: 'For example, with respect to the principle of the responsibility to protect, which we wish to endorse from this podium, even if it appears in the Millennium Declaration, it nevertheless remains open to very different interpretations. It is in contradiction with a principle enshrined in the Charter, namely, respect for national sovereignty and States' primary responsibility for the protection of their civilians.' UN Security Council, *S/PV.7109: Protection of Civilians in Armed Conflict*, 80.
81. References to primary R2P: China (7); South Africa (7); Germany (4); Colombia (3); France (3); Guatemala (3); European Union (3); Malaysia (3); the UK (3); Chile (2); India (2); Ireland (2); Kenya (2); Lithuania (2); Portugal (2); Switzerland (2); Armenia (1); Australia (1); Bangladesh (1); Benin (1); Bosnia and Herzegovina (1); Botswana (1); Brazil (1); Ecuador (1); Egypt (1); Estonia (1); Hungary (1); Indonesia (1); Iran (1); Italy (1); Japan (1); Jordan (1); Latvia (1); Morocco (1); Namibia (1); Nicaragua (1); Nigeria (1); Norway (1); Russia (1); Rwanda (1);

Slovakia (1); South Korea (1); Sri Lanka (1); Sudan (1); Syria (1); Thailand (1); the US (1); Venezuela (1); Head of UN PKO in Cote d'Ivoire (1); UN DPKO (1); and UN OCHA (1).

82. References to shared responsibility: Guatemala (3); France (3); Brazil (3); Turkey (3); Australia (2); Croatia (2); UN Secretary-General (2); the US (2); Nigeria (2); Armenia (1); Chile (1); Denmark (1); Estonia (1); European Union (1); Fiji (1); Germany (1); Israel (1); Japan (1); Kuwait (1); Lebanon (1); Luxembourg (1); Namibia (1); Norway (1); Rwanda (1); Saudi Arabia (1); Slovenia (1); Sweden (1); the UK (1); and UN Special Adviser on the Prevention of Genocide (1).

83. References to UNSC responsibility: France (3); Rwanda (3); Organization of Islamic Cooperation (2); Turkey (2); Armenia (1); Azerbaijan (1); Chad (1); India (1); Lebanon (1); Namibia (1); Norway (1); and Portugal (1).

Protecting while not being responsible: the case of Syria and responsibility to protect

Heidarali Teimouri

School of Law University of Leeds, Leeds, UK

This article seeks to dissect the doctrine of responsibility to protect, which consists of two other international law concepts, namely protection and responsibility, both long desired goals of international law. The article will discuss why this doctrine is not working properly. Here the focus is on the case of Syria; while the previous case of Libya was declared to be this doctrine 'came of age'. Here the problem will be discussed based on the inherent contradiction in this doctrine's formulation, and the related weakness of international law. Since, when one speaks about responsibility to protect, the notion of 'protection' trumps the other one and many ask for more intervention, while the other component of this doctrine, 'responsibility', will be eclipsed. Thus it tries to depict the problem of inconsistent application of responsibility to protect in a more general pattern of international law, as this phenomenon is nascent in the sense of legal responsibility. In this regard, the article is based on interactional international law, which is more focused on practice, since this doctrine has not been firmly legally codified; this theory better suits us to portray the inner contradiction of responsibility to protect.

1. Introduction

In a situation like Syria, I have to ask: can we make a difference in that situation? Would a military intervention have an impact? What would be the aftermath of our involvement on the ground? Could it trigger even worse violence or the use of chemical weapons? ... What offers the best prospect of a stable post-Assad regime? And how do I weigh tens of thousands who have been killed in Syria versus the tens of thousands who are currently being killed in the Congo? These are not simple questions.[1]

The prohibition of mass atrocity crimes, mainly including genocide, crimes against humanity and war crimes, is now recognized to be the peremptory norm of general international law.[2] This status of mass atrocity crimes is significant since it places responsibility on the international community, or perhaps on the UN Security Council as the best embodiment of it, to respond to the commission of these crimes, while, sadly speaking, history testifies the opposite. In this regard, the Syrian crisis as an ongoing case relating to international law to date highlights the uncertain legal status of the doctrine of responsibility to protect.

This article seeks to argue why applying the secondary responsibility of international community after the host state's primary duty failure is difficult, and thus far this type of responsibility does not enjoy concrete sanction within the international legal system. Therefore, recourse to coercive measures as the most controversial aspect of responsibility to protect comes to the fore, how to apply and monitor its protective nature.

It should be borne in mind that this article is not aiming to account for the (il)legality of intervention/non-intervention in the case of the Syrian crisis, but rather it is directed to look at this crisis from a different perspective. To dissect this doctrine, the question is whether the 'responsible protection' has taken place, or could take place at all. As a result, the debate of this article is not based on the classical clash of pro-interventionism (pro-human rights) and pro-sovereignty (non-interventionism), whereas the argument springs totally from an inside review of the responsibility to protect: how states understand and apply it. This approach tries to find this doctrine's genesis in a more general pattern of obligation and accountability in international law. In this regard, the above mentioned quotation can portray the problematic nature of protection and responsibility in our era.

Furthermore, the legal status of protection of people (humanitarian protection) in contemporary international law is problematic too. In fact, non-protective elements doubtlessly prompt interveners to have recourse on military or other types of intervention.[3] Therefore, one can acknowledge that it is hard or even impossible to find a case with *pure* or *exclusive* protective motives/reasons. Hence motives in all cases are mixed, and for whoever is analysing the protective phenomenon this point must always remain in their mind. Consequently, 'we must be very careful not to create academic concepts which might faithfully describe a single aspect of international law only to attribute to them afterwards the status of a legal provision ... without requiring detailed evidence for a "hard law" foundation'.[4] In this regard, owing to the absence of any hard law evidence of the legality of responsibility to protect thus far, this article is trying to analyse this doctrine based on interactional law theory, which best suits us in terms of its rootedness in reciprocal practices of states among themselves rather than mere reliance on treaties and formal documents.

Therefore, the first part of this article is concerned with a brief account of responsibility to protect formation, and the second section offers a short account of interactional international law theory, while the third part will go through the Syrian crisis and international community inaction/limited intervention. And finally, in conclusion, it will depict the legal status of responsibility to protect based on the practice of states.

2. Responsibility to protect: sovereignty as responsibility

Literally speaking, responsibility to protect consists of *responsibility* and *protection*, two rather controversial and also long-sought goals/principles of international law. Here this part will briefly account for the problem of responsibility and protection notions in this doctrine's trajectory.

> The [responsibility to protect] is viewed by its supporters as a milestone in the *protection of human rights* and a significant development from the initial idea of *state human rights obligations*, through the idea of humanitarian intervention and to the notion of a collective responsibility to protect. (emphasis added)[5]

This quotation can best epitomize the challenge ahead of this doctrine to gain international legality, i.e. the problem of human rights protection and states' obligation to act.

In fact, the responsibility notion was introduced to the protection of human rights by the ICISS (International Commission on Intervention and State Sovereignty) Report based on the distinction between internal and external responsibilities of states; the primary responsibility which each and every state has toward its own people (internal) and the secondary responsibility of the international community as a whole (consisting of all states) toward other states (external).[6]

While the notion of protection has its longstanding pedigree in history,[7] the notion of the responsibility of states, particularly a secondary responsibility of the international community to halt mass atrocity crimes, has recently emerged; it came out of the notion of a *right* to humanitarian intervention, and this issue appears to be the most innovative/transcendental feature of this doctrine (responsibility to protect).[8] In this regard, the emphasis on the issue of *sovereignty as responsibility* and the primary responsibility of host states was due to an attempt to shift this doctrine away from exclusively a rights-based formulation of humanitarian intervention. Therefore, responsibility to protect was mainly understood a duty-based doctrine, unlike humanitarian intervention;[9] i.e. to promote this doctrine one should lay stress on the notion of *responsibility* within international law.

After the adoption of responsibility to protect within the Outcome Document in 2005, the hostility against it among states seemed to ebb away with different legal or political arguments, generally trying to embolden it as a doctrine within pre-existing international law principles.[10] However, there seems to be an unrecognized perplexing problem here.

As was mentioned before, with regard to the entwinement of responsibility to protect with four international crimes, namely genocide, war crimes, crimes against humanity, and ethnic cleansing, seemingly this doctrine should gain the status of peremptory norm and invoke *erga omnes* responsibility,[11] but this is only one side of the coin.

To illuminate, in the process of the Outcome Document adoption in 2005, this issue that states are not ready to accept any kind of legal responsibility to protect other states' people in the face of mass atrocity crimes commission resurfaced, and some states even doubted the compatibility of this secondary responsibility of the international community with the UN Charter.[12] The famous letter of US ambassador John R. Bolton dated August 30 2005 can encapsulate the above-mentioned problem, since it manifests the general understanding of the responsibility notion among states, particularly powerful states. In this letter he mentioned that the US would 'not accept that either the United Nations as a whole, or the Security Council, or individual states, have an obligation to intervene under international law'. Accordingly, to remedy this total rejection of responsibility-based formulation of this doctrine, he proposed that international responsibility to protect be sought in the form of *moral responsibility* of the international community to 'use appropriate diplomatic, economic, humanitarian and other peaceful means, including under Chapters VI and VIII of the Charter to help protect populations from ... atrocities.'[13] Retrospectively, this *moral duty* argument to justify military intervention has its predecessor in the case of the Kosovo intervention when NATO states (with the exception of Belgium) had recourse to it to legally justify their behaviour.[14]

Considering that assessment of morality is subjective in the first place, this implies states escape any kind of hard law mechanism to guarantee their accountability in respect of exhaustion of their secondary international responsibility. This reflects the interrelation between *responsibility*, *accountability* and *institutionalization* in international law.[15]

Furthermore, the sense of particularly positive responsibility of states in case of peremptory norms violations is not a well-sanctioned issue in international law. Generally speaking, 'contemporary international law imposes only limited positive duties on states'.[16] The most prominent international document in this respect is the ILC Draft of States

Responsibility,[17] in which the commission designates that in case of 'a gross or systematic failure by the responsible State' to respect peremptory norms of general international law[18] two sets of consequences would ensue:[19] (1) the positive obligation of states 'to cooperate to bring [the serious breach] to an end through lawful means'; and (2) the negative obligation of states neither to 'recognize as lawful a situation created by a serious breach ... nor render aid or assistance in maintaining that situation.'[20] In this regard, the cautious articulation of the Outcome Document ('[W]e are prepared to take collective action ... on a case-by-case basis')[21] in fact resulted partly from the unwillingness of states to concede that the Security Council has a positive duty to act.[22]

On the other hand, in terms of the legality of responsibility to protect, the secondary legal obligation of the international community seems the most crucial part still requiring clarification and consensus to guarantee its application. Owing to the unauthorized intervention in Kosovo, which worked as a catalyst for the introduction of responsibility to protect by the ICISS Report in 2001:

> It is very important to keep in mind that the [responsibility to protect] has been born not only as an aspiration of the international community to protect civilian population from the most cruel and mass violations of human rights but equally as *an expression of the will of the international community to put an end to the practice by some states and alliances to use armed force for 'protection' in an unilateral manner, ignoring the UNSC and often promoting in reality their own interests.* (emphasis in original)[23]

Therefore, the most crucial aspirations were to curb the irresponsible unilateralism and promote human rights protection concomitantly, and this urged the birth of this doctrine upon the international community first and foremost.

To delve into this, it reveals that the responsibility to protect people from four international crimes 'rests on the foundations of the law of state responsibility'. In the case of peremptory norms violations, the law of state responsibility *should* instruct that states are not merely *entitled* to demand to stop the commission of crimes, but are under an *obligation* to cooperate to halt them.[24] Therefore, the credibility, authority, and thus the effectiveness of the doctrine's promotion are dependent on *consistent compliance* with its requirements among states.[25]

3. Interactional law theory: obligation and responsibility to protect

International law is imbued with legal inconsistency, deviation and violation if one takes a glance at the history. To speak about law, one should keep in mind that international law is a different kind of law in which states as its main originators/subjects are both executors and lawmakers simultaneously. Therefore, it is impossible to come up with a flawless theory to answer all these deficiencies and inconsistencies comprehensively.

In this regard, the interactional international law theory as an argumentative basis in this article is basically concerned with the *practice* of international law players,[26] and also with the distinction between social and legal norms[27] which could be translated in this respect as the distinction between political norms and fully-fledged legal norms. It should also be borne in mind that this theory is aimed at preserving and respecting the diversity and plurality of the international arena,[28] and thereby better explain the inconsistencies facing international law instead of dissolving it all in one universal understanding, which seems unrealistic and impractical in the contemporary world.

To be brief, to qualify an interactional norm process, essentially 'relatively stable patterns of expectation', or – to use constructivist terminology – shared understandings, must emerge. According to this theory, shared understandings 'are only likely to arise from repeated social practice' (a horizontal portrayal of law).[29] Therefore, the authoritative rules are formed by 'mutually constructed' (reciprocal) interactions rather than by 'power over' others.[30] Therefore, reciprocity takes priority in this theory. To reach a *shared understanding,* repeated behaviour is needed, which can only be sustained through *reciprocity* among different players. In this regard, legal norms 'can only emerge when they are rooted in an underlying set of shared understandings ... [and on the other hand] Shared understandings are collectively held background knowledge'[31] to form further norms and practices.

In sum, to depict interactional law theory a quotation from the founders of this theory can best serve us here:

> [t]hey are shared understandings precisely because they are intersubjective – generated and maintained through social interaction. On the one hand, actors generate and promote particular understandings. ... On the other hand, once in existence, shared understandings shape how actors perceive themselves and the world, how they form interests and set priorities, and how they make arguments or evaluate others' arguments.[32]

In a real sense, *legal obligation* will be generated based on *reciprocal/collectively practiced* shared understanding.

To introduce the next part addressing the uneven application of interventions in past practice, the failure of the international community in the case of the Syrian crisis is discussed to illustrate that 'there is merit in identifying patterns of practice in order to facilitate *'shared' normative understandings'* (emphasis added).[33]

4. Syrian crisis: ambivalent inaction/intervention

The Syrian upheaval followed the so called Arab Spring domino effect of autocratic governments' collapse, which began in Tunisia at the end of 2010, followed in February 2011 by peaceful demonstrations demanding reforms in Syria. Chronologically, a turning point came when the peaceful demonstration of Dar'a in mid-March received a brutal response from the government and caused the rapid spread of protest against the Syrian government.[34] Whilst the situation in Syria was worsening and brutality continuing in May 2011, France, Germany, Portugal and the UK brought a draft resolution to the table at the Security Council to condemn the Syrian government crackdown and *stress this government's primary responsibility to protect its citizens.* This draft faced strong opposition from Russia, China, India, Brazil, and South Africa, since they expressed their concern that this resolution was an intervention in matters which fell within the internal jurisdiction of the state of Syria. Finally, after five months of intense negotiations among the members of the Security Council, the final version of the resolution was concluded and put to the vote. To reconcile with its critics, they removed the paragraphs related to the imposition of sanctions, while not completely denying the probability of sanction enforcement should the Syrian government not comply with the resolution's provisions in the future. The resolution was vetoed by Russia and China, and therefore this first attempt foundered.[35]

Again, while the Syrian tragedy was continuing and the situation seemingly manifesting the government's failure to exercise the responsibility to protect its citizens, the Security Council engaged in renewed negotiations to respond to this situation, this time based on the Arab League's draft, which appeared more controversial and unacceptable to states like Russia. Prominently, the draft asked President Assad to step aside and call for a national unity government. Generally, the way this draft was articulated was similar to the Libyan resolution, particularly in that unspecified measures could be taken, so there was little chance this resolution would be adopted.[36]

Nevertheless, the efforts to reach a consensus to respond to the Syrian tragedy did not cease. Next, Morocco presented a draft resolution backed by 18 other states to try hard to encourage Russia and China into alliance; in its preamble the resolution explicitly rejected any kind of coercive measure authorization ensuing from this resolution to guarantee non-repetition of the Libyan case, but unfortunately the resolution was again vetoed by only two negative votes by China and Russia, while the rest unanimously voted in favour of it.[37]

In the drama of ceaseless proposition and rejection of resolutions between the Security Council members, a third vote was held in July 2012, again in a version friendlier to Russia and China, which was unsurprisingly faced with their veto once more.[38]

One reason Russia set out as a basis for its veto was the case of Libya and the way that military operation was implemented, which ended with regime change instead of following its protective mandate:

> The demand for a quick ceasefire turned into a full-fledged civil war, the humanitarian, social, economic and military consequences of which transcend Libyan borders. The situation in con-nection with the no-fly zone has morphed into the bombing of oil refineries, television stations and other civilian sites. The arms embargo has morphed into a naval blockade in western Libya, including a blockade of humanitarian goods. Today the tragedy of Benghazi has spread to other western Libyan towns – Sirte and Bani Walid. These types of models should be excluded from global practices once and for all.[39]

The lack of accountability regarding the scope and impact of the intervention in Libya, while it was launched ostensibly to protect the Libyan people, worked retrospectively to create a backlash against any lesser intervention in Syria.

Nonetheless, on 21 August 2013 the scene of the Syrian crisis changed dramatically; as documented through video evidence, civilians were killed, allegedly by chemical weapons, in the Ghouta area outside Damascus. This fact urged the US President to take action even without UN authorization since it was a red line which had been set previously by the American government which if crossed would result in intervention as had been plainly communicated to the Syrian regime.[40] In this case, Barack Obama tried to bolster the legal justification for *unilateral* use of force based on four arguments, namely deterrence, threats of further attacks, collective self-defence and enforcement of norms (prohibition of use of chemical weapons).[41]

This conduct, use of chemical weapons against civilians, as a breach of well-accepted customary international law,[42] qualifies both as a crime against humanity and as a war crime. It can trigger the application of responsibility to protect, as embraced in paragraphs 138 and 139 of the Outcome Document.[43] But the perplexing point here again gives rise to the issue of intervention. In fact, the question is not about whether to intervene or turn a blind eye and stand idle, but rather the critical point here is *how* to respond.[44]

In the same vein, punishing a regime for its unlawful behaviour through resorting to the threat or use of force without an authorized mandate is flawed. In fact, this argument con-flates to some extent two conflicting legal layers, namely: (1) the breach of an international peremptory norm (the universal ban on the use of chemical weapons in armed conflicts); and (2) the response method (accountability). This argument overlooks that there are other competing, important 'red lines' that deserve respect, i.e. the prohibition on aggres-sion and working through a collective security system: Articles 2(1) and (4) of the UN Charter.[45] In fact, the UN was established among other purposes to restrict and delimit the use of force among states and bring more legal transparency in this respect. In this regard, the use of force was exclusively restricted to self-defence (article 51) and the Security Council authorization in case of any threat against international peace and security (article 42). In the case of the Syrian crisis and the US response, owing to a lack of any firm excuse of self-defence (Syria has not launched an *armed attack* or threatened to attack any American target) and also a lack of Security Council authorization, to have recourse to use force or the threat of it is beyond the legal prescriptions of the Charter, hence it could be labelled as aggression or intervention in the domestic jurisdiction of Syrian sovereignty (Article 2[4]).[46]

Therefore, to overcome this contradiction, other tools for holding states accountable for their actions could be preferable here. The responsibility of states for their actions and individual criminal responsibility both come to the fore in consideration of any kind of intervention and application of responsibility to protect, legally speaking.

Unfortunately, recently it has become increasingly common to merge the language of punitive war with protection of people, and criminal responsibility of individuals and state responsibility in the case of human rights violations. This tendency is threatening the rationale behind the responsibility of states to protect their people and the responsibility of the international community to shoulder its secondary responsibility.[47] In this sense, the disagreement and boycott of referring the case of Syria to the International Criminal Court (ICC) to hold the Syrian government agents accountable for their alleged crimes against humanity demonstrate the reality, that although states are ready to cooperate at least to some degree to protect civilians from massacre, they totally reject supporting any kind of responsibility and accountability in this respect, such as resorting to the ICC as a neutral international institution to eliminate the commission of mass atrocity crimes with impunity.[48]

Finally, the US and Russia agreed to vote for the designation of an investigation committee in the case of alleged use of chemical weapons during the Syrian crisis. And concomitantly, on 14 September 2013,[49] the Syrian Arab Republic acceded to the Chemical Weapons Convention (CWC) as its 190th state party and agreed to cooperate in the elimination of its chemical weapon stockpiles.[50] Therefore, no military strike was launched based on transgression of that red line. But this never-launched intervention, accompanied by the elimination of chemical weapons storage by the Syrian government, brought the issue of accountability/responsibility of states in case of breach of peremptory norms and the way the international community should respond to a violation to the fore again.[51]

As the conflict in Syria continued, with the rise of IS (then ISIS) in 2014 and capture by IS of a swathe of territory in Syria and Iraq, the problem of *how* to respond to this Islamic group[52] and protect people against their brutality[53] was of central importance. In September 2014 John Kerry, the US Secretary of State, had a tour to enlist more allies in their fight against IS, particularly to encourage the cooperation of regional powers like Saudi Arabia, Turkey, EAU and Qatart.[54] The noteworthy point here is that ultimately the unauthorized limited military intervention of the US in this case happened nevertheless, particularly in the case of the Kobane resistance, which gained public attention. This recent episode of the Syrian tragedy involved military intervention to fight with the IS with justifications advanced based on the claim of helping Kurdish people entangled in Kobane. Again the protection rhetoric (to protect people against IS brutality) becomes prominent while this unauthorized (without Security Council sanction) limited intervention remains legally in limbo; i.e. holding accountable all sides of the conflicts for any international crimes committed; including the anti-IS coalition actions; the significant aspiration of doctrine of *responsibility* to *protect*.

5. Conclusion

Discourse on military intervention in Syria mainly relies on *protection* as a justification to attempt to achieve accountability of the host state through military force. It utilizes the core principles of humanitarian law to legitimize *jus ad bellum* claims. This is counterproductive and prone to being abused.[55]

The single-dimensional sense of responsibility to protect, stressing protection more than notion of responsibility, is still pervasive and it can find its predecessor and footholds in other international bodies, nevertheless. To epitomize, the Martic case of ICTY (International Criminal Tribunal for the former Yugoslavia) states that 'belligerent reprisals may "be considered lawful", subject "to strict conditions", including respect of "the principle of the protection of the civilian population in armed conflict and the general prohibition of targeting civilians".'[56] To make this reasoning more perplexing, even the articulation of the state responsibility draft in Article 50 states that taken countermeasures *shall not affect*:

> (a) the obligation to refrain from the threat or use of force as embodied in the Charter of the United Nations; (b) obligations for the protection of fundamental human rights; (c) obligations of a humanitarian character prohibiting reprisals; (d) other obligations under peremptory norms of general international law.[57]

Thus it is obvious that in the absence of any concrete mechanism to hold states accountable for their actions and for this to be implemented *reciprocally* among all states, the contradictory measures, on the one hand preserving non-interventionism and on the other protection of human rights, are always imbued with ambivalence and inconsistency.

The Syrian crisis illustrates that while 'international criminal law has evolved in parallel with [responsibility to protect]', evidently the power to hold states accountable for their actions, regardless of being the host state or states as representatives of the international community, is still weak and needs to be enhanced.

In the wake of IS's emergence in the Syrian and also Iraqi conflicts, it is difficult to speak about any kind of military intervention based on neutrality and not taking the side of any contending party, hence protective intervention in this case seems, if not impossible, awkward. As a result, to intervene to quell the systematic violation of human rights by all sides, if it is possible through military intervention at all, before establishing a responsible international communitarian mechanism can do more harm than good, and that such intervention would fulfil the protective promise of responsibility to protect seems unlikely. Additionally, with no precise prospect of a post-intervention stable legitimate government, and the fact that keeping the neutrality principle seems not to be protective, regime change strategy can abruptly end any protective military intervention based on the interveners' national interests or the financial and human costs, which could urge the intervener to end their war effort and exit the battlefield as soon as possible.[58] Sadly speaking, one can attest that this happened in the case of Libya and paved the way to some extent for the horrible scenes of the Syrian crisis, i.e. the changing strategy of the NATO states from supposed protective war to regime change or one-sided punitive war. In this regard, considering all these facts, it is far preferable for states to maintain their irresponsible position in their international relations.

Furthermore, any proposition to have recourse to regional organizations or coalitions of states in the face of the Security Council's inaction to respond to mass atrocity crimes, considering that in reality mostly all parties to the conflicts commit crimes, is inappropriate. This is due to the absence of any efficient mechanism to guarantee all parties, including interveners, are held accountable for their actions.[59] Even if a unilateral intervention is conceived of as being protective, since some states like the US believe that the Outcome Document does not exclude unilateral intervention as an option,[60] there is still the question of based on which international legal mechanism their action (intervention) can be judged and sealed as *responsible* protection.

Therefore, '[t]he very rationale of punishing the violation of a taboo ('red line') through unilateral military action appears to be incompatible with the underlying foundations of the [responsibility to protect] doctrine'.[61]

Although this article's argument is deeply influenced by the theory of interactional law and its authors, it is not in accord with the conclusion that there is a *shared understanding* of this doctrine among participants of international law.[62] As was outlined before, the confusion with regard to the concept of protection and responsibility is widespread. While states are ready to rely on pre-existing, and to some extent well-established, protection regimes of international law, they are not ready to relinquish their free hand of action to be subordinated to a mechanism of legal responsibility except in rhetoric. This mixed feeling must be overcome, otherwise no consistent practice of responsibility to protect will emerge. It should be noted that this ambivalence is common among permanent members of the Security Council as much as among other states;[63] the pending enforcement of a state responsibility proposed treaty is credible evidence for this. Therefore, according to the interactional law theory, it is hard to speak about *reciprocity* in terms of responsibility to protect, so no reliable *shared understanding* has emerged thus far.

As a result, as described above, since the protection notion still trumps the responsibility notion in international law, the responsibility to protect doctrine in its totality is limping along.

Notes

1. Zifcak Spencer, 'Is The Responsibility To Protect Dead? The Doctrine's Standing in the Wake Of Syria Massacre', in *Responsibility to Protect in Theory and Practice: Papers Presented at the Responsibility to Protect in Theory and Practice Conference Ljubljana,* eds. Vasilka Sancin and Maša Kovič Dine (Ljubljana: GV Založba, 2013), 254.
2. Paul R. Williams, J. Trevor Ulbrick, and Jonathan Worboys, 'Preventing Mass Atrocity Crimes: The Responsibility to Protect and The Syria Crisis', *Case Western Reserve University Journal of International Law* 45, no. 1&2 (2012): 490.
3. Peter Hilpold, 'Humanitarian Intervention: Is There a Need for a Legal Reappraisal?', *European Journal of International Law* 12, no. 3 (2001): 444.
4. Ibid., 453. Also look at Military and Paramilitary Activities in and against Nicaragua (*Nicaragua v. United States of America*), judgment 27 June 1986, ICJ, 206,207.
5. Alexandra Bohm, 'Why Do We Care? A Critical Look at the Responsibility to Protect' in Sancin and Dine, *Responsibility to Protect in Theory and Practice*, 143.
6. Carsten Stahn, 'Responsibility to Protect: Political Rhetoric or Emerging Legal Norm?', *American Journal of International Law* 101, no. 1 (2007): 104.
7. To know more about the history of humanitarian intervention look at: Brendan Simms and D.J. B. Trim, eds., *Humanitarian Intervention: A History* (Cambridge: Cambridge University Press, 2011).
8. Jutta Brunnée and Stephen J. Toope, 'The Responsibility to Protect and the Use of Force: Building Legality?' *Global Responsibility to Protect* 2, no. 3 (2010): 194–195.
9. Heather M. Roff, *Global justice, Kant and the Responsibility to Protect: A Provisional Duty* (London: Routledge, 2013), 10.

10. Brunnée and Toope, 'The Responsibility to Protect and the Use of Force', 201.
11. Ibid., 206–207.
12. Stahn, 'Responsibility to Protect', 108.
13. John Bolton 30 August 2005 Letter, http://www.humanrightsvoices.org/assets/attachments/documents/bolton_responsibility_to_protect.pdf. (accessed 12 January 2015).
14. Brunnée and Toope, 'The Responsibility to Protect and the Use of Force', 194.
15. To read more about the interrelation between morality and institutionalization look at: Grant Marlier and Neta C. Crawford, 'Incomplete and Imperfect Institutionalisation of Empathy and Altruism in the "Responsibility to Protect" Doctrine', *Global Responsibility to Protect* 5, no. 4 (2013): 397–422.
16. Stahn, 'Responsibility to Protect', 115.
17. Responsibility of States for Internationally Wrongful Acts; and its pending status to come into force after many revisions is the best example of problematic nature of responsibility notion in contemporary international law.
18. 'Responsibility of States for Internationally Wrongful Acts', Draft 2001, art 40.
19. Stahn, 'Responsibility to Protect', 115.
20. 'Responsibility of States for Internationally Wrongful Acts', art 41.
21. 'General Assembly World Summit Outcome', Summer 2005, UN Doc A/RES/60/1, para 139.
22. Stahn, 'Responsibility to Protect', 120.
23. Vladimir S. Kotlyar, '"Responsibility To Protect" The Hopes and the Crash of an Illusion. Is there any Chance to Revive it?', in *Responsibility to Protect in Theory and Practice*, eds. Sancin and Dine, 34.
24. Brunnée and Toope, 'The Responsibility to Protect and the Use of Force', 206–207.
25. Report of the Secretary-General, 'Implementing the Responsibility to Protect', 12 January 2009, UN Doc A/63/677, para 62.
26. Jutta Brunnée and Stephen J. Toope, *Legitimacy and Legality in International Law: An Interactional Account* (Cambridge: Cambridge University Press, 2010), 23.
27. Ibid., 33.
28. Ibid., 21, 30.
29. Ibid., 24.
30. Ibid., 24–25.
31. Brunnée and Toope, 'The Responsibility to Protect and the Use of Force', 203.
32. Ibid., 204.
33. Carsten Stahn, 'Between Law-breaking and Law-making: Syria, Humanitarian Intervention and "What the Law Ought to Be"', *Journal of Conflict and Security Law* 19, no. 1 (2014): 47.
34. Spencer, 'Is The Responsibility To Protect Dead?', 264.
35. Ibid., 255–257.
36. Ibid., 267–268.
37. Ibid., 268–269.
38. Ibid., 271.
39. 'United Nations Security Council 6627th meeting', 4 October 2011, UN Doc S/PV.6627, 4.
40. Carsten Stahn, 'Syria and the Semantics of Intervention, Aggression and Punishment', *Journal of International Criminal Justice* 11, no. 5 (2013): 957.
41. Stahn, 'Between Law-breaking and Law-making', 27.
42. Stahn, 'Syria and the Semantics of Intervention', 958.
43. Stahn, 'Between Law-breaking and Law-making', 29.
44. Ibid., 34–35.
45. Stahn, 'Syria and the Semantics of Intervention', 958.
46. To remind, one prominent reason for introduction of responsibility to protect by the ICISS Report in 2001 was states refrain from unilateral use of force after Kosovo crisis in 1999.
47. Stahn, 'Syria and the Semantics of Intervention', 956.
48. Thykier Moller, 'The R2P and the Sovereignty Game in the Security Council (UNSC): Syria Versus Libya', in *Responsibility to Protect in Theory and Practice,* eds. Sancin and Dine, 198–199.
49. Secretary-General Report of CW Investigation, http://www.un.org/disarmament/content/slideshow/Secretary_General_Report_of_CW_Investigation.pdf (accessed 3 February, 2014).
50. Ralf Trapp, 'Elimination of the Chemical Weapons Stockpile of Syria', *Journal of Conflict and Security Law* 19, no. 1 (2014): 7.

51. Stahn, 'Syria and the Semantics of Intervention', 956–957.
52. This Islamic group is regarded as a terrorist organization or/and in the eyes of some even as a quasi-government. For more idea about international legal status of IS look at: Joe Boyle, 'Islamic State and the Idea of Statehood', *BBC News Middle East*, January 6, 2015. 'United Nations Security Council Resolutions 2172 and 2178', 26 August and 24 September 2014, UN Doc S/RES/2172 and S/RES/2178. Secretary General Remarks to Security Council's open debate on International Cooperation in Combating Terrorism and Violent Extremism, 19 November 2014, http://www.un.org/apps/news/infocus/sgspeeches/statments_full.asp?statID=2439#.VNH60WisV8E. (Accessed 4 February, 2015). 'Transcript: President Obama's Speech on Combating ISIS and Terrorism', *CNN*, September 11, 2014. The League of Arab States Ministerial Council, 'Safeguarding the Arab National Security and Suppression of Extremist Terrorist Groups', and 'International Terrorism and Measures of Suppression', Res. no. 7804 – o.s. (142) – c. 3 – 07/09/2014 and Res. no. 7816 – o.s. (142) – c. 3 – 07/09/2014. And 'Special Meeting of the European Council', 30 August 2014, EUCO 163/14, 14–18.
53. To know more about IS violence and extremism look at: 'Islamic State: Can its Savagery be Explained?', *BBC News Middle East,* 9 September, 2014, and Paul Wood, 'Islamic State: Yazidi Women Tell of Sex-slavery Trauma', *BBC News Middle East*, 22 December, 2014.
54. Jonathan Marcus, 'Will Obama's global anti-IS coalition work?', *BBC News*, September 14, 2014.
55. Stahn, 'Syria and the Semantics of Intervention', 966–967.
56. Ibid., 968.
57. 'Responsibility of States for Internationally Wrongful Acts', art 50.
58. As happened in case of the US occupation of Iraq since the country is still in turmoil.
59. Williams, Ulbrick, and Worboys, 'Preventing Mass Atrocity Crimes', 490.
60. Stahn, 'Responsibility to Protect', 109.
61. Stahn, 'Syria and the Semantics of Intervention', 964.
62. 'The responsibility to protect, including its potential for collective action, is increasingly supported by globally shared understandings.' In Brunnée and Toope, 'The Responsibility to Protect and the Use of Force', 211.
63. Ibid., 212.

Responsibility to protect and 'peacetime atrocities': the case of North Korea

Serena Timmoneri

Department of Social and Political Sciences, University of Catania, Italy

Responsibility to Protect (R2P) has become part of the world's diplomatic language. The Security Council of the United Nations has mentioned the concept numerous times in the last decade and several non-governmental organizations have been established since 2005 with the purpose of advocating for R2P. This article focuses on the so-called 'peacetime' atrocities, defined as long-term situations that systematically destroy lives, communities and cultures without 'exploding' into armed conflicts. In particular, the author will use North Korea and the alleged genocide against Christians in the country, as a test case to analyse the effectiveness of R2P when dealing with 'peacetime' atrocities.

1. The responsibility to protect

During the 1990s, the international community has witnessed an array of humanitarian crises. Although at that time international law already proscribed specific kinds of state behaviours within national borders, genocide, ethnic cleansing, mass atrocities, and mass internal displacement of citizens were still happening. As a result, in 1999, Kofi Annan challenged the international community to develop a way of reconciling the twin principles of sovereignty and the protection of fundamental human rights. Purposefully, in 2001, the International Commission on Intervention and State Sovereignty (ICISS) provided a report on the new concept of the so-called 'Responsibility to Protect' (R2P), which was based on the 'responsible sovereignty' principle. This theory entailed a shift from the idea of 'sovereignty as control' to the concept of 'sovereignty as responsibility'. The underlying reason for sovereignty became the protection of people's most fundamental rights from egregious violations. This notion overcame the Westphalian concept of sovereignty, based on the 'non-interference' principle, conceived primarily as the right to act within national border without being internationally accountable for this. Although national governments are responsible for their citizens, when a state is unwilling or unable to protect its own people from gross violations of human rights, the responsibility shifts to the international community. R2P imposes a responsibility on states not to harm and also to pro-actively protect their populations, along with placing a responsibility on the wider international community to engage in an appropriately authorized and multilateral action (including, when needed, coercive force) to protect those populations if the particular states involved cannot or will not fulfil their responsibility. ICISS put forward six criteria for legitimizing intervention even without the consent of the state in question, i.e. right authority and intention, just cause, last resort, proportional means, and reasonable prospects of success. Intervention must follow the authorization of the UNSC and it must be triggered by a large-scale loss of life and/or 'ethnic cleansing', which is the product of a deliberate, state action or a failed state situation. It must require that all other paths for resolutions (such as the diplomatic and non-military tools) have been explored. Moreover, the intention behind the intervention must be to reduce human suffering and the military intervention should not be greater than that required to accomplish that objective. Thanks to the determination of UN Secretary General Kofi Annan and other R2P advocates, R2P became one of the topics at the 2005 UN Millennium Summit and it was included in the UN World Summit Outcome Document. This document introduced some changes. Firstly, it narrowed the focus on intervention (reducing it just to cases of genocide, war crimes, ethnic cleansing, and crimes against humanity), without mentioning explicitly the responsibility to rebuild present in the ICISS report. It did not adopt ICISS criteria for UNSC deliberations concerning the use of force. Moreover, it introduced a 'case-by-case' basis for deciding intervention and it used the term 'preparedness' rather than 'responsibility' in reference to UNSC action. In 2009, the UN Implementation Report on R2P clarified the concept of Responsibility to Protect and its various operational aspects. The goal was not to reinterpret or renegotiate the conclusions of the World Summit but 'to find ways of implementing its decisions in a fully faithful and consistent manner'[1] It introduced a 'three pillars' approach and military intervention lost much of its centrality. The first Pillar deals with the protection responsibilities of the state; the second one refers to the international capacity and state building, while Pillar 3 is about 'timely and decisive response'. The first two pillars delineated the preventive activities required by the state and the international community, while the third pillar put emphasis on pacific measures rather than military action. It described R2P as narrow in scope but deep in response, eliciting a wide variety of actions on the part of various agents in order to prevent the four crimes. In addition, it did not provide a sequence in moving from one pillar to another; R2P must be applied flexibly in the face of different circumstances. It is important to stress that R2P is not applicable to small-scale war crimes, institutionalized discriminations, disappearance, and sexual violence (all of which may occur during peacetime) but only to these crimes when they occur on a 'mass scale'. Furthermore, R2P does not seem particularly responsive to 'smoulder' situations of crimes against humanity, such as long-term situations that systematically destroy lives, communities, and cultures without 'exploding' into armed conflicts. For this reason, the aim of this article is to analyse the international response through R2P to 'peacetime atrocities', which are usually de-prioritized comparing to the crimes related to war mass scale killing. The main research question this article aims at answering is what the UN response to North Korea is, through R2P. The main hypothesis the author advances is that this response is not adequate to the current North Korean situation and that the UN is underestimating the scale and the gravity of crimes committed in the country. In order to support this thesis and analyse the validity of this initial statement the author will analyse the reports and the data, up to date, on the international response and on the human rights situation in North Korea, where besides crimes against humanity there is an alleged genocide of Christians.

2. Peacetime atrocities

As noted above, R2P applies to crimes against humanity, defined by their systematic and violent nature. Crimes against humanity involve gross violations of the fundamental human rights of a citizen population. Crimes against humanity were firstly explicitly formulated as a category of crimes in the Nuremberg Charter and they were considered as one of the most serious crimes under conventional and customary international law alongside genocide and war crimes. The definition of such crimes was developed by subsequent jurisprudence before various international criminal tribunals and national courts. Article 7 (1) of the Rome Statute states that a 'crime against humanity means any of the following acts, i.e. murder, extermination, enslavement, deportation or forcible transfer of the population, imprisonment or other severe deprivation of physical liberty, torture, rape, sexual slavery, enforced prostitution, forced pregnancy, enforced sterilization, or any other form of sexual violence of comparable gravity. Furthermore, other actions included are the persecution against any identifiable group on political, racial, ethnic, national, religious, and gender; enforced disappearance of persons, the crime of apartheid, and other inhuman acts of a similar character intentionally causing great suffering or serious injury to body, or to mental, or to physical health. The above-mentioned acts can be labelled as 'crimes against humanity' when committed as a part of a widespread or systematic attack directed against any civilian population, with knowledge of the attack. The difference with genocide is that, in case of crimes against humanity the perpetrators need not target a specific group. There is no need to show that they have an intention to destroy a group in 'whole or in part' (as proscribed in the 1948 Convention on the Prevention and Punishment of the Crime of Genocide), it is sufficient to prove that the crimes were committed as a part of a widespread or systematic attack against the civilian population. In addition, one of the peculiarities of crimes against humanity is that they do not have to be committed in the context of an armed conflict. In fact, there exist long-term situations that involves crimes against humanity but do not rise to the level of armed conflict that are equally destructive in the long-term and, actually, the relationship between armed conflict and crimes against humanity is highly complex and yet not well understood. The strong correlation between the two phenomena implies a direct link, however, not all conflicts give rise to crimes against humanity and many atrocities can occur in the absence of armed struggle. Among the great number of mass killing episodes observed since 1945, at least a third of these cases occurred outside the context of an armed conflict. A significant number of crimes against humanity are committed in peacetime, or after an episode involving conflict. Only one in 10 of every reported civilian death tends to occur in the context of armed conflict, while the majority takes place outside official combat zones (attributed for example to government repression or a state's failure to regulate violence). Besides, some crimes against humanity still occur 'under the cover' of armed conflicts, they are not directly linked to the causes of that conflict or civil war. Often crimes against humanity have been equated directly with war, with massive population losses caused through famine or disease, and other inhumanity and gross human rights violation (i.e. slavery). For the first thing that can come to mind thinking of crimes against humanity is the idea of killing on a vast scale and death (brutal death, massive of type, and uncompromising in its choice victim), often, in the popular consciousness, armies in war are the major vehicles by which this killing takes places. Undoubtedly, war can work as a catalyst for crimes against humanity, and probably more easily than in peacetime, however, war is not an essential element for crimes against humanity atrocities to occur; crimes against humanity do not equate with war and the two terms should not be employed interchangeably.

3. Test case: R2P in North Korea

In the last decade, the human rights situation in North Korea has increasingly come under international scrutiny, especially by the UN. UN bodies have issued over 60 reports and statements on North Koreas's human rights situation in the last 10 years.[2] In 2003, the United Nations Human Rights Council (UNHRC) adopted the first of many resolutions in relation to the Democratic People's Republic of Korea (DPRK). In 2004, the UNHRC established the mandate of an independent human rights expert as the Special Rapporteur on the situation of human rights in North Korea. Among the other things, the Special Rapporteur was in charge to establish direct contact with the government of North Korea as well as to visit the country. The government of North Korea stated their absolute rejection of this resolution categorically refusing to recognize, meet, cooperate with, or grant access to, the Special Rapporteur.[3] Since 2004, the Special Rapporteur has produced 18 reports and he has submitted Annual Reports to both the UNHRC and the UN General Assembly (UNGA). In response to these reports, the UNGA and UNHRC have repeatedly adopted resolutions voicing concerns about the human rights situation in North Korea. On 1 February 2013, the Special Rapporteur proposed to launch an international inquiry in respect of the situation in the DPRK. On 21 March 2013, with resolution 22/13, the UNHRC resolved to establish a three members' Commission of Inquiry (COI). The Council mandated the Commission to investigate the systematic, widespread, and grave violations of human rights in the State, with a view to ensuring full accountability, in particular for violations that may amount to crimes against humanity. The Commission mandated to investigate the systematic and widespread violations to the right to food, the full range of violations associated with prison camps, torture and inhuman treatment, arbitrary arrest and detention, discrimination, violation of freedom of expression, enforced disappearance (including in the form of abductions of nationals and of other states). In Resolution 22/13, the UNHRC urged the government of DPRK to cooperate fully with the Commission's investigation; to permit the Commission's members unrestricted access to visit the country, and to provide them with all information necessary to enable them to fulfil their mandate.[4] Immediately after the adoption of the resolution, the government of the DPRK publicly stated that it would 'totally reject and disregard it'.[5] The Commission based its findings on a 'reasonable ground' standard of proof, through first-hand testimonies and official visits and in its final report (UN Doc A/HRC/25/CRP.1 of 7 February 2014) invoked the R2P and called upon the international community to impose targeted sanctions and refer the situation to the International Criminal Court (ICC).

3.1 *Context*

North Korea is a 'Single Party State under a totalitarian familial dictatorship'.[6] Its history engendered an isolationist mindset and an aversion to outside powers that is used to justify internal restrictions.[7] The rule of a single party, led by a single person is elaborated on in the guiding ideology that its current Supreme Leader refers to as 'Kimilsungism – Kimjongilism'.[8] The State seeks to ensure that its citizens internalize this guiding ideology by indoctrinating them from childhood, suppressing all political and religious expression that questions the official ideology and tightly controlling citizens' physical movement and their means of communication with each other and with those in other countries. The authorities engage in gross human rights violations to crack down also on 'subversive' influences from abroad. North Korea has been a leader in human rights violations since the Korean War, when the North Koreans kidnapped and forced thousands of South Koreans to fight on the side of the North. The civil war, each side backed by a corresponding political superpower, led to the split of the peninsula along the 38th parallel. Since then, North Korea has used fear, torture, and propaganda to ensure the 'loyalty' of its citizens to the regime and the Kim family.[9] After the Korean War, Kim Il-Sung introduced the personal philosophy of

Juche (i.e. self-reliance) which became a 'guiding light' of North Korea's development. Kim Il-Sung died in 1994, but he received the nomination of president 'for eternity'.[10] The 1990s was a period known as the 'arduous march' in which North Korea's economy failed and the country fell into economic depression and famine. Since that time, the needs of the common people have taken a back seat to those who are members of the communist party and the military. These members are the first and often the last to receive the rations provided from foreign humanitarian aid. Two million people have died since the mid-1990s, because of acute food shortages caused by natural disasters and economic mismanagement. The country still relies on foreign aid to feed millions of its people. In addition, North Korea maintains one of the world's largest standing armies and militarism pervades everyday life. However, standards of training, discipline, and equipment in the force are reported to be low. Control over society by the state regime is absolute, information about the functioning of government is tightly controlled both to domestic as well as to the external audience, and corruption is endemic.[11] All domestic media are run by the State. Internet access is restricted. Although the Constitution guarantees freedom of religion, it does not exist in practice; intense state indoctrination and repression preclude free exercise of religion. There is no academic freedom and a huge network of informants monitors nearly all forms of private communications. Freedom of association and assembly is not recognized, and there are no known associations or organizations other than those created by the state. Moreover, strikes, collective bargaining, and other organized labor activities are illegal. The judicial system is not independent, and currently, 80,000 to 120,000 are held in detention camps in the country.[12] There is no freedom of movement and forced internal resettlement is routine. Access to Pyongyang, where the availability of food, housing, and health care is somewhat better than in the rest of the country, is tightly restricted and emigration is illegal. The country lives in an ideological isolationism and the economy is centrally planned and grossly mismanaged. The number of DPRK workers abroad has not been confirmed but some sources have put forward an estimate of up to 60,000–70,000 workers in 45 countries.[13] The DPRK sends labourers to work abroad under bilateral contracts with foreign governments. The 'export' of workers appears to be part of an official DPRK government policy, specifically to increase North Korea's reserves of foreign currency. Indeed, the majority of the foreign workers' wage, reportedly anywhere from 60% to 90% of their salary, is remitted directly to the North Korean government in taxes and 'loyalty' payments, as well as to the agencies that arrange for the workers to be sent to foreign countries and the agencies that domestically receive DPRK workers and liaise with North Koreans officials.[14] North Korea has used fear, torture, and propaganda to ensure the loyalty of its citizens to the regime and the Kim family. Atrocities committed by the communist regime include Nazi-like work camps, systematic starvation of non-party citizens and forced abortions. The North Korean criminal justice system and prisons serve not merely to punish crimes but also form an integral part of the State systematic and widespread attack against anyone considered a threat to the political system and its leadership.[15] The totalitarian state is also accused of systematic human rights abuses, i.e. torture, public executions, slave labour, forced abortion, and infanticides in prison camps. Hundreds of thousands of people are held in detention facilities in which torture is rampant and execution commonplace. The Freedom House Report (2014) described the crimes against humanity committed in North Korea, as more severe and widespread than any other in the contemporary world. They have arisen from 'policies established at the highest level of the state'.[16] The people of North Korea have the least freedom of any in the world. They are jailed for not dusting the pictures of the 'Great Leader' they must display in their home, for whistling

South Korean pop songs or for mentioning that the US won the war against Japan (their history textbooks explain that it was won almost single-handedly by the Great Leader).[17] The State does not allow them to think for themselves or to make up their own minds. If they do, they are dispatched to concentration camps where they are worked, in many cases, to death. Political enemies of the Dictator, even his uncle, are mercilessly and summarily executed. One general caught with a drink during the '90 days of no joy' following the death of the 'Dear Leader', was publicly executed, blown to pieces by a mortar.[18]

3.2 Main findings of the DPRK Commission of Inquiry

The COI is neither a judicial body nor a prosecutor. It could not make final determinations of individual criminal responsibility. It could, however, determine whether its findings constitutes reasonable grounds to establish that crimes against humanity have been committed as well as to deserve a criminal investigation by a competent national or international organ of justice. Its Report stated that crimes against humanity, pursued by policies established at the highest level of the State, have been committed in the DPRK and are still ongoing.[19] In many instances, the violations found entailed crimes against humanity based on State policies. The main perpetrators are officials of the State Security Department, the Ministry of People's Security, the Korean People's Army, the office of the Public Prosecutor, the judiciary, and the Workers' Party of Korea. They are acting under the effective control of the central organs of the Workers' Party of Korea, the National Defense Commission, and the Supreme Leader of the DPRK. According to the Report, North Korea is guilty of extermination, murder, enslavement, torture, imprisonment, rape, forced abortion and other sexual violence, persecution on political, religious, racial and gender grounds, the enforceable transfer of populations, the forced disappearance of persons and the inhumane act of knowingly causing prolonged starvation. Six groups of victims were identified, i.e. inmates of political prison camps and of the ordinary prison system (in particular political prisoners among them), religious believers and other considered to introduce subversive influence, people who try to flee the country, starving population, and people from other countries that become victims of international abductions and enforced disappearance.

3.2.1 Violations of the freedoms of thought, expression and religion

The government of North Korea claims to have an absolute monopoly over information and total control of organized social life. There is an almost total denial of the right to freedom of thought, conscience, and religion, as well as of the rights to freedom of opinion, expression, information, and association. There is an all-encompassing indoctrination and the Worker's Party of Korea controls all social activities undertaken by citizens of all ages. Through associations run and overseen by the Party, where citizens are obliged to be members, the State is able to monitor its people and to dictate their daily activities. Children and youth are indoctrinated through education, mass games, and other compulsory mass propaganda events. They are involved in regular confession and criticism sessions, obligatory participation in the activities of mass associations, as well as being subject to constant exposure to State propaganda. States surveillance permeates the private lives of all citizens to ensure that virtually no expression critical of the political system or of its leadership goes undetected. Citizens are punished for any 'anti-state' activity or expression of dissidence. There is a reward for reporting on fellow citizens suspected of committing such 'crimes'. The right to have access to independent sources is denied to citizens; State-controlled media are the only permitted source of information allowed in the DPRK. Telephone calls are monitored and mostly confined to domestic connections. North Koreans are pun-ished for watching and listening to foreign broadcasts (including foreign films and soap operas, the print media, the internet) and for the possession of foreign CDs and DVDs. The State considers the spread of Christianity a particularly serious threat since it challenges ideologically the official leader's personality cult and provides a platform for social and pol-itical organization and interaction outside the realm of the State. Apart from the few orga-nized State-controlled Churches, it is prohibited for Christians to practice their religion; they are severely persecuted. People caught practicing Christianity are subject to severe punishment in violation of the right of freedom of religion and the international law prohi-bition against religious discrimination.

3.2.2 *Discrimination*

State-sponsored discrimination in the DPRK is pervasive but it is also shifting. Discrimi-nation is also practiced on the basis of disability, although there are signs that the State may begin to address this particular issue. It is rooted in the *Songbun* system, which clas-sifies people because of State-assigned social class and birth, and includes consideration of political opinions and religion. Songbun determines where people are allowed to live, what sort of accommodation they have, their access to health care, and what occupations they are assigned to. It establishes whether they are effectively able to attend school (in particular university), how much food they receive, and even whom they may marry. Discrimination based on Songbun continues in particular through the stark differences in living conditions between the larger cities, where the elite of the highest Songbun is concentrated and the remote provinces to which people of the lower Songbun have been historically confined. Songbun intersects with gender-based discrimination that is equally pervasive. Discrimi-nation against women remains pervasive and is even increasing. In the political sphere, women make up just 5% of the top political cadre and 10% of the central government employees.[20] Women are victims of human trafficking, transactional sex, and prostitution. Another form of discrimination is the imposition of the payment of bribes or fines. Sexual and gender-based violence against women is prevalent throughout all areas of society. Victims are not protected by the State, not provided support services, and they have no recourse to the justice system

3.2.3 *Violations of freedom of movement and residence*

The State imposes on citizens where they must live and work violating their freedom of choice. State policies aim at isolating citizens from each other and from the outside world, violating all aspects of the right to freedom of movement. North Korean society is segregated socio-economically and physically. People considered politically loyal to the leadership can work and live in favorable locations, whereas families of people con-sidered politically suspect are relegated to marginalized areas. Citizens are not even allowed to leave their province temporarily or to travel within the country without official authorization. There is a ban on 'ordinary' citizens to leave the country. Repatriated woman who are pregnant are regularly subjected to abortion and babies who are born to repatriated women are often killed. These practices are driven by racist attitudes towards interracial children of Koreans, and the intent to punish further women who have left the country and their assumed contact with Chinese men. People found to have been in intimate contact with officials or nationals from the Republic of Korea or with Christians may be forcibly transferred into political concentration camps, imprisoned in ordinary prisons, or even summarily executed.

3.2.4. *Violations of the right to food and related aspects of the right of life*

The famine in North Korea is not a problem of food shortages and 'access to commodities'. The State has used food as a means to control over the population. It has prioritized those whom the authorities believe to be crucial in maintaining the regime over those deemed expendable. It has confiscated food from those in need and it has provided to other groups. State-controlled production and distribution of food has not provided the population adequately since the end of the 1980s. During the period of the famine, ideological indoctrination was used in order to maintain the regime, at the cost of serious aggravating hunger and starvation. The hiding of information prevented the population from finding alternatives to the collapsing public distribution system. It also delayed international assistance that, provided earlier, could have saved many lives. It criminalized people's moving within or outside the country in search of food and trading or working in the informal markets. Even during the worst period of mass starvation, the State impeded the delivery of food aid by imposing conditions not based on humanitarian considerations. International humanitarian agencies were subject to restrictions contravening humanitarian principles. Aid organizations were prevented from properly assessing humanitarian needs and monitoring the distribution of aid. The State denied humanitarian access to some of the most affected regions and groups, including homeless children. The DPRK has always prioritized military spending, even during periods of mass starvation, and the consequences are a disproportionately large army and ongoing malnutrition in children. North Korea has the fourth largest army in the world; an army comprised of 1.21 million soldiers.[21] The State has spent large amounts of State resources on luxury goods, the advancement of the Leader's personality cult, the development of weapons system, and the nuclear programme instead of providing food to the starving population. The State also used deliberate starvation as a means of control and punishment in detention facilities. This has resulted in the deaths of many political and ordinary prisoners. Decisions, acts, and omissions by the State caused the death of hundreds of thousands of people and inflicted permanent physical and psychological injuries on those who survived.

3.2.5 *Arbitrary detention, torture, executions, and prison camps*

The police and security forces of the DPRK systematically employ violence and punishment that amount to gross human rights violations in order to create a climate of fear that pre-empts any challenges to the current system of government and to the ideology underpinning it. Torture is widespread and starvation and other inhuman conditions of detention are imposed on suspects. The institutions and officials involved are not held accountable and impunity reigns. People who are found to have engaged in major political crimes 'disappear' without trial or judicial order, to political prison camps. They are incarcerated and held without their families knowing where they are. The State does not inform their families, even if they die. It is common that the authorities send entire families to political prison camps for political crimes committed by their relatives (to the third generation) on the basis of presumed 'guilt by association'. Inmate population has been gradually eliminated through deliberate starvation, forced labour, executions, torture, rape and the denial of reproductive rights enforced through punishment, forced abortion, and infanticide. According to the COI's report, 500,000 political prisoners have perished in these camps over the past five decades while, according to other various assessments, the total number of inmates who have died in the political prison camps may have been reached the million mark.[22]

In any case, the level of the atrocities committed inside these camps is reported to be the same as those committed inside Nazi camps.[23] Inmates are forced to carry out hard labour; they are tortured, and punished with severe beatings and other forms of inhuman, cruel, or degrading treatment for minor transgressions, often completely arbitrary.[24] North Korean authorities deny the existence of these camps, which is instead proved by satellite imagery and testimonies. Between 80,000 and 120,000 political prisoners (at the time of COI's inquiry) were detained in four large prison camps. However, gross violations are also being committed in the ordinary prison system and various types of short-term forced labour detention facilities. The detention is arbitrary and the inmates are subjected to deliberate starvation and illegal labour, torture, rape and other arbitrary cruelties in an environment of impunity. As a matter of state policy, the authorities carry out executions with or without a trial, publicly or secretly, in response to political and other crimes that are often not among the most serious ones. The policies of regularly carrying out public executions serves to instill fear in the general population.

3.2.6 *Abduction and enforced disappearance from other countries*

Since 1950, the DPRK has engaged in systematic abduction, denial of repatriation and subsequent enforced disappearance of people (200,000, including children) from other countries as a matter of State policy. The latter has prevented people from using effective remedies for human rights violations, including the right to the truth, the right to family life and to parents, and almost all of the foregoing victims remain disappeared. Human Rights violations continue against them and their families.

3.2.7 *Genocide*

The COI reported the possibility of three instances of genocide having been committed in the DPRK, i.e. political genocide, genocide in relation to children with Chinese ethnic lineage and, genocide against Christians. According to Article 2 of the 1948 Convention on the Prevention and Punishment of the Crime of Genocide, genocide is defined as the intent to destroy in whole or in part a national, ethnical, racial or religious group including by killing members of the group. The deliberate infliction on the group of conditions of life calculated to destroy the group physically, the infliction of serious bodily or mental harm to members of the group, and the imposition of measures intended to prevent births within the group and by forcibly transferring children of the group to another group constitute the material elements of the act of genocide. Article 3 describes as punishable the following acts: genocide, conspiracy to commit genocide, direct and public incitement to commit genocide, attempt to commit genocide and complicity in genocide.[25] Although the system of political repression targets political groups considered 'enemies' of the regime; not only the prisoners' conditions of life, but also the practice of targeting political prisoners fulfil most of the material elements of genocide, though political groups have been excluded from the list of protected groups under the Genocide Convention. Therefore, members of this particular group cannot under the Genocide Convention be considered victims of genocide even if they are victims of killing and serious mental and physical injuries. The children with Chinese lineage also are victims of acts constituting the material elements of genocide. In fact, forced abortions and infanticide, other acts with genocidal intent causing serious harm and imposing measures to prevent birth within a group all constitute acts of genocide. However, children with Chinese lineage cannot be considered a distinct national group under the Genocide Convention . In fact, they do not constitute a national minority given that the definition of nationality is 'the sharing of a legal bond based on citizenship, coupled with reciprocity of rights and duties'[26] Babies of mixed heritage do not constitute a 'racial group' given their fathers are Chinese in that the notion of race is not viable. At the same time, classifying the children as an ethnic group understood as a group 'sharing a common language or culture' is also problematic. Further, at this stage it is not possible to prove the evidence of the requisite 'genocidal intent'. The extent and the systematic nature of harms in North Korea intentionally directed to babies of mixed lineage are not entirely clear given the difficulties in accessing this information.

With regard to *Christians*, the COI noted that Christian Solidarity Worldwide had reported that there were indications that genocide had been committed against Christians in the past. In fact, Christians have been executed and sent to political prison camps that they cannot leave and where reproduction is prohibited. Evidence indicates that most or all of the acts specified in the Genocide Convention have been carried out against Christians who represent, as religious believers, one of the four protected categories under the Genocide Convention. Christianity has a long history in North Korea, with first contacts dating back to the seventeenth century. During the 1950s, under Kim Il-Sung, North Korean regime has embarked on a policy of rooting out religion.[27] The Regime aimed at forcing religious followers to abandon their own religious belief and practises through ideological indoctrination, by punishing religious leaders found to be engaged in 'counter-revolutionary' or 'anti-state' activities against the government policy, and by classifying those religious believers found incapable of being remade as ' targets of the dictatorship'.[28] The spread of Christianity has always been considered by the DPRK a particularly serious threat since it ideologically challenges the official personality cult and provides a platform for social and political organization and interaction outside the State realm. Religious persecution has been brutal, with the implementation of a very harsh programme of repression of religion, in the 1950s and 1960s. Protestants have been singled out, with virulent anti-Christian propaganda channelled through the Party, company, school and workers associations creating a culture of hatred and mistrust of Christians. Before the intense persecution of the Church, the Church in Korea was evangelistic, meaning that believers actively shared their faith. However, today believers trying to achieve this task are targeted (i.e. they are usually executed or sent to political prison camps).[29] Reports describe Christians being killed in brutal ways, such as being hung on a cross over fire, crushed under a steamroller or herded off bridges.[30] According to the policy of eliminating the seed of class enemies to three generations, family members including children, have also been targeted and incarcerated in political prison camps. Even though religious persecution wiped out virtually all religious believers and their family line, very harsh persecution of religious believers continues to occur today. In fact, although the number of Christians appears to have decreased significantly since the 1950s, Christianity continues to be practised principally in a clandestine manner and, despite the measures taken by the government, there is still a 'hidden' Christian population in North Korea. Apart from the few organized state-controlled churches, Christians are prohibited from practising their religion at the risk of severe punishment. Defectors systematically report that any Christian discovered are still sent to political prison camps or executed. Consistent accounts describe how, when religious activity is discovered by the authorities in their locality, the 'offenders' disappear, followed subsequently by their family members. A number of eyewitnesses' accounts exist of the *recent* execution of Christians. There is also evidence that families of religious believers are held in the political prison camps. A number of testimonies describe how Christians are particularly harshly treated in the camps, both because the guards target them and because the other prisoners demean and ostracize them, treating them as deranged because of their faith. Several accounts describe believers in the prison system who refuse to recant their faith being publicly trampled underfoot by guards and then by coerced prisoners, until they die. Other extremely brutal accounts of the Christians in the prison system have also been given. The COI Report refers to figures provided by the DPRK itself, which suggest that there has been a substantial drop in the number of religious believers between 1950s to 2002 from close to 23.69% to 0.16%. [31] The religious active population, in 1950, amounted to 200,000 Protestants and 57,000 Catholics. In 2002, the number of active Christians was of 12,000 Protestants and 800 Catholics. The number of the places of worship was reduced from 3000 to two Protestant Churches in the capital, which are state-sanctioned and exist just to give tourists the illusion of religious freedom. However, the COI suggests that there is insufficient factual evidence to come to any clear definite conclusions regarding genocide of Christians in North Korea though the available evidence is suggestive that this may be the case in that Christians may have been killed, caused to suffer serious physical or mental harm, or deliberately subjected to conditions of life calculated to cause their physical destruction. According to its report, the fact that the number of persons declaring to be religious followers in the DPRK is said to have dropped so dramatically cannot establish, by itself, an *intentional* extermination of Christians by the DPRK authorities. For the most difficult element to prove the crime of genocide is absolutely the specific intent, the COI concluded that it does not have sufficient evidence to make findings of genocide in this regard. It considered that it was not in a position to gather enough information to make a determination as to whether the authorities sought to repress organized religion by extremely violent means or whether they were driven by the intent to physically annihilate the followers of this particular religion as a 'group'.

4. Conclusion

During the last decade, the term R2P has been included in a number of resolutions. The UNSC has reaffirmed this concept in thematic resolutions and has referred it to numerous countries' situations. However, it is noteworthy that with the exception of the DPRK, the third pillar of R2P has only been invoked when there is an existing or imminent conflict. Therefore, even though there is still a lot of work to do and many situations like Tibet, for instance, remain almost totally ignored, the author considers 'positive' the fact that, for the first time, the R2P has been invoked for a 'peacetime' situation. This can represent a 'widening' of the R2P concept that has, so far, only been invoked and applied to mass atrocity situations related to armed conflicts. It represents a new awareness of the fact that long-term situations that involve crimes against humanity, but do not rise to the level of armed conflict like North Korea, can be in the long-term, equally destructive. In any case, the author considers the UN response through R2P to the North Korean situation as 'weak'. The COI's Report, in its conclusions, stated that 'the international community must accept its R2P the people of the DPRK from crimes against humanity because the North Korean government has manifestly failed to do so'. [32] It called upon the international community to impose targeted sanctions, to ensure that those responsible for the crimes against humanity committed in the DPRK were held accountable, and to reinforce a human right dialogue. However, UN sanctions against North Korea have achieved, so far, almost nothing and the DPRK continues to be a champion in gross human rights violations. Finally, the author disagrees with the COI's Report conclusion on the possibility of genocide against Christians in the DPRK. In fact, there is mounting evidence that genocide has been committed through the regime's action to eliminate these religious believers within the population. Christians have been defined as 'enemies' and 'agents of the imperialist forces'.[33] They were and still are, deliberately targeted as a group, which is the key issue in relation to the requirement to prove specific intent to destroy a religious group 'as such'. The drop in the number of Christians is significant enough to suggest that the DPRK may have committed harmful acts that are specifically targeting Christians. Available evidence demonstrates that Christians have been targeted and that various attacks or measures constituting the objective elements of genocide have been committed or imposed against members of the group. The discriminatory nature of the practice and the policy of subjecting members of this religious group to detention, inhuman prison conditions, torture, and in some cases, arbitrary killings is indicative of genocidal intent. The lack of any recent statements by the DPRK authorities that expressly demonstrate the intent to destroy Christians led the COI to its conclusions. However, a report by Christian Solidarity Worldwide (2007) contains several statements allegedly by Kim Il-Sung in the 1950s and 1960s, manifesting his intent to eradicate Christianity from the country. Intent is naturally difficult to prove, for the obvious reasons that a state may not wish to publish its genocidal intent. Moreover, even if such evidence of statements of genocidal intent exist there, this would have been hard to obtain. Moreover, the International Criminal Tribunal for Rwanda has recognized that the 'intent can be inferred from either words or deeds and may be demonstrated by a pattern of purposeful action.[34] In the past there were notorious situations like Rwanda (1994) and Darfur (2005) that were essentially 'ignored' and underestimated by the UN until after an *extraordinary* loss of lives happened. For these reasons, the author concludes that the COI has underestimated the situation in North Korea, where the deeds and the actions perpetrated by the regime prove the intention of exterminating Christians and where, what this group is suffering, constitute the material elements of the crime of genocide. Therefore, the analysis of the reports and the data up to date, confirm the initial hypothesis. Given the atrocious human rights situation in North Korea, the UN response, through R2P, is most definitively inadequate.

Notes

1. UN Secretary General, 'Implementing the Responsibility to Protect', report to the UN General Assembly 63rd session (12 January, 2009).
2. A list of the reports adopted can be found at Annex II to UNHRC, *Report of the Special Rapporteur on the Situation of Human Rights in the Democratic People's Republic of Korea, prepared by Marzuki Darusman* (UN Doc A/HRC/22/57), 1 February 2013.
3. Lovell Hogan, "Crimes against humanity – an independent legal opinion on the findings of the Commission of Inquiry on human rights situation in the Democratic People's Republic of Korea", a report commissioned by Human Liberty Center, Graduate School of International Studies – Yonsei University, May 2014.
4. UN Human Rights Council, Resolution on the situation of human rights in the Democratic People's Republic of Korea, UN Doc. A/HRC/RES/22/13 (9 April 2013).

5. UN General Assembly, Report of the Commission of Inquiry on Human Rights in the Democratic People's Republic of Korea (7.02.2015). Available at: http://www.ohchr.org/EN/HRBodies/HRC/CoIDPRK/Pages/CommissionInquiryonHRinDPRK.aspx (accessed 14 June 2015).
6. Freedom House – Freedom in the World 2014, North Korea. Available at: <https://freedomhouse.org/report/freedom-world/2014/north-korea#.VZDnp7cw9dg (accessed 10 June 2015).
7. Ibid.
8. Ibid.
9. Genocide Watch, Country Profile – North Korea. Available at: http://genocidewatch.net/2013/03/20/country-profile-north-korea-2/ (accessed 1 June 2015).
10. BBC News, North Korea Country Profile – Overview. Available at: <http://www.bbc.com/news/world-asia-pacific-15256929 (accessed 12 June 2015).
11. Freedom House – Freedom in the World 2014, North Korea (no. 6), 5.
12. Ibid.
13. Lovell Hogan, 'Crimes Against Humanity – An Independent Legal Opinion on the Findings of the Commission of Inquiry on Human Rights Situation in the Democratic People's Republic of Korea', (no. 3), 4.
14. Ibid.
15. Ibid.
16. Freedom House – Freedom in the World 2014, North Korea (no. 6), 5.
17. Ibid.
18. Ibid.
19. UNGA, Report of the Commission of Inquiry on Human Rights in the DPRK (no. 5), 5.
20. UNGA, Report of the Commission of Inquiry on Human Rights in the DPRK (no. 5), 5.
21. United Nations Development Programme, Human Development Report, Korea (Democratic People's Rep. of). Available at: http://hdr.undp.org/en/countries/profiles/PRK (accessed 29 June 2015).
22. Christian Solidarity Worldwide, 'North Korea: A Case to Answer, a Call to Act' (2007). Available at: http://www.csw.org.uk/2007/06/20/report/35/article.htm (accessed 14 June 2015).
23. UNGA, Report of the Commission of Inquiry on Human Rights in the DPRK (no. 5), 5.
24. Ibid.
25. UN General Assembly, Convention on the Prevention and Punishment of the Crime of Genocide (1948). Available at: http://www.oas.org/dil/1948_Convention_on_the_Prevention_and_Punishment_of_the_Crime_of_Genocide.pdf (accessed 12 January 2015).
26. International Criminal Tribunal for Rwanda, *Prosecutor v. Jean-Paul Akayesu* (Case No. ICTR-96-4-T), Judgment, 2 September 1998, para. 512–513
27. Christian Solidarity Worldwide, 'North Korea: A Case to Answer, a Call to Act', (no. 23), 10.
28. Ibid.
29. Christian Solidarity Worldwide, 'North Korea: A Case to Answer, a Call to Act' (no. 23), 10.
30. Ibid.
31. UNGA, Report of the Commission of Inquiry on Human Rights in the DPRK (no. 5), 5.
32. UNGA, Report of the Commission of Inquiry on Human Rights in the DPRK (no. 5), 5.
33. Christian Solidarity Worldwide, 'North Korea: A Case to Answer, a Call to Act' (no. 23), 10.
34. ICTR, 95-5-T *Prosecutor v Kayishema and Ruzindan*, Trial Chamber Judgement (21 May 1999).

Index

United Nations Human Rights Commissions
(UNCHR) 106
United Nations Human Rights Council
(UNHRC) 1–2, 257n, 295
United Nations Interim Administration Mission
in Kosovo (UNMIK) 194, 222–3
United Nations Security Council Resolutions
(UNSCRs) 215–21
United Nations Security Council (UNSC) 1–2,
28, 29n, 46, 76–7, 81–7, 92n, 104–5, 120,
126n, 128–9n, 150, 180, 206–7, 230, 281,
292; approved French-led intervention in
Mali (2013) 242
United Nations Supervision Mission in Syria
(UNSMIS) 105
United Nations (UN) 4–9, 17n, 28n, 62–3,
114–17, 127–9n, 165–8, 197n, 205–7,
229–30, 266–8, 288; Capstone Doctrine
232, 236–7; Charter 180, 205–8;
Commissions of Inquiry 37; Convention
against Torture and Other Cruel, Inhuman or
Degrading Treatment or Punishment (1984)
203–4, 208; Convention on the Prevention
and Punishment of the Crime of Genocide
(1948) 78, 107, 168, 177n, 181, 201–2,
202–9, 210n, 245–6, 300–1; Declaration for
Human Rights 236; Draft Code of Crimes
Against the Peace and Security of Mankind
33; Human Rights Due Diligence Policy
(HRDDP) 238; Implementation Report
of R2P 293; Millennium Summit (2005)
293; peace support missions 215; Special
Measures for Protection from Sexual
Exploitations and Sexual Abuse (2003) 238;
World Summit (2005) 5, 22–4, 47, 76–7,
88, 150, 167, 181–8, 262–9; World Summit
Outcome Document (2005) 33–5, 61–3, 76,
79–80, 100–4, 159, 198n, 242–3, 260–2,
266–7, 276n, 293
United States of America (USA) 7–12, 36–7, 78,
140–1, 172, 196–7, 247, 297; Congress 9;
National Public Radio (NPR) 69; National
Security Strategy (1994) 254n; New York 83,
90n, 141, 157; Obama 9, 25, 165, 286
universal consensus on genocide/ethnic
cleansing/war crimes and crimes against
humanity 32–4
Universal Declaration of Human Rights
(UDHR) 62, 67, 71
universal jurisdiction 244
universalization 102
Urquhart, B. 156
USSR 156

Vaughn, J.: and Dunne, T. 49
Venezuela 142, 267, 272–4
Verba, S.: and Almond, G.A. 64; Schlozman,
K.L. and Brady, H.E. 64

veto power 37–9, 114
victimization 54
Vienna Law of Treaties 117
vigilantes 132
violations of freedom of movement and
residence 298–9
violence 251–2; sexual 293, 298; structural
169
virtual communities (VC) 71
visas 60n; policy 199n
vulnerability 183

Waldron, J. 64, 67
Wallace, S.: and Mallory, C. 2, 215–28
Waltz, K. 155
war crimes 30n, 31–2, 102–3, 107–10, 124–5,
166–7, 181–4, 247, 257n, 283
War on Terror 167
We the Peoples: The Role of the United Nations
in the 21st Century (UN, 2001) 192
Weinert, M.S. 49
Weiss, T.G. 88–9, 102, 168; and Thakur, R. 52;
and Wilkinson, R. 47–9
Welsh, J. 247, 253n, 270, 274
West 141
West Asia and North Africa (WANA) region 83
West Bank 105–6
Western imperialism 95n
Western powers 32–4, 38, 53
Westphalia treaty (1648) 19–20, 28
Westphalian myth 179
Westphalian norms 157–9
Westphalian sovereignty 153–4, 247, 292
Wiener, A. 81; and Puetter, U. 81
WikiLeaks 71
Wilkens, J. 88
Wilkinson, R.: and Weiss, T.G. 47–9
Will to Intervene Project 139, 148n
Wilson, W. 70–1
Woocher, L. 168
Worker's Party of Korea 297
World Bank 173
World Heritage Sites 139
world politics 77
World War: I (1914–18) 70, 152; II (1939–45)
46, 67, 117, 179
world's armour 109–11

Yarmouk (Syria) 31
Yemen 6, 8, 76, 242, 271
Young, I.M. 67
Ypi, L.L. 68
Yugoslavia 10, 20, 62, 252, 254n

Zifcak, S. 218, 221
Zimbabwe 36
Zongze, R. 270
Zukin, C.: et al. 64